The Handbook of Counselling Children and Young People

SAGE was founded in 1965 by Sara Miller McCune to support the dissemination of usable knowledge by publishing innovative and high-quality research and teaching content. Today, we publish more than 750 journals, including those of more than 300 learned societies, more than 800 new books per year, and a growing range of library products including archives, data, case studies, reports, conference highlights, and video. SAGE remains majority-owned by our founder, and on her passing will become owned by a charitable trust that secures our continued independence.

Los Angeles | London | Washington DC | New Delhi | Singapore

The Handbook of
Counselling Children
and Young People

Edited by

Sue Pattison | Maggie Robson | Ann Beynon

Los Angeles | London | New Delhi
Singapore | Washington DC

British Association for
Counselling & Psychotherapy

Los Angeles | London | New Delhi
Singapore | Washington DC

SAGE Publications Ltd
1 Oliver's Yard
55 City Road
London EC1Y 1SP

SAGE Publications Inc.
2455 Teller Road
Thousand Oaks, California 91320

SAGE Publications India Pvt Ltd
B 1/I 1 Mohan Cooperative Industrial Area
Mathura Road
New Delhi 110 044

SAGE Publications Asia-Pacific Pte Ltd
3 Church Street
#10-04 Samsung Hub
Singapore 049483

Editor: Susannah Trefgarne
Assistant editor: Laura Walmsley
Production editor: Rachel Burrows
Copyeditor: Fern Bryant
Proofreader: Andrew Baxter
Indexer: Elizabeth Ball
Marketing manager: Camille Richmond
Cover design: Lisa Harper-Wells
Typeset by: C&M Digitals (P) Ltd, Chennai, India
Printed and bound by CPI Group (UK) Ltd, Croydon,
CR0 4YY

Contents

List of Figures and Tables

Figures

Tables

List of Abbreviations

AA	Alcoholics Anonymous
ADHD	Attention Deficit Hyperactivity Disorder
AFT	Adolescent-Focused Therapy
AN	Anorexia Nervosa
APA	American Psychiatric Association
ASA	Adoption Support Agency
ASCA	American School Counsellor Association
ASD	Autistic Spectrum Disorder
ASLI	Association of Sign Language Interpreters
BACP	British Association for Counselling and Psychotherapy
BACP CYP	British Association for Counselling and Psychotherapy Children and Young People
BAPT	British Association of Play Therapists
BN	Bulimia Nervosa
BPS	The British Psychological Society
BSL	British Sign Language
BTE	Behind-the-ear
CAF	Common Assessment Framework
CASE	Child and Adolescent Self-harm in Europe
CAMHS	Child and Adolescent Mental Health Services
CBT	Cognitive-Behavioural Therapy
CCS	Catholic Children's Society
CORC	CAMHS Outcome Research Consortium
CORE-OM	Clinical Outcomes in Routine Evaluation – Outcome Measure
CORS	Child Outcome Rating Scale
CPS	Crown Prosecution Service
CSRS	Child Session Rating Scale
CYP	Children and Young People
CYP IAPT	Children and Young People's Improving Access to Psychological Therapies
CYP PRN	Children and Young People Practitioner Research Network

DCHP	Deaf Children of Hearing Parents
DfE	Department for Education
DoH	Department of Health
DPM	Dual Process Model
DSM-5	The Diagnostic and Statistical Manual of Mental Disorders
EBD	Emotional and Behavioural Difficulties
EBP	Evidence-Based Practice
EDNOS	Eating Disorder Not Otherwise Specified
FBT	Family-Based Treatment
GCSE	General Certificate of Secondary Education
GP	General Practitioner
HCPC	Health and Care Professionals Council
HI	Hearing Impaired
IAPT	Improving Access to Psychological Therapies
IPT	Interpersonal Therapy
IQ	Intelligence Quotient
LA	Local Authority
LMS	Local Management of Schools
LSCB	Local Safeguarding Children Board
MCE	Manually Coded English
MHF	Mental Health Foundation
MUPS	Medically Unexplained Physical Symptoms
NAYPCAS	National Association of Young Peoples Counselling and Advisory Services
NDPT	Non-directive Play Therapy
NHS	National Health Service
NICCY	Northern Ireland Children's Commissioner for Children and Young People
NICE	National Institute for Health and Clinical Excellence
NSPCC	National Society for the Prevention of Cruelty to Children
OCD	Obsessive Compulsive Disorder
Ofsted	Office for Standards in Education, Children's Services and Skills
ORS	Outcome Rating Scale
PACE	Playfulness Acceptance Curiosity and Empathy
PBRN	Practice-Based Research Network
PBE	Practice-Based Evidence
PCA	Person-Centred Approach
PHA	Public Health Agency
PTSD	Post-Traumatic Stress Disorder
RBCSB	Rochdale Borough Safeguarding Children Board

RCT	Randomised Controlled Trial
SAN	Sub-threshold Anorexia Nervosa
SATs	Standard Assessment Tests
SBPCC	School-Based Person-Centred Counselling
SBN	Sub-threshold Bulimia Nervosa
SCIE	Social Care Institute for Excellence
SCoPReNet	School-Based Counselling Practice Research Network (now CYP PRN)
SDQ	Strengths and Difficulties Questionnaire
SE	Signed English
SEE	Seeing Exact English
SENCO	Special Educational Needs Co-ordinator
SIGN	Scottish Intercollegiate Guidelines Network
SPT	Individual Supportive Psychotherapy
SSE	Sign Supported English
TaMHS	Targeted Mental Health in Schools
UKCP	United Kingdom Council for Psychotherapy
UNCRC	United Nations Convention on the Rights of the Child
UPR	Unconditional Positive Regard
VA	Voluntary Action
WAG	Welsh Assembly Government
WHO	World Health Organisation
YCORS	Young Child Outcome Rating Scale
YIACS	Youth Information Advice Counselling and Support Services
YP-CORE	Young Person's Clinical Outcomes in Routine Evaluation
ZPD	Zone of Proximal Development

About the Editors and Contributors

Sue Pattison is Lecturer in Education and Counselling at Newcastle University and has strong experience of working in all four nations of the UK, Africa, the Middle East and Asia. She is Director of the Integrated PhD in Education and Communication. Her main research interests are the social and emotional health and well-being of children and young people and she is an accredited counsellor (BACP) in practice as a therapist and supervisor and trainer.

Maggie Robson is a senior teaching fellow at Keele University where she was responsible for the professional counsellor training programmes to Master's level. She is also a qualified play therapist and has a special interest in working with, and researching, children's bereavement. She has taught play therapy programmes in the UK, Kenya and the US and trained the first play therapy supervisors in Kenya. In her free time she is a bit of a water baby and enjoys sailing, canoeing and swimming. She also loves walking and bike riding and the occasional glass of wine!

Ann Beynon has worked as a teacher, counsellor, trainer and service manager for the last 40 years. She is convinced of the eclectic role of the counsellor in the development of effective learning relationships in educational and community settings. This conviction led her to focus on ways of developing integrated time for reflection, for teachers. To this end, she researched the application of a non-management therapeutic model of supervision within the educational context. Based on positive findings from this research, she has now established a service which provides regular Structured Time for Reflection, for head teachers and their staff.

Erica Allan has a background in psychology and is working as research assistant within the Eating Disorders Program at The Royal Children's Hospital, Melbourne, Australia.

As part of her involvement in the Eating Disorders Program, Erica has been involved in the management of a clinical trial for adolescents with anorexia nervosa.

Wilma Barrow is an educational psychologist working in Scottish Borders Council. She works with children and young people, their families, schools and other agencies to support learning and wellbeing through the application of psychology. She has been involved in postgraduate training of educational psychologists for ten years and is currently an Academic and Professional Tutor on the DAppEdPsy Programme at Newcastle University. She is interested in the role of dialogue within all aspects of educational psychology practice and particularly in its transformative potential for teaching and learning and participative practices.

Cathy Bell has worked with children and young people in statutory social services settings, within a voluntary organisation and in a residential setting in the developing world. While working with the NSPCC, Cathy set up the school counselling services in Northern Ireland, now Independent Counselling Services for Schools (ICSS) funded by the Northern Ireland Department of Education. Cathy is currently the ICSS coordinator, committed to advocating for a rights-based approach to services for children. Since September 2012 Cathy has been chair of the BACP's Children and Young People's Executive and has recently been awarded a Fellowship with BACP.

Edith Bell has worked for 14 years in schools and community practice with children, young people and parents. She is the Director of Counselling for Familyworks and has undertaken specialist CYP research and training as part of her CBT Master's. She has written and developed undergraduate courses and taught extensively at undergraduate and postgraduate levels, as well as in the voluntary and statutory sectors. She is a BACP Accredited Counsellor. She sits on the BACP CYP Executive Committee and was a member of the BACP Expert Reference Group in developing national competence standards for CYP counsellors.

Graham Bright is Senior Lecturer in Childhood and Youth Studies and Youth and Community Work at York St John University. He was formerly a lecturer in counselling on the Teesside University franchised FdA and BA (Hons) Counselling at Darlington and Redcar and Cleveland colleges, and is co-editor (with Gill Harrison) of *Understanding Research in Counselling* (Learning Matters/SAGE, 2013). His PhD study with Durham University is provisionally entitled: '*The Role of Personal Narratives, Vocation and Personal and Professional Development in the Formation of Youth Workers and Counsellors: A Comparative Narrative-Interpretative Phenomenological Inquiry*'.

Wendy Brown is an experienced trainer, supervisor and counselling practitioner having worked in charitable and social care settings, as well as private practice. Currently practising as an adult and young persons' counsellor and supervisor, Wendy also works within the care system, working systemically to support professionals around the child. Wendy runs groups, offers consultations, carer and child work, and develops and delivers trainings for social work staff and foster carers with the aim of helping understand behaviours and create attachment between the child and the carer. Wendy is a BACP Accredited Counsellor and has been a member of the BACP CYP Executive Committee since 2010, and Deputy Chair since 2012.

Divine Charura is a Senior Lecturer in Counselling and Psychotherapy at Leeds Metropolitan University. He is an adult psychotherapist in the NHS, voluntary sector, and in private practice. Divine is also an independent trainer, supervisor, and coach. He contributed various papers and to various books. His latest book contributions are two books on the therapeutic relationship: *The Therapeutic Relationship Handbook: Theory and Practice* (McGraw-Hill Open University Press, forthcoming, edited with Stephen Paul) and *An Introduction to the Therapeutic Relationship in Counselling and Psychotherapy* (SAGE, 2015, with Stephen Paul). In his spare time Divine is a lover of art, photography, music and outdoor pursuits.

Mick Cooper is a Professor of Counselling Psychology at the University of Roehampton, a chartered counselling psychologist, and a fellow of the British Association for Counselling and Psychotherapy. He has been involved in the evaluation of counselling with children and young people since 2003, leading on a range of quantitative and qualitative studies. Mick was Clinical Lead on the Counselling MindEd e-learning programme (www.minded. org.uk), and is author of a range of texts on humanistic and existential approaches to therapy. These include *Working at Relational Depth in Counselling and Psychotherapy* (SAGE, 2005, with Dave Mearns) and *An Existential Approach to Counselling and Psychotherapy* (SAGE, 2015). Mick lives in Brighton with his partner and four children.

Niki Cooper is Programme Leader for professional qualifications at Place2Be, which is the leading UK provider of school-based emotional and mental health support services, supporting 75,000 children in 200 schools. She is co-author of the Place2Be Postgraduate Diploma in Counselling Children in Schools and has also overseen the development of a comprehensive professional qualifications pathway from Level 2 to MA. Before joining Place2Be in 2002, she was a community-based counsellor in South London for London Marriage Guidance and a secondary school counsellor.

Karen Cromarty works for the British Association for Counselling and Psychotherapy and is their Senior Lead Advisor. In her role Karen works strategically with opinion formers, academics, governments, and service managers in all sectors, across all of the UK, to try to ensure that counselling services for children and young people are accessible, effective and based upon the most recent research. Karen is an experienced counsellor, supervisor, trainer and researcher, and in her spare time has worked for many years as a Chair of Governors of a large successful secondary school in the North East of England.

Ani de la Prida is a counsellor, lecturer and supervisor. She has worked to develop the DipHE in Counselling Children and Young People in her role as Course Leader at Anglia Ruskin University and Programme Leader at Renew Counselling, a charity based in Essex and East London. Ani is a person-centred therapist and arts counsellor who has worked with children and young people in schools, exclusion projects, foster care and drug treatment programmes since 1999. She has also worked as a foster carer for a number of years. Her special areas of interest include person-centred art therapy, looked-after children and digital media in therapy having recently completed research into the therapeutic use of digital media for her MA in Counselling & Psychotherapy at the University of East London. Ani was an author on the Counselling MindEd e-learning programme (www.minded.org.uk). In addition to her current work in private practice Ani is also an active member of the BACP Professional Education Development Forum, an Examiner for ABC Awards and Chief Examiner for AQA Counselling Courses.

David Exall studied counselling at Lewisham College. He has worked with children in the voluntary sector for 14 years and has worked in schools, further and higher education as a trainer and counsellor. He is a certified supervisor. David joined Place2Be as a School Project Manager in 2001 before becoming a full-time trainer, delivering training to staff, volunteers, professionals working with children and families, and trainee counsellors. He is currently Head Trainer and continues to deliver training, while developing new programmes and holding overall responsibility for the Quality Assurance of training. David continues to work therapeutically within schools and currently works with young people in a secondary setting.

Simon Gibbs is Reader in Educational Psychology at Newcastle University and is the Programme Director for the Doctorate in Applied Educational Psychology and Head of the Education Section. Before that he worked as a secondary school teacher, and as an Educational Psychologist in Cleveland, Hartlepool and latterly as Senior Educational Psychologist in North Yorkshire. He has an MEd in Human Relations, an MA in Child Psychology (Education) and a PhD in Psychology. His current research interests include the effects of teachers' 'Efficacy Beliefs' and attributions on their practice and the development of inclusion. He is also General Editor of *Educational and Child Psychology*.

Lisa Gordon Clark. After motherhood and six years as a primary school teacher in the London Borough of Hounslow, Lisa trained as a play therapist at Roehampton in the mid-1990s and has been in private practice ever since, recently transferring her therapeutic base from London to Wiltshire. For over a decade she was active on the Board of Directors of BAPT, chairing the Communications and Public Relations subcommittee. She remains Editor of the annual *British Journal of Play Therapy*. Since 2008 Lisa has taught on the Play Therapy MA at the University of Roehampton where she is now Senior Lecturer and Programme Convener.

Terry Hanley is the Programme Director for the Doctorate in Counselling Psychology at the University of Manchester. He is Editor of the British Psychological Society's *Counselling Psychology Review*, the lead author of *Introducing Counselling and Psychotherapy Research* (SAGE) and the lead editor of *Adolescent Counselling Psychology* (Routledge).

Belinda Harris is associate professor in the School of Education at the University of Nottingham, where she is responsible for undergraduate and postgraduate taught programmes, and led the Master's in counselling children and young people for several years. Belinda's original interest in counselling began through her experience of working as a modern languages teacher in an inner city school in very challenging circumstances. Following training in person-centred counselling and then Gestalt psychotherapy she established therapeutic services for students and their families, and worked closely with teachers and school leaders to enhance their capacity to create effective working relationships with the most vulnerable young people. This focus on the relationship between education and therapy is central to her work and research. She has published widely, and recently conducted a scoping review of school counselling in 105 countries for the BACP/DoH MindEd project. Belinda is a UKCP Registered Psychotherapist, an ICF Certified Professional Coach and has a small practice working with families and young adults. She is assistant editor of the *British Gestalt Journal*.

Elizabeth K. Hughes is a research fellow with the Eating Disorders Program at The Royal Children's Hospital and University of Melbourne, Australia. She received her PhD in Psychology from Monash University and holds honorary positions with the Murdoch Children's Research Institute and the School of Psychology and Psychiatry at Monash University. Dr Hughes' research focuses on the treatment of eating disorders in adolescents, particularly family-based treatment for anorexia nervosa. Her research interests also include co morbidity in eating disorders, emotion regulation, and family systems.

Sally Ingram is the Director of Counselling at Durham University. She is a qualified adult counsellor, child and adolescent counsellor, supervisor and trainer, with 15 years' experience of managing counselling services. During that time she has served as the deputy chair for the BACP's children and young people's division, as well as their journal editor. She was a contributor to the MindEd program with a focus on adolescent development and attachment experiences and how these impact on their well-being. Sally is passionately committed to the psychological and emotional well-being of children and young people and was awarded commitment to students in 2014 by the Student Union. In her spare time she enjoys hillwalking, photography and independent cinema.

Peter Jenkins is Senior Lecturer in Counselling at Manchester University. He has been a member of both the BACP Professional Conduct Committee and the UKCP Ethics Committee. He has extensive experience of training counselling practitioners and organisations on children's rights and legal aspects of therapy, and has researched and published widely on this topic. His publications include *Counselling, Psychotherapy and The Law* (2nd edn, SAGE, 2007) and, as co-author with Debbie Daniels, *Therapy With Children* (2nd edn, SAGE, 2010) plus a training DVD on ethics and law in counselling children, 'A Confidential Space' (Counselling DVDs/University of Wales).

Sue Kegerreis is Director of the Centre for Psychoanalytic Studies at the University of Essex, where she is a Senior Lecturer and Course Director for the MA Psychodynamic Counselling. She trained as a teacher; as a child and adolescent psychotherapist at the Tavistock; and later as an adult psychoanalytic psychotherapist with the Lincoln. She has practised privately and in a range of other settings: school, hospital and CAMHS, as well as teaching on many courses, both clinical and applied. She worked for many years as a school counsellor. She has published widely in professional journals and her book *Psychodynamic Counselling with Children and Adolescents* was published in 2010.

Daniel Le Grange is Professor of Psychiatry and Behavioral Neuroscience and Director of the Eating Disorders program at The University of Chicago Medicine. Dr Le Grange obtained his PhD in Psychology at the Institute of Psychiatry, University of London and completed postdoctoral training at the University of London as well as Stanford University School of Medicine, California. Dr Le Grange's research interests focus primarily on psychosocial treatment trials for adolescents with eating disorders. His peer-reviewed articles concerning these and other related topics number more than 150, and are published in prestigious journals such as the *American Academy for Child and Adolescent Psychiatry*, *American Journal of Psychiatry*, *Archives of General Psychiatry*, *Archives of Pediatrics and Adolescent Medicine*, and *Pediatrics*. Dr Le Grange has co-authored 7 books, more than 40 book chapters, and more than 150 abstracts and presentations for national and international scientific meetings. Dr Le Grange is a Fellow of the Academy for Eating Disorders, a Member of the Eating Disorders Research Society, Associate Editor for the *Journal of Eating Disorders*, serves on the editorial boards of the *European Eating Disorders Review* and the *International Journal of Eating Disorders*. Dr Le Grange is currently Principal Investigator on several National Institute for Mental Health-funded treatment studies in the United States.

Penny Leake started her professional life as a teacher, but later retrained as counsellor, social worker and clinical supervisor. She began counselling in 1980, and since 1992 has specialised in working with children and young people. She spent many years as practitioner, manager and clinical supervisor for therapeutic services in the North East of England, in both the statutory and voluntary sectors. She is BACP Senior Accredited as both Supervisor and Counsellor, and now works freelance in Derbyshire. Her supervisees have included several CAMHS workers and play therapists. She strongly believes that workers have to feel well supported themselves if they are to support others.

Tom McAndrew With over 10 years' experience in education in British and international institutions, Tom McAndrew has spent most of his teaching career working with deaf children. He holds an MA in Deaf Education from Leeds University and is a qualified Teacher of the Deaf. Passionate about British Sign Language, he is a keen traveller and aspires to build bridges between the hearing and deaf cultures, and empower young deaf and hard of hearing children from around the world. In 2011 he ran the London Marathon raising money for Deaf Child Worldwide. He has two young children and currently lives and works in Kuala Lumpur with his family.

Katherine McArthur is a research associate at the University of Strathclyde, currently undertaking action research on mentoring for looked after children. She practices counselling with adults in a research setting, and with young people in a Glasgow secondary school, using a humanistic approach. School-based counselling is her main research interest and the focus of her PhD from the University of Strathclyde. In 2013 she was awarded the British Association for Counselling and Psychotherapy's Outstanding Research Award for a pilot randomised controlled trial of school-based counselling. Her previous research interests include the needs and rights of disabled children in the UK child protection system. She is a core group member of the Children and Young People Practice Research Network developed by the British Association for Counselling and Psychotherapy, and a member of Psychotherapists and Counsellors for Social Responsibility. In 2012, she co-edited a school-based counselling symposium edition of the *British Journal of Guidance and Counselling*.

Nick Midgley is a child and adolescent psychotherapist and a lecturer at University College London, where he is Course Director of the MSc in Developmental Psychology and Clinical Practice, and Academic Director of the DPsych in Child and Adolescent Psychotherapy. He has written and edited several books, including *Reading Anna Freud* (Routledge, 2013) and *Child Psychotherapy and Research* (Routledge, 2009).

Richard Parker is an educational psychologist working in Newcastle University and a local authority. He has worked as an educational psychologist for more than 30 years, holding specialist and management posts in a number of local authorities and with responsibilities from pre-school to Further Education. Richard's interests focus on professional reflection and learning, how professionals' views affect their practice, developing professional supervision and the impact on life course development of relationships.

Peter Pearce is Head of the Person Centred Department at Metanoia Institute where, amongst other trainings, he runs a Post Qualification, Conversion Diploma from Adult to Adolescent and School Counselling. Peter has provided person-centred counselling with young people within NHS and education settings since 1989. He has worked as a school counsellor in secondary school settings since 1999. He has a 17-year-old son and four small daughters.

Mark Prever was a counsellor, trainer and supervisor. He was lead professional for Every Child Matters at Yardleys School in Birmingham; a Chair of Open Door Youth Counselling Centre; former chair of the BACP's Counselling Children and Young People division and a lecturer at Worcester University which he had hoped to carry on through his retirement. Mark wrote regularly and his books include *Mental Health in Schools: A Guide to Pastoral & Curriculum Provision* (SAGE, 2006) and *Counselling and Supporting Children and Young People* (SAGE, 2010). Mark passed away in March 2013.

Gwen Proud has been employed in educational organisations for the majority of her working life including being a secretary in local government and independent schools, counselling in secondary schools in the North East of England for a children's charity and later for the local education authority. She completed a Master's Degree in Counselling at Durham University, a Doctorate in Counselling Studies at the University of Manchester, and is a BACP Accredited Counsellor. Gwen has divided her working practice between primary care and school settings and is experienced in working therapeutically with groups of children of secondary school age.

Olga Pykhtina is doctoral student at Newcastle University. Under the supervision of Dr Sue Pattison and Professor Patrick Olivier, she is investigating how primary school children and therapists can use digital technology at different stages of play therapy. Her study aims to establish a paradigm of understanding as to what are the advantages and barriers for the use of multi-touch technology in therapeutic context. She is exploring whether there is a place within non-directive play therapy for the designed in her research application Magic Land. Her main research interest is the impact of digital toys for child–therapist therapeutic alliance.

Toby Quibell is a school teacher and drama therapist. In 1993 he set up The Learning Challenge, a charity that worked for 20 years in the most deprived schools in the North East of England. Over this time Toby initiated, piloted and tested a range of therapeutic group interventions designed to dovetail into the delivery of the school curriculum. Working between 2008 and 2010 with a team of specially trained teaching staff in two large secondary schools he co-ordinated the delivery of a combined package of therapeutic support as a timetabled slot for all Year 7 and Year 9 children.

Dee C. Ray is Distinguished Teaching Professor in the Counseling Program and Director of the Child and Family Resource Clinic at the University of North Texas. Dr Ray has published over 85 articles, chapters and books in the field of play therapy. Dr Ray is author of *Advanced Play Therapy: Essential Conditions, Knowledge, and Skills for Child Practice*, *Child Centered Play Therapy Treatment Manual*, *Group Play Therapy* and *Child Centered Play Therapy Research*. She is current editor of the *Journal of Child and Adolescent Counseling* and former editor of the *International Journal of Play Therapy*. Her research interests focus on effectiveness and mediator variables in play therapy.

Kaye Richards is Senior Lecturer in Outdoor Education at Liverpool John Moores University and a Chartered Psychologist of the British Psychological Society. She has worked and published widely across the areas of outdoor education, sport, adventure therapy, and counselling and psychotherapy, with a specialist focus on young people. She is a longstanding member of the Adventure Therapy International Committee, Chair of the Special Interest Group of Outdoor and Adventure Therapy for the Institute for Outdoor Learning and was launch editor of the academic *Journal of Adventure Education and Outdoor Learning*.

Ros Sewell is Primary Tutor for the Post Qualification Conversion Diploma from Adult to Adolescent and School Counselling at Metanoia and a BACP Accreditation Assessor. She has provided person-centred counselling with young people within NHS and education settings since 1989 and worked as a school counsellor in secondary school settings since 1997. She has two teenage children.

Caryl Sibbett is a Registered Member MBACP, a BACP Senior Accredited Counsellor/Psychotherapist and a BACP Fellow. Caryl is a Trustee of the BACP. She is also an Art Psychotherapist (HCPC Reg.). As an experienced trainer, she is also a Fellow of the Higher Education Academy and Chair of the Counselling Children and Young People Training Consortium (NI). Caryl works in private practice and sessionally in a Health and Social Care context. She supervises for a wide range of organisations providing services for children and young people. An experienced researcher, she has published and presented nationally and internationally.

Barbara Smith is Assistant Clinical Lead in the Children and Adolescent Mental Health Service at Alder Hey Children's Hospital, a UKCP registered Child and Adult Psychotherapist and a BACP (Senior) Accredited Counsellor. She works in private practice offering individual and group psychotherapy. She spent many years delivering counselling training, supervises practising counsellors and is a member of British Red Cross psychosocial support (disaster) team. She has a strong research background in cross-cultural psychotherapy having undertaken her doctoral research in the Maldive

Islands and has published in the areas of anti-discriminatory practice, adventure therapy, children's self-esteem and working creatively.

Paul Stallard is Professor of Child and Family Mental Health at the University of Bath and Head of Psychological Therapies (CAMHS) for Oxford Health NHS Foundation Trust. He trained as a clinical psychologist and works within a specialist child mental health team where he leads a Cognitive-Behaviour Therapy (CBT) clinic for children and young people with emotional disorders of anxiety, depression, OCD and PTSD. He is an active researcher and a leading figure in the development of CBT with children. He is the author of the much acclaimed *Think Good Feel Good: A Cognitive Behaviour Therapy Workbook for Children and Young People*.

Dave Stewart is a BACP Accredited Counsellor–Psychotherapist and registered social worker. With over 20 years' experience in therapeutic work with children, young people and families, Dave first trained and worked as a music therapist. He later worked as a child therapist in a community setting before taking up the post of senior trauma counsellor in the children's charity Barnardo's. Dave currently leads a team of Barnardo's school-based counsellors which won the BACP award for 'Innovation in Counselling and Psychotherapy' in 2012. His special areas of interest include therapy with younger children, children and young people with special needs and outcome-informed practice. Dave has many years' experience as a trainer and has presented and published widely. The last 5 years have seen him develop a relational, outcome-informed model of counselling practice specific to younger children.

Kelli Swain-Cowper is an HPC accredited art therapist, Co-Author and Lead Tutor of the Postgraduate Diploma for Counselling Children in Schools. She trained at NYU in New York City and specialised in working with children and adolescents at St. Luke's Roosevelt Child and Family Institute. In New York, she supervised, worked in and developed arts therapies programs in schools, clinics, emergency refuges and children's inpatient hospitals. Moving to London in 2001, she began work with Place2Be, project managing, supervising and training and maintains clinical work in schools and a private practice.

Beverly Turner-Daly is a qualified social worker, counsellor and clinical supervisor with over 25 years' experience in the field of post-abuse counselling and therapy. She works part-time as Senior Lecturer at Northumbria University where she is the Programme Leader for the Post-Qualifying Child Care Award and involved in several research projects focusing on child abuse and its impact on workers. Beverly also works as an independent supervisor, trainer and consultant, providing training and supervision to a wide-range of professionals who work with children and families.

Foreword

Mike Shooter

Round about my time of life, you start asking yourself what kept you in your career for so long – in my case, 30 years as a child and adolescent psychiatrist in the NHS. Well, here are a few good reasons why.

Working with children and young people is more directly about human beings and their lives than any other occupation I know. Rarely does the stethoscope, a packet of tablets or any therapeutic defence get in the way. And the corollary of that is that they present the therapist with the most difficult of challenges. Who are you? How did you resolve that in your own childhood? And can you cope with what I am about to throw at you from mine?

Answering those questions requires the most eclectic of approaches. Children, in my experience, rarely compartmentalise their lives. What misery they face in one bit spreads throughout. To tackle it, we must offer a package of approaches, tailored to the child's needs, not cram the child into whatever 'ism' suits us best. And that package, in turn, should be set within a holistic, multidisciplinary context that tackles the problems from every angle – home, school, peer group and community. The very process of working together can be healing to a shattered life.

Diagnosis, of course, may be important. But what children and adolescents may need most is the space to explore their life-story, where it began, where it might have gone wrong, and to re-tell it, with a different ending. All within the safety of the therapeutic structure. And that gives the therapist space too for a responsible creativity. Human beings again – exploring the problem together by whatever seems appropriate, not an all-powerful adult doling out treatment to a passive recipient.

And that means that this is the age group in which we can make most difference to their lives. By helping children and young people to voice their individual needs and their views of how services might best be organised to satisfy them, we can empower them to solve their life problems as they recur. For those too afraid, too downtrodden or too disabled, we can raise a voice for them until they are strong enough to find their own.

Finally, if all that sounds too glib, what kept me in the business most of all, was the element of surprise. I never knew from one day to the next what a child or adolescent might present me with, what fresh insights they might offer and how I might learn from them as much as I might offer in return. In the end, however skilled the consultants under whom I learned my trade, however skilled the supervisors I have used to guide me through the most difficult of situations, it is children and young people who have taught me most of what I know.

So why have I shared all those reasons with you? Because this book epitomises every one of them – the principles, the knowledge, the experience, the skills and techniques, and the sheer excitement of working with children and young people, and the challenges it entails. I wish I'd had it to hand when I started out those 30 years ago. Now it passes my ultimate test – 'damn, I wish I'd written that myself!'

Acknowledgements

We would like to thank all the contributors in this book for their generosity in sharing their knowledge, skills and experience for the benefit of children and young people worldwide and their counsellors.

We wish to remember Mark Prever with great respect and thank his brother for facilitating the publishing of Mark's chapter, sadly Mark died soon after writing it.

We would like to acknowledge the professionalism and editorial help given by Rachel Burrows, Laura Walmsley and Susannah Trefgarne from SAGE and for their patience and expertise.

We are grateful to BACP, the MindEd team and particularly, the Children and Young People's Committee for their ongoing support and the book reviewers for their valuable feedback.

Finally, it is important to acknowledge the relationships forged through the process of writing this book, between the authors and the editorial team. We have learnt much from each other.

Sue Pattison
Maggie Robson
Ann Beynon

Editors' Introduction

Sue Pattison, Maggie Robson and Ann Beynon

The ideas and impetus for this book came together as a response to the growing need for high quality training and reference resources in the expanding field of counselling children and young people. This book was waiting to be written – we had discussed producing a unique resource for counsellors of children and young people for some time. The opportunity to 'walk the walk' came when we were approached by SAGE as members of the British Association for Counselling and Psychotherapy's Children and Young People Committee. The timing was key, as BACP were developing the Counselling Competencies and the MindEd e-learning resources. The British Association for Counselling and Psychotherapy (BACP) have developed a set of competencies for therapists who work with young people. These are available on their website (www.bacp.co.uk/). These competencies were developed as humanistic competencies, but the further development of core and generic competencies, in our view, detail the general therapeutic skills relevant to all practitioners working both with children and young people, regardless of theoretical orientation. Some of the issues identified in these core competencies are explored in detail within this handbook, reflecting the importance of these areas when working therapeutically with children and young people. Competencies identified by BACP (2014) include knowledge of child and family development and transitions, and knowledge and understanding of mental health issues. Knowledge of legal, professional and ethical frameworks is considered essential, including an ability to work with issues of confidentiality, consent and capacity. BACP (ibid.) suggest that therapists need to be able to work across and within agencies and respond to child protection issues. In addition, therapists need to be able to engage and work with young people of a variety of ages, developmental levels and backgrounds, as well as parents and carers, in a culturally competent manner. They also need to have knowledge of psychopharmacology as it relates to young people. The generic competencies relate to knowledge of specific models of intervention and practice, an ability to work with emotions, endings and service transitions, an ability to work with groups and measurement instruments and to be able to use supervision effectively. The ability to conduct a collaborative assessment and a risk assessment is paramount. Crucially, BACP (2014) suggest the therapist needs to be able to foster and maintain a relationship which builds a therapeutic alliance and understands the client's 'world view'. In our experience most proficient therapists, irrespective of their modality, work to achieve this trusting relationship necessary for human change. BACP are also developing a children and young people specialist training curriculum based on the competences. It is intended that this will be a post-graduate top-up for counsellors/psychotherapists who have a completed an 'adult' practitioner training and who want to develop knowledge and skills to work with children and young people.

This book dovetails smoothly with these developments. We use the term 'therapeutic work' as an overarching term for the range of therapies referred to loosely as 'counselling' or 'psychotherapy'. Although each professional body has their own definition of counselling and psychotherapy, they are all similar in nature. 'Counselling and psychotherapy are umbrella terms that cover a range of talking therapies. They are delivered by trained practitioners who work with people over a short or long term to help them bring about effective change or enhance their wellbeing' (BACP, www.bacp.co.uk/). However, we would like to add to this definition, which refers to 'talking therapies', to include creative forms of communication including artwork and play to address the therapeutic needs of the wide age range of children and young people covered in this book (3–18 years and beyond, for young people with developmental delays).

This handbook is unique as the only comprehensive resource for counsellors, trainees and trainers working in the field of counselling children and young people that is linked to high quality online resources developed by BACP. The book is designed to provide essential reading for all counselling trainees and a guide to curriculum for the trainers. Any counsellor working with children and young people, or aspiring to work with this client group, will be able to refer to the handbook and use it to contribute to their continuing professional development. There are challenges around improving the quality and provision of support for the mental health of children and young people. Statistics show that the suicide rate is rising and children and young people's levels of well-being are falling. The quality of counsellor training and the evidence base required to ensure effective provision are both issues addressed in this book. Each chapter provides references to research and the evidence base, further supplemented through links to the BACP/NHS MindEd e-learning resources, which are indicated at the end of each chapter, where appropriate. By far the most important aspects of this book are the unique contributions each author has made. Each is expert in their field and has their own approach to the chapter topics, which makes for overlap in places, but with a different perspective in each case. The handbook will invite you in as reader, hold your attention and entice you to read further, giving you flavours of approaches to counselling children and young people that may be new to you and insights into topics that stimulate and leave you wanting more.

We intend this handbook to provide a comprehensive guide to the complex field of counselling children and young people in the UK and as a resource in the international arena. As its intended audience, you may be a trainee, trainer, practitioner, a service provider or a commissioner of therapeutic work with children and young people. The level of your training programme may be introductory or more advanced. The book is based on a set of values and principles, the rights of the child, the need to keep the child at the centre of our therapeutic work, unconditional acceptance, trustworthiness and congruence. The book will help you as the reader to identify, clarify, reflect upon and work with the underpinning legislation, ethics and values; theoretical approaches; research evidence; interventions and techniques that apply to the practice of counselling children and young people. You will be introduced to the diversity of working with children and young people at different developmental stages. In order to achieve this, the handbook follows a structured and logical approach that introduces you to a set of underpinning values related to legislation, policy and professional practice, demonstrating how these are used in practice by providing you with case study material. Although each case study represents the therapeutic way of working, the actual cases are amalgams in order to protect client confidentiality and identity. The handbook is presented in four major parts with 28 chapters. Throughout the book there is evidence of how therapeutic work with children and young people and the related services have developed historically. Although a range of theoretical approaches and different ways of working are explored in this book, the philosophical base when translated into underpinning values and principles of working with children and young people includes trustworthiness of the counsellor, acceptance, empowerment and a belief in the power of relationship. These values and principles will be woven throughout the book and are present in every chapter to enable theory, research and practice to be linked and consolidated for you, the reader.

As the field of counselling children and young people has rapidly developed over the past few years, the delivery, approaches to counselling and the nature of interventions have increased in number and range and been applied across an increasing range of contexts. Counselling practitioners come from a variety of backgrounds and professions. They bring new ideas into the field and also adapt concepts, ideas and tools developed in their own professions, including theoretical approaches. The diversity of the field creates increasing opportunities for interdisciplinary work and cross-fertilisation of ideas. However, there is also a sense of counsellors requiring help to position themselves professionally in relation to theoretical approach, methods, techniques and tools, bearing in mind the increasing demand for practice based on research evidence.

Questions that you may ask as a counselling practitioner, trainer, trainee or commissioner of therapeutic work with children and young people may include: Which is the best counselling approach for working with young children in primary schools? How is a therapeutic relationship with an adolescent who has problem behaviour established and maintained? Is it possible to provide complete confidentiality for a child in therapy? Should a child be 'sent' for counselling? Is parental permission needed to offer counselling to an adolescent? Although not all of your questions will be answered, this book provides the answers to a range of questions that the authors have been asked over their many years of experience.

The structure of the book has been designed to enable you to access any section independently of the others, yet they intrinsically link together. The book comprises four overarching sections: Theory and Practice Approaches; Counselling Practices and Processes; Practice Issues; and Practice Settings.

In 'Theory and Practice Approaches', the authors discuss a range of therapeutic approaches aimed at helping children and young people at different ages and stages. This includes child development and attachment; the child-centred approach, psychodynamic, cognitive-behavioural, gestalt, transactional analysis, play therapy and other creative therapeutic approaches. Where appropriate, the chapters will look at brief therapy where it is included within each approach. Age-appropriate interventions in relation to each theoretical approach are examined, for example, brief therapy, play therapy and its theoretical perspectives; cognitive-behavioural approaches such as problem-solving, and solution focused therapy. Each chapter refers to the underlying principles fundamental to counselling work with children and young people and relevant research. 'Counselling Practices and Processes' examines the nature of the process that can take place when counselling children and young people and looks at referral and indications for therapy, including assessment; preparation for therapy and beginnings; the therapeutic alliance and the middle part of therapy; counselling skills; supervision; group work and endings. The section incorporating 'Practice Issues' looks at law and policy; ethics; diversity; bereavement; depression; suicide and self-harm; sexual abuse; and eating disorders. 'Practice Settings' identifies and examines working in a range of contexts, statutory health and social care services; non-statutory services, for example, the third sector. The chapters in each major part of the handbook have an established common structure, and all case material used in the book is anonymised, to preserve confidentiality. This is the structure, which organises information and acts as a guide for you, the reader. Each chapter includes a set of questions designed for your further reflection on the topic with suggestions for reading that will allow you to investigate topics in more depth. Therefore, it is hoped that after engaging with the informative review of each key topic you will not only have a good understanding of it but will be interested in investigating the topic further.

Part 1

Theory and Practice Approaches

1

Child Development and Attachment

Simon Gibbs, Wilma Barrow and Richard Parker

This chapter includes:

- Developmental theory
- The role of the primary caregiver in supporting development
- Attachment
- Implications for counselling

Introduction

In this chapter we outline some theories about children's development, and the role of the primary caregiver (and other adults) in supporting children's development.

We then summarise the development of attachment theory and outline findings in relation to the theory as proposed by Bowlby (2005). In so doing we recall that the origins of attachment theory lie in cognitive psychology. We also note the role of two behaviours relating to the development of attachment: *exploratory behaviours* associated with cognitive, social and communicational development; and *caregiving* associated with parental availability, responsiveness and intervention. These are, as we discuss later, also crucial characteristics of therapists.

Regarding *exploratory behaviours*, we acknowledge the importance of the work of theorists and researchers such as Vygotsky, Bruner and Wood (see Wood, 1998) in describing how parents scaffolding their child's play facilitate exploration and the development of physical, social and communicational skills. Discussing this, we note the *dialogic* nature of these interactions (Gratier and Trevarthen, 2007). Thus, according to attachment theory, with appropriate contingent parental interaction, the child will develop a representation of herself as able to help herself and as worthy of receiving help when necessary (Bowlby, 1977a; Thompson, 2000).

Before considering these theories in detail we offer a brief introduction to issues arising from child development studies. Child development psychology is complex, and as ideas about childhood and children have shifted, the emphasis on development in *childhood* has itself been criticised. The notion of the child as the 'unfinished' version of the adult has been questioned and attention has shifted to development across the life course (Spiel, 2009).

Child Development: A Critical Overview

Developmental psychology has, over time, included a range of theoretical positions. Historically, these have differed regarding the emphasis placed upon physical, psychological and social factors implicated in the process of development. Historically, too, emphasis has been on studying the child objectively with minimal attention to the child's subjective experience (Hogan, 2005). Current thinking tends to reflect the dynamic relationship between factors implicated in children's development. Development may be seen as a dynamic process of interactions between innate biological (the cortex, for instance) and psychological factors (such as temperament), and influences such as caregiver responsiveness (Sameroff, 2009). Such complexity and reflexivity is reflected in newer theoretical positions such as neuroconstructivism. While emphasising the importance of neural structures for our understanding of cognition, neuroconstructivists argue that the developmental trajectory results from interactions between biological and environmental factors that shape and constrain emerging neural structures (Westerman et al., 2010).

While development can, therefore, be understood as a process of dynamic transaction between multiple factors, a number of other findings have emerged from recent research in developmental psychology. We identify those that we consider of particular relevance for those therapeutically involved in work with children who have experienced difficulty or trauma in their lives. It is important to emphasise links between these findings and associated philosophical and methodological debates. The findings include the following:

- The role of experience in neurodevelopmental plasticity (Goswami, 2004; Van Ijzendoorn and Juffer, 2006). Although research suggests certain experiences can lead to long-term difficulty, the possibility of catch-up is recognised.
- The primary need for significant relationships (Bråten, 1998; Linell, 2007; Trevarthen, 2001). Early developmental theorists like Freud considered relationship to be a means of satisfying basic biological need. Increasingly the importance of relationship as a primary need has been recognised in research demonstrating the role of intersubjectivity and the attunement of the young infant to the other (Meltzoff and Moore, 1998; Newson and Newson, 1975; Trevarthen and Aitken, 2001). Research on motivation led Deci and Ryan (2000), for instance, to conclude that relatedness is fundamental to human psychological well-being.
- Understanding the environment within which the child develops as a complex *eco-system*. Bronfenbrenner (1979) theorised that children develop within nested systems. Microsystems include the people and organisations within which the child has most immediate contact, such as family, peer group or school class. The mesosystem refers to the interface between aspects of the microsystem such as the interactions between a child's parents and teachers. The exosystem involves the wider community and the systems which directly or indirectly affect the child such as parental workplace or local neighbourhood. Finally, the macrosystem involves culture, ideology and legal systems. The relationships between these systems are transactional, as is that of the child and the various systems.
- Linked to ecosystemic understanding is the need to recognise cultural diversity (Dasen and Mishra, 2000; Kağıtçıbaşı, 1996). Developmental psychology has been criticised for relying on European and American-based research, and there have been calls for a more inclusive approach to the discipline (Marfo et al., 2011). This is of particular importance given this book's purpose. Research looking at children's emotional reactions suggests differences between cultural groups' responses to difficult situations (Cole et al., 2002). While it seems to be the case that all children develop attachment behaviours, there is evidence (Göncü et al., 2012) that the meaning and salience of these behaviours may be culturally specific, and have implications for counsellors and therapists. There is debate about how psychologists respond to cultural diversity. On one side of the philosophical and methodological divide is the cross-cultural comparative or etic approach. On the other lies cultural-psychology or emic approaches (Dasen and Mishra, 2000). The Turkish developmental psychologist Kağıtçıbaşı (1996), for example, has taken a mediating position due to concerns that uncritical approaches to cultural relativism might lead to failure to intervene in the lives of children whose development is being compromised by adversity. She has suggested a synthesis of etic and emic approaches to inform the development of contextually sensitive interventions (Kağıtçıbaşı, 1996). This requires collaboration with those positioned within cultures and avoiding culturally imperialistic interventions. Spiel (2009) identified Kağıtçıbaşi's work as an example of how discussion may be re-focused on positive cross-cultural development.

- The development of strength-based theories of development (Lerner et al., 2005). This is based on the ideas of neuroplasticity noted above. Lerner et al. have studied the development of competence, confidence, connection, character and caring through appropriate programmes of activity and social policy. Their focus is upon the contextual appropriateness of interventions, with sensitivity to cultural diversity.

It is also important to recognise that the development of young people is an emotive topic. The factors contributing to 'good' and 'bad' outcomes for children and the implications of these outcomes for wider society are fiercely debated within the media – as was evident during the aftermath of the UK 2011 riots (Channel4News, 2011). Ideologically-driven sound bites often reflect notions of development based on outdated, linear models of causality. Contemporary theories of child development can help by countering and reframing these. This is also important to those involved in therapeutic work who attempt to support the well-being and attunement of children, young people and their families.

Following this broad introduction to the field of child development we now turn to specific theories and consider their role in explaining cognitive and social-emotional development.

Theories of Children's Cognitive Development

We see daily the range and diversity of evidence of how children and young people develop physically, psychologically and socially. We may also see a range of parental behaviours toward children. These range from appearing to embrace warmth of care and support, to those seeming to engender anxiety, wariness, frustration or hostility. Thus we may witness how we consciously (or less consciously) shape the way babies are handled, how children learn from adults and each other, and how culturally we manage the processes of development into adulthood.

Some of the mechanisms that support children and young people's development are undoubtedly biological and genetic (Fonagy and Target, 2002; Schore and Schore, 2008) and the importance of these for the understanding of attachment is becoming clearer (see, for instance, Galbally et al., 2011). Although we do not underestimate the salience of the biological and physical factors that affect development, we will not deal with these extensively here. The present context demands attention to the sociocultural factors shaping the way we interrelate and interact with children's development.

We have already indicated that the history of developmental psychology involves a range of theoretical perspectives that reflect differing emphases. These have ranged across varying paradigms. In the early 20th century much research was associated with the psychoanalytical work of Freud and his followers (most notably his daughter Anna and Melanie Klein). Their work was an attempt to understand the impact of underlying *instinctual, emotional* and *intra-psychic factors* on children's development. One of Klein's insights was in recognising that children's play was a means to communicate feelings and instincts that, at an early age, children were otherwise unable to communicate. Of significance for later in this chapter, when we consider attachment theory in detail, is Anna Freud's belief that, in the psychoanalysis of children, the analyst represents and takes on aspects of the role of a parent (Freud, 1946; Keinanen, 1997).

However, in a deliberate reaction to the subjective, intra-personal nature of the psychoanalytical perspective, the work of psychologists such as Watson and Skinner was devoted to the development of psychology as an objective science. In that paradigm studies were carried out to establish how children's *behaviour* might be 'conditioned' or moulded – as had been evidenced in animal studies. Skinner proposed that children's learning would be significantly enhanced through the application of appropriate reinforcements (Skinner, 1968). Thus, specific behaviours (for example reading words correctly) may be reinforced by a smile from the parent. These ideas were adapted by Bandura to form the basis of his social learning theory (Bandura, 1977). In Bandura's view children learn by observing and imitating behaviours which, if appropriate, are then reinforced by significant others. On the basis of this feedback, children develop a belief in their 'self-efficacy' (Bandura, 2001).

Such theories have helped inform work with children. However, they have been criticised for their objectification of children. They have also been regarded as both underplaying children's own agency and contribution to their development, as well as ignoring how exploring their environments enables children to construct knowledge and understanding (Gillman et al., 1997; Hogan, 2005; Radin, 1991).

Our understanding of children's *cognitive development* has been greatly influenced by the work of Piaget and of Vygotsky. While their work has been of significance in its own right, we also suggest it is important to consider these (and other) theories here, since the way children's thinking develops and how adults understand that process of development play a major part in shaping the relationships between carers and children. It is, however, important to recognise that while Piaget's work provided illumination of the development of children's cognition through a series of stages, this story is incomplete. Children develop through interaction with their biological selves and the physical, social and cultural world (Wood, 1998). Understanding of this came from Vygotsky (1962), whose work demonstrated how adults in communicating aspects of the cultural context influenced the development of children's thinking.

Piaget's work is still important for its insights into children's perceptions and how we may conceptualise children's development. It has little to say, however, about how or why children develop as they do. Piaget (1953) charted the development of children's thinking as a series of stages. In the earliest stage (from birth to two years), in which children use their senses and motor abilities, Piaget held that children explore reflexively and do not consciously 'think'. However, they do show different reactions in differing situations – for example 'stilling' when the caregiver approaches; beginning to show they 'understand' that although out of sight, objects still exist – though challenge is emerging (see Kagan, 2008). It is in the next 'preoperational' stage (from around two to seven years of age) that children start to form mental representations and label these using words. During this stage they start to show they can see things from another's perspective and distinguish between animate and inanimate objects. As they progress, their ability to think logically and to formulate abstract thoughts develops. Piaget found that between seven and 11, children began to realise the logical nature of operations and classifications. More recent research, however, has suggested that these abilities do not necessarily emerge spontaneously but arise in association with certain cultural and contextual factors (see Donaldson, 1978; Maynard and Greenfield, 2003). Through creative adaptations to Piaget's methods and attention to how tasks were communicated, Donaldson, for instance, was able to demonstrate young children's ability to perform cognitive tasks earlier than predicted by Piaget, so long as the context was meaningful. Such work showed that the way tasks were constructed and communicated could be critical in determining children's success or failure. Cross-cultural research has reinforced the importance of this by demonstrating that rates of cognitive development can vary across cultures, dependent on cultural and environmental factors (Dasen and Mishra, 2000). While Piaget's work provided a framework for viewing the development of children's cognitive abilities and provided the concept of 'readiness', the work of Vygotsky has enabled greater understanding of the tools (including language and cultural heritage) that mediate development.

Vygotsky (1962) differed significantly from Piaget in his concepts and methods by showing the importance of communication as a crucial factor and providing clues about how children progress in their development. Thus, Vygotsky considered that when talking to themselves (in their 'self-talk') children used language as a tool to help them overcome problems (Vygotsky, 1978; Winsler et al., 2006). In the 'zone of proximal development' (Vygotsky's term), while a child may be unable to succeed with a task or problem on their own, with the help of someone more expert (a child or adult), the child could be more successful. Vygotsky suggested that when acting on her own, the child may be heard commentating on her activity, expressing both curiosity and puzzlement – essentially to herself. With her parent it was possible to see how the child's self-talk became a dialogue with a more expert other. This other, if sufficiently skilful, could help 'scaffold' the child's problem-solving of a task confronting her (Keen, 2011; Wood et al., 1976). Through such skilful (spontaneous and contingent) verbal and non-verbal intervention, the parent, in dialogue with her young child, also facilitates the development of intersubjectivity and synchrony (Newson and Newson, 1975; Trevarthen, 2011). Through such processes adults help regulate children's active and purposeful exploratory engagement with their surroundings (David et al., 2012;

Sroufe, 2005). With the reassurance and guidance of such 'scaffolding' the child may feel safer in exploring and, almost literally, extending their grasp to take on new challenges. Thus, the child's exploratory play can be seen to be reciprocated by their carer's behaviour. It is with this theoretical basis that we now turn to a consideration of the role of 'attachment'.

Attachment Theory

Attachment theory describes and predicts the dynamic effects of long-term relationships between humans. Most especially the theory deals with the relationship between the 'primary caregiver' and child from birth through childhood. The theory provides a means of understanding the way that we form strong emotional bonds with particular others and the distress that may ensue when these bonds are disrupted.

In developing the theory of attachment, Bowlby (1977a, 1977b) was heavily influenced by two quite disparate sets of observations: first, the work of clinicians who, in the 1930s and 1940s, had observed the consequences for children of institutionalisation and disruption of stable parenting; second, the ethological studies of Konrad Lorenz (Ainsworth and Bowlby, 1991; Lorenz, 2002). Lorenz had noticed the instinctual behaviour, imprinting, that emerged spontaneously in many animal species between mother and offspring. Counter to prevailing theory, this appeared unrelated to feeding (Lorenz, 2002).

Although acknowledging inheritance from psychoanalytic and behavioural theories, Bowlby (1977a) was at pains to differentiate the instinctual nature of the attachment bond from the drives and reinforcements postulated by those other theories. Attachment behaviour was conceived as

> … any form of behaviour that results in a person attaining or retaining proximity to some other differentiated individual, who is usually conceived as stronger/wiser. While especially evident during early childhood, attachment theory is held to characterise human beings from the cradle to the grave. (Bowlby, 1977a: 203)

However, in combining ideas from psychoanalytic, cognitive, biological and ethological approaches, Bowlby provided a clearly delineated conceptual framework (Bowlby, 1977a) for testable hypotheses in relation to children's development and mental health. This has led to many detailed studies confirming significant relationships between attachment and, for instance, the development of children's behaviour (Fearon et al., 2010), or later anxiety disorders (Esbjørn et al., 2012). However, it is important, as Thompson (2008) cautioned, to avoid taking a view that 'attachment' can account for all aspects of later development. It is clear, as Fonagy and Target (2002: 328) stated:

> Attachment relationships are formative because they facilitate the development of the brain's major self-regulatory mechanisms, which ... allow the individual to perform effectively in society [but] they offer no guarantee the individual will achieve this, and they can place powerful limits on the individual's chances of coping with major adversity.

We also note a high probability that adverse circumstances, such as poor socioeconomic conditions, may prove the foundation for a circularity of perpetuating, if not deteriorating, patterns of poor attachment and adult mental health problems (Stansfeld et al., 2008). It is thus important to understand how patterns of attachment are established and what may be done to enhance these proactively, or at least therapeutically.

The infant's attachment bond starts to form at birth (Zeanah et al., 2011), if not earlier (Rackett and Holmes, 2010; Walsh, 2010). The young child develops selective attachments with a small number of adults who are most closely involved in her care (Rutter, 1995). The key caregivers have a critical, responsive, role throughout the first year to 18 months of the child's life (Fonagy and Target, 2002; Thompson, 2000). As we noted above, this is effected through the ongoing processes of contingent and synchronous dialogue between caregiver and baby (Bowlby, 1977a; Fonagy and Target, 2002; Newson and Newson, 1975). The provision of early and sensitive care by key caregivers is one factor in supporting secure attachment (that serves to control distress and facilitate the development of neural self-regulatory mechanisms). This helps provide foundations in adulthood of secure relationships and social behaviour (Crespi, 2011; Fonagy and Target, 2002; Johnson et al., 2010), though this has been disputed by Rutter et al. (2009). However, it is also evident that levels of caregiver affect are in a reciprocal relationship with children's own emotional security (Murray et al., 1999). In less fortunate circumstances, if the crucial caregiver role is not fulfilled, the child may not develop a sense of security and confidence in exploration and socialisation. There is evidence to indicate that inconsistent care in infancy may be predictive of certain outcomes in adulthood. It has been suggested that resultant attachment styles can be conceptualised on two dimensions: attachment-related anxiety and avoidance (Mikulincer et al., 2013). The first relates to doubts about self-worth and that others will not provide support when needed; attachment-related avoidance, in contrast, relates to distrust of others' motives and goodwill, causing behavioural and emotional detachment. Those who are either highly anxious or avoidant – or both – may 'suffer from attachment insecurities, self-related worries, and distrust of others' goodwill and responsiveness in times of need' (Mikulincer et al., 2013: 607). However, according to Bowlby (2005), attachment behaviours, such as seeking support, may be evident throughout life (see also Ainsworth, 1989). Bowlby (2005) also maintained it is possible to experience relationships later in life that provide a sense of secure attachment. (As we discuss below, this may be seen as an integral component of therapeutic relationships.) There is also some encouraging evidence that intervention in schools and early years settings may help counteract initially unfavourable factors (Kennedy et al., 2010; MacKay et al., 2010; Roggman et al., 2009).

Despite the importance of attachment to the development of the young child it is important to emphasise, however, that attachment does not provide a comprehensive explanation for all social relationships and behaviour, and that other factors need to be considered (Rutter et al., 2009).

Discussion and Synthesis: The Implications for Counselling

As we have shown, children's development may be conceptualised and studied within a range of paradigms. We now bring these ideas together to provide a possible foundation for professional work with parents and their children.

It is evident that children's development and long-term well-being are the product of genetic, biological and environmental (including parental) factors. Therapeutic involvement is unlikely to be sought before a child is born. It is more likely to revolve around the relationship formed with parents and the relationship they have with their children. Within that nexus, the first and most crucial relationship is that between caregiver and infant. The security of well-formed attachment, and the implicit contingent regulation of emotions and exploratory play that should be found, forms the basis for the child's social, cognitive and communicational development (Meins and Russell, 1997; Thompson, 2000; Trevarthen and Aitken, 2001). It is within the unconscious, instinctual dialogue between caregiver and baby that begins at birth and develops and changes over time that the infant develops. This relationship provides a safe environment in which the infant can develop the confidence to explore, and the caregiver can develop the confidence to provide care and support. In turn, that reciprocal, attuned, relationship forms the basis of further development from which emerges the child's increasing physical and oral communication (Bowlby, 1977a, 2005; Vygotsky, 1962). Gradually and contingently, the child's oral utterances and physical gestures are guided, reinforced and commented on by the caregiver (Keen, 2011; Wood et al., 1976).

Just as the child has to explore to develop and the primary caregiver has to be 'available and responsive as and when wanted, [and be able] to intervene judiciously should the child or older person who is being cared for be heading for trouble' (Bowlby, 1977a: 204), so does the therapist need to provide attuned interaction with her client (Bowlby, 2005: 159; Mallinckrodt, 2010; Mikulincer et al., 2013). As Bowlby (2005: 172) also maintained, 'The therapist strives to be reliable, attentive, empathic and sympathetically responsive to his patient's exploration, and also to encourage his patient to explore the world of his thoughts, feelings and actions'. These are qualities to be found in the counselling relationship, however brief.

It is also worth considering the relationships children have with significant others such as grandparents and siblings, as these may offer support through periods of transition or trauma (Lussier et al., 2002). Furthermore, Dunn (2004) summarised evidence that relationships with peers can provide support through transition. Dunn considered that relationships with parents can affect peer relationships but importantly also demonstrated that relationships with peers can influence a child's relationship with her parents. It is therefore important to assess the quality of the child's relational network in considering any form of intervention. There is evidence that some difficulties require work to be conducted with the child or young person and their family (Fonagy et al., 2002).

Therapeutic endeavours are not without risk. For example, some who seek counselling will also be seeking security and attachment. If, as may happen, the client experiences yet another failure to form a secure attachment (perhaps because the therapeutic sessions are prematurely curtailed), she may place even less trust in any other relationship – personal or therapeutic. This may be particularly problematic in direct therapeutic work with children and young people (Allen, 2011). For children who show clear signs of insecure or disordered attachment it is, therefore, considered more appropriate to work with the primary carer first, before then working with the carer and young person together (Allen, 2011).

Conclusion

In this chapter we have given an overview of current notions about children's development and the development of attachment bonds. In our synthesis of these ideas we have considered what these ideas might imply for those, such as school counsellors, who engage in therapeutic work with children and young people.

The findings from research are informative. In relation to the formation of attachment bonds, most salient is the evidence from developmental psychology that has given insight into the importance of contingency, availability, synchrony and dialogue. In the absence of at least some of these features in an infant's development, attachment bonds may be impaired. Likewise, the presence of parental warmth, care and support that enable the child to explore and learn is critical for development.

Therefore, rather than predicate the purpose of this chapter as a foundation for therapeutic intervention, it would be better, we think, to be pre-emptive. Thus, as Fonagy and Target (2002: 328) have said:

> The target for early intervention becomes clear: no child should be deprived, through lack of adequate support in his earliest relationships, of the opportunity to develop his interpersonal, interpretative capacity to a level that will enable him to tackle the adversities that life is likely to bring him.

However, in the same vein we can conclude that understanding that children and young people's development is facilitated by appropriate care and attachments is important for those responsible for the provision of help for anyone whose early life was adversely affected.

Case Study   Lise

Lise's mother, Sara, 23, is a single parent. Lise is six and her only child. It seems Sara never speaks about Lise's father. In school Lise is said to be quiet and withdrawn. Her class teacher is concerned because she appears rather isolated from her peers and sometimes wets herself. Her attainments in school are said to be well below the average of her class. Her drawings of people, for instance, are very simple; her understanding and use of language is said to be more like a much younger child.

Summary

In this chapter we examined:

- Current notions on children and young people's development
- Development of attachment bonds and primary carers
- A synthesis of the above ideas and how they are relevant to counsellors
- Findings from research

Reflective Questions

1. In your work do you notice children or young people forming an 'attachment' with you? If so, what do you notice and how do you respond?
2. In considering work with children or young people, how important is it for you to also explore the relationship their parents or carers might have with you?
3. Which of the theories about children's cognitive development have greatest resonance for you in your practice? What do you see as the theory's strengths and how do you see the theory at play in your work?
4. What parental behaviours might you seek to encourage and how?
5. What do you find most helpful when engaging in work with adolescents and how might the ideas in this chapter influence your future practice?

There are no specific answers to the questions – you are asked to reflect and use your own experiences.

Learning Activities

Read the case study: Lise. The school would like your help.

1. What hypotheses do you already have?

   o What is the basis of these?
   o In these, can you differentiate between the effects of factors that might relate to 'development' and those that might relate to 'attachment bonds' and, if so, how?

2. What other information would you like to have?

   o How would that affect your hypothesising?

3. In relation to the case details (above), who else would you like to meet, and why?
4. What rationale can you provide for what you might do next?

Further Reading

Bowlby, J. (2005) *A Secure Base: Clinical Applications of Attachment Theory*. London: Routledge.
Sameroff, A. (2009) *The Transactional Model of Development: How Children and Contexts Shape Each Other*. Washington, DC: American Psychological Association. pp. 3–21.
Vygotsky, L.S. (1962) *Thought and Language*. Cambridge, MA: MIT Press.
Wood, D. (1998) *How Children Think and Learn*. 2nd edn. Oxford: Blackwell.

Online Resources

The MindEd e-learning resource CM 5: Developmental Themes in Children and Young People could be useful, especially: CM 5.1 – Becoming Independent; CM 5.2 – Developing Relationships; CM 5.3 – Developing Sexuality.
Counselling MindEd: http://counsellingminded.com.

Child and Young Person-Centred Approach

Graham Bright

This chapter includes:

- The origins and key tenets of the person-centred approach (PCA)
- Rogers' core conditions
- Person-centred practice with children and young people

History and Background

The person-centred approach (PCA) to therapy is grounded in Carl Rogers' formative work with children and young people; it seems right, therefore, as a means of introduction to this chapter, to recover some of that history here. Carl Rogers (1902–87) was born near Chicago. His family moved to live and work on a farm when he was in high school. Rogers was by all accounts a studious but shy boy who did not have many friends outside the family circle. Growing up, he had a keen interest in science, and his formative years were significantly influenced by his family's Christian beliefs. Rogers studied agriculture at college for two years before briefly exploring a vocation to Christian ministry. During this period he attended the International World Student Federation Conference in Beijing, which he described as 'a most important experience for me' (Kirschenbaum and Henderson, 1989: 9). Here Rogers observed a good deal of disagreement and even animosity amongst delegates, which led him to conclude that pluralistic divergence was phenomenologically inevitable. As a result, he began to question some of the more affixed doctrine that he had grown up with (Barrett-Lennard, 2013). The result – to his parents' despair – was that the newly-married Rogers chose to attend a highly liberal seminary, where he was exposed to heuristic forms of inquiry which enabled Rogers and his fellow students to reach their own very personal conclusions regarding matters of faith and experience.

These student-led seminars helped Rogers to clarify his own beliefs; as a result, he felt it incongruous to continue pursuit of the ministry to which he could no longer profess. It was at this time that Rogers felt drawn to the field of child guidance, an arena which at that time was saturated by Freudian thinking. He was appointed to a team of three psychologists working with the Society for the Prevention of Cruelty to Children in Rochester, New York. Rogers recounted his time at Rochester in the psychoanalytical diagnosis and treatment of young people as being a period of deep learning, yet one which left him re-evaluating the prescriptive nature of psychoanalytical diagnostic formation and treatment. One particular incident with a mother of a challenging young boy proved to be seminal. Rogers recalled trying (without success) to offer psychoanalytical interpretation regarding the underlying nature of the family's symptomatic behaviours; later, however, the mother began to detail her own distress regarding her marriage. Rogers cited this incident as:

> one of a number which helped me to experience the fact – only fully realized later – that it is the *client* who knows what hurts, what directions to go, what problems are crucial, what experiences have been deeply buried. It began to occur to me that unless I had a need to demonstrate my own cleverness and learning, I would do better to rely upon the client for the direction of movement in the process. (Kirschenbaum and Henderson, 1989: 13; emphasis in original)

Rogers' first book, *The Clinical Treatment of the Problem Child*, was published in 1939 and viewed as a welcome contribution to an emergent field. In it kernels of what we have come to understand today as the PCA can be seen. Relational qualities between practitioner and 'patient' are described and accentuated, most notably that of non-judgemental acceptance. Here too we see the emergence of Rogers' ideas on the 'actualising tendency'. Barrett-Lennard (2013: 35) notes that 'by the time his first book was completed, what was to become non-directive client-centred therapy was germinating strongly in the thought and practice of its founder'.

Theoretical Underpinning

Over the ensuing years, Rogers refined his theory, arguing that the quality of relationship between therapist and client was central to facilitative growth and change.

In Rogers' view it is unnecessary to engage in therapeutic formulation drawn from the client's past; rather, he emphasised the import of empathically experiencing *with* the client the subjective, transcendent essence of their here-and-now reality as it is fluidly experienced. In this way, Rogers' work related to Husserl and Heidegger's ideas of phenomenological construction (Cooper and Bohart, 2013) and posited a distinct shift from directive forms of therapy which draw upon therapist interpretation and expertise towards non-directive, facilitative work in which the client – motivated by their actualising tendency – instinctively 'understands' at different levels of their being what is needed for their own healing and growth (Rogers, 1959). Here the therapist seeks to enter and understand the Other's subjective reality as they experience it, and to offer particular conditions which enable the fluidity of the Other's experience of being and becoming as determined by their congruent response to what is happening within their field of reality (or environment) to be realised. What Rogers emphasised, therefore, is a 'way of being' with another which enables that Other to intrinsically nurture their own organismic processes without recourse to technicised therapeutic interventions which draw upon more prescribed theoretical formulations (Merry, 2008; Rogers, 1951). The PCA has oft been criticised for a lack of theoretical rigour and therapeutic wizardry associated with other psychotherapeutic approaches; yet proponents would argue that it is theoretically rich and necessitates advanced levels of practitioner discipline, integration and growth – it requires, perhaps more than any other approach, that therapists bring and use their whole being to assist the client on their therapeutic odyssey (Mearns and Thorne, 2013).

Rogers' work itself was based on certain theoretical underpinnings which he described throughout his career as particular hypotheses. This ongoing experiential work led Rogers to develop and iterate his own theory of the person. Central to his postulation was that each human being has an 'actualising tendency', which Gillon (2007: 27) describes as:

> an inherent, biological tendency towards growth and development. This tendency is located at the level of the organism as a whole and is seen as the single, basic motivational force driving each human being toward the fulfilment of their unique potential.

The Rogerian vision of the person is positive and hopeful. It views with optimism the possibilities of human potential (Reeves, 2013), observing the self as changing and dynamic, and as responsive to different stimulae within its environment. This fluidity, however, is underpinned by particular characteristics which might be viewed as relatively consistent at given moments of time and more generally across the lifecourse (Merry, 2008). For the infant, there is no experiential division between what they perceive as internal and external to the self (Cooper et al., 2013). As they grow, babies become aware through reflective interactions with others of their separateness, resulting in experiential differentiation. Infants begin to recognise the 'I' or 'me' or 'self' as being separate from others, from which a concept of the self begins to emerge (Gillon, 2007). The self requires two principal needs to be met in order to develop higher actualised outcomes. We can, according to Merry (2008), consider these as needing positive regard from self (internal regard) and others (external regard). External regard tends to manifest itself as we grow and develop through our need of acceptance, praise and recognition from those close to us, including parents, other caregivers, and those whom we admire in some way. At the same time, each individual needs to develop trust in their own intrinsic organismic processes in order that a diversity of needs are met in nourishing the potential of the actualising tendency, which Gillon (2007: 28) describes as 'an on-going, biologically-driven valuing process which allows each of us to assess experiences that are enhancing to, or maintaining for, our organismic needs and potentialities'. Such is our need, however, for others' approval that over time we adapt our intuitive feelings and behaviours and conform to meet others' expectations to the detriment of our organismic needs and processes. We become subtly, and sometimes not so subtly, subjected to and imprisoned by particular messages which become imbibed deep within us: messages of conditionality – 'I will accept you if you conceal this or "change" that ... I will love you if ... I like this about you, but not that ... If you want my approval, then don't do the other ...'. The result, as Mearns and Thorne note, is that people:

> struggle to keep their heads above water by trying to do and be those things which they know will elicit approval while scrupulously avoiding or suppressing those thoughts, feelings and activities that they sense will bring adverse judgement. ... They are the victims of *conditions of worth* which others have imposed on them, but so great is their need for positive approval that they accept this straightjacket rather than risk rejection by trespassing against the conditions set for their acceptability. (2013: 9; emphasis in original)

Such is the assault on the person's core and the onslaught against their very being that their humanity is threatened; no longer able to trust their own inner voice, they resort to consulting external loci of evaluation and living by others' ideas, values and practices. Yet, however fragile, the actualising tendency retains the potential of hope and healing.

Self and Self-Concept

For Rogers (1959), the self was the totality of human experience as it is subjectively understood by each individual from their own unique phenomenological worldview. An individual builds their self-concept as a result of their interactions with their world and with others in that world; the extent to which the self-concept is constructive is determined by the positive regard the individual receives from others when engaging in behaviours that are aligned with their organismic core. The individual who introjects others' wishes and values into their self-concept in order to maintain their love and affection risks such osmoses being at odds with his own organismic valuing process. The child who draws conditionality into himself increasingly locates his loci of evaluation externally, feeling decreasingly able to trust his own inner voice (Prever, 2010), thereby generating a corrosive effect on the self-concept. The result is an individual who feels progressively detached from his own organismic reality and who increasingly internalises a negative self-concept which tends to perpetuate and reinforce 'negative' behaviour and emotional-belief patterns (Mearns and Thorne, 2013). The experiential disorientation which results in the dissonant incongruence between a self-concept which has been infiltrated by a drip-feed of conditionality and the individual's resilient capacity to remain wired to their organismic potential is tangible. It is the work of the person-centred therapist to permit and enable the client to reconcile himself to that potential.

Nowhere, perhaps, are these processes more acutely noticeable than in the formative experiences of the young. They are dependent on others for their care, less able to filter out negative personal messages concerning them individually from significant adults and peers, and they are often tyrannised as groups by insidious attacks from politicians, the media and society at large. Such messages are subtle, yet strong and clear.

The Core Conditions

In 1957 Rogers published a seminal paper which famously declared that there are six 'necessary and sufficient' conditions required for therapeutic change:

1. Two persons are in *psychological contact*.
2. The first, whom we shall term the client, is in a state of *incongruence*, being vulnerable or anxious.
3. The second person, whom we shall term the therapist, is *congruent* or *integrated* in the relationship.
4. The therapist experiences *unconditional positive regard* for the client.
5. The therapist experiences an *empathic understanding* of the client's internal frame of reference and endeavours to communicate this experience to the client.
6. The communication to the client of the therapist's empathic understanding and unconditional positive regard is to a minimal degree achieved.

Conditions 3, 4 and 5 later became known as the 'core conditions' and are viewed by many therapists across modalities as the *foundation* for therapeutic work. The PCA hypothesises, however, that it is *solely* these qualities within the therapeutic relationship that matter in catalysing the client's inner resources. By inference, how the therapist embodies the core conditions is of deepest concern; rather than being something that is 'switched on' when entering the therapy room, such embodment becomes a way of life. This demands that the therapist takes seriously her commitment to personal development, attunement and attending to self in supervision in order that she can fully 'be' with the client.

Whilst for the sake of discussion it is necessary to consider the core conditions separately, the nature of their seamless, triune integration cannot be ignored (see Figure 2.1). Empathy, for example, cannot be understood or 'practised' on its own without reference to its dynamic interrelationship with congruence and unconditional positive regard (UPR). Together, they offer a potent way of being with oneself and with others.

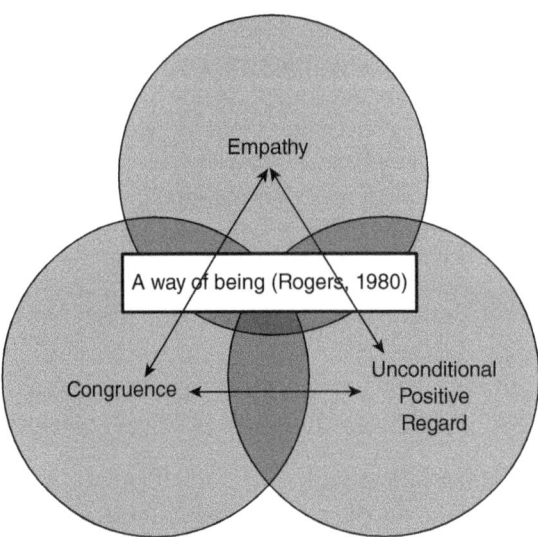

Figure 2.1   A way of being (Rogers, 1980).

Congruence

The task of person-centred therapy is to nurture congruence in the client, to permit him to reconnect with the congruent experiencing of his organismic self and to re-enable trust in his internal locus of evaluation. Therapy seeks to minimise the distorted gap between the client's idealised self-concept and their real self. Here, the therapist's congruence becomes a counterpoint to the client's incongruence, a mirror held up to the client that indicates not only its possibility but its desirability also. Congruence builds trust in the therapeutic relationship (Mearns and Thorne, 2013); it expresses something of the wholeness of the person, the consistency or genuineness that exists between outward expression and inward experiencing – a gestalt, if you will. Congruence is therefore concerned with being oneself in the moment and accurately and appropriately representing the significance of that to and for the benefit of the client. The therapist who is able to be in touch with herself at some deep level, and to be accepting of that self, has a greater capacity to be attuned to the Other's process. There is no pretence; the therapist is a person willing to accompany the client on their journey, not an expert in the client's life. This message when 'conveyed' through the therapist's way of being moves the client from a reliance on external loci to re-building trust in their own inner experiential voice. Congruence therefore requires the therapist to nurture high levels of reflexive self-awareness through personal development and supervision. Mearns and Thorne (2013: 115ff) contend that whilst the therapist must remain intuitively aware of what is happening within her, the expression of congruent awareness to the client must be based upon what is appropriate, relevant and persistent. This is not to deny what is within the therapist's stream of consciousness, thereby unleashing incongruence; rather, it is beholden on the therapist to judiciously decide what might be important to explore in her own personal development or supervision and what should be shared with the client as a means of fostering benefit and realness in the therapeutic relationship.

Children and young people require their relationship with their counsellor to be trustworthy, in order that they can feel safe to explore the things they need to; secure, in order that they can go to those often difficult, painful and challenging places with the surety that they will be accompanied by someone real who can anchor their own quest for reality. Congruence fosters trust. Young clients are adept at recognising those playing a therapeutic role which is at odds with the rest of their character (Geldard and Geldard, 2010; Geldard et al., 2013); such insincerity dissipates therapeutic value and further undermines the client's capacity for self-trust. Congruence is therefore central to therapeutic work with children and young people.

Unconditional Positive Regard

Unconditional positive regard (UPR) is founded in a deep-seated regard for others' fundamental humanity. Rogers frequently referred to UPR as 'prizing' the client. UPR is the persistent attitude of *actively* accepting and valuing the totality of each client's unique being and becoming, which, although it may be challenged, is not swerved by the client's attitude or behaviour. UPR therefore goes beyond the conditional nature of 'liking' to embrace a more essential attitude that deeply and warmly accepts the client for who he is (Mearns and Thorne, 2013). Setting the client free of conditionality is central to the process of person-centred therapy. Indeed, for Bozarth (2013: 183), UPR is the 'curative variable' in the therapy. The counsellor therefore must nurture acceptance of the client's process wherever that may take them. For the therapist, embodying UPR as part of her way of being is a challenge. She needs to be congruently aware of her true feelings regarding her clients; where persistent attitudinal conditionality exists, she must examine this with the support of her clinical supervisor.

As we noted earlier in this chapter, young people in particular are one of the most judged groups in western societies. Developmentally they are locating through experience their own values, beliefs, ideas and practices through which they construct both their sense of self and their place in the world (Corsaro, 2011). At times, however, children and young people's values and behaviours can appear to be at odds with normative adult conventions; the result is that many experience conditionality in a range of domains. In order for therapy to be an effective counter-ballast which enables the dissolution of conditionality and its symptoms, those working with young clients must foster and effectively convey UPR if they are to be successful in enabling their clients' therapeutic progress (Geldard and Geldard, 2010).

Empathy

One of the key facets of the person-centred therapeutic relationship is empathy. The counsellor's ability to lay down (without disconnecting from) her own phenomenological reality and to enter the unique perceptual world of her client, to move around in that world and to feel at home in the ebb and flow of the client's lived experiencing of it is arguably one of the most potent therapeutic capacities (Freire, 2013; Prever, 2010; Smyth, 2013). Empathic expression has often been caricatured as the therapist repeating the essence of what the client has just said. Whilst empathic understanding must be conveyed in order to be of value to the client and to meet the requirements of Rogers' sixth condition, it is so much more. It is perceiving with accuracy the subtlety of the client's feelings and meanings in the totality of their emotional, spiritual, psychological and physical being. It is conveying that understanding with tentative sensitivity to the client in a way that enables them to absorb that their experiences and meanings have been deeply understood and accepted by another, thereby releasing the client to do the same on their journey towards a congruent integration of their totality. Empathy strengthens the therapeutic alliance and enables that which is on the edge of awareness to be made known. Empathy enables the conscientisation of therapeutic material: sometimes this is as a result of 'apparently sudden light bulb moments of realisation, and sometimes through the slow burning of unconscious materials and meanings which gradually slot into place in a way that gives crystallised panoramic understanding' (Bright and Harrison, 2013: 42). Empathic understanding speaks with lucidity over the confused din of incongruence. Whilst conditions of worth lead to detachment and isolation from the self and others, empathy's gift is to enable clarity in the client's configured selves (Mearns and Thorne, 2013) and to offer connection to another who both deeply understands and accepts the client in their being and becoming. Empathy rehumanises the client; for Rogers (1986: 129, as cited by Freire, 2013: 167), it 'releases [and] confirms, it even brings the most frightened client into the human race'.

The challenge to the therapist of continually suspending her own perceptual reality in order to live within each client's internal frame of reference 'as if' it were her own is unmistakable. Such a 'task' requires time, energy, discipline, intuition, deep listening, compassion, highly developed awareness and a willingness to take risks. It requires a continual attunement to each client's 'experiences in the here-and-now' (ibid.: 168) in which the therapist must learn to flow with the client's narrative, meaning and emotions whilst remaining attentive to the changing landscape of the client's inner world.

Rogers' Seven Stages of Process

Rogers (1961: 125ff), as summarised by Casemore (2006: 11–12 in Table 2.1), offered his view of how clients tend to process through therapy. Not all clients enter therapy at stage one and leave at stage seven; hence the seven stages of process should be regarded as a direction of travel in therapy rather than a matter of rigid linearity. However, it can be used as a reference point to consider where a client might be and might be heading in the therapeutic process; where appropriate, it might even be used with clients to discuss how they feel therapy is progressing and how they might like it to proceed.

Table 2.1 Rogers' seven stages of process.

Stage	Description
1	The client is very defensive, and extremely resistant to change.
2	The client becomes slightly less rigid, and will talk about external events or other people.
3	The client talks about him/herself, but as an object, and avoids discussion of present events.
4	The client begins to talk about deep feelings and develops a relationship with the counsellor.
5	The client can express present emotions, and is beginning to rely more on his/her own decision-making abilities and increasingly accepts more responsibility for his/her actions.
6	The client shows rapid growth towards congruence, and begins to develop unconditional positive regard for others. This stage signals the end of the need for formal therapy.
7	The client is a fully functioning, self-actualising individual who is empathic and shows unconditional positive regard for others. This individual can relate their previous therapy to present-day real-life situations.

Expressing Person-Centredness

The chapter to this point has sought to emphasise person-centred counselling's distinctiveness as a therapeutic way of being. However, to be effective, not only must the essential nature of the therapeutic relationship be experienced, but the embodied qualities of the therapist must also be expressed if therapeutic change is to occur (Rogers, 1957). Such ideas are, however, elusive. Person-centred therapists need to 'practise' a way of being which is congruent to them without recourse to mechanistic forms of response which might be perceived as 'wooden' and ultimately counter-intuitive. Person-centred practice is fundamentally about being able to capture the essence of the client's experience as it is lived in the moment; to congruently and unconditionally accept the client in their individual process of being and becoming. Deep listening to narrative and meaning is required in order that the therapist can 'lock into' the client's internal frame of reference; however, this understanding must also be shared with the client to facilitate their process. Perhaps the key *skill* associated with this way of being is reflection. Reid and Westergaard (2011: 48) describe reflection as 'the counsellor "holding a mirror" to their client by ensuring that responses are appropriate and that they reflect accurately the words and feelings that the young person is expressing'. Thus, the counsellor reveals their understanding of the essence of the client's lived experience. Person-centred therapists who are able to synchronise their being with the client's experience are not, however, limited to words. For some, empathic understanding is 'received' through mental pictures or felt bodily sensations which, when congruently and sensitively conveyed, can facilitate powerful therapeutic movement.

Working in a Person-Centred Way with Children and Young People

Accompanying the client on *their* particular journey of growth and change is, perhaps, most accentuated in person-centred practice with children and young people who by the maturational nature of lifecourse experiences are *very* much in the process of developmental change. Geldard and Geldard (2010) and Geldard et al. (2013) contend that therapists of all hues are most effective in practice if they are able to empathically get in touch with their own inner child or adolescent. This, they argue, enables the therapist to understand the child or young person's phenomenological experience more vividly.

Person-centred practice seeks to put the client at the centre of practice. Such an assertion means that those working with children and young people must appreciate the particular needs of these age groups, to become attuned to the appropriateness of language and expression. It has often been said that 'play is the language of the child', and whilst more significant coverage of this claim is offered in Chapter 7, it seems right to offer some discussion here. Döring (2008: 41) argues that 'Play is spontaneous, self-initiated learning; it enables a child to acquire new abilities, problem-solving strategies and skills for coping with emotional conflicts'. Person-centred practice provides space for being and exploring; for children and young people these processes take on a variety of expressions. Behr et al. (2013) note the distinct processes in practice with children, contending that whilst adults are able to verbalise and reflect on their experiences, children symbolise their inner world via creative media like play, art, puppetry, stories, sand-play, dressing up and music (the term 'play' will be used hereafter as shorthand for all these creative media). Perhaps it is Rogers' student and colleague Virginia Axline (1989 [1969]: 69–70) who is best known for developing eight key principles for person-centred play-therapy, positing that person-centred play therapists must become attuned to the child's process; offering empathic reflection of the child's symbolisation, rather than psychodynamically-founded interpretation of the child's play (see Box 2.1). The language of play privileges and beckons the therapist to enter the child's world; it must therefore be honoured. Play must be treated with the same dignity that is afforded to adult clients' verbalisations. Children will only trust the counsellor and advance in the therapeutic process when they are joined in play and experience the being of the core conditions through the therapeutic interactions which they initiate. The therapist needs, therefore, to follow the child's lead, to be moulded by what the child does. So, when a child sits on the floor, perhaps the counsellor should to do the same. Such practice also begins to mitigate inherent power differentials that can exist between client and counsellor; it emphasises the value the counsellor has for the child and fosters equality in the relationship (Smyth, 2013).

Box 2.1

James is busy lying on the floor, drawing a picture. The therapist lies next to him, supporting his chin in his hands.

Therapist:	'It looks like you are drawing a playground with a swing, a roundabout and a climbing frame?'
James:	'Uh-huh.'
Therapist:	'The playground looks as if it's in a park?'
James:	'Yes.'
Therapist:	'There's a boy playing in the park?'
James:	'That's me.'
Therapist:	'You've drawn a bench?'
James:	No reply (silently concentrating)
Therapist:	'It looks as if you are sitting on the bench on your own?'
James (smiling reflectively):	'Yes, I like to be alone. I like the peace.'

(Continued)

> (Continued)
>
> Therapist: 'Peace?'
>
> James: 'Yeah, I never get it at home – mum and dad are always arguing and then I have to share a room with two of my brothers …'

Adolescence is a time of profound emotional, social, physical, sexual, psychological, familial and educational change (Coleman, 2010). During this period, the process of being and becoming is perhaps highlighted more than any other. Person-centred work affords young people the space to be, to individuate, to clarify perspectives, to gain new insight and to manage relational boundaries between self and others (Bright, 2013). Working with young people during this period of their lives can be both challenging and richly rewarding as together counsellor and client observe the person who begins to emerge from the chrysalis. During this phase, young people often change their communication preferences, becoming increasingly likely to talk rather than use creative media. Adolescent communication is affected by a range of factors including culture, environment, age-related development and even time of day. Many young people feel a distrust of adults, who they perceive don't understand them (Hawkins, 2008); counsellors working with adolescents therefore must learn to empathically enter each client's phenomenological and linguistic reality and to convey their understanding of the client's internal frame of reference by paralleling the young person's communication processes (Geldard and Geldard, 2010). Such practice fosters relational security between client and therapist and builds the young person's sense of inter-connectedness (Smyth, 2013).

Short-Term Work

As we have noted, the PCA is concerned with placing the client at the heart of practice. It expresses empowerment, democracy and the promotion of client autonomy as foundational principles. Merry (2008: 12) contends that the PCA above all others affirms an 'enduring commitment to encounter clients in a direct, person-to-person manner without providing a set of rules … that control the process'. Indeed, Smyth (2013: 163) argues that time-limited work in person-centred practice is 'anathema'. Externally imposed time constraints potentially limit the client's capacity to engage fully in the therapeutic process, and may result in 'rushing' the client towards a premature ending, thereby undermining hard-won therapeutic gains. The PCA holds that the decision to end therapy should be the client's in *conjunction* with the therapist. Externally imposed time restrictions can place counsellors under significant pressure to direct clients towards conclusions before they are ready, resulting in practice that may be unethi-cal. The PCA therefore finds itself increasingly at odds with the assimilated wisdom of other approaches and funders' preferences for time-limited work. Pragmatically, Mearns and Thorne (2013) suggest that counselling agencies might seek to negotiate an average of, say, six sessions per client; doing so, they argue, allows practitioners to manage caseloads more effectively whilst maintaining the integrity of the approach. In practice, 'surplus' sessions from one client can then be allocated to others.

Case Study   Sarah

Sixteen-year-old 'Sarah' was referred to me for counselling by 'Des', her Connexions Adviser. She had found school educationally disengaging and socially difficult. Sarah was also coming to terms with the recent break-up of her parents' relationship. Living with her dad, she had hardly left the house since leaving school three months previously. Sarah didn't want to engage with friends, and despite her love of drama felt una-ble be part of any group activity.

I saw Sarah for six sessions. During the first two, she was unable to look at me and spoke very little. I was aware, however, of a very damaging self-concept. As the sessions progressed, I began to ques-tion what help I (as a trainee counsellor) could be to a client who would barely speak and offered very little eye contact. I wondered whether I should integrate other approaches into my work with this client. In truth, I found the experience of working with Sarah quite disarming. In exploring this with my supervisor, I became aware of *my need* to rescue my client, of *my need* for my client to 'improve' in order to validate *me*. I was encouraged to trust the client's process, to be with her as she was, to listen empathically to her in her speaking and in her silence. I had come to realise that my expectations of Sarah's processes were counter-therapeutic, and were compounding the conditions of worth that she had experienced. To my amazement, Sarah continued to come willingly each week, slowly saying more about her experiencing and owning more of her own story. Sarah allowed me to listen beyond words, to experience empathy in the silence.

Weeks later Des called me to say that Sarah was a 'different person'. She was volunteering at a local youth project, involved in a drama group and enrolling on a training course. Des asked Sarah what had made the difference. 'Counselling', she replied. 'Graham just allowed me to be there.'

I learned to trust the client's process!

Research

The person-centred world appears engaged in some considerable debate concerning its involvement in particular forms of evidenced-based research, which some argue are counter-intuitive to its humanistic-phenomenological axiology. Others, meanwhile, contend that Rogers himself was an empiricist who engaged in rigorous forms of research which were concerned with both process and outcomes in therapy. Whilst there have been recent moves to produce efficacy studies via randomised controlled trials and meta-analyses on wider population studies, little has yet been specifically developed regarding the efficacy of the person-centred approach with children and young people. This picture, however, is slowly changing, thanks to the pathbreaking work of Professor Mick Cooper and colleagues who are generating interesting evidence bases regarding the efficacy of humanistically-based therapies in secondary schools (see Cooper, 2009a, 2013; Cooper et al., 2010, 2013; McArthur et al., 2013).

Summary

This chapter has:

- Outlined the central ideas of the person-centred approach
- Considered the Rogerian postulation that particular qualities expressed within the counselling relationship are the singular requirement for therapeutic change and growth
- Explored the challenge of these relational qualities as a 'way of being' for the counsellor in accompanying the client in their journey of being and becoming
- Offered application of these principles to therapeutic practice with children and young people with particular reference to Axline's ideas on creativity and play as symbolisation of the child's inner world

Reflective Questions

1. Rogers contended that the six conditions that he outlined in his 1957 paper were 'necessary and sufficient' for therapeutic change. What is your view of his assertion?
2. How effective are you in offering the core conditions to clients? What might your clients say? What might be different?
3. The person-centred approach is concerned with therapist embodiment of a way of being. What are the particular challenges of this idea within your own personal development and professional practice?
4. Rogers (1961) proposed his seven stages of process. Map the process of a client you have been working with. What might be learned here?

There are no specific answers to the questions – you are asked to reflect and use your own experiences.

Learning Activities

Theory suggests that psychological distress occurs when we adapt our being and behaviour to meet others' demands, values and expectations. This generates disconnects between our organismic or core self and our self-concept. This, as I have argued, is particularly pertinent in work with children and young people.

Answer the following for yourself, then discuss appropriately with others (a peer, personal therapist or supervisor perhaps).

1. What conditions of worth or introjected values can you identify as having influenced your own way of being?
2. Thematically, what conditions of worth might you identify as salient for clients with whom you have worked? Where do these originate?

The PCA is a 'way of being' with self and others.

Explore with another:

3. How this challenges you, personally and professionally.
4. How accessible is your own inner child/adolescent?

Further Reading

Cooper, M., O'Hara, M., Schmid, P.F and Bohart, A.C. (eds) (2013) *The Handbook of Person-Centred Psychotherapy and Counselling.* Basingstoke: Palgrave Macmillan.
This excellent and recently revised compendium on the person-centred approach examines theoretical concepts, underpinning values and contemporary debates and practices.

Mearns, D. and Thorne, B. with McLeod, J. (2013) *Person-Centred Counselling in Action.* 4th edn. London: SAGE.
This classic text, now in its fourth edition, from these doyens of the approach is known as 'the Bible'.

Merry, T. (2008) *Learning and Being in Person-Centred Counselling,* 2nd edn. Ross-on-Wye: PCCS Books.
A warm, accessible introduction to the person-centred approach.

(Continued)

(Continued)

Prever, M. (2010) *Counselling and Supporting Children and Young People: A Person-Centred Approach*. London: SAGE.

Mark Prever's book is a much needed addition to the literature. It examines the person-centred approach with clarity and offers excellent application to practising counsellors and other professionals working with children and young people.

Smyth, D. (2013) *Person-Centred Therapy with Children and Young People*. London: SAGE.

David Smyth's book is written with rigour and warmth. This is a text that draws wisdom from the wells of practice.

Online Resources

BACP website: www.bacp.co.uk/, especially the BACP Children and Young People Division and the Competences for Working with Children and Young People.

Counselling MindEd: http://counsellingminded.com, especially Modules CM 07: Relational Skills, and CM 08: Therapeutic Skills.

3

Psychodynamic Approaches

Sue Kegerreis and Nick Midgley

This chapter includes:

- An outline of the history of psychodynamic ideas
- An account of the particular features of the psychodynamic approach to work with children and adolescents
- Suggestions regarding the applications of psychodynamic thinking in different settings
- A brief description of a case illustrating the key concepts and elements in use in psychodynamic practice
- A description of recent research into the efficacy of psychodynamic treatment with children and adolescents.

Background and History

Psychodynamic psychotherapy with children and young people has its origins in the work of Sigmund Freud. First in *The Interpretation of Dreams* (1900) and then in *Three Essays on the Theory of Sexuality* (1905), he suggested that our behaviour is governed by unconscious processes, and that mental disturbances (and indeed the core of our personality itself) can often be traced back to key aspects of early childhood experience. He also argued that mental and emotional difficulties can be addressed through a therapeutic relationship that assumes that behaviour has meaning, and that exploring and coming to some understanding of one's 'internal world' is a key element of emotional well-being.

Although he worked primarily with adults, Freud was interested in the way his ideas could be used to help children, although at first he thought this was best done by supporting parents. In his famous case study of 'Little Hans' (1909), he offered a series of 'parent consultations' to the father of a five-year-old boy with a phobia about horses, in which he encouraged the father to pay attention to his son's anxieties and to take seriously the way in which this worried little boy was making sense of the world around him. Freud demonstrated that taking the child's view of the world as genuinely meaningful and taking time to listen to him was in itself therapeutic, although he thought at the time that only a parent would have the kind of relationship that would make this type of work possible.

It was left to the next generation of psychoanalysts – including Hermine Hug-Hellmuth (1921), Melanie Klein (1932) and Anna Freud (1974 [1927]) – to demonstrate the possibilities of direct work with children. These early analysts differed on many points of theory and technique, but they were all agreed that children's difficulties could be understood by paying attention to the 'internal world' of the child, and that establishing therapeutic settings in which this internal world could be explored safely was key to therapeutic change. They agreed that play was central to the way in which children communicated about their internal worlds, and that children often play out in their relationship to the therapist (the transference) some of the key elements of their internal drama. Later psychoanalysts also came to see that the emotional experience of the therapist him- or herself (the counter-transference) could be a source of information about the child's inner world and, furthermore, that being able to manage strong counter-transference feelings was a key to successful therapeutic work (Heimann, 1950).

Many of the most influential psychoanalysts of the second half of the 20th century developed their ideas through working with children. Winnicott (1958) recognised the role of the parent–child relationship in supporting healthy emotional development. He also saw that not all unconscious mental processes had to be verbally interpreted in order to be therapeutic. For Winnicott, play itself had therapeutic value – an idea that builds bridges with the work of play therapists such as Axline (1990 [1971]). Meanwhile, Anna Freud was coming to see that not all childhood disorders were necessarily based on internal conflicts (as Sigmund Freud had supposed). In *Normality and Pathology* (1965), she came to the opinion that for some children their difficulties were based on 'deficits' in their early experience (whether due to trauma and neglect or to genetic or biological causes – or indeed a combination of both). Meanwhile Bion (1962) introduced the important concept of 'containment', i.e. that a child's development depends on the capacity of the adults to receive and metabolise the child's powerful emotional experiences, and return them to the child in a way that could be properly processed. Without this the child's inner experiences are more likely to be overwhelming and manifest as emotional or behavioural problems.

> ## Case Study   Paolo
>
> Paolo,[1] eight, was referred to the school counsellor because he was hitting other children, constantly distracted in class and lacking the concentration to learn effectively. Staff felt that he was intelligent but was underachieving. A psychologist found him to have a mild degree of attention deficit disorder but not to be hyperactive. Paolo's parents were caring and concerned, seeing the problem mainly in terms of him not applying himself – although they were aware also of him preferring to be in a world of his own. He resisted attempts to be taken out on family outings, preferring to play games on his phone or computer. He had always seemed 'different', but they had not seen him as having problems until the demands of school began to bite.
>
> In the assessment meetings, Paolo played rather formless games with the cars and other toys. Some had a narrative of sorts, with animals gobbling each other up or attacking each other in shifting alliances, but relationships between the toys were perfunctory or unclear, and the play meandered without much focus. After a while, the counsellor felt completely at sea, beginning to think that she had lost her expertise in understanding children or maybe never had any. Although she was an experienced counsellor who had worked with many hard-to-reach children, she felt unable to make a link with Paolo, who related to her in an affable but impersonal way.

What does this tell us about psychodynamic counselling or therapy? And why would it help the therapist – and, more importantly, Paolo himself – if the therapist is able to think psychodynamically to try and make sense of what was going on in these assessment meetings? Below we will set out key elements of psychodynamic counselling and psychotherapy,[2] and show how this way of thinking and working can be of value when facing situations such as this.

Contemporary psychodynamic therapy with children and young people builds on many of these key ideas, and has developed in somewhat different ways in different cultures (see Geissmann and Geissmann, 1998). Psychodynamic therapists also integrate findings from other disciplines such as developmental psychology, attachment theory and neuroscience to enrich their clinical and research work (e.g. Green, 2003;

---

[1] For reasons of confidentiality this case is a fictionalised and disguised amalgamation of several actual cases.

[2] In this paper 'counselling' and 'therapy' will be used interchangeably although the authors are aware that these terms have different histories and are often linked to different trainings and professional groups. The term 'psychodynamic' is used to cover a broad range of approaches, all of which have their roots in psychoanalytic thinking, but which have developed in a number of different directions. As described in this chapter, most contemporary psychodynamic thinking is also integrated with findings from other disciplines, such as attachment theory, neuroscience and developmental psychology.

Horne and Lanyado, 2012; Alvarez, 2012). Psychodynamic child therapists are also influenced by systemic thinking, in particular the idea that understanding a child's problems involves an appreciation of the system in which they live; and that working with that system is as important as working with the child's internal world.

Skills, Attitudes and Beliefs Necessary for a Psychodynamic Practitioner

The core skills and attitudes needed in a psychodynamic practitioner follow directly from the set of beliefs on which they are based. As indicated above, the central idea is that behaviour, emotions and responses have an inherent logic and meaning – a way in which the child's problems, despite their apparent unhelpfulness, make some kind of emotional sense. Their roots lie in the internal world of the child that has been built up from his earliest experiences and relationships.

If a child has been presented with experiences that are hurtful, frightening or which engender internal conflict (which will always be the case to some degree), he or she will have built up defences to make the emotional pain less overwhelming, and to keep out of awareness whatever is more than can be coped with. This is often related to how difficult his beginnings have been, but not inevitably or simply, as some children are more resilient than others – making surprisingly good progress in relatively impoverished or damaging circumstances – while others are much more sensitive and vulnerable.

The real relationships and circumstances in children's lives are, of course, crucial influences on how they feel about themselves and others, and family or parental work is often indicated to help address ongoing difficulties in home relationships. However, in psychodynamic work the focus will be on how children have internalised a 'cast of characters' in their mind, a set of 'ways of being with others' (Stern, 1985) and a set of ideas and beliefs about themselves and relationships which powerfully dictate how they behave and respond. They need new, good experiences, but for some this is not enough, and they can be held in these patterns because of the greater vulnerability they would have to manage and the pain they would have to face if they were to lower their defences and experience the world more as it actually is, rather than through the lenses established from earlier experiences. Of course if the world is still unsafe then it may not be appropriate to expect the child to make such changes, and the priority is to work with the network around the child to help create a more supportive environment. In reality, this is not usually an either/or situation, as changes in a child can impact on the environment around them, as well as vice versa.

From this underlying set of ideas follows the key elements of psychodynamic practice. First, the practitioner has to observe extremely carefully how the child acts, reacts, responds and relates, as expressed in the way the child speaks, plays and behaves but also, crucially, in how it appears he is experiencing the therapist. This emotionally sensitive and informed observation will reveal information about the internal world of the child. The therapist will be alert to clues as to what anxieties the child is most affected by, what defences he is using to keep vulnerability at manageable levels, what sorts of experiences appear to have been indigestible and what inner conflicts are causing the child's development to have stalled or become disrupted.

Putting observation first does not preclude the counsellor interacting in a lively way with the child – far from it. The counsellor offers a thoughtful presence, perhaps putting into words what he is doing and showing or commenting on what the play is conveying. However, it does mean that the counsellor will most likely let the child lead the session, usually avoiding setting agendas or dictating activities. She might join in play with the child, but would take care to remain reflective and alert to the emotional dynamics, seeking guidance from the child as to what part she is supposed to play, and all the time keeping one foot outside the game, reflecting and maybe commenting on what is being brought into focus through the play. As the main aim is to find out what is going on in the child's mind and emotional life, it is essential that the child's own preoccupations are allowed to emerge rather than that the practitioner impose a shape on the sessions.

Alongside observation, the counsellor looks for ways of putting words to the child's experience. Giving children an emotional vocabulary is often of key therapeutic value, partly because this offers acceptance and validation of often shaming or painful emotions the child may have, but also because the act of naming a feeling makes it accessible to thinking, giving it a shape and substance that can render it less overwhelming and more available to be processed. Feeling understood is in itself a powerful therapeutic agent.

So the counsellor observes and is perhaps able to comment or put into words something that the child is revealing but may not be consciously able to think about. This might, as already indicated, be about the child's inner feelings and emotional conflicts and anxieties, but it might be more explicitly about the relationships the child habitually experiences.

This brings us to another central plank in psychodynamic thinking – the transference. The way the child responds to us in the therapy room is often a direct communication about how they have internalised their earlier experiences with others. We get information from them as the relationship develops as to how they see us, what issues they have with us (feeling badly treated, wanting to be the sole focus of our attention, being afraid of disapproval, expecting us to be punitive, seeing us as useless and so on) which are good indications of the perceptions they are prone to have of others in their lives and clues as to how they have experienced aspects of their first and most important relationships. Some of this may be of relatively recent origin, but a psychodynamic practitioner will also be attentive to indications of the nature of the infantile transference – that is, feelings in relation to the therapist that hark back to the child's earliest experiences, when they were at their most vulnerable and when their capacity to process experience was at its most primitive.

Alongside this the therapist will be paying attention to their own emotional state, reactions and responses, using these to provide another level of information about the child – the counter-transference. The child may be relating to the therapist so that the therapist feels something the child himself feels consciously or unconsciously, such as fear, despair, frustration, vulnerability, stupidity. The therapist here is being asked to register and bear feelings which the child himself may not be able to manage. Or, in a variation on this theme, the therapist may find herself responding as if she is a figure from his inner world, perhaps feeling rejecting, detached, mindless, punitive or placatory. This can carry vital information about the unhelpful responses the child engenders in those he meets – based on experiences of his first relationships.

So the psychodynamic therapist is constantly using this binocular vision, monitoring both the child's way of relating and her own emotional state. First she has to manage the impact of these, then she has to work out whether, when and how to put some of this into words for the child. If she manages to remain curious and thoughtful while registering and digesting the impact of the child – without getting caught up in the urge to respond in kind or retaliate – she is offering him 'containment' (Bion, 1962). This can be therapeutic in itself and is of great value in both clinical and non-clinical settings. The therapist's processing and understanding may be sufficient to free the child, without this having to be interpreted. However, sometimes a timely and simple interpretation of what she has understood will help the child make sense of his own feelings and liberate him from being driven endlessly to repeat the same dynamics.

It becomes clear from these considerations that some personal attributes are essential for working psychodynamically. Practitioners need to have a high level of self-awareness and self-knowledge, as they are using themselves as the central tool of the therapy. They need to be substantially in charge of their own feelings, so they can use their responses as a sensitive barometer for the dynamics in the room, without resorting to reaction or blocking the impact of the child on them. They need to be endlessly curious as to what might lie behind a child behaving or relating as they do, and above all be prepared to manage receiving the child's negative as well as positive responses.

Using Psychodynamic Approaches across the Age and Ability Range

One of the beauties of the psychodynamic approach is that it can be adapted to work with such a wide range of children, both in age and in intellectual capacity. Psychodynamic work can take place in classrooms, children's homes or in hospitals, as well as in consulting rooms, with individuals or with groups (see Lanyado and Horne, 2009; Kegerreis, 2010; Schmidt Neven, 2010). Because of its focus on emotional communication and interpersonal dynamics, and because so much of the work can be done through art and play, and through the capacity of the therapist to process the relationship dynamics brought to life by the child, much can be done with children who are not particularly verbal as well as those who want to talk and who can understand at a sophisticated level.

The kind of language used and the means of expression for the child will of course vary depending on the age and developmental stage of the child. With younger children a great deal of the work will be conducted through art and play, with much of the processing done within the practitioner's mind and any interpretation geared sensitively to the child's level of linguistic ability and understanding. With older children and adolescents more will be done verbally, and interpretations may be more elaborate, making more explicit the patterns observed and their links with those from the family or from the past.

Whatever the age of the client, however, what is therapeutic and brings about change is often less the explicit working out of a narrative link between past and present but more the way in which, during the therapy, the old and now out-of-date relationships are recreated, but this time worked through differently, with the therapist able to be thoughtful about the dynamics, reflecting on and having insight into and curiosity about their meaning, rather than just responding or retaliating. In Anna Freud's words, the therapist is both a 'transference object' but also a 'new object', offering the child a different kind of experience and thereby promoting the child's own capacity to accept and welcome new experiences (Hurry, 1998).

As it focuses so closely on the way in which the world is subjectively experienced by the child, the psychodynamic approach can be also used helpfully across cultures, encouraging genuine curiosity about cultural differences and how they are experienced by each individual. Undeniably a therapist must be sensitive to how a different culture may have shaped the child's start in life and current milieu. She also needs to be alert to her own limitations in understanding how different their experiences might be, including the child's perception of her and the therapeutic setting. She must register and process the 'cultural transference' (e.g. Gibbs, 2009), and pay attention to real differences in terms of cultural and social inequalities. The psychodynamic counsellor also needs to explore her own cultural positioning and recognise her own 'internal racism' (e.g. Davids, 2011). However, the emphasis on the sense the child is making of their individual world means that psychodynamic approaches can be used to address whatever conflicts and vulnerabilities are getting in the child's way, as well as assisting the child in processing the meaning of their own cultural journey.

Using the Psychodynamic Approach in Short-Term Work

If the essence of psychodynamic therapy is the reconfiguring of a child's inner world, removing unhelpful defences and installing more benign inner objects, then it is true that this work can take a long time, as it involves major restructuring of the child's way of relating to the world, itself dependent on making it first safe enough to do so.

However, another central element in the psychodynamic approach is the bringing of unconscious elements to the surface and becoming aware of internal conflicts. Particularly with older children and adolescents, it is possible to help a client swiftly by helping them see what internal conflicts lie hidden in their presenting problems. They feel stuck, trying to change a behaviour which they can see is unhelpful to them, but unable to change because they are not in touch with the underlying reason for, and meaning of, the behaviour. For example, Sam, 15, was consciously desperate to do well in his GCSEs, so as to impress the father who had left two years earlier and to be in a position to follow in his footsteps. But he found himself endlessly procrastinating and avoiding his revision. In therapy it was quickly possible for the first time for his deep hurt and anger with his father to come to the surface, making him aware of the unconscious sabotage going on. Once this was conscious he found it much easier to make himself work, on his own behalf rather than in an attempt to resolve his emotional difficulties with his father. Longer-term work might have led to deeper levels of meaning and other kinds of changes. But short-term work enabled Sam to deal with the specific problem he was facing – his problems preparing for his exams – and also awakened in him a curiosity about the links between his behaviour and his deeper thoughts and feelings about the people around him.

Uncovering patterns, making links that are as yet unacknowledged and recognising ambivalent feelings are ways in which psychodynamic work can be effective even though brief. Sometimes it is enough for a child or adolescent to have their feelings recognised, named and validated. Many young people are in families where, for whatever reason, the way they feel or how they are experiencing things is difficult for their carers to acknowledge. Maybe it is too painful for a parent to see their child's distress, or the parent's own past is so vivid in their mind that they find it hard to see their child clearly in their own right. Coming to therapy can give a child a chance to have their real feelings witnessed, accepted as real, named and understood in a way that is immensely healing in its own right. This can be helpful in a short intervention, making space for the child's own developmental drive to reassert itself.

Returning to Paolo

At the start of this chapter we introduced Paolo, and left him at the point where he was being assessed by a psychodynamic counsellor at school, who was left feeling rather de-skilled after her initial meetings with him, in which his play seemed to be formless and without meaning. But the therapist was, after the discomfort of these initial feelings, able to draw on her psychodynamic thinking and to process her counter-transference in a number of ways. First, she realised that her lack of connection with Paolo was not just her own failure but was similar to how the staff at school and, to some extent, his parents felt. Second, she realised that her experience of nothing making much sense and the links between things being obscure and/or arbitrary was an indication of how this child experienced his world.

In treatment with Paolo, she put these experiences and thoughts into words. He let her know how much difficulty he had in getting properly in touch with, let alone making sense of, his feelings. His recourse to repetitive games was in part a retreat from what baffled and perplexed him in the real world of other people. He sought distraction and excitement in a fantasy world that offered escape from his sense of disconnection and disarray. Given his difficulty in staying in touch with reality, it was not surprising that applying himself to learning was a challenge.

One important strand in the work with Paolo consisted in the therapist helping him grasp and identify his own feelings. Another consisted of her first registering, then processing and bearing, then being able to feed back to him the experience – clearly one he had himself struggled with – of not being emotionally connected. His parents were kind, but for a range of reasons had not been consistently able to reach out and try to understand this little boy. They were very practical in outlook, pragmatically unwilling to address their own emotional agendas and troubled marriage, and coped by addressing behaviour but not emotions. Paolo responded strongly to the therapist's interest in his emotional life and week by week built better links both inside himself and between himself and others. His play became more coherent, with clear narratives and consistent relationships. He calmed down, as he no longer needed to distract himself so much from his own confusion. As he became more at ease inside his own head, as it were, he began to be able to learn. He was also increasingly able to mentalise, which meant that his capacity to relate to other children improved (Midgley and Vrouva, 2012). Regular meetings with his parents also helped them to see the importance of looking beyond Paolo's behaviour and seeing him as a child with his own mind and his own feelings. When the counsellor was able to help the parents recognise their own resistance to doing this, they were also able to acknowledge their own need to address issues in the parental relationship, and made a decision to attend a service that offered counselling for couples.

Research, Including Evidence-Based Practice and Practice-Based Evidence

A case example such as the one about Paolo, above, might suggest that psychodynamic counselling or therapy can be helpful for children, but there is always a danger that we generalise too much from specific experiences, or that we remember those interventions that were helpful and find reasons to forget or excuse those times when our approach did not seem to be so useful. For many years psychoanalytic and psychodynamic therapies have been considered to lack a credible evidence base and have consistently failed to appear in lists of 'empirically-supported treatments'. Partly this has been due to a degree of reluctance among psychodynamic practitioners to support the kind of empirical research that could establish such an evidence base, whilst other approaches – especially cognitive-behavioural therapy – appear to have been more active, but it is also due to the fact that the research which has been done has not been gathered together and widely disseminated.

In the field of psychodynamic treatment of adults, recent years have seen the publication of a series of important reviews and meta-analyses culminating in the landmark publication of Jonathan Shedler's paper on 'The efficacy of psychodynamic psychotherapy' (Shedler, 2010). This paper brought together the evidence from a number of randomised controlled trials, showing that effect sizes for psychodynamic therapies are at least equal to those of other forms of treatment long regarded as 'evidence-based', and that patients who receive such treatment not only appear to maintain their therapeutic gains after treatment ends but in many instances continue to improve.

Research examining the efficacy and effectiveness of psychodynamic treatments for children and adolescents has lagged behind the equivalent with adults, although there exist a rich clinical literature and a strong tradition of qualitative, practice-based research (see Midgley et al., 2009). However, this situation is changing, with many more studies now being completed. A systematic review of the evidence base for psycho-dynamic therapy with children (Midgley and Kennedy, 2011) used 34 separate studies, including nine randomised controlled trials (RCTs), to provide as complete a picture as possible of the existing evidence base for individual psychodynamic psychotherapy for children aged between three and 18.

Key conclusions of the review included the following:

- Studies of psychodynamic therapies indicate that this treatment can be effective for a range of childhood disorders, as measured by well-validated, standardised research instruments.
- Psychodynamic treatment of children and adolescents appears to be equally effective when directly compared to other treatments, with mixed findings across studies – some suggesting psychodynamic therapy is more, some less, and some equally effective as other forms of therapy.
- Psychodynamic treatment may have a different pattern of effect to other treatments. For example, depressed children appeared to recover more *quickly* if given family therapy, whilst improvements for those receiving individual psychodynamic therapy appeared to be *slower but more sustained*, with some young people continuing to improve after the end of treatment. A similar pattern of more gradual improvement, but with improvement continuing beyond the end of treatment, was found in a study of children with emotional disorders, giving some evidence of a possible 'sleeper effect' in psychodynamic therapy.

- Younger children appear to benefit more than older ones, with the likelihood of improvement during treatment declining with age. However, older children and adolescents can also benefit from psychodynamic therapy.
- Children with emotional or internalising disorders seem to respond better than those with disruptive/externalising disorders, with an especially strong evidence base emerging for the treatment of children and young people with depression.
- Children and adolescents with disruptive disorders are more difficult to engage and more likely to drop out of psychodynamic treatment; but where they have engaged in treatment there is some evidence that it can be effective.
- A range of studies suggests that psychodynamic work is effective with children who have experienced abuse, maltreatment and trauma, although the group is too diagnostically diverse for this to be reflected in empirically-supported treatment guidelines.
- In samples that apparently had lesser degrees of difficulty either because of the setting or selection criteria, short-term and even minimal interventions were shown to be effective.
- There were some indications of potential adverse effects, especially if therapy was offered to children without parallel work with parents or if it added to an adolescent's sense of 'stigma'.

One positive message taken from this review is that the amount of research investigating the efficacy and/or the effectiveness of psychodynamic psychotherapy with children and adolescents has increased decade by decade from the 1970s. This is a promising sign that we are beginning to gain some understanding of 'what works for whom' in regard to psychodynamic treatments for children and young people.

Concluding Remarks

The psychodynamic approach emphasises three main distinctive features:

1. the power of unconscious dynamics at work in all of us;
2. the central importance of early experiences in shaping how we perceive, experience, behave and relate;
3. the use of the therapy relationship itself in bringing about both insight and change.

Out of these core features come key techniques and attitudes. The therapist uses her own observational skills to elucidate the inner world of the child. The child may play, use art materials and/or talk, and from this and the evolving relationship with her, the therapist gains insight into what conflicts, anxieties and defences are at work and how these are interfering with the child making the most of their opportunities and relationships. She processes all this and feeds back to the child where appropriate, while appreciating that the receiving and understanding of the child's feelings and providing the child with opportunities for emotional expression and exploration may be powerfully therapeutic in themselves.

While it has its roots in psychoanalysis, psychodynamic work with children has been modified and extended to meet contemporary challenges. In response to theoretical refinements, clinical experience, different client groups, new knowledge about child development and input from many other kinds of psychological and therapeutic understanding, it now offers a flexible yet powerful tool to help a wide range of children.

Furthermore, because it also offers so much understanding of the impact of troubled children and families on those who work with them, and the complexity of professional interactions around challenging cases, it can be used effectively in non-clinical as well as clinical settings and to help staff as well as children and families (Nicholson et al., 2011; Kegerreis, 2011).

Summary

- Psychodynamic work with children and adolescents has evolved from its psychoanalytic origins into an adaptable and practical approach to the problems of young people
- The psychodynamic approach requires from practitioners particular qualities of observational skill, self-awareness and emotional sensitivity
- Psychodynamic therapy enables children to experience and identify their feelings more fully and have these feelings witnessed, validated and understood
- Psychodynamic therapy aims to help children develop more benign inner worlds, which in turn can foster better feelings about themselves and better relationships with others
- There is increasing evidence that psychodynamic therapy can be helpful for a wide range of children and adolescents, but there is a need for more high-quality research in this area

Reflective Questions

1 How does the psychodynamic approach enable children to gain greater control over their behaviour?

The therapist helps the children become aware of unconscious factors influencing how they perceive, behave and relate to others. Once conscious, these factors lose some of their power and are more susceptible to conscious control. Thought and/or talk can then take the place of action. The psychodynamic approach would suggest that a child's difficult behaviour arises from defences which have outlived their usefulness and are, in fact, causing greater problems and/or cutting the child off from internal resources and external support. The therapy will help the child relinquish some of these defences so they can develop more creative and mutually enriching relationships with those around them and have better access to their own resources.

2 Does psychodynamic thinking suggest that children with abusive pasts are bound to get into abusive relationships later in life?

Psychodynamic thinking helps explain repetitive patterns in relationships (e.g. Klein's concept of the 'inner world' and 'projective identification', Freud's view of 'repetition compulsion' and Anna Freud's ideas about 'identification with the aggressor'). Unconscious factors can lead children who have abusive pasts to find themselves in abusive relationships later in life. However, while our past influences our future, this is not deterministic. Good relationships mitigate the effects of damaging ones and our inner worlds are constantly changing.

3 Why is it useful in psychodynamic work for the setting and the time of sessions to be kept as much the same as possible?

It takes courage for a child to engage with us, lower their defences and allow themselves to open up and become more vulnerable in their work with us, so it is vital that we create a containing environment, with safety and regularity essential. If we are to make it safe for them to experience and work through difficult feelings, including re-encountering relationship difficulties through their experiences with us, then we have to make sure they know we will be there for them in a regular and reliable way, whatever comes up in sessions. Second, if we keep the 'frame' as stable as possible, it is easier to perceive what it is that they themselves are bringing into the situation. The specific emotional environment brought into being by each child can more accurately be discerned if everything else is kept constant.

4 Why would a psychodynamic practitioner pay a lot of attention to how they were feeling in their interactions with clients?

It is a central tenet of psychodynamic understanding that we project difficult feelings into one another, to get rid of them and/or in the hope that someone will be able to process them and help us manage them. Therefore we as therapists monitor the way a client makes us feel (the counter-transference) as it may contain important information about their emotional world, as well as our own. We consider that our capacity to register, process and make sense of how our clients make us feel and react is a key element in working through their emotional difficulties.

5 Why is the psychodynamic approach applicable to children of all ages?

We concentrate on the subjective reality of the child, with particular attention paid to early experience and the quality of the relationship created between child and therapist, so there is no age of child – or adult – with whom the psychodynamic approach is not relevant. Most psychodynamic practitioners' training includes the observation of an infant from birth, so we are used to thinking about the earliest levels of experiencing. Work can be done with both verbal and non-verbal communication. Understanding child development and the particular tasks of each stage are central to all trainings, as is the capacity to communicate with children of all ages. At the other end of the spectrum psychodynamic work has also been applied to work with all ages of adults, including the elderly.

Learning Activities

- With a friend or colleague, take it in turns to play with a range of small dolls and toy animals for 10 minutes while the other observes – then share thoughts and understandings about how it felt to 'just play', what was observed and what narratives/themes emerged.
- Reflect on three important figures in authority over you in your adult life – are there any similarities in the way you see them or in the way you relate to them? If there are, think about where these patterns might come from in your early life.
- With a friend or colleague, take it in turns to tell each other a story from your life, something important but not too powerful. The listener should concentrate not on what is said but on how they themselves feel, both physically and emotionally. Then feed back to each other and discuss.

Further Reading

Blake, P. (2011). *Child and Adolescent Psychotherapy*. London: Karnac.

French, L. and Klein, R. (2012) *Therapeutic Practice in Schools*. London: Routledge.

Kegerreis, S. (2010) *Psychodynamic Counselling with Children and Young People: An Introduction*. London: Palgrave.

Lanyado, M. and Horne, A. (eds) (2009) *The Handbook of Child and Adolescent Psychotherapy: Psychoanalytic Approaches*. 2nd edn. London: Routledge.

4

Cognitive-Behavioural Therapy

Paul Stallard

This chapter includes:

- An historical overview of CBT and the underlying theoretical model
- The therapeutic process of CBT and phases of treatment
- How CBT is adapted for use with children and young people

Introduction

Although developed from work with adults, cognitive-behavioural therapy (CBT) can be used with children from seven years of age if it is carefully adapted to the developmental level of the child. With younger children CBT may need to be simpler, made concrete through the use of familiar everyday metaphors and involve less verbal and more visual techniques. Adolescents will have more developed cognitive and verbal skills and may be able to engage in more sophisticated and abstract verbal discussions.

CBT provides an evidence-based approach to the treatment of emotional problems in children and adolescents.

- It is based on the premise that psychological problems arise from dysfunctional and unhelpful cognitions which are maintained by attention and memory biases, emotional responses and maladaptive behaviours.
- Through the process of collaborative empiricism dysfunctional cognitions are subject to objective evaluation through techniques such as Socratic dialogues and behavioural experiments.

- These result in the discovery of new or overlooked information and alternative meanings about events, which leads to the development of more functional and balanced cognitions.
- Coping is enhanced through the development of emotional literacy and management skills and performance through behavioural and problem-solving skills.
- Enhanced coping and performance results in greater reinforcement of positive and adaptive behaviours.

Historical Development

CBT was heavily influenced by the pioneering work of Albert Ellis (1994) and Aaron Beck (1963, 1964) and their models of rational emotional therapy and cognitive therapy. These models built upon the success of behaviour therapy by attending to the meanings and interpretations individuals make about events. Initially CBT was developed for adults, and it was not until the 1990s that descriptions of the way CBT could be used with children began to emerge (Kendall, 1991). Many early studies applied CBT programmes developed for use with adults to older adolescents, and how these were adapted for children received comparatively little attention. However, the new millennium heralded the arrival of a number of publications that described how CBT can be adapted for use with children (see Further Reading).

One of the first randomised controlled trials to evaluate the effectiveness of CBT with adolescents was published in 1990 (Lewinsohn et al., 1990). The following 20 years saw an explosion of empirical studies that have established CBT as the most extensively researched of all the child psychotherapies (Graham, 2005). Early research compared CBT to waitlist control groups and found large treatment effects. The next wave of trials compared CBT with other active interventions and, unsurprisingly, treatment effect sizes were smaller but nonetheless positive. For example, when CBT was compared with medication, CBT was not found to be superior, although the results confirmed that CBT offers an effective psychological intervention (Goodyer et al., 2007; Treatment for Adolescents with Depression Study (TADS) Team, 2009; Brent et al., 2008; Walkup et al., 2008). Similarly, CBT programmes provided in schools as prevention or early interventions for the treatment of anxiety or depression have demonstrated very positive results (Calear and Christensen, 2010; Neil and Christensen, 2009; Mychailyszyn et al., 2012). This extensive research has resulted in CBT being recommended by expert groups such as the UK National Institute for Health and Clinical Excellence and the American Academy of Child and Adolescent Psychiatry for the treatment of children with emotional disorders including depression, obsessive compulsive disorders, post-traumatic stress disorder and anxiety. This growing evidence base has also prompted the development of national training programmes in CBT and the extension of the UK Improving Access to Psychological Therapies Programme to children and young people (IAPT, 2012).

Theoretical Model

CBT is concerned with the relationships between cognitive, emotional and behavioural processes.

Behavioural theory is based on the premise that maladaptive behaviours are learned and draws upon the principles of classical and operant conditioning. Classical conditioning focuses upon the role of antecedent conditions in which neutral stimuli or situations (e.g. a shop) become associated with an involuntary response (e.g. anxiety). Interventions involve techniques such as learning relaxation skills to counter anxiety; the development of a hierarchy of situations that elicit anxiety; graded exposure and systematic desensitisation whereby anxiety is controlled whilst feared situations are faced and mastered.

Operant conditioning focuses upon the role of consequences in maintaining maladaptive behaviours. It assumes that behaviours that are rewarded (positively reinforced) or are followed by the removal of an aversive consequence (negative reinforcement) are more likely to be repeated. For example, a child who is anxious about leaving the house to go to school may be allowed to stay at home (i.e. staying at home is positively reinforced). If their anxiety is reduced by avoiding school, then school non-attendance is negatively reinforced (i.e. avoidance reduces anxiety). In both cases the consequences will result in the child being less likely to leave the house and go to school. Interventions involve contingency management whereby adaptive behaviours are reinforced.

Whilst behaviour therapy is effective, it fails to consider the personal meanings and interpretations that are made about the events that occur. Cognitive therapy emerged to address this issue and is based on the premise that mental health problems arise when dysfunctional and biased meanings and interpretations are made. The cognitive model proposed by Beck et al. (1979) suggests different levels of cognitions with the deepest being schemas which are strong, global, fixed ways of thinking that underpin the meanings and interpretations that are made. Schemas can be functional and adaptive but some are overly rigid, negative and dysfunctional. They are assumed to develop during childhood as a result of significant and/or repeated experiences. Poor attachment, maltreatment or overly critical and demanding parents may, for example, lead a child to develop a cognitive schema that they are 'unlovable' or a 'failure'.

Schemas are activated by events reminiscent of those that produced the schema. Once activated, attention, memory and interpretation processing biases filter and select information that supports the schema. Attention biases result in attention being focused upon information that confirms the schema whilst neutral or contradictory information is overlooked. Memory biases result in the recall of information that is consistent with the schema whilst interpretation biases serve to minimise any inconsistent information.

The most accessible level of cognitions are automatic thoughts or 'self-talk' and represent the involuntary stream of thoughts that run through the mind providing a continuous commentary about events. These are functionally related to schemas, with dysfunctional schemas producing negative automatic thoughts. Negative automatic thoughts tend to be biased and self-critical and generate unpleasant emotional states, e.g. anxiety, anger, unhappiness and maladaptive behaviours such as social withdrawal or avoidance. The unpleasant feelings and maladaptive behaviours associated with these dysfunctional cognitions and processing biases serve to reinforce and maintain them as the individual becomes trapped in a self-perpetuating negative cycle, as highlighted in Figure 4.1.

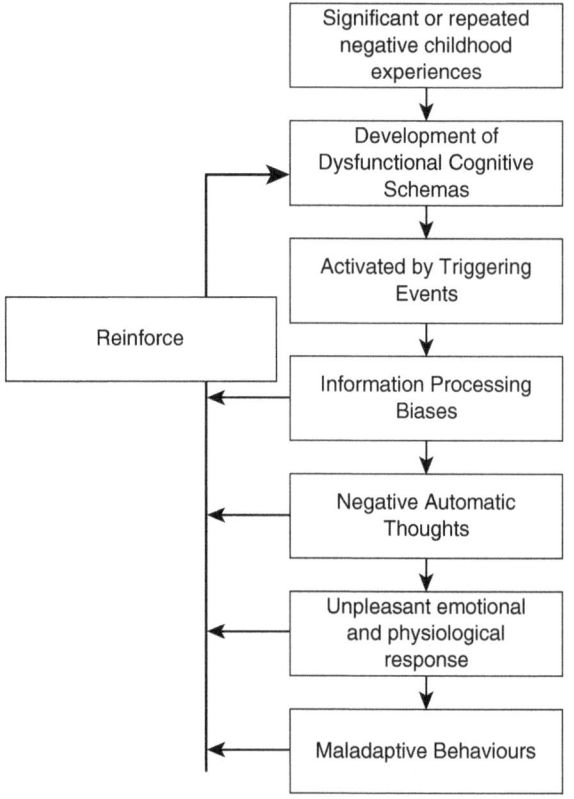

Figure 4.1   Reinforcing behaviours.

In addition to the different levels of cognitions, CBT is concerned with the specific content of dominant cognitions which vary according to the particular psychological problem. Depression, for example, tends to be related to cognitions concerning loss, deprivation and failure; anxiety to cognitions of personal threat, vulnerability and inability to cope; obsessive compulsive disorder with cognitions of personal responsibility for harm; PTSD with current threat and panic with catastrophic interpretations of physiological symptoms.

The aim of CBT is to identify, test and reappraise dysfunctional and unhelpful cognitions. Testing involves challenging selective attention biases by attending to overlooked information, challenging memory biases by recalling contradictory experiences and challenging interpretation biases by exploring alternative explanations. Two key methods of achieving this are Socratic dialogues and behavioural experiments.

Socratic dialogues help to discover new information which questions or contradicts the meanings or interpretations that are made. Attending to new or overlooked information challenges internal, stable and global beliefs (e.g. I am stupid; no-one likes me) and helps to develop functional cognitions by establishing limits (e.g. maths is hard but I am good at art; none of the people I know have the same interests as me).

Behavioural experiments provide an objective way of testing assumptions and beliefs. A belief that 'no one likes me' could be tested by recording how many times a young person receives a text, email, Facebook hit or phone call in a week. A prediction is made at the start of the experiment about what will happen (e.g. no-one will contact me) which is compared with the outcome. Through this process limits are placed around global schemas, which helps to promote more balanced and functional cognitions.

Therapeutic Process

CBT occurs within the context of a strong therapeutic relationship. The relationship needs to be open, honest and non-judgemental and is conveyed through a genuine, warm and respectful rapport. The process is one of collaborative empiricism in which the therapist and child actively work together to test the child's beliefs and interpretations. Stallard (2005) has defined the key elements of this process with children by the acronym PRECISE.

- P: highlights the need to develop a therapeutic **partnership** based upon collaborative empiricism and emphasises the central role of the child and their parents/carers in securing change.
- R: draws the therapist's attention to developmental considerations and the need to ensure that the intervention is **right** for the child's cognitive, linguistic, memory and perspective-taking abilities.
- E: highlights the need to develop and maintain an **empathic** relationship which conveys warmth, genuine concern and respect.

- C: identifies the need to be appropriately **creative** in conveying the concepts of CBT in ways that match the child's developmental understanding and interests.
- I: highlights **investigation** and the need to adopt a curious, open and inquisitive stance in which thoughts are subject to objective evaluation through Socratic dialogues and behavioural experiments.
- S: encourages the development of **self-efficacy** and learning through reflection and assimilation of new information.
- E: highlights the importance of engagement and **enjoyment** and the need to ensure that the child's interests and motivation can be maintained.

Phases of CBT

CBT typically involves the four phases of psycho-education and relationship building, skills development, consolidation and relapse prevention.

Psycho-Education and Relationship Building

During this initial phase, the primary focus is upon engagement, developing the therapeutic partnership and socialising the child and their family into the cognitive model. Information is provided about the cognitive model (the link between events, thoughts, feelings and behaviours) and an overview of what therapy will involve. The idea of learning together (collaborative empiricism) and the active role of the child in testing ideas and undertaking experiments is emphasised. A shared understanding of the child's problem within a CBT framework (a cognitive formulation) is jointly developed and treatment goals are identified.

The therapist has a fairly active role during this stage as they provide information and develop the therapeutic alliance. This is a key task since typically children are referred because of concerns from others, and they may have no ownership of the referred problem or little motivation to change. Engaging and motivating the child is a prerequisite to the subsequent stages of CBT. The therapist therefore presents as open, understanding, positive and hopeful as they elicit commitment from the child to 'give it a try'.

Skills Development

The second phase focuses upon the development of skills to counter dysfunctional cognitions and processing, unpleasant emotional states and maladaptive behaviours.

The particular skills and domains of the intervention will be informed by the formulation. In the cognitive domain, cognitive enhancement will help the child assess the accuracy and usefulness of their cognitions and to develop more helpful, balanced cognitions. Different types of cognitions (helpful and unhelpful thoughts), processing biases (thinking traps) and common dysfunctional cognitions will be identified through thought monitoring. Behavioural experiments and Socratic dialogues will be used to systematically test these unhelpful cognitions and processes in order to identify new or overlooked information. This process results in limits being placed around dysfunctional global beliefs and negative thoughts and provides alternative interpretations which are more balanced and functional.

Emotional skills may be enhanced to promote better understanding, awareness and management of unpleasant emotions. Emotional monitoring can help to identify links between emotions, events and thoughts and those situations that are associated with particularly strong, unpleasant or prolonged emotional states. Emotional management may be developed through relaxation training, positive imagery or activity rescheduling to reduce the intensity or frequency of unpleasant emotions.

In terms of behaviour, the intervention may involve developing more adaptive behaviours in which problem-solving and social and personal effectiveness skills such as assertion and negotiation are enhanced. This may involve techniques such as roleplay, observational exercises, graded exposure, behavioural activation or response prevention. Finally, the child is encouraged to notice and reinforce positive attempts to change.

During the skills development phase the therapist adopts an open and curious approach to encourage the child to experiment and discover skills and strategies that are particularly helpful for them.

Consolidation

The third stage is consolidation, where the new skills are practised and integrated into the child's everyday repertoire. By this stage the child has a good understanding of the key elements of the cognitive model, their key cognitions and thinking traps. Regular practice of session assignments is a particularly important aspect of CBT at this stage. Through these assignments the child is encouraged to systematically face and cope with increasingly difficult situations and problems as they use their new skills to regain control of their life.

The therapist becomes more reflective as the child is increasingly encouraged to take a lead role in analysing difficult situations and finding solutions. The therapist reminds the child of the core elements of the CBT model and the skills they have acquired and encourages them to apply this framework and these skills.

Relapse Prevention

The final stage is relapse prevention where the child is encouraged to reflect on those aspects of the intervention that have been most helpful, prepare for possible relapse and to develop a contingency plan in case problems re-emerge. Their own specific thinking traps are highlighted and the skills and techniques that have helped to challenge dysfunctional internal, stable and global cognitions identified. The child is prepared for relapse and a plan developed to deal with short-term problems, and triggers for seeking further help are identified. During the final phase the therapist is a facilitator who encourages the child to process their learning and apply it to future situations and events.

Adapting CBT for Children

CBT was originally developed for work with adults. It relies heavily on verbal and memory skills and involves advanced meta-cognitive skills which require individuals to be both aware of their cognitions and able to reflect upon them. Through this process the individual is helped to find overlooked information and new meanings, which lead to the development of alternative, more functional cognitions.

Childhood and adolescence are characterised by significant and rapid development of cognitive, linguistic and memory skills. It is generally recognised that children from seven years of age can engage in CBT, although the content and process will need to be adapted to reflect their developmental level. Younger children, for example, may have problems with some cognitive tasks such as identifying and appraising cognitions. This does not necessarily imply that they cannot engage in CBT but indicates that some preparatory psycho-educational work may be required to help them identify and find ways to communicate their cognitions. This may involve use of worksheets where the child is given a picture with a single thought bubble (e.g. footballer preparing to take a penalty) and asked to identify what the person may be thinking. Extra thought bubbles can be added to introduce the child to the notion of alternative thinking, i.e. there may be different thoughts about the same situation (for example, a picture of someone receiving a present, with two or three thought bubbles).

Whilst younger children can typically generate some cognitions, they may not necessarily be able to understand general or overarching cognitive patterns, their cognitive processes or generalise dysfunctional patterns from one situation to another. The therapist may need to be more focused and use the cognitive framework to increase their understanding of specific events or difficulties.

Young children may also find the process of cognitive appraisal difficult, although they can be helped to engage with this if provided with a clear framework. They could be encouraged to become detectives and to actively seek 'evidence' for and against their way of thinking. Once the evidence has been collected the child can be encouraged to 'weigh it up' and to decide how well their thinking fits the evidence. Phrases such as 'catch it, check it, change it' can be helpful. This reminds the child to 'catch' their common dysfunctional thoughts and to 'check' them to see if they make them feel good and help them to face challenges. If not, the final step is to 'change' them into more functional and activating thoughts that make them feel good.

Metaphors can be a helpful way of relating abstract concepts to familiar, everyday situations. A washing machine can be used to explain the way some thoughts tumble around and around in our heads. 'Computer spam', 'thought invaders' or the metaphor of a CD playing in one's head can be used to explain automatic thoughts and how they just pop up without being requested and are difficult to ignore. These can be developed into coping strategies. For example, children could be encouraged to develop a computer firewall and shoot down their invading thoughts or to turn the volume down on the CD so they can stop listening to their negative thoughts. The metaphor of an anger volcano can help children understand the cognitive and emotional build-up that occurs before they lose their temper. Once the stages have been mapped, strategies can be developed to stop the volcano from blowing. Finally, a metaphor of traffic lights can be used to discuss dysfunctional and functional thoughts and how they affect our behaviour. Red (dysfunctional) thoughts stop us from doing things whilst green (functional) thoughts are empowering and activating.

Adolescents have more developed cognitive abilities and often enjoy the debate of the Socratic dialogue. Most are able to identify, test and challenge their cognitions and many are able to engage in more complex cognitive work in which common themes and processes are identified. It is not, however, uncommon to find that adolescents hold very strong beliefs and are unable to see alternative explanations. This can result in the therapist becoming increasingly active in generating alternative views which are simply dismissed by the adolescent as the Socratic dialogue becomes lost. It is therefore important that the therapist remains open, non-judgemental and curious and maintains an objective focus to help the adolescent reflect upon and question their beliefs.

Non-Verbal Methods

CBT with children also requires greater use of non-verbal methods. Drawings can be helpful and provide a useful way of externalising problems and separating them from the child. For example, children with OCD can be encouraged to draw and give a name to their OCD which they can then learn to boss back. Games such as emotional charades can be used to act out different emotions to help children identify facial expressions associated with different emotions. Brightly coloured worksheets provide engaging ways to help children map physiological changes associated with different emotions onto outline body shapes. The development of a feelings scrapbook can be a fun way for young children to establish a library of pictures expressing different emotions.

Puppets can provide an engaging way to help young children talk about their worrying thoughts and feelings. Problem situations can be acted out and children encouraged to suggest what the puppets might be thinking in order to identify potentially important cognitions. They can also be used to develop skills by encouraging children to coach their puppet through a difficult situation

With adolescents a greater use of technology can be helpful. Video or YouTube clips can provide a visual introduction to many of the key areas of CBT and can be used to introduce, highlight or facilitate discussions. Computer logs can be used as methods of self-monitoring and email as a way of reminding young people about out-of-session assignments and for providing feedback. The internet provides a rich source of information which individuals can be encouraged to use to seek evidence that might challenge their beliefs, e.g. fears about contamination or transmission of disease. Pie charts provide useful visual ways of challenging and reappraising beliefs about responsibility or blame. Similarly, quizzes can help young people identify different types of thinking traps.

Finally, visual diagrams depicting a problem formulation or the link between events, thoughts, feelings and behaviours can provide helpful ways of reinforcing the cognitive model. Printed material can supplement the session and provide a fuller and more accurate record of discussions and key points, while visual rating scales help to quantify belief in thoughts or strength of feelings and provide a useful way of demonstrating change over time.

Case Study   Sarah

Sarah, 13, was referred by her GP with severe anxiety. She had a long history of anxiety but this was increasingly interfering with everyday life to the extent that she was now reluctant to go out and was experiencing panic attacks.

Psycho-Education and Relationship Building

The first assessment session was with Sarah and her mother. Sarah presented as bright, articulate, readily engaged with the meeting and appeared very motivated to control her anxiety.

The second session completed the assessment with information from standardised anxiety measures complementing the clinical interview. This confirmed that Sarah had a generalised anxiety problem that was resulting in panic attacks in public. At the end of the session Sarah agreed to complete a mood diary and to record any times she became anxious

The diary was reviewed in session three and identified three anxious situations. All occurred when Sarah was invited out (to the cinema, to sleep at a friend's, shopping) and resulted in her being unable to go. This information was used to map a formulation which highlighted the connection between her thoughts ('I won't be able to cope') with her emotions (anxiety) and behaviour (avoid leaving home). Finally, the process of CBT was discussed and how the therapist would help Sarah to discover ways to manage her anxious feelings. Sarah agreed to complete another diary describing the bodily signals she noticed when she became anxious.

Skills Development

The fourth session focused upon emotional recognition. The physiological anxiety reaction was explained and the signals that Sarah recorded in her diary were discussed (racing heart, difficulty breathing, hot and sweating). Sarah was then asked to record any thoughts she noticed when she became anxious and what she did.

Session five focused upon the development of anxiety management skills. A number of anxiety management skills were identified and potentially useful ideas practised. In particular controlled breathing, listening to music and visualising a relaxation place were identified as potentially useful. Sarah agreed to practise these methods at home each day and agreed to record her thoughts when she became anxious.

The diary was reviewed in session six. Controlled breathing was helpful when Sarah began to feel anxious, whilst listening to music and visualisation helped her to prepare for potentially worrying situations. There was one situation when Sarah was invited shopping but was unable to control her anxiety. She recorded her thoughts ('I will become anxious and won't be able to cope'; 'I always panic when I go shopping'; 'I will make a fool of myself'). This led to an exploration of processing biases and how Sarah had fallen into the 'fortune teller' thinking trap where she was predicting failure. Sarah agreed to keep the diary for another week.

In session seven Sarah reported that she had gone to the school dance. She had become anxious before she went ('I look awful in this dress') but successfully managed this with her visualisation. However, whilst at the dance she was constantly looking for signs that she did not look nice. The 'negative glasses' thinking trap was discussed and a Socratic dialogue used to help Sarah find information that she had overlooked (e.g. comments from her best friends; postings on Facebook). This provided a direct challenge to Sarah's thoughts and helped her to recognise that others thought 'she looked nice'. This event also challenged Sarah's belief that she was not safe and unable to cope when she was out. The session ended with Sarah agreeing to develop a list of activities that she would like to do.

Consolidation

In session eight Sarah was encouraged to use her skills to cope with challenging situations. The activity that Sarah felt would be the easiest to manage was to go with her best friend to the local coffee shop. Sarah was asked what she thought would happen (have a panic attack) and she rated her belief that she wouldn't be able to cope (80/100). A behavioural experiment was agreed to test her belief. Helpful skills were rehearsed: relaxing visualisation before she went and controlled

(Continued)

(Continued)

breathing if she felt anxious whilst out. Functional cognitions were practised ('I have done this before so I can only give it a go and see what happens') and a way of countering her thinking trap (negative glasses) by focusing upon what she was achieving rather than what she felt she could do better was rehearsed.

Session nine revealed that Sarah had successfully been to the coffee shop with her friend. She did not become unduly anxious and rated the belief that she wasn't able to cope as 40/100. Over the next three sessions further experiments were agreed, culminating in Sarah going out one Saturday shopping with her friends.

Relapse Prevention

The final sessions were monthly and encouraged Sarah to reflect on what she had discovered and the skills she found useful. Possible setbacks were discussed and a written coping plan developed. She continued to face and cope with increasingly difficult situations, and six weeks after the final appointment she sent a postcard from London where she had gone shopping with her friends.

Summary

This chapter has focused on:

- Historical development of CBT
- Theoretical model
- Therapeutic process
- Phases of CBT
- Adapting CBT for children
- Non-verbal methods

Reflective Questions

1 How might you incorporate more non-verbal techniques into your practice?

Younger children: cartoons and thought bubbles can be used to identify and discuss what someone might be thinking; pictures and worksheets can stimulate and emphasise key aspects of the CBT model; games like emotional charades can highlight the different facial and bodily signals associated with different emotions. Older children: diagrams and summary sheets (explaining the link between thoughts, feelings and behaviours) provide a useful way of summarising the cognitive model; video clips can be a useful way of presenting ideas and stimulating discussions (e.g. around thinking styles and errors).

2 When you ask a child or young person 'what were you thinking?' they reply 'nothing' or 'I don't know'. Does this mean that they are not able to engage in CBT?

It is not uncommon for young people to reply to direct questions in such a way. This does not mean that they are unable to identify their thoughts but suggests that alternative methods might be more productive. You can help them tune into their thoughts by talking about positive or familiar events (e.g. preparing for something they like) or by talking about what a third party could be thinking. With younger children you could describe an event and ask them to write or draw a picture in a blank thought bubble to show what someone might be thinking about it. Alternatively, you may discover a child's thoughts by simply listening very carefully to what they say. Descriptions often include thoughts and assumptions which we are not always very good at noticing.

3 What tends to be the content of negative automatic thoughts associated with anxiety and depression?

The content of anxious cognitions tends to be about threat ('people are looking at me'), danger ('everyone will make fun of my new trainers') or an inability to cope ('I won't know what to say if they ask me any questions'). Depressive cognitions tend to be about loss ('everyone I get to know leaves me'), deprivation ('I am sure I'm not as interesting as everyone else') and failure ('I am useless at talking to people').

4 What are the key characteristics of functional and dysfunctional thoughts?

Functional thoughts can be described as 'green thoughts' because they are motivating and encourage you to do things. They are positive ('I can do it'), balanced ('this might be hard but I have done it before') and enabling ('I've got nothing to lose by giving it a try'). Dysfunctional thoughts are 'red thoughts' which stop you from doing things.

They are negative ('I will get this wrong'), biased ('I can never get this right') and are disempowering ('there is no point in trying').

Learning Activities

1   How would you explain CBT to a 9- or 10-year-old child with an anxiety disorder?

Keep the explanation very simple. You could say that 'people who worry often think in ways that make them feel frightened. When they feel frightened they want to avoid the things that scare them. We will work together to see if this happens for you by looking at the way you think, how you feel and what you do'.

2   You would like to find out more about the negative thoughts a 14-year-old boy is having and think that a thought diary would be helpful. How would you go about doing this?

You would need to provide a rationale and explain why this was important and negotiate whether he would be able to undertake this task. The 'diary' could be a paper record, computer log, text or email so the boy can choose a method that he finds most attractive. Check that the diary is achievable, e.g. you may agree to record a whole week or the next three negative thoughts. If the boy feels unable to keep the diary then respect his decision. You will still be able to find out about his thoughts by talking through any situations during your next meeting.

3   Design an experiment to test a belief that 'I never get my school work right'.

Ask the young person to predict what they think would happen if this was true, i.e. I will get D grades or lower. Ask them to rate how much they believed this thought on a 1–100 scale. The young person could then record all their school marks over the next week. What actually happened is then compared with what they predicted, to test their belief. How much they believed the original thought can then be re-assessed to see whether the experiment had helped them discover any new information which challenged their original belief (e.g. 'I seem to get better marks in history').

4   Think about some Socratic questions you could use with adolescents

Socratic questions are designed to encourage self-refection with the aim of helping the young person find new information and meanings which challenge their existing thoughts. The therapist adopts an open and curious stance and uses questions to draw the young person's attention to exceptions ('have there been any times that this didn't happen?'), reflect on different perspectives ('what would your best friend think if this happened to them?') and to consider different meanings ('are there any other explanations for what has happened?').

Further Reading

Adapting CBT

Friedberg, R.D. and McClure, J.M. (2002) *Clinical Practice of Cognitive Therapy with Children and Adolescents.* New York: Guilford Press.

Friedberg, R.D., McClure, J.M. and Hillwig Garcia, J. (2009) *Cognitive Therapy Techniques for Children and Adolescents.* New York: Guilford Press.

Kendall, P.C. (ed.) (2012) *Child and Adolescent Therapy: Cognitive-Behavioral Procedures.* 4th edn. New York: Guilford Press.

Stallard, P. (2002) *Think Good – Feel Good: A Cognitive Behaviour Therapy Workbook for Children and Young People.* Chichester: John Wiley.

Stallard, P. (2005) *A Clinician's Guide to Think Good – Feel Good: The Use of CBT with Children and Young People.* Chichester: John Wiley.

Verduyn, C., Rogers, J. and Woods, A. (2009) *Depression: Cognitive Behaviour Therapy with Children and Young People.* London: Routledge.

Examples of CBT Programmes

Barrett, P. (2012) *Friends for Life: Group Leaders Manual.* 5th edn. Available at: www.friendsinfo.net/uk.htm (FRIENDS anxiety prevention programme).

Clarke, G., Lewinsohn, P., Hops, H. and Grossen, B. (1990) *Leader's Manual for Adolescent Groups.* Available at: www.kpchr.org/research/public/acwd/acwd.html (Adolescent coping with depression course).

Kendall, P.C. and Hedtke, K.A. (2006) *Cognitive Behavioural Therapy for Anxious Children: Therapist Manual.* 3rd edn. Available at: www.workbookpublishing.com/ (Coping Cat anxiety treatment programme).

Rohde, P., Feeny, N.C. and Robins, M. (2005) *Characteristics and Components of the TADS CBT Approach.* Available at: www.ncbi.nlm.nih.gov/pmc/articles/PMC1894655/ (Programme used in the Treatment for Adolescents with Depression Study – TADS).

5

Gestalt

Belinda Harris

This chapter includes:

- Key gestalt concepts and relational processes that inform a gestalt understanding of human development
- The research evidence for gestalt practice with children and young people
- The development of gestalt theory, and significant influences on its formulation and evolution
- Key features of and relational processes involved in gestalt practice, illustrated by thickly disguised case vignettes
- Gestalt as a brief therapy

Introduction

As a humanistic teacher and counsellor working with adolescents in schools in challenging circumstances, I was drawn to gestalt because of familiarity with its underlying philosophical approach, including a focus on the whole person (holism), on awareness of immediate, present-centred experience (existential-humanism), and on the way the individual perceives and engages with reality (phenomenology). Gestalt's particular appeal, however, lay in the emphasis placed on the young person in their situation, its field theoretical orientation.

Field Theory and the Evolution of Self

The concept of field has two meanings here: the first focuses on the way the person organises their inner experience (*perceptual field*) to make meaning of their situation; the second (derived from Lewin's (1935) field theory) recognises that the person and their world are inseparable and interdependent parts of a dynamic whole, or *gestalt*. Gestalt recognises human development as a lifelong, co-creative and inter-subjective process. The self-experience of the infant and the self-experience of the parent therefore co-evolve within a dynamically unfolding relational field. It is the present moment experience (sensory, physical, emotional and cognitive) *between* adult and child that enables the child to differentiate between the 'I' and the '*not I*', and the adult to develop their felt sense as a parent (e.g. competent or incompetent) in relation to the child.

This energetic meeting at the '*contact boundary*' (Goodman, 1951) leads to an iterative, vibrant integration of experience; a perspective that is consistent with Stern's infant observation research (1985), and with recent findings in affective neuroscience (Lee, 2007). The gestalt therapist's focus, therefore, is on the young client within their situation, and may involve working with members of the child's relational field to enhance their ability to support the child.

The Relational Field

The relational field has two elements:

a) the *ground* of the relationship, which includes, for example, the child's unique characteristics (e.g. health, temperament, etc.) and the parents' mental model of parenting, values and support systems;

b) the *figure* – the dominant need informing the relational contact (e.g. the child is tired and needs to be carried).

These elements combine in the embodied, present-centred experience of child and adult at the contact boundary, as each makes a '*creative adjustment*' (Goodman, 1951) to the other. If the need is met and assimilated, the gestalt is closed and a state of balance is restored (i.e. the child is rested and re-energised). McConville (2007) argues that two ground conditions are particularly important in supporting child development, namely the extent and ways in which power is exercised to influence the child's choices and behaviours, and the way the boundaries of the relationship are organised and transformed over time to meet the child's emergent developmental needs.

When the use of power and boundaries is sufficiently attuned to the needs and capabilities of the child *and* the here-and-now situation, then the child's organismic self-regulation process (Perls, 1948: 576) is activated and their evolving sense of self is supported. For example, when a toddler moves towards danger (e.g. an electrical socket), the parent acts decisively but gently to divert their attention elsewhere. Such contact alters the ground of the child–adult relationship and the toddler trusts the relational field to meet their need for safe, self–environment exploration.

Conversely, if the toddler's needs for safety and containment are ignored or responded to with harshness or contempt, then the flow of their experiencing is interrupted. Where neglect or abuse persists, the creative adjustment needed to manage and make meaning of the situation is likely to result in a fixed gestalt, or rigid way of being at the contact boundary when similar situations occur. This is evident, for example, when a distraught, sobbing boy is scornfully told to 'stop being a sissy and act like a man'. If repeated over time, he learns not to approach another for support when he is distressed, then he learns to stop himself from crying, and eventually he becomes unaware of his need to cry when he is hurting. A *fixed gestalt* therefore is often indicative of an unfinished situation.

Unfinished Situations

Perls (1969 [1947]) identified a physiological–biological 'cycle of interdependency of organism and environment' (p. 45) which Goodman (1951) subsequently categorised as fore-contact, contact, final contact and post-contact. If followed sequentially, these stages of contact between the child and others in their environment enable them to create a meaningful whole (gestalt) from their experience. The sense of completion and closure of the gestalting process is experienced intuitively as 'right', and is accompanied by a sense of calm, satisfaction, peace or fulfilment. However, if progression through the cycle is thwarted in some way, and the gestalt remains incomplete, then unfinished business results.

The therapeutic relationship provides a here-and-now situation in which closure (Perls, 1975 [1959]) can be experienced viscerally and emotionally. For example, a child whose parents are over-protective may need support to define and express their own needs and wants. The parents may also need help with unfinished situations (e.g. traumatic experience in childhood) to manage their hyper-anxiety about safety and reduce the power they exert over the child's choices within the relational field.

The Relational Field of Childhood

In early childhood the child's primary need is for 'embedding' (McConville, 1995), a sense of connection where they feel safe and protected enough to explore the environment, to express themselves physically and emotionally, and to trust in others for stimulation, comfort and support. During the embedding phase the child needs a 'porous relational boundary' (McConville, 2007: 9) where significant adults are intensely involved with the child's physical growth and well-being. Adults use their power to soothe and support the child's affective experiencing, as well as to firmly and decisively inhibit behaviours that could do harm, and refuse to accede to the child's excessive or inappropriate wants. In other words, the child experiences support whilst also learning to manage their emotions (fear, sadness, anger, joy) and tolerate disappointment.

The Relational Field of Adolescence

In contrast, the adolescent is focused on the process of 'disembedding' (McConville, 1995) from the family and other adult systems of support. This involves a major reorganisation of the field, based on differentiation of self from others and integration of the evolving self into new *Gestalten* or wholes. The adolescent is actively involved in stretching and redefining their power and boundaries, and needs significant adults (and their therapist) to support a 'safe emergency' (Perls et al., 1951) of the adult self, *and* of their worlds, whether family, social, or educational. 'Safe emergency', a term coined by Perls et al. (1951), highlights the importance of *just enough* support to risk experimenting with new behaviours, in service of 'becoming' whole.

McConville (2007) highlights the key role of negotiation in this process, so that adult and adolescent meet at the contact boundary as separate individuals. Here they discuss what actions are reasonable and acceptable according to the adolescent's immediate wishes, and in the context of the environmental situation. Handled well, such negotiations are characterised by and nourish mutual respect and a flexible, rather than rigid, responsiveness. The adolescent is held accountable for their behaviours and there is a positive shift in the ground of the child–adult relationship, whereby the adolescent disembeds from the family without losing their sense of belonging, and the family slowly adjusts to and appreciates the emerging adult without a loss of connection to their child or sibling.

The Shame–Support Dynamic

The reader may have noticed the frequent use of the word 'support', and gestalt therapists are curious about the quality and quantity of support in the person–environment field. Where, for example, the demands of the environment and the needs of the child conflict, then the creative adjustment required of the child and/or the environment to accommodate the other may be costly. For example, for children and young people with complex trauma, the behaviours required of them in school settings constitute a 'big ask' (Bomber, 2011), and without sufficient support the student is likely to fail in some way and experience further punishment, rejection and humiliation.

From a gestalt perspective such situations manifest as shame, which is '*a major regulator of the boundary between self and other*. It is a field variable, a ground condition that is the opposite of *support*' (Lee, 1996: 10; emphasis in original). Shame is an excruciating sense of self-disgust and isolation, in which the individual's yearnings for connection are unmet. This creates a 'shame bind' (Kaufman, 1989), whereby the individual withdraws from the environment rather than reaching out. This is often as true of parents, who feel judged and blamed for their child's misdemeanours, and therefore avoid contact with the school. The shame bind not only inhibits the awareness and expression of vital, positive energy but also creates strong neural pathways for experiencing self-disgust and rejection in early childhood (Philippson, 2004).

In this situation the therapeutic process involves novel experiences that foster the development of new neural pathways. A gestalt therapist develops an in-depth appreciation of shame dynamics and uses the relational field within and beyond the therapy room to support the young client's connection with self and others. Such long-term work requires a therapist who has enough self-support to lean into the shame – experiencing the client's resistance to being accepted and to stay present at the contact boundary. Despite being repeatedly mistrusted, verbally attacked and rejected, the therapist remains solidly present until there is 'at least a thread of a relationship' (Oaklander, 2006: 20), when the therapeutic work can begin.

History and Background of the Gestalt Approach

The early 20th century saw major developments in science and technology and a rise in radical socialist movements, challenging the prevailing order. New movements in the arts also challenged bourgeois values and norms, as evidenced by expressionist paintings depicting the subjective feelings and fantasies of the artist. The founders of gestalt therapy embraced the creativity, spontaneity and intuition of expressionism alongside the existential focus on 'being' (what is) and 'potential being', which is experienced through the exercise of choice with self-responsibility.

Fritz Perls is considered the father of gestalt therapy, yet his two co-founders, Laura Perls (dancer and philosopher) and Paul Goodman (radical thinker, activist and writer), were significant contributors to its evolution. The Perls were trained as Freudian analysts (Wulff, 1966) and critiqued Freud for refusing to evolve his theory further in the light of new influences and information. In contrast, the founders eschewed dogmatism in favour of 'the experimental, insecure, but creative, pioneering attitude' (Perls, 1948: 586). The Perls broke their ties with psychoanalysis (Perls, 1969 [1947]), and having escaped German fascism, settled in New York in 1946, joining with Goodman to develop their theory of gestalt practice. For this, they drew on direct experiences of working with key professionals over previous decades.

Of particular relevance for this chapter are the influences of Martin Buber, Laura Perls' teacher; the neuropsychologist Kurt Goldstein, in whose clinic for soldiers with traumatic brain injuries Perls worked (Goldstein identified the concept and process of self-actualisation two decades before Abraham Maslow popularised it); Jacob Moreno, who emphasised the client 'showing' and experiencing rather than talking 'about'; and Wilhelm Reich, whose breath- and body-oriented approach illuminated the processes of working holistically.

Violet Oaklander is responsible for developing a comprehensive account of gestalt therapeutic process with children. Originally trained as a teacher, in the 1960s she found her niche with emotionally disturbed children. In childhood Oaklander experienced long-term hospitalisation and major surgical interventions. As a parent she was further traumatised when one of her children was diagnosed with terminal lupus. While he was dying in hospital, she attended a one week gestalt group experience, which she described as life changing (Elsbree, 2009). She attributed this impact to the quality of the relationship with the group therapist, Jim Simkin:

> He got me working on my grief, on my anger, on my avoidance ... my denial of what was happening ... everything, but at the same time he was always with me. Talk about an 'I–Thou' relationship, he was with me. ... He really got me working. When I say it changed my life, I mean it somehow transformed me. (p. 205)

Oaklander then trained as a gestalt therapist and began to present and write up her work. *Windows to Our Children* (1988) was adapted from her doctoral thesis, and has been translated into 13 languages. Her experience with Simkin and other gestalt trainers, including Laura Perls, who she described as a 'loving presence', informed her understanding of therapeutic process, which is characterised by contact, awareness and dialogue on the bedrock of a safe, trustworthy, engaged relationship.

Whilst Oaklander still dominates the field, other gestalt therapists continue to evolve the theory and practice of gestalt (e.g. Harris, 2011; Wheeler and McConville, 2002), to acknowledge and incorporate the neuroscientific evidence, that affirms gestalt's original emphasis on the embodied (e.g. Tervo, 2007) and relational fields (e.g. Lee and Harris, 2011) with reference to a range of presenting issues (e.g. eating disorders, sexuality, grief, trauma, learning disabilities) and age groups (e.g. Blend, 2007; Blom, 2006). In the next section I will illuminate the theory–practice relationship with reference to case vignettes from practice.

Translating Theory into Practice

The Person of the Therapist

Perls (1970: 15) recognised that talking *about* issues inhibits awareness and that it is sensory, embodied experiencing within the therapeutic relationship that opens the door to change. Using their awareness as a searchlight, the gestalt therapist endeavours to tune into the field, noticing their own experiencing (e.g. sensation, physicality, feelings, fantasies) and moment by moment changes in the client's contact (e.g. skin tone, eye contact, posture, breathing, emotional expression), to be fully present to *what is*.

Case Study   Meera

Meera is eight years of age, and I notice my throat and chest tighten as she looks vacantly round the room, before choosing to sit on a beanbag. Her breathing is shallow and her chest looks collapsed, as if defeated. I sense that she needs me close, so I softly offer her the choice 'Do you want me to join you or sit over here?' She shrugs her shoulders, and yet moves over to create space, so I sit down alongside her. We are quiet and there is a sense of calm between us. After a few minutes like this, she turns to look up at me and quietly says 'Jodie, my dog, died'. I notice my throat and chest relaxing, and tears welling up behind my eyes. She swallows hard and her chest tightens, so I gently offer, 'It's ok to cry when someone you love dies', and she bursts into tears.

This deliberate use of the embodied self is predicated on self-awareness, and gestalt training is an intensive experiential process supported by ongoing in-depth personal therapy. The trainee becomes acutely aware of their own embodied presence and impact on others. Therapy requires humility and awareness that within the co-emerging field anything can happen. There is no room for complacency or grandiosity.

Creativity lies at the heart of gestalt practice and the therapist must be imaginative and comfortable playing in an uninhibited way with children and young people at all developmental levels. Within the creative play the therapist is a willing participant in the individual's efforts to define themselves, express their emotions, and gain some sense of their potency and efficacy.

Oaklander (2006) describes vividly participating in games where she was bossed about, handcuffed or tied up by young clients who needed an embodied experience of feeling powerful and in control. I have certainly played the cowering pupil of a shaming, angry 11-year-old teacher, in the service of completing an unfinished situation. In this process clear limits and boundaries are vital, as is modelling 'No' appropriately.

Rigorous attention to self-care, self-support and use of supervision are essential when the therapist is committed to supporting the young client within their field. Working with children and adolescents requires stamina and emotional resilience.

The Nature of the Relationship

For many young people, the therapist is just another adult who will let them down. Therefore, being met at the contact boundary in a new way enables the client to re-sensitise their awareness of the *now*, and of the totality of their experiencing, e.g. their likes and dislikes, their similarity to and difference from the therapist. Such awareness helps the young person to define themselves and develop self-support, and is built on solid ground.

Establishing the Ground of the Relationship

Oaklander (2006: 27) compares therapy with children to a dance – 'sometimes I lead and sometimes the child leads'. There is movement between directivity and non-directivity according to the demands of the situation. In the early stages of the relationship the focus is on safety and trust-building through the dialogic 'I–Thou' relationship (Buber, 1959 [1937]). Here the therapist's authenticity and equanimity meet the child where they are, as an equal and separate individual.

Through their embodied presence and ability to honour and respect the client's resistance, contact style, rhythm and pace, they lay foundations for the work. They are not interested in creating dependency or being a surrogate parent, but commit to being a caring, supportive presence, holding an attitude of '*creative indifference*' (Friedlander, 1918), or neutrality. This attitude supports 'responding' (Parlett, 2000), whereby the client develops response-ability and responsibility for their choices through a gradual expansion of experiences they can assimilate.

Case Study   Syed

Syed, aged 12, was referred for therapy by his teacher because of his constant distracting of others and inability to sit still. Initially I copied his running and darting around the room, and voiced my experience out loud, e.g. 'I'm enjoying this pace'; 'I'm hot and stopping for a moment'. Each week the amount of time we spent in this cat and mouse game gradually decreased and he slowed down, becoming interested in exploring other games we could play together.

Developing the Client's Sense of Self

Once the relationship is established, then we work together to develop the child's 'embodying' ability (Parlett, 2000), including awareness of their senses, their breathing, the way they use their body and express their thoughts and feelings. In all this the therapist is a playmate or friendly companion who is genuinely interested in and welcoming of the whole child, however they present.

Having fun is part of childhood and helps to build the relational field. If a child is anxious and their breathing is shallow, I may suggest that we blow bubbles or play tin whistles to see how much noise we can make. I may offer pieces of fabric doused with aromatherapy oils, to support choosing between two scents, or tasting two different fruits. I may ask adolescents to bring their favourite music CD, or use fashion magazines to create a collage of their ideal personal wardrobe. Guided imagery and meditation techniques serve as strategies to calm and settle themselves in times of stress. Such work also supports self-definition, and Oaklander (2006) gives numerous examples of helping clients to use 'I' statements, as they clarify who they are and who they are not.

Opportunities for play and 'experiencing mastery' (p. 28) are also important for clients who have had insufficient support and grown up too quickly. Even adolescents can become absorbed in tidying the doll's house, building lego scenes or writing a poem. Through such activities they gain a sense of satisfaction in their achievement and consolidate their evolving capacity for self-support.

Expanding the Client's Sense of Self

Once the sense of self is sufficiently robust, the experience of imaginative play enables the therapist to support the client's imaginal world. Using whichever creative materials they are drawn to, the client is encouraged to create a scene, and these scenes are often representations of their situation. Listening intently, the therapist invites the client to describe what they have created, and to 'be' one or more of the characters, e.g. 'I am the fat controller and I decide where the naughty engines go'. The therapist encourages the client to say more, and asks questions, e.g. 'Which engine is the naughtiest?'; 'What do they do that is naughty?'. These projections offer the therapist a sense of the client's world and the client experiences being heard, accepted and responded to in their fantasy world. They also practise 'experimenting' (Parlett, 2000), where they begin to risk novel ways of being, acting and thinking.

Completing the Gestalt

The fantasy is a kind of a bridge into aspects of the self that they don't even know are parts of the self. The child begins to relate to those parts and gets to the point where they can own them. It's like they're looking into a window of the self. (Oaklander, in Mortola, 2011: 346)

Oaklander does this by inviting the client to dialogue with the characters in their picture or sand-play, e.g. 'How could you help the fat controller?'; 'What would you like to tell him?'. She emphasises, however, that such work is founded on the therapist's relationship with and support for the child, which enables them to engage in the fantasy, relate to different aspects of self and own them. Such work strengthens 'self-recognising' (Parlett, 2000), or knowing one's own truth, and young clients may use the relationship with the therapist to develop and embody new competences, such as exerting power and control over others in the service of completing *Gestalten*.

This stage also supports 'interrelating' (Parlett, 2000), the ability to relate to others according to the needs of the situation. The process of gestalt completion may happen within one session or take many sessions. The therapist needs to stay alert to the client's resistance surfacing at any stage, as expressed through a change in energy, or suddenly diverting attention elsewhere. Such resistance is honoured and respected, so clients learn to trust their natural cycle of contact and withdrawal. The therapist has faith that that they will return to complete the gestalt when they are ready.

Brief Therapy

Houston (2003) provides a powerful rationale for the relevance and value of brief gestalt therapy with adults. She offers the reader a useful framework for supporting the client through their contact cycle towards completion of their need, and case studies which illuminate how individual and group gestalt practice may enhance clients' abilities to impact and respond to their environment. Here I focus on three aforementioned aspects of gestalt practice that support the relevance and value of gestalt for brief work with children and young people.

First, gestalt emphasises process, or what is happening in the here-and-now between therapist and client, whereby the client's dominant need organises their perceptual field. The therapist stays open to the totality of the experience of the young person's impact on them and uses this awareness to inform their way of being with the client in the present moment. Second, the therapist is willing to enter their client's world as an attuned playmate or companion and meet them exactly where they are. This experience of support helps to interrupt any shame processes, and affects the client's self-experiencing at the contact boundary, potentially opening them up to new possibilities. Third, the therapist is committed to support the client's potential for creative experimentation so they may try out novel experiences (e.g. being the centre of loving attention, expressing anger) as a means to complete their dominant need or unfinished situation. Such work may take place within one session, or over a number of sessions, depending on how successfully the ground of the relationship is established.

Oaklander's reports of her work with young clients demonstrate that brief work can be effective for many children and young people, and in some cases may be as much as they can assimilate at a given stage in their own developmental process. In the final section I offer a brief account of contemporary research evidence for a gestalt approach to working with children and young people.

The Research Evidence

Greenberg (2008) argues that process–outcome research studies have proved a valuable way of generating evidence-based data on gestalt therapy with adults over many years. Recently, gestalt practitioners working in the NHS found a practice-based research network (PBRN) approach to collecting methodical, rigorous, clinically-based, mostly quantitative data to be more workable in a context where minimum funding and voluntary effort is required. Their three-year study found gestalt psychotherapists to be as effective as therapists trained in other modalities working in the NHS and in primary care (Stevens et al., 2011). Although an equivalent study of gestalt therapy with young people in the NHS is feasible, one is yet to be conducted.

Barber and Brownell (2008: 37) argue that 'Gestalt therapists are practitioners who work with direct perception to discover how a person is sensing, thinking, feeling and imaginatively projecting information to constellate the world ... they are well on the way to conducting qualitative inquiry'. Trustworthiness is a key criterion when assessing the reliability and validity of qualitative research (Krefting, 1991), and Oaklander's collected works are a prime example of such trustworthiness in action. Her subsequent papers in *Windows to Our Children* (1988) and her latest book, *Hidden Treasures* (2006), added to the practice-based evidence in the original volume, and more recently set out the theoretical framework she created and developed over 60 years of practitioner-research.

Case Study   Eze

Eze was 15 years old when she was referred for counselling as an alternative to exclusion from school. Her tutor reported that Eze had arrived aged 14 with a glowing report of her academic and social skills. However, neither had been evident since then and her attitude to authority, behaviour and academic work had caused concern, despite teachers' best efforts to engage her and hold her to account. Her parents had apparently been uncooperative.

Initially Eze seemed hesitant, peeking a glance at me before plonking herself down on the chair closest to the door. I sensed her resistance, 'I guess you don't want to be here with me. I understand … you didn't choose to come. So we both need some time to check each other out'. She looked askance at me, so I continued, explaining that I would meet her parents separately and explain our contract together, including issues of confidentiality. When asked if she had any questions she sat up and informed me that speaking to her parents would be a 'waste of time'. I thanked her for her honesty and asked 'how are you feeling now you've told me that?'. 'Fine' came the prompt reply. 'Are you willing to try something with me?' I inquired. 'You can stop whenever you want'. She looked non-plussed but nodded. 'Okay, let's take in some short, shallow breaths, like this. How was that?'. 'Easy'. 'Good, shall we try another way now?'. Eze nodded, so we took some longer, deeper inhalations and exhalations. I noticed her face soften and her upper body relax as we did this, and we ended the session with an agreement to 'do more stuff like that' the next week.

On meeting Eze's parents, they insisted I get her 'back on track'. When I inquired whether anything had happened that would account for the changes in her behaviour, they were quiet and looked away. Her mother abruptly stood up and proclaimed, 'it's just puberty, it's normal!' before walking out.

Eze and I continued to work together on sensory activities to deepen awareness of herself and her preferences. One day she expressed some muted anger towards her parents and I invited her to choose some objects to represent her parents and place them in the sand tray. She became totally absorbed creating a scene with four figures, a lion cub lying in the sand with a lion on each side, and another cub hidden from view behind a mud wall. She poured sand over the lying cub until it was completely covered. I suggested she 'be' one of the figures in the scene and speak 'as if' she were them. She looked embarrassed, so I encouraged her to focus on the breathing and grounding techniques we had practised. Tuning into her growing capacity for self-support, she was able to speak as the buried cub: 'I want to live. Help me'. As the cub behind the wall she said, 'I am so lonely. I wish I had died, not you'. I was touched by the agony in her voice and took a moment before asking her what this scene meant for her. Tearfully, she told me her twin sister had died of a congenital disease 18 months earlier. She had neither been allowed to visit her bedside towards the end, nor to attend the funeral. Since then, it had been taboo to speak of her sister at home, as 'it would kill her mother'. Within six months of their bereavement her parents had sold the family home and moved to a new suburb.

Summary

- Gestalt works with the totality of the child's relational field, and recognises the dynamic interplay of field variables. These are experienced at the *contact boundary* between adult and child. Here, both co-evolve in response to one another and the demands of the situation

- It is assumed that everyone is doing the best they can with the resources they have in the moment. This involves making *creative adjustments* to the situation in order to achieve a satisfactory ending, or *complete gestalt*
- Shame and belonging are key field variables affecting experience at the contact boundary. Two ways of being at the contact boundary are of particular importance for child development: the way power is exercised and the way boundaries are organised to meet the child's emergent needs
- The therapist is a fully *embodied, energetically available presence* and meets the child where they are, offering an 'I–Thou' experience at the contact boundary. It is recognised that no therapeutic work will occur until the relationship is established
- Gestalt therapy may be *directive or non-directive* depending on the demands of the situation and the present moment. The therapist partners with the child and *co-creates* what happens with as much support as possible and as little support as possible, to activate the client's organismic self-regulatory process
- Gestalt is a *creative* therapy and uses multi-sensory media to support the client's experiencing of self at the contact boundary, and hence self-definition. From this ground the client can explore other aspects of self that have been neglected, become fixed or disowned in some way
- Clients are helped to understand and own their feelings, offered opportunities to unblock emotions that interfere with their capacity to function healthily, and to learn how to express difficult feelings safely

Reflective Questions

1 There is a field between you the reader and the text. How are you experiencing this field? What did you bring to the field by way of your previous experience of gestalt? How did this affect your reading? How, if at all, has your view of gestalt changed as a result of reading the chapter?

This question provides an opportunity to explore what is co-created between the author and reader. The aim is to support you in identifying your own cherished values and beliefs, and also to notice how you respond to the similarities and differences between your own theory of practice and gestalt.

2 How do you currently engage with the relational field in your own work with children and young people? How do you manage the relational ethics within the field?

Working with adults in support of the child or young person can feel challenging, and therefore it is important to establish the relational ethics involved at the outset. The young person's needs and voice are paramount, and unless contravening my legal responsibilities, I would not disclose any information shared with me unless the young person had given their express permission to do so. This is also true when working with both parties, as with Eze in the case vignette. When working separately with a parent or teacher, my key focus is on supporting their process, and helping them to develop the attributes and skills needed to support the young person more sensitively and effectively.

3 How do the concepts of embedding and disembedding work for you when thinking about the child's and adolescent's relationship with significant others? How might the way you exercise your power and hold boundaries change over time as a child moves through the school years?

Young child: power is exercised to support the child's engagement in co-created experiences to meet their dominant need at the time. In this way pressing or unmet needs (e.g. for attention and care, self-definition, control, mastery) can be met. Within this process the therapist holds boundaries conducive to novel experiencing whilst keeping the child safe at all times.

Adolescent: power is exercised to support the young person's capacity for making responsible choices, and then behaving appropriately and in accordance with their choices. Boundaries are negotiated with the young person to support their growing ability to hold appropriate boundaries themselves. If a young person fails to behave appropriately, then the boundaries are collaboratively redrawn between the pair to support their joint learning from the situation, and without activating debilitating shame.

Learning Activities

1. If you reflect on the relational field in your family of origin, or your current family, what is the ground of the relationship? Consider individual and cultural factors, including roles, values, norms related to social, emotional behaviour, etc. How do these affect the quality of your relating with significant others at the contact boundary?

2. What memories do you have of adults playing alongside you to give you experiences of mastery, power and control? How were you supported by adults to find your voice (thoughts and feelings) as a child or adolescent?

3. Given the above, how might you respond to a young person's desire to handcuff you or confine you to a chair under their orders? What further work might you need to do to be able to enter a child's play world and meet them where they are as a character in their fiction or drama?

4. Think of a young person or client you know well. What is the balance of shame and support in their life? Are you aware of any unfinished business that might affect their way of being with you at the contact boundary?

5. How well equipped do you feel to work with parents to support their capacity to support your client? How would you manage the key issues of power and boundaries in this situation?

Further Reading

DeMille, R. (1997) *Put Your Mother on the Ceiling: Children's Imagination Games*. Cambridge, MA: The Gestalt Press.

Kanner, C. and Lee, R.G. (2005) 'The relational ethic in the treatment of adolescents', *Gestalt Review*, 9 (1): 72–90.

Lampert, R. (2003) *A Child's Eye View: Gestalt Therapy with Children, Adolescents and Their Families*. Cambridge, MA: The Gestalt Press.

Oaklander, V. (1979) 'A gestalt therapy approach with children through the use of art and creative expression', in E.H. Marcus (ed.), *Gestalt Therapy and Beyond*. Cupertino, CA: Meta Publications.

Oaklander, V. (1992) 'Gestalt work with children: Working with anger and introjects', in E.C. Nevis (ed.), *Gestalt Therapy: Perspectives and Applications*. New York: Gardner Press.

Oaklander, V. (1999) Group play therapy from a gestalt therapy perspective', in D.S. Sweeney (ed.), *Group Play Therapy: Theory and Practice*. New York: Charles C. Thomas.

Online Resources

BACP website: www.bacp.co.uk/ especially the BACP Children and Young People Division and the Competences for Working with Children and Young People.

Counselling MindEd: http://counsellingminded.com.

6

Becoming an Integrative Practitioner

Niki Cooper and Kelli Swain-Cowper

This chapter includes:

- Common features of integrative practice
- The challenges and benefits of becoming an integrative practitioner
- An integrative practice-based model which uses a developmental perspective to integrate aspects of attachment, psychodynamic, person-centred, play therapy and systemic thinking
- A case history to illustrate core principles of theoretical synthesis

Child practitioners, especially those working in settings with a socially and culturally diverse client group, often find themselves making use of a variety of therapeutic models and techniques to meet the needs of the children they work with (Warr, 2009).

It is hoped that what will emerge is an understanding of how the different schools of counselling are essentially, as Castonguay (2006) said, 'trying to make sense of the same beast'. As such, they do not always contradict each other but can offer helpfully complementary perspectives which give a fuller dimension to our understanding of the children and young people with whom we work.

Introduction

The world of counselling and psychotherapy has a tradition of warring schools of thought or 'schoolism', which took root in the earliest days of its development. At present, the accrediting bodies are still structured along model-specific lines. As Mick Cooper (2008) bemoaned, much energy has been wasted in writing and research which simply seeks to prove which model is best and most effective. In fact, the most consistent finding in therapeutic research suggests that the models are equal in terms of effectiveness and that there are other variables which are much more predictive of positive change (Cooper, 2008). We are a long way from having all the answers about best practice with children. Our commitment must be to keep the dialogue alive and practice-led. 'Schoolism' is perhaps an understandable strategy to manage the uncomfortable muddle that is the human psyche, yet it limits the creative possibilities in evolving our understanding and practice.

There are many ways to feel better and more functional in the world. As practitioners we are not doing anything extraordinary. We are simply, as Lomas (1981) suggested, manifesting 'creative human qualities in a facilitating setting'. Everyone can be helpful to some people some of the time. Our mission as counsellors, especially for children and young people, is to strive, with humility, to develop and broaden these 'creative human qualities' so that we can more accurately attune to the needs of a diverse range of others. That way we can be helpful to more people more of the time.

History and Background

Although the name 'integrative' is a relatively new title for a way of working, in fact practitioners have been continually integrating new concepts to existing frameworks throughout the history of psychotherapeutic work. It is, however, the legacy of 'schoolism' that many innovative clinicians and theorists have been eager to be associated with or set directly against existing historical positions. It is a recent development that clinicians have openly acknowledged finding a variety of theories from different historical lines relevant to practice and have coined the term 'integrative' practice.

What do we really mean by 'integrative' practice and how does this differ from what some might describe as 'eclectic' or 'pluralistic' practice? Eclecticism is where different tools and techniques from different schools are used without any particular regard to their philosophical underpinnings (Hollanders, 1999). A pluralistic model suggests that each client needs different interventions at different stages of their therapeutic journey (Cooper and McLeod, 2007). Integration is where diverse theoretical concepts and techniques have been synthesised together to form a new coherent theoretical position (Hollanders, 1999). Arguably, 'integrative' practice itself could be viewed as the formation of yet another 'school' of thought. The difference may be that 'integrative' practice directly pays homage to each of the historical evolutions from which it borrows.

Some research suggests that although just 42 per cent of experienced counsellors declare themselves to be eclectic or integrative, as many as 98 per cent make use of techniques from different theoretical orientations (Cook et al., 2010; Hollanders and McLeod, 1999; Schottenbauer et al., 2007). A recent national scoping report of counselling in primary schools (Thompson, 2013) estimates that 61 per cent of the child practitioners would call themselves integrative and that play-oriented, art, and psycho-educational techniques are used by at least half of all responding individuals and organisational providers. This research implies that the reality of the work with children requires elements of theoretical and technical integration. Even if practitioners openly acknowledge the integrative nature of their practice (Cook et al., 2010), it is hard to know what exactly these therapists 'really do in practice'. Identifying core principles which define how theories can be woven together to connect and co-create a therapeutic relationship is the topic of this chapter.

The process of synthesising different frameworks into a coherent position presents a number of challenges to both the individual and training programmes. It is dependent upon defining an underlying philosophy which will consequently influence which theories one uses to conceptualise the very nature of what it means to be human (Gilmore, 1980). There are an infinite number of possible combinations of theory and the specific manner in which they are interwoven will, necessarily, be affected by the personality of the training, the tutors, the supervisors and that of the practitioner. In support, McLeod (2004) argues that good counselling – and, by inference, training – must be authentically grounded in our own experience and values rather than a wholesale adoption of a set of skills and techniques. Being familiar with the assumptions that we bring to the work can enable us to ensure that our practice is not limited or confined by our own social or cultural constraints, yet assist us in finding an authentic presence in the work. Together, these are perhaps some of the influences which come together to define what Stern et al. (1998) refer to as the 'therapist's personal signature'.

There are a number of examples of therapists who have created integrative models for work with children. Dowling and Osborne (2003) combine the systemic family theory and traditional psychoanalytic thinking to a child in the context of home and school.

Grehan and Freeman (2009), Holm-Hadulla et al. (2011) and Geldard and Geldard's (2010) models generally support the idea of a:

- person-centred approach for the therapeutic relationship
- psychodynamic thinking for processing and surviving the complexities of the relationship

- systemic thinking for looking at the social and cultural context of the child to locate obstacles to change and conflicts in cultural norms
- cognitive-behavioural approaches to change behaviour and/or thinking.

These approaches see the components working together in different ways. The creative challenge for an integrative practitioner is to find and identify the underlying philosophy that will make for a 'coherent' theoretical position that is helpful in practice (Gilmore, 1980).

Hollanders (1999) identifies what may be another challenge to becoming an integrative practitioner, suggesting that integration is an ever-evolving process rather than a fixed position. This makes for a journey of perpetual uncertainty and, conversely, possibility. Lowndes and Hanley (2010) highlight the difficulties for trainees on integrative training programmes in tolerating the anxiety raised by theoretical contradictions and ambiguity. However, they agree with Ladany et al. (2008) who propose that 'tolerating ambiguity is an important aspect of any counselling practice' and that managing ambiguity and not-knowing leads to a more collaborative client-led practice. Perhaps the challenge of becoming an integrative practitioner is ultimately a benefit in working with the 'untameable nature of clinical reality' (Castonguay, 2006). It is the integrative practitioner who has developed a capacity to manage the inevitable ambiguities, uncertainty and not-knowing who can remain open to the creative potential and the possibility of meeting the child in a collaboratively defined intersubjective moment.

Theoretical Underpinning: Theory into Practice

Identifying Practice-Led Core Principles

The integrative model we are presenting views each therapeutic journey as a unique series of co-created moments. However, we have identified core factors which facilitate growth and resilience in children and young people and bring about therapeutic change (Lee et al., 2009). These consist of:

- building a therapeutic relationship
- the ongoing development of self-awareness in the counsellor and the child or young person
- engaging with children, young people and adults through the medium of play or playfulness in its broad sense

Use of these core factors in our integrative practice has yielded positive outcomes, with 82 per cent of teachers and 74 per cent of parents noting positive changes for the child as a result of the therapeutic intervention (Lee et al., 2009).

The identification of these core factors which affect change is not, however, a 'coherent theoretical position', as earlier defined. Yet it becomes clear that any relevant model for working with children and young people must address these core principles.

A Practice-Led Integrative Model

This chapter presents our model for working with children. This model has been influenced by the work of diverse practitioners across the field working with children and young people for the last 20 years. Gilmore (1980) states that any integrative model for practice must begin with a general theory of human behaviour built over a foundation of philosophical assumptions. The model of integration presented here begins with the 'general theory' that children and young people are oriented toward growth, development and forming relationships, and that the nature of these relationships will affect the development of the self. We believe that, from birth, humans are driven to form secure bonds with others and that the capacity to make and build helpful relationships is the cornerstone for sound mental health (Holmes, 2010). Play, in its widest definition, is an integral language to facilitating this process of development. And finally, it is through these relationships and experiences that children develop and evolve a sense of themselves which influences their way of functioning in society.

Transcultural Challenges

An evaluation of this general theory will reveal that the underlying 'philosophical assumptions' (Gilmore, 1980) place an emphasis on a relational-based self-understanding and identity, the importance of play, the social context of mental health, the primacy of early carer relationships and an implicit valuing of a child's experiences. Many assumptions which underpin counselling trainings, both in the content and structure, have a Euro-American cultural standpoint (Watson, 2011). For example, some cultures may place a greater emphasis on the 'we' rather than the 'I', more importance on the community or intergenerational aspects of carer relationships over the mother (Music, 2011), or privilege religious or spiritual philosophy over social context in the understanding of mental health. Music (2011) poignantly exemplifies the subtleties and power of such differences when he cites a study where mothers of two different cultures are shown videos of each other's caretaking styles, resulting in each group's cringing bewilderment at the other. Given the vastness of cultural differences, we cannot hope to achieve a fully global perspective, but perhaps, as McLeod (2004) argues, being explicit about our beliefs and values, aware of a tendency toward ethnocentricity and acknowledging the cultural limitations of our assumptions, we can remain more flexible and open to a dialogue that will aspire to greater inclusivity, open acknowledgement of difference and increased accessibility.

Relationship, Self-Awareness and Play: Using a Developmental Perspective to Weave Together an Integrative Approach

Our understanding of an integrative model is a weave of attachment and child development theory; person-centred presence, regard and empathy for the other with the offering of relational depth; a psychodynamic understanding of the conscious and unconscious forces within therapeutic transference relationship; and an understanding of the early childhood 'dance' of intersubjectivity which influences the child's dance of life and the dance within the therapeutic space. The model we have presented is but one way of integrating different therapeutic understandings, theories, experiences, research and philosophies into a working model of practice, and we include it here as an illustration of integration. Many child psychotherapists argue that the traditional case study remains a useful form of research which most clearly demonstrates effective ways to practise (Reid, 2003; Rustin, 2003) and most accurately represents the qualitative, investigative and interpretive nature of therapeutic work. We continue with an illustration of how our model is applied in practice.

Case Study   Abdi

Background and Referral

Abdi is 10 years old. He is Somali and arrived in Britain when he was five years old. He lives with his mother and two older sisters. Abdi has attended a primary school in South London where there is a well-established Somali community. It was four years before the family were granted leave to stay in Britain. All of the teachers in the school are white British and female. Abdi has been referred to the school counsellor by the inclusion manager in the school because he is often in trouble for fighting on the playground, does not appear to have formed any close friendships and the rest of the class seem wary of him, and his attainment is below expectation for his age.

Goals and preferred outcomes are influenced by one's philosophical assumptions and judgements. Each adult involved with Abdi will have differing perspectives on what would be a positive change for him and different ideas about how this change might be achieved. Counselling may

(Continued)

(Continued)

not be the preferred method for achieving change for each of these individuals. By acknowledging personal preferences it is more possible to see where assumptions may be limiting the possibilities of connecting helpfully with Abdi and the systems around him. Behaviour support or extra tuition could possibly also address the priorities and beliefs of his teacher or his mother. As integrative practitioners, we would want to support this and hold in mind his relational needs as well.

Assessment

Mother

The counsellor, John, met with Abdi's mum for an assessment session and learnt the family's story. Mother described the family in Somalia, her husband and two daughters, as being secure, settled and thriving. She recounted being excited about the idea of having their third child when she discovered she was pregnant. She described the shock and fear when a sudden outbreak of war ravaged a nearby village. Her husband had quickly organised for her and the girls to flee to a Kenyan refugee camp. He had planned to send for them when the trouble had passed, but she had never heard from him again. She confided that she had suspected he had been killed, but that as she was not sure she didn't ever talk about it to the children. The uncertainty around her husband's whereabouts and the rudimentary facilities in the refugee camp had made her depressed and unsettled in the time following Abdi's birth until their move to London. Abdi had always been very difficult and demanding and she felt he had missed out on having a man about to discipline him. Things were still difficult for the family as they had only recently been given leave to stay in the UK, but she was feeling more settled and optimistic now. She explained that his two sisters were doing well at school and had formed good relationships both in and outside of school. She had friends and family in the area and was volunteering for a local Somali family project. She wanted Abdi to settle down at school so that he could learn and behave more respectfully at home. She expressed concern that he might get into more serious trouble when he moved to secondary school.

Abdi

In the assessment session Abdi moved constantly and flitted excitedly from one play activity to the next, leaving a trail of toys and mess behind him. He spoke English well, but described his activities in short, fragmented sentences. He did not make much eye contact and did not appear to want to talk about his life outside of the room. When the counsellor gently spoke of the concerns of his teacher and mother, Abdi looked fleetingly out of the window and continued to move around the room. Abdi seemingly ignored the counsellor at first, then later said that he was good at football, but that he was always treated unfairly by everyone. He said he liked coming to the lunchtime self-referral sessions because he liked playing and drawing. He was delighted to be offered more time in the playroom.

Formulation

An understanding of the importance of the early mother–child relationship in the development of the self influenced the counsellor's thinking. The work of Bowlby (2005), Winnicott (1965), Bion (1965) and Stern (1985) places importance on the capacity of the mother to emotionally attune to the infant's communications in order to help the baby manage and make sense of the chaotic array of stimulation from within and without that he is as yet unable to do himself. Stern (2004) viewed the mother's repertoire as offering vitality, experiences of being with an other and a co-regulating other. The dance between a mother and baby would be responsive to the baby's innate senses of self, which Stern referred to as the emergent self, the core self and the core self with an other. These selves are described as a newborn baby's sense of its own integrity as sensing, experiencing, continually existing beings with some awareness of and readiness to experience and engage with an other. He saw these domains of self as co-existing and forming the basis for relationship, or what he referred to as core-relatedness. It was also the foundation upon which other domains of self, e.g. the intersubjective, verbal and narrative self, would later be layered on top. Stern saw these selves as existing together like strings on a violin and viewed our interactions and activities as activating or attending to different selves at different times. He viewed it as possible to have them all vibrating in harmony, or simply one or two at a time.

The counsellor thought that the dislocation, trauma and hardship of securing basic needs would have likely affected Abdi's mother's sense of self, which in turn would impact on her capacity to provide such emotional attunement, playful and co-regulating experiences with her baby – perhaps, at times, leaving Abdi with a sense of overwhelming anxiety and a feeling of 'falling to pieces' (Horne, 1999). In light of Bowlby's (2005) attachment theory and Erikson's (1965) ideas on child development, a fundamental sense of trust and security would have been at stake in these early experiences. Abdi's domains of self and first experiences of being with and co-regulated by an other, the very foundations for intersubjective experiences, may have thus been affected (Stern, 1985).

Taking a systemic perspective, the counsellor was also aware of how isolated Abdi was becoming in the school by being 'sent out' of both his class and his football games. He had become the 'excluded' one. Culturally, his family had been uncertain of their 'right to belong' in Britain for their first four years of living there. While his mother and sisters were achieving and thriving, Abdi held a place within the family system of being undisciplined and reckless with his educational and social opportunities, which were deemed by his mother as very important. He compared Abdi's mother's belief that what her son was missing was a 'man to discipline him' with what the school was offering – an empathic counselling relationship. This made him aware of the potential for culturally-conflicting messages between the predominantly white British female school staff and Abdi's Somali,

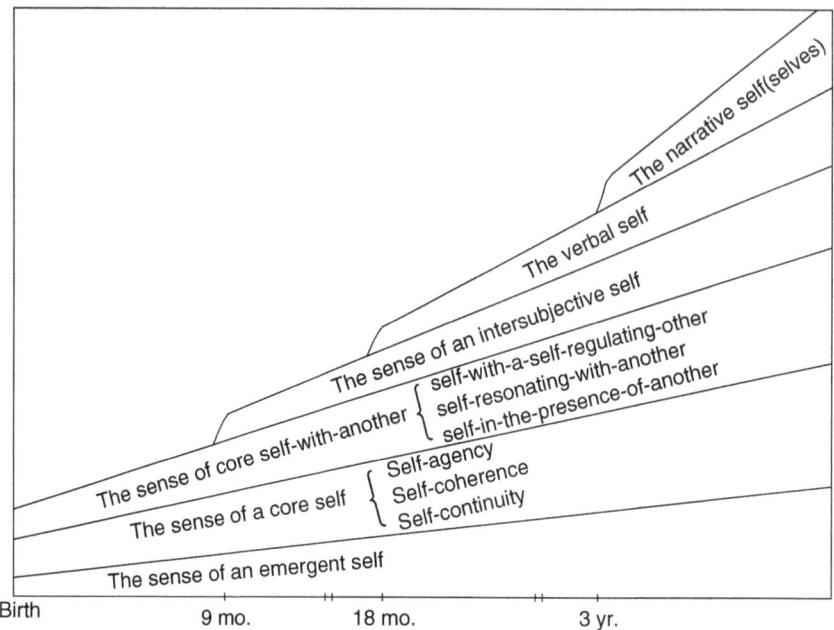

Figure 6.1 The interpersonal world of the infant (Stern, 1985: xxv).

Muslim, first-generation immigrant home culture. His presentation as the 'one who does not belong' made sense in the context of his worlds.

Abdi did have resiliencies to build on. He had made use of the self-referral lunchtime service and enjoyed the play and artwork that he had done in the room. He had used this service repeatedly, demonstrating that his internal expectations of relationships did allow for the identification of some helpful relationships and a willingness to seek them out. Although he had found the assessment difficult, he had been able to stay in the room for the whole session, suggesting that he might be able to find a safe place in the room for one-to-one work. His engagement in artwork showed his capacity to create which, according to Winnicott's (1991) idea of transitional space, necessarily indicated some aspects of 'good enough' early parenting. The family was now settled and his mother cared deeply about Abdi's success at school. He was part of a supportive community and motivated to play football. The counsellor decided that he would continue to work with Abdi's mum and teacher to ensure that their perspectives were honoured and that there was consistency in the adults' approach to him. He also offered Abdi one-to-one weekly counselling and hoped that having his story heard would create a secure enough base from which Abdi could begin to experience the world in a less uncertain way. This would, in turn, make him less anxious in the learning setting and more able to concentrate and maintain helpful relationships with his peers and other adults.

Beginning the Relationship

The play room was equipped with a range of play and art materials, including a sand tray, an array of small world figures, paints, modelling material, coloured pens and pencils, and puppets. John, the counsellor, spent the first session with Abdi drawing up a contract for their work together which named the basic boundaries of safety for them both, the times and days of their sessions, and an explanation of the limited confidentiality that John could offer. Abdi chose to draw pictures to represent the contract but finished as quickly as he could, saying that he wanted to come for counselling so he could be captain of the football team and so he could miss numeracy. John told him that he was a person in the school who listened carefully to the children's feelings and the things they think about. He explained that play and art are sometimes a good way of working things out and making sense of things together and that when he came here he could choose what he might like to do. They agreed to use the time together to think about how he could get better at football and what he would need to do to become captain.

John, inspired by person-centred play therapy, offered warmth, a positive regard and empathy to Abdi (Axline, 1990 [1971]). He viewed Abdi's process of development as driven by an actualising tendency and felt that if he offered the right conditions to Abdi, he could fulfil his potential. He allowed the child to lead the play and choose what he wanted to do in the room. However, forming a helpful relationship with Abdi was challenging.

John sat alongside Abdi while he moved from one activity to another. Abdi would use fragmented sentences to describe some goodies or baddies, but this seemed more inwardly directed. Using his knowledge that play involving 'goodies and baddies' was a common strategy for middle childhood management of anxiety (Canham, 2006), Abdi's play seemed developmentally appropriate. John observed Abdi carefully and noticed that they rarely made eye contact. John felt invisible, bored, and found it difficult to stay focused on Abdi's play. Abdi enacted one battle after another. At the end of each story everyone died and no-one came to the rescue. John reflected aloud on the stories, offering some emotional and narrative reflection on the battles. He got no response and the battles continued on in the same manner. This persisted for a number of weeks.

Supervision

In supervision John and the supervisor considered Abdi's apparent rejection of John's verbal reflections and John's sense of being bored, invisible and useless. They discussed the possibility that John's sense of not mattering and being invisible was a projection from Abdi describing his own internal experience. John's lack of attentiveness may have been a counter-transference response to Abdi's transference to John as a preoccupied and disconnected parent.

John and his supervisor were making use of an understanding of transference and counter-transference, developed from psychoanalytic and attachment-oriented therapy, which understands that a client's internal relationship models will be consciously and unconsciously communicated in the therapeutic relationship. They considered John's withdrawal and disconnection as a counter-transference response which, by thinking about it together, meant John could respond to the boredom and inattentiveness in a helpful way rather than acting it out. Awareness of the transference led John to realise that despite the warmth and good intention that he thought he was offering, Abdi's internalised expectations of relationships, expressed in his verbal and non-verbal communications, were pressuring John to repeat these earlier caregiver experiences. This realisation allowed John to stay alive and empathic to Abdi's vulnerability being expressed in the endless battles.

They also considered Abdi's metaphorical play of endless repeated battles with no helpful or organising authorities. The supervisor assisted John in linking this to Abdi's history, and both posited that the circumstances around his early childhood made it probable that his mother's availability to offer a 'co-regulating other' may have been at least partially jeopardised, leaving Abdi's core sense of self with a co-regulating other disrupted, fragmented. This could make him easily overstimulated in moments of relating. They also considered the absence of his father and Abdi's mother's feeling that order, albeit in the form of discipline, had left Abdi without a sense of structure (Horne, 1999). In reference to the transference relationship in the here and now, they considered the likelihood that Abdi was currently experiencing a doubtfulness that John could offer any help in making sense of things.

They concluded that Abdi's lack of response to verbal interventions appeared to show that Abdi was not ready for an intersubjective moment that was expressed verbally and narratively. In referring back to Stern's (1985) layered domains of self, they viewed John's rejected attempts to narrate the play in order to attune to Abdi as 'plucking the wrong string'. They felt that Abdi's non-verbal selves, particularly the core self with another, would need to be attuned to before any experiences of intersubjective meeting could happen.

Deepening the Relationship

In the following sessions John felt a deepened sense of empathy for Abdi and observed him more closely and spoke less. He mirrored Abdi's body language and breathing and when Abdi vigorously threw a tiger down into the sand, John mirrored him. Abdi looked at him wide-eyed and grinned. He picked up another figure and did the same. John followed him and this continued for the rest of the session. At times John ventured into a cross-modal sound reflection, offering a playful hmph or grrr when it matched his movements, gently bridging the domain from Abdi's non-verbal selves to a verbal self. This time Abdi was delighted and they experienced an intersubjective moment, a sense that an inner experience had been shared. This represented a significant step forward in their relationship. John had attuned to Abdi's pre-verbal senses of self. Like a mother in the early infant dance, he used his body, his expression, his deeply felt empathy to offer Abdi a chance for his core selves to be in the presence of, resonating with and co-regulated by an other. At the next session the battle of the goodies and baddies continued – only this time an ambulance arrived to tend to the wounded. The work with Abdi was slow and painstaking. John continued to deepen the relationship by focusing on Abdi's pre-verbal domains of self and by being consistent and holding the boundaries of the contract.

By the end of the first term Abdi had invited John to join in with his storytelling, and was using a wide variety of media to tell his stories. He would spend more time on one activity before moving onto the next. He enjoyed painting different characters and asking John to give voices to them. At first John checked everything he did with Abdi before he did it (What kind of a noise does the evil T Rex make? How fast does he move?). Later on, when John was confident that he was properly attuned to Abdi, he was able to make bolder interpretations and connections. He did this either in the metaphor by giving voice to the experience of one of the characters or by stepping out of the play to wonder how a character might deal with a situation. John's invitation into the storytelling began to address the narrative self by co-creating a literal metaphorical narrative. Abdi's use of John to fill in the narrative corresponds to the role a parent takes in co-creating a coherent narrative for a toddler. John was also aware of Abdi's still fragile sense of pre-verbal self and continued to be mindful of when this needed attention.

Ending

As the work was coming to an end, John and Abdi were firmly venturing into Abdi's sense of verbal and narrative self. There were occasions when Abdi talked about home, Kenya, or his classmates, and they wondered together about Abdi's thoughts and feelings. John remained aware that Abdi might still need additional support in building a more coherent narrative about himself and his experiences at some point in his future. He was aware that Abdi's verbal and narrative self had been affected by sudden changes in language and culture and that the absence of Abdi's father had only been touched upon when it had been present in the transference. John felt that Abdi might one day need to make greater sense of the loss of his father and incorporate it into his narrative understanding of himself. However, John felt confident that Abdi was taking with him a different kind of 'good enough' experience of a helping relationship and would be more likely to seek out this kind of help when he needed it.

Behavioural Change

John met with Abdi's teacher and together they thought about Abdi's difficulties in experiencing others as helpful in regulating his experiences. She began to notice when he was likely to become anxious and unregulated and could intervene earlier by responding to his pre-verbal needs immediately with a touch of his shoulder or an offering of eye contact. Her physical attentiveness enabled him to engage with the mostly verbal tasks on offer. She found that he was more focused in class and more able to engage with help to raise his achievement levels. By the end of the year, she reported that Abdi had managed three matches in the football team without being sent off and appeared pleased with himself and able to survive the moments of tension and excitement.

Practice-led models require us to truly listen to the children and young people that we work with and when we do, we believe, an integrative approach is inevitable. Abdi benefitted from an integrative approach which made use of a developmental perspective which wove together person-centred, psychodynamic and systemic interventions. Play, music, drama, art and movement are essential tools in work with children and young people because they can offer a language to explore pre-verbal aspects of the self. John's use of this integrative framework gave him the tools and the thinking to find a way to offer Abdi both non-verbal and verbal ways of making sense of himself and his world and experiencing an empathic connection. A brief therapy approach would not have been appropriate for Abdi because he needed time to build the foundations of his pre-verbal self. Brief therapy requires the pre-existence of this solid foundation.

Summary

This chapter has argued that:

- Integrative models require a sound, coherent theoretical basis within the practitioner, but are flexible and responsive to each co-created therapeutic relationship. An integrative intervention is tailor-made and not duplicatable
- The integrative practitioner's capacity to connect with children is enhanced by attending, attuning to and communicating with the verbal *and* non-verbal layers of self in relation to communications from the child and by using self-awareness helpfully
- Maintaining coherence, authenticity and flexibility to co-create unique therapeutic relationships requires the integrative practitioner to have a commitment to ongoing training and self-development in order to stay open to an ever evolving approach to the work

- Continuing to articulate what we do and why means that good practice can be shared and the dialogue can continue
- Qualitative studies of therapeutic work with children offer useful insights into best practice across all modalities (Day et al., 2006; Carroll, 2002; Green and Christensen, 2006). The insights gained from qualitative investigation of what actually happens in the counselling room may then be shaped into questions for larger qualitative and quantitative studies to establish its effectiveness

Reflective Questions

1 From a systemic perspective, what might a more extensive, supporting intervention by the counsellor look like?

In his assessment, John may become aware and focus on the relationship that home (mum and family) and school (school staff, ethos, and their responses to cultural requirements/laws/standards) have with each other. Very often in such cases as Abdi, there exist some undercurrents of blame between the two systems which make it difficult for the two systems to come together in their thinking about change (Dowling and Osborne, 2003). Dowling and Osborne (2003) warn against 'blaming' and the search to pin down 'who *must* change' and instead support the idea that a person in a 'meta' position, outside of, yet connecting, the systems can provide an impetus which invites a shift in perspective. The counsellor, in a 'meta' position between the two systems, could be just this sort of impetus for a change in the interactions and, ultimately, allow Abdi more opportunity to widen his experience beyond being the 'excluded one'. Each small shift in the perspective or experience of any of the key people in Abdi's story may lessen the possibility of Abdi remaining in the position of the 'excluded' one, but this is only possible if each system can move away from a position of blaming the other. Enabling this shift in perspective is something the integrative practitioner may be able to effect.

2 What might a follow-up intervention look like for Abdi?

Transitions and changes, especially the transition from primary to secondary schools, are anxiety provoking and difficult for many children and families to manage, even for the most resilient and supported ones. This is even more so for children who have had disruptive events in their lives or difficult early relationships, as in the case of Abdi. Good practice has shown school staff building links, ensuring that information regarding a child's educational, emotional and behavioural needs is passed on. Many secondary schools provide an induction morning, allowing Year 6 students to visit their new school. In Abdi's case, identifying key named people (such as a Year 7 head of year) or support services (such as a drop-in service or school counsellor) to both mum and Abdi may assist them in identifying helpful people to go to when in need of support. Such communication, seemingly simple, but at times technically difficult to carry through, goes a long way toward trying to hold the child in mind in the gap between the primary and secondary school systems.

3 What race, culture and age did you picture John to be?

The race, ethnicity and age of John are not mentioned in the case study. If you had an impression or image of him, it may be useful to examine what it was like. We generally associate characteristics of benevolence, altruism, thoughtfulness and hopefulness with counsellors, and it is useful to think about the race, ethnicity and age that you may associate with these general characteristics. We believe that this is an important aspect of developing self-awareness to recognise your own assumptions and biases. Lanyado (2004) reminds us of the importance of our presence as a therapist in the room, especially when working with children where you will be face to face and sometimes physically interacting in play. While some theories may suggest that your individuality should be kept out of the room, we suggest that this would be impossible and that self-awareness should be developed to ponder such things as: How might an other see me? What labels might they give me? How might this child see me, my clothes, my haircut, my race, my accent, my age, my class, my ability/disability, and what might their associations be with 'someone like me'?

Learning Activities

Activity 1: Practise Being with Another, Focusing on the Non-verbal 'Domains of Self'

When we have a conversation with a friend, our focus is on connecting and communicating with the other through our 'narrative' and 'verbal' selves. At times, many new child counsellors are less aware of and sensitive to both their own and others' non-verbal ways of being and communicating.

Sit with a willing other and try, without using words, to connect and attune to them.

Experiment with your body positions:

- sit side by side
- move closer and then further apart
- sit facing each other
- move closer and then further apart
- one of you sit on a chair, the other on the floor
- adjust how you are sitting
- monitor your physical and emotional responses to the different positions and distances
- reflect together on the 'dance' between you and discuss what made you feel connected and understood and what was uncomfortable
- did your perceptions differ?
- how aware were you of your partner's felt experience?

Activity 2: Supervision Activity for Abdi

Daniel Stern's child development model suggests that both verbal and pre-verbal aspects of self need to be attended to in order for a child to thrive emotionally. This activity helps to articulate how Abdi's layers of self are being addressed.

- Choose one small world figure to represent Abdi's verbal layers of self and another to represent Abdi's pre-verbal layers of self. Think about which object or figure you choose for each and where they are placed in relation to each other.
- Choose more small world figures to represent Abdi's mother, his father, his sisters, his peers, his culture, his teacher and John.
- How might these figures relate to each other, what might they say or need from each other? Would another constellation of figures be more helpful to Abdi's well-being? What would need to change?

Activity 3: Becoming an Integrative Practitioner

The integrative practitioner also needs to attend to both verbal and pre-verbal aspects of themselves in order to fully attune with all aspects of their child clients. This activity helps to articulate how the counsellor is addressing their own layers of self.

- Choose one small world figure to represent your verbal layers of self and another to represent your pre-verbal layers of self.
- Then choose figures to represent your training, your supervisors, your course tutors, one of your current clients and your other non-professional sources of support.
- What relationships exist between these figures? What might they have to say to each other? To develop as an integrative practitioner are there any figures that need to change or move?

Further Reading

Alvarez, A. (2012) *The Thinking Heart: Three Levels of Psychoanalytic Therapy with Disturbed Children*. London: Routledge.
Recommended to begin to conceptualise different levels of intervening in the therapeutic work with children, which we believe bridges very well with Stern's different layers of self.

Geddes, H. (2005) *Attachment in the Classroom*. London: Worth Publishing.
Recommended to build an understanding of how attachment patterns in children affect their classroom behaviours and approaches to learning.

Kalff, D. (2003) *Sandplay: A Psychotherapeutic Approach to the Psyche*. Cloverdale: Temenos Press.
An introduction into the world of sand-play and small world figures in psychotherapeutic play.

Kegerreis, S. (2010) *Psychodynamic Counselling with Children and Young People: An Introduction*. London: Palgrave.
A good introduction to the dynamics of the counselling relationship and understanding transference and counter-transference.

Landreth, G. (2002) *Play Therapy: The Art of the Relationship*. New York: Brunner-Routledge.
An overview of a person-centred approach to play therapy.

Lanyado, M. (2004) *The Presence of the Therapist: Treating Childhood Trauma*. Hove: Routledge.
A sensitively written book which acknowledges our 'presence' as therapists and as an individual person and how who we are affects the work in the room. This book uses descriptions of powerful case material to illustrate this.

Wilson, P. (2004) *Young Minds in our Schools: A Guide for Teachers and Others Working in Schools*. London: YoungMinds.
A guide for school staff describing how children may bring their life experiences into the school in their behaviour and interactions.

Online Resources

BACP website: www.bacp.co.uk/, especially the BACP Children and Young People Division and the Competences for Working with Children and Young People
Counselling MindEd: http://counsellingminded.com.

Play Therapy

Lisa Gordon Clark

This chapter includes:

- Play therapy's theoretical underpinnings and evidence base from a historical perspective
- A continuum of play therapy approaches from non-directive to directive
- Suggestions regarding setting up play therapy in a school setting
- A case study to illustrate a fairly typical play therapy process

What Is Play Therapy?

Following several years as a primary school teacher, latterly supporting children with special educational needs, I trained as a play therapist at Roehampton under Ann Cattanach in the mid-1990s and since then have worked both in private practice and as resident play therapist at a child and family centre in London. I am currently programme convener of the Play Therapy MA at the University of Roehampton. In this chapter I will describe the increasingly recognised, reputed and respected therapeutic approach with children and young people: play therapy.

In 1996 The British Association of Play Therapists adopted the following definition of play therapy:

Play Therapy is the dynamic process between child and play therapist in which the child explores at his or her own pace and with his or her own agenda those issues, past and current, conscious and unconscious, that are affecting the child's life in the present. The child's inner resources are enabled by the therapeutic alliance to bring about growth and change. Play Therapy is child-centred, in which play is the primary medium and speech is the secondary medium.

Play Therapy encompasses many approaches but the foundation of all approaches is child-centred. (www.bapt.info/aboutbapt.htm)

Whilst there is a spectrum of approaches in current play therapy practice within the UK, all share the understanding that play is the natural, instinctive means through which all children learn, communicate and explore their worlds and gain a sense of identity. Play is universal and vital to every child's social, emotional, cognitive, physical, creative and language development. It is generally held that conventional talking therapies are inappropriate for young children who struggle to find the words to describe complex feelings. Rather than having to explain what is troubling them, as adult therapy and more cognitive approaches usually expect, in play therapy children use play to communicate at their own level and pace, without feeling pressurised or interrogated. The symbolic distance of play enables children to express their feelings, thoughts and beliefs surrounding difficult life experiences. These experiences are explored and made sense of through the dynamic interaction between the child and the play therapist.

Play therapy utilises metaphors inherent in children's play, art and narratives; therefore it feels less threatening for a young person than the expectation that they explain, describe or depict factual reality. This symbolism has been termed 'aesthetic distance' and is critical for the safety of the abused child (Cattanach, 1997). Play therapy is not a quest to elicit some objective factual truth – 'what really happened'; rather, the play therapist works with the subjective meanings that the child has made of their experiences and the feelings generated – meanings and feelings which are made manifest in their play and responded to by the therapist in the same metaphorical mode. 'The therapist acknowledges that the child has had life events which might need some sorting and the play will not be to talk about these experiences but to make up stories in which the characters might have had the same thing happen to them as have happened to the child' (Cattanach, 1997: 11).

The plots, themes and storylines the child creates may indeed have links to real world experiences, but the play therapist will not interpret back to the child along the lines of: 'I see – what you really meant in that story was that the dragon is your stepfather and you are like that hedgehog', but will instead work safely and playfully with the metaphors the child has chosen, for example: 'That tiny hedgehog is so scared of that huge dragon when he roars fire! He has to curl up in a little ball to try and make sure the dragon won't see him. I wonder if he hopes that might keep him safe?', etc. The child is thus enabled to explore feelings and experiences, make sense of them and cope better thereafter, without it ever being made explicit that the story is 'really' about them and their lives. Indeed, a critical assumption for play therapy is that therapeutic change may occur without a conscious awareness of the association between the life experiences that relate to the child's difficulties and the symbolic manner in which these are expressed. Dighton (2001) proposed that this therapeutic process enables children to alter their perspectives on their life experience – what he termed 'first order changes' – and, furthermore, that these may translate into changes of behaviour, cognition, affect and attitudes ('second order changes').

Since play therapy uses the child's natural 'language' – play – the level of sophistication of this language will reflect the child's age and developmental stage. A typical play therapy session with a 3-year-old will inevitably be rather different from that with a 13-year-old – although the teenager may very well need to regress back to missed earlier play experiences, so there may also be many similarities! Jennings (1994) proposed a continuum along which children's play may be described: the earliest type of play (both in normal childhood development and as featuring in a play therapy session) is 'embodiment play' whereby the child explores the world through their senses and in which their own physical being is central. Sensory or embodiment play allows the child literally to 'get in touch with' their physical selves, to differentiate what is 'me' and 'not me', to get a sense of what they like and dislike on the sensory level as a prerequisite to being able to understand and express their emotional feelings. Sensory play taps into primitive parts of the brain accessing pre-verbal experiences. All too many children who come to play therapy have not had adequate embodiment play opportunities and the chance to indulge in regressive sensory play: running their hands through wet sand, poking holes in soft clay, exploring the 'puerile' delight of slime and fart putty can be liberating and cathartic – and provide an awareness of the bodily self perhaps hitherto suppressed or undeveloped.

The next stage on Jennings' continuum is that of projective play – when objects (the toys or play materials) and images take on metaphorical significance as the child projects meaning onto them: a simple stick can be a sword, a magic wand or a fishing rod, and symbolic potential is limited only by the child's imagination. In projective play the child makes use of objects other than their own bodies to externalise their inner worlds.

Finally, in role-play, the last stage on Jennings' continuum, the child – and often the therapist too, at the child's invitation – assumes roles within dramatisations which may also be metaphorically rich. In dramatic play the child takes on roles in stories from texts or through improvisation, and may involve the play therapist in the scene. Dramatic role-play gives permission to do things that in everyday life would not be permissible or 'socially acceptable'.

Working therapeutically with young people in a school context, elements of all three play types may well feature: the young person may feel more comfortable in one play mode but it is likely that there will be movement back and forth along the continuum as the intervention progresses.

Play Therapy: History, Background and Context

The use of play in therapy was pioneered in the field of child psychotherapy in the early 20th century. Anna Freud (1928) and Melanie Klein (1932) were among those who proposed a theoretical premise for the use of play. Freud used play to maximise the child's ability to form a 'therapeutic alliance' with the therapist, introducing games, toys and magic tricks to interest the child patient in the therapy and in the therapist. Klein claimed that a child's spontaneous play was a direct substitute for the free association used within adult psychoanalysis. Whilst theories and practice surrounding play differ within each child psychotherapy tradition, they share the common central proposition that play communicates the child's unconscious experiences, desires, thoughts and emotions. However, it could be argued that these analytical approaches use the medium of play to indicate the source of the problem, rather than viewing play as a curative or healing factor itself.

Whilst play therapy emerged from these elements of child psychotherapy, its specific theoretical foundation owes much to the work of Carl Rogers (1951), who established a new model of psychotherapy – client-centred therapy (later termed person-centred therapy), a humanistic psychology tradition born out of a protest against the diagnostic, prescriptive perspectives of his time. Rogers emphasised a relationship between therapist and client based upon genuineness, acceptance (or unconditional positive regard) and trust (see Chapter 2 for further details).

Influenced by this person-centred approach, Virginia Axline (1989 [1969]) developed a new and succinct therapeutic approach for working with children – non-directive play therapy (NDPT). Like client-centred counselling, NDPT holds a central hypothesis of the individual's innate capacity for growth and self-direction and a belief in the child as the chief agent in his/her own therapy. Axline's eight principles, which emphasise the core importance of a warm, accepting relationship, underpin the work of most play therapists today.

American play therapists such as Moustakas (1953), Schaefer (1979) and Landreth (2002) progressed Axline's formulations and devised differing models, integrating elements of systemic family therapy, narrative therapy, solution-focused therapy and cognitive behavioural therapy. One of the most significant developments has been an increasing emphasis on the role of the environment in the formation of children's personality and mental/emotional health and, pivotal within this, the role of attachment.

Recent advances in neuroscience have also informed the theoretical and clinical development of play therapy: the more that is understood about how early experiences shape and impact on brain structures and neural functioning, the better play therapists are able to comprehend resulting behaviour and to demonstrate the importance and efficacy of early interventions. Of particular fascination to play therapists practising today are enhanced insights into the neuropsychology of attachment and trauma such as Perry's (2001) findings that children raised in environments characterised by domestic violence, physical abuse or other persistent traumas develop an overly active midbrain/brainstem, resulting in an over-reactive stress response and predisposition to impulsiveness and aggression. Such evidence confirms that therapy must do more than talk if the child is in a persistent hyper-arousal state, for the child's brain may well be unresponsive to verbal interactions. In order to heal a 'damaged' brain, interventions must activate those portions of the brain that have been impacted.

Play therapy is now increasingly available in clinical and statutory settings in the UK, for example within CAMHS (Child and Adolescent Mental Health Services), bereavement organisations, 'looked-after children' teams of social services departments and in the voluntary sector. Whilst several charitable organisations offer packages of play therapy to clusters of local authority schools, it is still relatively rare for a referral to be funded by schools themselves. However, it is common for a play therapist to work with a child on school premises. At present this is predominantly within the primary school age range, but play therapists do work in secondary school settings too – particularly, perhaps, EBD (emotional and behavioural difficulties) schools or in specialised units within mainstream schools. One of play therapy's strengths is its universality: the approach can be adapted to suit different developmental levels and is appropriate for children of all ages, and those from different cultures, genders and abilities. Play therapists generally work with individual children, but some have experience of working with groups and with siblings.

Play therapy is an effective intervention for children with a variety of presenting problems and childhood difficulties (Bratton et al., 2005; BAPT, 2009). These include children:

- who have been abused: physically, sexually or emotionally
- who have experienced loss through bereavement, family breakdown or separation from culture of origin
- who are terminally ill or disabled, or who cope with carers or siblings with disabilities or illness
- who have witnessed violence or the abuse of substances
- who are displaying behaviour that is regarded as a problem by those who care for them: they may be difficult to control, withdrawn or not reaching their potential
- who externalise their difficulties with antisocial, aggressive, bullying behaviours
- who internalise their problems: the often-overlooked victims, prone to low self-esteem, anxiety, depression or self-harm.

LeBlanc and Ritchie (2001) conducted a meta-analysis of 42 research studies of play therapy which demonstrated that it is also a viable intervention for children with various additional emotional and physical needs. Further evidence has demonstrated play therapy is effective in a number of areas, including: prevention programmes (medical);

conduct disorder (Davenport and Bourgeois, 2008); oppositional/defiant disorders; social skills problems; sexual behaviour problems (Ciottone and Madonna, 1996); attachment disorders (Ryan, 2004); and children in divorce. Other research points to probable efficacy in prevention programmes (early childhood mental health); with children experiencing peer relationship problems; chronic illness (Jones and Landreth, 2002); anxiety; separation and loss; fears and phobias; PTSD (Ogawa, 2004; Ryan and Needham, 2001); witnesses to domestic violence (Kot et al., 1998); sexual, emotional and physical abuse (Scott et al., 2003); ADHD; and with autistic spectrum disorders (Josefi and Ryan, 2004).

Play Therapy Theory and Application to Practice

The format of exploration of the child's difficulties is determined by a variety of factors, including the child's needs, the therapist's theoretical perspective and their work setting. Most play therapists adhere to child-centred principles in that the child is given significant choices about how to use the time and the play materials, but there is a continuum from pure non-directive approaches to more focused techniques.

Non-directive play therapists abide by the humanistic principles prescribed by Axline (1989 [1969]) and emphasise the child's ability to choose those materials which make most sense to him or her, and to utilise the play experience and therapeutic relationship in their own way and in their own time: the child is in control of the process and directs the agenda, focus and timing. The non-directive play therapist follows the child's lead, verbally tracking what they are doing, acknowledging non-judgementally the choices they make and voicing ongoing empathic reflections of the feelings they convey. A core aim of the non-directive play therapist is simply to 'be with' the child (Landreth, 2002) and to provide the optimum conditions that allow the child to develop their inherent potential.

Some play therapists take a somewhat more prescriptive approach, using focused techniques with defined goals in which it is the therapist who formulates the agenda, with greater emphasis on 'doing' than 'being'. Therapist-directed interventions influenced by structured approaches, such as cognitive-behavioural therapy, have specific aims such as helping bereaved children to explore grief and loss, or aggressive young people to manage their anger.

In the middle of this continuum fall play therapists who follow a more eclectic or collaborative approach, utilising both non-directive and directive methods, allowing the child and therapist equal power to direct the agenda, focus and timing of the play therapy. Cattanach (1997), for example, advocated storytelling techniques in the co-creation or 'co-construction' of a narrative of the child's experiences that evolves in the interaction between therapist and child.

Central to all play therapy approaches, however, is the relationship between therapist and child. The development of a constructive, trusting therapeutic relationship is a vital component of the play therapy process.

In any play therapy intervention, the efficacy and legacy of the work with the child client will depend greatly on liaison with parents/carers and on important inter-professional communication. A child does not exist in isolation – the family and social systems in which they live and function can compound or perpetuate their difficulties, and if significant adults in the child's life are supportive of the play therapy, the child is more likely to engage. The work has a better prognosis when there is a sense of team commitment. Most play therapists will therefore meet with key adults such as parents, teachers, social workers and learning mentors to gather a thorough understanding of the child's background and needs from their varied perspectives before commencing therapy and will maintain this relationship via regular review meetings throughout the intervention. Whilst adherence to client confidentiality is imperative, insights can be shared and advice given which can help to shift others' perspectives too and extend the benefits.

Play Therapy in Schools and Brief Play Therapy

Whether the approach is non-directive, directive or collaborative, many factors may be involved in the decision for brief or longer-term play therapy to happen in a school setting. The security of the familiar could be important for a young person who may be intimidated by being taken to a clinic or strange venue. It is less disruptive to be removed from one room to another for an hour than to leave school early or arrive late, or to have an extra two-way journey during the day. Perhaps the child's home is not an appropriate place to work – maybe through lack of confidentiality or space, or the need for a more emotionally neutral setting. Some children receiving play therapy may be in transition from the birth family to a foster or adoptive placement, so that the school environment may be a key element of consistency.

Play therapists will commence their intervention with a careful assessment, building up a comprehensive profile of the child, their early history, family background, and the nature of the difficulties as perceived by others as well as by the child him/herself. When working in school contexts the play therapist may require several referral meetings with staff and parents/carers and ask for access to reports and existing assessments before actually introducing themselves to the child. This assessment process, which begins at referral, does not stop once the clinical work begins but is ongoing, with speculations and hypotheses remaining open to re-evaluation as the therapeutic relationship develops.

It is crucial that the room where the therapeutic work takes place is free of interruptions. It can be immensely disruptive to a child in the middle of a session to have a teacher enter to retrieve forgotten resources or for another child to burst in and wonder curiously what is going on. It need not be large or have any existing equipment – peripatetic play therapists will usually bring their own play materials. Some will also bring a mat as a wipeable playing surface which both minimises the impact of any mess and defines the therapeutic space, differentiating it from the room as it is normally used. Access to a sink is an advantage, especially when several children are seen in succession.

The selection of toys and play materials should facilitate children's expression by providing a wide range of play activities at their developmental level. These may include:

> *Toys for sensory/embodiment play:* A sand tray (and water), clay, playdough, slimes, putties, bubbles, assorted stretchy and tactile balls, etc.

> *Toys for projected/symbolic play:* A dolls house, miniature human figures (various ages and ethnicities), hero and monster figures, toy soldiers, cars and other vehicles, animal families, miniatures of current popular film and TV characters (it is important to keep abreast of trends), etc.

> *Real life toys for role-play:* Dressing-up clothes, realistic dolls and baby accessories, puppets, masks, pretend food, toy 'weaponry', play mobile phones, doctor's kit, etc.

> *Toys for creative expression:* Paper, paints, finger-paints, felt-tip pens, crayons, chalk, collage materials, glues, scissors and sticky tape, percussion musical instruments, etc.

These lists are not exhaustive and the range of equipment may be conditional on storage/ transportation factors.

The security of a predictable, consistent time for the play therapy session aids the development of therapeutic trust. It is also imperative that all appropriate members of school staff are apprised of the nature of the work and understand that attendance at play therapy is not conditional on good behaviour. The misconception that play therapy is a treat and that when a child has misbehaved in class they do not 'deserve' to have this 'reward' can be hugely counterproductive.

Once initial assessments have been undertaken and practical logistics organised, the play therapist will meet the child for the first time. Depending on the context of the referral, and on the young person's age and level of cognitive understanding, it may be supportive for a key adult to be present at this first meeting. For some children knowing that significant adults in their life endorse the idea of play therapy can be most positive. For others, of course, it may be quite the reverse!

It is critical that the child knows why they are there, so some discussion about the reason for play therapy needs to be addressed at an age-appropriate level. It is important to emphasise that the referral has not been made because the young person is 'in trouble' – if it is perceived as a punishment then the intervention is tarnished from the outset. Naturally the request for play therapy may be linked to a prevalence of 'unacceptable behaviour' in school or at home, but the play therapist will need to stress that the therapeutic support is to help the child with the feelings that underlie the behaviour.

To reduce the negative perception that the referral is to meet an adult behaviour modification agenda, it is helpful to get a sense from the young person themselves of what they hope for from the therapeutic support.

Early sessions may well involve some limit-challenging as the child tests out the boundaries that the play therapist has outlined. Equally, many young clients are sceptical about the confidential nature of the therapy, and this is another aspect of the play therapist's credibility and trustworthiness that may be questioned and challenged. A young person whose previous relationships with adults have been characterised by negativity, abuse, inconsistency or punitive criticism, will have developed an 'internal working model' (Bowlby, 1969) to expect the same from all relationships, so establishing and consolidating therapeutic trust may take several weeks.

The expectation for child-centred play therapy is that, through the play therapist's consistent, empathic acceptance and respectful reflections, the young person will develop *self*-respect and *self*-acceptance, and that improved self-esteem and capacity for self-regulation will generalise to outside the play therapy space. Ongoing liaison with key adults in the child's life will help determine when the therapeutic goals have been met sufficiently to close the work. Endings must be carefully planned: many young people will have experienced these as traumatically abrupt in the past, so preparation for the end of play therapy must be sensitively managed. The efficacy of the play therapy intervention can be ascertained by qualitative or quantitative outcome measures, and reports provided. The requirement for brief working tends to be more budget-driven and thus more goal-orientated and the pressure to prove efficacy is increasingly acute in such contexts.

Case Study   Elijah

Elijah was 10 years old at referral. Concerns from infancy about his speech and language development had led to a Statement of Special Educational Needs which ensured ongoing in-class learning support. He struggled to make sense of lessons, did not cooperate with teachers and found social situations, e.g. playtime, difficult to manage. His emotional well-being was connected to contexts that he found challenging to interpret: his responses could appear impulsive and unpredictable so that interactions with peers often escalated to conflict. He would sometimes express his frustration in screaming and lashing out and often labelled himself negatively: 'I'm really bad'. Elijah's mother told me he occasionally 'zoned out' when overwhelmed and that he had obsessive 'specialist interests' – then predominantly basketball. Whilst there had been no formal diagnosis, there was an unvoiced implication in these behaviour patterns that Elijah might be on the autistic spectrum and there was heightened concern about his impending transition to secondary school. Play therapy was introduced with the aim of increasing emotional stability and coping strategies, and thus decreasing inappropriate behaviour. It was envisaged that it would also improve understanding of self and

(Continued)

(Continued)

others (especially around feelings and the link to behaviour), thus building empathy, and would strengthen his self-esteem.

At the introductory meeting in the presence of his mother and the SENCo, Elijah was initially subdued and chose to lie on the floor rather than sit on a chair – I joined him there, which immediately helped put him at ease. He listened attentively while I explained the reasons for play therapy. He was particularly fascinated by the sensory materials and spontaneously involved us by showing his discoveries. I drew attention to his reactions, and to those of his mother and teacher where these might differ from his own: he was able to guess that Mummy would think the slime was 'disgusting' whereas he was enthralled by it, suggestive of an unexpected potential capacity for empathy.

In the first session alone with me, Elijah asked many interested questions in an evident bid to build a relationship. He also showed a surprising facility for dramatised role-play: playdough became a delicious pizza which he invited me to share. Whilst we carefully clarified that this was all pretend – 'Don't eat it for real!' – Elijah's ability to initiate and sustain an imaginative mime required an awareness of 'other ways of being' and an understanding of non-literal meaning, which ran counter to the suspected ASD label.

As the intervention progressed Elijah blossomed. Whilst obviously hampered by language-processing difficulties, he seemed desperately needy to engage with other people, greeting me each week with garrulous enthusiasm. He soon began drawing, and the metaphors in his prolific and skilful cartoons of basketball players in action provided rich therapeutic material. Themes of competition and rivalry, of fairness and unfairness, of triumph and failure, of pride and shame/despair were all vividly symbolised in his basketball imagery. Later the drawings broadened out to enactments of imaginative scenes – he role-played post-match interviewers, jubilant winners and despairing losers, describing their supposed emotions in powerful language. He was even able to understand the inherently contradictory concept of sarcasm, which had been the trigger of many a playground dispute in the past.

After six sessions, teachers reported that Elijah had started to behave more like his peers and that he was better at completing educational tasks. Towards the end of the second term there were no further incidents of being sent 'on referral' and he had been able to stay calm throughout his Year 6 SATS tests.

The focus of my work shifted towards preparing Elijah for the move to secondary school – having been at the same school since nursery, this was a major transition so a specially devised statement included the provision of ongoing play therapy in the new educational context. Written reports and advance liaison with the new school facilitated this.

As the end of his primary schooling loomed, Elijah's mixed feelings of excitement and fear were expressed in the metaphors of basketball players preparing to transfer to different teams for the new season: what would their new coach and team-mates be like? Would they like the huge training facilities? Elijah's basketball players conceded that their feelings might change as they familiarised themselves with the new environment. By addressing this apprehension and ambivalence within the safety of play therapy, Elijah coped with it in reality – in the event, the loss of all his primary school friends and surroundings was not as traumatic as many had anticipated.

After one term at secondary school, feedback was so positive that just five further fortnightly sessions were scheduled. At the final review the SENCo reported: 'We are pleased with his progress. Elijah is a popular member of the class and staff report he is pleasant and attempts work set. He interacts appropriately with his peers and has a good sense of humour. He is functioning well and has had no detentions.' Elijah's mother was grateful: play therapy had helped her son understand his own and others' feelings and had enhanced his self-esteem. My empathic reflections, unconditional acceptance and playful, empowering child-led approach were held to have been key mechanisms of change. Play therapy also highlighted the potential for Elijah to develop further in his social competence than early assessments had implied and thus facilitated his adjustment into secondary school life.

Summary

- This chapter has summarised the historical development of play therapy in the United Kingdom, tracing its theoretical underpinnings and evidence base
- A continuum of play therapy approaches was described, from non-directive to therapist-directed, stressing that in all a trusting therapeutic relationship is as crucial as the play itself, as is appropriate recognition and involvement of the wider system in which the child lives
- Some practicalities of setting up play therapy in a school setting were outlined, including the environment and selection of appropriate resources
- A detailed case study, based on real client material (anonymised to protect the identity of the client), illustrated a fairly typical process and progress of a young person receiving play therapy in school, bridging the transition from primary to secondary education

Reflective Questions

1 Non-directive play therapists need to be unconditionally accepting of the young person – why do you think this is important and what obstacles within a school context might there be for you in achieving this non-judgemental attitude?

Rogers (1951) argues that if the person can feel fully accepted, constructive personality change will occur. Unconditional positive regard (UPR) may feel difficult to offer in a school setting because we are used to judging children and young people in terms of achievement and behaviour, so UPR would feel contrary to the prevailing culture. We need to consciously resist the ingrained adult inclination to praise a child for 'being good' and saying 'nice things' and instead allow them to voice negative, potentially shameful feelings without fear of judgement or criticism.

2 Whilst play therapy is relatively free of 'rules', unlike much of the school environment, there are certain boundaries that do need to be in place – what is the justification for this and what limits might you establish?

Limit-setting ensures a safe and secure environment for children – indeed a child can feel scared if left totally 'free'. Clear boundaries also reduce anxiety for the play therapist. Limits structure, teach self-control and self-responsibility, serve to protect the child, the therapist, the toys and the room and also help to minimise socially unacceptable behaviour (whilst still demonstrating acknowledgement and acceptance of the feelings that may underlie this behaviour). Whilst there are individual variations in approaches to limit-setting, most play therapists clarify that children are not permitted to hurt themselves or the therapist and that the toys and the room are not damaged on purpose. Adherence to time limits is also important.

3 If children are deprived of opportunities for self-directed play, what impact do you think this may have on their creativity, self-confidence and capacity to relate to others?

Childhood play that is self-directed can lead to self-assurance, mastery and creative problem-solving skills. Children whose play is limited to interactions with equipment where there is a 'right' way to complete specified tasks and where opportunities for meaningful social relationships are negligible, may grow up lacking the capacity to think for themselves.

4 What long-term value do you think there may be in messy play and in role-play?

Children who have restricted messy play opportunities may remain disconnected from their physical selves and may become more inhibited in creative or physical self-expression in later life. Those who engage in lots of pretend role-play may be better able to manage different adult roles with more confidence.

Learning Activities

1. Think back to your own earliest play memories: what do you recall that was especially pleasurable or significant in your childhood play experiences? Consider the type of play you remember most fondly – was it messy or orderly? Creative/imaginative or structured and rule-bound? Solitary or with peers/siblings or in a team? Contemplate how this play has influenced how you behave as an adult.
2. Rediscover your 'inner child' and nurture your own playfulness: inspired by activity 1, do something playful or creative that you have not made time to enjoy for too long. It is important that play therapists are comfortable with all types of play so maybe also try something new – and relish the excuse to get messy!
3. Observe a group of young children at play – note who takes the initiative and how the game evolves. Do the boys play differently to the girls? What happens in a mixed gender group? Consider how power and status are negotiated through play and how peer relationships are developed.
4. Practise your tracking skills: watch a television programme with the sound muted and give a running commentary of the key action you see. Label the emotions you can perceive in the facial expressions and body language of the actors.
5. Go to a charity shop or car boot sale and build up your collection of small toys and play resources: other people's discarded 'junk' can be a play therapist's treasure trove!

Further Reading

The following core texts elaborate on some of the theoretical underpinnings to play therapy outlined in the sections above and will enhance and deepen understanding of this clinical approach and the contexts in which it is practised

Axline, V.M. (1990 [1971]) *Dibs in Search of Self*. London: Penguin Books.
Carroll, J. (1998) *Introduction to Therapeutic Play*. Oxford: Blackwell Science.
Cattanach, A. (2003) *Introduction to Play Therapy*. Hove: Brunner-Routledge.

(Continued)

(Continued)

Cochran, N.H., Nordling, W.J. and Cochran, J.L. (2010) *Child-Centred Play Therapy: A Practical Guide to Developing Therapeutic Relationships with Children*. New York: John Wiley & Sons.

McMahon, L. (2009) *The Handbook of Play Therapy and Therapeutic Play*. 2nd edn. East Sussex: Routledge.

Schaefer, C.E. and O'Connor, K.J. (eds) (1983) *Handbook of Play Therapy*. New York: John Wiley & Sons.

Van Fleet, R., Sywulak, A.E. and Sniscak, C.C. (2010) *Child Centered Play Therapy*. New York: The Guilford Press.

West, J. (1996) *Child Centred Play Therapy*. 2nd edn. London: Arnold.

Wilson, K., Kendrick, P. and Ryan, V. (2001) *Play Therapy: A Non-Directive Approach for Children and Adolescents*. London: Bailliere Tindall.

Woolf, A. and Austin, D. (2008) *Handbook of Therapeutic Play in Schools*. Chester: A2C Press.

Online Resources

BACP website: www.bacp.co.uk/, especially the BACP Children and Young People Division and the Competences for Working with Children and Young People.

Counselling MindEd: http://counsellingminded.com.

BAPT (British Association of Play Therapists) *Play Therapy in Action*. Available at: www.bapt.info/trainingdvd.html. This is a 3-minute clip of play therapy and the page has links that will enable you to order the whole DVD, more than 2 hours in length.

8

Other Creative Approaches

Barbara Smith, Kaye Richards and Toby Quibell

This chapter includes:

- A number of creative approaches that can be integrated into counselling and psychotherapy practices, many of which have longstanding traditions and are underpinned by a wide range of theoretical perspectives and have been developed over many years
- An insight into alternative ways of engaging children and young people in counselling and psychotherapy with the integrated use of creativity. This will draw upon the experience of the authors who use a range of modalities (person-centred, transactional analysis, and cognitive-behavioural therapy) and creative approaches (drama, sand-play, outdoor adventure, art, clay-work, music, dance, etc.)
- Case study material to illustrate creative working in action, to serve as a reminder that sometimes talking alone isn't always enough
- Questions and activities for exploration and discussion

Elsewhere in this book are valuable accounts of important issues of ethics, boundaries and the law, as well as other significant aspects of working with young people. It is not the intention to include these concerns here, but instead to explore the practical matter of helping children and young people to open up through a variety of creative and 'alternative' methods. In examining creative ways of working, this chapter will by no means be an exhaustive account of these approaches, and some are covered in more detail in other parts of the book.

Introduction

> Even a minor event in the life of a child is an event of that child's world and thus a world event.
>
> Gaston Bachelard (1884–1962)

Being allowed into the world of a child or young person is a privilege and an adventure. Every encounter provides an opportunity for healing: every smile; every greeting; each time we laugh at a child's humour; sharing aspects of our own experience; and offering a safe space in which to explore past experiences and worries goes a little way to healing the hurts that bring them into therapy. As adults, we often focus on the 'problems' that children bring: trauma, bereavement and other transitions; the effects of bullying, depression and all manner of anxious states (Bailey and Shooter, 2009). In this chapter, as well as acknowledging children's distress, we want to also highlight the strengths that children and young people bring: resilience; power; humour; imagination; experience and creative possibilities that help them to overcome difficult life experiences or worries.

The title of a recent strategic plan supporting the government's 'No health without mental health' agenda is *Talking Therapies: A Four-Year Plan of Action* (DoH, 2011). Such a title clearly indicates a preference for therapies which use language as a central construct to address the various issues that children and young people bring to therapy. This chapter offers alternatives to solely talking; indeed, many of the young people that the authors have worked with have been unable or unwilling to express themselves in the more traditional verbal way.

Creative work is particularly relevant when working with children and young people. Axline (1947) believed that because they express themselves through play, it is a natural therapeutic medium for children. As a student of Rogers' person-centred approach, she saw that the child would direct the play in a way that is productive in helping them to work through their struggles. Children dealing with particular issues will 'play out' what they can't 'talk out' about difficult life events (e.g. parental separation, conflict and bereavement), enabling them to resolve issues that they cannot express through words.

Malchiodi (2005) distinguishes between those therapists who have in-depth training in various creative therapies and those who integrate expressive therapies into their psychotherapy work. This chapter focuses on the latter group, in that it introduces ideas that have been successfully integrated into the authors' own practice, and in doing so is not offering a detailed examination of specific creative therapies, such as art, drama and dance therapy. Carson and Becker (2004), however, refer to 'creativity in counselling', describing the therapist's willingness to respond in a flexible and creative way, attuning to client's creative possibilities. It is hoped this chapter explores, therefore, the broader creative potential of therapeutic practice.

Some creative approaches are more readily available for the everyday therapist (e.g. art and creative writing), whereas others require more specialist skills (e.g. outdoor adventure therapy). That said, as pointed out by Malchiodi (2005: 6), when using creative therapies to complement other psychotherapy theories we should 'be mindful of the current standards of practice in the particular modality [we] are using'. So it is important to refer to the list of relevant professional bodies and organisations to find those related to the approaches discussed here. And of course the old maxim of 'never ask a client to do what you wouldn't do yourself' applies in creative therapies. At the end of the chapter there are a number of simple exercises to encourage the reader to explore some of the creative themes addressed.

Taking Creativity into Therapeutic Practice

The value of creativity in the therapeutic process is not a new phenomenon; McNiff (1981) discusses the use of art in healing throughout the ages and Malchiodi (2005) builds on this, highlighting how artistic activity was used in ancient Egypt to help people with mental illness. She describes how the Greeks used drama and music for healing, and how Goodenough (1926) was analysing children's drawings early in the last century. In 1939 Margaret Lowenfeld developed the 'Lowenfeld World Technique' from her work with sand trays, toys and models. The children Lowenfeld worked with called her 'wonder box' of play materials 'the world' and started to create scenes and worlds in the sand box in her playroom (Lowenfeld, 1993). Alongside this, dance therapy can be traced back to the 1930s with dance teacher Marian Chace (see Sandel et al., 1993). She encouraged her students to express their emotions through dancing. Local doctors, seeing the benefits of the approach, started sending patients to her classes. Founded on the assumption that movement and emotion are directly related, the principle behind dance and movement therapy is to find a sense of wholeness and balance (Payne, 2006).

The use of creative therapies is increasing its standing in the statutory mental health field. In 2009 the National Institute for Health and Clinical Excellence (NICE) recommended that art therapy be considered as a supplement to standard care in patients with schizophrenia, and Crawford and Patterson (2007) highlight the emerging evidence base for using arts therapies for people with schizophrenia. A systematic scoping review undertaken by Harris and Pattison (2004) revealed a range of evidence-based studies supporting the use of creative therapies with children and young people: group drama therapy for children with behavioural and emotional problems in the school setting (McArdle et al., 2002), group work and role-play for improving levels of acting out, distractibility and sociability with learning-disabled children (Omizo and Omizo, 1987), humanistic play therapy effective in reducing anxiety in children whose parents have divorced (Dearden, 1998) and play therapy to reduce anxiety and build self-esteem and cognitive skills in schoolchildren (Sherr and Sterne, 1999). What follows are illustrative case study examples of how, as authors, we have used creativity in our therapeutic work with children and young people, employing a variety of media.

Working in the Sand Tray and Storytelling

Sand tray work is a creative and popular approach, especially in working with younger children. The use of small toys and figures in sand tray work is highlighted by Geldard and Geldard (2002). They describe a goal of sand tray work as giving children an opportunity to tell their story with symbolism and metaphor, using model trees, fences, cars, soldiers, heroes, dragons and animals. This enables the child to express fears and fantasies in the small safe 'world' of the sand tray. Children use their imagination and subconscious to create a microcosm of their inner world. Below is an example of sand tray work with 'Tom'.

Case Study   Tom

Tom, aged 10, was in care and had been referred because of his withdrawn behaviours, enuresis and occasional aggressive physical outbursts. He found it hard to regulate his feelings and would often seem to be 'in a world of his own' – disconnected – and finding it difficult to express himself verbally. He was significantly developmentally delayed in his speech, cognitively, and in his social and emotional skills. Before meeting Tom I had read a comprehensive referral document detailing some of his early experiences. It was heartbreaking to read. He and his siblings had been severely neglected from an early age and he had taken a great deal of responsibility for his three young brothers and little sister. He had been denied food, water and stimulation. He had also been physically and emotionally abused by his stepfather. Tom had had a number of fostering placements.

Tom was invited to explore the play room and to choose what media he would like to use. He loved the sand tray. He chose a variety of toys, including trees and wild animals. Over the weeks as he played in the sand, his story of abuse and fear unfolded as the giraffe shouted at the monkey 'Get in there *you*'… 'don't you get out of that bed'… 'stand *there*'. Other times animals would be buried deep in the sand – 'disappeared'. These scenes were played over and over until he moved onto another theme from his difficult past.

During the early stages of our work together he had been told that he was moving to another placement. While therapeutic work can be contra-indicative for a child who is not in a settled placement, this was another unexpected twist in his troubled and unsettled life. Whilst waiting for his new placement, Tom continued his sand tray work. One day he drew a line down the middle of the sand. One side was his old life and one side was his new life. In exploring his old life, he made several purposeful trips to the imaginary skip, throwing out all the 'old stuff'. In his new life he created a veritable little paradise, speaking about his hopes and expectations of his new placement.

While Tom never spoke verbally about his experiences prior to coming into care, he took the opportunity, through the sand, to communicate his distressing feelings of fear and anger. Tom is now thriving in his new placement; he is dry day and night, and expressing his thoughts and feelings in more helpful ways within the nurture and care of a loving family.

There are other ways in which therapists can be creative in enabling children to work playfully and tell their stories. One author uses miniature plastic toy figures – Gogo's (also referred to as Crazy Bones) – in her storytelling with children. After discovering Gogo's by accident, she now keeps a collection of the tiny, brightly-coloured figures in her therapy room. All have different colours and features, and the children and young people are able to project their own characters onto the figures, sometimes telling stories about who lives in their house or who's who at school. They have been particularly helpful in life story work for looked-after children, with each different household they have lived in being portrayed by small groups of Gogo's as the child's story unfolds. The popular little figures are immediately recognisable to the children and seem to be 'of their world'. Children often leave with a handful of Gogo's to represent qualities that they have, e.g. 'Choose one that fits with your being really kind. Now choose one that shows how strong you are when you play football. Now choose one that shows your funny side.'

Working with Art

Art is commonly used across a range of psychotherapies as a vehicle for self-expression and understanding and can employ a variety of media. In a discussion of working therapeutically with clay, Geldard and Geldard (2002) emphasise its pleasant texture when 'feeling, stroking, pressing, punching, squashing and shaping'. They highlight the benefits of being able to change its shape, allowing the exploration and development of emerging themes to symbolically express held-in feelings. Emotionally blocked children are able to contact and express their feelings through working with clay. Sherwood (2010) suggests that using clay in therapy provides therapists with a powerful medium to help clients work through many core issues such as anger, grief and fear.

> ## Case Study   Jess
>
> Jess, a black child, aged five, was referred by her social worker after becoming 'looked-after' because her mother's partner had pushed her down the stairs. Other physical abuse became apparent during the investigation, and despite the man being convicted of the assault, Jess's mum refused to acknowledge the danger that he posed to her daughter.
>
> Jess was placed with her maternal aunt but was distressed and confused about not living with her mum. She was an anxious little girl who sometimes had distressing 'outbursts' where she was clearly overwhelmed by her difficult feelings. Jess had no understanding of how to regulate her difficult emotions.
>
> *(Continued)*

(Continued)

When Jess was invited to work with the clay, she built a fort with no doorway. She also built a jail. In exploring the jail, she was able to talk about where the bad man went, whether he might come and 'get her' and who would save her. Jess was expressing her fear of the man who abused her and letting me know about her precarious sense of safety. We were able to explore who was there to look after her (safe adults, police, social worker, the judge) and how the bad man would have to learn his lesson in jail about how to be good. As the session progressed, Jess created a door in the fort 'for the people to get in and out' (the jail stayed firmly locked). As Jess's anxieties were addressed, she was able to contemplate allowing others into her clay refuge and also to venture outside.

During another session, Jess was talking about her life when she distractedly began to scrape cobs of clay up and down her little arms until her beautiful black skin was covered in the pale grey clay. When I commented about it she said, 'if I drink milk will the rest of my body be white like my feet?'. This presented an opportunity to explore Jess's black identity, discovering how she related to her blackness and how she coped with this in a largely white community. In addition to the work in the therapy room, the work also presented the opportunity to support her aunt in developing a positive black identity. (For more on black identity see the work of Esther Ina-Egbe, 2010.)

Gestalt therapist Violet Oaklander (1997) talks of the endless possibilities for freeing our creative process through drawing. She describes how the very act of drawing, even with no therapist intervention, 'is a powerful expression of self that helps establish one's self-identity and provides a way of expressing feelings' (ibid.: 306). Whilst many children enjoy messy play with clay, poster paints, etc., others enjoy the ordered world of mandalas (see Figure 8.1).

Mandala is a Sanskrit word meaning 'circle'. Within Buddhism and Hinduism they have spiritual and ritual significance. Some therapists have used mandalas to work with

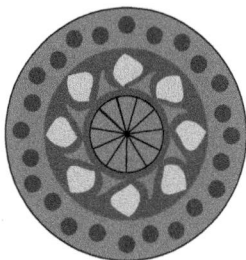  

Figure 8.1 Mandala images.

young people and their teachers in the school setting for personal growth and relaxation. In a study by Curry and Kasser (2005), 84 undergraduate students, after having a brief anxiety induction, were randomly assigned to colour a mandala, a plaid form, or to colour on a blank piece of paper. They found that anxiety levels declined similarly for the mandala and plaid colouring, and that both of these groups experienced more anxiety reduction than the unstructured colouring group. The findings suggest that structured colouring of quite complex geometric patterns may induce a meditative state that benefits people with anxiety.

Poetry and Song Writing

In thinking about creative approaches, Oaklander (1997) makes use of storytelling and poetry, as do Cattanach (1997) and Hedges (2005) in their therapeutic practice. The National Association for Poetry Therapy (2014) tells of the first poetry therapist on record, a Roman physician, Soranus, who practised in the first century AD. They identify how he prescribed tragedy for his manic patients and comedy for those who were depressed. They also note how during the 17th century Dr Benjamin Rush, known as the 'father of American psychiatry', introduced poem writing to patients who went on to publish their work in the hospital newspaper, *The Illuminator* (ibid.). One of the authors of this chapter uses 'bio-poems' when training foster carers to work creatively with looked-after children. These draw upon a child's biography, and an example can be seen in Table 8.1.

Table 8.1   An example of a 'bio-poem'.

Bio-poem formulation	A bio-poem example
Line 1 Your first name only	Caitlin
Line 2 Four traits that describe you	Petite, bubbly, happy and energetic,
Line 3 Sibling of ... (or son/daughter of)	Sister of Gemma,
Line 4 Lover of ... (three people or ideas)	Lover of gymnastics, chocolate and horses,
Line 5 Who feels ... (three items)	Who feels happiness with friends, loneliness at night, and joy at the gym,
Line 6 Who needs ... (three items)	Who needs friends, love and acceptance,
Line 7 Who gives... (three items)	Who gives friendship, love and encouragement,
Line 8 Who fears ... (three items)	Who fears not winning, bullies and losing friends,
Line 9 Who would like to see ... (three items)	Who would like to see the world, Justin Bieber and the summer holidays,
Line 10 Resident of (your town or street)	Resident of Liverpool,
Line 11 Your last name only	Jones

Others highlight the role of song-writing therapeutically, for example in palliative care (O'Callaghan, 1996), promoting pro-social behaviours in aggressive adolescent boys (Rickson and Watkins, 2003) and reducing anxiety and distress in traumatised children (Mayers, 1995). One author uses the notion of 'boasting songs' (a song-writing pastime of adolescent Maasai girls in Kenya) in her work with young people. Drawing on the concept of 'strokes' in transactional analysis, where we embrace other people's qualities and talents, as well as our own, she helps young clients to engage with and highlight their attributes and potentials through the playful process of boasting songs. This can be particularly helpful using rap music in group work with teens, as described by Hadley and Yancy (2012).

Drama

In her work with 'creative dramatics', Oaklander (1997: 298) describes how children, when play-acting, 'never actually leave themselves; they use more of themselves in the improvisational experience.' A connection between drama and healing was proposed by Aristotle, who coined the term 'catharsis'. While Aristotle never defined this in his work (*Poetics* 335 BC), it has been interpreted by others as purgation, purification and clarification (Aristotle, 1895). Essentially, drama therapy is a group of action techniques (drama games, improvisation, masks, puppetry and role-play) which helps with personal growth and behaviour change. Drama therapy is often used in schools, and Schneider (2006) promotes the use of drama therapy with autistic children to enhance self-confidence, not only in performing but in interactions. She also suggests that the work increases children's self-esteem, recognition of emotions in others, skills for functioning as part of a group, and improved interaction with other group members.

The provision of therapeutic interventions in schools is clearly a key agenda for addressing the mental health of children and young people, as discussed in other chapters. For example, School Counselling: The Action Group Skills Intervention programme (McArdle et al., 2002, 2011), developed by one of the authors, is one of many examples of integrating therapeutically-based drama approaches into intervention work with young people. This approach specifically focuses on four areas of work within a school setting (traumatised children, classroom situations and behaviours, creative curricula and systemic change within the organisation), using drama to help groups of young people in schools who are troubled and troublesome. It aims to help children to recognise destructive patterns in their behaviour, and by reflecting on their roots in social, emotional and behavioural habits, to change these patterns. It is grounded in attachment theory, object-relations theory, and psychodynamic theory. The intervention comprises creative-expressive (Jennings, 1992) or psychodrama

(Moreno and Moreno, 1969) approaches, including role-play (Bolton and Heathcote, 1999), and using a range of dramatic techniques to either heighten the experience or to contain it (Emunah, 1994).

All sessions begin with a 'talking forum', an opportunity for each child to speak out and be heard. The earlier sessions are characterised by co-operative and competitive games, so that talk can focus on common themes or experiences within the group. These also serve the purpose of creating a group identity, mutual trust and the setting of boundaries for behaviour. The middle sessions use a range of self-expression and controlled physical activity, as well as artistic work such as painting and mask-making. Later sessions utilise the material from the expressive phase to create dramas, enacted by the group for the group. The nature of the drama varies from group to group, depending on their experience and the way each group approaches expressive materials. For instance, a group might develop a fantasy play drama using predominantly their mask work or real-life role-plays with children taking on the characters of figures from their world. In the final phase, the sessions are characterised by reflection on the learning and developmental points offered by the group experience and integration of individual insights into ideas for behaviour outside the group.

Case Study   A Brief Encounter

A smartly-dressed man sits alone in a circle of chairs waiting for eight Year 9 pupils. 'Why is it always Year 9?', he wonders, feeling nervous and uncharitable. The door opens and he gets up to greet the young men and women who crowd the room in all the glory of their ruckus and aftershave. As the session progresses, the young people run through a practised repertoire of hormonally-fuelled bonding and conflict behaviours, most of which are fielded by the smartly-dressed man, who works hard to engage the noisy, energetic group in simple group games.

Using six-part story-making (Lahad, 1992) as a structure, we were working in a very cold room in a portakabin and the group was not going well. Too many big characters with too much bravado and too much knowing adolescence to let go and re-enter childhood. We were looking for a spark as the group went through the motions, first drawing their stories and then sharing them. We had the idea to make masks with card, each child making a mask relating to a character in their story – the young people taking control of the creative process. We then put three seats out front and waited for them to fill with children and their masks. It could go either way – my sense was that one of the young people might put on a silly voice and mock the process.

Maria pulled the mask down over her face and took a 'isn't this a waste of time' pose. She started to talk and something amazing happened – she was speaking gobbledegook. It was wonderful. It was like she had accidentally made a leap into hyperspace – she scarcely knew what was happening herself. I grabbed a pencil sharpener from the desk behind me, pressed it into her hand and we spoke

(Continued)

(Continued)

into this 'decoder'. We heard that she was alien to this planet and she did not understand any of its rules. She was lonely, although she had learnt how to pass herself off as one of the crowd. Maria's body shape had changed, her breathing was full of attention, and we could almost feel the adrenalin of hyper-awareness. The room was rapt and the magic began to happen.

At the end of the session one of the pack leaders begins the feedback. The man leans forward to listen – 'this is alright actually; because at first we thought you were some random banker'. The man smiles in a friendly fashion and straightens his tie. He thinks he heard it right.

Creative Risk-Taking: Outdoor Adventure Therapy

There has been a long tradition of using outdoor adventure activities for the personal and social development of young people (Hopkins and Putnam, 1993; Ogilvie, 2011). The psychological and physical demands of outdoor and adventure settings are often so different and so much more intense than those experienced in everyday life that they offer psychological, sociological and physiological benefits (McCormick et al., 2003). Research suggests that self-concept and self-esteem are key benefits of outdoor programmes (Martin, 1983; Washburn, 1983) and recorded benefits for young people include reducing problem behaviour (Pommier, 1994), reducing recidivism rates (McNutt, 1994), increasing self-efficacy (Hughes, 1993) and improved social functioning of outdoor programme participants Gibson (cited in Gass, 1993: 44). Ewert (1989) argues that outdoor activities can provide benefits to mental health, as an adjunct to clinical therapeutic techniques, and this is evident in the treatment of addictions and post-traumatic stress disorder (Ragsdale et al., 1996), substance abuse (Gass and McPhee, 1990), survivors of sexual abuse (Pfirman, 1988), young offenders (Reddrop, 1997), problems with marital intimacy (Hickmon, 1993), eating disorders (Richards et al., 2002) and psychiatric patients (Gilliam, 1990; Blanchard, 1993). So the range of identified benefits has clearly been used for addressing a range of clinical and health conditions and reflects the growing development of outdoor adventure therapy, with approaches including wilderness therapy and nature-based therapies (Richards et al., 2011). These developments are reflected in the regular international adventure therapy conferences and related publications overseen by the International Adventure Therapy Committee (see Itin, 1998; Richards and Smith, 2003; Bandroff and Newes, 2005; Mitten and Itin, 2009; Pryor et al., 2012).

The elements of novelty and challenge are key ingredients that differentiate adventure and wilderness therapy from more conventional experiential therapies. A young person's perception of the risk involved may be such that they have an additional emotional level of arousal to manage. The key concept here is of inviting young people to step outside their comfort zone and in so doing examine the experience they have of themselves, in a new zone of disequilibrium (Gass, 1993). The significance of this novelty is that it provides clients with an opportunity to examine their pre-existing beliefs about themselves. Gass (ibid.) describes this as 'edge work'. It is largely a process-oriented approach based on a number of assumptions about the process of therapeutic change. It holds the view that clients may find it difficult to achieve change in the context of their normal everyday circumstances. In such settings, much in their lives and thinking will conspire to keep things the same. Thus, if clients stay within their comfort zones change is unlikely. However, if clients are facilitated to work at 'the edge', or even step over the edge of their comfort zone, then they are likely to experience, at best, new aspects of themselves and new ways of coping, or at least gain some insight into their habitual coping behaviour.

The role of risk-taking in the therapeutic agenda of young people has particular significance. Geidd (2008) suggests that adolescence is a time of substantial neurobiological and behavioural change. The behaviours that accompany these changes include separation from family of origin, an increase in risk-taking and increased sensation seeking. 'These changes and the plasticity of the teen brain make adolescence a time of great risk and great opportunity' (Geidd, 2008: 341). Similarly, Hasset (2012: 70) suggests that 'increased risk-taking in adolescence is normative, biologically driven and inevitable'. Speaking of the adaptive role of adolescence, he states that a biological wedge is naturally driven between young people and their parents to aid transition to independence. He also states that 'you need to engage in high-risk behaviour to leave your village and find a mate' (ibid.: 72). Adventure therapy enables young people to engage in creative risk-taking, allowing the experience of authenticity and subsequent psychological change.

Case Study   Danny

Danny, aged 14, had been diagnosed with ADHD some years ago and had had a troubled past. He was being raised by his dad, his mum having died when he was eight. Since his mum's death Danny had become difficult to manage at school and at home. He had been referred for bereavement support through his school counsellor, but did not return after the first session. He had begun to seriously self-harm by cutting his arms, was hanging around with much older boys and was drinking alcohol harmfully. He did not want to access the Child and Adolescent Mental Health Service (CAMHS), as is common with young people who are at this level of risk. A range of professionals were trying to support Danny, and he was reluctantly placed in a single occupancy residential placement with 'round the clock' care.

(Continued)

(Continued)

As the staff team began to win Danny's trust, he would talk to them about his mum and his past, but he continued to harm himself and put himself at considerable risk in the community. An offer was made to work on a one-to-one basis with Danny in the outdoors, and while initially giving a flat refusal, he was shown the website of the venue where the work would be undertaken. This seemed to 'hook' Danny's adventurous spirit. After meeting with Danny, it was evident that there were areas that could possibly be impacted by the use of a variety of outdoor adventurous activity, including rock-climbing, mountaineering and high ropes courses. The therapists agreed to offer opportunities to experience issues of 'trust', safe 'risk-taking' and 'accepting support'.

Danny arrived at the outdoor venue and was introduced to the activities for the two days. The first was a ropes course where we invited Danny to engage in a childlike way, quite different from the moody adolescent façade we were used to. In the paradoxical experience of fear and excitement, Danny showed his authentic feelings of enjoyment, unable to maintain the indifferent and disconnected persona which had kept him 'safe' and others at bay for many years. As the outdoor trainer and therapist worked together to enable Danny to express his feelings more openly, he began to acknowledge his fears and uncertainty about the future. His sense of self-efficacy was compromised due to his early life experiences. Offering him opportunities to experience his capabilities was crucial in the outdoor adventure work.

Given this, the team decided to facilitate Danny on a mountainous rock climb to build a sense of competence and resilience. At first Danny was doubtful about the task in hand – he had never climbed roped on a mountain before; he felt unsure about his ability and anxiety about entering an unknown environment.

This was the kind of risk Danny had never previously encountered. During the climb, a number of pivotal moments occurred. As he became more confident in the climb, Danny began to connect more openly with the therapists, sometimes offering support and even requesting support – something that Danny had previously resisted. Importantly, he began to play, making Tarzan noises as he became more relaxed and playful. Hearing Danny's laughter and Tarzan cry echoing across the mountains was a joy for the therapists. Danny had resumed his journey.

Research Issues

The creative endeavour offers opportunities for therapists to engage with their young clients on a range of levels and through a wide variety of media. Recently, Cooper and McLeod (2010) presented the concept of pluralistic counselling and psychotherapy. Citing Lazarus' (2005) multimodal approach, they suggest that different clients are helped by different methods. They also highlight the development of practice which incorporates the whole range of concepts and therapeutic methods. Two key principles underpin the pluralistic approach: 1) lots of things can be helpful to clients; and 2) if we want to know what is most likely to help clients, we should talk to them about it (Cooper and McLeod, 2010: 6). Alongside this, we need to also ensure that the relevant research agendas are developed in order to examine the impacts and effectiveness of such work. The research priorities for creative approaches obviously cross a wide range of priority areas of counselling and psychotherapy research per se – too many to discuss here. However, the role of creative approaches for certain types of presenting client issues and the dynamic nature of key aspects of the therapeutic process need consideration and raise challenging research questions. For example, the changing dynamic of the therapeutic relationship in an outdoor setting is one of many examples (Harper, 2009). As practitioners we need to ensure we look to research findings to guide us on the application of creative approaches in our work and also to understand more fully the potential of these approaches for achieving longstanding psychological change.

Summary

In conclusion, the key points for consideration when thinking about the role of creative approaches for counselling and psychotherapy are:

1. Engaging young people means communicating in ways that they understand and *enjoy*. The sensory nature of creative work supports this endeavour, enabling children and young people to express their feelings in their own language
2. Having access to a broad range of creative media enhances therapeutic possibilities and gives children a wider choice in how therapy is conducted
3. Employing creative media and techniques requires the therapist to be able to connect with the symbolism and imaginative essence of the child's world
4. Working creatively with children and young people teaches us how to re-connect with aspects of ourselves perhaps long-forgotten

Finally, it is well documented that children and young people contact the world through play and creativity – our task is to harness the therapeutic potential that these things bring and thus embrace more of a pluralistic approach to our creative practices. In the words of Picasso, 'Every child is an artist – the problem is staying an artist when you grow up'.

Learning Activities

So now time to get creative yourself. The invitation is to simply take some time to do some of the creative activities as highlighted in the chapter. As with any creative approach, the goal is not to overthink it – just create a quiet space, gather the relevant resources and allow yourself some creative time.

1. Writing a bio-poem: Write a bio-poem, following the format example in the text, about a child you care about.
2. Creating a mandala: Sit quietly and breathe deeply. Ask yourself these questions: what shapes do I like – curves, angles, circles, straight lines? What do I like in nature – trees, water, animals, birds? What symbols do I like – light, dark, candles, flowers? Draw a circle on a large sheet of paper. Choose a few colours to use – about four or five. Divide the mandala intuitively into sections, e.g. your past, present, future, hopes, dreams, family, friends, faith. Now let your mind wander and let the colours find their own way onto the paper. Daydream. Be open to insights and new awareness. Access your own wisdom, creativity, love, and truth and see what unfolds.
3. Mould clay to music: Letting your creativity flow in response to music can have a meditative quality. Let your feelings out or just relax and enjoy the sensory experience of moulding clay. See what textures, shapes and images emerge.
4. Go outdoors: Take a walk outside in a local green space area. As you walk, take notice of natural things that you see – take time to look, sense, touch and smell these. As you do, take notice of thoughts and feelings that these natural things stir in you. Do they provide symbols to you, do you notice metaphors that relate to you – feelings, dilemmas, thoughts, hopes, etc.? After a short time find a suitable safe spot to sit down. Take time to reflect more on your experience of nature, jot down thoughts, images, feelings, etc. If you collected any natural things replace them after you have made some notes. Do the same walk for a number of days or weeks. Allow your journey each time to unfold and don't let rain deter you from going outside!

Further Reading

Axline, V. (1947) *Play Therapy*. Boston: Houghton Miffin.
An older but nevertheless classic text for play therapy with children. Always good to read the key foundational books, and this one certainly still stands strong today.

Emunah, R. (1994) *Acting for Real: Drama Therapy Process, Technique and Performance*. London: Brunner-Routledge.
This offers a good overview of the field, so will set the scene well for a range of key areas.

Karkou, V. (ed.) (2010) *Art Therapies in Schools: Research and Practice*. London: Jessica Kingsley.
This deals specifically with practice in schools, which helps to focus on approaches for young people. It gives context to work in both mainstream and special schools, and across the different art therapies (e.g. music, dance and art).

Gass, M.A., Gillis, H.L. and Russell, K.C. (2012) *Adventure Therapy: Theory, Research and Practice*. London: Routledge.
Although it has a North American slant, this offers a good overview to key areas related to this developing field, with good signposting for key ideas and literature.

For a wider overview of international practices and developments see the published texts from each of the International Adventure Therapy Conference Proceedings (all cited in the chapter), as this provides an excellent account of diverse international theory and practices and emerging practices.

Online Resources

BACP website: www.bacp.co.uk.
BACP Children and Young People Division – see Competencies for Working with Children and Young People.
Counselling MindEd: http://counsellingminded.com, especially CM 4.4: The Range of Creative and Symbolic Methods with CYP.

Part 2

Counselling Practices and Processes

Referrals and Indications for Therapy

Ani de la Prida and Wendy Brown

This chapter includes:

- Background to child and adolescent mental health policy
- Legislation relevant to referral
- Referral forms and relevance to assessment
- Influence of counselling modality on referral process
- Indications for therapy
- Potential dilemmas and good practice

Introduction

This chapter is designed to inform referring agencies, practitioners and counselling services. It raises points for discussion and highlights a number of aspects influencing referral. It explores the background to UK child and adolescent mental health policy alongside influential legislation relevant to referral. We consider referral forms and their relevance to assessment, highlighting the influence that the counselling modality can have on the referral process. We discuss indications for therapy and explore a variety of settings before highlighting potential dilemmas and good practice.

Referral is an important part of the counselling process, although one that in our experience may be overlooked at times. When considering the counselling process as a whole, it is perhaps difficult to determine the most significant aspect that enables change to occur for each client. Of recognised importance to the counselling process are the therapeutic conditions (Prever, 2010) and therapeutic alliance (Muran and Barber, 2010), but the referral is where we really start the work with each client. It is where we begin to develop a relationship, where we gain a 'picture' of the client in context and where we have an opportunity to create dialogue that can contribute towards therapeutic change.

Policy Background and History to Referral System

Currently there is no single UK system or policy for referral, but a variety of ways in which children and young people come to counselling, further complicated by the variation in legislation and policy within each of the of the four nations. Although not an inclusive list of all legislative policy, the following key points have a focus on the health and emotional well-being of the UK's children and young people, influencing the commissioning of services.

Table 9.1   CAMHS' four-tier system.

Tier 1 – provides treatment for less severe mental health conditions, such as mild depression, while also offering an assessment service for children and young people who would benefit from referral to more specialist services.
Services at this level are not just provided by mental health professionals, but also by GPs, health visitors, school nurses, teachers, social workers, youth justice workers and voluntary agencies.

Tier 2 – provides assessment and interventions for children and young people with more severe or complex health care needs, such as severe depression.
Services at this level are provided by community mental health nurses, psychologists and counsellors.

Tier 3 – provides services for children and young people with severe, complex and persistent mental health conditions, such as obsessive compulsive disorder (OCD), bipolar disorder and schizophrenia.
Services at this level are provided by a team of different professionals working together (a multi-disciplinary team), such as a psychiatrist, social worker, educational psychologist and occupational therapist.

Tier 4 – provides specialist services for children and young people with the most serious problems, such as violent behaviour, a serious and life-threatening eating disorder, or a history of physical and/ or sexual abuse. Tier 4 services are usually provided in specialist units, which can either be day units (where a patient can visit during the day), or in-patient units (where a patient will need to stay). Depending on the nature of the condition, this could be a stay of several days to several months.

Child and Adolescent Mental Health Services' (CAMHS) provision in the UK is organised around a four-tier system of assessment and delivery of services first outlined in an NHS Health Advisory Service review (1995). However, not all CAMHS offer counselling services; Richardson et al. (2010) point out that differing interpretations of the tiers have resulted in the very confusion that the system was designed to resolve. Referrals may be assessed in terms of the four tiers (see Table 9.1), although outside of the NHS many organisations do not make reference to it at all.

The need for clear referral and acceptance systems is recognised by practitioners, with specialist CAMHS and counselling services largely agreeing on criteria for appropriate referral (Spong et al., 2013). However, a clear route for communication, referral and consultation between counselling services and specialist CAMHS is not always available or seen as appropriate or supportive (ibid.). Spong et al. (2013) also highlight that at times there are difficulties between counselling services and specialist CAMHS where counsellors are critical of the rationale of specialist CAMHS, which is likely to have an impact on referrals from counselling services.

The Youth Justice Board Mental Health Report (Harrington and Bailey, 2005) points out that the CAMHS framework necessitates a holistic assessment approach, and that local and regional partnerships are necessary for consistent provision of services. Provision and assessment, however, are inconsistent (Mulley, 2009), and dependent on partnerships with public, private and voluntary organisations which are at times disjointed (DoH, 2005; Spong et al., 2013).

Recent research highlights that children and young people are more likely to be referred to a professional for behaviour than for emotional difficulties, with mental health support being provided principally by teachers (DfE, 2011). More worryingly, the DfE report states that in their study 'no primary or secondary schools reported using approaches that involved following a rigorous protocol' (2011: 10). This picture suggests children and young people may not always be referred when appropriate or needed.

A BACP scoping report points to recent figures which suggest that the numbers attending school-based counselling are similar to the numbers attending specialist CAMHS services (Cooper, 2013). The report suggests that counselling is currently available in approximately 60 to 85 per cent of secondary schools in the UK, whilst there is mixed provision in primary schools (Spong et al., 2013). Cooper (2013) highlights that sources of referral to school counselling services include parents, school staff, and self-referral, although the most common source of referral is school staff. In particular, pastoral care teachers were reported to be involved in approximately two-thirds of referrals.

Counselling services in the community and voluntary sector are an important part of mental health provision for children and young people. A recent report estimates that there are approximately 100,000 referrals per year for children, young people and young adults (Street, 2013).

Referral Forms and Assessment

It is difficult to separate referral and assessment as the two are linked and often intertwined. Different theoretical orientations have different ways of assessing (or not assessing) clients, which will discernibly influence the information sought as well as the referral process. The structure of the setting will also shape the referral process both in terms of information requested and also who is seen or referred on. Therefore there is a huge diversity in terms of referral and assessment practices in the UK, and localised referral policies and forms will naturally reflect this.

Some settings prefer a written referral to be completed before seeing a client, for example specialist CAMHS require written referrals from a GP, social worker or other professional. Drop-in centres, schools-based counselling services and community-based services may not require referral or assessment documentation, whilst other counselling services may ask clients to meet with a counsellor to complete a referral or assessment form during an initial session.

Reflective Question

Imagine you are a counsellor working in a school-based service. You receive a referral form. What information would you want the form to contain that would enable you to make an informed choice about accepting the client or referring on?

Discussion

Ideally, information on a referral form would include the client's voice, whether the client wants to come to counselling, the nature of the problem, how long the difficulty has been experienced, and any information considered relevant to the issue. For example, in the case of bereavement the form should include details of the loss. Information about the context of the client may be useful, for example if the child has just moved to the school or local area.

The form should also contain information about any serious issues, such as child protection. Decisions to accept referrals would be informed by modality, limits of competency and counselling service policy.

Referral forms could be considered inherently flawed in that they are predominantly created for the needs of the setting rather than the client, they often contain other people's perceptions – and the younger the child the less likely that they will contain the client's words or view.

Although a referral form can contain much information about a client, it is important to remember that it may not be the client's opinion. It may contain biased opinion, for example one teacher may see behaviour as unmanageable that others, and the client, would view as acceptable. Referral information may not be accurate, for example informal assessments and diagnoses such as 'Jane has low self-esteem' may be inaccurate. It is important to be able to hold the information on a referral form in mind without allowing it to prejudice your view or opinion of the client before you have even met.

Relevant information may also be missing at referral, for example a recent bereavement may not be mentioned unless the referrer is prompted. Perceptions of those referring may be distorted by their own difficulties, for example a mother who is unable to process her own grief at the loss of a partner may consider their child's grief problematic or abnormal – whereas the child's expressed grief may be the healthier response.

The requirements and structure of settings will often create dilemmas, challenging ethical boundaries, theoretical stance and counsellor competence – for example a counselling service policy to decline referrals for pre-trial therapy for children involved in court proceedings because of the risk and complexity of managing the counselling without prejudicing the client's evidence (for further discussion see Chapter 17: 'Law and Policy'). This may not be in the client's interest, however, and could be seen as contrary to the ethical principles of autonomy and beneficence (BACP, 2013).

Theoretical stance can also give rise to dilemmas with referral. For example there is anecdotal evidence that specialist CAMHS services, particularly when working from systemic and integrative perspectives, will decline referrals for counselling for looked-after children on the basis that they must be in a stable environment before engaging in therapeutic work. Other service providers working from modalities such as person-centred therapy do not see this as a barrier to therapeutic work. In fact it could be argued that the child's need is greater during periods of instability than when their environment is stable. Declining requests for therapy on this basis could also be seen as contrary to the ethical principles of autonomy and beneficence (BACP, 2013).

Good Practice

At referral it can be useful to include or have information on:

- Client's voice
- Current family status (both parents, lone parent, step-parent, carer, adopted)
- Is the child subject to a child protection plan/order?
- Is the child a looked-after child – if so, placement history?

(Continued)

(Continued)

- Any current medications?
- Behaviours or issues causing concern?
- What is the hoped for outcome of therapy?
- Any recent losses, bereavements, or major changes?

Case Study   Josh

Referral from Greenwich Town High School to ABC Counselling Services

Josh, DOB 6.6.97. 15 years old – Year 10

Lives with mum and dad, no siblings. No medication.

Josh's behaviour is causing concern. His previously good grades are rapidly in decline and he has poor attendance. We are concerned he is truanting, although mum says Josh's absences are due to illness recently and she forgets to inform school. No GP evidence to support any illness.

Josh had been a pleasant but quiet student, but is increasingly defiant and disruptive in class. He is tired and easily distracted, and has fallen asleep in class. He seems to be getting into fights, and recently had a black eye which he said he got from 'walking into a door'. There are allegations of bullying by Connor, a Year 7 boy, although Josh denies this. Recently Josh was excluded for three days for punching Connor in the face.

We are concerned that Josh may be using drugs or alcohol and that he may be stealing as a number of items have gone missing in PE.

Our initial suggestion for counselling was refused by Josh. We contacted Mum, and Josh has now agreed to counselling

Reflective Question

What are your initial thoughts on working with Josh? Which ethical principles would you specifically consider with this case?

Discussion

It is important to notice that the referral information is based entirely on information from those surrounding Josh. It is not clear if Josh wants to attend counselling.

In terms of the BACP Ethical Principles (2013) this would highlight the need to pay attention to autonomy to ensure that Josh's right to be self-governing is supported.

Below is an example of the notes that Josh's counsellor made in response to the referral, and the first two sessions with Josh.

Denise   Josh's Counsellor

Case Notes

Initial Reflections

Josh's voice is entirely absent from the referral form – has anyone asked Josh how he is feeling? Can he open up? He sounds angry – why?

His behaviour could suggest drug use – is he stealing? I can feel my assumptions forming of a rude, aggressive teenager – he reminds me of my nephew. Can I put these feelings aside and open myself up to see the real Josh?

Josh refused counselling initially – did mum insist he attend? If he has been coerced is it ethical to start sessions? No mention of dad – why? How can I enable Josh's voice and support his choice to not attend if he wishes?

I need to pay attention to Josh's autonomy at the start.

Supervision Notes

Session 1

Josh was very angry and reticent at our first session, 'Everyone has it in for me', he said. I explained he could choose to not come, and that I would support his choice – hopefully this will help him build some trust with me. He was concerned about confidentiality – I wonder why? I agreed to discuss with him first anything I might need to disclose. He was very angry about Connor and said they had a fight.

Session 2

Josh opened up and told me that dad is alcoholic. There is violence at home, Josh is angry and protective of mum – does he get hurt trying to protect mum? His absences from school are when mum is 'ill' – she refuses outside help. He is often awake at night because he is worried. Connor, who gave Josh a black eye, is bullying Josh. Josh has asked me not to tell anyone, says he'll deny it. He feels stupid because Connor is younger. I am concerned – if I break confidentiality now I think Josh will disengage, leaving him more vulnerable. I need to explore further in supervision.

> ## Reflective Question
>
> How accurately did the referral capture Josh's situation?
>
> ### Discussion
>
> Referrals often may not accurately capture the client's situation. Looking at Denise's initial reflections and supervision notes, notice where you made assumptions or judgements. How able would you have been to meet Josh without prejudice after reading the referral? Past experiences, culture and even media images shape our perceptions of children and young people (Prever, 2010), and recognising these is important in order to see the client beyond the referral form.

Initial Referral Meeting

Initial referral meetings often include the child and parent. This meeting gives the counsellor an opportunity to hear where the difficulties may lie, and how these are being felt and displayed by the child or young person. This is also an opportunity to ensure that both parties fully understand what counselling is, and just as importantly, what it is not. With an older child or young person who doesn't have an adult present, it is important to ensure that you check their understanding throughout the process.

With a younger child the initial consultation session can be a transitional space for parents and child to traverse the space from parental authority to having individual sessions. At times it can also be a difficult session for the child. He may not want the adults to share information about him, or he may not agree with what is being said. It is important to ensure that the child has a voice at these meetings. It can also be a difficult session for the counsellor, who may experience the parent as judgemental or punitive towards the child. This can be a tricky scenario to manage, particularly when a counsellor is in private practice, as payment can create an additional dynamic with a parent. Managing boundaries and expectations is important, and this initial referral meeting can help build a therapeutic relationship and ensure clear understanding of the boundaries of the counselling work.

There are particular issues around client agenda that are complex to balance at times but which need careful attention at referral. The reason for referral may be a parent's, but the parent's agenda may be different to the client's. For example, a young person may be referred by a parent for being angry at home, but the young person may choose to explore their sexuality rather than their anger, and they may only disclose this to the counsellor in private. Paying attention to this possibility is important to ensure an autonomous space for the client.

Difficulties can also arise around expectations at referral. Clear information and contracting at referral can support the work by informing realistic expectations and verbalising therapeutic aims. For example a parent who brings a child who is 'sad' to counselling may become disturbed if their child appears to become angry or unhappy through counselling. Changes that occur as part of the client's therapeutic growth process – for example, because the child is revealing previously hidden feelings – can make it seem that counselling isn't working or is even making things worse. Discussing this at referral can help support the therapeutic work. It is important therefore to give clear information at the outset for parents/referrers, explaining what may occur as part of the counselling process.

Different Modalities' Perspectives

It can be difficult to separate referral and assessment as the two are intrinsically linked. A referrer in a sense has already made an assessment that a child or young person would benefit from counselling. The information required from a counselling service or practitioner at referral will seek to explore this further and may even include an assessment before a child or young person is accepted for counselling. It is important to recognise that there are a wide variety of referral systems and practices, which are also influenced by modality.

Systemic

Some therapies – particularly attachment focused, family therapy and systemic – are likely to carry out more lengthy assessments as part of the referral or initial assessment. Observational assessments often include all family members and a team of professionals either in the child's home or at the clinic, and may last for a whole day or over a number of sessions. Referral information sought can include details such as chronology, nurture-trauma timeline, health, diary of daily routine and behaviour, formal reports from parents, professionals, school, examples of schoolwork, and details of previous assessments. Examples of questionnaires that may be used at referral and assessment include:

- the child behaviour checklist
- an executive functioning questionnaire
- a child trauma checklist

- a parental stress checklist
- the ACC
- Connor's questionnaire

For further information see the Comprehensive Multi-disciplinary Child Assessment (Family Futures, 2014).

Cognitive-Behavioural Therapy (CBT)

CBT therapists use structured assessments to develop individualised treatment plans designed to help children restructure their thinking and learn new problem-solving skills. Tests may be used at referral to measure symptoms, and a clear idea of issues to be worked on will usually be agreed as part of the assessment. CBT with children and young people may include books or manuals designed to teach the client about the relationship between thoughts, feelings and behaviours (The Centre for Cognitive Behavioural Counselling, 2014).

Psychodynamic

Psychodynamic practitioners consider that assessing at referral requires specialised skills, and that the assessment process itself can be a helpful 'exploration which leads to a variety of treatment possibilities' (Rustin and Quagliata, 2000: 1). The psychodynamic model uses observation and pays attention to the transference and counter-transference (i.e. feelings elicited in the therapist). The therapist may use questionnaires to gather information, and may ask to observe the child with parents and interpret behaviours. At referral the therapist will be seeking to understand the child's current situation and past experiences, particularly attachment experiences (ibid.).

Person-centred

For person-centred practitioners the focus is on the client as expert, or at least equal in the referral process with the therapist. Assessment is seen primarily as an opportunity to explore with the client the appropriateness of counselling and not as a tool to diagnose or determine treatment options (Gillon, 2013). Based on Rogers' six conditions being necessary and sufficient (Rogers, 2003), person-centred practice considers that the treatment is the same whatever the diagnosis, i.e. the six conditions, and therefore information and assessment at referral hold much less importance.

Person-centred counsellors will generally ask fewer questions, want less background information, and will be aiming to understand the difficulty from the client's point of view. Therefore the person-centred therapist may hold information from other parties at referral lightly. They will pay attention to their own reactions and feelings, as well as their client's, to inform an assessment of risk. A common difficulty for many person-centred therapists is how to balance organisational requirements at referral that require a more objective assessment without abandoning their own therapeutic stance (Prever, 2010).

Client's Environment

At referral it can be important to understand the circumstances and relationships surrounding the child or young person. Dilemmas can arise when the client's difficulties are being created by parents, whether because of abuse or because of poor parenting. A child may disclose abuse or neglect at referral. This can be difficult in any setting, but particularly when challenging the parent could result in them ending counselling for the client. Working with a child or young person's issues when the parent is contributing to or compounding a child's difficulties is difficult and demanding for a counsellor to manage, therefore supervision is an essential support. Reflecting on the dynamics in

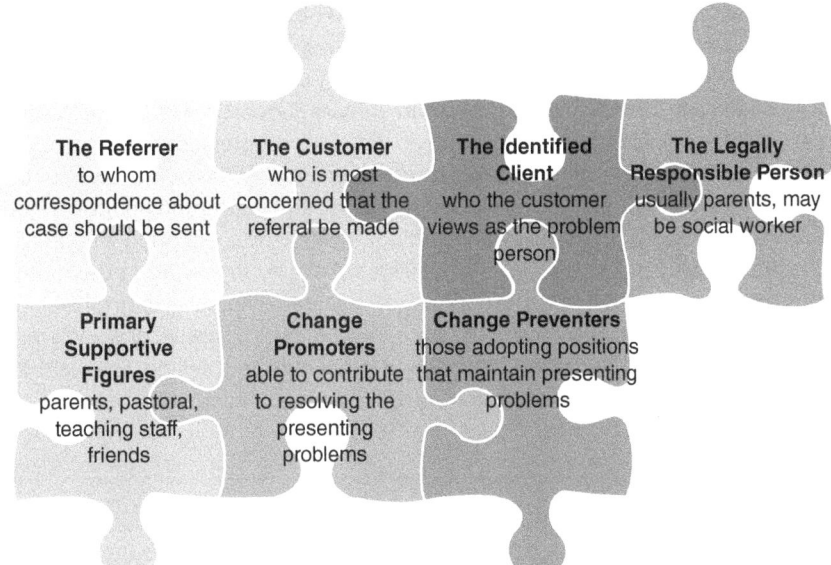

Figure 9.1   Puzzle grid.

the child or young person's world can help deepen your understanding. The puzzle grid (Figure 9.1), adapted from a systemic model, can be a useful and easy-to-use reflection tool for the counsellor (Carr, 2004).

The puzzle grid tool can be used as a guide to identify key people in the referral process who can help the counsellor gain an overview of the structure surrounding the child or young person. In using the tool it is important to ask the following questions:

- Who has decided the child needs therapy?
- Who is referring them?
- Why are they referring this child?
- Does the child know about the referral?
- What does the child feel about the referral?

The case study below illustrates how one counsellor used the puzzle grid tool to enable a deeper understanding of the client's context, and of the therapeutic process.

Case Study   Phillipa

Phillipa was an extremely shy 12-year-old girl living alone with her mother after Dad left nine months ago. Phillipa was refusing to go to school and was referred by her GP after seeing her at an appointment with her mother, who was described in the referral letter as 'beside herself with worry'. During the first contracting session Phillipa seemed anxious and tearful a lot of the time. Using the puzzle grid, Phillipa is The Identified Client and Mum is in the role of Customer and Legally Responsible Person. Counselling began and a teacher was identified as Primary Supportive Figure. The counsellor recognised two of Phillipa's friends as Change Promoters. Sessions progressed and the work flourished with Phillipa improving and returning to school on a phased basis. At this point, Mum contacted the counsellor, worried that Phillipa was being bullied at school, and concerned about her getting the bus to school in the mornings. There had been a minor incident, but exploring with Phillipa it become clear that Mum's distress was the cause of Phillipa's difficulty in leaving in the mornings. Using the grid, Mum was identified as in the role of Change Preventer – Mum's anxiety following Dad leaving was possibly being unconsciously projected onto Phillipa. The counsellor showed empathy and compassion towards mum and suggested she engage in her own counselling. She went ahead with this and became able to separate her anxieties from Phillipa, and moved from being a Change Preventer to a Change Promoter for Phillipa.

Indications for Therapy and Presenting Problems

Below are some examples of indications that children and young people may benefit from counselling. The list is not exhaustive, and although most children do the things on this list at some time or other, it is the degree, persistence and proportion of symptoms that should guide a referral. Age is an important factor to consider, for example mood swings and difficult behaviour are developmentally appropriate in a teenager but less so in a six-year-old.

Persistent feelings of sadness or hopelessness

Children may not be able to talk about being sad, or even identify how they are feeling as sadness, but may express this through their actions. This can include rudeness, difficult or defiant behaviour, breaking rules, withdrawing or isolating themselves, not being able to stop crying, refusing food, needing constant reassurance or clingy behaviour.

Persistent or unexplained anger

Children and young people may express anger verbally in temper tantrums, persistent refusal to cooperate, aggression or arguing. Anger may lead to aggressive behaviour such as hitting, biting, shouting, breaking or destroying things or self-harm.

Persistent anxiety or worrying

Children may become anxious because of parenting experiences or a recent event, for example illness or death, separation, divorce, or a major change or move. Presenting issues connected to underlying anxiety can include a preoccupation with physical illness or appearance, performing routines obsessively, or changes in patterns of sleeping or eating.

Loss

Children may struggle with processing loss following events such as death, their parents' divorce, or a move, and may need to have some time to work through this in counselling. They may present as constantly wanting to talk about the past, or seem unable to separate past and present. They may also present as tearful, disengaged, with poor concentration and memory, anxiety and difficulty sleeping.

Withdrawal or isolation

A child may become reclusive, preferring to be alone all the time and isolating themselves from peers and family. Presenting issues can also include anxiety, depression, not laughing or joking, not enjoying activities they once enjoyed, or a sudden, unexplained drop in grades at school.

Other indicators include:

- Expressing thoughts of suicide
- Seeming very low or depressed
- Family difficulties
- Behaviour difficulties
- Repetitive or obsessive thoughts or behaviour
- Eating problems
- Bullying or being bullied
- Difficulties with peers and friendships
- Self-harm
- Alcohol or drug use
- Dieting obsessively, or bingeing followed by vomiting or taking laxatives
- An inability to concentrate, think clearly, or make decisions
- Returning to younger behaviours
- Seeking or asking for counselling
- Experiencing regular nightmares

Presenting issues

In terms of presenting issues recent research has identified that the most common difficulty that young people seek referral to counselling for is family/relationship difficulties (Cooper, 2013; Street, 2013). In the voluntary and community sector, Street (2013) described the most common reasons as:

- General mental health issues
- Challenging behaviour
- Self-harm
- Abuse/neglect
- Bullying
- Bereavement
- Suicidal feelings

- Eating disorders
- Substance misuse

In addition to these, referral issues included depression, lack of self-esteem, rape, pregnancy, panic attacks, lack of self-confidence, paranoia and eating disorders. Of the concerns or issues presented at referral some clients have multiple issues, and most of those with multiple issues present with three to five issues.

Cooper's (2013) research in secondary school counselling found similar concerns or issues at referral:

- Anger
- Behaviour
- Bereavement
- Bullying
- Self-worth
- Relationships in general

Anger was significantly more common for young male clients, with approximately 25 per cent reporting this as a difficulty at referral. He also noted that presenting issues tended to change as therapy progressed, from anger towards relationships and self-worth difficulties. In addition to these presenting issues, secondary school counsellors' records also included depression, self-harm, abuse, and eating disorders.

A similar pattern of referral issues was reported in a report on primary school counselling, with Thompson (2013) citing Webb et al.'s list of most common referral reasons as:

- Family problems
- Trauma and abuse
- Friendship and bullying
- Bereavement
- Anxiety

This report highlighted a worrying issue of inappropriate referrals, where referrals for counselling have been made for classroom behaviour management difficulties rather than the child being in need of counselling.

Specialist CAMHS

Referral to specialist CAMHS services can be dependent on local provision, relationship between CAMHS and counselling service, counselling service policy and counsellor competence. The four-tier system can be used as a guide to enable appropriate referral.

Cooper's (2013) research found that '92% of counsellors feel clear about when to refer a young person on to specialist CAMHS or other services' (2013: 5). Spong et al.'s report includes a table (2013: 10), reproduced here as Table 9.2, showing accepted referral criteria to specialist CAMHS as identified by CAMHS staff. School counsellors, however, see clients with a wide range of difficulties, and there are no set criteria for who is considered an appropriate referral for schools (Cooper, 2013). The list below is not conclusive and is open to interpretation and further discussion. However, it usefully illustrates a broad view of when a CAMHS referral may be appropriate.

Table 9.2 When a CAMHS referral might be appropriate.

Specialist CAMHS should take referrals	School- or community-based counselling should take referrals
Moderate to severe mental health problems	Mild to moderate mental health problems
A clinical diagnosis	Emotional health and well-being problems
Where risk needs to be 'held'	Those who are not at risk
When multi-disciplinary skills are needed	Those whose lives are too chaotic to attend regular clinic appointments
Where social care elements are needed	When services only available in community agencies are needed (for example, drop-in)

In secondary school-age clients, Cooper (2013) found that specialist CAMHS in 2008–9 recorded the most common referral issues as:

- Emotional problems
- Self-harm
- Eating disorders
- Conduct difficulties
- Hyperkinetic problems
- Autistic spectrum problems
- Developmental difficulties
- Psychotic problems

Counselling Settings

Counsellors work in a variety of settings, and the setting in which the client is seen will impact on the referral and on the therapeutic work. Whether in private practice or within service providers such as voluntary or statutory agencies and schools, surprisingly children's rights – and consequently their rights within a therapeutic relationship – vary. The diagnostic labels used to describe children's behaviour and distress can vary between agencies (Malek, 1991, 1993), and it is not unusual, therefore, for counsellors and therapists to become confused as to the limits of their work with the child. Knowing when to refer on to specialist CAMHS, or when specialist CAMHS should refer on to counselling, is therefore not always clear.

Schools

Counsellors in schools can find that some children perceive counselling as stigmatising or as part of the disciplinary system, although the opposite can also be true with children finding school counselling less stigmatising (Cooper, 2013). Work may be needed to overcome a negative perception at referral, particularly drawing attention to the child or young person's autonomy to choose whether they wish to engage with counselling. Provision of school counsellors is increasing (Cooper, 2004, 2006; McGinnis, 2006), and drop-in sessions within schools are becoming more common. There is, according to independent legal opinion, no specific requirement in law for parents' prior permission to be obtained before a child makes confidential disclosures to a teacher (Beloff and Mountfield, 1994), but Gillick competency should be determined (Children's Legal Centre, 1997) when working with children in the UK.

Statutory Agency

A significant level of therapeutic work is provided by statutory agencies, such as Children's Services departments, specialist CAMHS, the NHS, and youth services of local authorities. Provision is variable, although a more comprehensive and integrated provision is being developed in response to guidance and directives (Spong et al., 2013). Assessment-focused, time-limited, and risk-averse policies are likely issues for counsellors in practice in statutory agencies, all of which can influence the referral process.

Voluntary and Community Sector

Given current constraints affecting statutory bodies, some of the greatest opportunities for child-centred therapeutic practice are in the voluntary and community sector (Daniels and Jenkins, 2010). Clients highlighted strength of this provision as the non-stigmatising settings, holistic approach and initial contact at referral (Street, 2013). However, agencies may have limited administrative ability to gather data on outcomes or referrals, and agencies may be reluctant to engage with routine monitoring (Street, 2013). Agencies will have their own specific referral policies in place and practitioners need clear understanding of these to ensure they work with cases appropriate to the agency's work. For example, some agencies work only with sexual abuse, whilst others may decline referrals from young people who are using drugs. Each individual agency will also have policies relating to confidentiality and child protection, for example information about self-harm may be sought at referral with one agency whilst another may not require this.

Private Practice

There are many counsellors and therapists working with children and young people within their own private practice. Rather confusingly, these practitioners are not necessarily bound by the same requirements, such as referral policies or specific requirements related to their therapeutic work, as those working in statutory or voluntary agencies. For example, in terms of child protection, there is no legal requirement to report suspected child abuse to the authorities, although the therapist would be justified in doing so in the 'public interest' (Daniels and Jenkins, 2010). The increased freedoms in private practice run parallel to an increase in responsibility and complexity the practitioner carries. The self-referral process can leave practitioners vulnerable. For example, risk assessment may be more difficult when working in isolation. Additionally, working in your own home carries vulnerability for the counsellor that can affect the referral process. For example, a counsellor working alone at home may choose not to see clients with a history of violence, and therefore this may form part of the information sought at initial referral. Boundaries and risk need to be clearly and ethically explored by the practitioner.

Good Practice Issues

Referring on to Other Agencies

Know your limitations and other clinicians' strengths. (Lazarus, 2002)

There are various reasons for referring a child or young person onto another agency and at the core of this action is recognition that this is in the child's best interests. Onward referral should never be viewed as a sign of a practitioner's weakness, or lack of skill, but in fact quite the opposite. There are a number of possible reasons for referring a child or young person onto another agency. These may include:

- The child's presenting problems are outside the remit of the agency or counsellor
- The counsellor knows the child or the family on a personal basis
- It is appropriate for the child to access additional sources of support
- The child requires more specialist intervention, or a clinical assessment for a mental health difficulty

It is important when referring on to check that the parent and the client clearly understand the reason and do not interpret the referral as being because they are 'too difficult', 'too complex' or 'too ill'.

Abuse and Investigations

There are difficulties with a referral for children and young people when there are issues of abuse under investigation. There are risks and fears associated in seeing clients in this situation – for example, that a counsellor may potentially damage the case by influencing a client's testimony (see Chapter 17 for further discussion). This situation in itself is not a reason to decline a referral, although many agencies may wrongly believe this to be the case.

There may be fear around the possibility of notes being requested, or of a counsellor being required to give evidence. A disproportionate fear of the risk means that services may decline referrals until after the court case rather than risk damaging the prosecution, or opening a counsellor to scrutiny. However, a client may be in great need of support at this time, and *The Cleveland Report* states: 'there is a danger that in looking to the welfare of children believed to be victims of sexual abuse the children themselves may be overlooked. The child is a person and not an object of concern' (Butler-Sloss, 1988: 245).

Children have a right to influence decisions made about them (HMSO, 1989, The Children Act), and before declining a referral the potential impact on a client in this circumstance must also be considered in terms of the ethical framework (BACP, 2013).

Careful assessment, understanding of legal issues and clear and open communication with referrers can help ensure good practice.

Looked-After Children

There are particular issues and contexts surrounding referrals for looked-after children. In 2011 there were over 83,000 children in the UK care system (Royal College of

Paediatrics and Child Health, 2012). Looked-after children's mental health difficulties are exacerbated by their experiences, for example loss, poor parenting, abuse, poverty, neglect, insecurity or a combination of these issues. There is a statutory duty to ensure that looked-after children's health needs are assessed at regular reviews and that they have access to a range of services (ibid.).

However, referrals to counselling often take longer to be made because a number of professionals, e.g. child's social worker, team manager, foster carer, supervising social worker, school, child's guardian, as well as the parents, will need to be consulted. Referring information may be substantial, complex and at times inconsistent, partly due at times to the fragmented history of care around the child or young person. For example, a complete history of the child's behaviour might be provided whilst details of a close family bereavement might be missing. The issue of different agendas at referral is compounded here with the potential for a variety of agendas to be at play. At referral it is important that the therapist takes extra care to ensure that the voice of the child is heard amongst the competing agendas and substantial referral information.

Looked-after children are often in unstable settings, for example having multiple placements. Referrals to specialist CAMHS may be declined if a child or young person is in an unstable setting. The reason for this is primarily one of modality. Although a stable environment may be desirable, this in itself is not a reason to decline a referral for therapy for many modalities, for example person-centred. The interest of the client should be paramount and the potential impact of declining a referral should be considered in terms of the Ethical Framework (BACP, 2013). If a referral is declined on this basis, then a client in need of therapy should be referred on to a service that is able to provide counselling. Sadly, many children in care experience years of instability, and the risk in declining a referral in this situation is that it may take years before a child receives the support they need.

Case Study   Amanda

Amanda, aged 11, is the elder sister of two brothers, aged three and five. All siblings were taken into care 18 months ago, due to severe neglect, parental drug and alcohol use and failure to keep the children safe. When living at home Amanda looked after Mum and did most of the cooking and caring for her brothers. The siblings were separated when Amanda's brothers were placed with a foster family 15 miles away.

Amanda lived with foster carers for seven months, but they struggled as she refused to attend school, became violent and kept running away to try to return home. A referral to specialist CAMHS was sought, but following assessment the referral was declined, advising that Amanda needed to be in a more stable placement before therapeutic work was undertaken. There was no onward referral made by the CAMHS team at this time. The carers were unable to contain Amanda's violent outbursts and the placement broke down.

Amanda moved to foster carers 40 miles from her family. Amanda settled somewhat, but after four months the carers reported that Amanda was becoming withdrawn and aggressive, and had difficulty making friends following a change of school. A referral was made to the specialist CAMHS team in her new area, which had a waiting list of 12 months. A referral was also generated to a national children's charity counselling service that was able to offer an initial appointment within four weeks. The counsellor met with the social worker and foster carer to begin with, to enable clear contracting and obtain consent from the social worker to start counselling. This gave everyone an opportunity to speak about their current concerns and reflect upon the behaviours that Amanda was currently displaying and what they might be indicating. The social worker decided that due to Amanda's recent chronology it would not be in her best interest to be at the referral meeting as she wanted to give the counsellor a full history. The foster carer also completed a Strengths and Difficulties Questionnaire, which the counsellor scored. Once the parameters of the counselling had been contracted it was arranged that Amanda be invited in with her foster carer to meet the counsellor.

Amanda's first session included the foster carer. The counsellor advised Amanda that she had already met the carer and her social worker, and listed some of the concerns they had. She expressed that these opinions may or may not be 'correct' in Amanda's eyes and her role was to understand how things were for Amanda, and to offer her a space each week. Amanda avoided eye contact and shrugged her shoulders. During contracting the counsellor acknowledged Amanda's disengagement, and offered Amanda six sessions, with a planned break at session five in order for Amanda to identify for herself whether she wished to continue. The counsellor felt that Amanda's overall presentation showed signs of avoidant attachment rather than being resistant towards counselling.

The counsellor used YP-CORE in each session, mapping scores onto a graph each week to show any change. The building of trust was slow, and the main focus for Amanda each week was anxiety about how her mum and brothers were coping without her to 'look out for them'. Amanda was unhappy at having monthly contact with her mother and siblings and she worried constantly about them. The counsellor took account of the Getting It Right For Every Child (Scottish Government, 2008) principles and, with Amanda's knowledge and consent, sent a letter to her Local Authority social worker, stating that such lengthy periods between seeing her siblings and mother were impacting on her emotional well-being. She requested that this be considered at Amanda's next review meeting. The counsellor noticed that from session four onwards Amanda was disengaging, and she felt this was likely to be due to the sessions drawing to an ending. She knew that it was common for some children to 'shut off' when there was a change approaching. The counsellor worked hard to ensure Amanda understood she had the choice to return to sessions after the sixth session, as they had agreed when contracting. After the break Amanda chose to continue with counselling. The counsellor noticed that Amanda seemed more willing to engage.

Summary

To sum up, it is important for referrers to aim to provide clear, unbiased and accurate referrals. The referral system surrounding the child or young person can be complex at times. Policies, organisational settings, and theoretical stance can influence the process in ways that may not be in the client's interest. Information received at referral may be incomplete, inaccurate or biased. For the practitioner, remaining able to meet the child without a prejudiced view caused by information at referral isn't easy and can be challenging. Experience, supervision and reflection can help to develop the counsellor's capacity to manage the challenges of referral when counselling children and young people.

Key Points

- There is no single referral system in the UK
- Child and Adolescent Mental Health Services' (CAMHS) provision in the UK is organised around a four-tier system of assessment and delivery of services which influence referral
- Referral is influenced by counselling setting, service provider policy, modality and client's context
- It is important to recognise that the information received at referral may be inaccurate or incomplete and the child or young person's views may not be present
- Referrals to specialist CAMHS that are declined for looked-after children due to placement instability should be referred on to an alternative counselling service

Learning Activities

1. Using one of your clients, apply the puzzle grid to identify the various roles surrounding the child in order to gain a deeper understanding of the client's situation. Then discuss with a peer, tutor or supervisor.
2. Design your own referral form, and then discuss with a peer, tutor or supervisor.
3. Work through the Counselling MindEd module CM 2.6 on risk assessment, available at www.counsellingminded.com.

Further Reading

Richardson, J. (2002) *The Mental Health of Looked-After Children. Bright Futures: Working with Vulnerable Young People*. London: Mental Health Foundation.

Spong, S. Waters, R., Dowd, C. and Jackson, C. (2013) *The Relationship between Specialist Child and Adolescent Mental Health Services (CAMHS) and Community-Based Counselling for Children and Young People*. Lutterworth: BACP/Counselling MindEd. Available at: www.counsellingminded.com.

Online Resources

Counselling MindEd: http://counsellingminded.com, especially CM 2.1: What Is Assessment in CYP Counselling?; CM 2.2: Engaging the CYP in Collaborative Assessment; CM 2.3: Areas to Consider Assessing with the CYP.

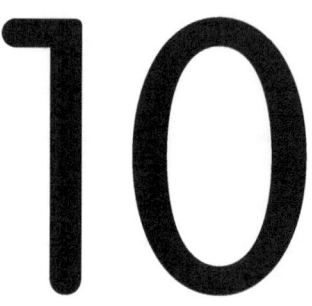

Preparation for Therapy: Beginnings

Dave Stewart and Edith Bell

This chapter includes:

- The primary importance of listening to children and young people in the preparation for therapy process
- The need to tune-in to different ages, developmental presentations and preferences to help children and young people access and articulate their thoughts and feelings in the preparation phase
- The importance of a more 'active counsellor' stance in assisting young clients to feel more confident in expressing emotion and more at ease in the therapeutic relationship
- 'Collaborative assessment' as a new development within the CYP counselling field
- Seven collaborative assessment tasks that together create a 'preparation for therapy map'
- Some of the key constructs from within child development theory that underpin safe and effective preparation for therapy: Piaget's (1936) theory of cognitive development (including 'schema' formation), Bronfenbrenner's (1979) 'ecological systems theory', Gardener's (1983) 'multiple intelligences' and Vygotsky's (1934) ideas about the 'zone of proximal development'.

Introduction

Listening to Children and Young People – the Critical Preparation Task

In his book *Equals*, child psychotherapist Adam Phillips (2003) provocatively invites us to reconsider therapy as a 'listening' – rather than 'talking' – 'cure'. Few of us would argue about the prime importance of listening in our work. Why then can it be so difficult to *really* listen to children? Why do we sometimes find it hard to let go of 'counsellor-knows-best' when deciding how to shape work with young people? What barriers do therapists face in trying to centralise the voice of a child/young person in therapy? In hearing the views of key adults in a child's world – often an important part of the initial listening process and especially with younger children – how do therapists hold and contextualise the potential 'clash' of voices? What templates and structures might helpfully scaffold the preparation listening process to enable a young client to define what they want from counselling? And – what theories should counsellors be aware of when preparing a CYP for therapy?

Preparation for Therapy – Unexplored Territory within CYP Counselling

A search of BACP journals over the last five years confirmed that this has not been a priority area to date. While *Therapy Today, Counselling and Psychotherapy Research* and *Counselling Children and Young People* host a good number of articles on research, theory and practice with CYP, there are only two pieces specific to the preparation therapy phase. First is an interview with Ruth Schmidt Neven (2010) exploring her book *Core Principles of Assessment and Therapeutic Communication with Children, Parents and Families*; however, it comes from a sister therapeutic tradition – psychoanalytic child psychotherapy – as opposed to CYP counselling. The second is a short article by Liana Lowenstein (2011) looking at creative assessment techniques, in-tune with counselling within an integrative orientation.

Overall, however, it would appear that preparation and assessment with CYP from a humanistic orientation is a neglected area within the literature. Perhaps counselling preparation and assessment are unexplored territories because they are seen as places *outside* the core humanistic counselling map. With historical roots within the 'anti-medical model' movement, assessment can be seen as antithetical to what counselling stands for. Its seeming need to label, prescribe and diagnose places it beyond counselling's horizon. Indeed some counsellors might agree with Worrall (2006) that the only task during preparation/contracting is 'to create with them [the client] a relational climate that will most effectively facilitate their self-directed exploration and development' (p. 52). For others there is a conviction that it is even contrary to Rogers' 'core conditions':

> within the person-centred domain the question of assessment is ridiculous: the assessor would have to make a judgement not only about the client but on the relational dimensions between the client and the counsellor. (Mearns, 1997: 91)

Contemporary Developments and Their Impact on Preparation Practice in CYP Counselling

However, the ever-growing field of CYP counselling is pushing at historical boundaries of what is necessary and feasible within the counselling map. As it does so it is articulating more clearly what it does and how its work, of necessity, differs from adult counselling. For instance, BACP's 'CYP Competency Framework for Humanistic Counselling' (2014) – a landmark document in our development as a profession – has 'ability to conduct a collaborative assessment' as one of its generic therapeutic competencies. To create safe and effective practice counsellors must scaffold the preparation process in developmentally-attuned ways that both facilitate each CYP to draw a map of *their* territory and enable the counsellor to fine-tune the picture to illuminate any areas of risk or vulnerability.

Inevitability this means donning a more active role in the preparation phase. Katy McArthur's (2013) qualitative research of secondary school counselling highlights that 'emotional expression' is seen by young people as the most helpful aspect of their therapy, with difficulties in talking about emotions the key hindering factor.

Young people in the study also preferred a more 'active counsellor' approach: asking questions, offering advice, providing psycho-education and self-help strategies. These counsellor-led activities are seen to reduce anxiety, overcome barriers to emotional expression and create a sense of ease in the relationship.

Similarly, research carried out by Barnardo's (Regan and Craig, 2011) with primary school children indicated that 'talking about feelings' and 'counselling activities' were the two aspects children mentioned the most in interviews.

Activities – carefully attuned to the client's developmental presentation and preferences – help mediate the content of these critical preparation phase conversations. The right activity helps a child get beyond some of the barriers to accessing and expressing emotion. Perhaps what looks like non-engagement is really crying out for a less verbal, more 'right-brain' approach. Here we might find that introducing something visual, like a series of 'feelings faces' to map responses to key areas in a client's life, can break the silence. Or maybe an invitation to use the sand-tray to 'tell a story of me and my world' will unlock the communication pathway.

For others, the winning activity is more 'left-brain' and verbal, with structured questions establishing grounds for conversation: 'In your family … who is the safest person to talk to when you've had a hard day? Who is the best at being angry? Who is the one who sorts out fights between you and your brothers?'. Scaling might also help a child with a more cognitive preference: 'On a scale of 1–10, where 1 is the worst and

10 is the best, how would you score your relationship with your teacher … the two friends you mentioned … your new step-dad?'. A client's self-perception in relation to the reason(s) they are seeking support is another area often requiring a lateral approach from counsellors. Here asking a child/young person how their 'best friend … mum … favourite teacher' might describe them, their strengths and qualities, can help access a useful self-perspective.

By adopting this flexible, adaptable approach counsellors can scaffold their input, moving 'up and down' a framework of activities until they find the right 'fit' for each client's developmental presentation and preferences. This 'back-and-forth' movement calls for a capacity to 'learn from our mistakes and mis-attunements' in a creative listening process that ultimately helps access the CYP's voice and story.

Our experience is that none of this need be at odds with counselling's commitment to the therapeutic alliance, client autonomy and self-determination. Assessment *can* be a highly collaborative activity, a rich opportunity to get to know a CYP, establish a strong partnership and through this catch a view of their map of the territory. It is about generating 'constructive understanding' (Sharry, 2004) to inform preparation for therapy and its development at each successive phase. We will now go on to look at preparation process and practice in more detail.

Making the 'Preparation-for-Therapy Map': Seven Key Tasks

We have identified seven key tasks in making the 'preparation-for-therapy map' (see Figure 10.1).

---

1. *Pre*-preparation – therapist and environment
2. Facilitating the C/YP to create a personal preparation-for-therapy map
3. Mapping risk
4. Mapping the context
5. Integrating the standardised measures map
6. Reviewing the 'assessment meta-map'
7. Contracting

Figure 10.1 Seven key tasks of the preparation-for-therapy map.

First Preparation Task: *Pre*-preparation – Therapist and Environment

The preparation process begins before client and counsellor meet. In her article 'Therapist as Host: Making My Guests Feel Welcome' (2006), Jodi Aman notes the importance of attending to the physical environment within which we meet clients, hypothesising that 'a calm space supports a person in getting distance from the immediacy of their experience, therefore enhancing the effectiveness of the conversations' (p. 8).

Leaflets, voicemail messages and websites need to sound a warm, welcoming approach, and Aman gives examples of children's art work and a child-friendly introductory letter from her website. Her 'therapist as host' metaphor is useful for shaping therapists' own preparation before work with a new client:

> treating someone as a cherished guest addresses the power differential undisputable in a therapeutic relationship by elevating the status of the person who comes to consult the therapist. (p. 4)

Addressing the power differential is of particular importance in CYP counselling, where elevating the status of the CYP serves as an essential guard against a 'therapist-knows-best' attitude, itself a subtle but insidious barrier to listening.

Second Preparation Task: Facilitating the CYP to Create a Personal Preparation-for-Therapy Map

The territory to cover here involves accessing CYP's views on why they are coming to therapy and the impact the perceived problems, issues and situations are having on each aspect of life – personal, family, school, friendships/relationships, hobbies, values/beliefs. Crucially, we also ask the CYP to map the strengths and resources they identify in themselves, family, peer group, school, and wider community. Identifying strengths provides a bridge from problem perception to goal setting.

The map should also include specific goals – usually no more than three – creating a transparent baseline for what change will 'look like'. Goals are best expressed as the presence of something new or different in the child's life as opposed to the absence of something difficult (e.g. 'I want to start doing X' rather than 'stop doing Y').

There are a range of approaches and techniques here, from the strengths-based information gathering outlined by Sharry (2004) to the creative techniques indicated by Liana Lowenstein (1999, 2011), to structured therapeutic games such as *All About*

Me (Hemming/Barnardo's). Age, developmental level and temperament/specific interests will dictate the right blend of methods for each child/young person.

Third Preparation Task: Mapping Risk

Issues of safety are central within CYP counselling. Historical, existing or potential risk therefore needs to be part of the mapping process. When working with children under 12, this includes engaging with parents/carers in risk identification and assessment. Areas for inclusion on the risk map include:

- parent/carer or young person with mental illness, current or historical;
- child/young person on the 'at risk' register;
- young person indicating wish or intent to harm self or others;
- history of abuse, neglect, domestic violence, other trauma;
- misuse of alcohol and/or other drugs;
- parent/family member in prison;
- newcomer/immigrant black/ethnic minority family
- multiple bereavement;
- poor school attendance;
- poor parental involvement (for children 6–12);
- impact of learning or other disabilities;
- emotional communication difficulties;
- significant life-cycle transition in combination with any of the above.

Risk assessment informs whether counselling is a feasible support at a particular time in a young client's life. It contextualises other key preparation phase decisions too, including the counselling goals agreed – *what is realistically possible given the risks identified?* – the timeframe for reviews – *should reviews occur more often in the light of assessed risk?* – and any safety planning required for safe, effective counselling to occur.

Risk assessment entails enquiring about other services involved with the family – social services, CAMHS, etc. – and explicitly contracting to liaise with these services as part of the overall assessment. With identification of risk comes an increased need to triangulate services so that counselling is contextualised within a network of supports.

Fourth Preparation Task: Mapping the Context

To fully appreciate the unique circumstances shaping the CYP's personal map we must contextualise it within the larger territory of family, school and community maps. From a developmental perspective this is particularly important in work with under-12s and with young people who present as 12 or under, due to learning or other disabilities.

Supporting adult carers during the preparation phase – including school staff where the service is school-based – recognises the key role they play in defining and, sometimes, constraining the maps children live by (Perry and Szalavitz, 2010). An assessment with parents/carers can happen with the adults only or with the child/young person present for all or part of the meeting(s). Covering the same ground as outlined in the child/young person assessment, it invites caretakers to be part of the change process and to be 'change allies' with the child (Freeman et al., 1997).

Encouraging caretakers to shift their own map boundaries – in terms of compassion and understanding, relationship, or behaviour – can in turn free the child to make the changes that they want. In some instances the adults *must* make a change before change is a possibility for the child, e.g. an acrimonious divorce where parents' hostility increases pressure for their child to 'take sides', or where a school has a too-entrenched negative view of a pupil and cannot see the efforts she is making to change (see Example 1 below).

Example 1   How a Change in Perspective for Adults Increases the Possibility of Change for a Child

Simon is 10 years old. He is identified as the school 'trouble-maker', invariably at the tail-end of a story of conflict and dispute. Early in the counselling preparation phase Simon indicated that he was always in conflict with his brother and peers at school. He was distressed by this, particularly how he was blamed as instigator on every occasion. As a result Simon was feeling very down on himself, though few recognised this part of him hidden behind the conflict. In the school's opinion he *was* the trouble-maker.

During the pre-therapy assessment Simon identified how he wanted to both change his behaviour and how he saw himself. He wanted others to think more positively of him too. As part of the assessment the counsellor invited Simon's teacher to closely observe how many times he got into trouble and what led up to it. The teacher was quite surprised to discover that Simon's behaviour was often a reaction to someone else's taunt. This change in outlook saw the teacher become more compassionate towards Simon. She started to notice changes in his behaviour and encouraged him. In turn this helped Simon to more frequently step back from situations of conflict. A new story about Simon was emerging, possible only through the involvement of a key adult during the preparation phase who was willing to rethink an established and defeatist story that could have really hindered counselling progress.

As a young person increases in age there is less reliance on direct adult involvement in recognition of their developmental capacity for increased autonomy and personal problem-solving. However, it is worth bearing in mind that young people may wish to continue to involve parents/carers at key points in the work, especially where relational difficulties are a source of distress (see Example 2 below).

> ### Example 2   Re-connecting Family Relationships in the Face of Suicidal Thoughts
>
> Mark was 16 when he self-referred to the Barnardo's school-based counselling service where he attends a school for pupils with mild to moderate learning disabilities. At his first session Mark presented with high levels of emotional distress, finding it hard to verbalise his thoughts and feelings. However, he was able to indicate that things had got so bad for him recently that he had been thinking of taking his own life. Given Mark's level of distress and his difficulty in articulating it, the counsellor tentatively suggested completing the 'young person's stress profile'. Mark agreed and found it useful to communicate and clarify his distress this way.
>
> It emerged later that Mark greatly valued the relationship with his parents but felt it had been going through a difficult patch lately. He began to identify this as a key contributor to his current feelings of stress and isolation. Taking Mark's lead, the counsellor indicated it would be possible to meet with his parents in a counselling session. Mark was very interested in this idea. The next session was a four-way conversation between Mark, his parents and the counsellor. During the session the counsellor facilitated a discussion about how much the whole family valued the close relationship they had and the things they did together to maintain it. Mark also got to hear directly from his parents what it was they particularly valued about him and their hopes for his future.
>
> At the following session Mark completed the stress profile again only to find significantly reduced scores. Mark saw the conversation with his parents as pivotal to his change in personal outlook. Given Mark's age, it would have been easy to overlook the relevance of parental involvement in the counselling assessment.

Fifth Preparation Task: Integrating the Map of Standardised Measures

Standardised measures are not incompatible with relational counselling practice. Using them does not require counsellors to resolve a clash between the 'art' (relational practice) and 'science' (standardised measures) of preparation/assessment. Rather, it's about how to interconnect the more emotionally-distant, analytical perspective of a measure with the more inter-subjective, relational knowledge of a therapeutic conversation. This interconnection enriches potential for a fuller understanding of all the assessment material. The counsellor's task is to hold together the different – sometimes clashing – emerging perspectives, while centralising the voice of the CYP.

Several standardised measures have gained prominence within UK CYP counselling, namely the Strengths and Difficulties Questionnaire (SDQ) (Goodman, 2001) [available at www.sdqinfo.com] and the YP-CORE (Twigg et al., 2009).

The use of session-by-session measures has emerged as a key trend over the last five years. Collecting outcome information at each session is a great way of gathering 'practice-based evidence' (PBE). Session-by-session measures improve effectiveness, reduce drop-out and prevent deterioration (Duncan and Sparks, 2010) and, remarkably, without asking counsellors to make any other changes to how they work. In addition to the popular ten-item 'YP-CORE', there is also a suite of measures called the Outcome Rating Scale (ORS) (Miller and Duncan, 2006) which tracks distress/well-being and the therapeutic alliance session-by-session. ORS is validated for use with young people 12 and up; there is a version for children aged 6–11 called the Child Outcome Rating Scale (CORS) (Duncan et al., 2003), and one for children under six called the Young Child Outcome Rating Scale (YCORS). Quick to complete and useful as a clinical as well as an outcome tool, Barnardo's Northern Ireland has used these measures in its school-based counselling service since 2008. They are available at www.heartandsoulofchange.com, and more information can be found in Stewart (2012).

Scoring the measure and sharing the result with the client – including an outline of its meaning in relation to the clinical cut-off – provides a final reference point in the collaborative preparation process. It further informs its outcome and decisions about counselling suitability.

Sixth Preparation Task: Reviewing the 'Assessment Meta-Map'

The endpoint of the preparation listening process will be the creation of a larger 'assessment meta-map'. Therapist and client – including key adults with younger children – need to review the meta-map together and agree on the suitability of counselling.

Seventh Preparation Task: Contracting

If a period of counselling is agreed a contract should be drawn up with the young client covering the following areas:

1. *Who will be involved?* Agreeing the level and extent of systemic involvement (if any).
2. *Where and when will the counselling happen?*
3. *What will happen in sessions?* Outlining the range of approaches and activities the counsellor can offer and ascertaining any immediate client preferences (e.g. sand-tray work; psycho-education; therapeutic assessment game).

4. *Why might counselling be useful?* Establishing focus/purpose/goals; this includes talking with younger children (4–12 years) about why key adults feel it would be useful and checking this against their views.
5. *What about confidentiality?* Establishing confidentiality and its limits.
6. *What about counselling records?* Outlining the policy on record-keeping and gaining consent from the young person (or parent/carer if not 'Gillick competent').
7. *What about complaints?* Outlining the complaints policy and agreeing whether a nominated 'trusted adult' is required to represent the child's views.

Theoretical Underpinning

It is a pleasure to listen attentively to children because listening opens windows on the child's world. As therapists, as we accept their invitation to explore their world, we quickly understand our dependency on them as our guides. This is because the CYP's understanding of their world differs from the adult experience in a myriad of ways. I am reminded of the CYP who was exploring the experience of loss of a much loved adult with a parent. The parent had explained euphemistically that the adult had 'gone to be with Jesus'. The CYP thought for a little moment, and then helpfully clarified, 'So they're in Bethlehem then'. A charming anecdote or a sharp reminder of the way children understand the world. Listening to the client involves not only what our clients say but also being attuned to their age and stage of development. In laying the theoretical foundations for sensitive and autonomous therapy we believe that focusing on developmental theories will provide clear signposting and guidance. We would advocate a framework for integration of counselling theory and child-centred practice as the basis for preparing CYP clients for therapy. We also believe that, given the CYP's embedding within their family system, it is essential to take the widest possible view of who and what needs to be prepared if children and young people are to gain all they can from their experience of therapy. To assist us in laying a theoretical basis for the work, we propose briefly to explore Piagetian theory, Bronfenbrenner's ecological systems theory, schema theory and the application of Vygotsky's theories to the process of preparation for therapy.

Age and Stage

Piaget asserted that childhood is not just *quantitatively* but *qualitatively* different from adulthood as shown in the example given above. As the counsellor enters into the process of preparing themselves for working therapeutically they must actively engage with the age-appropriate aspects of the CYP's voice. The counsellor must be listening so actively as to hear variations in the range of development between children/young people within ages and stages. The counsellor must understand the normative issues that development itself generates, whilst also being aware that every child is part of a particular complex familial and societal system.

> ## Example 3   Listening to the Developmental Voice
>
> Samira, aged nine, self-referred to a school counsellor after her mother had slipped into a diabetic coma in the early hours of the morning. Her mum had managed to call the emergency services when she felt unwell. The police had to break into the house and Samira was worried about her mother dying in the future. She had talked to mum about this but mum said she was being silly. Mum felt Samira should be over it by now and didn't need counselling. Samira's view of illness and death differed markedly from her mum's. At nine, Samira was on the cusp of developing a more mature concept of death and dying. She had begun to recognise that death is permanent and irreversible and felt fiercely protective of mum and did not want to distress her. Her mum had talked to her about diabetes as a manageable illness but Samira was unable to understand this because she had not yet developed a scientific view of illness as a process. Preparation for therapy involved acknowledging Samira's fears and concerns whilst helping mum understand the need for a safe place for Samira to ask potentially upsetting questions and explore different ways of understanding how human beings with illness survive with an intact sense of self. The developmentally aware counsellor should be actively engaged with understanding development and its effect on the client.

Individual Variation

Children and young people are not a homogeneous group, despite the fact that we often talk about them as if they are. Individual children and young people differ markedly from each other in temperament, experience, life setting, understanding and capacity to process the many elements that represent the beginning of the therapeutic experience. Practitioners and teams employ different skills and tools working across the age range and we should be respectful of other ways of working than our own model. Counsellors can also benefit from a more global understanding of how CYPs engage with taking information from their environment. Gardener's theory of multiple intelligences alerts us to the fact that 'the brain has evolved over millions of years to be responsive to different kinds of content in the world. Language content, musical content, spatial content, numerical content' (Gardener, 1983). Learning styles theory also encourages us to engage with the CYP styles of encountering the world, so preparation for therapy should include auditory, visual, read/write and kinaesthetic ways of introducing the therapeutic process. CYP counsellors value the CYP client, their right to autonomy, and to safe, sensitive and appropriate access to therapy that makes human sense to the client (Donaldson, 1978). In order to ensure this, we must always take the CYP as our guide for the start of the therapeutic process, committing to setting aside our adult assumptions, frameworks and language. General history-taking and specific measures like YP-CORE or SDQ can support this.

Context is Everything

Ecological systems theory illustrates the complex systems in which the CYP lives and helps us conceptualise the interacting and reciprocal effects of these systems on the client and counsellor whilst also allowing for change due to the impact of time (Figure 10.2). While Bronfenbrenner (1986, 2005a) does not offer a counselling theory, he reminds us of the who, what and how of assessment and preparation as we engage in the pre-therapeutic process.

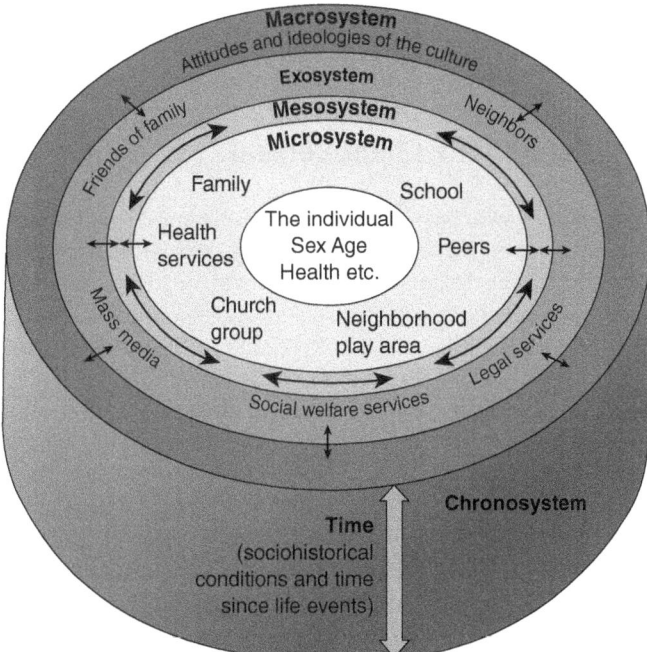

Figure 10.2   Bronfenbrenner's ecological model of development.

Whilst children are regarded as autonomous beings from the counsellor's perspective and within the BACP ethical framework, not everyone within the child's social system may understand or accept this. The counsellor may have a differing view of autonomy from parents, social workers, teachers or other adults who have an interest in the therapeutic process. The CYP may have an unexplored understanding of their autonomy. The counsellor may therefore need to prepare the CYP or others within the setting for this. Views of autonomy and control may differ between the multi-disciplinary team in a school or CAMHS. Theoretical orientation may also place demands on how counsellors prepare CYPs for therapy work. The counsellor should also move beyond this normative preparation by engaging with the legal and ethical framework within the CYP's system. In doing so the counsellor must hold the CYP's needs and rights as paramount. In practice this is rather like engaging in a complex multi-player video game in which the counsellor is central because it involves the counsellor in mediating intra-personal issues like competence, capacity and consent, interpersonal issues such as risk, safeguarding, confidentiality, and societal issues like legal requirements regarding disclosures, role limits and boundaries. For example, CYPs can often disclose safeguarding issues at assessment. As many young video gamers tell us, when dealing with complexity, a clear, simple plan is often best. Therefore many of these issues can be dealt with at the outset of the preparation for therapy phase by clear communication with the CYP, their carers, and any other interested parties, for example social services.

Example 4   Holding the Client Central

Cody is a 15-year-old boy who has cancer. He and his parents know that his disease is terminal. He has been offered a place on a palliative drug trial which may extend his life by a few months. His parents desperately want him to agree to the trial and have asked him to spend time considering this in counselling. Cody has made it clear that he has made the decision to decline taking part in the drug trial. He wants to spend his time in counselling discussing how to tell his parents and plan for the last months of his life.

Cody's case is just one example of many where competing expectations, hopes, needs, desires and interests can benefit from open, thoughtful and honest preparation for therapy. Preparation for therapy involves the counsellor in the process of actively engaging with competing interests whilst advocating for the client. It requires counsellors to use age-appropriate, high-level skills to establish excellent psychological contact with the client. Once this has been established, respectful, collaborative assessment of the CYP's developmental ability and potential, reasoned professional

(Continued)

(Continued)

judgements about their ability to understand and consent to counselling, and honest communication can be entered into. Only by doing so can we ensure that young people have opted to attend counselling freely (not because mum, dad or their social worker felt it would be good), understand the consequences of counselling and can openly speak and own the therapeutic space as theirs. Through a process like this Cody was able to own the counselling space and his parents were helped by him to let go. Preparation for therapy for the parents was an essential adjunct to this process.

Developing a Schema for Therapy

CYPs, carers and other interested adults usually have no idea of what counselling is. Just as we have no schema for astrophysics (unless somebody helps us acquire one!) so CYPs, carers and interested adults need the counsellor to help them develop a schema for therapy. It is therefore the role of the counsellor to provide a window into the world of therapy. This builds engagement and provides a narrative for the process. Clear information leaflets and website statements need to be offered. Pre-therapy conversations need to be had with CYPs and adults that emphasise that the CYP, and not the parent or carer, is the client. Clear, picture-based, verbal, age-appropriate descriptions of what counselling is, and is not, need to be provided for CYPs and interested others (Arnold, 2010). Expectations on all sides need to be elicited and explored. In Cody's case this was essential. To do this a counsellor may meet with the CYP and with parents either separately or together in pre-therapy. Interested adults need to be freed up from the 'counsellor as fixer' paradigm because CYPs are not 'broken'. They are themselves and we respect them as such. Counsellors also need to establish clear confidentiality, safeguarding and risk boundaries to the preparation for therapy schema so that young people are not shocked or disappointed when, during or after assessment, a counsellor must report a disclosure or take action because a CYP is at risk of significant harm. A positive view of standardised and session-by-session measures should be built from the outset. We are strongly of the opinion that measures are there to resource the client in their understanding of self, change and development. However, in order for the client to be positive the counsellor must have honestly explored and engaged with their barriers and biases to the use of such resources. It is fascinating to see even very young clients take skills they have learned, to develop positive personal evaluation skills that build their confidence in school, with friends or at home.

Preparing for Good Outcomes – The Zone of Proximal Development (ZPD)

This leads us to the final girder in our theoretical underpinning of preparation for therapy. Vygotsky (1934) postulated that the work of development can be described as the acquisition of cultural tools. As counsellors we might describe the process as a gateway to more useful ways of being for the client. He postulated that understanding and meanings are acquired through interactions between adults and children and that this begins 'first as an interpersonal process before it appears in the child as an intrapersonal process' (Vygotsky, 1988, cited in Lee and Das Gupta, 1995: 13). He also introduced the concept of the ZPD (Vygotsky, 1934). This means that children can get a certain way on their own initiative but the presence of a respectful, listening and engaged adult increases the child's developmental reach. The difference between where they are and where they can get to is the ZPD. This is the counselling space.

Summary

- A 'collaborative assessment' is essential for safe and effective preparation for therapy with children and young people
- There are seven key collaborative assessment tasks that make up a 'preparation-for-therapy' map:

    i. Pre-preparation (therapist and therapy environment)
    ii. Facilitating a personal preparation-for-therapy map with a child/young person
    iii. Mapping risk
    iv. Mapping the context
    v. Integrating outcome measures
    vi. Reviewing the assessment 'meta-map'
    vii. Contracting

- Counsellors should have a working knowledge of developmental theory if they are to provide safe and effective therapy
- Counsellors need to draw on this knowledge in order to tune into the age and stage of each client's developmental presentation
- Children and young people are not a homogeneous group and the counselling approach should reflect awareness of 'multiple intelligences' and cater for a range of 'learning styles' – visual, auditory, read/write, and kinaesthetic – to help scaffold a schema for therapy
- In the presence of a respectful, engaged and attuned therapist the counselling space can become a 'zone of proximal development' for children and young people where they can extend their developmental reach and make positive life changes

Reflective Questions

Reflection 1

> The purest form of listening is to listen without memory or desire. (Wilfrid Bion, 1897–1979)

How might the counsellor's experience of their own childhood or their experience of parenthood have an impact on their understanding of how to prepare children, young people and parents for the experience of therapy?

Reflection 2

The process of counsellor reflection is vital to preparing ourselves for undertaking therapeutic work with any client group. It is particularly important in working with children and young people because the counsellor may find themselves 'staring into the mirror of (their) own grief' (Formica, 2009). A consideration of the potential for parallel processes in the room can and should be explored when a referral is first made. What memories or desires might I need to deal with?

Reflection 3

What knowledge, skills, attitudes and values do I have in assessing the capacity, competence and ability of CYPs to give consent to counselling? What knowledge and skills do I need to acquire? What personal and professional attitudes and values do I need to reflect on and process, to assist myself, children, parents and other concerned adults in the process of understanding the autonomy of children and young people?

Learning Activities

Activity 1 – Hearing Your Own Voice

Record yourself explaining the process of counselling to a child, adolescent, parent. Play it back and reflect on what you have learned from listening.

Activity 2 – Preparing the Setting

You are a counsellor in a school setting. A teacher comes to you with the dilemma below and asks for advice. A client's parent has made it explicit that they want to withhold consent for their 14-year-old to attend counselling. The young person is clear in their own mind that

(Continued)

(Continued)

they do wish to attend. What processes would you as a counsellor have to undergo to prepare yourself to work with this situation? What might you as a therapist be able to say to the teacher, the young person, the parent, that might add clarity to the pre-therapy process?

Activity 3 – Preparing the Client

Consider the following clients:

An eight-year-old who is described by a parent as being very anxious

A 14-year-old newcomer who is a refugee from ethnic violence

A 10-year-old who has been exposed to domestic abuse at home

A 15-year-old who is wanting to explore issues around gender identity and sexuality

What preparation might you need to set in place that is specific to these clients as you consider working with them?

Further Reading

CYP Counsellors require a developmental meta-rationale for how they begin, engage in and work with their clients. Learning about development as a precursor to preparing for therapeutic work is both a joy and a challenge. For CPD reading on development we would recommend:

Music, G. (2011) *Nurturing Natures: Attachment and Children's Emotional, Socio-cultural and Brain Development*. Hove: Psychology Press.
Santrock, J. (2010) *Child Development: An Introduction*. New York: McGraw Hill.

For texts related to counselling assessment we recommend:
Lowenstein, L. (1999) *Creative Interventions for Troubled Children and Youth*. Toronto: Champion Press.
Sharry, J. (2004) *Counselling Children, Adolescents and Families*. London: SAGE.

Online Resources

BACP website: www.bacp.co.uk/ especially the BACP Children and Young People Division and the Competences for Working with Children and Young People.

Counselling MindEd: http://counsellingminded.com, especially modules CM 0103: Presenting Issues and CM 06: Using Measures.

The Therapeutic Alliance and Counselling Process

Mark Prever

This chapter includes:

- Therapeutic alliance
- Counselling process and the middle stage
- Monitoring client process and progress

Introduction

This chapter explores the concept of the 'therapeutic alliance', so critical in counselling, but especially so in work with children and young people. When I go to meet a new young client, it is the issue that concerns me most. Will I get on with this young person? Will I be able to establish a climate of trust and respect? Will we agree as to what counselling is for and, ultimately, will they like me and I like them? In essence, will we get on? In a sense, I am expressing concern about my ability to establish an alliance which ensures that therapy can take place and, without which, any attempt at growth or change is near impossible. The relationship we build with clients impacts on the counselling process and the client's process and progress. Although this chapter overlaps with some of the material from other chapters, the material is focused in relation to: the therapeutic alliance, counselling process and the middle stage, monitoring client process and progress

Therapeutic Alliance

The therapeutic alliance may also be referred to as the 'working alliance' but, put simply, the therapeutic alliance indicates the degree to which the child or young client trusts and believes in the counsellor and whether they 'like' them or not. It refers to the collaborative aspect of the relationship between a young client and their counsellor. Forming such an alliance is especially important when working with children and young people who may come for counselling having already experienced a range of 'interventions', where a therapeutic outcome has been second to behavioural or attitudinal change.

The importance of the relationship in therapy and counselling with children and young people did not begin with Carl Rogers, although his substantial work remains a very important component and the essence of any discussion about the relationship between client and counsellor. In his seminal article published in 1957, Carl Rogers set out his understanding of the relationship in therapy as well as its centrality. The 'conditions of therapeutic change' influenced all his subsequent works and the development of what later became known as 'person-centred therapy'. Rogers argued that therapy is less about what the therapist does to a client and more about the quality of that relationship and the therapeutic conditions, which he felt were essential in any therapeutic work. These were defined as empathy, unconditional positive regard and congruence; that is, being yourself, non-judgemental and real with a client. It is worth noting that empathy is seen as an important component of the therapeutic alliance across all models of counselling theory and practice (Feller and Cottone, 2003). Rogers also emphasised the need for what he termed 'psychological contact' by which he meant that both client and therapist need to be aware of the presence of each other for a relationship to occur. It is hard to see how a therapeutic alliance can be formed with a young client where such contact does not exist.

The concept of the therapeutic alliance has its roots in psychoanalytic theory with its emphasis on the transference relationship between therapist and client where the work is based around the client's previous experiences of relationships such as with parents or significant others. A comprehensive and detailed history of the concept of the therapeutic alliance can be found in Horvath and Luborsky (1993). This analysis stretches as far back as to the work of Freud where, according to the authors, he makes reference to the analyst maintaining 'serious interest' in and 'sympathetic understanding' of the client to allow for the client to attach themselves positively to the analyst. Greenson (1967) has also added to the discussion around the concept of the working alliance in psychoanalytic theory (see also Kanzer, 1981). Focused discussion of the concept begins with the work of Bordin (1979), who suggested that the working alliance in therapy was comprised of three elements: *tasks*, *goals* and *bonds*. These were later developed by Dryden (1989), who included a new component, 'views', which he felt should be included in any expanded discussion of the therapeutic alliance. Bordin believed that the therapeutic alliance was an essential component in counselling and was possibly the most important factor in bringing about change in the client.

Goals are the outcomes which the client and counsellor have agreed to work towards together. In other words, a mutual understanding of what might be causing the client's problems or unhappiness. Such an agreement is more likely to lead to a successful outcome for the client. In contrast, differences in expectations and understandings with a young client or where the counsellor has a different agenda or is under pressure from an organisation having been sent a particular role in relation to the counselling, which is different to the client's, is likely to undermine a successful outcome.

Tasks are the things that the counsellor actually does to help the client achieve their goals. Again, these may be problematic where there has been a lack of contracting with the young client or where there are misunderstandings around the way the work will proceed.

Bonds refer to the interpersonal and are harder to describe but will include respect, trust and hope. These themes are well developed in the person-centred literature. Dryden (1989) sees the client's attitude to the counsellor as important. This might include things like trust in the counsellor and feelings of safety in the relationship. He also refers to the client's faith in the counsellor to bring about change in their lives. He notes that clients will often bring with them to the counselling room 'pre-formed tendencies' which have the potential to impact markedly on the counselling process. His reference to 'client reluctance' may be relevant to work with children and young people who may have developed preconceived ideas about adults in their lives and whether they can invest trust in them.

Dryden is clear that the establishment of a therapeutic alliance is most likely to occur where the views held by both client and counsellor are convergent, and where they are not they need to be explored as part of the counselling work. Views held by both client and counsellor around issues such as the nature of the client's problems, how these are best addressed and how this will happen also require exploration leading to common understanding.

In drawing on the work and extending it to children and adolescents, Campbell and Simmonds (2011) found that empathy and trust were highly valued by young people as bond indicators whilst an additional parental support dimension was identified as of particular importance, especially where the counsellor was able to show understanding, reassurance and support. It is not surprising to find that research has shown a strong correlation between the establishment of an effective working alliance and 'success' in therapy. An excellent and detailed analysis of the arguments around this can be found in Muran and Barber (2010). Equally, it follows that where there are obstacles to the establishment of an effective working alliance, client progress will be limited – if, indeed, the child or young person continues to regularly attend sessions. Most research into the therapeutic alliance has related to work with adults, but this is changing, and some useful papers can be found in the further reading section below.

So what can hinder the therapeutic alliance? Ackerman and Hilsenroth (2001) looked at the personal attributes of the therapist which might interfere with the therapeutic alliance. These included: rigidity; uncertainty; being critical, distant, tense and distracted. He also noted that the therapeutic techniques of the counsellor were an important factor and a negative influence on the working alliance where sessions were over-structured, where there was inappropriate self-disclosure, an over use of transference interpretation and an unhelpful use of silence. In recent years there has been increasing academic discussion around the concept of 'ruptures' or a 'weakening' in the therapeutic alliance and their repair. Interested readers might want to look at Eubanks et al. (2010) and Safran and Muran (2000). We know when a therapeutic alliance has been established with a young client; we have a sense that our young client is engaged with the process, and we seem to understand each other. The client is open and appears to trust us. We have a feeling that progress is being made. We feel a sense of rapport and that we are doing what we are meant to be doing. Conversely, where there is a lack of understanding and communication between counsellor and young client, it is likely that a working alliance has not been established. Where the client becomes frustrated with the counsellor expressing anger or anxiety or, indeed, a lack of interest, it might be suggested that the working alliance is in difficulty.

Returning to the influence of Carl Rogers, there exists a consensus that regardless of counselling orientation, it is hard to see how without the 'core conditions' a therapeutic relationship can be established. It doesn't matter how much training a person has done or what counselling qualifications have been achieved, it is difficult to see how these professional developments alone are sufficient for the building of a therapeutic working relationship. This is even possibly more marked when working with children and young people who may already have suspicions about professionals and who desire a helping relationship that is characterised by warmth, acceptance, trust, realness and an empathic ability to feel what they are feeling.

My own experience of working with children and young people has shown that a therapeutic alliance is more likely when the counsellor is able to remove issues of power and authority and bring some equality and mutual respect into the relationship. Other important dimensions to the relationship are that it should be characterised by warmth, friendliness, honesty, openness, a lack of judgement, real empathy, showing energy and interest in the child and their story. Children and adolescents need to feel that their counsellor is a real person and not somebody in a role.

Bryant-Jefferies (2004: 6–7) draws our attention to the work of Everall and Paulson (2002) and their 2002 study which focused specifically on the needs of adolescents. Based on a series of semi-structured interviews, three themes were explored in relation to the therapeutic alliance: therapeutic environment, uniqueness of the therapeutic relationship and therapists' characteristics. They observed that a therapeutic alliance was characterised by acceptance, supportiveness, trustworthiness and the appropriateness of the therapeutic tasks and goals. Bryant-Jefferies notes how it is important for the young client to see the therapeutic relationship as special, and indeed the counsellor as their 'special friend', and the relationship experienced by the young person as being different to those normally experienced with an adult. In this sense, there is the expectation that the counsellor will adapt their working style to suit the age of their client.

At the relational level, I believe that it is important that the counsellor can help the client to find a sense of meaning and hope, allow the child to talk about what is important to them and not show frustration or impatience when the young person has lost hope, is sad or despairing. The literature reveals an acceptance that the therapeutic alliance or its equivalent is an essential part of any therapeutic work, regardless of orientation or modality. Muran and Barber (2010) refer to Wolfe and Goldfried's (1998) description of it as 'the quintessential integrative variable' and most quoted 'common factor' in psychotherapy as discussed by Wampold (2001). However, they also refer to a growing number of writers who have challenged this assumption or see the matter as being of greater complexity than first understood. Some of these points are explored in the literature listed in Further Reading. You will also see I have included a growing body of work around the therapeutic alliance in relation to children and young people that had previously been largely neglected.

Counselling Process and Middle Stage

Whilst it is possible for the therapeutic alliance to be established in a first session with a child or young person, for others it may occur over a period of time. It is equally important to note that once this alliance has been established, it does not remain static or 'established' but will continue to develop and deepen in what might be referred to as the 'middle' stage of counselling. For an analysis of the therapeutic alliance over time, see Stiles and Goldsmith (2010).

Gerard Egan's (1998: 190) successful books set out clearly a model of counselling where there are clearly identifiable steps towards helping people to become more competent in helping themselves in their everyday lives. However, not all counselling modalities see the counselling process structured in such a formal way. In a person-centred approach for example, the counsellor does not see the client in such definable ways. Mearns and Thorne (1988: 190) write: 'Instead, she recognises that each client is unique, and that the therapeutic process he experiences will be different from any other individual.'

However, Mearns and Thorne do recognise that counselling is a 'process' and understand that in the middle phase of counselling relational depth should develop alongside an increase in trust. They also see the middle stage of counselling as being characterised by increasing intimacy, the creation of a sense of mutuality and increasing self-acceptance by the client. As the counselling develops with the young client, we might expect to see a deepening of the relationship which may offer the counsellor more confidence to challenge the young person and a willingness by the young person to accept these kinds of interventions. As the counsellor displays qualities of acceptance, the young person may be more inclined to take risks and show a preparedness to explore and express feelings which may be difficult or disturbing.

In my work as a supervisor with counsellors who work with children and young people, it is not uncommon for counsellors to refer to a feeling of 'stuckness' to emerge within later sessions and either a sense of 'going round in circles' or for the work to appear to regress. It is at this time that counsellors can sometimes question the process or their own skills. Nelson-Jones (2002: 255) refers to the dangers of the middle phase of counselling experiencing 'session drift' where the work with a client becomes aimless with little progress being made. Counsellors working with young people may increase the pace of the counselling during this phase, depriving future sessions of their rightful place in the counselling process.

Horton (2000: 126) notes that the middle phase of counselling is usually the most lengthy. This is not surprising as it can be seen as the work phase, when problems are clearly defined and hopefully worked through. It is also where 'unexpected memories, discoveries and obstacles, crises and ambivalence or defences may arise'.

Horton (2000) goes on to describe a number of process goals of this middle phase of counselling, which include: seeing patterns and important themes, affirming and using the client's strengths to help the client move towards new perspectives, leading to increased self-awareness and ultimately new ways of thinking, feeling and behaving. The problem with seeing the middle phase of counselling as the primary working phase is noted by Nelson-Jones (2002) because it detracts from the working potential of the beginning and ending phases. The middle phase of counselling with children and young people will of course be affected by the orientation of the counsellor. The centrality of the relationship as a necessary aspect of change within a person-centred approach has been explored above. In their book *Cognitive Behavioural Counselling in Action*, Trower et al. (1988) clearly set out a three-stage model where the first is concerned with getting started, while the final phase seeks to develop independence. The middle phase, with which we are particularly concerned here, has a focus around the client learning the method of change inherent in the CBT process and theoretical framework.

In psychodynamic counselling, the middle phase is more likely to focus on the relationship between counsellor and client. This may involve exploring defences, transference and feelings, behaviours and patterns of thinking, which may be contributing to the client's problems. Holmes (1999: 35) looks specifically at the role of the relationship in relation to psychodynamic work. He suggests that people who turn to a psychodynamic counsellor often have relationship difficulties and therefore these can be addressed through the relationship between counsellor and client. He argues that the relationship itself becomes the 'object of scrutiny and a vehicle for change'. He accepts that the approach does also attempt to address issues outside of the therapeutic relationship but, ultimately, the 'principles learned' will appear within the counsellor–client relationship. In this way, whilst the nature of the therapeutic alliance within the psychodynamic field may be different, it remains crucial if there is to be sufficient trust to allow the client and counsellor to explore what Holmes refers to as the 'key to change'.

Gaston et al. (1995) offer us an interesting insight into the therapeutic alliance from three differing theoretical orientations, that is: cognitive-behavioural, psychodynamic and experiential. The aim of their work was not to arrive at some 'true definition' of the alliance, but to explore similarities and differences of the alliance from three theoretical perspectives. In a similar way, the middle stage of counselling will be influenced by the number of sessions. Time-limited counselling has become more common where sessions are being paid for and formed as part of a service-level agreement by an organisation such as a company, or in the case of children or adolescents, in a school or youth setting. The reality is that for those working with young clients there is now an increasing pressure of time in terms of the number of sessions or, indeed, the length of sessions. Some schools may expect a session with a student to last around 30 minutes, which is hardly adequate for quality work to take place.

Feltham (1997: 1–28) offers a fascinating insight into the relationship between time and counselling. He challenges the criticisms made of time-limited counselling which assert that the result is a far more superficial activity than long-term or open-ended work. Feltham recognises that despite the time set aside for counselling, most models revolve around the idea of sequential stages, which include a beginning, middle and end. Indeed, it could be argued that all human encounters follow this process, whether they are long or fleeting. Feltham also suggests that the essence of all modalities is that the counselling offered in some way allows for a number of therapeutic processes to take place, thereby accelerating the change or improvement that might have occurred, had that passage of time been unaided. In his book, Feltham explores a range of arguments for and against the move in the profession towards time-limited work. Whilst these are interesting, we do not have the time or space to discuss them here. However, he does suggest that all counselling is time-limited in one way or another. There may exist a danger that a young client may feel unable to explore serious issues where time is limited, or as Feltham draws our attention to the arguments set out by Rowan (1993), where he suggests that it threatens to 'short-change' clients, 'robbing them of the deeper layers of work on themselves they may need'. In a sense, the argument here is that this is all academic, since whether our work with children and young people is short-term or time-limited, it will still have a beginning, middle and end.

Monitoring Client Process and Progress

Counsellors working with children and young people often want to carry out regular reviews with their young clients as a way of informing the counselling process, measuring the health of the therapeutic alliance and, indeed, the effectiveness of the counsellor's work in the room. Reviews provide the counsellor with important indicators as to whether the client is making progress, is experiencing the counselling as a positive and useful intervention and whether the child's needs are being met.

Reviews may be important because, as counsellors, we cannot assume we are offering the young client the kind of help they need at this particular time in their life; this would be our perception alone and there has to be some discussion. Reviewing in this way gives the client a sense that their views matter and they are part of a relationship and not simply on the end of another adult helping intervention. Client reviews with children and young people often ask the young client to comment on matters such as counsellor behaviours which they find helpful, or not, whether sessions are enjoyable and meaningful and whether they feel able to talk to their counsellor about their most difficult feelings. By stating from the start that reviews will be carried out periodically, the young client sees these times as natural and part of the process as opposed to an adjunct, which might have the feel of assessment. Indeed, some counsellors keep review informal and they are smoothly slipped into sessions and are therefore less threatening to a young client. Some counsellors find the idea of reviewing their work with children and young people not necessary, either because they feel they are monitoring feedback from the client throughout the counselling, or because they feel that it interrupts the flow of the work. It has been argued that formal reviews do not provide useful information about the feelings of their client as young people are more inclined to show conformity and not want to upset their counsellor. They may feel that negative feedback might lead to the ending of the contract and that the work is likely to finish as a consequence. For an overview of the process of reviewing therapeutic progress in counselling, see Sutton (1997).

If one function of a review with a young client is the monitoring of client progress, then it is important to be clear about what we are actually measuring. I have written elsewhere (Prever, 2010) about the difficulties associated with measuring outcomes in therapy with children and adolescents. Voluntary agencies keen to attract funding are required to show client progress whilst service-level agreements mean that the receiving organisation often needs to provide evidence of change. Often, organisations will use scaling systems that enable comparisons of clients' perceptions of progress over time. However, just because a young client's scores may not have improved is not necessarily an indicator of the counselling being ineffective, as the client might have deteriorated had counselling not been offered. It is also clear to me as a counsellor that much change will be at an emotional and feelings level often associated with new insights and meanings rather than overt behavioural changes often demanded by funders. It may also be possible that the effects of counselling will not be felt immediately but returned to in later months and years as a personal resource. This is not of course to suggest that regular reviews designed to monitor change and progress in our young clients should not be attempted, but rather an indicator that any such reviews should be used with caution and in the context of the wider counselling work with the child.

The most widely used review tool is The Young Persons Clinical Outcomes in Routine Evaluation (YP-CORE). The measure consists of 10 items to be used by 11–16-year-olds and is easy to administer. The items which are completed by the young person focus on areas subject to change and invite the young person to respond on a five-point scale. YP-CORE is designed as an outcome measure but can be used regularly in sessions to measure change and progress. A description of the rationale and development of YP-CORE can be found in Twigg et al. (2009) and is discussed elsewhere in this book.

Case Study   Aaron

Aaron is 12 years old and lives with his mother, Diane, and new stepfather, Colin. This is a relatively new arrangement, perhaps only six months after his previous stepfather, Dean, had been forced to leave home as part of an informal arrangement with social workers. Aaron has a sister and younger brother – Rebecca, who is 15 years old, and Ben, aged seven. Mum is also expecting a fourth child. It is likely that Colin and mum will marry in the near future.

Aaron and Rebecca have had almost no contact with their biological father, who left home within 18 months of Aaron being born. Dean was convicted of a physical assault on Rebecca that had been described by the judge, in court, as particularly vicious.

There had been a history of domestic violence in the family from the outset and police had been called to the home on numerous occasions. Both children had witnessed some very brutal attacks on mum and both children had been offered counselling at school but only Rebecca had taken up the offer of this kind of support. However, this work was short-lived.

The attack by Dean on Rebecca was outside the norm, since all of Dean's attention had previously focused on mum. Dean claimed in court that he was only disciplining Rebecca for her rudeness to her mother after an argument around keeping her room tidy and staying out late. However, the court had decided that the 'discipline' was indeed beyond acceptable and had occurred over a period of time and had the feel of a ritual. There was a suggestion that persistent alcohol and substance misuse had been a factor in the assault and, whilst not raised in court, professionals working with the case had agreed that there may have been a sexual element to the attack.

Rebecca's behaviour and achievement at school had deteriorated and staff at her school were already concerned before she began cutting her wrist and arm. The cuts were superficial and caused by a paper clip and later by a pencil sharpener blade, but sufficient to alarm her friend Eva, who informed pastoral staff at the school. It was events around this that resulted in the school making a child protection referral, after which further disclosures were made.

Aaron's behaviour had already been affected by the domestic violence he had witnessed, but the trauma suffered by his sister had resulted in Aaron fighting at school, rudeness to staff and his eventual 'managed move' to a nearby school. An attempt to allocate a mentor, Steve, to work with Aaron to address his unwanted behaviours proved brief and fruitless.

By the time Aaron was referred to a counsellor by his social worker he, like his sister, had been involved with a large range of professionals. In addition to children's services in the borough, Aaron had been involved with a number of behavioural support workers and a range of behavioural interventions had been introduced by his head of year. There had also been an assessment by an educational psychologist when suspicions had been raised that he might have some characteristics associated with ADHD. When Aaron was referred for counselling at a voluntary youth counselling agency, he had no sense of what counselling was. Whilst he agreed to the counselling, no one had explained to him what these sessions were for. He believed them to be 'compulsory', as a way of avoiding yet another move to a new school or alternative provision. Aaron turned up to his first counselling session accompanied by his mother, who insisted on explaining to Hamza, the counsellor, why Aaron needed to be there.

Hamza, having read the referral notes, knew that establishing a working therapeutic alliance with Aaron was going to be difficult. In the first session, Hamza experienced Aaron as polite, pleasant, and not quite as described in the notes, which had emphasised aggression and anger. However, what was clear to Hamza was that Aaron could not see the purpose of the counselling if, indeed, he had an idea of what to expect. Hamza was also aware of the many professionals who had played a part in his life, but his arrival at the agency suggested that very little therapeutic work had been carried out; rather, there had been attempts to modify his behaviour which had been causing so much concern. Hamza felt no connection with Aaron and it was clear that, if the work with Aaron was to be meaningful, then a working relationship needed to be established.

Aaron shared few common goals, or any joint understanding or purpose to the work. At this stage, Hamza was wrestling with the uncomfortable feeling of not liking Aaron, as all attempts at inviting him to speak resulted in only a few words, leaving Hamza feeling de-skilled and doubting his own abilities as a counsellor. Hamza discussed with his supervisor his frustrations in working with his young client and how he felt he was becoming increasingly rigid in his approach, more inclined to resort to 'techniques' and questions, disinterested, aloof and distant.

In the third session, Hamza decided to re-establish the contract discussed in the first session. He said that he reassured Aaron that there was no expectation that he would talk about his very painful past. He said that he recognised that a lot of adults had tried to help in the past and had possibly let him down. Hamza made it clear that he was not here to change Aaron's behaviour unless he wanted that too, but stressed that this was Aaron's time and he could talk about anything he wanted to. As Aaron began to disclose a little more in each subsequent session, Hamza worked hard not to make

(Continued)

(Continued)

any judgements about what others had classed as anti-social behaviour. He strove to communicate to Aaron that he was genuinely interested in him as a young man and not as a 'case'. As Aaron opened up a little more, Hamza saw glimpses of the hurt and anger that his young client had previously been unable to express.

By the middle stages of counselling, Hamza described in supervision how he felt a sense of rapport and warmth towards Aaron. Perhaps most importantly, Hamza believed that trust had been established. It would not be true to say that this trust was never tested, because it was. School holidays were a problem, as it sometimes felt that the therapeutic alliance had been lost in some way and needed re-establishing each time. From initial assessment through a series of periodic reviews, there was a clear sense that progress had been made and the feedback from Aaron was that the counselling was 'useful for getting your feelings out'.

The sessions shared by Aaron and Hamza lasted for 16 sessions. It was clear to Hamza that more work was yet to be done, but he recognised that at this time this was the limit for Aaron, and he had shared all he could at this particular stage in his life. Aaron continued to experience a range of difficult emotions, of which guilt at not protecting his mother and sister was paramount. He remained confused, torn, angry and feeling helpless, but possibly a little more in control of what had felt decidedly out of control. Hamza hoped that Aaron would have further opportunities for counselling and that the trust and common understandings, beliefs and warmth shared could be carried over into any new counselling relationship.

Summary

- This chapter has shown that the therapeutic alliance is critical to any work with a child or young person. Without this qualitative aspect of the therapeutic relationship, counselling with a young client becomes something else. Whilst different models of counselling place a different emphasis on the importance of this relationship, most see is it as an essential component and pre-requisite for therapy
- The chapter has also shown that as counselling moves through a number of phases, the therapeutic alliance has to be maintained and nurtured to ensure that client and counsellor remain in contact with each other and with some shared understanding of the work and the way an outcome can be achieved, whatever form that takes
- Whilst many organisations working with children and young people are required to submit detailed statistics on the work of the service as a whole, individual reviews with clients provide the kind of feedback and mutual exploration for the work to grow and develop

Reflective Questions

1 Are there differences in the nature of the therapeutic alliance when working with children and young people and with adults?

You may want to read the first chapter of this book on development and attachment. Children and young people relate to adults differently, dependent upon their stage of development and previous experiences of attachment. The counsellor will need to focus on building up trust and being aware of power dynamics related to the counsellor and client.

2 In your work with young clients, how would you know if a strong therapeutic working alliance had been established?

You would be monitoring the relationship through the risks the young person was taking in sharing their material. If they share easily and have built up this through gradually sharing more personal and revealing material, you can be sure that the therapeutic relationship is strong. A child or young person may act out within a strong relationship to test the boundaries.

3 How might a counsellor working with a child or young person build trust?

Think around the development of the counselling contract and the limits of confidentiality. If a counsellor is to be trustworthy, they will need to keep to the contract, stick to boundaries and be accepting and unconditional in the relationship.

Learning Activities

1. Think about and describe examples from your own practice where you have felt a rapport and common sense of purpose with a young client. Also, a time when there were barriers to establishing a therapeutic alliance; were these difficulties overcome and, if so, how?
2. If you have personally been in the role of client, reflect upon your experiences of the therapeutic relationship, or otherwise. What were your feelings at this time?
3. Consider some of the cross-cultural dimensions to the establishment of the therapeutic alliance.

Further Reading

Clarkson, P. (2003) *The Therapeutic Relationship.* London: Whurr Publishers.

Cooper, M. (2009) The young person's CORE: Development of a brief outcome measure for young people. *Counselling and Psychotherapy Research* 9 (3): 160–168.

Feltham, C. and Horton, I. (2000) *The SAGE Handbook of Counselling and Psychotherapy.* London: SAGE.

Levy, S. (2000) *The Therapeutic Alliance.* Madison, CT: Psychosocial Press.

Mearns, D. and Thorne, B. (2013) *Person-Centred Counselling in Action.* 4th edn. London: SAGE, chapter 8.

Nelson-Jones, R. (2002) *Essential Counselling and Therapy Skills: The Skilled Client Model.* London: SAGE, chapter 12.

Online Resources

BACP website: www.bacp.co.uk/, especially the BACP Children and Young People Division and the Competences for Working with Children and Young People.

Counselling MindEd website: http://counsellingminded.com, especially: MN 12.01: Empowerment, Activation, and Tackling Passivity and Stigma; CM: Establishing a Therapeutic Alliance; CM 2.2: Engaging the CYP in Collaborative Assessment; CM 2.4: Establishing a Therapeutic Goal/Focus with CYP; CM: Using Process Measures in Counselling.

12
Therapeutic Skills
Sally Ingram and Maggie Robson

This chapter includes:

- Generic therapeutic skills we utilise when working with children and young people rather than describing the skills used in a specific modality
- A brief review of the research into the types of counselling and psychotherapy interventions which appear to work the best
- A definition of therapeutic skills
- An outline of the BACP (2014) Competencies for Working with Children and Young People
- The argument that active listening is a generic therapeutic skill relevant across modalities
- Identification of the differences between working with children, young people and adults
- A discussion of the issue of working briefly

Introduction

This chapter focuses on the therapeutic skills we use when working with children and young people. These skills are related both to our knowledge and also our beliefs about what we feel is effective. These beliefs often rest upon our theoretical orientation. So, the first question we may need to ask is 'what works best?'. This is addressed in Chapter 16 of this handbook, 'Evaluating Counselling'. However, probably the most comprehensive overview of research into the efficacy of working with children and young people is to be found in the recently published BACP scoping review on research on counselling and psychotherapy with children and young people by McLaughlin et al. (2013). The study examined evidence from meta-analyses, systematic reviews from controlled trials, cohort studies, case studies, observational and exploratory studies, and 'methodological papers that raise issues for future research in this field' and so gives an exceptional overview of research in this area.

The review builds on the previous scoping review by Harris and Pattison in 2004 and asks the same question: Is counselling and psychotherapy effective for children and young people? Three sub-questions were also explored:

1. Which types of counselling and psychotherapy interventions work?
2. For which presenting problems?
3. For whom?

In terms of techniques, CBT, psychodynamic, play therapy, humanistic therapies and interpersonal psychotherapy were all found to be beneficial, with some approaches seeming more beneficial than others with particular presenting problems.

Contained within the review is a report of a study by Bratton et al. (2005), who conducted a meta-analysis into the efficacy of play therapy. They found that the results were more positive for humanistic approaches and that inclusion of parents in play therapy was associated with a positive outcome.

Part 1 of this handbook explores the therapeutic techniques of these different theoretical approaches, whilst this chapter considers the knowledge and skills that underpin all therapeutic encounters with children and young people, regardless of orientation. It focuses, in part, on the therapeutic relationship and the skills utilised to offer this. Rather than repeat the content of other chapters, the reader is advised to read the relevant chapters to support understanding of this chapter. Chapter 1 is relevant to the discussion of child development and attachment. Chapters 2 to 8 outline different theoretical approaches. In addition, the reader is also advised to read Chapters 17 and 18 when considering law and policy and ethics and Chapter 16 when curious about evaluation.

Lambert and Barley (2001) identified four factors that influence the outcome of therapy: These were:

> extra therapeutic factors, expectancy effects, specific therapy techniques, and common factors. Common factors such as empathy, warmth, and the therapeutic relationship have been shown to correlate more highly with client outcome than specialized treatment interventions. (p. 357)

And they suggest that:

decades of research indicate that the provision of therapy is an interpersonal process in which a main curative component is the nature of the therapeutic relationship. (p. 357)

They argue that we need to tailor our relationship to our individual clients, in this case children and young people, and improve our ability to relate to them.

What Are Therapeutic Skills?

Therapy is a process of relationship building and trust acquisition between the therapist and the client. To facilitate this relationship counsellors need highly developed therapeutic skills. Therapeutic skills are verbal and non-verbal ways of engaging with clients in order to establish an emotional environment where a therapeutic alliance can be created, maintained and safely terminated. This relationship is vital if we are to assist clients in exploring how their life experiences have informed their way of being and, if they choose, find new meanings and ways of relating to self, others and life.

Corey (2001) reminds us that irrespective of one's core therapeutic model, effective counselling skills should be a carefully balanced blend of attention to our client's emotions, thoughts and actions. In this way, we can enable our clients to reflect upon their belief systems, experience the emotional depths of their internal and external struggles and use these to aid new ways of being.

Rather than detail specific therapeutic skills, The British Association for Counselling and Psychotherapy (BACP) have developed a set of competencies for therapists who work with young people. These are available on their website (www.bacp.co.uk/). These competencies have been developed as humanistic competencies but the core and generic competencies, in our view, detail the general therapeutic skills and knowledge relevant to all practitioners working both with children and young people regardless of theoretical orientation. Some of the issues identified in these core competencies are explored in detail within this handbook, reflecting the importance of these areas when working therapeutically with children and young people.

Competencies identified by BACP (2014) include knowledge of child and family development and transitions, and knowledge and understanding of mental health issues. Knowledge of legal, professional and ethical frameworks is considered essential, including an ability to work with issues of confidentiality, consent and capacity. BACP (ibid.) suggest that therapists need to be able to work across and within agencies and respond to child protection issues. In addition, therapists need to be able to engage and work with young people of a variety of ages, developmental levels and backgrounds as well as parents and careers in a culturally competent manner. They also need to have knowledge of psychopharmacology as it relates to young people.

The generic competencies relate to knowledge of specific models of intervention and practice, an ability to work with emotions, endings and service transitions, an ability to work with groups and measurement instruments and to be able to use supervision effectively. The ability to conduct a collaborative assessment and a risk assessment is paramount. Crucially, BACP (2014) suggest the therapist needs to be able to foster and maintain a relationship which builds a therapeutic alliance and understands the client's 'world view'. In our experience most proficient therapists, irrespective of their modality, work to achieve this trusting relationship necessary for human change. Four broad areas of the therapist's intent within this relationship are described below:

Attention-Giving

This is where we actively demonstrate to clients through verbal responses, facial expressions, eye contact and body posture that we are in a supportive, respectful, accepting and authentic relationship with them. This builds respect and trust in the therapist–client relationship.

Observing

This is where we observe the client's verbal and physical expressions to enable us to more fully understand our client's experience, their relationship with the therapy process, their life experiences and us. We believe that by noticing these, it leads to greater relational depth (Mearns and Cooper, 2005). This relational depth allows the client to feel safe enough to try out new ways of being, which can be a prelude to trying these outside of the counselling relationship.

Listening

This is where we are *actively listening* (Rogers and Farson, 1987) to the content and emotional experience of a client's story, while listening out for indicators of how the client defines their experience. At the same time, we are continuously communicating back to the client that we have heard and understood their phenomenological perspective. Active listening and affirming what we have heard imbues in the client a sense of being understood and accepted.

Responding

This is where we are responding to a client's core communication. This involves reflecting the content and feeling of the client's expressions while offering summaries that can lead to further expression or exploration of how the client wishes to move forward from current or historical experiences. This also gives the client the opportunity to modify the internal view of their external experience, as they hear it reflected back to them. As we discuss later in the chapter, the way we respond will need to be developmentally appropriate and may use other mediums of communication such as play.

Although specific orientations, for example CBT, will have specific skill sets, the four broad areas described above are often seen as the basis for therapeutic work with children and young people. Taken together, these four areas can be described as demonstrating the skill of active listening. Rogers and Farson (1987: 1) argue that:

> People who have been listened to in this new and special way become more emotionally mature, more open to their experiences, less defensive, more democratic, and less authoritarian.

The fundamental premise is that these therapeutic skills span all client groups irrespective of age, gender, sexuality, cultural background and life experiences. What is key is how we adapt attention-giving, observing, listening and responding to meet the unique needs of the client before us. This is true for all client groups but never more so than for those of us working with children and young people. For younger children, we may adapt our active listening by communicating through play whereas older young people may be more able to tolerate a more adult type of counselling experience.

Rogers and Farson (1987) describe the skills required for active listening. They argue we need to really understand what the speaker is saying from their perspective and communicate that we have done this. When we listen, we have to listen for 'total meaning' – both the content of the communication and the feeling and/or attitude underneath this. We need to 'respond to feelings'. The feelings can be much more important than the content. Finally we must 'note all cues'. This means attending to non-verbal as well as verbal communication and being aware of how something is communicated, hesitantly or confidently for example. Again, we will adapt our skills to the age and developmental level of our client and communicate through appropriate mediums. For work with children, play is often the preferred way of working and this is described in Chapter 7, 'Play Therapy'. Young people and adults can also find play therapy very powerful but may feel it's babyish so age-appropriate ways of working need to be employed. Younger adolescents may find it difficult to tolerate the focused attention of the therapist so a third focus, often creative work, can be offered.

Using age-appropriate mediums will make the communication of active listening more accessible. It is acceptable to be creative and not be fearful of inviting the client to consider working in this way. Chapter 8, 'Other Creative Approaches', offers some ideas and it may also be useful to offer life simulation computer games as a powerful vehicle for the client to express their world. Clients may choose to use mobile phone texting to share some of the toughest experiences they are not able to verbalise. This may require a service phone specifically for this purpose and some pretty fast texting skills on the counsellor's part.

In addition to offering active listening skills which can be viewed as one of the underpinning skills of all interpersonal encounters, there is also a need for the specialist skills that fit with different modalities and relationship needs of the client. Therapeutic skills when working with children and young people will be used to orperationalise the philosophy of the particular modality. Person-centred counsellors will focus on offering a relationship characterised by the core conditions (Rogers, 1951). Cognitive-behavioural therapists will be looking to develop the therapeutic alliance in order to help the client make connections between thought, emotions and behaviour (Beck, 1995). The psychoanalytic therapist will be aiming to develop a relationship in which transference can occur and where unconscious material can be made available to the conscious mind (Corey, 2001).

What Are the Differences between Working Therapeutically with Adults, Children and Young People?

Although there are similarities between all therapeutic work, there are some important differences. These include:

- Differing stages of development – emotional, moral, physical and cognitive: see Chapter 1 of this handbook, 'Child Development and Attachment'
- Ethical and power issues: see Chapter 17 ('Law and Policy') and Chapter 18 ('Ethics') of this handbook, and Daniels and Jenkins (2010)

Therefore, as has been suggested in the BACP (2014) Competencies for Working with Young People, a knowledge of child and family development is essential, as well as a knowledge of legal frameworks and an ability to work with issues to do with confidentiality and capacity.

Therapeutic skills that enable us to work with adults are not necessarily suitable for work with children and young people. In addition, those suitable for young people (adolescents) are not necessarily suitable for working with children (primary school aged children and younger). Those commissioning therapy for children and young people share this understanding (Pattison et al., 2007). We need to appreciate what separates children from young people and young people from adults, and how having a therapeutically differentiated strategy can be the crucial element in providing safe yet effective therapeutic outcomes. What should inform this strategy is an understanding of the developmental stages young people grow through and which are described in Chapter 1.

Counsellors need to be aware of the significant impact these developmental stages have on childhood understanding and communication and must be willing to adapt their way of work to accommodate these variants (Churchill, 2011). Particular skills in working with children and young people need to be developed. Part 1 of this handbook, particularly Chapters 2 to 8, describe the theoretical base and skills needed for a number of modalities for working in this field.

The key stages of development include physical, emotional and cognitive functioning. These stages are rarely synchronised with each other and we would argue that the chances of them being disharmonious is greater in young people who have suffered early life trauma, This means that many of our clients may present as being under- or overdeveloped physically, emotionally and/or psychologically in relation to their expected stage of development. Client presentations of development will often not parallel each other; a client could be physically overdeveloped and emotionally underdeveloped. The case study is an example of this, the issues it may cause and the skills a therapist may employ to manage this.

Culture may also affect the development of children and young people and how we view their development. The age at which a child becomes a young person or an adult varies from culture to culture and so we need to move away from adopting one static theory of child and adolescent development and select one that can form a 'baseline starting point from which to modify and improve upon so that they maintain their relevance in a rapidly changing multicultural society' (Walker, 2005). He maintains:

> We also need to reflect upon our own perceptions and beliefs concerning child development and avoid rigid understandings. We need to ensure that we come from an open, curious and culturally pliable position. (Walker, 2005: 15)

Another difference when working with children and young people is that of boundary keeping, especially confidentiality. Children and young people are, in general, much less autonomous than adults and have several groups of people interested in, concerned for and responsible for their welfare (parents, relatives, carers, teachers, social workers, dinner nannies for example). In our experience, to stick to the normal adult limits of confidentiality can risk alienating the people responsible for the care of the child or young person and may ultimately put them at risk. The carer may feel that the child or young person is sharing 'secrets' that they feel threatened by or that you have an intimate connection with your client that could jeopardises the relationship they have. In order to keep this boundary sensitively, we need to develop communication skills that will allow us tell the carers enough to keep them involved but not enough to violate the child or young person's privacy. Generalities such as 'Things seem to be going well' or 'How are you feeling about the therapy?' may suffice but thought needs to go into what it is OK to say and what not. Supervision can help with these decisions and, if possible, the client should also be involved. Sometimes the client wants you to act as a spokesperson for them to their carers so a careful discussion of what is to be shared is vital.

The mechanics of therapy may also be different when working with children and young people. Adults usually refer themselves for therapy but children and young people may be referred by others, usually carers or teachers. If this is the case, both the client and referrer need to understand what therapy is and the client needs to want to engage. It may be appropriate to offer a home visit to explain both the purpose and procedure of therapy to both the client and the carer. In the case of a teacher referral, a programme of education and information would ideally have been undertaken within the school.

In our experience, in private rather than school settings, we feel it may be better if a carer could accompany a younger child and wait outside the therapy room as the child may want to leave early. Also, having the carer involved in the practicalities of therapy can help the therapist maintain a positive relationship with them.

As with adult clients, it is important to work and plan for the ending of therapy right from the beginning (Robson, 2008) and, if possible, to include the client in planning the final session. It is also helpful, in our view, to try and finish therapy at a time which would resonate with a normal end, for example, the end of school term.

Relationship of Personal Qualities or Attributes to Therapeutic Skills

It has been suggested that the therapist needs particular qualities or attributes when working with children and young people (Geldard et al., 2013; West, 1996). These qualities or attributes are conveyed through the use of therapeutic skills. They, and the associated skills, will depend, to a certain extent, on the therapist's theoretical orientation. West's (ibid.) description, although quite dated, is one that would be familiar to child-centred play therapists. She suggests personal qualities should include the ability to

- Relate to, through and with feelings
- Understand and come to terms with what has happened in their own childhood, adolescence and adulthood, including child-rearing and parenting issues
- Work within a child-centred framework
- Communicate with children
- Play
- Work alongside troubled children without being damaged by the children's pain
- Act as an advocate for the children they have in play therapy. (p. 150)

Geldard et al. (2013), working from a more CBT stance, suggest four attributes for therapists:

1. Congruence
2. In touch with own inner child
3. Accepting
4. Emotionally detached. (p. 21)

The final one, 'emotionally detached', may be shocking for some therapists but they do qualify this by saying that this 'does not mean that the counsellor needs to be limp, lifeless and remote. On the contrary, the child does need to feel comfortable with the counsellor' (p. 23).

Whatever personal qualities or attributes we develop to further our work will be communicated through the use of therapeutic skills. Each modality will dictate what we are trying to convey to our clients and how we use our skills to do that. The use of active listening skills can express empathy and attention giving and are qualities commonly valued by all approaches.

Working Briefly

Working briefly with children and young people will not necessarily change the skill set employed by the therapist but can put pressure on the therapist to 'solve' the problem rather than concentrating on building a strong relationship with the client. As has been suggested earlier, clients, particularly younger children, can find it helpful to end therapy where a break in their routine would occur naturally, for example the end of a school term. Brief or time-limited therapy may not allow this to happen.

Case Study   Andrew

This case study demonstrates work with a client whose physical development had overtaken his cognitive and emotional development and the skills the therapist used to help her client explore the meaning of his experiences.

Andrew was 14 when he was referred to Liz, his school counsellor. He'd been at his new school only five months after his mother had moved to the area seeking a fresh start after the end of another violent relationship. Andrew had two younger female siblings and none of them shared the same father. Andrew was not in contact with his father but his sisters' fathers kept in sporadic contact. Overall their life had been fairly nomadic since Andrew was about two years old.

Prior to the referral, at least three teachers had reported that Andrew's behaviour was becoming more and more disruptive in class and one teacher had asked that Andrew be excluded permanently from his class, after Andrew had 'faced him off in front of other pupils'.

Other staff and pupils had reported that they found it hard to warm to Andrew and that he had done little to integrate himself into his new school community. Andrew's year head accompanied him to his first counselling session to, as the year head put it, 'make sure he bothered to turn up'.

(Continued)

(Continued)

The first thing that struck Liz about Andrew was his physical presence. Andrew was incredibly tall and broad for his age and could easily have passed for a baby-faced adult man. Andrew's posture, attitude and general manner was one that seemed to demonstrate nonchalance bordering on arrogance. Liz opened the early stages of her work with Andrew by congruently reflecting the path by which he had arrived at counselling. Liz explained it felt their coming together had been coerced. She disclosed her own dissatisfaction about this, and explained that one of the fundamental tenets of counselling was that it had to be a voluntary process that both parties wished to freely engage in.

Andrew said he had no problem attending counselling but he did not know why others thought he would benefit from it. Referring to his teachers, he stated that the only thing that would be gained by counselling was that others would be pleased because he would be 'out of the way as usual'. Despite his physical stature, Liz noticed that when Andrew said this, he seemed small and diminutive; his posture was hunched and almost foetal like. Liz reflected back to Andrew that he didn't seem pleased by the idea that people wanted him out of the way and asked if his teachers were the only people that seemed to enjoy his absence.

Andrew then gave an outline of his life, explaining that it was only men who wanted him out of the way – male teachers, mum's boyfriends and male peers. Most of Andrew's early years had been deeply fractured; he could report no consistent male role model, just a series of men who drifted in and rather violently out of his family's life. Despite his apparent physical maturity, it was clear that Andrew carried a rather young and naive sense of blame for the patterns in his mother's relationships. 'They get sick of me you see'; 'They don't mind my little sisters'; 'It is only my dad doesn't keep in touch'.

Liz invited Andrew to explore how he felt about 'being out of the way' and he explained that sometimes it was for the better. For many years there had been multiple violent incidents that he had heard and observed. These culminated in his mother being so badly beaten that she had a punctured lung and was unconscious. Andrew was deeply disturbed by this incident, explaining he regularly 'saw' it when he closed his eyes and he 'daydreamed' about it. With the help of supervision Liz began to realise that Andrew was describing early signs of post-traumatic stress and that his daydreaming appeared to be an indicator of intrusive daytime imagery. Liz's supervisor encouraged her to give Andrew more space to explore his daydreams.

Andrew explained daydreaming was why he had been excluded from class. He was being seen as uncooperative and had been described as blatantly ignoring classroom instructions. In fact what Andrew said was happening was that he was 'zoning out' in thinking about what had happened to his mum.

In his own language, prompted by accurate reflections from his therapist, Andrew began to articulate the internal conflict he experienced between physically appearing as an adult while internally feeling young and fearful. 'I'm built like a brick shit house'; 'I should be able to protect my mom. I'm big enough but I'm a pussy'.

Andrew's stature was a real hindrance to him as he was regularly perceived as being an adult. This led others to place unrealistic expectations upon him in terms of his behaviour, attitude and emotional resilience. Andrew had internalised many of these expectations, especially when it came to protecting his mother. His inability to live up to these internalised standards ultimately led Andrew to feel a great sense of shame and physical and emotional impotence. Andrew's arrogance, nonchalance, and burgeoning aggression, seemed to be his way of covering what he felt sure others could see in him.

Liz recognised initially she had also been a little blinded by Andrew's stature and that she had the challenge of building a relationship with a vulnerable young man whose sense of self was incredibly fragile. The work began to focus on what attributes Andrew wanted people to see. Andrew said he wanted people to see his sporting and artistic skill, although he wrestled with the latter as this was 'a wussie's game'. The remainder of Liz and Andrew's work focused on attending to the common question that is present for many adolescent clients (Horne, 1999): 'Who will I be?'.

Over the following weeks Liz and Andrew returned to Andrew's image of who he might be and explored which elements of this could be facilitated through change within his life and which elements needed to be accepted as currently unachievable. During one particularly difficult session, Andrew became distressed when he realised that he could never have protected his mum from domestic abuse as for many years he'd been physically unable to because of his youth and small stature. His recent physical development had left him with a feeling that he should have done something to protect his family. This led Andrew to look at the limits and scope of his own personal responsibility. Andrew found this frustrating but was willing to accept on a cognitive level that he had not had the capacity to protect his family and because of this, he could not be responsible. Throughout the counselling encounter Liz used active listening to try and enter Andrew's world and congruently worked with the dissonance between his developmental levels.

Summary

In this chapter we have:

- Argued that we need different therapeutic skills and knowledge when working with children and young people
- Detailed the competencies required and highlighted the importance of the skill of active listening.
- Considered the impact of the developmental stage of the client on the therapy
- Explored the differences in working therapeutically with children, young people and adults
- Provided a case study to demonstrate the dissonance that can occur between different elements of development and how the therapist uses her therapeutic skills to attend to the whole client experience

Reflective Questions

- Can you think of a child or young person where their physical, emotional, cognitive or behaviour development is not synchronised? Does this cause issues?
- Are there any special attributes or qualities that you feel a therapist working with children and young people should have? If so, what are they and why?
- Why might it be important to communicate to carers of the child or young person something of what is happening in your therapy sessions?
- What do you think are the most important skills for a therapist when working with children and young people?

Learning Activities

- Think about your school days and about your teachers. Think of one good teacher and one bad teacher. What were their qualities/behaviours/attributes that made them good teachers? What were their qualities/behaviours/attributes that made them bad teachers? Can you list them? Think about your 'good' list. Does it connect in any way to the suggestions made by Rogers and Farson (1987) about how to listen actively?
- Write a list for yourself of the different skills required to work with children and young people. If you do not already have these skills, where could you learn them? Do a search for training providers.
- West (1996) suggests that in order to work with children and young people we need to 'understand and come to terms with what has happened in [our]/their own childhood, adolescence and adulthood, including child-rearing and parenting issues'. How could you do this?
- West (ibid.) also suggests that we 'work alongside troubled children without being damaged by the children's pain'. What sort of strategies can we put in place for ourselves to help us manage this?

Further Reading

Baruch, G. (2001) *Community-Based Psychotherapy with Young People: Evidence and Innovation in Practice*. Philadelphia: Taylor and Francis.

Bowman, R.P. and Bowman, S.C. (1998) *Individual Counselling Activities for Children*. Chapin, SC: Youth Light.

Harris, B. and Pattison, S. (2004) *Research on Counselling Children and Young People: A Systematic Scoping Review*. Rugby: BACP.

Lines, D. (2002) *Brief Counselling in Schools: Working with Young People from 11 to 18*. Thousand Oaks, CA: SAGE.

Luxmoore, N. (2000) *Listening to Young People in School, Youth Work and Counselling*. Philadelphia, PA: Taylor and Francis Group.

McLaughlin, C., Holliday, C., Clarke, B. and Llie, S. (2013) *Research on Counselling and Psychotherapy with Children and Young People: A Systematic Scoping Review of Evidence for its Effectiveness from 2003–2011*. Rugby: BACP.

Mapes, K. (2000) *Stop! Think! Choose! Building Emotional Intelligence in Young People*. Tucson, AZ: Zephyr Press.

Ponterotto, J., Casas, M.J., Suzuki, L.A., Alexander, C.M. (2001) *Handbook of Multicultural Counselling*. 2nd edn. Thousand Oaks, CA: SAGE.

Schaefer, C. (ed.) (2003) *Foundations of Play Therapy*. Hoboken, NJ: John Wiley & Sons.

Simpson, A.R. (2001) *Raising Teens: A Synthesis of Research and a Foundation for Action*. Boston: Center for Health Communication, Harvard School of Public Health.

Online Resources

BACP website: www.bacp.co.uk/, especially the BACP Children and Young People Division and the Competences for Working with Children and Young People.

Counselling MindEd: http://counsellingminded.com, especially Modules CMD 02: Participation and Empowerment; CMD 03: Legal and Professional Issues; CMD 04: Cultural Competence; CMD 05: Initiating Counselling; CMD 07: Relational Skills; CMD 08: Therapeutic Skills; CMD 10: Concluding Counselling.

Children and Young People's Improving Access to Psychological Therapies (CYP IAPT): www.cypi-apt.org.

Griffiths, G. (2013) *Helpful and Unhelpful Factors in School Based Counselling: Client's Perspective*. Counselling MindEd Scoping Report. Available at: http://counsellingminded.com/wp-content/uploads/2013/12/griffiths_MindEd_report.pdf.

13

Supervision

Penny Leake and Ann Beynon

This chapter includes:

- A general introduction to the role and definition of supervision
- A presentation of a working model of practice
- A history and background to this professional development
- A theoretical underpinning of the supervisory relationship
- A case study
- Research
- Questions and activities for reference and discussion
- Further reading
- Summary

Introduction

In this chapter we will look at the supervision of therapeutic work with children and young people, examining its history, theory and practice. We shall look at a working definition of such a supervisory relationship and examine how the supervisor has to take account of how work with children and adolescents is different from work with adults. We will explore the issues of creativity and of power, and suggest activities and reflective questions for both practitioner and supervisor. The chapter also contains a case study, some suggested reading, and thoughts about what research exists and what more is needed.

Therapeutic work with children and young people can be undertaken in many settings, and practitioners may espouse a variety of models of working. The latter may largely be influenced by the age/developmental stage of the child or young person. The supervisor chosen by the practitioner (if choice is possible) will need to be comfortable with the variety of needs the supervisees will therefore bring, as well as having a good understanding of the ways in which supervision of work with children and adolescents is different from supervision of work with adults.

There have been many working definitions of the triple function that supervision serves in work with adults, and we have chosen Houston's (1995) description of 'policeman, plumber and poet' to look at in the context of child and adolescent work. Houston's use of metaphor in her definition seems very appropriate when we think about work with children, their communication being so rooted in symbolism. This creative aspect of the work, so frequent in the therapy itself, can get forgotten about as a tool in the supervisory process.

Policeman

The 'policeman' metaphor reminds us that the ultimate function of supervision is to benefit and protect the child client, even though the practitioner is likely to experience it as a benefit to themselves. In their extensive writing on supervision of adult work, Proctor and Inskipp conclude that it is not possible to have an exact parallel of Rogers' core conditions in the supervisory relationship, because the need for rigour is not compatible with a completely non-judgemental attitude. A clinical supervisor, just like a line manager, has a vicarious liability for the standard of work being done. The version of the core conditions which Proctor and Inskipp therefore describe is one of empathy, respect and genuineness.

The kinds of duties which the 'policeman' may have to fulfil are best discussed between the supervisor and the practitioner at the outset and set out in a written contract in order to model good boundary-keeping and to avoid any later discomforts. Examples of items in the contract would be the extents and limits of confidentiality, the keeping of records and serious concerns about the standard of work. One of the important ways in which supervision of child and adolescent work is different from supervision of adult work is the need to keep in mind the legal framework that surrounds practice. Sometimes the practitioner can lose sight of this in the midst of the therapeutic relationship. Legal issues (such as safeguarding, parental responsibility or the child's competence to make decisions) can lead to very difficult dilemmas for the practitioner around confidentiality. It is good to have reference in the supervision contract to what kind of issue can stay within supervision and what may need to go outside. If the practitioner works for an agency there will be times when agency policy must be followed quickly and the line manager consulted rather than the clinical supervisor.

The level of experience of the supervisee is likely to affect how frequently the 'policeman' function comes to the fore, and this can also affect the character of the 'plumber' aspect.

Plumber

Here Houston is referring to looking at the nuts and bolts of the day-to-day work, the discussion of individual sessions, the progression of the series, the need for additional training, etc. If the supervisee is on a qualification course, or if s/he feels the need for some minute attention to a session, this may take the form of looking at a video recording together. The supervisor might give straightforward advice in a case like this. Supervisors of work with children and adolescents need to have experience in the field themselves. Sometimes drawing on this to make practical suggestions may be helpful, but too much may interfere with the collegial exploration which is likely to be the most successful. Houston believes that her best work as a supervisor is when the therapist supervises herself in front of her.

This 'plumber' work may well be done cognitively, but there will be times when the supervisee brings feelings of 'stuckness' which s/he finds elusive and difficult to describe. This is an ideal opportunity for the supervisor to invite the supervisee to use creative ways of exploring, such as by using stones, sand, art, play therapy figures, etc. In so doing, the supervisee's emotions about the work are likely to come to the fore, and parallel processes may emerge. This is where the third function of supervision, the 'poet' work, is crucial.

Poet

The 'poet' in the supervisor listens out for themes and patterns, but above all listens to the music under the words, which gives clues to the supervisee's feelings about the child and those in the child's system. Sometimes the supervisee knows all too well how she feels, and can say so given the right atmosphere. Our feelings when working with children can go beyond counter-transference, as we are working with an actual unhappy child in real time, and this may bring out natural protective instincts which can lead to rescuing and unhelpful mothering behaviours. The practitioner needs to stay with the child's pain, and this is very difficult to do. She needs to be able to bring these feelings to supervision in order to lessen them, both for her own sake and for that of the child.

When working with adolescents, more negative feelings may be triggered, if hostility and attachment difficulties are being directed towards the counsellor. Practitioners may find working with self-harm and disordered eating particularly anxiety-provoking.

Other people in the child's system may cause the practitioner to feel professionally isolated, angry or inadequate. It is the feelings of inadequacy and other vulnerabilities that cause practitioners to want external clinical supervision rather than any that may be contracted within their agency. This is the effect of the power issues inherent in any supervisory relationship, irrespective of how good the agency's supervisor (or, indeed, line manager) may be. The reality may be that choice may not be possible, as agencies may wish to have a tight accountability for the work, although a clear three-way specimen contract from a potential clinical supervisor may help here.

Sometimes, however, a carefully boundaried in-house supervision programme can be useful – such as when both group co-facilitators can be supervised together, or as a way of getting insight into the tricky systemic issues that are so central to work in this field.

History and Background

In the 1960s and 1970s, the 'birthing period' of counselling for children and young people in education, approaches to counselling practice learnt much from the developing fields of child psychiatry and social work, not least in terms of the integrated models of management supervision in delivering effective practice. In Anne Jones' visionary and practical account of her work as a counsellor in Mayfield Comprehensive School in London, she recognises the integral purpose of supervision.

> For a counsellor to deny the emotional repercussions a counselling interview may cause within him may block any growth and development in his work and possibly indirectly to his client. To face and accept his limitations and to make the best of them, the counsellor needs help – systematic, structured and specific help. (1970: 170)

She talks of finding 'our own unofficial channels of support and supervision' to meet this need, a practical exercise which many counsellors, nationally, were engaged in during this period. Individual and group supervision contracts were explored with the psychological, psychiatric, welfare and education services, building the understanding and acceptance that 'to appoint supervisory personnel specifically for counsellors is not an extravagance but an essential.'

During these early years supervision, or tutorial sessions, had become an integral part of generic counselling training programmes and finally became recognised as a requirement for professional accreditation by the British Association for Counselling and Psychotherapy (BACP) and other professional bodies. Thus the need for specific training for counselling supervisors as a distinct professional role and function became increasingly apparent and a number of training courses were developed in the 1980s and 1990s based on a variety of theoretical models.

The BACP/NHS MindEd online training for counselling with children and young people coming on-stream in 2014 has designated modules on the supervisory relationship.

In recent years many counsellors have initiated peer mentoring services in their schools, working in partnership with other members of staff. Provision for integrated supervision for both mentors and staff is crucial to sustained service development. Helen Cowie and Patti Wallace (2000) go as far as to say: 'If there is really not enough time to supervise peer supporters regularly, perhaps it is not the best time to set up a peer support service.'

They describe the function of supervision in this context as follows:

> it can be a forum for monitoring the effectiveness of the service, a forum in which ideas for further training can be generated and, if done in a group, it can help to develop cohesiveness within the group of peer supporters. (Cowie and Wallace, 2000: 134)

Thus with an infrastructure of consistent and creative management and supervision the value of these outreach services alongside a counselling provision can actively influence an ethos of mutual awareness and openness in a school community.

Theoretical Underpinning

Supervision of therapeutic work with children and young people has to take account of how this work is different from that with adults.

Systemic Thinking

A fundamental difference is that children, in particular, and young people, to a large extent, do not have personal autonomy. They are part of a system that includes parents, foster-carers, culture, school and possibly other agencies. If a parent is hostile to the idea of therapy for a younger child, they have the power to forbid it, sabotage it, withhold it as a punishment or turn it into a scapegoating process. A Fraser-competent young person may be able to have counselling in a school setting without their parents' knowledge, but here the system of the school could itself cause tensions. The supervisee can find that many people besides the child are taking up her headspace. She may need the supervisor's help to sort out which of these extra players need to be centre stage and which can be in the wings.

She may also need a safe place to vent frustrations about parts of the system, and a containing supervisor can help with any accompanying issues of splitting and activation of Karpman's drama triangle (see below). The supervisor may be able to spot if the agency is mirroring the issues of the client group they work with, if practitioners are mirroring family dynamics, or if a parallel process is emerging in the supervisory relationship. Anything that can be done to get the system on board is likely to make the therapy more effective.

Sometimes family therapy is needed rather than individual, and this need may become clear through discussion in supervision. Sometimes the supervisor has to support the therapist in facing the fact that his or her work can only be damage limitation, and that a good therapeutic relationship now may enable the child to seek therapy again when an autonomous adult.

Information-sharing within the system is always a tricky business. The looked-after system may expect frequent sharing. If a practitioner was originally trained in adult counselling, the principle of tight confidentiality may still be firmly rooted in them, and the supervisor can help with the discomfort that information-sharing may bring. It may be helpful to look during the supervision session at the written ethical guidance that is produced by professional bodies such as BACP and BAPT, and to think through together how far and in what ways ethical principles such as non-maleficence, autonomy and fidelity can apply to work with children. Age and developmental issues will be crucial here.

Developmental Issues

Many of the complex threads which distinguish child and adolescent work from adult work come together in the subject of age and stage of development. Both practitioner and supervisor need to have a good understanding of child development, especially emotional development. A framework such as that of Erikson (1965) can be helpful, combined with an understanding of how trauma and disability can skew these stages.

A young person who is considered Fraser-competent can reasonably expect that his or her issues will be kept confidential, with the usual exceptions of harm to self or others. However, degrees of harm may cause grey areas that need to be explored in supervision. The thought of the law, parental anger, cultural opposition and possible court appearance can make the practitioner feel very precarious. Consultation with the Children's Legal Centre may be helpful here. On the other hand, a therapist trained in adult work may need reminding that promises of confidentiality to a young child can have resonance of, for example, 'our special secret', which can cause confusion rather than healing.

Embedded in person-centred work is Rogers' concept of 'the wisdom of the client'. Practitioner and supervisor may wish to discuss how far this concept can apply to work with children and young people. They may well have perfect wisdom over the pacing of their sessions and the methods of communication they will use. There will, however, be some decisions, depending on age and understanding, that they cannot make and, sometimes, should not be asked to make. A practitioner may have to think about who should be present at any feedback meetings with parents or carers. Whilst a young person may well want to be present, it would be counterproductive for a young child to hear their unconscious symbolic play being decoded for the benefit of adults.

The supervisee, too, has stages of development, and the supervisory relationship may need to adapt accordingly to advancements and to any regressions caused by professional or personal insecurity.

Attachment Issues

The children and young people whom therapists see are likely to have difficulties with attachment. This may be because early attachment was skewed through abuse or neglect or because it was disrupted through bereavement or separation. These attachment patterns are likely to be acted out in the therapy room, and may cause a variety of discomforts for the practitioner.

The early stages of the work are likely to echo the anxiety, hostility, avoidance or ambivalence of a child's insecure attachments. Ambivalent attachment can manifest itself in anxiety to please. The child may need a period of being securely attached to the practitioner before being able to move on, and judging when this time has come can be difficult. The subjects of dependency and endings are likely to be brought to supervision, and the supervisee's own feelings may well need to be disentangled from the needs of the child, especially if the attachment has started to become mutual. The supervisor can help the practitioner to feel that the child is getting a good, predictable ending rather than the many unpredictable ones they have had in the past.

The attachment issues of adolescents are additionally complex because of their need to begin attaching to peers and push away parent figures. Moving from individual work to group work is therefore ideal here. If the supervisee is facilitating a group, there are many people, issues and powerful feelings that will be present in the supervision room. The use of creative methods of supervision, such as with stones or Russian dolls, can help to make this feel more clear and manageable.

The Supervisee's Feelings

It is difficult for a counsellor to stay with the pain of adults, but staying with the pain of children is especially difficult. There is a great temptation to minimize, distract and rescue. Landreth suggests that anyone who wants to be a play therapist should ask themselves several searching questions, such as how much they need to be needed and whether they feel guilt about limit-setting.

Supervisees can bring complex and overwhelming feelings to supervision. Issues of counter-transference may be at work, or real-time sympathy or despair for a vulnerable child. A child can silently call to the supervisee's inner child, or evoke feelings about children in her family, or lack of them. Through projective identification, the therapist may get an unbearable feeling of what it is like to be this child. If the feeling is one of guilt and inadequacy, the supervisor may be able to point out the process that is happening, and so normalize what the therapist may be feeling about her work, disentangling what is hers and what is the child's. The supervisor, too, may experience strong feelings, and generally these can be brought into the room so that an exploration of parallel processes can help with the clarification.

Counsellors and therapists are constantly having to swallow down children's pain, and this needs to be assuaged in supervision and in other replenishing activities. If it is not, it can become toxic to the practitioner, or lead to defences which protect the therapist but can give a subtle message to the child that there are some no-go areas in therapy.

We know from neuroscience that a practitioner can be simultaneously flooded with the same unhealthy cortisol as is the child they are listening to. Equally, the child can pick up the opioids generated by calmness and containment. The supervisee needs a containing supervisor to increase her own opioids and diminish cortisol. So, too, the supervisor has to hear pain and contain splitting, and he or she needs to keep up their own regular supervision for identical reasons.

The supervisor's overview of many cases can help him or her to remember that children heal more quickly than adults given the right circumstances, and this can help to keep the therapist's optimism alive. Sometimes, however, the supervisor may sense that the supervisee's usual resilience is being chipped away by too much pain, and the subject of time out and/or burn-out may have to be raised, with the help of a diagnostic questionnaire if necessary. Sometimes there are so many personal issues impacting on the work that it becomes clear that the supervisee may need personal therapy in addition to clinical supervision. Here the supervisor can model good boundaries, signposting the supervisee elsewhere for this and not letting supervision become a kind of counselling.

Legal Issues

This has been referred to under 'policeman' in an earlier section of this chapter. It is the practitioner's responsibility to be very familiar with all issues of safeguarding children, Fraser-competence, the basics of current Children Acts, the latest assessment framework, and his or her own agency's procedures. However, the supervisor also needs knowledge on these matters. There needs, for example, to be a clear understanding about when a child's wish for confidentiality has to be overruled, whilst at the same time minimizing any harm from this. Acting on disclosures of abuse can be distressing for both child and practitioner, and there will also be a need for the therapist to seek legal advice on how soon play therapy or counselling can be resumed after legal proceedings have been begun. With both children and adolescents there is a greater danger of the practitioner being accused of 'coaching' the child in their evidence than there is in equivalent adult work. The supervisor can model the careful record-keeping that is always necessary in child therapy, and there can be discussion on the complexities of this. Any court appearance is likely to be stressful for the practitioner, and he or she will need support from both supervisor and line manager.

Symbolism and Creativity

Older children and adolescents may communicate in a counselling relationship like adults do, using words and perhaps art. They may also be disconcertingly silent. For younger children, however, it is not natural to them to talk about what troubles them. The play therapist and supervisor are likely to spend much time discussing hypotheses about symbolic play. If this is done mutually, without the supervisor doing all the interpretation, it can be fascinating and rewarding for both, even if the material is sad. Sometimes the therapist will have to continue explaining to impatient people in the system that the child is not 'just playing', and this can make her feel frustrated and professionally isolated.

The supervisor and therapist together can look for the signs that the urgent symbolic play is diminishing, and ordinary playfulness is increasing – a sign that the work is nearing its end.

Ideally the supervisor will offer creative methods in supervision so that the unconscious and the right brain are as active for the therapist as they are for the child.

Power Issues

The supervisor will have been congruent in the contract about the power issues inherent in the supervisory relationship. A clause about regular review of both the contract and the relationship may help to avoid some of the dangers of long-term supervisory relationships.

Karpman's drama triangle (1968) of victim, rescuer and persecutor can be activated especially easily in therapy with children and young people because children have little power and we frequently see them as victims. It would be easy for this dynamic to be mirrored in the supervision process, and supervisors need to be on their guard against acting on such feelings, especially that of wanting to rescue. That is not to say that supervisees do not need to hear their good work regularly praised to keep up their enjoyment of what they do. A containing adult-to-adult atmosphere will make drama triangle dynamics less likely.

The power/powerlessness issues of difference and diversity are important here. Amongst the many conscious and unconscious triads which feature in supervision, there can be a sub-system of two and an odd one out. Already the practitioner and supervisor are adult, and the client is not. If in addition the supervisee and supervisor are, for example, white and the child is black, it is possible for unconscious filtering and collusion to occur. Equally, there could be times when child and therapist are in a sub-system which is causing boundary difficulties, and the objectivity of a supervisor from a different grouping might be helpful.

Case Study   Pippa

Pippa had worked for three years in a CAMHS Tier II community team, which mainly took referrals from social workers. She had been trained in adult counselling, but had had in-house training in therapeutic work with children and adolescents.

Pippa was allocated a new case, where even the referral details made her feel overwhelmed. Adam was a nine-year-old boy, a looked-after child living with his grandparents. By the time he was six, he had been physically, emotionally and sexually abused and had seen his mother die of a cerebral haemorrhage as she was cooking the tea in front of him. For three years he had been quiet and no-one had thought he needed therapy, but now he was being oppositional and destructive at home, and his Nana was not sure that she could continue to look after him if his behaviour did not improve

Pippa took her feelings of being overwhelmed to supervision even before her first session. She had never known a child suffer so much, and even his system, which included complex reconstituted families, was more than she could grasp. Jane, her supervisor, suggested using Russian dolls to clarify this, and this externalizing and miniaturizing helped Pippa to feel less submerged.

Pippa had to use a room mainly used for adult work. Adam's Nana had said he liked art, and when preparing the room Pippa had put out very many large tubes of poster paint. She realised later in supervision that this was her 'rescuer' at work. Adam had squirted paint wildly, which had stained the carpet, and made much mess with sand and water. He had also banged loudly on the walls. Pippa found herself worrying about what other people would say, and was powerfully reminded of when her own toddler made a mess in someone else's house. She had coped with boundary-testing before, but realised there was rightly no mention of mess or noise in the ground rules which she had outlined to him earlier. He was very excited when his Nana came to collect him, and Nana looked worried. She wanted to talk to Pippa in front of him, but Pippa gently put her off. Pippa went home worrying that she might have done more harm than good in letting him be so wild.

(Continued)

(Continued)

She had lots of unease to share at her next supervision. Jane made the practical suggestion of asking if Pippa could change the therapy day to one when no-one was using the room next door. This was simple but extremely effective 'plumber' work. Jane also contained Pippa's feelings in a calm and respectful way. They reflected together on what mess might mean to Adam, and Jane suggested slightly re-stating the ground rules to 'no damage that can't be put right'. This later proved to be a deep insight on Jane's part.

Pippa stayed with the process with more confidence over the next month. Adam's mess began to focus itself into a game of a naughty, messy baby. He sucked on a baby's bottle, and wrenched Pippa's heart by crawling round saying someone had taken his bottle away and he couldn't find it. She did, however, feel this was progress – until the phone calls started coming in.

Nana had been worried by Adam telling her he was drinking from a feeding bottle, and she had shared her fears of regression with a liaison teacher. The teacher had rung Pippa and said, 'He needs to be made to talk', and had advised immediate referral to one of Pippa's colleagues. After a moment of indignation, Pippa went into self-doubt, and suddenly felt inexperienced. Luckily, her supervision was the next day. Jane was able to help her to see that the good therapeutic relationship meant she was the right person to do the work, but that she had not taken enough account of systemic issues. Pippa quickly arranged a programme of regular feedback meetings, which Adam had no objection to, some just with Nana and some with the professional system as well. Pippa came to realise how deep Nana's anxiety went, and how she also needed signposting to counselling for her own grief. After that, the system was fully supportive of the therapy, and enhanced it by making adjustments in the outside world.

Pippa had to contain Adam's splitting of his vulnerability and his anger in many dizzying role reversing dramas, which she took for her own containment to supervision. Just as she was beginning to gain more confidence, she heard from Nana that Adam had recently exposed himself at a family party and put his head up a girl's skirt.

Pippa was used to working with victim issues, but not with sexually harmful behaviour. She needed all Jane's 'policeman, plumber, poet' functions, together with line management involvement. Pippa's growing attachment to Adam tempted her to minimize what had happened, but Jane was clear that the behaviour had to be addressed at once and mainly cognitively, both supportive and challenging. She helped Pippa to see that it was important neither to under-react nor over-react to what had happened, and to use an age-appropriate assessment process, including other members of the system, to see if this was an 'amber light' or a 'red light' situation. Because they concluded it was the former, it was felt Pippa could do the work herself with Jane's supervision and some further reading

Pippa was enabled to do this, and Adam showed no more sexually harmful behaviour. He resumed his symbolic play, acting a kick-boxing baby who integrated his earlier splitting. He invited Pippa to be 'the Mam'. Over the weeks, he directed Pippa in dramas in which the mother was angry with the messy baby, and their mutual anger and rejection escalated to the point where the mother died – died whilst cooking the tea. Pippa knew the theory of children's magical thinking about their own responsibility, but she had never felt it in her stomach until that day. She needed to discharge her pain in supervision, and also to talk about the way forward, whether it was right to stay indefinitely with this bleak pain or intervene to move it on in some way. Jane pointed her in the direction of literature which suggested that repeated post-traumatic play does need to be interrupted.

At Adam's next repetition of this scene, Pippa was able to use what she had learnt, together with her own intuition, to make the dying mother say words of reconciliation and reassurance that he was not to blame. After that, Adam's play showed themes of forgiveness, hope and growing self-esteem, and ordinary interactive games began to appear

Adam was by now halfway through the third reviewed series of six sessions. Pippa knew that the journey they had been through together made her reluctant to let him go, even though she knew the work was done, and that he was behaving well at home and starting to transfer his attachment to his Nana. Jane reminded her that it is the therapist's job to make herself unnecessary. Pippa took comfort from this and kept it as a mantra. She was able to do a good ending, and she and Jane looked back together with satisfaction on what had eventually been achieved from such a daunting beginning.

Research

From our experience of researching the nature of therapeutic supervision, we can verify the scarcity of research undertaken to evidence the value and nature of the role and function of supervision, particularly for counsellors working with children and young people. In this chapter we have summarised the theory and history of the integral place developed and held by supervision within the delivery of good and safe counselling practice. Recent evaluations of school counselling, such as the Counselling in Schools Project in Scotland (Cooper, 2004) and the Welsh School-based Counselling Strategy 2011 (Hill et al., 2011), provide encouraging evidence of the effectiveness of counselling in schools, based on detailed qualitative and quantitative evidence but, and maybe appropriately for their focus, with little or no reference to the need and place of the supervisory relationship in the service delivery. Similarly in 'Research on Counselling Children and Young People: A Comprehensive Systematic Scoping Review', undertaken by Belinda Harris and Sue Pattison in 2004, the function and training requirements for supervision is absent.

In the BACP's supervisors' workshop devised for circulation by Francesca Inskipp and Brigid Proctor in response to the need to introduce the re-framed Ethical Framework for Good Practice in Counselling and Psychotherapy in 2003, key statements for consideration under the heading 'Supervising and Managing' were as follows:

- Practitioners (supervisors) are responsible for clarifying who holds responsibility for the work with the client.
- General obligation for all supervisors to receive supervision/consultative support independently of managerial relationships.
- Supervisors' responsibility to maintain and enhance good practice by practitioners, protect clients from poor practice … acquire attitudes, skills and knowledge required by their role.

The above statements might well form the focus for much needed research projects; to justify their importance through practice-based evidence, indeed supervisors themselves are in a prime position to take up this initiative. The recent BACP research initiatives SuPReNet, Supervision Practitioner Research Network, and SCoPReNet, School-based Counselling Practice Research Network, which provide support to practitioners to undertake practice research projects, are a welcome resource to build this research base into the future.

Without comprehensive research for this dimension of counselling practice, commissioners of counselling services can be forgiven if they underestimate the need for supervision in their budget proposals – a serious professional concern in these straitened times.

Summary

This chapter has explored the role and development of supervision when working with children and young people, focusing on the following key issues:

- The supervisor of work with children and young people fulfils the same functions of 'policeman, plumber and poet' as for supervision of adult work, but has to bear in mind the ways in which these client groups are different
- Account has to be taken of the legal framework, systemic issues, child development, attachment patterns and the communication styles used by children and young people
- The power/powerlessness issues of any therapeutic relationship, and hence any supervisory relationship, are likely to be accentuated in this field
- A crucial difference of this work is that it is even more difficult for the practitioner to stay with the pain of children than it is to stay with that of adults, and the supervisee is likely to bring powerful and complex feelings to supervision
- Children's healing can be faster than that of adults, however, and seeing this brings great reward to both practitioner and supervisor

Reflective Questions

1 As a supervisor how much do I need to be needed?

If you find yourself regularly providing, or wanting to provide your answers to your supervisees' practice situations, whose needs are you meeting? This response could be an alert to considering how you are using your own supervision or peer consultation.

2 Do I feel uncomfortable setting limits?

As a supervisor you have a dual responsibility for the safety and potential for the well-being of your supervisees and their clients, while holding a safe, open working space with your supervisee. Monitoring limits of time, place and role becomes part of this duality – have you considered this responsibility in your supervisory role?

3 What are the key elements of a supervision contract with a supervisee working with children and young people?

Key elements of a supervision contract are the following:

For the supervisor and supervisee:

- Your membership of a professional body
- Your professional liability cover

Shared agreements:

- Time, place, frequency and payment for sessions
- Conditions of confidentiality
    - In what circumstances must confidentiality be broken, how will the client be informed?
- Name the key professionals and other adults with shared responsibility for the client, e.g. link teacher, parent or carer.
- Identify the line of management accountability, e.g. service manager and/or head teacher.
- Stages of a complaint's procedure:

    a) Mutual discussion to resolve the issue
    b) If no resolution possible, refer the situation to management personnel and/or the appropriate professional body, with the knowledge of each party.

Learning Activities

For supervisor

Think of one of your supervisee's clients and construct his or her family system as you understand it at this moment, using objects or drawing a map with the client in the central position. Use this in your supervision, or peer consultation, to clarify your own reactions and ownership of issues.

For supervisor and supervisee

Evaluation Exercise:

- Design and use a questionnaire to focus on the purpose, model and outcomes of your work in supervision for an agreed period, perhaps six months or a year.

Suggested Questions:

- What issues were raised in the supervision session?
- What approaches, exercises were used?
- How useful were they?
- How did the supervision session affect the work with the client?

Further Reading

Houston, G. (1995) *Supervision and Counselling*. London: The Rochester Foundation.
A small book, full of wisdom, in which more can be read on the 'policeman, plumber, poet' metaphor.

Landreth, G.L. (2002) *Play Therapy: The Art of the Relationship*. New York: Brunner-Routledge.
A very practical 'Bible' of non-directive play therapy, which combines theory with feeling and which highlights the importance of self-awareness.

Karpman, S.B. (1968) 'Fairy tales and script drama analysis', *Transactional Analysis Bulletin* 26 (1): 39–43.
Here more can be read about the power dynamics of the drama triangle.

Cowie, H. and Wallace, P. (2000) *Peer Support in Action*. London: SAGE.
For teachers and counsellors considering a school-based, peer support service. The chapter on supervision is constructive, detailed and hands-on.

Online Resources

BACP website: www.bacp.co.uk/, especially the BACP Children and Young People Division and the Competences for Working with Children and Young People.
Counselling MindEd: http://counsellingminded.com, particularly Module CMD 11: Using Supervision.

14

Group Work

Peter Pearce, Gwen Proud and Ros Sewell

This chapter includes:

- An outline of some of the key applications of group work with children and young people
- An exploration of some of the benefits and advantages of this work
- A description of some of the considerations necessary for setting up group work
- Identification of many of the attributes required of a group facilitator as well as behaviours that are not facilitative
- Details of some of the theoretical ideas about group work and group dynamics
- A summary of the history and background for group work
- A picture of current research on group work

Introduction

In a climate of limited resources, particularly one which can be dominated by concerns about results and statistics, as within a school environment, therapeutic group work can be seen as cost effective and time efficient. It can be attractive to stakeholders to know that 12 people are being seen in a group. Groups might also be seen as a way to address particular issues, for example bullying or anger management. So there may be considerable pressure for group work to be offered. The key benefit of therapeutic group work is that it results in interaction and social contact which does not occur in the individual client and therapist model. In this way therapeutic groups can offer participants the potential to develop their understanding of themselves and others by being in relation to other group members. The social, interpersonal context for issues is played out live through embodied experiencing. Groups can also become rich feedback environments where any participant can be facilitative, not only the therapists, and this can support increased self-awareness and awareness of what others see. It can be very validating and potentially developmental for a participant who, because of previous experiences, may feel they have nothing to offer others to begin to experience that they can be facilitative and that they might receive something valuable for themselves in return.

In a group new responses and ways of being can be tried out in relative safety. Participants have the opportunity to be more than the person they have come to be known as, providing the opportunity for harsh introjects and conditions of worth to be dissolved and offering important preparation for using newly learned behaviours in other areas of their lives.

The facilitative conditions can begin to be 'held' and communicated by the group, as participants begin to challenge and keep each other on track. Participants may also be triggered by others' material into a range of emotional responses, giving the opportunity for vicarious learning and, particularly with young people, for building on emotional literacy. The effect of working in this way therefore can have a profound impact on personal awareness and development. All of this makes group work a suitable choice for effective work with children and young people in a variety of contexts such as schools and children's services, particularly when the problems are recurring, isolating and stigmatising.

Therapeutic group work involves the bringing together of a carefully selected group of individuals to meet regularly with a therapist. The purpose of such work may include to assist each individual in emotional growth and personal problem-solving to identify and increase the use of strengths and to increase well-being.

Generally, therapeutic group work will be adopted for children and young people whose problems relate to social and/or relational difficulties. It is about helping people within a social setting to grow and develop their social skills, personal resources and their relationships with other people. In the school setting, therapeutic group work can have a variety of applications including prevention (e.g. peer pressure), problem-focused (e.g. parental separation) and information-focused (e.g. study skills) with the decision to offer group work often influenced by time constraints (Steen et al., 2007).

Small group work, facilitated by a mental health professional with knowledge and experience of how to use the group process to promote the individual, can be a useful intervention to attend to self-esteem and social difficulties. Within the group context the group process is viewed as an integral agent for change in individuals. Although beneficial outcomes can be achieved from educational and guidance group interventions, a counselling/therapy approach, which addresses internal difficulties in an environment of support and group cohesiveness and enables freedom of self-expression, has the potential for greater intra-personal gains relating to self-esteem and locus of control.

The culture of group work is somewhat informal, every member sitting in a circle, though there will usually be in-built safe working practices, including mutually consented boundaries and meeting in the same room, that provide privacy, appropriate space for movement, light and resources.

Carl Rogers describes the group as an organism with an inherent actualising tendency which means that, given a reasonably healthy psychological climate (i.e. characterised by the presence of Rogers' six conditions), the group will move towards health. Facilitation of group work ensures a climate that is psychologically safe for the participants through being authentic, offering empathic understanding and acceptance of each individual, and the group itself.

During therapeutic group work, participants can begin to see that they are not alone in experiencing difficulty in life and can find it comforting to hear that others have similar difficulties, or have already worked through an issue that is problematic for another group member. Yalom and Leszcz (2005) describe this therapeutic factor as 'universality'. Other therapeutic factors of group work identified by Yalom (Yalom and Leszcz, 2005) include:

Therapeutic factor	Definition
Altruism	Participants gain a boost to self-concept through extending help to other group participants
Instillation of hope	Members recognise that other participants' success can be helpful and they develop optimism for their own improvement
Imparting information	Education or advice provided by the therapist or group participants
Family re-enactment opportunity	To re-enact critical family dynamics with the group; the corrective recapitualisation of the participant's primary family experience
Development of socialising techniques	The group provides participants with an environment that fosters adaptive and effective communication
Imitative behaviour	Participants expand their personal knowledge and skills through the observation of group participants' self-exploration, working through and personal development

Therapeutic factor	Definition
Cohesiveness	Feelings of trust, belonging and togetherness experienced by the group participants
Existential factors	Participants accept responsibility for life decisions
Catharsis	Participants' release of strong feelings about past or present experiences
Interpersonal learning input	Participants gain personal insight about their interpersonal impact through feedback provided from other participants
Interpersonal learning output	Participants provide an environment that allows participants to interact in a more adaptive manner
Self-understanding	Participants gain insight into psychological motivation, underlying behaviour and emotional reactions

Yalom's therapeutic factors are consensually accepted and remain widely debated and researched.

Therapeutic Group Work as an Economic Intervention

A considerable benefit of the group modality is that professionals can work with a larger group of young people at one time. This possibility offers a degree of relief in child-based health-care systems which are often bound by restrictions on time and resources. A particular benefit is the opportunity to alleviate pressure on waiting lists, allowing clients to be seen sooner and helping prevent difficulties increasing or a decline in coping that may occur during a long waiting period (Freeman et al., 2004).

Selecting Participants for Group Work

It is important to consider the basis on which individuals are brought together to work in a group. Candidates for therapeutic group work should be offered a group that is best suited for their identified needs. This is different from forming a group based on a diagnosis or label. Consideration of the rights of children and young people, including full and appropriate consent, need to be an integral part of the recruiting process.

In order that a therapeutic group is able to function effectively some care needs to be given to group selection. Aspects that might need to be considered could include that need is compatible with the goals of the group, that the group is mixed (i.e. not a group of young people all of whom have behavioural difficulties – which might be in danger of entrenching existing self-images and become the 'naughty boys' group), motivation to participate and capacity to perform given group tasks. It is also useful to have a balance between those who speak easily in a group and those who find it more difficult.

The size of groups can range from between five and 12 participants, but eight participants would generally be considered as the optimal size. Whilst therapeutic groups will normally have one or two group facilitators, it is worth considering the benefits from having two facilitators. Greater opportunity for observing and noting the group dynamics is afforded, improved access to adult support when needed for certain tasks, less chance of disruption should a facilitator be unable to be present for any reason and less chance of leaving a group unattended in a situation that might require a facilitator to seek help.

It is recommended that prospective group work participants meet in advance with group facilitators to determine suitability. This provides the opportunity for the group facilitators to explain the purpose and format of group work and answer any questions that will help in deciding whether to participate.

Attributes of a Group Facilitator

We have found that to be effective group facilitators with young people we have had to be:

- flexible, willing to start where the participants can
- willing to really hear the young people and honour each person's unique contribution and frame of reference
- willing to allow conflict in the room and support others to be okay with this too
- unafraid of the process and non-defensive
- able to stay in relation
- attentive to the process and sensitively observant
- open to welcome different parts of participants and open to people changing
- 'in the moment'
- equipped with a sense of humour
- willing participants in the group ourselves and consider self-disclosing when it feels appropriate
- good advocates for the group outside of the group setting and represent it positively to others
- mindful of child protection issues and safety in the group
- consistent in maintaining a quietly positive invitation to participants that signals hope and welcomes potential
- warm, accepting and able to set clear boundaries

We have found that these attributes, that might all be part of one-to-one work or other group work too, have needed to be developed further in this setting which can feel more intense and issues amplified.

Corey (1981) identifies some behaviours which he sees as non-facilitative. These include, giving frequent interventions, pushing or manipulating the group towards their own unspoken goal, judging the success of a group by the dramatics (how many people cried), acting as an expert with superior knowledge and withholding of self, using 'we' statements, implying there is no free choice – 'now we will do an exercise', etc.

Life Cycle of the Group Dynamic in Group Work

Many theories exist about group work dynamics and life cycle. Though there is no definitive model of group stage development it is generally considered that the group process is fairly predictable and that therapeutic groups change and evolve over time (Arrow et al., 2005). This process of change can help the therapist to determine personal and group development as well and provides opportunity to evaluate and formulate specific interventions. Tuckman (1965), Slavin (1997) and Lewin have been highly influential in providing insight into the possible factors involved in group dynamics.

Rogers believed that therapeutic potentiality was influenced by having trust in the group process – 'I rely on the wisdom of the group' – with the group facilitators becoming participants and having influence but not control. Rogers trusted in the group's potential for recognising and dealing with unhealthy elements.

Studies of group development are generally consistent with the Tuckman model which considers the developmental stages (from conception to the end) to be the most significant dynamic. Tuckman identified five stages through which groups progress. The first stage is 'forming' and involves a number of group participants experiencing levels of uncertainty and anxiety, whilst others will experience feelings of positive anticipation or even excitement. Expectations about what might happen in the group will vary from member to member. Participants will be appraising how trustworthy or safe the group feels for them and will generally be looking to the facilitator for guidance. The second stage, 'storming', involves the formation of a group identity and is more challenging in character than the forming stage because of increased active participation and the emergence of personalities ranging from dominant to withdrawn. This is the time when the boundaries and skills of the facilitator will be tested and the importance of tolerance and patience, and being able to demonstrate firmness, fairness and support, will be imperative for the future triumph of the group. Tuckman's third stage, 'norming', involves participants having a sense of belonging, giving up their own interests to the interests of the group, and establishing group 'norms' that enable a sufficient sense of trust and safety. The resulting shift in the power dynamic means that participants will begin to feel comfortable enough to work together on given tasks with less reliance on the facilitator and will in effect be 'performing'. The final 'adjourning/ mourning' stage of the group process is concerned with the phase that includes ending the group work when the work is completed and the group breaks up. This will present varying levels of emotional challenge for participants depending upon their experience of change and former endings in their lives. Great consideration and care needs to be given to participants during this phase. Preparing participants for the end of the group work may include an acknowledgement and celebration of work accomplished and completed, facilitating the expression of feelings about ending and engaging in some kind of evaluation process.

The perspective of the group dynamic of Slavin differs from that of Tuckman with its emphasis on the importance of individual behaviours of group participants and the effect they have on the group dynamic. Individual participants begin to adopt roles that influence the direction of learning and group process that will be significantly impacted, for example, by the absence of a particular group member.

Lewin's approach to therapeutic group work focused on group behaviour. Lewin was responsible for coining the term 'group dynamics' and suggested that the individual exists in a psychological field of forces. He revealed the impact of the group on the individual and consequent change in behaviour followed by the individual then impacting on the group, which he defined as 'group pressure'.

History and Background

The therapeutic power inherent in groups was recognised in the early 1900s by Boston physician Joseph Pratt working with impoverished sufferers of tuberculosis. Pratt initiated group intervention for his patients for efficiency purposes and learned from observations that healing qualities emerged from the group process involving mutual concern and learning. The efficacy of the work demonstrated by Pratt sparked an interest in group work as a therapeutic intervention in the field of psychology based on the dual belief that many individual problems are social in origin and that people sharing a common problem can be helpful to each other. The formation of Alcoholics Anonymous is a notable example. The ensuing widespread practice of group therapy and the growing body of literature commending the benefits of group work resulted in firmly establishing its practice across populations and settings.

The developmental roots of therapeutic group work with children and young people are founded in the social and theoretical changes relating to psychology. A noteworthy example is that of S.R. Slavson and his role in the establishment of the American Group Psychotherapy Association. Slavson became interested in social group work within his New York neighbourhood in 1911. His educational convictions, viewed as progressive, determined the nature of the group work. In 1934 he introduced a child guidance clinic for small groups of socially-alienated girls. Structured activities using arts and crafts materials allowed complete freedom of self-expression devoid of any didactic or judge-mental elements in the belief that self-expression and creativity are the key to human happiness and constructive social adjustment.

From the 1950s great strides were made towards the development of group therapy with increasing focus extending to other areas including education and child guid-ance. A humanistic approach was brought to group psychotherapy by Dreikers, Adler and Rogers and significant contributions by Corsini, Rosenberg and Berne, amongst others, helped to illuminate the role of group dynamics and environment in successful therapeutic outcomes.

Theoretical Underpinning

A person-centred or child-centred theoretical orientation provides an appropriate context for group therapy and is in line with contemporary guidance and policy for psychological interventions with children and young people (e.g. the UN Charter on Children's Rights). Therapeutic group work with children and young people is rooted in the humanistic tradition of psychology and Carl Rogers' theory of person-centred practice which centres on the individual's potential to be self-directive within a facilitative environment. A doctoral student of Rogers, Virginia Axline (1947), out-lined important child-centred principles for providing an effective framework for group therapy practice. They include: that the therapist develops a warm, friendly relationship with the child; the child is accepted exactly as he/she is; that only those limitations that are necessary to anchor the therapy to the world of reality are estab-lished; that the child is made aware of his/her responsibility in the relationship; that a deep respect is maintained for the child's ability to solve his/her own problems if given an opportunity to do so; that the responsibility to make choices and to institute change is the child's.

Models of Group Contracting and Maintenance

As in all therapeutic work it is imperative to establish clear boundaries. At the outset of group work the boundaries can be incorporated into a contract which involves participants of the group, including the facilitators, working together to produce a statement, usually in writing, of the general responsibilities and expectations for the course of the group work. As the group develops, it is possible that the contract may need to be reviewed and revised to reflect altering conditions and expectations. Revisions happen as a result of increased meaning and significance of the contract for participants brought about from experiential learning and group process. Some group contracting models require participants to sign the contract, agreeing to abide by its conditions. A copy of the group contract is generally available for reference at every session.

The content of the group contract should reflect that it is designed to provide a safe and cohesive environment for participants including the valuing of one another. It may include agreements about conflict resolution, attendance expectations, terms of withdrawal from the group, confidentiality, physical contact limits, the right to 'pass' on an activity and how feedback, evaluation and information are handled and shared.

Regular attendance and punctuality increase value for participants and contribute to creating a climate of cohesiveness and purpose. Participants may need to be helped to appreciate that their participation makes an important contribution to the group process and is therefore helpful not only personally but also to the other group participants. Leaving a group is an important process because of the feelings involved. The terms might usefully encourage discussion of any concerns a member may have initially within the group so that efforts can be made to find a satisfactory resolution.

An atmosphere of trust is essential for group participants to feel safe enough to share material and disclose their feelings and problems. Participants should be asked not to discuss anything outside the group, using the principle of 'what is said in the group stays in the group'. It is the group facilitator's job to help each member understand that it is their responsibility to protect the names and identities of fellow group participants. At the same time, because sharing themes of the group work and their personal material with significant others can be an important element of personal growth for participants, the facilitator should not discourage it as long as it does not contravene confidentiality boundaries. An element of safety can be provided by including the right to 'pass' on any activity that may cause a member of the group to feel uncomfortable and helps to establish trust that may enable fuller participation as confidence grows.

Contracting will also need to make clear the limitations of what can remain private and that the group facilitators have an obligation under child safeguarding requirements to share with relevant parties any disclosures that indicate serious risk of harm.

Generally group contracts will specify that there should be no uninvited physical contact. This is important because young people will have different personal histories and interpretations of what touch means. Exceptions include drama and dance groups where touch will form a natural and normative part of the group work.

Context of the Group

Therapeutic group work acknowledges that personal well-being depends to some extent on how the individual constructs the self in social terms and the strong relationship between emotion and social interaction. This approach takes a holistic view of the complex range of human need, conceiving human problems in context.

Methods of Outcome Evaluation

Evaluating the outcomes of group therapy can be useful to determine whether the intervention is suitable to a child's needs and is achieving the goals that were identified at assessment. An evaluation can provide important information on the effectiveness of the content of group work as well as ideas for improvements. Essential characteristics of outcomes evaluation include the use of reflective practice, clinical supervision, gathering feedback from participants about their experience of the intervention, and overall authoritative monitoring and assessment.

Evaluation may involve measuring numerous outcomes such as behaviour changes, attainment of skills, group process, goal attainment, and participant satisfaction. It may take the form both of quantitative and qualitative assessment measures and in work with children and young people may also involve taking into account assessments obtained from significant others such as parents and teachers. Debate surrounds this practice because of the potential for bias and personal interest influencing assessment.

An Example of Therapeutic Group Work

The group was a closed group of 12 students and we met together for one and a half terms. All the students were aged 14 to 15 years old and had been selected by their year head for a variety of reasons. The presenting issues from the school's perspective were mainly behavioural issues which affected the school, for example 'challenging behaviour', 'withdrawn', 'violent', 'rude to staff', 'aggressive' and 'silly in class'. With only this information about the students the group was formed, so our beginning point with this group was knowing their behavioural history at school but very little about them as people. What unfolded in the group were the group members' individual stories. These were moving and helped us to make sense of their behavioural issues.

One of the challenges in this setting is to collect and assemble a group in the designated room. These particular students were drawn from a pool of students who were seen as 'problem students' – those who the staff found 'difficult to work with'. It was our task to try to move the students through the school in a group. Moving around the school together caused problems for other classes as the group were often shouting, disruptive and knocking on classroom doors en route. This can present problems for counsellors working within a school environment as the role of group facilitator may become compromised by enforcing discipline, and of course the rules of the environment need to be respected if any group is to go ahead. The tension between these attitudes is always present for a school counsellor and working with groups seems to highlight this issue.

Our experience with this particular group was that once we had arrived at the room it was always difficult to begin. We would invite an opening circle. We found that by asking each member of the circle to share the best and the worst part of their week this helped to invite them to a reflective place. This process was a struggle to achieve. During the opening circle, we modelled trying to listen respectfully whilst openly acknowledging the difficulties of speaking over each other and striving to manage this without being critical or telling the participants off. We were seeking to invite a different experience of mutual respect for each other in the group, helping to create a safe space where all the participants could share openly.

C:	The best bit of my week was …
D:	The best bit of his week was shagging his girlfriend.
	(all the group participants laughing and commenting 'whooo, yeah', etc.)
D:	Yeah – he thinks he's fit, innit?
	(all the group participants laughing and commenting 'whooo, yeah', etc.)
C:	Shu' up.
D:	No, you shu' up!
	(the whole group just began taking sides and shouting 'shu'up' at each other)
	We waited for a break in the shouting.
Peter:	(to C, said with warmth) It didn't feel like you really got a chance to speak C … do you want to carry on?
	The therapist's response here was just enough to create some space and allow the group to continue, and we were able to complete the opening round. L was the first person to speak after the opening round. She told the group that she had noticed how dark it was this morning on her way to school and said how she hated it and it made her feel a bit 'rotten'.
J:	What d'you mean rotten?
L:	Well … a bit sad I think.
Ros:	You feel a bit sad.
L:	Yeah sad, because it was in the winter when I had to go and live with my Nan and she lives so far away from the school that I had to leave early when it was dark … (silence) and I think the dark reminds me of that time.

F: Why were you living with your Nan?

L: It was when my Mum died.
        (There was absolute silence while the whole group watched and listened attentively and a palpable feeling of warmth and empathy entered the room)

C: I didn't know your Mum had died.
        (Various group members said 'nor did I', 'how sad', 'that's awful')

C: I don't know how to say this ... I just feel so sad for you ... and I want to say ... I'm here for you.

L: (sat quietly for a while – then cried – L got up and moved towards C and they hugged each other and the whole group cried together).

This example demonstrates the capacity that group members have for listening to each other and for reaching out with empathy. The group moved from all shouting at each other in the early part of the session to being able to be empathic without the need for 'facilitation'.

Research

A systematic scoping review for BACP (Harris and Pattison, 2004) reviews a number of controlled trials and meta analyses that include group therapy interventions for children and young people. Group play therapy (Bratton et al., 2005; Danger and Landreth, 2005), group CBT (Kaufman et al., 2005; Carpentier et al., 2006), school-based group psychotherapy (Layne et al., 2008) and group humanistic and interpersonal therapies (Shechtman and Pastor, 2005; Rosselló et al., 2008) all show some evidence of effectiveness. Baskin et al. (2010), examining data from 107 studies, found that treatment groups that were predominantly male or female did better than mixed gender groups and suggest that the flexibility of schools to offer multi-faceted interventions seemed to demonstrate an advantage of the school setting over mental health clinic settings. In a randomised controlled trial by Stice et al. (2010), adolescents with mild to moderate depression were randomised to either supportive group therapy vs. CBT group therapy vs. CBT bibliotherapy vs. controls. In this study those who received supportive therapy showed comparable benefits to those in CBT. These benefits were sustained at two year follow-ups and were much better than the control group.

The BACP scoping review also identifies that future research needs to be rigorous and transparent to capture the complexity of routine practice with this client group. The authors recommend a wider range of research methodologies, attention to the transfer of research findings into clinical settings, consideration of the relationship between age and treatment outcome specifically adapting interventions to the different developmental stages of adolescence and pre-adolescence, and research into the long-term impact of interventions with children and young people. They also note the relative absence of research relating to certain issues, particularly self-harm and eating disorders.

In a recent research review of school-based counselling in UK secondary schools, Cooper (2013) highlights that, both for young people themselves and other stakeholders, there tends to be a preference for school-based counselling services that offer a wider array of interventions beyond the one-to-one counselling setting. It further identifies that there is evidence to suggest that mental health and well-being interventions are more helpful when a 'whole school' approach is adopted, targeting interventions at the wider school context and the groups within it, rather than just the individual young person's problems and needs.

Cooper identifies how the extent to which counsellors can expand their services will depend on the resources available but also identifies that there may also be issues of training, and of how the school-based counsellor role is conceptualised.

Summary

- The key benefit of therapeutic group work is that it results in interaction and social contact which does not occur in the individual client and therapist model
- The group context offers a method of intervention that acknowledges individual problems in relation to the wider social world
- Therapeutic group work is a suitable intervention in a variety of contexts such as education and family work for problem-solving, social skills building and addressing socially-constructed problems
- An understanding of issues for children and young people and related mental health problems is necessary for implementing effective support
- Awareness of the emotional and social aspects of child development is important for understanding how social situations impact on child well-being
- Therapeutic group work acknowledges the relevance of group process as a helping technique in personal development
- There are a variety of methods for measuring the outcomes of interventions. The choice of method may be governed by available resources
- Preliminary discussion and preparation are key factors in conducting successful group work
- The environment in which therapeutic group work takes place needs to be supportive, with a therapist whose approach is sensitive and respectful
- Feedback from group work participants and other interested parties is a necessary part of the evaluation process and provides a cross-reference against group work aims and objectives

- Therapeutic group work has a proven record of significant benefit and is becoming a common choice for therapeutic use. If introduced at a grass-roots level, such as within schools, it can provide a great opportunity to address specific social and emotional needs preventatively to support healthy development as part of a school well-being service

Reflective Questions

1 What kinds of characteristics are common to group work development across different theories?

Common characteristics across theories include:

- that each group experience will be unique
- that each participant will experience group work in their own unique way
- that the culture and environment in which the group is set will impact on the experience.

2 When might therapeutic group work not be suitable?

If a child or young person is unable to engage because of issues of significant risk of self-harm or suicide, or if the group setting cannot provide sufficient support to contain their distress or behaviour this may preclude them from being able to engage with or benefit from a therapeutic group setting.

3 What might be some of the advantages of the therapeutic group?

As therapeutic group work is a social activity it has intrinsic advantages on two levels. Humans are by nature social beings and working in a group is therefore within the realms of natural human experience. Being part of a group provides access to a variety of insights and experiences not possible in an individual setting. Working in a group represents in microcosm the family, society, and civilisation.

4 What are some of the ethical considerations of group work?

Group facilitators have responsibility for protecting the welfare of each individual group member and for ensuring that the group as a whole functions in a way that benefits everyone involved. The ethical concerns relevant to individual psychotherapy apply in the same way in group work. Ethical issues specific to group work involve the group selection process, screening, diversity and social contact amongst group participants outside of the group. An important ethical consideration is to determine member compatibility with the goals of the group and for the potential member to determine whether the group is compatible with their personal goals.

Group facilitators should be fully familiar with the ethical frameworks and guidance of associated professional bodies. They are required to be sufficiently competent to lead a group, have the adequate training, experience and qualifications necessary to understand group process and be able to respond appropriately to the inevitable conflicts and challenges of group work. Adequate supervision needs to be sought by group facilitators for the duration of the work. Great care needs to be given to planning the work and recruitment of participants including ensuring their informed consent. A clear understanding of how to deal with confidentiality and disclosure is needed along with establishing and maintaining boundaries, minimising risks, managing premature withdrawals from the group and ending the group in an ethically sound manner. Group facilitators should be aware of their power in a group and careful not to impose their own values on the group. They need to be mindful of the limits and appropriate use of personal disclosure. Group session notes should not make reference to individual group participants by name or other identifying information. There should be adequate provision for follow-up of any issues arising out of the group work.

Learning Activities

Scenarios – how would you respond?

1. The head has asked you to organise a group to address an escalation in bullying that has been identified within the school.
2. A year head has given you a list of boys who really need to 'work on their anger' and asks you to sort it out.
3. A group of girls, including one of your current clients, asks if they can all come together to talk in a group.
4. A teacher who you know really values your work asks you to help her with her class tomorrow after registration as she needs to address their disruptive behaviour.

Group facilitator self-evaluation

Ask yourself the following questions:

- Am I genuinely interested in people?
- What personal needs are met by my being a group facilitator?
- Am I authentically myself in the group, or do I have a need to direct the participants' lives?
- Am I willing to take time to understand others, or do I force them to follow my agenda?
- Do I offer a proper model for what I hope and expect the members in my group to become?
- What kind of model am I? (derived from Corey, 1981)

Further Reading

Bratton, S.C., Ray, D., Rhine, T. and Jones, L. (2005) 'The efficacy of play therapy with children: A meta-analytic review of treatment outcomes', *Professional Psychology: Research and Practice*, 36 (4): 376–390.

Carpentier, M.Y., Silovsky, J.F. and Chaffin, M. (2006) 'Randomized trial of treatment for children with sexual behaviour problems: 10-year follow-up', *Journal of Consulting and Clinical Psychology*, 74 (3): 482–488.

Cooper, M. (2013) *School-Based Counselling in UK Secondary Schools: A Review and Critical Evaluation*. Glasgow: University of Strathclyde.

Danger, S. and Landreth, G. (2005) 'Child-centred group play therapy with children with speech difficulties', *International Journal of Play Therapy*, 14 (1): 81–102.

Kaufman, N.K., Rohde, P., Seeley, J.R., et al. (2005) 'Potential mediators of cognitive-behavioral therapy for adolescents with co-morbid major depression and conduct disorder', *Journal of Consulting and Clinical Psychology*, 73 (1): 38–46.

Layne, C.M., Saltzman, W.R., Poppleton L., et al. (2008) 'Effectiveness of a school-based group psychotherapy program for war exposed adolescents: A randomized controlled trial', *Journal of the American Academy of Child and Adolescent Psychiatry*, 47 (9): 1048–1062.

McLaughlin, C., Holliday, C., Clarke, B. and Llie, S. (2013) *Research on Counselling and Psychotherapy with Children and Young People: A Systematic Scoping Review of Evidence for Its Effectiveness from 2003–2011*. Lutterworth: BACP.

(Continued)

(Continued)

Rosselló, J., Bernal, G. and Rivera-Medina, C. (2008) 'Individual and group CBT and IPT for Puerto Rican adolescents with depressive symptoms', *Cultural Diversity and Ethnic Minority Psychology*, 14 (3): 234–245.

Shechtman, Z. and Pastor, R. (2005) 'Cognitive-behavioural and humanistic group treatment for children with learning disabilities: A comparison of outcomes and process', *Journal of Counseling Psychology*, 52 (3): 322–336.

Stice, E., Rohde, P., Gau, J.M. and Wade, E. (2010) 'Efficacy trial of a brief cognitive-behavioral depression prevention program for high-risk adolescents: Effects at 1- and 2-year follow-up', *Journal of Consulting and Clinical Psychology*, 78: 856–867.

Westergaard, J. (2009) *Effective Group Work with Young People*. Berkshire: Open University Press.

Yalom, I.D. and Leszcz, M. (2005) *The Theory and Practice of Group Psychotherapy*. 5th edn. New York: Basic Books.

Online Resources

BACP website: www.bacp.co.uk/, especially the BACP Children and Young People Division and the Competences for Working with Children and Young People.

Counselling MindEd: http://counsellingminded.com, especially the modules on the Counselling Context, CMD 0104–0108, and CMD 0110.

15

Endings

Dee C. Ray

This chapter includes:

- A review of outcome goals to guide the ending process in order to improve intentionality when approaching the ending of the counselling relationship
- Unique themes encountered by therapists in ending therapy with children, including developmental and attachment considerations
- Types of endings encountered in most counselling relationships and how to manage endings when they come too soon
- Affective elements that impact a therapist's decision-making and approach to ending and children's affective and behavioural responses to ending counselling
- Skills, scripts, and activities to facilitate the process of ending

Introduction

The purpose of this chapter is to explore the closing phase of the counselling relationship specific to the developmental level of children and review attitudes, obstacles, and skills related to effective approaches to ending.

As a therapist for over 20 years, I have experienced ending a great number of therapeutic relationships with children. In my early career I worked with young adolescents in a residential setting where endings varied from abrupt runaways to very satisfying completion of therapeutic relationships. In later years, as a school counsellor, my endings were often softened by the reassurance that I would see the children throughout the school day, even if I no longer engaged in counselling with them. And in recent years, I have worked at a university-based counselling centre where I teach, supervise and facilitate the counselling of children in an agency setting and a school outreach programme. Currently, my role entails ending counselling relationships on a weekly basis. As I supervise the ending of counselling relationships facilitated by my supervisees and students and as I experience my own endings with children, I recognise and honour the emotional process involved in this final stage of the counsellor–child relationship.

Endings start at the beginning. The therapist's job is to facilitate expression and functionality so that each child can move toward optimal development. The ending of therapy must be part of the therapist's vision at initial contact with a child. The therapist visualises the child at a point in time when obstacles to growth are removed and the child progresses to a state of interdependent and healthy functioning. The therapist sees the end as the real beginning for the child. Ironically, the goal of therapy is to end therapy.

Ending is typically viewed as the resolution of the counselling process. However, closing therapy may possibly be an active part of the counselling process that allows children to create meaning (Harrison, 2009) or experience new ways of coping with loss (Many, 2009). Within the process of ending, the therapist and child collaborate to make sense of the counselling relationship and develop new directions for growth. Ending is the catalyst for the child's movement into the world minus the extra emotional and behavioural supports provided by the therapist.

Although the closing phase is critical to all endings of counselling with children, the level of emphasis or time spent on ending is affected by several factors. First, endings in more relationally-oriented treatment relationships necessitate more emphasis by the therapist on the ending and loss of a meaningful relationship (Joyce et al., 2007). Brief and skill-oriented therapies may require less reflection by both therapist and child. Additionally, younger children may require less verbalisation and reflection on the counselling process usually addressed in endings. Extensive talk and requests by the therapist to verbally address the closing of therapy may be confusing and disconcerting to young children due to their limited ability to grasp timelines. Finally, premature ending initiated by a parent or managed care entity may influence a therapist's presentation and processing of ending with a child. Timing, emphasis, and approaches to endings are addressed throughout this chapter.

Outcomes of Endings

Because ending is a phase of the therapeutic process, there are goals to guide this phase just as there are goals for other stages of treatment. Joyce et al. (2007) identified three outcomes related to successful endings in adult therapy that can be applied to working with children, including the consolidation of therapy, resolution of relationship and preparedness for progress.

Consolidation of Therapy Process

The first outcome is consolidation of the therapy process and gains made in treatment. When described within the context of adult therapy, this phase requires a review of the therapeutic relationship since the beginning of therapy and self-assessment by the client regarding changes in functioning. Although a verbal review of therapy would be a meaningless task for a young child, this outcome can be addressed through skilful therapist introduction of ending and the child's natural response.

Case Study   Seth

Seth was a seven-year-old client who I saw over eight months for selective mutism. I introduced ending in the following way, 'Seth, do you remember when you first came here and you never talked at school?' Seth nodded. I continued, 'And now you figured out how to feel good about talking at both home and school? Also, you used to never talk to me but now you talk to me a lot?'. Seth nodded. He said, 'Now I talk all the time.' I responded, 'Yep, you sure do. Now that you're feeling good about yourself and you can figure out ways to feel good about talking, I think that it's time for us to stop seeing each other. We'll have four more playtimes together.' Seth nodded and then responded, 'I also used to act like a dog but I don't do that anymore. I talk instead of bark.'

The brief verbalisation by reviewing Seth's progress served to consolidate Seth's view of the changes he made. Seth further acknowledged his growth by identifying a previous coping skill that kept him from connecting to others (barking) that he replaced with a more functional skill (talking).

Resolution of Therapeutic Relationship

The second outcome of endings is the resolution of issues within the therapeutic relationship. In most cases, children develop intimate relationships with their therapists. During the ending phase, the child will experience a sense of loss and will respond to that loss. The success of this outcome is related to the child's view of the therapist and view of self outside of the relationship with the therapist.

In the session following the announcement of ending to Seth, I gave a five-minute warning for the end of the session. He threatened to cut my neck with a rubber knife if I stood up from my chair to leave. After threatening me a few times, I responded, 'You don't want me to leave, but our time is up for today.' He said, 'I guess you can go.' In our second to final session, Seth painted a picture of a woman handing a bouquet of flowers to a child. He did not describe the picture but he presented it to me by saying, 'This is for you.' Both the threats and painting were new behaviours for Seth in which he had not engaged until ending was presented. These behaviours appeared to be his attempt to let me go and acknowledge what he had been given in our relationship.

Preparedness for Progress

The third outcome of endings is related to the child's preparedness for continuing progress and functioning following counselling (Joyce et al., 2007). For this outcome, the child internalises the counselling process and the therapist's role in that process. In other words, the child reveals self-reliance and confidence in abilities to work through future challenges.

In Seth's final sessions, he initiated a new type of play with a toy he had not used prior to the endings phase. Seth picked up a turtle and placed it in the sandbox. Seth drowned the turtle in the sand and then brought the turtle back to the surface over and over again. He verbalised, 'This turtle just keeps coming back to life'. The continued resurgence of the turtle seemed to imply that Seth knew he was resilient and could thrive when things get tough. He acknowledged his readiness to face the challenges before him.

Considerations for Child Endings

Development

A child's understanding of ending is directly related to age and developmental stage. In the preoperational stage of cognitive development (ages 2–6; Piaget, 1965 [1932]), a young child has difficulty grasping the permanence of loss and timelines set for an impending loss. Giving a young child a five-week notice for ending of therapy may be understood as a lengthy time period. If not reminded, the child is surprised by the quick end of therapy and has difficulty managing the processing of ending. Yet, a child in concrete cognitive operations (ages 6–12) may assume that if the counselling relationship is ended, then logically she will never be able to see her counsellor again, leading to significant grief. A therapist may need to reassure the child that the relationship can be continued at a later point or the child can contact the therapist after ending.

Due to egocentricity states of children, children may feel that therapy is ending due to something they have done wrong or that they have been bad in some way. Helping children understand the reasons for ending therapy, and reminding them as needed throughout the closing process, is one way to address a child's tendency to interpret events negatively (Moore et al., 2008). Also, young children may often misunderstand the permanency of ending or they may come to understand permanency only after weeks of not seeing the therapist. They may gleefully run out of the therapist's office with no goodbye after the last session. In these cases, the therapist may send a note following the final session or suggest the parent facilitate a note from the child to the therapist if the child needs to send a last goodbye.

Another factor related to endings and development is acknowledgement of the child's need to revisit issues related to treatment as they reach new developmental stages. Even if children have progressed well through therapy, meeting all treatment goals, it is likely that they will revisit old issues with each new developmental phase. In a case where a six-year-old child has been sexually abused and the child has worked through fear and pain related to the abuse, it is likely that the same child will revisit issues related to cognitive understanding of those events when he reaches a concrete level of operations, attempting to make cognitive sense of the situation. And again, when the same child reaches puberty, there may be a need for extra support as the child attempts to understand self as a sexual being. Therapists help parents understand that many issues related to child challenges are not simply resolved in one period of time. There is a need to encourage parents to seek therapy when they see their children struggling at subsequent developmental stages. In the ending phase of child treatment, the therapist emphasises the fluidity of development and the likelihood of additional therapy.

Attachment

Endings are addressed sporadically and incompletely in the literature and endings in child therapy are even less addressed. However, one element that is emphasised in the few manuscripts addressing endings is the relationship between ending, attachment, and loss. Joyce et al. (2007) claimed that a history of serious loss during critical developmental periods increases the importance of endings for adult therapy. In humanistically and psychodynamically-inclined therapies, the therapist works with diligence to facilitate a relationship with a child that emphasises trust, acceptance, genuineness, and warmth. If a child is able to perceive these therapist attitudes, an attachment bond is formed and valued. Ending is a direct threat to this bond and may cause feelings of grief, loss, abandonment, anger or rejection (Moore et al., 2008).

Due to the fact that children presented to therapy typically have multiple risk factors, often related to significant histories of loss and abandonment, the issue of attachment is a key feature of treatment and endings (Many, 2009). Children seek the stability of a therapeutic relationship and are often positively responsive to such a relationship. When such a relationship is established and treatment goals are met, a conflict ensues regarding how therapy can end while the child maintains relational gains. Additionally, the child does not just lose the therapeutic relationship but also loses the stability of therapy itself, such as the therapy room, materials, rituals, and people related to therapy, such as administrative staff (Zilberstein, 2008). The loss is relationally intense and structurally broad.

Historically, the ending phase signified a definitive end to therapy. Therapists were seen as crossing over professional boundaries with clients if they maintained contact following the completion of therapy. In recent literature, it is suggested that a therapist consider ending as transitional, not resolved (Zilberstein, 2008). Suggestions related to addressing attachment issues within the ending phase offer the therapist various opportunities for contact with the child. A therapist may taper sessions from once a week to once every two weeks to once a month as a move toward ending. Therapists may provide follow-up sessions at various intervals to check-in with the child, such as once every six months or year. Providing children with transitional objects such as pictures and crafts during the ending phase is suggested. Additionally, a therapist may want to provide the child with a way to contact the therapist following the closing of therapy through notes or phone calls. With opportunity for subsequent contact, the therapist allows the child to transition from the therapeutic relationship on a timeline that fits the child's needs.

Both Many (2009) and Zilberstein (2008) suggest that a gradual and transitional approach to ending offers a child with attachment difficulties an experience outside of her reference, an opportunity for non-traumatic loss. While preparing the child for loss, the therapist will also want to prepare the parent for the child's loss. Collaborating with parents regarding time and structure of closing offers parents an opportunity to face their own losses and prepare to support their children. The parent's acceptance of the end of therapy helps them to model acceptance for the child.

The process and structure of endings has not been explored in the research. The field of psychotherapy lacks knowledge on clients' responses to endings or its effects on counselling outcome. Although some counsellors believe that endings should be final with no contact between therapist and clients, others believe that tapering of sessions or continued contact after ending is the most effective way to close the counselling process. Yet, there is no research to substantiate either practice.

Types of Endings

Natural Endings

In the ideal therapy world, therapy is completed when a child, parent, and therapist agree that treatment goals have been met, emotional needs have been addressed, and the child is ready to operate independently from the therapist. This leads to a natural ending. Most child therapists experience natural endings in a minority of cases. Rarely do therapists, parents and children come to the same conclusion at the same time. Natural endings may be initiated by any of the three parties involved in therapy. Therapists are probably the most likely to initiate a natural ending by highlighting therapeutic progress with the parent and child. Children will often initiate ending through verbal or behavioural signs such as 'I want to go to football practice instead of coming here', or being bored in session. Parents are often hesitant to end therapy if progress has been made due to fears of regression. They tend to address the topic of ending hesitantly: 'I think he's doing better but I'm just not sure if this is the right time to end.'

Premature Endings

Client/Parent-Initiated

Premature ending initiated by the client, more typically initiated by the parent in child therapy, is also referred to as dropping out of therapy. The dropout rate is cited with a substantial range depending on individual studies but, on average, appears to be hovering at approximately 50 per cent (Venable and Thompson, 1998). Often, therapy ends abruptly at the will of the parent without therapist or child consent. The abrupt ending to therapy is disconcerting for a child and may result in the child's interpretation that she did something wrong or that the therapist no longer wants to see her (Ray, 2011). Child therapists first address endings in initial parent consultations, explaining the need for a planned approach to ending therapy. When parents decide that ending is in order before the therapist or child agrees, the therapist makes a concerted effort to contact the parent to plead the case for one last session with the child. If parents do not concede to bring the child in for a last session, the therapist may decide to send a note as one method of ending.

> **Example Note**
>
> Dear Michael, I am writing this note to tell you that I cherished our time together for the last few weeks. I enjoyed talking with you and getting to know you. I hope that you enjoy your karate lessons. Please take care of yourself and remember how special you are. Thank you for sharing time with me. Suzanne

Research has focused on variables related to premature endings with children, emphasising characteristics of clients that lead clients to end therapy early. Kazdin and Mazurick (1994) found children at one site were more likely to prematurely end therapy at early stages (six or fewer sessions) if children had higher impairment in conduct, academic and social behaviours, parents were younger, children came from a single-parent home, parents identified with a minority group, or parents reported higher levels of stress. Children were more likely to prematurely end therapy at later stages (7–14 sessions) if mothers were younger, children had a history of antisocial problems, children had lower intellect scores, children were in a household with a non-biological parent, or children had poor adaptive functioning reported at school. Venable and Thompson (1998) found that caregivers who were highly self-critical or held personal guilt for the predicament of the child were more likely to initiate premature endings. It appears that reasons for ending prematurely are cross-cultural, as found by McCabe (2002), who reported that Mexican-American children were more likely to drop out of therapy if parents had a lower level of education, perceived barriers to treatment initially, believed that increased discipline addressed emotional problems, or experienced lack of client–therapist ethnic match.

Children who dropped out of play therapy at one site were more likely to be from single-parent homes, have younger mothers, or have mothers with lower levels of education (Campbell et al., 2000). And parents at another site who had very high or very low expectations for therapy were more likely to complete therapy while parents with moderate expectations were most likely to end prematurely (Nock and Kazdin, 2001). Overall, children with higher levels of behavioral problems were more likely to end therapy prematurely (Tsai and Ray, 2011). This extensive research on premature endings offers explanations for why child clients drop out from therapy early but it offers no insight into best practices for the process of endings. Because endings are a significant stage of therapy, there is a need for researchers to focus on variables related to process and structure of the final stage of therapy.

Therapist-Initiated

When therapists initiate premature endings, typically referred to as forced endings, a client is informed by the therapist that counselling will be ended even if treatment goals have not been met. Forced endings are usually triggered by professional and personal changes in the therapist's life such as moves, new professional opportunities, or changes in family situations. Although forced endings are to be expected, they are particularly difficult to address in child therapy. It is often hard for a child to understand that he will be losing his therapist because she is having a baby or moving with a new partner. Forced endings are more likely to be met with feelings of rejection by the child and feelings of guilt by the therapist.

Pearson (1998) and Bostic et al. (1996) suggested several implications for counselling related to forced endings. Forced endings require the therapist to conduct a thorough review of each child's case and consider the child's response to an unexpected ending. If a therapist is open in sharing why he is leaving and where he is going, such openness helps to soothe the child's personalisation of the ending. Genuineness on the part of the therapist by sharing emotions about leaving helps a child feel valued. Additionally, a therapist should expect a child to respond in a variety of ways from apathy, to anger, to sadness. The therapist is open to the child's response and need for expression of the loss. Wittenberg (1999) emphasised the therapist's emotions of guilt, followed by defensiveness, that sometimes interfere with the therapist's ability to hold the child's emotions. Therapists benefit by recognising their own ambivalent feelings and consulting with colleagues. Additionally, allowing children to have subsequent contact through notes and letters can be helpful to the separation process. In the case of child therapy, Moore et al. (2008) cautioned against accepting children with attachment disruptions in therapy if the therapist knows that treatment will end early due to forced ending situations.

Managed Care

Often, ending of therapy is decided by a third party who is uninvolved in the process yet a decision-maker about length of therapy. In these cases, the therapist is typically aware of the limited time for therapy at the beginning of the relationship. Although children may be developmentally limited in their understanding of time, facilitating therapy under management of an outside entity requires that children are fully informed of therapy time limits from the beginning of the relationship. If only eight sessions are allowed, the therapist should emphasise in the first session that 'we will meet together eight times'. Clarity helps children understand the concreteness of the limitations. Just as in adult therapy, children will make a choice consciously or unconsciously regarding how they will use their time in therapy and the limitations of the therapeutic relationship.

Avoiding Endings

Child therapy is particularly susceptible to a therapist's or child's desire to prolong therapy and avoid the ending of the relationship. Because children are in a constant state of development, therapists might aspire to be involved in each developmental stage or issue to ensure the child is progressing well. There is a tendency for some therapists to prolong therapy until the child's situation is 'perfect' – waiting for the parents to establish complete stability or the school to offer a perfect learning environment. Moore et al. (2008) warned that prolonging therapy may be motivated by a therapist's personal issues and may inadvertently undermine the independent functioning of the child and parent. Boyer and Hoffman (1993) found that counsellors were more anxious regarding endings if they had a personal history of loss or if they perceived the client would be sensitive to loss. Knowing that almost all children are sensitive to loss, especially children with attachment issues, may inspire therapists to continue therapy beyond necessity. In supervision of new therapists, I often find that they must be prompted to end therapy when it appears that treatment goals have been met. Often therapists feel that they provide the only predictable stability in the child's life and hesitate to end the relationship. Such feelings prompt discussion about the therapist's role in the child's life and counter transference issues. With supervision or consulting support, therapists work through their hesitancies and intervene for the benefit of the child.

A child's hesitancy or reaction to ending therapy is complicated. As a normal reaction to ending, a child might regress in behaviour and emotions, reverting back to negative coping skills used in the beginning of the relationship. Often, the therapist can be reassured that this is a natural response to ending the relationship and the child will return quickly to the new behaviours acquired during therapy. Yet, children often seem to organically know what is in their best interests when provided with a stable and emotionally-supportive environment. Hence, when it appears that a child does not want to end therapy, the therapist needs to ask if she should take the child's lead and extend the relationship. A close attunement between therapist and child, along with the therapist's trust in the child, typically result in most effective therapeutic judgement. If consideration of all factors does not clarify the therapist's direction, a therapist may want to offer ending as a break for a few weeks instead of ending therapy permanently. Interrupting therapy for one or two months may provide clarity regarding the child's readiness for ending.

Approaches to Endings

Timing

There is no clear timeline suggested for the ending phase of child counselling. Some have suggested two to three sessions (Moore et al., 2008), yet others encourage four to six months (Wittenberg, 1999). Adult therapy guidelines tend to indicate that the longer a therapy relationship has been established, the longer time is needed for termination. Yet, developmental considerations of children indicate that drawn out periods of endings may actually induce anxiety. Knowledge and attunement with the child, as well as a collaborative relationship with parents, help inform the therapist in decision-making about ending timelines. However, a minimum of three to five sessions is encouraged for most children. Additionally, the view of endings as a transitional period for children may also influence a therapist's approach to timing. For example, an endings phase of frequent weekly sessions may be shorter if the therapist plans to taper to monthly sessions.

Preparing Parents

Parents are often hesitant to end therapy, especially if they have established a trusting and stable relationship with the therapist just as their child has. In these cases, the therapist has become part of the family system and it is difficult for the parents to visualise themselves without the support of the therapist. The therapist presents the subject of ending to the parent before the subject is approached with the child. The therapist may need to provide several sessions of support to the parent in preparation of ending. During this time, the parent is advised to not inform the child of impending ending until the parent is confident about the ending of therapy.

In some cases, the ending phase will consist of reminding the parent of the skills s/he acquired over the time of therapy and continuing to bring up the inevitability of ending. Meetings with the parent may become more frequent to provide emotional support for ending. Once the parent agrees to ending, the therapist will introduce ending to the child. Therapists are very encouraging during this phase of therapy, reminding parents of their growth that correlated with the child's development. The therapist will discuss options for returning if the parent feels that the child is in need of therapy following closure of therapy.

Preparing the Child

The therapist needs to offer a developmentally appropriate explanation for ending therapy. Although some children may be unable to process extensively, they may be able to connect behaviours with new situations, indicating that they have integrated a newly revised sense of self. Child therapists are often surprised, sometimes disappointed, by a child's reaction to endings. A child may respond with a simple 'okay' and it is never spoken of again. At the last session, the child may simply wave goodbye to the therapist without any demonstrative sadness or upset. Although this may be hurtful to the therapist's feelings or bruising to the ego, this type of ending is developmentally appropriate. In addition, a simple ending to the relationship indicates that the child was ready to end and progress to the next stages of self-actualisation without dependence on the therapist.

Activities and Gifts

Child therapists will often ask if they should give the child something or do something different in session to mark endings. If the therapist decides to do something to mark the ending of therapy, it is purely for the therapist, not for the client. Creating crafts, exchanging gifts, and hosting parties are common rituals indicating the end of the therapeutic relationship. Generally, large gifts are discouraged but sharing small gifts is often understood as a cultural custom. The most essential element to activities that address endings is a focus on the ending of the therapeutic relationship. An ending activity should represent the value of both people within the relationship and a celebration of what each has contributed to the relationship. This celebration may include shared drawings, photographs, or notes.

Children may want to give something to the therapist to mark an ending. In these cases, if the child asks first, 'What do you want me to give you for our last time?', I will respond, 'Anything that you make is something I will like.' If a child wants to celebrate the ending of the relationship with a symbolic token, I truly want to participate in that celebration. I attempt to avoid any encouragement for the child to buy a gift but if a child arrives at our last session with a gift (of small monetary value), I will usually accept such a gift as a way of honouring the child's intention. Whether the child acknowledges ending or not, I commemorate our relationship by taking a few minutes to review the child's file by reading through all the documents in a personal way before filing my final treatment summary.

Summary

Ending counselling with children is a significant undertaking within the therapeutic relationship. Endings involve the consideration of specific outcomes such as the need for integration of changes adopted by the child during counselling, synthesis of the counsellor–child relationship, and acceptance that closing of therapy is the beginning, not the end. Some key points to remember from this chapter include:

- Due to developmental and attachment factors, counselling endings with children require a high level of personal awareness by the therapist, as well as ability to respond affectively and effectively to children's reactions to the endings phase. Emphasis and timing of endings are influenced by the significance of the therapeutic relationship and the counsellor's attunement to child needs
- Endings involve goals that address the affirmation of the counselling process, resolution of the relationship between counsellor and child and preparation for the child's progress following counselling
- Types of endings include natural endings, that take place when therapeutic goals are met and a child is ready for ending, and premature endings, which may be required when a parent withdraws a child from counselling or a counsellor ends therapy prior to a natural ending. A counsellor seeks to prepare a client according to the experienced type of ending
- In contrast to historical approaches to endings, new ways of conceptualising the ending of counselling involve possible ongoing contact between therapist and child to address issues of loss and independence
- Activities or shared gifts may be ways to help a child and counsellor commemorate their shared relationship and offer a symbolic gesture of care to one another when ending a therapeutic relationship
- The ending of the counselling relationship can be the catalyst for effective relationships over the lifetime of a child. Hence, a counsellor is most therapeutic when acknowledging the ending of counselling as an essential part of the therapeutic relationship

Reflective Questions

1 What are the implications of working with children who have significant attachment problems regarding endings? How might a past history of attachment disruptions negatively affect the ending process?

In the process of therapy, children with a history of attachment disruptions are slow to develop meaningful and effective therapeutic relationships with counsellors. When they finally develop these types of relationships, it may be their first time to have such a relationship with anyone. Endings with children with attachment disruptions may likely be characterised by a child's tendency to withdraw, become depressed or angry, or revert to apathy toward the counsellor.

2 How do endings of counselling with children differ from endings with adults? How would a therapist approach endings differently with children?

Endings with children are different from endings with adults due to developmental stages of life. First, the child's understanding of time is different from an adult's. Secondly, the context of endings is new to a child. Because of greater experience, an adult is more likely to understand circumstances such as a therapist moving to another job. Even if a therapist explains the necessity of ending, the child is more likely to interpret the ending as being related to something the child has done or said. These types of interpretations need to be worked through during the final sessions as the child comes to understand that ending of therapy does not mean that there is something wrong with him or her.

3 How can a therapist react in an effective way to premature endings in the three identified situations: parent-initiated endings, managed care endings, and therapist-initiated endings?

A therapist is more effective when endings are addressed at the beginning of the counselling relationship. At first contact, the therapist emphasises the need for parents to share concerns as soon as they develop. The therapist also emphasises the importance

of allowing several sessions for endings to occur. If parents are certain about ending, the therapist will ask for at least three to four more sessions for a proper closing to therapy.

4 What is your history of personal loss? How might this affect your approach to endings?

A therapist's personal history of loss has great impact on the therapist's approach to termination. If a therapist has experienced multiple losses but has not undergone personal therapy, the therapist may transfer these experiences to the counsellor–client relationship.

5 What is your reaction to conceptualising endings as a transition, not an ending? What effect, if any, will this conceptualisation have on your approach to endings?

A therapist may be impacted by the structure of endings. The finality of a closing session with no further contact will feel disruptive to some therapists while the tapering of sessions or further contact after therapy will cause some therapists to feel that the relationship is deteriorating, not ending.

Learning Activities

1. Imagine you have been seeing a child for six months in therapy. The child had a significant history of loss and abandonment and has made great gains in therapy. Write an ending note to the child.
2. With a partner, practise presenting the ending phase to the same child.
3. With a partner, practise presenting the ending phase to a parent of a child you have seen for three months.
4. Imagine you have seen a child for six weeks in therapy and the parent meets with you to tell you that she is dissatisfied with therapy and will not be bringing her child back. With a partner, practise what you would say to that parent.
5. Create a shared ending activity and role-play the activity with a partner.

Further Reading

Joyce, A., Piper, W., Ogrodniczuk, J. and Klein, R. (2007) *Termination in Psychotherapy: A Psychodynamic Model of Processes and Outcomes.* Washington, DC: American Psychological Association.

Landreth, G.L. (2012) *Play Therapy: The Art of the Relationship.* 3rd edn. New York: Routledge.

Novick, J. and Novick, K. (2006) *Good Goodbyes: Knowing How to End in Psychotherapy and Psychoanalysis.* Lanham, MD: Jason Aronson.

O'Donohue, W. and Cucciare, M. (eds) (2008) *Terminating Psychotherapy: A Clinician's Guide.* New York: Routledge.

Ray, D. (2011) *Advanced Play Therapy: Essential Conditions, Knowledge, and Skills for Child Practice.* New York: Routledge.

Wilson, K., Kendrick, P. and Ryan, V. (2001) *Play Therapy: A Non-Directive Approach for Children and Adolescents.* London: Bailliere Tindall.

Online Resources

BACP website: www.bacp.co.uk/, especially the BACP Children and Young People Division and the Competences for Working with Children and Young People.

Counselling MindEd: http://counsellingminded.com, especially Module CMD 10: Concluding Counselling.

16
Evaluating Counselling
Katherine McArthur and Mick Cooper

This chapter includes:

- The experience of evaluation for clients and therapists
- The impact of evaluation on therapeutic outcomes
- The inter-relationship between research and practice
- Evidence-based practice and practice-based evidence
- Outcome and process feedback
- Qualitative and quantitative evaluation methods

Introduction

Across both child and adult services, there are many counsellors – particularly those of a more relational orientation – who are disinclined to participate in formal outcome evaluation (Daniel and McLeod, 2006); and this reluctance has been noted by the Department of Health's Improving Access to Psychological Therapies (IAPT) programme (Wheeler and Elliott, 2008; DoH, 2008b). In spite of this, evaluation of therapeutic outcomes is often necessary for counselling services to secure and retain funding, and is often seen by stakeholders as essential.

The Experience of Evaluation for Clients and Therapists

Research suggests that the evaluation process may be a positive experience for both clients and therapists. Recent studies in the context of school-based counselling, for instance, have shown that young people report positive responses to completing psychometric measures at regular intervals before, during, and after counselling (Hanley et al., 2011; Cooper et al., 2010). Indeed, a recent interview study of young people allocated to the waiting list condition of a randomised controlled trial of school-based counselling (Daniunaite et al., 2012) found that these participants were able to make substantial progress from participation in the research project alone – without an active counselling intervention.

From the practitioners' perspective too, a Northern Irish study showed that the process of participating in a large-scale school counselling evaluation garnered considerable benefits for practice and professional development, although the experience was described as challenging (Tracey et al., 2009).

The Impact of Evaluation on Therapeutic Outcomes

There is also growing evidence that evaluation improves therapeutic outcomes. In the field of adult psychotherapy, Lambert and Shimokawa (2011) recently published a meta-analysis of studies investigating the effects of providing systematic feedback to clients. Their results showed that clients who are given systematic feedback on progress were 3.5 times more likely to experience reliable positive change, and had less than half the chance of deteriorating, when compared with clients who received no formal feedback.

The potentially therapeutic effects of research also appear to extend to young people in counselling. For example, Saunders and Rey (2011) found that screening and assessment procedures contributed to improvement for 12–25-year-olds with alcohol problems. A recent evaluation study (Cooper et al., 2014) on school-based counselling for young people obtained a substantially larger effect size for counselling (1.26; see Box 16.1) than the mean weighted effect size (0.81) calculated in a comprehensive meta-analysis of UK audit and evaluation studies (Cooper, 2009b). The key difference between this and previous evaluation studies was that counsellors administered weekly session by session outcome measures. This suggests that completing measures at every session, as opposed to only at the beginning and end of the entire counselling period, may improve outcomes for young people in school-based counselling. In fact, the results of another recent study of school-based counselling using systematic feedback with children as young as seven suggest that feedback may as much as double the impact on reducing psychological distress (Cooper et al., 2012).

The Inter-Relationship between Research and Practice

Research activity among counselling practitioners is now widely encouraged, and counsellors in training are expected to develop interest in research evidence and understanding of methods with a view to actively participating and securing the future of counselling as a profession (Dunnet et al., 2007; Wheeler and Elliott, 2008). Outcomes of counselling with children and young people, in particular, has seen a flourish of research interest, and the BACP (British Association for Counselling and Psychotherapy) have recently launched a Practice-Research Network specifically dedicated to this area: CYP PRN. Its aims and objectives include promoting the inter-relationship of research and practice and creating a sustainable network of practitioner-researchers to engage in ethical practice-based research.

Wheeler and Elliott (2008) outline three key questions for the evaluation of practice: 1) Do clients change substantially over the course of counselling? 2) Is counselling substantially responsible for these changes? 3) What specific aspects of counselling contribute to client change? Adequately answering these questions, and the many further questions that they inspire, requires that they are addressed from a range of different perspectives, using a range of different tools.

Evidence-Based Practice and Practice-Based Evidence

Although the counselling and psychotherapy field requires rigorously controlled research, designed to meet the demand for *evidence-based practice*, this must be balanced with the real world perspective provided by *practice-based evidence*. Evidence-based practice is a philosophical approach used in medicine and gaining ground in counselling and psychotherapy, whereby empirical research is systematically reviewed to develop practice guidelines, on which clinical decisions are based. Research studies are selected and interpreted according to specific methodological criteria governing what constitutes 'evidence'. Research is considered on a spectrum of rigorousness, typically leading to qualitative data (which may be considered anecdotal) being disregarded in favour of quantitative studies conducted according to strict methodological criteria.

Practice-based evidence is one way of informing evidence-based practice, rather than an opposing concept. It is the exercise of drawing evidence from practice settings in order to take this into account along with data from controlled experimental studies to form the basis for clinical decision making. In other words, rigorous research is conducted in routine clinical practice, and this evidence feeds into decisions about clinical practice.

In established counselling services for children and young people, outcome measures can easily be incorporated into everyday practice, resulting in the potential to generate a large body of evaluation data which can be a powerful aid to the interpretation and application of evidence.

Outcome and Process Feedback

Outcome feedback is the process of monitoring change in individuals, with the aim of using this information systematically to improve practice. In counselling, it is complicated by the fact that practitioner-researchers from different theoretical approaches may have different aims and different concepts of 'improvement' for clients. For instance, cognitive-behavioural therapy aims to address specific problems, such as obsessive-compulsive behaviour, and measures its outcomes accordingly. Conversely, person-centred counselling focuses on the client's intrinsic needs and wants and may be more appropriately tested by measuring overall well-being. Typically, outcome measures used to evaluate counselling interventions focus on constructs such as psychological distress, or difficulties. Some have a more 'positive' focus, attempting to measure well-being or achievement of personal goals.

Box 16.1   Effect Sizes

Even when different outcome measures are used in evaluation studies, direct comparisons can be made between them by calculating standardised 'effect sizes', which is a way of reporting the amount of change observed. The most common effect size in the counselling and psychotherapy literature is Cohen's d, which is the amount of difference between two groups on some variable (for instance, pre- and post-counselling scores on the CORE-OM), divided by their 'standard deviation' (a measure of the amount of variability across scores).

Cohen (1988) proposed that in the social sciences, standardised effect sizes can be understood in the following way:

Small effect ≥ .2

Medium effect ≥ .5

Large effect ≥ .8

In addition to the specific outcome measure used, decisions regarding when and how to administer these measures influence the results of outcome studies, and must be carefully considered. Traditionally, measures are taken before counselling begins, and immediately after it ends. This approach allows practitioner-researchers to assess the amount of change that has occurred in a given domain (according to the specific outcome measure used) during the counselling period. However, a key recommendation for practice research networks like CYP PRN is for members to routinely collect data from all clients on a session-by-session basis (Parry et al., 2010; Clark et al., 2008) rather than only at the beginning and end of counselling. One reason for this recommendation is that weekly monitoring allows practitioner-researchers to collect more robust evaluation data than pre–post measurements alone. The majority of practice-based evidence is limited by the problem of missing data (Stiles et al., 2008), and this is true of school-based counselling studies too (Cooper, 2009b). Crucially, when measurements are taken at the beginning and end of counselling only, the endpoint data collected comes exclusively from clients who participated in a planned ending with the counsellor. Cooper (2009b) found that in school-based counselling studies, the mean response rate was less than 65 per cent, suggesting that a large proportion of young clients are not represented by these studies due to dropping out of counselling before completing endpoint questionnaires. This means that calculated effect sizes cannot accurately reflect the whole population of young people in school-based counselling. This is a particularly pressing problem given that those who complete counselling tend to have better outcomes (e.g. Wierzbicki and Pekarik, 1993). Using weekly outcome monitoring ensures that data is available for all clients, producing more reliable evidence. Therefore, studies which use weekly session by session monitoring overcome one of the major limitations of practice-based research and have a greater chance of influencing clinical guidelines.

Some of the most frequently used tools for evaluating counselling with children and young people are detailed in Table 16.1.

As noted, clients in general tend to respond positively to outcome measures, and some may have additional benefits. For instance, the opportunity to collaborate on goals with a counsellor, which is part of completing the Goal-Based Outcome Record, has been shown to improve outcomes for clients (Tryon and Winograd, 2002).

As well as outcome measures, questionnaires are available to investigate the therapeutic *process* and clients' experiences in counselling. One of the most commonly used tools here is the Child Session Rating Scale (CSRS), which invites children and young people to rate the extent to which they felt listened to in the therapeutic work, and the degree to which the work met their personal needs and preferences (Duncan et al., 2006). In addition, satisfaction questionnaires such as the Experience of Service Questionnaire (developed for children and young people by Bury NHS Trust) can give valuable insight into clients' views of counselling. This measure asks young people to rate their experience of a service on 12 items related to satisfaction, such as 'I feel that the people who saw me listened to me'. Both of these measures are available to download from CORC (CAMHS Outcome Research Consortium) at www.corc.uk.net/resources/downloads/.

Table 16.1 Most frequently used tools for evaluating counselling with children and young people.

Name	Acronym	Key Publication	Age Range	Prevalence	Strengths	Limitations
Young Person's CORE (Clinical Outcomes in Routine Evaluation) Outcome Measure	YP-CORE	Twigg, E., Barkham, M., Bewick, B.M., Mulhern, B., Connell, J. & Cooper, M. (2009) The Young Person's CORE: Development of a brief outcome measure for young people. *Counselling and Psychotherapy Research* 9(3): 160–168.	11–16 years	Most widely used in UK school-based counselling	Sensitive to change Appropriate for brief interventions Concise User-friendly; simple, easy scoring system Suitable for weekly use	Not suitable for use with children <11 years Clinical norm data not currently available
Strengths and Difficulties Questionnaire	SDQ	Goodman, R. (2001) Psychometric properties of the strengths and difficulties questionnaire. *Journal of the American Academy of Child and Adolescent Psychiatry*, 40(11): 1337–1345.	Self-report version: 11–16 years Parent- and teacher-rated versions: 3–4 years and 4–16 years	Most widely used in specialist CAMHS (Child and Adolescent Mental Health Services)	Four distress-related subscales allow comprehensive view of difficulties; one subscale dedicated to pro-social behaviour Excellent evidence of reliability and validity Translated into a range of languages	Not suitable for brief interventions Not suitable for weekly use Relies on adult caregivers' perceptions for children <11 years

(Continued)

Table 16.1 (Continued)

Name	Acronym	Key Publication	Age Range	Prevalence	Strengths	Limitations
(Young) Child Outcome Rating Scale; from Partners for Change Outcome Management System (PCOMS)	CORS / YCORS	Duncan, B.L., Sparks, J.A., Miller, S.D., Bohanske, R., Claud, D.A. (2006) Giving youth a voice: A preliminary study of the reliability and validity of a brief outcome measure for children, adolescents, and caretakers. *Journal of Brief Therapy,* 5(2): 66–82	CORS: 6–11 years YCORS: children <6 years	Used internationally, with growing popularity in UK	Focuses on child's own perception of well-being Concise User-friendly Appropriate for brief interventions Designed for session-by-session use	Psychometric validity yet to be well-established
Goal-Based Outcome Record	G-BOR	Law, D. (2011) Goals and Goal-Based Outcomes (GBOs): Some Useful Information. Internal CORC publication. Available at: www.corc.uk.net	11–16 years Can be completed by parent/care-giver for children < 11 years	Growing use in specialist CAMHS in UK	Measures what child or young person wants to achieve Incorporates collaboration with counsellor on therapeutic goals Concise Appropriate for brief interventions Suitable for weekly use	Relies on adult caregivers' perceptions for children < 11 years

Name	Acronym	Key Publication	Age Range	Prevalence	Strengths	Limitations
Revised Children's Anxiety and Depression Scale	RCADS	Ebesutani, C., Bernstein, A., Nakamura, B.J., Chorpita, B.F., Weisz, J.R. (2010) A psychometric analysis of the Revised Child Anxiety and Depression Scale, The Research Network on Youth Mental Health. *Journal of Abnormal Child Psychology*, 38(2): 249–260.	6–18 years, (both self-report and parent/care-giver report versions)	Increasingly widespread use in specialist CAMHS	Evaluates changes in anxiety symptoms across range of subscales Includes assessment of depression symptoms Can be completed by both child/young person and adult caregiver	Limited to specific disorders (based on DSM-IV Diagnostic Criteria for range of anxiety disorders)
Health of the Nation Outcome Scales for Children and Adolescents	HoNOSCA	Gowers, S.G., Harrington, R.C., Whitton, A., Beevor, A., Lelliott, P., Jezzard, R., Wing, J. (1999) Health of the Nation Outcome Scales for Children and Adolescents (HoNOSCA). Glossary for HoNOSCA score sheet. *British Journal of Psychiatry*, 174: 428–431.	3–18 years	Estimated use of <10% among CAMHS in UK	Sensitive to change Good validity, reliability and feasibility 15 scales allow comprehensive view of difficulties	Primarily relies solely on clinician's report, though self-rated and parent-rated versions are available Designed to be used only by clinicians who know the child or young person well

Qualitative and Quantitative Evaluation Methods

While outcome studies focus on quantitative data taken from psychometric measures, qualitative data can also have a role in evaluation. Conducting semi-structured interviews is a potential way of collecting clients' views about the outcomes of therapy, and can provide a more in-depth perspective than psychometric measures. While outcome measures give valuable information about effectiveness and appear to have benefits for young people in their own right, combining this kind of data with qualitative records from children and young people can enrich and support findings, providing crucial depth and context to our understanding of the counselling process. This form of interviewing generally involves using a pre-set series of open-ended questions and prompts, and allowing the respondent to take the conversation in new directions as they come up. Robert Elliott (1999) designed an interview schedule entitled the Client Change Interview, which asks clients whether and how they feel they have changed since beginning counselling, to what they attribute the change and how much it has impacted on their lives, as well as covering the client's overall experience of counselling. This has recently been adapted for use with young people in school-based counselling (Lynass et al., 2012).

Once semi-structured interviews have been conducted and transcribed, they can be analysed in various ways. Thematic analysis is a commonly employed method, and involves searching text for emerging themes and categories of responses (Guest et al., 2012). Using this approach, Lynass et al. (2012) found that young people in school-based counselling tended to experience positive changes in emotional, interpersonal and behavioural domains. When asked about the helpful aspects of counselling, young people mentioned talking and 'getting things out', as well as specific counsellor qualities.

A different approach to qualitative data is discourse analysis, which investigates a text on the level of underlying meanings as opposed to face value. A recent example of this method is Prior's (2012) investigation of how young people manage stigma in relation to accessing a school counselling service. He described how young clients demonstrated critical views of help-seeking, which they had internalised, before going through a process of reformulating those critical views, so that they came to see their own behaviour (seeking counselling) as a sign of strength and self-empowerment.

Randomised controlled trials (RCTs) are the most politically powerful method of evaluation in health research, since clinical guidelines groups (such as NICE, the National Institute for Health and Clinical Excellence, and SIGN, the Scottish Intercollegiate Guidelines Network) primarily draw on RCTs to develop guidelines for evidence-based practice. The basic principle is that quantitative measures are taken from a sample of participants (the larger the sample, the more powerful the trial), who are then randomly allocated to two or more conditions: the treatment under investigation, and a control (or controls), which either involves not receiving the treatment, or receiving a comparative treatment. Then measures taken from both groups at the end of the trial period are compared to assess differences, which are assumed to be solely caused by the treatment(s) under investigation, since random allocation is assumed to control for individual differences. One recent RCT (McArthur et al., 2013) compared YP-CORE scores from young people who attended school-based counselling with those of young people who were on a waiting list, and found that those in counselling showed significantly more improvement in psychological distress.

Summary

- Measuring outcomes of counselling is increasingly necessary to secure funding
- Outcome research appears to have considerable benefits for clients and counsellors
- Weekly outcome monitoring has further benefits for creating a robust evidence base
- A wide range of measures are available for children and young people
- Evaluation methods available to counselling practitioner-researchers are both qualitative and quantitative
- Counsellors interested in becoming more involved in research can benefit from practice-research networks

Reflective Questions

1 How and why might research in various forms contribute to therapeutic change for children and young people?

Some young people say that being asked about their experiences in a research interview, or on a questionnaire, makes them start to reflect on their lives in a way that they hadn't before, and that this leads to realisations about themselves and what they want, which helps to make positive changes. It may also be that taking part in research makes people feel that they are contributing something positive, helping the researchers and the wider population, and that this helps young people to feel better about themselves.

2 How easy is it to incorporate an evaluation project into an existing service? What might be the impact of this for a service?

Evaluation can be incorporated in different ways, and to different degrees. As a minimum, completing an outcome measure before and after a period of counselling can provide useful information on change. Using measures at every session gives much more in depth data, which can be used to give detailed feedback to clients and/or counsellors.

3 What might be the barriers to introducing evaluation to a service, and how might they be overcome?

Some counsellors may feel that evaluation of outcomes impedes their work with clients. It is important that counsellors feel confident with any evaluation tools before using them with clients, and have the opportunity to discuss and explore their experience of evaluation with a supervisor.

> **Learning Activities**
>
> 1. Join the BACP CYP Practice Research Network (PRN): www.bacp.co.uk/schools/
> 2. Work through the three Counselling MindEd e-learning modules on Using Measures (CMD 06, freely available through www.counsellingminded.com)
> 3. Download some examples of measures from www.corc.uk.net/resources/. What do you think of them? How do you feel about completing them? Do you prefer some to others, and if so why? If possible, role play how you might use these measures while counselling a child or young person. What impact do you think they might have?
> 4. Download the Goal-Based Outcome Record from www.corc.uk.net/resources/measures/practitioner/. Imagine you are a client beginning therapy, being asked what things you would like to achieve by the end. What kind of goals would you set yourself? How does it feel to compose and rate these life goals?
> 5. Try to design a research project to investigate any aspect of counselling children and young people. This could be a project to evaluate an entire service, or focus more specifically on your own practice. What would you want to find out? How would you go about it? What ethical issues might it raise?

Further Reading

McLeod, J. (2003) *Doing Counselling Research*. London: SAGE.

Sanders, P. and Wilkins, P. (2010) *First Steps in Practitioner Research: A guide to understanding and doing research for helping practitioners*. Ross-on-Wye: PCCS Books.

For counselling practitioners or trainees who are new to research, and interested in getting involved, these introductory texts are ideal. They explain the basic principles in an accessible manner, covering quantitative and qualitative methods, and include practical advice on ethical considerations, getting started, and ways of presenting research to others.

Fraser, S., Lewis, V., Ding, S., Kellett, M. and Robinson, C. (eds) (2004) *Doing Research with Children and Young People*. London: SAGE.

This text provides information and advice on the specific issues relating to research with children and young people.

McLaughlin, C., Holliday, C., Clarke, B. and Ilie, S. (2013) *Research on Counselling and Psychotherapy with Children and Young People: A Systematic Scoping Review of the Evidence for its Effectiveness from 2003–2011*. Rugby: BACP.

This report provides an excellent grounding in counselling research conducted with children and young people, which is essential to planning future research projects and addressing gaps in knowledge.

Deighton, J. and Wolpert, M. (2009) *Mental Health Outcome Measures for Children and Young People*, CAMHS Evidence-Based Practice Unit. Available at: www.corc.uk.net/resources/downloads/.

An overview of outcome measures, including those discussed in this chapter and many others, is given in this report. The CAMHS (Child and Adolescent Mental Health Services) Outcome Research Consortium (CORC) website (www.corc.uk.net) is an excellent resource for practitioner-researchers interested in work with children and young people.

Hill, A., Cooper, M., Pybis, J., et al. (2011) *Evaluation of the Welsh School-based Counselling Strategy*. Cardiff: Welsh Government Social Research.

This is a landmark piece of research evaluating the Welsh Assembly Government's School-based Counselling Strategy, employed since 2008. The study incorporates outcome measurement, interviews and surveys with key stakeholders such as counsellors and link teachers. The findings showed reduction in psychological distress associated with counselling, with greater improvements than in previous studies of UK school-based counselling services.

(Continued)

(Continued)

Cooper, M. (2011) Meeting the demand for evidence-based practice. *Therapy Today* 22(4): 10–16.

McArthur, K. (2011) 'RCTs: A personal experience', *Therapy Today* 22 (7): 24–25.

Rogers, A., Maidman, J. and House, R. (2011) 'The bad faith of "evidence-based practice": Beyond counsels of despair', *Therapy Today* 22 (6): 26–29.

These three articles published recently in *Therapy Today* give an introduction to the debate surrounding evidence-based practice and the use of randomised controlled trials (RCTs) in relational counselling.

Online Resources

Counselling MindEd: http://counsellingminded.com, especially Module CMD 06: Using Measures.

Children and Young People's Improving Access to Psychological Therapies Programme (CYP IAPT): www.cypiapt.org.

Griffiths, G. (2013) *Helpful and Unhelpful Factors in School Based Counselling: Client's Perspective.* Counselling MindEd Scoping Report. Available at: http://counsellingminded.com/wp-content/uploads/2013/12/griffiths_MindEd_report.pdf.

Part 3

Practice Issues

17
Law and Policy

Peter Jenkins

This chapter includes:

- A framework for categorising the legal rights held by children and young people
- Information on some of the key areas likely to cause anxiety, both to novice and more experienced therapists, their supervisors and managers
- Policy and law relating to children and young people, e.g. school-based counselling; mental health services; and pre-trial therapy
- Key aspects of the law, such as the rights of children and parents, confidentiality, safeguarding, information-sharing, contracting, record keeping and appearing in court

Introduction

This chapter starts by acknowledging the very real concerns held by many therapists about the impact of law and policy on their therapeutic work with children and young people. It is designed to be read in tandem with the accompanying chapter in this book on 'Ethics' and outlines:

What Is the 'Law'?

The term 'law', in this context, refers to all legal systems applying in the UK, with particular reference to England and Wales. Reference will also be made to the law applying to Scotland and Northern Ireland, where relevant. The law includes statutes, i.e. Acts of Parliament, or devolved legislation, such as via the Welsh Government, common law and case law. (For a more detailed discussion of these terms, see Jenkins, 2007.) 'Policy' refers to the statutory and voluntary provision of counselling services, including relevant mental health services. This is based on legal requirements, codes of practice, government reports, and established 'custom and practice', in relation to counselling services.

The law can seem complex and intimidating at first sight. This chapter takes an explicitly *rights-based approach*, as a way of making sense of the (sometimes conflicting) legal pressures weighing upon the individual counsellor. A rights-based approach considers the entitlement of children and young people to specific responses by counsellors, social workers, parents, etc., regarding young people's rights to welfare, participation and autonomy. A right is defined as 'a claim to treatment which an individual can make, by reason of law, code of practice or otherwise' (Jenkins, 2013a: 5). A child, in legal terms, is defined as a person under the age of 18, as per section 105, Children Act 1989. While not a legal definition as such, it can also be useful to bear in mind the distinction between *children*, of roughly primary school age, i.e. 6–11 years, and *young people* of secondary school age, i.e. 11–18 years, respectively. These broad age bands may carry differing levels of legal entitlement to autonomy, in terms of decision-making by younger people.

A Rights-Based Model of the Law Regarding Young People

The following approach categorises rights held by children and young people as being of four types. In the first, children and young people are effectively *denied* a claim to counselling or psychotherapeutic 'treatment', either by the law, or as the effect of existing policy. In the second, children do hold rights within counselling and the wider society, which are determined by adults *in their best interests*. In the third, children and young people can exercise their *rights to a say*, in any decisions being made on their behalf. In the fourth, children and young people can exercise their *rights to autonomous decision-making*, independently of adult parents and care-takers.

Briefly, this model therefore suggests four types of rights for children and young people with regard to counselling:

Level 1: Children have *no rights* to counselling;

Level 2: Children have rights to *welfare and protection, decided by adults*;

Level 3: Children have a right to *participate in decisions* made about them;

Level 4: Children have rights *independent of their parents*.

Level 1: Children have no rights to counselling

One example of this would be the denial of young people's rights to freely access information on sexual orientation during the operation of 'Section 28', i.e. from 1988–2003, forbidding local authorities from actively promoting homosexuality as 'a pretended family relationship'.

Level 2: Children have rights to welfare and protection, decided by adults

Children have a right to be protected from 'significant harm', under Section 47 of the Children Act 1989, and under Articles 19 (protection from abuse) and 24 (protection from sexual abuse) of the United Nations Convention on the Rights of the Child 1989.

Level 3: Children have a right to participate in decisions made about them

In deciding whether a child witness in a case of a criminal prosecution for alleged abuse should have pre-trial therapy, 'due consideration should be given to ascertaining the wishes and feelings of the child, in a manner which is appropriate to the child's age and understanding' (CPS, 2001: 16).

Level 4: Children have rights independent of their parents

Young people under the age of 16 of 'sufficient understanding' have a right to confidential medical treatment, *without* parental knowledge or consent, under the *Gillick* case [1986], or via the Age of Legal Capacity Act 1991 in Scotland. This right can logically be extended to include access to confidential counselling.

This model can be useful in helping therapists to distinguish between rights which are driven more by *adult perceptions*, e.g. (Level 2: Protecting a child from harm), and those which are more about the *empowerment of young people* (Level 4: Promoting autonomy). A rights-based approach to the law and policy may have its weaknesses. It may appear to over-emphasise the position of individuals, such as an entitlement to confidentiality, at the expense of wider social considerations, e.g. the value of having mandatory reporting systems for abuse. However, the advantage of this model is that it permits a useful point of cross-over with ethics, as a decision-making aid, as the concept of rights embraces *both* formal legal entitlements *and* the corresponding ethical obligations for counsellors.

Ethical Dimensions of Legal Practice in Counselling Young People

Legally informed therapeutic work with children and young people clearly has an *ethical* dimension, just as ethical practice also has a *legal* aspect to it. However, there are relatively few specific references to the law in the BACP Ethical Framework, in contrast with the particular injunction that: 'Working with young people requires specific ethical awareness and competence' (2010b: 6).

The key BACP statements regarding the law relate to:

- counsellor knowledge of the law and accountability to it;
- client rights of access to information;
- disclosure of information to third parties *without* client consent, under mandatory reporting requirements.

The BACP Ethical Framework (2010b) does not offer specific guidance regarding the complexities of the law in relation to working safely with children and young people. Nevertheless, it is clear that practitioners need, as with any client group, to be fully *aware* of the law, *understand* it, and be accordingly *accountable* for their own professional practice.

Research on Law and Policy for Counselling Children

The limited research base on counsellors and the law tends to be drawn primarily from practice-based evidence. Brown identified critical ethical dilemmas for generic counsellors (n: 20), which broadly relate to issues of risk of harm/child protection issues, information-sharing and record-keeping (2006: 101). Confidentiality emerges, unsurprisingly, as a key, but still problematic, issue in counselling young people in particular. Confidentiality is highly valued by young people working with voluntary agencies (LeSurf and Lynch, 1999; n: 42), and in schools (Cooper, 2009b). It is seen by young people as being particularly important in relation to the provision of counselling and treatment on sexual health issues (Carlisle et al., 2006; n: 18). This expectation appears to have carried some weight in the judge's decision in the *Axon* case in 2006.

Policy and Law Relating to Counselling Children and Young People

The term 'policy' with regard to counselling for children and young people has two main dimensions in this context. One refers to a hierarchy of sets of official guidance to therapists, and the other to the actual provision of counselling services. It may be tempting to see the law and policy as being completely 'black and white', with no room for professional discretion over decision-making, but this is far from being entirely the case. It is also important to understand that law and policy may be 'out of synch' with each other. It may be the case that children and young people are entitled to certain rights according to the *law*, but these are not afforded in practice by counselling providers, due to the operation of a particular *policy*. One example of this would be where young people under 16 in England and Wales are afforded autonomy rights via the law, in terms of the *Gillick* case, but providers actually insist on evidence of parental consent, due to their policy. This would be an example of young people's Level 4 autonomy rights being overridden by reference to paternalistic Level 2 rights (see section above for the corresponding framework of children's rights).

Law Relating to Counselling Children and Young People

The law, as suggested above, refers to all systems of law in the UK. The law varies between different parts of the UK, so that child care law for England and Wales is determined by the Children Acts of 1989 and 2004, in Northern Ireland by the Children (NI) Order 1995 SI 1995/755 (NI 2), and in Scotland by the Children (Scotland) Act 1995. Common legal principles may apply in each legal context, but, equally, there may be significant differences. This discussion will cover mainly the law relating to England and Wales, on the basis that much will also be common to the other jurisdictions in the UK. However, therapists will need to check the detail of the law applying to their own practice, as the law is subject to constant updating and change.

The term 'law' includes statutes, i.e. Acts of Parliament, such as the Data Protection Act 1998. Statute law has an added significance for therapists, in that some therapists, such as psychologists, are subject to statutory regulation, via formal bodies such as the Health and Care Professions Council. In addition, some forms of counselling provision are provided on a statutory basis, i.e. school counselling in Wales. This may help to protect its resource base and impose a greater degree of public scrutiny of appropriate professional standards.

The term 'common law' refers to law which is decided by judges on a custom and practice basis over centuries, such as the law relating to confidentiality. Case law refers to key legal decisions, such as the *Gaskin* and *Gillick* cases. In the first case, Graham Gaskin, a young man formerly in care of Liverpool Social Services, sought to gain access to his own social work file. He partially won his case at the European Court of Human Rights at Strasbourg, opening the door for client access to social work, education and medical files, a decade before the Data Protection Act 1998 came into force (*Gaskin v. UK* (1988) [1990]; Jenkins, 2007: 140). In the second case, i.e. *Gillick*, it was decided by the House of Lords that a young person under 16 could receive confidential medical treatment without parental knowledge or consent, if judged to have 'sufficient understanding' by a health practitioner. This decision was confirmed in the subsequent *Axon* case in 2006.

Table 17.1   Legal sources and their application to counselling practice.

Hierarchy of legal sources (in descending order of importance)	Examples potentially applying to counselling practice
Statute, i.e. Act of Parliament	Children Act 1989; Data Protection Act 1998; School Standards and Organisation (Wales) Act 2013
Common Law	Law relating to confidence/confidentiality
Case Law	*Gaskin* case [1990]; *Gillick* [1986]; *Axon* [2006]
Statutory Codes of Practice	Health and Care Professions Council Code (2012); Mental Health Act Code (2008)
Statutory Guidance	*Working Together* (2013) (England) and equivalent guidance on child protection for Wales and Scotland; Practice Guidance on pre-trial therapy for children (2001, 2002)
Government Reports	Laming Report on Victoria Climbie Inquiry (2003)
Professional Codes of Ethics	BACP Ethical Framework (2010)

Hierarchy of Legal Authority Relating to Counselling Practice

In terms of a hierarchy of law and policy, there are also statutory codes of practice, which derive from specific Acts of Parliament. For example, the Code of Practice for the Mental Health Act (MHA) 1983 sets out authoritative guidance for practitioners working with adults and young people under 18, within the mental health services in England and Wales (DoH, 2008a). The HCPC Code, Standards of Conduct, Performance and Ethics (2012) set out a clear duty for its registrants, in relation to protecting children from harm. Arguably, statutory codes such as the HCPC (for HCPC registrants only) and MHA 1983 (for mental health practitioners) would carry significant weight in a court of law, in determining a judge's perception of the appropriate professional responses made by a therapist.

In terms of a hierarchy of guidance, the next level would include statutory guidance, government circulars and statutory instruments. For counsellors, the key examples here would include the relevant guidance on child protection and safeguarding, such as *Working Together* (DfE, 2013), and its equivalent versions for Wales and Scotland. A second example would include practice guidance on the provision of pre-trial therapy, which is further discussed below (CPS, 2001). Other levels of this hierarchy of authority and influence, regarding legal perspectives on good professional practice, could also include influential reports, such as Lord Laming's report on failures of child protection in the Victoria Climbie Inquiry (Laming, 2003) and, not least, professional codes of ethics by therapist organisations (BACP, 2010b), setting out ethical principles, values and minimum standards of therapist competence.

Policy and Provision of Counselling Services

This section covers three key areas of counselling provision for children and young people, i.e.:

- school-based counselling
- counselling as part of mental health services
- pre-trial therapy (i.e. counselling for a child witness prior to a criminal trial)

School-Based Counselling

Historically, counselling has mainly tended to be provided on a voluntary, non-statutory basis within the UK, by a wide range of providers. This has included provision by voluntary or third-sector agencies (Street, 2013) and by private and independent therapists. Counselling has been long established within the Further and Higher Education sectors as an element of pastoral care, for students moving from adolescence into young adulthood. School counselling within secondary schools saw a decline from a peak of influence in the 1960s, but has since undergone a resurgence, with an estimated 80 per cent of secondary schools in England now providing counselling for pupils, and 100 per cent in Wales (Hanley et al., 2012). Secondary school counselling is now a statutory requirement in

Table 17.2   School-based counselling: Comparison of current and potential future patterns of counselling practice (adapted from Jenkins and Polat, 2006: 11).

	Current pattern	Potential future pattern
	Child-centred orientation.	Family-centred orientation.
Model of Confidentiality	Exclusive model of confidentiality.	Inclusive model of confidentiality.
	Limited sharing of client information.	Routine sharing of client information.
	Role-based professional boundaries.	Task-based professional boundaries.
Professional Orientation	Individual focus of therapy.	Systemic and community focus of therapy.
	Status as individual practitioner.	Member of inter-disciplinary team.
Relationship to Other Professions	Loose integration with other support services.	High levels of integration with other support services.

Wales, under Section 92, School Standards and Organisation (Wales) Act 2013. Increasing numbers of primary schools also provide counselling for children.

The rapid expansion of school-based counselling has made this provision available to a growing number of young clients, in a non-stigmatising and accessible format (Cooper, 2013). However, it has also brought with it some major challenges to the counselling profession, particularly that of integrating therapy within schools, as highly complex, bureaucratic organisations, with their own distinct ethos and culture. In addition, it could be argued, perhaps controversially, that the traditional model of child-focused counselling has been strongly challenged by the safeguarding agenda (see below). This may have led to pressures for the adoption of a more multi-disciplinary, team-based approach, with different expectations about confidentiality and information-sharing (see Table 17.2).

Not least, in terms of policy, the growth of school-based counselling has raised key questions about its relationship towards other, related forms of provision, such as mental health services.

Counselling as Part of Mental Health Services

Counselling can also be provided as part of mental health services. The Mental Health Act 1983 Code of Practice for England shows strong signs of influence by the *Gillick* case. It confirms the rights of young people under 16 to confidentiality, if of sufficient understanding (DoH, 2008a). Provision of mental health services for children and young people is determined within England and Wales by the National Service Framework, setting out relevant standards (DfE/DoH, 2004). This has identified problem areas, such as the relative lack of provision for 16–17-year-olds, the perceived gap between adolescent and adult services, and the inappropriate placement of some adolescents on adult psychiatric wards. Other weaknesses include problems transferring between adolescent and adult services, and the lack of provision for self-referral by young people, in order to access mental health services.

Counselling provision within mental health services within England is provided via Child and Adolescent Mental Health Services (CAMHS). This operates on a four-tiered level of service:

Tier 1:   Primary level of service, such as initial assessment and referral by GPs;

Tier 2:   More specialised provision, by child psychologists and some school counsellors;

Tier 3:   Specialist provision via multi-disciplinary teams, such as CAMHS;

Tier 4:   Highly specialist out-patient and in-patient services for severe mental health problems, such as eating disorders.

Mental health services provide medication and psychological therapy. Both are governed by reference to NICE guidance, for example regarding the use of anti-depressants for under-18s. It also applies in relation to evidence-based therapies, such as cognitive-behavioural therapy (CBT), for a wide range of presenting problems, such as anxiety, depression and self-harm.

Access to CAMHS is governed by referral gateways, such as via GPs, school counsellors and social workers. Increasingly, CAMHS services are mapped onto the tiered system used by Children and Young People Improving Access to Psychological Therapies Programme (CYP IAPT) (Spong et al., 2013). This was initially aimed primarily at adults and has now been extended to include children and young people (see Table 17.3). Counselling services within CYP IAPT are closely evaluated via a battery of outcome measures. CYP IAPT services for children and young people may provide a wider range

Table 17.3   Stepped care model for the CYP-IAPT service (Bala et al., 2011: 24).

Stage/step	Services	Interventions available
Step 5	CAMHS psychiatrist Inpatient CAMHS services	Specialist services (Tier 4 CAMHS)
Step 4	Core CAMHS team	Secondary care services (Tier 3 CAMHS)
Step 3: High intensity interventions	Core CAMHS team CAMHS outreach team (Children in Need/Looked After Children) Primary Care Children and Young Persons worker team Bereavement service	Systemic, narrative and solution-focused therapies CBT Face-to-face counselling Family counselling Bereavement counselling Play therapy Psychology Specialist parenting groups Psycho-educational and psychotherapeutic groups Signposting/assessment/step up/step down
Step 2: Low intensity interventions	Streetwise Action for Children Targeted Adolescent Mental Health Services Team Psychological well-being practitioners 16–19	Guided self-help based on CBT Parenting groups Behavioural activation Structured physical activity Computerised cognitive-behavioural therapy (CCBT) Bibliotherapy Psycho-educational workshops and groups Signposting/assessment/step up/step down
Step 1: Primary care	GP Children's health services Education Social care services	Watchful waiting Advice and information Local parenting groups

of types of therapy than their adult equivalent. However, cognitive-behavioural therapy may hold a key position in terms of recommended treatment, given its privileged, evidence-based status within NICE guidelines.

The above model is based on the work of Bury NHS Primary Care Trust. It is included simply as an illustration of CYP IAPT provision for children and young people, rather than claiming to be either representative, or prescriptive. The CYP IAPT model in general may well be significant for the future of counselling provision for children, in adopting a systemic, tiered approach, using a wide range of therapeutic interventions, for targeted treatment and therapy for assessed psychological difficulties, which are then subject to comprehensive outcome measurement.

Pre-Trial Therapy

Where a child or young person is potentially a witness in a criminal trial, for example, as the victim of alleged abuse, therapy is governed by practice guidance issued by the Crown Prosecution Service and other agencies (CPS, 2001). This sets out very clear and specific parameters for the provision of counselling. Any pre-trial counselling must be provided in close liaison with the Crown Prosecution Service (CPS) and avoid rehearsing evidence, or revisiting the original alleged abuse. This is in order to pre-empt future claims by the defence solicitors that the child's evidence has been 'contaminated' by the therapy, or that the child has been 'coached' by the therapist. The counsellor is required to keep careful records of therapy, which are accessible to the CPS. Any fresh disclosures of abuse, or material changes to the child's evidence, must be reported to the CPS. The guidance lists certain types of therapy, including hypno therapy, psychodrama and group therapy, amongst others, which are identified as presenting particular problems for the child later giving evidence in court. Anecdotal evidence suggests that some children are still being actively discouraged by the authorities from attending counselling before the criminal trial, despite this advice running directly counter to the ethos of this guidance. Pre-trial therapy for child witnesses and victims of abuse has received relatively little research attention, despite its prominence as a complex and significant issue for many practitioners and clients. Plotnikoff and Woolfson (2009; n: 182) found continuing delays in child abuse cases going to court, and high levels of anxiety amongst young witnesses.

Key Aspects of the Law Relating to Counselling Children

There are a number of key aspects of the law relating to counselling children and young people. These include:

- rights of children and parents
- confidentiality and privacy
- safeguarding and child protection
- information-sharing with other professionals
- contracts and contracting
- record-keeping and data protection
- appearing in court

Rights of Children and Parents

Children and young people under the age of 18 in the UK have extensive rights to the provision of counselling (Level 2 rights), to participation in decisions (Level 3 rights) and to autonomy (Level 4 rights). (For a detailed outline of this framework, see Jenkins, 2013a; for its application to counselling, see Jenkins, 2013b, and Daniels and Jenkins, 2010.) The rights of parents were substantially recast by the Children Act 1989, to assume the much narrower form of 'parental responsibility'. This legal power is not limited to biological parents, but can be legally acquired by other significant figures in a child's life, such as a grandparent. The notion of 'parental rights' has been radically reframed and slimmed down, to now include essentially, parental *duties* to provide for, educate and protect children (see Daniels and Jenkins, 2010: 18). Counsellors should therefore be wary of accepting at face value any claim to 'parental rights' as affording a parent the authority to intervene into the counselling space where the client is a child or young person.

Confidentiality and Privacy

Young people aged 16 to 17 years have the same entitlement to confidentiality as would an adult, under Section 8, Family Law Reform Act 1969. Under the age of 16, young people in England and Wales, with 'sufficient understanding', are deemed capable of consenting to medical treatment by a health practitioner, following the *Gillick* case. Confidentiality is an essential pre-condition for exercising such consent, according to the *Axon* case in 2006. This confirmed that '*Gillick* remains good law' (*Axon* [2006] at 24). Following the principles set out in *Gillick,* it follows that parental consent is, therefore, *not* a legal requirement for counselling a young person under 16 with 'sufficient understanding'.

Children of any age also have the right to respect for their private and family life, under Article 8 of the Human Rights Act 1998. In 2003, Naomi Campbell won a key legal case and was awarded damages for breach of privacy, when the *Daily Mirror* published photos of her leaving a meeting of Narcotics Anonymous. Following the *Campbell* case [2004], it could be argued that this right of *privacy* extends to the very fact of actually *attending* counselling. This may be true even for those primary school-age children, who may be considered as too young to qualify for confidentiality under the *Gillick* criteria (Daniels and Jenkins, 2010: 135).

Safeguarding and Child Protection

There is now an extensive safeguarding and child protection agenda in place, designed to protect children under 18 from abuse. Child abuse is defined as 'significant harm', under Section 47 of the Children Act 1989 for England and Wales. Children and young people within these jurisdictions are protected via the Children Acts of 1989 and 2004, the safeguarding provisions of the Education Act 2002 and the vetting provisions of the Safeguarding Vulnerable Groups Act 2006 and Protection of Freedoms Act 2012. These are then set out in detail, at an operational level, by statutory guidance, such as *Working Together* (DfE, 2013) and the equivalent guidance applying variously to Scotland, Wales and Northern Ireland.

There is, however, a widening gap between the formal *law* on this issue and the *policy* of many agencies, with regard to the *reporting* of alleged abuse. It is quite clear that 'there is no mandatory reporting law in England and Wales', according to Hoyano and Keenan (2007: 444). However, many agencies operate on the basis of an obligatory abuse reporting *policy*, which is imposed as a term of the counsellor's contract of employment. This can clearly be justified by appeals to the concept of social justice and by being demonstrably 'in the public interest'. Nevertheless, it can also raise acute ethical and professional dilemmas for counsellors working with mid- to late-age-range teenagers. Such clients may be making highly conflicted disclosures of abuse, but might not be perceived by the counsellor as being at *immediate* risk of exposure to current or continuing significant harm.

This issue of mandatory reporting of child abuse has been the subject of several research reports relevant to current debates about safeguarding. Goldman and Padayachi (2005) found a tendency for school counsellors in Australia (n: 122) to *under-report* their suspicions of child sexual abuse, possibly due to their lack of confidence in accurately identifying symptoms of abuse. Bryant and Baldwin (2010) found a similar reticence regarding reporting abuse amongst school counsellors in the US (n: 193), which has a similar system of mandatory reporting. These research findings would suggest that counsellors' abuse reporting practice relies on more than a simple legal requirement to do so, and is, in part, mediated by professionals' own perceptions and practices.

Information-Sharing with Other Professionals

In legal terms, information-sharing with other professionals can be justified by obtaining the consent of the child or young person. It can also be carried out *without* consent, if it can be justified as being 'in the public interest', i.e. in preventing significant harm to the child or young person concerned. On information-sharing practice within safeguarding, Bunting et al. (2010) provide an extensive literature review. Brown's research (2006) has identified some of the role-strain experienced by counsellors between, on the one hand, respecting client confidentiality and, on the other, becoming involved in information-sharing with other professionals. Cromarty and Richards (2009) found less evidence of this difficulty amongst school counsellors (n: 16). However, they identified a preference amongst counsellors for sharing information with trusted individuals, rather than in a group setting, where there was less control over its subsequent use. Rees et al. (n: 24) found similar concerns about retaining control over information amongst young people, in making disclosures of abuse to social workers. 'For young people, the relationship with social work practitioners was central to disclosure and protection' (2010: 52).

Contracts and Contracting

In England and Wales, young people under 18 (under 16 in Scotland) are not usually deemed capable of entering into a legally binding contract, with certain rare exceptions (Mitchels and Bond, 2010: 64). Where counselling is being directly paid for, then the contract would often be between the counsellor and the parent concerned. The terms of the contract need to specify the limits to confidentiality applying to the therapeutic work and any restrictions on the nature of the counsellor's reporting back to the parent(s) of the process and content of therapy. In other contexts, it may be that the counsellor is carrying out their work under contract to an *agency*, such as children's services. Again, the specific terms of the contract may include provisions for returning completed case files to the agency purchasing the service, and an obligation to report any disclosures of abuse made during therapy.

Mitchels and Bond (2010: 65–6) discuss the capacity of children and young people to make 'therapeutic contracts', according to their age, understanding and legal jurisdiction. Where these are not properly legally binding contracts, these might be more accurately described as 'consent agreements', or even as 'working charters'. This is precisely to avoid any potential confusion over their legal status. Such an agreement can set out clearly practical arrangements for therapeutic work, any limitations to confidentiality, data protection requirements and provision for client complaint, in the event of dissatisfaction

Record-Keeping and Data Protection

Record-keeping in counselling children and young people is covered by the somewhat complex guidance derived from the Data Protection Act 1998 (ICO, 2009). The law essentially parallels provision for record-keeping for adult clients, but with significant differences relating to access to records by younger clients (see Jenkins, 2007). Data protection requirements cover all processing of personal data, i.e. client recording, in electronic/computerised, including audio, video and digital recording, and manual/handwritten formats. Records must be accurate, relevant, not excessive for their purpose and kept no longer than necessary. Health, social work and education records comprise a special sub-set of client records. This is based on the successful case brought by Graham Gaskin for access to his own social work file in 1988 (*Gaskin v. UK* (1988)). Counselling records in health, social work and education contexts will therefore comprise a sub-set of the child's corresponding health, social work or education file, with certain specific implications for school counsellors.

Record-keeping in therapeutic work with children may be governed by agency policies, regarding their content and time-limits. Generally, as with adult clients, the Data Protection Act (DPA) 1998 has seen a marked shift away from the keeping of therapist- and process-focused recording, towards much briefer, primarily factual, records. Records of therapy with pre-trial child witnesses need to follow this approach and are, in principle, accessible to the Crown Prosecution Service (2001). Children and young people have rights as data subjects to access their own files. There are some limitations to access, based on the contextual setting of therapy and the nature of the record kept (Jenkins, 2007). A child under 16 can exercise their rights under the Act, if possessing 'a general understanding of what it means to exercise that right' (s. 66, DPA 1998), which is assumed to apply from the age of 12. Conflicts can arise when parents seek to access health, education and counselling records, independently of the child, as may happen in contested cases concerning divorce, or medical treatment.

Appearing in Court

All counselling records are potentially accessible to the courts via a court order. Counsellors do not possess legal privilege in the UK, with the limited exception of marital relationship counsellors (Jenkins, 2007: 105). Equally, a counsellor may be called upon to write a report for the court, as either a professional witness, or as an expert witness. The tasks of report writing, or appearing as an expert witness, for the court require substantial professional experience and, ideally, specialist training. Where therapists are asked to provide court reports, these are often related to the assessment of attachment, parenting, child development, trauma, or child abuse. This may be in the context of proceedings connected with divorce, separation, parental contact, domestic violence, adoption, or child care proceedings.

Counsellors called to court can obtain expert legal advice from their employer, if applicable, and from their professional indemnity insurance society, or psychologists' protection society. Counsellors employed by large organisations may have an advantage over colleagues in private practice, in having easier access to the legal resources of the relevant employing Local Education Authority or NHS Trust. Legal and professional advice can also be obtained from professional associations, such as BACP, UKCP, BABCP, or BPS, as appropriate. Counsellors providing pre-trial therapy for child witnesses in alleged abuse cases need to be particularly mindful of the practice guidance governing therapy in these circumstances and to follow it closely (CPS, 2001). Advice for counsellors on appearing in court is aptly summarised as 'Dress up, stand up, speak up and shut up!' More generic suggestions for giving evidence in court are outlined in Jenkins (2007: 52–73).

Case Study   Parveen

Parveen worked as a counsellor in a secondary school run by the local authority, and developed a particularly close therapeutic alliance with Simon, aged 12 years, who came from a fairly chaotic family background. There was some evidence of poor parenting by his mother, a single parent with multiple domestic and housing problems. Parveen met with Simon on a regular basis, with no missed sessions. She was actively supported in this work by the head teacher, who saw the counselling as enabling Simon to engage as well as he could with his studies, as an 'oasis' in an otherwise stormy life. Simon's social worker was also highly appreciative of this therapeutic work, but respectful towards the ongoing therapy as a 'private space', while also trying to support his mother with her daily struggles.

The situation changed drastically when Simon's case was taken over by a new social worker, with a very different attitude towards the counselling. The new social worker instructed Parveen to attend a 'CAF' (Common Assessment Framework) meeting, where she would be expected to update the professionals attending on the fine detail of what Simon was discussing in therapy. Parveen was concerned at this, as Simon was not prepared for the detail of the counselling session to be shared in

(Continued)

(Continued)

this way. The social worker's view was that the school counsellor was now part of a multi-disciplinary team, and that Parveen was duty-bound to share all relevant information about Simon, as a 'child in need', under the *Working Together* guidelines. Parveen's referring to the BACP Ethical Framework was dismissed as being 'just a code of ethics', even though the head teacher supported Parveen in her defence of client confidentiality. Parveen was informed in no uncertain terms by the social worker that, if she failed to attend the meeting and share all relevant information, Simon would be referred to CAMHS, with the result that the school counselling would cease forthwith.

Summary

- Law and policy may be perceived by practitioners as being highly complex, but they provide a framework for working therapeutically with children and young people in the UK
- The legal framework consists of a hierarchy of law, ranging from statute, case law, codes of practice, to statutory guidance, official reports and voluntary codes of ethics
- Policy overlaps with this legal framework, in setting out the requirements for counselling provision, e.g. within mental health services, YP IAPT and NICE guidelines
- Much counselling provision, for example in schools or in voluntary organisations, currently sits outside these statutory frameworks, but is heavily influenced in practice by statutory provision, such as in CAMHS, or by the safeguarding and child protection agendas
- A rights-based model offers a way of grasping the rights of young people, and protecting the 'confidential space' in which counsellors do their valuable work

Reflective Questions

1 What are the rights of the child in the situation discussed in the case study?

Simon has a number of rights in this situation. He has a right:

- to a say in decisions being made about him, under Article 12 of the UN Convention on the Rights of the Child (UNICEF, 1989)
- to confidentiality, if of 'sufficient understanding', under the *Gillick* case [1986], confirmed by *Axon* [2006]

- to therapeutic privacy, under the *Campbell* case [2004]
- to services from the local authority, if deemed to be a 'child in need', under Section 17, Children Act 1989

2 What is the legal situation for the counsellor in this situation?

The school counsellor's legal position is influenced by safeguarding policy and by employment law, i.e.:

- the local authority has a duty to safeguard and promote the welfare of children, under Section 175, Education Act 2002
- the local authority is required to cooperate with social services in providing services for 'children in need', under the Children Acts 1989 and 2004
- the counsellor is obliged to comply with school and local authority policy with regard to attending safeguarding meetings, under the terms of her contract of employment

3 What are the options available to the counsellor in this situation?

The counsellor has a number of options here, i.e.:

- seek professional guidance from the BACP Ethical Framework and the BACP Information Office
- clarify her professional and therapeutic options, through supervision with a suitable qualified counsellor with experience in working with children and young people
- obtain expert legal advice from her professional indemnity insurance provider, or professional protection society
- review school policy on confidentiality and information-sharing with the head teacher, in order to protect school counselling confidentiality as far as possible

---

Learning Activities

1. Check online for the latest version of *Working Together* (DfE, 2013) or its equivalent and read the sections on:

   o information-sharing
   o a child in need
   o safeguarding

(Continued)

> *(Continued)*
>
> 2. Check the safeguarding policy of your own counselling agency, and how it might apply in this situation
> 3. Construct a possible solution which might offer a way forward in this complex situation and discuss it with your tutor, supervisor or line manager

Further Reading

Daniels, D. and Jenkins, P. (2010) *Therapy with Children: Children's Rights, Confidentiality and the Law*. 2nd edn. London: SAGE.

Jenkins, P. (2011) *A Confidential Space: Ethical Considerations When Counselling Children and Young People*. DVD: University of Wales. See: http://hss.newport.ac.uk or https://sites.google.com/site/counsellingdvds/a-confidential-space.

Jenkins, P. (2013) *Children's and Young Persons' Rights to Counselling*. 2nd edn. Brighton: Pavilion.

Online Resources

See Counselling Mind-Ed session on 'Applying the Law'.
Counselling MindEd: http://counsellingminded.com/.

Legal Cases

Axon, R (on the application of) v. Secretary of State for Health and Anor [2006] EWHC 37 (Admin).
Campbell v. MGN Ltd [2004] UKHL 22
Gaskin v. UK ECHR 2/1988/146/200, [1990] 1 FLR 167.
Gillick v. West Norfolk AHA [1985] 3 All ER 402; [1986] AC 112.

18
Ethics

Peter Jenkins

This chapter includes:

- An exploration of some of the different approaches to ethics within counselling and psychotherapy, and the particular issues of concern with regard to counselling younger and more vulnerable clients
- The value of adopting a rights-based approach to addressing ethical dilemmas in therapy with children and young people, and an exploration of a number of key areas of concern to therapists, including contracting, and undertaking research with children
- A discussion of recent research evidence on how practitioners actually work in practice with some of the key issues confronting them in their day-to-day practice with children and young people

This chapter is designed to be read in conjunction with Chapter 17, 'Law and Policy', in this volume.

Counsellors often tend to see the subject of ethics as a topic which is dry and academic, or as being worthy, but slightly dull, or even as an 'add-on' to the more *central* task of actually working in therapy with children and young people. This is a real misreading of the importance and value of ethics, which is defined as 'a generic term for understanding and examining the moral life' (Beauchamp and Childress, 2008: 1). Ethics is concerned with addressing, and attempting to find answers to, key therapeutic dilemmas such as:

- a child's parents *insisting* on knowing what is said in the therapy session;
- an agency requiring *all* under-age sexual activity to be reported as a risk factor;
- defining the *age* at which a child becomes self-determining and acquires a right to greater autonomy.

Ethical Practice and Codes of Ethics

The counselling profession attempts to support, monitor and reinforce ethical practice amongst its members, by providing codes of ethics, or ethical frameworks, for decision-making, and by implementing complaints procedures, in order to offer redress to aggrieved parties. Codes of ethics are, in turn, not set in stone, but change over time. They are influenced by changing professional perceptions, broadening experience, key cases or complaints, and by the changing legal and policy context. Codes attempt to embody the current professional wisdom of the time, but they cannot realistically seek to answer every issue confronting a counsellor or supervisor. Instead, codes offer a *framework* for responding to both everyday and more complex and unusual challenges to therapeutic practice.

Professional approaches to ethics also vary between professional associations and change over time. A key moment in the development of the counselling and psychotherapy profession was marked by the decisive shift by the British Association for Counselling and Psychotherapy, from the former *Code of Ethics* (1998), to the *Ethical Framework for Good Practice in Counselling and Psychotherapy*, in 2002 (BACP, 2010b). It is often not fully appreciated that codes or frameworks speak with different tones or authority, in setting out, for example, what counsellors *may* do (or may *not* do), and what they *must* do. These tones, or requirements, can be described as including the following:

- *advisory*: Psychologists '*should* practice within the boundaries of their competence' (BPS, 2011 [2009]: 16)
- *supportive*: 'Practitioners are *strongly encouraged* to ensure that their work is adequately covered by insurance' (BACP, 2010b: 7)
- *prescriptive*: 'You *must* keep accurate records' (HCPC, 2010: 3)

The BACP Ethical Framework contains a variety of different authoritative tones, but marks a distinct shift away from the earlier binding set of prescriptions. It recognises that counsellors need a more flexible set of ethical guides, where there are competing claims for action, and there is not necessarily one single, right answer to a pressing ethical dilemma.

Within philosophy, there is a wide range of different approaches to the study of ethics. These different approaches include the following:

- *deontological*, i.e. *rule following*, prescriptive: 'You *must not* break client confidentiality'
- *teleological*, i.e. based on achieving a positive *outcome*: 'You *may* decide to break confidentiality, *in order* to avert client suicide'
- *rights-based*, i.e. based on an active appreciation of the *rights* of all parties involved, e.g. 'You need to *balance* the child's right to privacy, *versus* their right to protection from harm'

The approach taken in this chapter follows an explicitly *rights-based model*, while acknowledging the valuable contribution of both rule-following and outcomes-based approaches. It also needs to be borne in mind that the practical application of ethics in counselling does not solely revolve around the ethical stance adopted by the counsellor. It is increasingly clear that children and young people also bring their own expectations and a strong sense of ethics and fairness to therapy, which can become a key factor in the unfolding of the therapeutic work (Jenkins, 2010).

Ethical Approaches to Work with Children and Young People

Discussion of ethical approaches to work with children tends to have a distinct nature, marking it apart from more generic discussions about ethics in counselling with adult clients. This is so for a number of reasons. The terms 'children' and 'young people' cover a wide range of age groups and situations; the 'child' in question may be aged 17 (using the term 'child' in a strictly legal sense); or the 'young person' may be aged 12 or 13. The terms children and young person/young people are used here to denote persons of roughly primary school age, i.e. 6–11 years, or secondary school age, i.e. 11–18 years, respectively. This follows a broad distinction, between *children*, who are assumed not to be mature enough to make decisions for their own care, and *young people*, who may have developed sufficient maturity to do so. However, this broad distinction is no more than a very rough guide, as there will emerge situations where these categories are not particularly useful in guiding ethical decision-making by the counsellor.

Counselling work with children and young people is also considered to be a distinct field in terms of ethics, because of the child or young person's developmental, physical and emotional vulnerability. The long-term adverse effects of child abuse, trauma, bullying and emotional abuse are by now well-established. Children and young people may also be more subject to manipulation by powerful and respected adult authority figures, perhaps lacking an adult's wider experience of relationships, on which to judge a counsellor's influence. By definition, children and young people are also heavily dependent upon adults for their everyday care, protection and control, whether in a family, hospital, residential care home, or in a custodial setting. It is also probably much more likely that counselling will involve potential contact by the counsellor with *adult third parties*, who take an active interest in the process and outcomes of therapy, whether as parents, foster-parents, social workers, teachers, or judges, than would normally be the case with an adult client. This vulnerability to harm, and corresponding dependence upon adult care-takers, is recognised by specific provision for children and young people under the law, which then becomes a further crucial element, in terms of ethical decision-making by counsellors.

There is limited counselling-based research on how counsellors work with ethical dilemmas in their practice, mostly drawn from practice-based evidence, such as work by Brown (n: 20), in exploring the uncertainties experienced by counsellors in confronting issues which relate to young people, such as child protection (2006: 102). Research on the nature of the therapeutic alliance in working with young people has emphasised the key role of the therapeutic alliance, and within this, confidentiality as a central component of the therapeutic environment (Everall and Paulson, 2002). This latter small-scale survey (n: 18), carried out in Canada, found that many young clients did not grasp that the *context* of therapy radically influenced the limits of confidentiality, hence underlining the need for careful initial contracting to set out the limits of confidentiality. This finding is echoed by LeSurf and Lynch, in their research with young clients of a counselling agency (n: 42). They found with young people that 'their desire for confidentiality related not so much to concerns for privacy, but to a wish to retain control over the material which they disclosed' (1999: 237). A study by Finkenauer et al. (2002; n: 227) found that the provision of client confidentiality, in essence the keeping of secrets from parents and authoritative adults, had an additional and unexpected *developmental* value, in promoting a stronger sense of autonomy amongst young people.

BACP Ethical Framework

The BACP Ethical Framework (2010b) will be taken as the main reference point for discussion, while acknowledging that there are other, equally valid, ethical codes available for practitioners belonging to other professional associations. The Ethical Framework refers to values, ethical principles and (often overlooked) the *personal qualities* of therapists, as components of informed ethical decision-making. These separate elements amount to a kind of 'scaffolding', which supports and empowers counsellors, in making often difficult decisions. The Ethical Framework identifies a number of key areas for special attention in therapeutic work with children and young people (BACP, 2010b: 6):

- *specific ethical awareness* in therapeutic work with children and young people;
- *competence* in therapeutic work with children and young people;
- assessing the *balance* between a child or young person's *dependence* on adults and carers and their progressive development towards *acting independently*;

- the child or young person's *capacity to give consent* independently of adults with parental responsibilities;
- the *management of any confidences* disclosed by the child or young person.

These areas, which are identified as especially sensitive, or even problematic, could easily occupy a special ethical framework simply for work with children and young people. The complexity of devising a set of ethics for work with children and young people is further recognised in discussion of the possible constraints to a key ethical principle, i.e. that of autonomy. The Ethical Framework sets out key principles, including respect for autonomy, i.e. 'a client's capacity to be self-directing within therapy and all aspects of life' (2010b: 3). It notes, however:

> An obligation to act in the best interests of the client may become paramount when working with clients whose capacity for autonomy is diminished because of immaturity, lack of understanding, extreme distress, serious disturbance or other significant personal constraints. (BACP, 2010b: 3)

As with adult clients, the counsellor may be working to promote the client's developing sense of autonomy, or ability to make decisions for themselves. However, this quality of autonomy may be radically compromised by the immaturity of a child, or young person, in the role of client. For example, a 10-year-old client may be exposed to, or encouraged to drink, alcohol in their home by older peers, or by parents. The child's autonomy, in choosing to experiment in this way, may be in conflict with their lack of maturity in making such a decision, which then places them at risk of harm.

Regard for client autonomy, in the case of children and young people, may be framed by respect for 'their progressive development towards acting independently', as above (BACP, 2010b: 6), or by the related concept of the 'evolving capacities of the child', drawn from the UN Convention on the Rights of the Child 1989 (UNICEF, 1989: 5). However, in some cases, a child or young person's assumed rights to autonomy may be assessed to be significantly impaired, or even malignant in nature. This process can be observed in the case of a sexually exploited young person, still under the age of consent, mistakenly being deemed by social workers, or police, to be evidently making 'their own choices' to become involved in 'consensual sexual activity' with adult males (RBCSB, 2012: 9).

A Rights-Based Approach to Therapy with Children and Young People

The field of ethics in therapy with children and young people is often seen as being hugely complex and risky, not least for practitioners. The advantage of a rights-based approach is that it offers a way of categorising a wide range of conflicting material, of identifying key underlying ethical principles in decision-making and of linking ethical choices with the often closely-related legal framework underpinning such decisions. This framework is developed in more detail elsewhere (Daniels and Jenkins, 2010; Jenkins, 2011).

Within this model, a right is defined as 'a claim to treatment which an individual can make, by reason of law, code of practice or otherwise' (Jenkins, 2013a: 5). Thus a child may have a right to *privacy*, regarding accessing therapy, which is both an *ethical* imperative for the counsellor and agency, and also, arguably, a *legal* right under the Human Rights Act 1998. In some cases, a child may require the proper support of an adult, in order to claim such a right, whether in the role of advocate, solicitor, or social worker.

Briefly, the model suggests four types of rights for children and young people with regard to counselling:

Level 1: Children have *no rights* to counselling;

Level 2: Children have rights to *welfare and protection*, decided by adults;

Level 3: Children have a right to *participate in decisions* made about them;

Level 4: Children have rights *independent of their parents*.

Level 1: Children have no rights to counselling

This category relates to children effectively being denied access to counselling, or having their access severely and unjustifiably constrained. Examples would include a requirement for parental consent to access counselling provided in secondary schools; proposals for the mandatory reporting of under-age sexual activity by counsellors in sexual health clinics; constraints and limitations on the discussion of sexuality in state schools; age limitations on referrals to counselling services in primary care; and refusal of self-referrals by young people to mental health services.

Level 2: Children have rights to welfare and protection, decided by adults

Within this category, children and young people have rights to the provision of counselling, for example, for gay and lesbian young people in care, and for children with a disability, under Guidance and Regulations for the Children Act 1989; for children and young people in schools in Wales; for children who have broken the law, under the UN Convention; and to access pre-trial therapy, when awaiting court action as a witness in the case of alleged abuse. In addition, children and young people have a right to be protected from significant harm, including physical and sexual abuse, under the Children Act 1989.

Level 3: Children have a right to participate in decisions made about them

Under the Children Act 1989, children in care, or those appearing in civil court, have rights to be consulted about decisions being made about them, depending on their age and level of understanding. This right is extended to *all* children by Article 12 of the UN Convention, ratified by the UK government in 1991. This right would include an entitlement to be actively consulted in the contracting process within therapy, for example, regarding the proposed limits to confidentiality; it should also include young people being consulted about school policies on parental permission for accessing counselling, and on proposed closures of youth counselling services by local authorities.

Level 4: Children have rights independent of their parents

Children and young people also hold substantial rights in relation to counselling, which are independent of parents or adult care-takers. Young people aged 16 to 17 have rights to consent and confidentiality equivalent to adults. Young people under 16 have rights to counselling confidentiality and to consent to medical treatment, if of 'sufficient understanding', in the view of the relevant medical practitioner, and, arguably, of the counsellor. Some of these rights are non-age dependent, in that the child has rights to confidentiality of personal data, and to privacy, regardless of age.

In ethical terms, these sets of rights correspond to key ethical principles. Level 1 concerns the *denial of rights* to children and young people, presumably on the basis of age, thereby contradicting the ethical principle of justice. Level 2 rights relate to *classic welfare rights*, including the ethical principles of beneficence, or welfare, and non-maleficence, namely the avoidance of harm to the client. Level 3 rights directly express the broader social value of the child's *participation in decision-making*, which can be linked to the ethical principle of fidelity, or trust. Finally, Level 4 rights are primarily concerned with *autonomy*, and promoting the developing capacity of the child, or young person, for greater independence and acknowledging, in the words of the UN Convention, the 'evolving capacities of the child' (UNICEF, 1989: 5).

In practice, the rights of the child or young person might well be in direct conflict with each other. A child may be entitled to confidentiality (Level 4), but also require immediate protection from harm (Level 2). The age of the child and an assessment of the degree of perceived risk are crucial here. Conversely, a young person may be entitled to privacy in attending a sexual health clinic (Level 4); a parent may claim, however, to be entitled to be informed of this, given their (assumed) rights as a parent (Level 1). The model offers an initial way of recognising complementary, competing and sometimes *conflicting* rights by all the various parties, who are frequently involved in accessing counselling services for children and young people.

Clearly, a rights-based approach to ethics has its own weaknesses. Critiques might point to the implicit emphasis on the value of *autonomy*, as betraying either gender-informed assumptions about desirable developmental norms, or a narrow, cultural bias towards Western expectations for family life. However, a rights-based approach does also offer a way of understanding a major anomaly within the field of counselling provision for children and young people. This is the pronounced influence of *context and institutional setting* on professional and ethical approaches to therapy with children and young people. Practitioner approaches, for example, to confidentiality, can vary enormously between school, medical centre, voluntary agency and private practice, in a confusing range of apparently inconsistent policies. Given that the rights of children and young people are heavily determined by institutional context, a rights-based approach can clarify why the same young person can be offered confidentiality for contraceptive treatment in a general practitioner setting, but be effectively denied confidentiality in a secondary school, via a policy-based requirement for prior parental permission to access counselling (Jenkins, 2013a, 2013b).

Current Issues within *Rule-Based* and *Outcome* Approaches to Ethics

There are a number of crucial ethical principles contained in the BACP Ethical Framework, drawn from a wider tradition of discussion on ethics. These principles include *beneficence*, i.e. promoting welfare, and *non-maleficence*, i.e. avoiding harm. Given some of the factors referred to previously, such as the vulnerability of children and young people, their developmental immaturity and their dependence on adult care-takers, ethical discussion about work with this client group often seeks to emphasise the need to promote welfare and avoid harm, at the expense of limiting autonomy. A consequent shift towards a rule-following approach seems to be explicit in BACP-endorsed literature on safeguarding, with the strong recommendation that 'All therapists should comply with child protection law' (Mitchels and Bond, 2010: 38). This tendency also seems evident from recent BACP policy statements on therapeutic work with children and young people:

> BACP believes that the physical safety of a young person is paramount and that young people in counselling will be led to understand that there are certain limits to confidentiality. (BACP, 2010b: 46)

> BACP believes that counsellors who work with children and young people should pay due regard to current legislation, policy and procedures in education. (BACP, 2010b: 46)

The first of these statements seems uncontentious, except that the term 'paramount' carries a certain added persuasive authority in any ethical and legal discussion. Taken literally, this would mean that *any* risk of physical harm to a person under 18 would entail a limit to confidentiality, regardless of the expressed contrary wishes of the young person concerned. The second statement appears to present safeguarding law and practice in education as the template for good practice for *all* work with children and young people, rather than considering how best practice needs to take account of differing opportunities and constraints for promoting adolescent autonomy, as, for example, can be found in the third, or voluntary, sector.

Ethical Challenges to Maintaining Counselling Confidentiality

No conscientious counsellor would want to place, or leave, a child or young person at evident risk of harm. However, the reality is that many young clients are already engaged in risky behaviour, or have a history of being abused, *before* coming into therapy. Adopting an ethically-informed stance of always reporting such risk or harm, against the client's expressed wishes, runs the risk of breaking the therapeutic alliance, and even of the client later retracting, or minimising, their original disclosures. Daniels and Jenkins present a sustained argument for providing 'confidential spaces' in working with children and young people and suggest possible factors to consider, in deciding whether to initiate a report to the authorities (2010: 99). This stance receives support from a perhaps surprising quarter. The NSPCC presented evidence to the Laming Review (2009), which argued for a 'mixed economy' of services for children, offering differing levels of confidentiality, in order to provide a range of choices and appropriate support for children and young people (2008: 32).

Confidential counselling can offer a safe space for young clients to disclose very private material, often relating to risk of harm or experience of abuse. Research by Rees et al. (n: 24) emphasises the key *relational dimension* to such disclosures, i.e. 'a consistent relationship with a professional they felt they could trust' (2010: 52). This finding is paralleled by Ungar et al. (2009) researching patterns of disclosure of abuse by young people in Canada (n: 1621). They describe such disclosure as 'an interactive process', a 'co-construction'. Disclosure of abuse depended heavily on the young person's perception of the *quality* of their relationship with a trusted adult.

Brown (2006) found that school counsellors (n: 30) were often challenged by dilemmas around confidentiality, with competing demands for information from head or class teachers, and parents. Jenkins and Palmer (2012) found, in a relatively small-scale survey (n: 6), that counsellors worked to protect client confidentiality as far as possible, with the exception of overt child protection incidents, in order to manage high levels of risk for young clients, without breaking the therapeutic frame. In a relatively rare piece of research, on the perceived benefits of supervision for school guidance counsellors in Australia, McMahon and Patton (n: 51) reported on the value of supervision as ongoing support, in 'reducing the professional isolation' of counsellors facing ethical and professional dilemmas (2000: 344).

Key Issues and Concerns in Ethical Practice with Children and Young People

It is, perhaps, evident from the foregoing discussion, that there are no easy answers, in exploring ethical dilemmas in therapy with children and young people. This discussion will now focus on key areas presenting a major challenge to therapists, i.e.:

- ethical issues in contracting
- ethics in counselling research with children and young people

Ethical Issues in Contracting

The process of contracting with the child or young person is important, for clarifying mutual expectations in therapy. This needs to be done in age-appropriate language, geared to the child or young person's level of understanding and verbal ability. For a younger child, starting play therapy will require a very different type of explanation than an older teenager entering into therapeutic work with a mutually agreed focus. The younger the child, the more likely it is that parents, or adult care-takers, will be party to the therapeutic contract. In law, children and young people cannot enter into a contract, with certain very specific exceptions, so any contract for payment will need to be made with parents, or those with parental or other formal responsibility for the child. The contract then essentially requires all three parties, i.e. the child, therapist and those paying for the therapy, to agree the form, focus and duration of the therapy, with discussion obviously taking account of the child's level of understanding. Child psychoanalysts have pointed out that contractual therapy is usually initiated by the parents, as the child may have limited understanding of their own distress, or that their behaviours are becoming problematic for others, or, indeed, of what therapy itself entails. As Anna Freud expressed it, with regard to therapy for younger children: 'The situation lacks everything which seems indispensable in the case of the adult: insight into illness, voluntary decision, and the wish to be cured' (1974: 6).

Contracting, from a rights-based approach, is consistent with honouring the child's right to participate in decisions, within the limits of their understanding. From an ethical point of view, the counsellor needs to work within the limits of their own professional competence, to refer to more a specialist service if necessary, not prolong the therapy beyond the point at which it appears to be of value to the client and to clarify limits to confidentiality regarding any disclosures of abuse, or parental access to detailed information on the therapy itself. Geldard and Geldard set out this aspect of contracting with some clarity:

> We think it is important for parents to understand that it is preferable for the child–counsellor relationship to be exclusive. Therefore, we tell the parents that for counselling to be effective their child will need to feel free to talk openly and confidentially with us. We also say that we realise that it may be uncomfortable for them not to be kept fully informed of what their child is telling us. However, we assure them that we will keep them informed with regard to the overall process. Further, we tell them that if information emerges which they, as parents, have a right to know, we will talk to the child about the necessity of sharing this with them. (2002: 45)

With older children, it is important to spell out the limits to confidentiality very clearly within the contracting process, as young people may not fully appreciate the contextual constraints on reporting disclosures. Research suggests that retaining some element of *control* over disclosures is very important to this older age group, in terms of maintaining their trust in the therapeutic alliance (Rees et al., 2010).

Ethics in Counselling Research with Children and Young People

Counselling research activity with children is driven by the need to promote the well-being of children. However, research with children is also heavily influenced by the need to avoid causing harm to them, on account of their age and vulnerability, both physical and emotional. The major safeguard employed, to promote the rights of children within research and to protect them from harm, is via applying the concept of *informed consent*. Children, and their parents or care-takers, need to be able to give valid consent, on the basis of being provided with sufficient information, so as to make a reasoned choice as to whether or not to participate in any research activity.

Following the Inquiries at Alder Hey Hospital in Liverpool and at Bristol Royal Infirmary, more stringent conditions have been introduced, to protect the rights of parents and children taking part in both medical and social research. Department of Health guidance defines informed consent as being 'at the heart of ethical research' (2005: 7). This concept is also emphasised by relevant professional codes of ethics (BACP, 2010b). The *age* of the child taking part in research is seen as a key factor. The BPS code on research ethics requires that children and young people under 16 need to have *additional* consent from their parents, in order to participate (BPS, 2009:

16). However, it also suggests that this parental consent may be dispensed with, if the result would be to severely constrain significant research, as long as this approach has approval from the relevant research ethics committee.

Research ethics committees have been heavily criticised for introducing bureaucratic procedures into the research process. These procedures can also be notoriously risk averse, regarding research with children. The effect has been, arguably, to limit couns elling research with some marginalised groups of children and young people, seen to be 'high-risk' in research terms, such as lesbian, gay, transgendered, bisexual, queer, or questioning their own sexuality (McDermott, 2010), or young women with eating disorders (Halse and Honey, 2005). From a *rights-based perspective*, research committees may thus be in danger of adopting a paternalist or protectionist approach, but at the cost of denying the potential for *autonomy* of young research subjects.

Seen from a narrowly legal perspective, research codes may also be in danger of making a number of errors with regard to children taking part in counselling research. Firstly, the law requires only the lower standard of *consent* for research participation (other than clinical trials), rather than the higher, ethically-driven standard of *informed consent* (Masson, 2004: 50). Secondly, children under 16 in England and Wales can consent on their own to taking part in research, on the basis of their demonstrating 'sufficient understanding', following the *Gillick* decision. This view is also clearly stated in the Mental Health Act Code of Practice (DoH, 2008a: Para 36.38).

Best practice in counselling research ethics continues to rest on the process of obtaining informed consent from children, and, in the case of younger children, also from their parents or care-takers. The process of obtaining informed consent from a younger research participant is illustrated below. Here, the researcher was looking at adoption support services, and initially explained the research to the child's parents, leaving an information pack for the eight-year-old daughter. In a later phone call made by the researcher with the permission of the girl's parents, the girl asked the following questions about the research itself (DoH, 2005: 12):

- How long do you want to talk to me?
- Will you tell anyone what I say?
- Will you write down what I say?
- Will anyone reading the book know me?
- Will you all come to speak to me?
- What if I'm not sure? Can I change my mind?

In essence, this girl is covering, in her own way, the essential features of confidentiality and informed consent. Greig et al. (2007: 175–6) define this for children, as consisting of the following characteristics, depending on their level of understanding:

- knowing they have a choice;
- knowing they have the right to withdraw;
- knowing exactly what their role is in the research;
- knowing what will happen to the research data.

Case Study   Richmond Moves to Reassure Critics over Catholic 'Counselling' Body in Schools

The London Borough of Richmond upon Thames has tried to reassure critics about its decision to award an £89,000 contract to the Catholic Children's Society to offer counselling and support to children in the borough's schools. It comes after Baroness Jenny Tonge – an ex-MP for Richmond Park – said: 'It is unfair and irrational for the council to impose Catholic thinking on the entire population of young people in this borough, the vast majority of whom are not Catholic or may have no religion at all.'

But Richmond Council insisted that staff from the Catholic Children's Society were committed 'first and foremost' to their professional standards and 'not by standards of the Catholic Church'. The Society, which is accredited by the British Association for Counselling and Psychotherapy, said in a statement that its counsellors respect other beliefs and would not try to convert or pass judgement on children.

It said: 'Issues raised in counselling are therefore explored in a way which respects the autonomy of the individual receiving counselling. On matters pertaining to sexual health, such as contraception and teenage pregnancy, we ensure that young people are referred to medical health services where the appropriate professional advice and guidance can be given. In particular, young people who come to our counsellors because they are unsure about their sexuality and may be frightened and confused are treated with sensitivity. On the matter of homophobic bullying in schools, we work with students to use the appropriate policies and procedures within schools to address this.'

The Society was required to sign the Council's equalities policy before it won the contract in February (20 May 2011; abridged. Reprinted with the kind permission of the National Secular Society. Available at: www.secularism.org.uk/richmond-moves-to-reassure-criti.html accessed 12/11/12).

Summary

- Ethics is concerned with addressing, and attempting to find answers to, key therapeutic dilemmas
- Professional codes of ethics, such as the BACP Ethical Framework (2010b) offer a *framework*, to support counsellors in responding to both everyday and more complex and unusual challenges to therapeutic practice

- Approaches to ethics can include rule-following, outcomes-based and the explicitly rights-based model underpinning the arguments put forward in this chapter
- This chapter follows a very broad distinction, made between *children*, i.e. 6–11 years, who are assumed not to be mature enough to make decisions for their own care, and *young people*, i.e. 11–18 years, who may have developed sufficient maturity to do so
- Counselling work with children and young people is often considered to be a distinct field in terms of ethics, because of the child or young person's developmental, physical and emotional vulnerability, requiring correspondingly higher levels of ethical awareness and therapeutic competence from practitioners

Reflective Questions

1 What are the rights of children and young people in the situation discussed in the case study?

Children and young people have a number of rights in this situation. They have a right to:

- a say in decisions being made about them, under Article 12 of the UN Convention on the Rights of the Child (UNICEF, 1989);
- confidential access to information and medical treatment on sexual health and counselling

  o depending on their having 'sufficient understanding', if aged under 16;
  o on the same basis as an adult if aged 16–17;

- not to be discriminated against in the provision of their rights, under Article 2 of the UN Convention.

2 How can the rights of children and young people be maintained and protected in this situation?

- by providing children and young people with full information about their rights, as required by the UN Convention, under Article 42;
- by independent monitoring and evaluation of the referral patterns, outcomes and satisfaction levels of children and young people accessing the service;
- by actively involving children and young people in the management of the service, in ways consistent with their age and understanding.

3 How might the rights of children (i.e. aged 6–11 years) be different from those of young people (i.e. aged 11–18 years) when accessing counselling from this agency?

- differing levels of understanding, leading to more limited entitlement to confidentiality for children, on the *Gillick* principle;
- a heightened balance for *welfare* considerations for children, compared with *autonomy* considerations for young people;
- potentially greater scope for counsellor risk-taking with young people, based on ethically-informed practice.

Learning Activities

1. Read the case study above:

   o should counselling services be awarded to faith-based organisations?
   o what ethical issues might this faith-based counselling provision raise for children and young people accessing this service?
   o how might the professional and ethical standards of a faith-based counselling service be monitored, in order to ensure compliance with equal opportunities principles?

2. Look at the ethical principles contained in the BACP Ethical Framework (2010b)

   o which of these principles are potentially *consistent* with faith-based provision of a counselling service for children and young people?
   o which principles might potentially *conflict* with faith-based counselling provision for children and young people?
   o how might any such ethical conflicts be addressed and resolved?

3. Review the material in this chapter on approaches to ethics, i.e.

   o rule-following
   o outcomes-based
   o rights-based

   How might each of these ethical approaches be applied to this situation? Where would the significant differences, if any, be found between these approaches?

Background Material on Activities and Case Study

- In 2009, the Catholic Children's Society withdrew from the process of approving same-sex adopters, on the grounds that this was incompatible with the teachings of the Church. This requirement was brought into law by the Equality Act (Sexual Orientation) Regulations of 2007.
- The decision by Richmond Council to award a contract for the provision of counselling services to the Catholic Children's Society was criticised by gay, secular and humanist organisations, as being likely to lead to potential bias against, or exclusion from, helping services, of young people, given the religious beliefs of the provider.
- The Catholic Children's Society is accredited by the British Association for Counselling and Psychotherapy, and must comply with its Ethical Framework (2010b). It is also subject to the complaints and disciplinary procedures of the BACP.
- The Catholic Children's Society (CCS) has agreed to comply with the Council's equalities policy, as a necessary part of the process of being awarded the contract. The CCS has also stated that it will respect the autonomy of children and young people, make appropriate referrals to medical and sexual health centres, and respond sympathetically to young people experiencing homophobic bullying in schools and elsewhere.

Using Different Models of Ethics with the Case Study

Rule-following approach: The counselling provision could be monitored by the Council and by BACP, or by an independent body, to ensure compliance with the existing equalities policy and with key ethical principles, such as autonomy and justice, drawn from the BACP Ethical Framework.

Outcomes approach: The provision could be monitored and evaluated by the Council, BACP or by an independent body, to ensure a continuing rate of referrals to gay counselling organisations, and to sexual health clinics. Rates of access (or non-access) by young people from a range of religious backgrounds, race, ethnicity and sexual orientation could be audited, to identify the effects of faith-based provision.

Rights-based approach: The ongoing practice of the agency could be monitored and evaluated, to identify the extent to which attitudes and professional counselling practice reflected particular models of rights, e.g. potential denial of rights to gay and lesbian young people; welfare rights of provision and protection from harm; rights to participation in decision-making; and rights to autonomy consistent with the *Gillick* decision.

Further Reading

British Association for Counselling and Psychotherapy (2010) *Ethical Framework for Good Practice in Counselling and Psychotherapy*. Lutterworth: BACP.

Daniels, D. and Jenkins, P. (2010) *Therapy with Children: Children's Rights, Confidentiality and the Law*. 2nd edn. London: SAGE.

UNICEF (1989) *The United Nations Convention on the Rights of the Child 1989*. London: UNICEF.

Online Resources

Counselling MindEd: http://counsellingminded.com., especially Module CMD 03: Legal and Professional Issues.

19

Diversity

Sue Pattison, Divine Charura and Tom McAndrew

This chapter includes:

- The importance of transcultural working with children and young people
- Neurological development and damage due to traumatic experiences related to diversity such as disability, discrimination or asylum and its causes
- Communicating with deaf young people
- Communication with children and young people who have learning disabilities

Introduction

Working with children and young people in therapeutic settings is specialist work, which has many dimensions of influence. Children and young people are a heterogeneous group with diversity in language, culture, family histories, social classes, and experiences of life events. For those who come for counselling or are in contact with services, their experiences may include abuse, adoption, death of a loved one, and other multiple levels of loss and trauma. Such diversity of experiences and backgrounds has led to the development of specialist transcultural and diversity practice. It is not possible to cover the full range of diversity and related counselling practices.

This chapter can be viewed as a taster, something to whet your appetite for the overt and covert aspects of diversity. The authors have knowledge and experience in the field of counselling, psychotherapy, education and working in practice with the diverse range of young clients referred to in the text. Divine and Sue are researchers, therapists and educationalists, while Tom is a qualified and experienced teacher of the deaf. Each of us has developed a range of skills and techniques to aid communication and we have learnt from each other through collaborating on the writing of this chapter. At the heart of our work we share fundamental values, those of acceptance, empowerment, the rights of the child, inclusion and a love of humanity.

The Importance of Transcultural Working with Children and Young People

Transcultural and intercultural therapy was pioneered as a result of dissatisfaction of therapists trying to apply Eurocentric models of training and practice in their work with non-European migrants and their families (Kareem and Littlewood, 1992; Lago, 2011). Recognition of cultural, racial, ethnic and the wider impact of socio-political and economic influences on the therapeutic relationship are important aspects of therapy.

Within the last two decades many parts of the world, including within the UK, have become increasingly multicultural. This has influenced further development of transcultural counselling and multicultural practice within therapy (Lago, 2011). As such, this way of working has permeated not only in working with adults in therapy but also in working with children and young people whose wider experiences are reflected in therapy, and they show how they are increasingly influenced and affected by not only personal but also wider societal and cultural issues. Several factors are central to transcultural counselling, including the importance of the development of skills in meeting the needs of children and young people from diverse backgrounds in the therapeutic relationship and counsellor self-reflection in responding to dynamics and interventions specific to working with diversity and within transcultural settings. This will inform practitioners' thinking when assessing children, exploring issues of race and cultural discrimination, and will influence decision-making as well as the therapeutic process when issues of race, culture, disability, and ethnicity are taken into account. The role of therapy with children and young people is to provide a safe and ethical way to explore their experiences, unpack their problem story and its cultural underpinnings, explore their concept of self as a result of the experience and also to make visible information or perspectives that are neglected through the problem story filter (Beaudoin, 2004, 2005).

Lago (2006) noted that clinical practice and research indicates just how important it is for the therapist to both respect and acknowledge diversity and difference in the therapeutic setting. That is, the capacity of therapists to recognise and value unconditionally the (diverse) clients and their circumstances. Smith and Widdowson (2003) highlighted the importance of child-centred practice. They identified the disadvantages and experiences faced by black, disabled or working-class children. They postulated a framework to work from and stated that children who are different will be acutely aware of their difference and hence will need affirmation for that difference. Children and young people from minority ethnic groups have specific identity needs relating to knowledge about their cultural roots/identity and hence it is important to respond to this as to ignore it may disadvantage them in later life in their understanding and acceptance or comfort of self (Smith and Widdowson, 2003). Furthermore, Charura (2012) highlighted the importance of therapists and professionals carefully considering the hypersensitivity and the skills necessary in working with children and young people. When working with difference, transcultural counselling is an example of working with diversity in children that embraces the child's diversity/ difference. It uses the recognition that within the therapeutic relationship the child can be helped to integrate their experience and accept their identity and cultural roots (Charura, 2012).

Counselling Children Impacted by Abuse or Trauma Related to Their Difference

Unsurprisingly, the children and young people who access therapy or services are often referred because they have experienced abuse or trauma related to their difference, which has had a negative impact on their lives. At times they may want to deal with existential experiences such as disability, discrimination, or other experiences affecting them. Therefore, it is important for us to be aware of the growing range of modalities to support children and the research evidence of their effectiveness. As with any therapeutic approach, such new approaches need to be viewed with caution and the first intention should be 'to do no harm'. There is a large body of literature and research pointing out the dangers of re-traumatising children by involving them in a retelling of their story, including traumatic experiences (Adam-Westcott and Isenbart, 1995; White and Epston, 1990; Durrant and White, 1992; White, 2004a). Many of these articles are drawn from family therapy theory [narrative therapy] which engages people in a process that distances them from their experience of problems in ways that can allow them to re-examine, reflect and deconstruct problems' influence over their lives (Freedman and Combs, 1996; Beaudoin, 2005).

Scott and Stradling (2006) provide information on another approach to working with children and young people experiencing post-traumatic stress. They suggest four goals that counsellors can work towards:

1. Developing a strong therapeutic alliance/relationship of safety with the child/young person
2. Obtaining a clear description of the trauma
3. Focusing on working with problematic behaviours
4. Helping the young client to understand the connections between thoughts and feelings

As with all interventions which value anti-discriminatory practice, this way of working should also at all times consider the differences in children and young people and influences of culture/experiences on the articulation of emotions and feelings, along with the child's willingness to engage with the therapeutic process.

Therapeutic interventions for children who have had difficult and traumatic experiences can be invaluable and it is important that counsellors can offer supportive and therapeutic interventions that are reparatory and can respond to the needs of a diverse young population. Engaging children and young people in therapy or services is specialist work, which needs to be carried out with expertise, caution and care in order to avoid further damage or re-traumatisation, leaving both the young person and therapist stuck. Professional organisations such as BACP, UKCP and BPS provide good practice guidance for working with children and young people and ethical frameworks that can help counsellors to make decisions about their practice based on judgements made in relation to potential harm weighed against the benefits of individual therapies. The issues discussed in this chapter therefore raise important points for therapeutic arenas in the offering of therapeutic modalities that employ a true valuing of diversity in helping children and young people.

Case Study   Tarie

Tarie is a young black African girl, aged 14 years. She came to the UK from Rwanda as an unaccompanied minor over three years ago following serious political violence aimed against her, which included rape and torture. Tarie also witnessed most of her family members being killed. She was referred by a health professional in the UK to an organisation which works with refugees and asylum seekers following serious concerns of depression and an episode of self-harm. This episode followed reports of being bullied in school and being called names because she is black.

Initially in therapy, despite being supported to communicate by a translator, Tarie was unwilling to talk about her experiences. However, as the weeks went on Tarie referred to her life prior to coming to the UK and in particular her childhood experiences. She was forced to be a war rebel's sex slave, a child soldier, and described nearly being killed on two occasions. In counselling, she often described how she felt that she was no longer the person she thought she would

(Continued)

(Continued)

be. She stated that she had discussions with two adult women from her country she met at the church she now goes to and told them about her family and her situation. She was informed by them that that all her life experiences were influenced by voodoo, and transgenerational misfortune. She shared some of her cultural metaphors with the counsellor, including the historical practices of voodoo and witchcraft in her family, which she had witnessed when she was much younger. Tarie told her counsellor that a child psychiatrist/psychologist who had worked with her in the past had suggested that any connotations of voodoo practices were not scientifically founded and were hallucinations and paranoia. Tarie shared with the counsellor how she believed that her parents and grandparents whom she had witnessed being killed were now ancestors who looked over her and helped her in times of crisis and that at times she could hear her grandmother speaking to her.

Issues raised in this case study include working with trauma, depression, rape, multiple levels of loss and bereavement, cultural practices, such as voodoo and witchcraft, religion, beliefs on death and life and also working with a young person who hears voices. It also raises questions and issues regarding the type of support that can be provided for such a young person, including the need for a translator.

Neurological Development and Damage Due to Traumatic Experiences Related to Diversity

Developmental processes are discussed more fully in Chapter 1. However, a brief look at neurological development here is intended to refresh the reader's memory and make the material more accessible when applied to aspects of diversity. The importance of love and attachments within primary relationships and their impact on children's mental and physical well-being is well documented (Joseph, 1999; Gerhardt, 2004). Joseph (1999) highlighted the relationship between children's experiences and neurological development at different age stages.

Van der Kolk (1994, 2005) describes the neurological impact of trauma in childhood and how the child's detachment is expressed in their body, by a 'shutting down' of sensation, the body protecting itself from trauma, for example, rape, torture and natural disasters, as experienced by some children and young people from war-torn countries who may access our counselling services as refugees. This 'shutting down' affects how the child or young person feels, learns and moves in the world as they are developing their vital physical skills. This highlights the neurological impact of trauma on children's behaviour and self-concept. This can continue to be evident in early adulthood manifesting as disruptive behaviour, inability to connect emotionally, and personality complexities if therapeutic change does not occur. Cook et al. (2005) identify a wide range of areas in which deficits arise after early relational trauma: cognition, self-concept, affect regulation, attachment, biology, behavioural control and dissociation. Goldfinch (2009) concurred with this and further states that when children experience trauma early in life, when their nervous system is immature, then the development of their concept of self and of others is disturbed (Drell et al., 1993). She further argues that young children are more vulnerable to trauma because they are more dependent on their environment and less able to self-regulate than adults.

Communicating with Deaf Children and Young People

Although there are many types of disability that can affect communication in the couns elling context (the section following this focuses on young people who have learning disabilities), hearing impairment can fundamentally affect how a child or young person communicates and the quality and type of communication possible. Communicating with young deaf people can be challenging and in order to be effective and make couns elling accessible, a range of skills, some knowledge and experience is very useful. In this section we look at some of the considerations you will need to take into account. Over 40 per cent of deaf people have additional special needs, such as autism, Down's syndrome or other congenital disorders, and they may have physical disabilities or may be deaf-blind. This section refers specifically to young deaf clients without additional complex needs.

Terminology

The term deaf is often used to refer to people with a hearing loss. However, Deaf with a capital 'D' refers to people who identify themselves as part of the sign language using Deaf Community. In the UK, the Deaf Community communicates in British Sign Language (BSL). In reality, there is a spectrum of hearing loss across the frequency range and it is rarely uniform: hearing loss can be mild, moderate, severe or pro- found. People with mild to moderate hearing losses may refer to themselves as hearing impaired or hard of hearing. The latter term is more widely acceptable internation- ally, although both are used in the UK. For counselling purposes it is important to be aware of these basic differences in terminology so as to minimise the risk of offence (Marschark and Hauser, 2008).

Cultural and Educational Backgrounds

Over 90 per cent of deaf children are born to hearing parents (Knight and Swanwick, 1996) and for most of these hearing parents it comes as a shock to have a deaf child, especially if there has been no history of deafness in the family. They often go through a grieving process and may have difficulties accepting their child's deafness. Hearing parents of deaf children rarely have sign language skills at the time of diagnosis and although some parents may take on board learning about deafness, baby signing and British Sign Language (BSL), others may choose not to learn BSL – they may not have the necessary motivation to learn this language or indeed be advised not to learn it by some, otherwise well-meaning professionals.

Many deaf children of hearing parents (DCHP) take an oral pathway in education and are fully integrated into mainstream schools or go to mainstream schools with a hearing impaired (HI) unit attached. Consequently these children have not grown up as members of the Deaf Community and may not have developed the sign language skills to communicate that enable communication with this community. They do not necessarily share the same cultural values and could feel they belong more to the wider hearing community, an issue around diversity that counsellors may need to be aware of.

Many of the 10 per cent of deaf children of deaf parents (DCDP) are members of the Deaf Community from birth since they more are likely to grow up with BSL as a preferred/first language and have contact with Deaf Clubs and organisations associated with the Deaf Community from an early age, which helps to nurture a distinctive Deaf culture. Deaf parents are more likely to opt for a sign-based educational pathway (e.g. Total Communication or Sign Bilingual Education) for their deaf children. However, it needs to be emphasised that some DCDP take oral pathways in education and some DCHP take sign-based educational pathways, which means that forms of communication cannot be assumed by the counsellor. The pathway taken depends on the level of hearing loss, aids used (e.g. hearing aids or cochlear implants) and the availability/type of specialised deaf education institutions near to where they live and, of course, parental choice.

Deaf children, especially teenagers and young adults, could be very confused as to whether they belong to the Deaf Community or not. A deaf child whose preferred language is spoken English and has more of an affinity with the wider hearing society may join the Deaf Community through later association with its members. It is also important to realise there are different sign languages for each country and there are regional variations within countries too. Deaf people from ethnic minorities in the UK will also have been exposed to their parents' native language (whether through speech sounds or writing) as well as another sign language. Deaf and young people who have sought refuge in the UK with or without their families may be more vulnerable regarding lack of communication than others due to their exposure to trauma, loss and unavailability of sign language translators from their linguistic or cultural background. In addition to these difficulties, some young people may have been deafened through the violence of armed conflicts without any opportunity for treatment or education in forms of communication. Their experience can be extremely traumatic and enduring.

Methods of Communication

There are various ways of communicating with young deaf people. BSL and other sign languages have already been mentioned as well as speech for mild to moderately deaf people (or deaf people with cochlear implants). However, there are also other sign systems that can aid communication with young deaf people. Although the examples presented here cannot be detailed, there is much information available through a range of internet websites. Examples of other sign systems include: Sign Supported English (SSE), Manually Coded English (MCE), Seeing Exact English (SEE), Signed English (SE), Cued Speech, Paget–Gorman, Makaton and Finger-spelling (Knight and Swanwick, 1996). These systems are mainly used in deaf education to help support and encourage speech, written grammar, spelling (Finger-spelling) or to communicate on a basic level with deaf people with complex needs (Makaton). It must be emphasised that they are not languages; they are methods of communication used by professionals and deaf people in specific contexts.

This section does not describe the full variety of communication systems in detail. However, if a young client does express a wish for one of the above systems to be used then the counsellor may consider learning more about this particular method or contacting a competent user to act as a form of interpreter. Another aid to communication includes lip-speaking. A trained lip-speaker can use facial expression and clearer lip patterns to make the speaker more easily understood. This is an option that also needs taking into consideration by the counsellor.

Long-Term Preparation for Communicating with Deaf People

Going on a Deaf Awareness course is a fundamental starting point for counsellors who want to work with young deaf clients. The next step would be to start learning BSL, ideally progressing to a highly competent level but at least to a basic level so that introductions and basic conversations can be held. This would reassure the young deaf client that their counsellor is aware of their language and culture and have the effect of putting them at ease and promoting the development of a stronger therapeutic relationship.

Eventually being a fluent signer of BSL will enable a counsellor to directly communicate effectively to young members of the Deaf Community without recourse to booking an interpreter. Two-way rather than three-way communication will lead to more effective counselling and safeguard against confidentiality issues (interpreters, by the very nature of their job, will be privy to very personal information about the deaf client). However, counsellors cannot assume that young deaf clients value confidentiality in the same way that hearing clients do; by the very nature of the world in which a deaf young person operates, familiarity may foster greater trust and confidence. If a BSL-English interpreter is required, BSL users usually have a preferred interpreter who may be a family member or someone they use on a regular basis in contexts other than counselling. The young deaf person may feel more comfortable with an interpreter they are familiar with. Many parents and guardians of deaf young people will book an interpreter themselves but it is wise to check just in case the family expects the counsellor to organise this service. Also, it is prudent to have the contact details of one or two BSL/English interpreter agencies in case the client's usual interpreter is not available. The issue of funding for interpretation services should be addressed by all counsellors prior to beginning a therapeutic intervention. The initial assessment stage of counselling may need to be longer to make sure that the needs of the young client are met in the most effective and appropriate way.

There may be other difficulties around the provision of communication support for young deaf clients, for example, family members who take on the role of interpreters for their children may not be ideal during counselling sessions because their signing skills may not necessarily be of a high enough level. In addition, the child's trust or confidence in their family members, especially when discussing sensitive personal feelings, cannot be guaranteed. Most competent BSL/English interpreters will be members of the Association of Sign Language Interpreters (ASLI) and work to a Code of Practice that includes confidentiality in relation to the content of their interpretation.

Deaf Awareness

The following guidance cannot replace a course on Deaf Awareness but it can help counsellors with the basics. Regardless of the client's level of hearing loss, it is good practice to always face the client whilst talking/communicating, to speak clearly and evenly rather than exaggerating facial expressions. The background environment is also important, with the counsellor being more visible when sitting in front of a plain background, rather than, for example, highly patterned wallpaper or pictures. It is more difficult for a young deaf client to lip-read the counsellor or interpret signs, if using BSL, with an irregular background.

It is useful for counsellors to have an awareness of the range of technology to help deaf young people maximise the use of their residual hearing (remember, most deaf people are not profoundly deaf). For many, a particular model of behind-the-ear (BTE) digital hearing aid or one of the other types of hearing aid will be worn. More and more deaf young people have cochlear implants and the recent trend is for young people to have cochlear implants for both ears. However, these are simply aids to using residual hearing – not cures for deafness.

When using a BSL/English interpreter, it is good practice for the counsellor to always address the client, not the interpreter. It is useful to be aware that there will be a short time delay between the words you have spoken and the interpreter's signed translation. BSL interpreters work to a strict Code of Practice and if there is only one translator, the counsellor should make sure they give the interpreter short breaks every 15 minutes since it is a very intense and tiring activity. If you want to get your client's attention, tap them on the shoulder or give a hand signal that is appropriate and clearly visible (mainly for severe to profoundly deaf clients; for mild to moderately deaf clients this may not be required). This may go against some counsellors' practice of not touching clients. However, in order to provide an appropriate service to young deaf clients, flexibility rather than rigidity is essential.

Counselling Young People with Learning Disabilities: A Proactive Process

In this section we put forward a proactive process through which counsellors can 'step out, reach out and move out' to include young people with learning disabilities in mainstream counselling. The concept of being proactive was addressed by Viktor Frankl in his book *Man's Search for Meaning* (1946) and has at its heart a process of taking responsibility, not looking to others or outside circumstances, but having the courage, perseverance, awareness of the existence of choices, regardless of the situation or context. Martin (2001) refers to Frankl's work in his assertion that 'the active choice is to play the game; the proactive choice is to change the rules of the game, especially when the rules of engagement are unfair'. The rules of 'the game' are inherently unfair for young people who have learning disabilities, by definition present during childhood, impacting on developmental processes and manifesting in a variety of ways including the presence of a significantly reduced ability to understand new or complex information, to learn new skills (impaired intelligence, usually an IQ below 70; WHO, 1999), with reduced ability to cope independently leading to impaired social functioning (APA, 1994; WHO, 2003). The major argument for specifically including young people with learning disabilities in counselling rests on four major premises. Firstly, the low level of perceived well-being among young people with learning disabilities in the UK (UNICEF, 2007) and their high level of emotional distress and psychological problems (NSPCC, 2007; WHO, 2001); secondly, and more specifically, the high level of mental health problems in young people with learning disabilities referred to as 'dual diagnosis' (Raghavan and Patel, 2008; NSPCC, 2007; Allington-Smith, 2006; Royal College Psychiatrists, 2004). Thirdly, the international human rights movement and literature on human rights (Morrall and Hazleton, 2004; Shakespeare, 2006) and national social inclusion policies (HM Government, 2006; Social Exclusion Unit, 2004; Ofsted, 2004). Finally, national policies aimed at addressing the needs of children and young people in contemporary society (DfES, 2003, 2004a) form the political canvas against which practices may be funded and developed. How can school counsellors become more inclusive? Human rights policies that provide the impetus for inclusive counselling are the Disability Rights Commission Act (1999); Human Rights Act (1998); United Nations Declaration of the Rights of Disabled People (1975); United Nations Convention on the Rights of the Child (1989); United Nations Standard Rules in the Equalisation of Opportunities for Persons with Disabilities (1993); and the National Advisory Committee on Creative and Cultural Education (1999).

Research carried out by Pattison (2010) indicates that counsellors who are proactive in raising awareness of the service to young people, their parents or carers, and within organisations working with young people (reaching out) and who provide inclusive initial assessments, found that the level of inclusivity in their practices and processes increased and they saw more young people with learning disabilities in their counselling rooms. Similarly, a proactive use of advocacy through the young person's teacher, support worker, parent or peers improved inclusivity. Moreover, an integrated partnership approach, including building relationships with parents/carers, school staff, statutory health and social care professionals, and/or voluntary agencies and charitable trusts, raised inclusiveness in counselling. This can be aligned with national polices supporting the needs of young people (DfES, 2003, 2004a); DoH/HO, DfEE, 1999) and provides the 'bottom-up' approach that can make 'wrap around care' policies work in practice. In order to support these processes counsellors may require specialist training in learning disability issues leading to the paradoxical position of specialist training leading to more inclusive practices in the mainstream context. In Pattison's (2010) study, linked to counsellors' expressed need for specialist training was the need for experienced supervision. In the school context counsellors' requirement for supervisors experienced in working with children and young people, along with knowledge and experience of the school context, is well documented (WAG, 2008; BACP, 2006). However, no mention is made of the value of knowledge and awareness of learning disability issues. This highlights the poor visibility of this client group in mainstream policy documents.

The most inclusive counsellors are clear about what works for them and they proactively include young people with learning disabilities in both their practices and processes. By far the most effective factor is building relationships, with the client, with members of staff who have enabling roles in schools, health and social care services, and parents/carers. In terms of specific client work, the engagement and process of counselling is enabled through proactive relationship building and communication. Pattison (2010) found that by trying out various imaginative and creative approaches and the use of simplified language, most importantly at the initial assessment stage, counsellors discovered ways of communicating that worked. The barriers to inclusion were largely located in systems, for example, resources, time, money, and training. In order to overcome these barriers, a proactive approach to the operationalisation of equal opportunities policies is recommended, and this brings us back to the quote at the beginning of this section by Martin (2001) with reference to Frankl's (1946) work. The overt rules of the game appear inclusive, supported by policies and legislation. However, the hidden organisational, social and political discourses, or covert 'rules of the game', may differ and relate more to resource management and educational, health and social care agendas that are adopted by organisations in response to central policies, for example meritocratic goals and league table achievements in schools and a hierarchy of resource distribution in the NHS and social care services (DfES, 2004b, 2008). These dual discourses and agendas may extend into the counselling service, impacting on practices and processes in ways that can exclude some young people from counselling when they may benefit from the service, for example, referral for behavioural programmes when the young person's behaviour is an external expression of their emotional distress. Martin (2001) proposes that Viktor Frankl's proactive stance builds upon foreknowledge (intelligence) and creativity to anticipate and see situations as opportunities and to influence systems constructively for the good of the client.

Summary

As identified in the introduction to this chapter, working with children in therapeutic settings is specialist work. We identified that children and young people are not a homogeneous group and display diversity in language, culture, family histories, social class, and life experiences. The reasons for therapy are also diverse, and young people's experiences may include abuse, adoption, death of a loved one, and other multiple levels of loss and trauma. It has not been possible to cover the full range of diversity and related counselling practices. Therefore, this chapter has focused on:

(Continued)

(Continued)

- transcultural working with children and young people
- neurological development and damage due to traumatic experiences related to diversity such as disability, discrimination or asylum and its causes
- communicating with deaf young people
- communicating with young people who have learning disabilities

Reflective Questions

1 What challenging issues can you identify in the case study – Tarie?

The challenging issues are those that any counsellor could face with a young client: working with risk in terms of psychological holding and self-harm, listening to stories of severe trauma and violence and being 'with' Tarie, yet keeping self safe. There are also issues of spirituality that may be in line with or against your own belief systems.

2 What therapeutic approach would you take in supporting Tarie?

A transcultural approach would involve listening to and accepting Tarie's accounts of her experience within a framework of cultural and spiritual material that may be very different to your own.

3 How could you prepare for future work with deaf children and young people?

By taking a Deaf Awareness course in the first instance, you will become more aware and knowledgeable in respect of issues that may impact on your young deaf clients and learn more about methods of communication. Further preparation would include courses in British Sign Language, or the sign language of your own country.

Learning Activities

1. Make contact with your local Deaf Club – the College of Further Education in your area will be able to provide contact details. You may be able to visit and get to know some useful contacts, building up a network to draw upon when you need a BSL translator or advice and guidance on deaf issues.
2. Look at the anti-discrimination policies in your counselling setting and assess accessibility for children and young people of difference.
3. Get to know the local community where you are based for your counselling work, and get a feel for issues around diversity that impact generally in that community.

Further Reading

Glickman, N.S. (2013) *Culturally Affirmative Psychotherapy with Deaf Persons*. New York: Routledge.

Lago, C. (ed.) (2011) *The Handbook of Transcultural Counselling and Psychotherapy*. Maidenhead: Open University Press/McGraw-Hill.

Zand, D.H. and Pierce, K.J. (eds) (2011) *Resilience in Deaf Children: Adaptation through Emerging Adulthood*. New York: Springer.

Online Resources

BACP website: www.bacp.co.uk/, especially the BACP Children and Young People Division and the Competences for Working with Children and Young People.

Counselling MindEd: http://counsellingminded.com. MN8 Cultural Competence and Equalities Issues for CYP and Families, MN 8.01, MN 8.02, CM.

20

Bereavement

Maggie Robson

This chapter includes:

- Loss and bereavement
- Whether therapeutic interventions can help children and young people who have experienced significant loss
- The differences when working with children and young people
- The theoretical underpinning of the experience of grief and its relationship to attachment and developmental stage

Terminology and the Loss Experience

Bereavement and loss are terms which are often used interchangeably but which have slightly different meanings. Bereavement is commonly used to mean mourning after the loss by death of a significant person in our life. Loss may be described as any loss experience that causes an individual to re-evaluate their worldview, as well as their past, present and future, as a result of that experience. Loss can thus encompass bereavement and can include the results of other experiences such as divorce, abuse, death of a pet and moving house. This re-evaluation means that we can no longer take for granted assumptions about our world; our assumptive world changes (Lewin, 1935; Parkes, 1993). For example, if a young girl's mother dies, she can no longer assume that her

Mum will greet her at the door on her return from school. She can no longer assume she can share the ups and downs of her day with her. A small boy can no longer assume that his older brother will be there to protect him in the playground or to play football. However, we need to have assumptions in our internal world in order to function as a psychologically healthy people. The process of bereavement, therefore, is about adapting to these losses in our internal world and restoring a degree of denial that life is transient and fragile.

Loss is strongly connected to change as most change involves some loss and loss always involves change. Parkes (1993) argues that bereavement may be viewed as a process of adaptation to change (a psychosocial transition) whilst also acknowledging the role of attachment in shaping our responses to loss. The significance of the loss experience may not necessarily be confined to physical loss but can be symbolic in nature, depending on the meaning the individual attributes to the experience, for example, lost childhood due to abuse.

Grief is the result of experiencing both bereavement and loss and is the process we go through when mourning. In bereavement, we may be consumed by images and thoughts of the dead person, feel overwhelmed by sadness and also experience more unexpected emotions such as guilt that we have survived or that we did not prevent the death, anger at the dead person for dying and leaving us, relief that the dead person is no longer in pain or even relief that the dead person is no longer able to harm us. In other losses we may experience a similar complex and possibly ambivalent mix of thoughts and feelings which may have an effect upon our behaviour.

The emotions we experience when we are bereft can be overwhelming – we can feel that we will never be able to function 'normally' again or be the same as we were before the experience. Although most theories of loss and bereavement (Bowlby, 1980; Worden, 1991; Stroebe and Schut, 1999) tend to talk about adjusting to the loss and disengaging from the deceased in order to reinvest our emotional energy in others, Silverman and Klass argue that the process of mourning is about maintaining the relationship with the deceased, albeit in a different form:

> rather than emphasising letting go, the emphasis should be on negotiating and renegotiating the meaning of the loss over time. While the death is permanent and unchanging, the process is not. (1996: 18)

If our loss is significant, it may be that part of us always remains grieving (Hunt, 2004). This does not mean that we cannot still lead satisfying and fulfilling lives but that our grieving self will always be with us, sometimes very much in the background of our lives, but sometimes in the forefront, and can feel as raw as when first experienced. This rawness, however, may be present less and less as time passes. The effects of loss can be imagined as being like ripples in a pond after a stone has been thrown in with the biggest waves nearest the stone and getting smaller and gentler as they get further away. However, big waves can come and take us by surprise! The effects of loss can also be physical – we can feel as if our heart is breaking and, in fact, the experience of grief can be linked to depression, somatic symptoms and interpersonal problems (Goodman and Brown, 2008).

Is Therapeutic Intervention Helpful when Children and Young People Experience Loss?

All human beings are driven to try and make sense of their experiences even though, in the case of significant loss, there may seem to be no sense to it, and the grieving process is a way of making this sense. Counselling can help us to do this but may not always be the most appropriate response for children and young people.

Bereavement and loss can be viewed as a 'natural' part of our experiencing. There is, therefore, a debate about whether counselling is appropriate for people who have experienced loss as loss is a normal and natural part of our life, not something pathological or unusual (Bonanno and Lilienfeld, 2008). Parkes (1998) suggests that there is:

> no evidence that all bereaved people will benefit from counselling and research has shown no benefits to arise from the routine referral to counselling for no other reason than that they have suffered a bereavement.

However, just because these may be universal experiences, it doesn't make them less painful or individual. Grief is a process that is both unique to the loss we experience and to us as people.

Counselling, both for children and young people and for adults, can be helpful if normal social support is either not available or if it is limited in some way, and/or if the grief is complicated or the effects last for a long time. Adams (2012) argues that:

> Grief is not an illness or a condition, it is normal, as are extreme responses to it. It is when these responses continue into the long term that there may be cause for concern. A young person will not get over their grief, but with timely and appropriate support, they will hopefully learn to live with it. If it is preventing them from engaging with normal life, do not hesitate to seek help. Most young people will not need professional help but some will need a bit of extra support. Others will require a more in-depth approach with bereavement counselling, or therapy.

Children and young people may have a very supportive social network but often the most intimate supporters (family and friends) are also devastated by the same loss and so are unavailable. Sometimes, the young people are afraid to utilise the family support for fear of upsetting the people around them and sometimes the people who could be of most support feel as though they haven't the knowledge or expertise to help. Adults may find it easier to deny the idea that the child might be grieving. Perhaps, because we all share a knowledge of the impact and pain of loss on ourselves, we can find it difficult to witness this in children and young people and are tempted to downplay the effect that it may be having on them. 'She's too young to understand what's happening' is not an uncommon response to a bereaved child. It can sometimes feel overwhelming for us to witness the pain of a young person and can feel more comfortable if we minimise, in our minds, the pain we are seeing.

Additionally, it is important to acknowledge, children and young people do understand death differently and grieve differently to adults and this is sometimes misinterpreted as them being unaffected by the loss. Although they may experience the same range of feelings as an adult and process the loss in a similar way, they may lack the conceptual skills to talk about it and their distress may become apparent through their behaviour (Pennells and Smith, 1995: 9). In my experience, therapeutic help can be of benefit when this occurs.

In situations where carers lack the confidence to work with the child or young person, perhaps the most helpful thing a professional therapist can do is to support the family/friends to support the young person. This can be done through information giving and talking through what may be helpful.

Counselling may also be helpful if the grief is complicated by unsureness about how we felt about the deceased. Although we are often taught not to speak ill of the dead, some of the significant losses we experience are of people with whom we had an ambivalent relationship and perhaps even hated. This can lead to a complicated grief response. The type of loss can also trigger more difficult grief responses; for example sudden, unexpected loss, loss by suicide, murder, and loss where the body is unrecoverable or not found. Children and young people may also need to mourn a loss at different stages of their lives. For example, a young girl whose mother died when she was six may mourn the loss again when she goes to secondary school, gets married, has her first baby and at other significant points in her life. Also, we may not recognise the full impact of the loss at the time but may come to recognise it gradually or at a later date. For example, a child who has been adopted and has no details of their birth family's medical history may grieve anew when a doctor asks if some condition 'runs in the family'.

History and Background

In its present form, counselling has only been available in the UK since the 1950s although helping with psychological distress has historically been a part of the function of all societies (McLeod, 2009). Bereavement counselling similarly has a short history. Perhaps the best known charity offering bereavement counselling in the UK is CRUSE, founded in 1959. Its initial remit was to help bereaved adults although it now offers a website for bereaved young people. Initially, bereavement support services rarely extended their work to children and young people but recently these services have been developed (Rolls and Payne, 2003). Some local therapeutic services are available and schools who offer access to counselling often find bereavement and loss to be a common issue brought to therapy. Cooper (2013) reports that bereavement issues make up about 10 per cent of the concerns that young people attending counselling in schools present.

There is little research into the efficacy of therapeutic interventions with children and young people who have been bereaved (Wilkinson et al., 2007). The lack of research using randomised control trials (RCT) is perhaps understandable given the ethical issues raised in denying some of the population support during bereavement, but qualitative research is sparse too. Wilkinson et al. (2007) attempted a RCT trial but had to abandon it due to lack of participation, but they did conduct a study of parents' perceptions of a family bereavement support service in seven UK hospices. They concluded that 'support interventions can have a positive impact on post-bereavement adjustment'. It is an interesting study but has quite a limited scope and more research needs to be developed to examine more fully the efficacy of bereavement work with children and young people and also needs to include the views of the children.

Theory that Tries to Explain Responses to Loss in Children and Young People

Why do we grieve? We grieve because we have lost something or someone with whom we had formed an attachment. Parkes suggests 'that it is the nature and quality of the attachment that determines the intensity of the grief, rather than the magnitude of the psychosocial transition that results' (1993: 246). In other words, it is the importance we attach to the loss rather than the disruption in our lives that affects the depth of our grief. This seems to be true whether the attachment experienced is positive or negative or, in Bowlby's (1969, 1973, 1980) terms, secure or insecure. This concept is explained in detail in Chapter 1, 'Child Development and Attachment'.

The idea that early relationships are important in healthy development permeates all development theory, and it is interesting to note that attachment theory implies a causal relationship between loss and our responses and is seen, as Fraley and Shaver report, to determine our grief responses:

> whether an individual exhibits a healthy or problematic pattern of grief following separation depends on the way his or her attachment system has become organised over the course of development. (1999: 740)

Bowlby (1969, 1973, 1980) conceptualises grief as separation anxiety (caused by separation from an important attachment figure), so the way we manage grief is dependent upon our attachment style and whether the 'internal working models' we hold in mind are positive or negative. Broadly, secure individuals are believed to be able to recognise their losses and be able to deal with them and able to seek support. Anxious-ambivalent individuals are thought to focus on their distressing thoughts and feelings more in order to maintain contact with the person or thing they have lost. They may have difficulty 'moving on'. Avoidant individuals are thought to be more likely to minimise their grief and to 'move on' quickly (Cassidy and Shaver, 1999).

There do seem to be some commonalities within models of the grieving process, as seen below, but the intensity, duration and experience is a very individual one. Most models of the process suggest that it is either phased (moving through various phases of grief, e.g. Bowlby, 1980; Parkes, 1986), tasked (having to complete a variety of tasks to successfully negotiate the process, e.g. Worden, 1991) or an oscillation between grieving and coping, as in the Dual Process Model (Stroebe and Schut, 1999).

Bowlby's phase model is derived from his attachment theory and has similarities with the phase model proposed by Parkes (1986), where the following phases are identified: numbness (denial and shock), pining (yearning and protest), disorganisation and despair, reorganisation (recovery).

Stroebe and Schut's (1999) DPM describes our grieving process as an oscillation between focusing on the emotions surrounding our loss and avoiding the loss. We engage in restorative behaviour as well as experiencing the meaning of our loss. Stokes et al. (1999) suggest this model is useful in helping us understand the behaviour of children and young people in managing their grief. They suggest, for example, that if the child or young person senses the adult is distressed when talking about the dead person, they may attempt to distract the adult or avoid talking about the dead person themselves. This can be a helpful strategy but can also be misconstrued by the surrounding family and friends as an indication that the child or young person is not affected by the loss.

How Children and Young People May Grieve

Although all of these models may help our understanding of the process of bereavement and loss children may experience, we need to remember that grief is unique. Children and young people understand death differently at different developmental stages and are likely to deal with it in a different way to adults (Slaughter, 2005; Himebauch et al., 2008).

Four concepts are commonly used in the literature (e.g. Willis, 2002; Orbach et al., 1986) to judge whether children and young people understand death or not. These are:

1. Do children understand that death is irreversible?
2. Do they understand it is final?
3. Do they understand it is inevitable, that all living things die?
4. Do they understand causality, that there is a physical cause to death – the body stops working?

There are huge differences of opinion about the age at which a child can understand these concepts, with some authors believing that children as young as six months can understand and others believing understanding only emerges in adolescence (Willis, 2002: 222). Broadly, however, understandings that children and young people have relate to the developmental stages they have reached which are, in turn, related to the development of cognitive understanding. As suggested in Chapter 1, Piaget (1965 [1932]) argued that children's thinking is structurally different from that of adults and suggested a theory of cognitive development based on the way that children and young people at different ages function. These ideas can be used to understand children's developing concept of death and dying (Himebauch et al., 2008).

The Development of the Concept of Death in Children and Young People Related to Developmental Stage

Sensory Motor Stage: 0–2 years approximately

Normally, there appears to be little cognitive understanding of death or loss but the child does respond to separation and is often very in tune with parents' emotions. However, Raphael (1984) suggests that we may be unconsciously aware of our losses:

David, a young man of 22 who saw a dead woman being taken from the site of an accident on a stretcher. Her arm was hanging over the edge and her breast was partially exposed. This awakened a vivid and previously repressed, memory of his attempts to suckle the breast of his dead mother when he was 10 months old. (p. 79)

Pre-operational Stage of Development: 2–7 years approximately

Up to around five years, a child is usually able to use words about death relatively appropriately but really it seems to be 'pretend' and there is little concept of the irreversibility or finality of death. It is common to confuse death with sleeping and death may be seen as a punishment. They may feel they have caused the death although guilt is a common feeling associated with grief right through life, including adulthood. We need to be very careful with the language we use to explain death as the misunderstanding reported by Raphael (1984) demonstrates:

Jason (2½) … He and his father used to go to a nearby airport to see planes together. When his father, to whom he was intensely attached, died, he was told he had 'gone to Heaven to be with Jesus' … he ran away on many occasions and was found … [near the airport] where he had gone to 'get in a plane to go to the sky to Daddy'. (pp. 86–7)

Between the ages of around five to eight years, children gradually see death as possible but not for them, and usually associate death with old age. They begin to accept that death is an end and begin to realise death is not reversible. They often have a real curiosity in the idea of death.

Concrete Operational Stage: 7–11 years approximately

Children are much more able to see death in abstract terms and can understand as much as people will tell them. They begin to realise death may include them and to understand the irreversibility of death. They are able to differentiate between living and non-living.

Formal Operational Stage: 11–16 years approximately

The young person begins to have a more adult understanding. Because they are able to think more abstractly, they understand implications of death more fully. It is possible that some may think suicide is a means of getting back at someone, but they may also see it as reversible (as some survive) and re-occurrable (as some try more than once). Desperate young people can engage in risk-taking behaviour which can result in death.

The descriptions of Harry Potter's experience of Dumbledore's death provide an illustration of the range of emotions an adolescent might experience – sadness, mirth, regret, curiosity, suppression of emotion, accumulation of grief and loss, isolation (Rowling, 2005: 599–600).

Case Study   Sharon

Sharon was nine years old and was referred because her older brother was killed in a car accident which Sharon witnessed. She, understandably, was having difficulty processing this experience.

Her mother, because of her own distress, felt unable to offer Sharon appropriate responses to her questions about the death of her brother, and because Sharon's 'supporters' were also bereft they were unable to help her to find a voice for her feelings of loss.

Sharon and I met for ten sessions of play therapy where the purpose was to use the child's natural medium of communication, 'play', to make some sense of her experience. Rather than interpret the meaning of the play, I look for themes and the themes in her play were predominantly about making order out of chaos and about nurturing. She rarely talked directly about her experiences or acknowledged her feelings.

The major theme of Sharon's play was nurture. She played most of the time with the doll's house which 'Mammy' or 'Daddy' kept clean and where they looked after the children. In session two, a new theme occurred through her stories, that of sudden happenings, then things returning to normal, but nothing ever being the same again.

Sharon's play became much more expressive in the seventh session and she spoke for the first time of the things that had happened to her. She again played with the doll's house and the theme of creating order out of chaos was apparent.

Session eight seemed to mark a change in Sharon's behaviour. She was much more assertive and more playful. The themes included being in control and, although terrible things happened in her stories, they had a happy ending and seemed less chaotic. This continued in session nine.

In session ten, themes of order and normality were very apparent and the session seemed very peaceful. Her play was still very ordered but seemed less stressed. The children in the doll's house did not seem to need quite so much looking after and could be very independent.

The final session was a very tranquil session and old themes and play were re-visited. The chaos seemed to have receded and some sort of order established in her life. Perhaps the therapeutic play space had allowed her to make some sense of her experience.

Summary

How a counsellor works therapeutically with children and young people who have been bereaved will depend upon their theoretical orientation (see Chapters 2–8 in this handbook). However, in this chapter I have suggested:

- The meaning associated with the loss is what is central in understanding the loss and to working with grieving children and young people
- Reactions to loss are individual and range from feelings of sadness to serious physical, emotional, behavioural and cognitive reactions
- Responses are dependent both on the meaning of the loss and the development stage of the child or young person

In addition:

- To understand how children and young people perceive loss and grieve, it is important for us to appreciate how working with this issue with this population may affect us. It is often very difficult to witness pain in others, especially if we see the others as vulnerable children. This may make us reluctant to 'hear' the children, so we need to make sure we are well supported
- How we work therapeutically with our young clients will depend upon our training, orientation, work setting and experience, but we all need to be aware of the possible effects on us. Working with loss can make us aware of our own mortality and the mortality of those we care about, and we can become supersensitive to risk, which can be paralysing
- We need good supervision and good self-care in order to keep ourselves open to our clients and safe

Reflective Questions

Some of these activities, as with all personal development work, may be upsetting, so make sure you are well supported if you choose to do them.

1. Think about a loss you have experienced; write down an account of your process. Does it fit in with any of the models of grief described in Table 20.1? Where is it the same, where different? Why might that be?
2. How well do the descriptions of how death is conceptualised at different developmental stages in the Box above fit with your experience of children and young people? Where is it the same, where different? Why might that be?
3. Why is it important to keep parents and carers 'on board'?
4. What strategies would you use to do this whilst still maintaining confidentiality?
5. When do you think it would not be appropriate to offer a therapeutic intervention to a bereaved child or young person?
6. You are working with children and young people who are bereft. What support do you have? How will you look after yourself so you can be open to listen to your clients?

Learning Activities

Again, some of these activities, as with all personal development work, may be upsetting so make sure you are well supported if you choose to do them.

Theory suggests that our response to loss is associated with our attachment style. When working therapeutically with loss, our own attachment style as a therapist can impact upon our work, so the first two activities are designed to help us explore our own styles.

1. Answer the following questions by yourself, then discuss with a partner:

   i. Who do you like to spend most time with? Why?
   ii. Who do you miss most during separations? Why?
   iii. Who do you feel you can always count on? Why?
   iv. Who do you turn to for comfort when you're feeling down? Why?

2. Is there any particular type of loss you think you would find hard to work with; death by suicide, murder, road accident, cancer, for example? With a partner, discuss why you think this may be difficult.

3. Sit quietly by yourself. Let an image of death and/or dying come into your head. Does it have a size, a shape, colour, texture, smell? Does it change or remain the same? Is there anything else about it? When you feel you know your image, then draw, sculpt, make a collage or write about it. Share with a partner.

Further Reading

Gerhardt, Sue (2004) *Why Love Matters: How Affection Shapes a Baby's Brain*. London: Routledge. She argues much of our brain and connections develop after birth, ready to be shaped and learn from the environment we are born into.

Gersie, Alida (1991) *Story Making in Bereavement: Dragons Fight in the Meadow*. London: Jessica Kingsley.
This is a lovely book which introduces stories connected to death which can be used therapeutically or just enjoyed.

Golding, Kim (2008) *Nurturing Attachments: Supporting Children Who Are Fostered or Adopted*. London: Jessica Kingsley.
This book contains good descriptions of attachment types

Mallon, B. (2011) *Working with Bereaved Children and Young People*. London: SAGE.
This is a comprehensive book which combines theory with practice and the latest research. Each chapter ends with a reflective exercise which adds interest.

All About Me. This is a game (currently £45) developed by Barnardo's which is designed for use in therapy to help children and young people talk about difficult feelings.

Pennells, M. and Smith, S. (1999) *The Forgotten Mourners: Guidelines to Working with Bereaved Children*. 2nd edn. London: Jessica Kingsley.
Although quite an old resource, this book offers very practical and straightforward advice about working with bereaved children and young people.

Online Resources

BACP website: www.bacp.co.uk/, especially the BACP Children and Young People Division and the Competences for Working with Children and Young People.
Counselling MindEd: http://counsellingminded.com.

21

Depression

Caryl Sibbett and Cathy Bell

This chapter includes:

- Prevalence of depression
- Risk factors
- Interventions
- Counsellor's practice
- A case study
- Reflective activities
- Key resources

Introduction

Whilst this chapter focuses on depression it should be noted that linking factors with self-harming and suicidality create significant overlaps with the ground covered in Chapter 22. All such conditions and experiences are complex, and whilst they can coincide and be inter-related, they each, including depression, may also occur independently of each other and at the same time also be related to wider difficult experiences, such as abuse, trauma, alcohol and drug problems, although again they may occur independently of these.

History and Background

Devaney et al. (2012: 51) note that 'Shaffer et al. (1996) found that the majority of young people who die by suicide have a mental illness, mostly depression'. The World Health Organization (WHO, 2013) reports that: 'Mental disorders (particularly depression and alcohol use disorders) are a major risk factor for suicide in Europe and North America; however, in Asian countries impulsiveness plays an important role' (see Chapter 22).

In counselling practice with such issues, duty of care to the client is of prime importance. Especially when dealing with such an often resistant and hidden condition as depression, the counsellor must always know, and practise within, their own professional boundaries and take care of themselves as professionals. Counsellors should remember and use the guidance and support available from their clinical supervisor and relevant professional bodies and, when working in an organisation, from managers and colleagues.

As Bronfenbrenner (2005b: 262) concludes: 'In order to develop normally, a child needs the enduring, irrational involvement of one or more adults in care of and in joint activity with that child. In short, *somebody has to be crazy about that kid*. Somebody has to be there, and to be doing something – not alone but *together* with the child.' Specifically in counselling practice, the counsellor needs to 'join with' the client to enable them to 'tell their story' (Geldard and Geldard, 2009: 21).

Counselling and Depression

Experiencing different emotions is natural and feeling low or sad is part of a normal response to life events that are upsetting or stressful. Generally, support and the passage of time help these feelings ease. However, in cases where a person feels very low and sad and such feelings do not ease and tend to dominate and hinder usual activities this can become an illness which is called 'depression' (Royal College of Psychiatrists, 2013). When a person has depression, they 'feel very sad or down, and the feelings don't go away or get worse. Depression is different from feeling a bit sad or down for a day or two, which is how everyone feels from time to time' (NICE, 2005: 7). Depression affects a person's mood and they often also feel: 'worried, tearful, moody, bored, tired most of the time' (NICE, 2005: 7). A young person with depression may also: 'find it difficult to concentrate; not want to see family and friends; have aches and pains; eat less or more than usual; have problems sleeping; injure or hurt themselves; feel as if life is not worth living' (NICE, 2005: 7).

Depression can be mild or more severe and the intervention should be tailored to the level of depression and age of the child or young person (NICE, 2005).

Depression: Prevalence

The Mental Health Foundation (2013) summarises that: 'One in ten children between the ages of one and 15 has a mental health disorder' (The Office for National Statistics, Mental Health in Children and Young People in Great Britain, 2005). Estimates vary, but research suggests that 20 per cent of children have a mental health problem in any given year, and about 10 per cent at any one time (Mental Health Foundation, 2005).

> Rates of mental health problems among children increase as they reach adolescence. Disorders affect 10.4 per cent of boys aged 5–10, rising to 12.8 per cent of boys aged 11–15, and 5.9 per cent of girls aged 5–10, rising to 9.65 per cent of girls aged 11–15. (National Statistics Online, 2004)

In its 2013 report, citing data for 2012–13, ChildLine (2013) stated that it created a new category of 'depression and unhappiness' (including feeling sad, low mood, lonely, low self-esteem, confidence or body image issues). ChildLine (2013: 56) reports that:

> In 2012/13, this new category was the top concern overall with 35,941 counselling sessions about this issue as a main concern, and a further 51,918 where it was mentioned as an additional concern – a total of 87,859 counselling sessions. This was also the top concern for girls, and for young people aged 16–18 (where age was known).
>
> Young people also talked about self-harming and feeling suicidal – both of which feature in the top five additional concerns where depression and unhappiness was the main concern.

Depression: Risk Factors

Risk factors for depression in children and young people are complex and there is general research consensus that there are multiple risk factors, both individual and social, that are often not independent of each other (NICE, 2005: 50). There are likely to be 'multiple risk pathways' that may lead to depression (p. 51).

These involve genetic predispositions, different types of adversities occurring during the first two decades of life and acute personally disappointing life events not a consequence solely of past difficulties in the weeks prior to onset (Kendler et al., 2002). Adolescents at high risk for depression are exposed to, or possess on average, three psychosocial risks in the 12 months before follow-up (Goodyer et al., 2000b). (NICE, 2005: 51)

Children and young people can experience depression particularly as a response to experiences like loss, family or school problems, family crisis or breakdown, major changes in life circumstances. Depression seems to be associated with chemical changes in the brain that affect mood control, and it may run in families (Royal College of Psychiatrists, 2013). NICE (2005: 8) lists the following reasons why young people may become depressed:

Being homeless, Being hurt at home, Being treated differently because of your race, Bullying, Death of a parent, relative or someone close to you, Having other illnesses, Moving away from your home country, Other members of your family being depressed, Parents splitting up, School problems, Trouble at home, Friendships going wrong.

Depression can have physical causes and may also be a side effect of medication. Counsellors need to be aware that depression may present in the sessions as physical symptoms being described. It is important that the counsellor really listens to the client and undertakes a comprehensive assessment.

Depression is more common in the teenage years than in children under 12 years of age and it is more common in girls than in boys (Royal College of Psychiatrists, 2013).

Very high risk groups include: 'looked-after children, refugees, the homeless and asylum seekers. Children and adolescent offenders, particularly those in secure institutions' and those with a physical or learning disability (NICE, 2005: 51).

Depression: Interventions

Helping factors can include protective factors, self-help strategies, family and parental support and education, social/environmental interventions, and psychological, pharmacological and physical treatment (NICE, 2005).

Protective factors that 'reduce the likelihood of depression in the presence of vulnerability and activating factors' include: 'a good sense of humour; positive friendship networks; close relationship with one or more family member; socially valued personal achievements; high normal intelligence' (NICE, 2005: 57).

As noted above, counselling interventions should be tailored to the level of depression and age of the child or young person and help provided should feature good information, a good relationship and advice about self-help strategies such as regular exercise, balanced diet, ways of coping with sleep problems and anxiety, and relevant treatment (NICE, 2005: 9–10).

Psychological approaches with children and young people affected by depression tend to differ from those with adults, indeed:

> children with depression are often not thought of as 'having' depression but as affected by a set of emotional, behavioural, learning, relationship and family problems which need to be considered together, and may still need to be addressed together, even if depression in the child is a primary concern. (NICE, 2005: 75)

NICE (2005: 14) recommends the following psychological therapies for young people with mild depression: non-directive supportive therapy, group cognitive-behavioural therapy (CBT), guided self-help – if working, for two to three months; and for those with more severe depression: individual cognitive-behavioural therapy (CBT), interpersonal therapy, family therapy – if working, for at least three months.

A meta-analysis and review of evaluation and audit studies by Cooper (2009b: 2) of counselling in UK secondary schools reports that school-based counselling was associated with large improvements in mental health (mean weighted effect size = 0.81), with around 50 per cent of clinically distressed clients demonstrating clinical improvement. Cooper (2009b: 33) notes that this is consistent with evidence that: 'a non-directive therapeutic intervention can be as effective as CBT for children and young people experiencing mild to moderate depression (Birmaher et al., 2000; Vostanis, Feehan, Grattan, & Bickerton, 1996)'.

Reporting on school-based counselling in UK secondary schools, Cooper (2013: 1) notes that 'non-directive supportive therapy is a NICE-recommended intervention for mild depression; and there is emerging evidence to suggest that school-based humanistic counselling – a distillation of common school-based counselling practices in the UK – is effective at reducing psychological distress and helping young people achieve their personal goals.'

A NICE (2005: 95) report found that, while a range of therapy approaches have been found to be effective by the end of therapy with reasonable follow-up benefit, minimally treated children tend to catch up over time. NICE (2005) found inconclusive evidence of the effectiveness of individual CBT, limited evidence of the efficacy of interpersonal therapy (IPT), some unpublished evidence for benefits from individual psychodynamic therapy, considerable evidence for effectiveness of group CBT with adolescents, and unpublished evidence for effectiveness of family therapy.

> Although little is known about therapist factors that influence outcome, there is some evidence that professionally trained therapists have better results than paraprofessionals

with this group. As there is some evidence that a positive treatment alliance predicts better outcome, therapists who are better able to create this alliance with depressed young people are likely to be more successful. (NICE, 2005: 98)

Giving guidance specifically for practitioners working with children and young people experiencing depression, NICE (2005: 4) states:

Children and young people with depression should have the opportunity to make informed decisions about their care and treatment, but this does depend on their age and capacity to make decisions. It is good practice for healthcare professionals to involve the young person's parent(s) or carer(s) in the decision-making process. Where a child or young person is not old enough or does not have the capacity to make decisions, healthcare professionals should follow the Department of Health's advice on consent and the code of practice that accompanies the Mental Capacity Act.

Psychological therapies, such as counselling and arts therapies, can be valuable interventions. For instance, family therapy, interpersonal therapy and CBT have been found to be useful (Royal College of Psychiatrists, 2013). If depression is severe, then medication prescribed by a specialist medical professional can be useful (Royal College of Psychiatrists, 2013). Devaney et al. (2012: 51) argue that:

There has been tremendous advancement in the treatment of adolescent depression and many studies have assessed the use of CBT, interpersonal psychotherapy (IPT) and medication (Jenkins, 2002; Scocco and De Leo, 2002; Conwell and Duberstein, 2001; Jenkins, 2002). A recent Cochrane systematic review of the research on psychological and educational interventions for preventing depression in children and adolescents (Merry et al., 2011, p.2) concluded that 'Compared with no intervention, psychological depression prevention programmes were effective in preventing depression ... We found data to support both targeted and universal programmes, which is important as universal programmes are likely to be easier to implement'.

There is literature indicating that whilst group therapy can be valuable, as with all forms of therapy, it may have risks if not managed appropriately. 'Group therapy may carry the risk of depression transmission, which may contribute to hopelessness', but the therapist can mediate such negative dynamics, although this takes careful handling (Winter et al., 2009: 35–6).

The BACP (2010a) notes that counselling for depression is 'a manualised form of psychological therapy as recommended by NICE' (NICE, 2009) and:

It is based on a person-centred, experiential model and is particularly appropriate for people with persistent sub-threshold depressive symptoms or mild to moderate depression. Clinical trials have shown this type of counselling to be effective when 6–10 sessions are offered. However, it is recognised that in more complex cases which show benefit in the initial sessions, further improvement may be observed with additional sessions up to the maximum number suggested for other NICE recommended therapies such as CBT, that is, 20 sessions.

A stepped-care model indicates the diverse needs children and young people may have depending on their circumstances and shows the services required at the various tiers, ranging from risk-profiling to intensive care (NICE, 2005: 18–19). Counselling is part of, and can be relevant across, all levels of a stepped-care model.

NICE (2005: 4) states that, when working with children and young people with depression, practitioners' 'treatment and care should take into account the child's or young person's individual needs and preferences as well as the wishes of the parent(s) or carer(s)'.

NICE (2005: 5) emphasises a number of key priorities for implementation, one of which is that 'psychological therapies used in the treatment of children and young people should be provided by therapists who are also trained child and adolescent mental healthcare professionals'. During assessment, health-care practitioners should routinely record:

> potential comorbidities, and the social, educational and family context for the patient and family members, including the quality of interpersonal relationships, both between the patient and other family members and with their friends and peers. (NICE, 2005: 5)

Practitioners should manage, in consultation with wider relevant social and education care, any co-morbid conditions and developmental, social and educational problems experienced by the child or young person and any parental mental health needs.

Counsellors' Practice

The literature on the topics of counselling for self-harm, suicide and depression indicate that the counsellor's practice should be evidence-based and should contribute effectively to a holistic partnership approach and joint working strategy that is informed by relevant current research, legislation and policy. Counsellors must also be mindful of their organisational policies and protocols.

Counsellors need to liaise appropriately with families and other professionals such as CAMHS, school staff, GPs, social workers, etc. Support may be needed for other individuals affected and the counsellor must be mindful of their limits and their role in signposting and referring. Counsellors also need to be mindful of their personal circumstances and the need to consult with their clinical supervisor and managers in evaluating their fitness to work with individual cases. Counsellors have a role in being a link to other agencies to facilitate referral.

Engaging in appropriate supervision is vital for all practice, and is particularly useful in helping counsellors manage the ethical and emotional issues experienced when working with children and young people who are experiencing suicidal tendencies, self-harm and/or depression. In counselling and psychotherapy, it is important to emphasise that the practitioner's professional self-care is an ethical imperative that is part of one's duty of care to clients. It is vital that counsellors working with such issues 'consider their own self-care strategies, or lack of them. Developing a plan of self-care can provide an important opportunity to model an approach to self-care that clients might feel unable consider' (Reeves and Howdin, 2010: 5). Counsellors should practise in a way that demonstrates their commitment to a relevant ethical code or framework, such as the BACP's Ethical Framework (BACP, 2013). The duty of care to clients is paramount and this also includes appropriately addressing safeguarding relating to the welfare of children and young people.

In general, counsellors' practice should involve the appropriate management of communication and informed consent. Gillick competence must be considered by each counsellor. 'Gillick competence is assessed to decide whether a child under 16 is able to consent to his or her own medical treatment without parental permission or knowledge: a child should fully understand the medical treatment that is proposed' (NSPCC, 2009: 8). Organisational policies must also be considered by the counsellor and this can include their employer organisation and a school context of practice.

Counsellors should be aware of relevant protocols, procedures and best practice when dealing with critical incidents. Some employing authorities may state that all issues of self-harm or depression must be reported under safeguarding guidance. It is a responsibility of the individual practitioner to make themselves aware of their employer's stance. The client's welfare is paramount and counsellors may have to take action in line with organisational policy that may mean the ending of the therapeutic relationship.

Comprehensive assessment and the provision of co-ordinated care and services are important. Practice should be provided in age/developmental appropriate ways and with the use of interpreters as needed.

Good practice in record-keeping has to be considered and implemented within the context of the counsellor knowing agency expectations. It is necessary to ensure that record-keeping is maintained with the awareness that, should there be sudden death of a young client, the notes will probably be requested, for example in the case of a child death review. Counsellors should adhere to good practice guidance on record-keeping and information management, such as works by Bond and Mitchels (2008).

In general, the management of endings and breaks must be handled according to best practice. Whilst counsellors strive to provide a good enough secure attachment for the client, breaks and endings can evoke feelings in the client and even in the counsellor that can resonate with ambivalent or avoidant attachment experience (Ainsworth et al., 1978) and these should be managed appropriately.

Counsellors should engage in routine evaluation, using appropriate outcome measures and audit tools as part of overall quality assurance. Counsellors' practice, training and supervision should also be informed by research. The following both exist in a complementary relationship:

- *Efficacy* research: often referred to as *evidence-based practice* (EBP) (*does it work?*);
- *Effectiveness* research: often referred to as *practice-based evidence* (PBE) (*does it work in routine practice?*)

Reporting on therapies and approaches for helping children and adolescents who deliberately self-harm, SCIE (2005b) notes that both more EBP and PBE is needed, particularly relating to younger children and on long-term effectiveness.

Counsellors can draw on a wide range of resources to inform their practice. The Counselling MindEd initiative is 'an evidence-based, e-Learning programme to support training of school and youth counsellors and supervisors working in primary, secondary, tertiary and community settings, as well as the independent sector' (Counselling MindEd, 2013). Resources are available at http://counsellingminded.com/ and www.rcpch.ac.uk/minded.

There is a growing literature on healthy schools initiatives, promoting emotional intelligence and literacy and building resilience. Professional bodies such as the British Association for Counselling and Psychotherapy (BACP) offer access to relevant specific interest groups such as the BACP Children and Young People division and the Counselling Children and Young People Practice Research Network. The BACP has developed a Competency Framework relevant for the 11+ age group and is considering the development of one for younger children pre-11. The associated development of curricula for the specialist training of counsellors to practise with children and young people is also vital. Such projects will contribute to ensuring safe ethical practice in counselling children and young people.

Case Study   Kevin

Kevin is 15. He is encouraged by his youth worker to attend counselling provided by a community provider with close links to the youth service and wider community activity. The youth worker has been worried about Kevin self-harming as this previously has been his way of coping with changes or upsets in his life.

Kevin agrees to go for, in his words, 'a checking out meeting with the counsellor'.

It soon becomes obvious during this 'checking out' meeting that Kevin is deeply troubled, and when he rolls up his sleeves because he 'is too warm', cuts are seen on both his arms.

Consider: How should the counsellor proceed?

Particularly consider:

What safeguarding issues are there and how can the counsellor manage them?

What ethical issues are there and how can the counsellor manage them?

Does the counsellor involve the youth worker?

For the counsellor, the young client's welfare is the most important issue in that counselling/therapeutic space. What are the implications for practice?

Joining with the young person is key to ensuring that their issues are allowed to surface in this safe place. What are the implications for practice?

The counsellor has to be aware of their own situation and be conscious of transference and counter-transference taking place. Is this serious self-harming, how often, using what, has the young client thought of suicide, do they have a plan? What are the implications for practice?

What are the implications for practice in relation to Gillick competency, client autonomy, and risk management?

What if the young person walks out, disengages, and what can a counsellor do in these situations?

How might it change implications for practice if the client was being seen in a school context?

How might it change implications for practice if the client was of another age, gender, culture, ability, context, etc.?

Summary

In conclusion, in counselling with children and young people affected by such issues, it is important to:

- Provide a quality therapeutic relationship
- Listen to the young person's story, understandings and feelings

(Continued)

(Continued)

- Tailor the approach to the individual and contextual needs
- Adhere to best practice guidance and ethical principles
- Demonstrate evidence-based practice, showing relational competence and empathic congruence
- Be informed by specialist training and supervision
- Engage in ongoing assessment, review, evaluation, quality assurance and continuing professional development

Reflective Questions

1. In addition to a capacity to communicate respect, understanding and acceptance (Winter et al., 2009), does research identify any other qualities, skills, competencies?
2. Some have suggested that depression might be due to changes in brain development in adolescence. In addition, adolescents (particularly young women) have higher rates of anxiety and depression than younger children, and self-harm is clearly associated with these kinds of mental health problems (Hagell, 2013: 2). Does research identify any other influencing factors?
3. Identify appropriate specialist training; utilise relevant outcome measures; identify relevant legislation; consult recent research; discuss with your supervisor.

Learning Activities

1. Discuss and create a plan to ensure evidence-based practice.
2. Arrange an outreach programme to raise awareness in your community of the prevalence of depression in the child population and the available interventions.
3. It is important to give yourself attention. Explore ways of pacing yourself and your energy output.

Further Reading

Ainsworth, M.S., Blehar, M.C., Waters, E. and Wall, S. (1978) *Patterns of Attachment*. Hillsdale, NJ: Erlbaum.

Geldard, K. and Geldard, D. (2009) *Relationship Counselling for Children, Young People and Families*. London: SAGE.

Online Resources

BACP website: www.bacp.co.uk/, especially the BACP Children and Young People Division and the Competences for Working with Children and Young People.
Counselling MindEd: http://counsellingminded.com.

22

Self-Harm and Suicide

Caryl Sibbett and Cathy Bell

This chapter includes:

Self-harm and suicide as relevant to counsellors working with children and young people, including:

- Prevalence
- Risk factors
- Interventions
- Reflective activities
- Key resources

Introduction: History and Background

As part of the UK context, ChildLine's (2013) report *Can I Tell You Something?*, citing data for 2012–13, indicates a significant increase in children and young people contacting ChildLine for support on high-risk issues, with main concerns being: depression and unhappiness (13%), family relationships (13%), bullying/online bullying (11%), self-harm (8%), suicidality (5%), problems with friends (5%), physical abuse (5%), sexual abuse (4%), puberty and sexual health (4%) and mental health issues (3%).

Hawton et al. (2012a: 2373) report that 'Self-harm and suicide are major public health problems in adolescents, with rates of self-harm being high in the teenage years and suicide being the second most common cause of death in young people worldwide'. Self-harm can be a suicidal act, but not everyone who self-harms is suicidal.

Suicide in adolescents 'has been identified as a serious public health problem worldwide' (Devaney et al., 2012: 7), and a growing incidence of suicide has been reported and high risk groups have been identified. For instance, young males generally are associated with greater rick of suicide, particularly those aged 15–25 (Reeves and Seber, 2010: 2).

The United Nations Convention on the Rights of the Child (UNCRC) puts a duty of State parties to ensure that children and young people are supported during childhood so that they can attain the highest standard of well-being and health, and to respond robustly where factors may impact on their welfare (Devaney et al., 2012: 7). Counselling in schools is part of the response in the UK and Ireland. The UK Children's Commissioners and the UN Committee on the Rights of Children share a concern that mental ill health and high rates of suicide and self-harm among children and young people is one of the key areas of children's rights that is being underplayed (Devaney et al., 2012: 7).

Government policy initiatives have aimed to promote suicide prevention and reduction, nationally and in the four UK countries, and an implication is that this should be a priority for all therapists (Reeves and Seber, 2010). Often, such initiatives can be part of wider well-being strategies.

When working with children and young people affected by such issues, it is vital that the counsellor ensures the good quality of the therapeutic relationship. Counsellors need to create positive therapeutic alliances with both the child or young person and with their parents, and this is especially important since maintaining these over time is predictive of successful treatment outcomes with youth (Shirk and Karver, 2010: 8).

Counselling and Self-Harm

It is important to note that self-harming is 'not the core problem but a sign and symptom of underlying emotional difficulties, used as a way of coping' (MHF/CF, 2006, cited in NSPCC, 2009: 3). The counsellor plays an important part in helping the client explore the underlying emotional trauma that has led to the point of self-harming.

The National Institute for Clinical Excellence (NICE, 2004) guidelines define self-harm as 'self-poisoning or injury, irrespective of the apparent purpose of the act', and adds that 'self-harm is an expression of personal distress, not an illness, and there are many varied reasons for a person to harm him or herself' (NICE, 2004: 7). MIND (2013c) states that 'Self-harm is a way of expressing very deep distress. Often, people don't know why they self-harm. It's a means of communicating what can't be put into words or even into thoughts'.

Self-harm is a broad term, often regarded as involving various specific behaviours such as overdoses, self-mutilation, burning, hitting the head or other parts of the body against walls, hair pulling, biting and/or reckless, risk-taking behaviour (National CAMHS Support Service, 2011: 2). Self-harm has also been deemed to range across a spectrum of activities from those causing immediate injury, to those where harm may not be apparent for some years (Reeves and Howdin, 2010: 1), including addiction, eating disorders, etc. (MIND, 2013c). Paracetamol overdose and cutting have been the two most common forms of self-harm reported for children and young people, with self-harm being more common after age 16 (SCIE, 2005b).

A recent study that examined epidemiology and characteristics of self-harm in adolescents who attended hospital at sample sites in England reported that self-harm in children and adolescents in England is common, especially in older adolescents, and paracetamol overdose is the predominant method (Hawton et al., 2012b). Hawton et al. (2012b: 369) found that relationship problems were the predominant difficulties associated with self-harm.

Self-harming responses have diverse motivations and are generally a response to a set of circumstances, rather than one isolated event (SCIE, 2005a). Self-harming may help someone cope with intense feelings that seem overwhelming.

> Self-harm may serve a number of purposes at the same time. It may be a way of getting the pain out, of being distracted from it, of communicating feelings to somebody else, and of finding comfort. It can also be a means of self-punishment or an attempt to gain some control over life. Because they may feel ashamed, afraid, or worried about other people's reactions, people who self-harm often conceal what they are doing rather than draw attention to it. (MIND, 2013c)

Self-harming behaviour is primarily a coping strategy for young people (Hagell, 2013: 2) and can be experienced by the child or young person concerned as 'soothing and relieving' and, 'As such, self-harm is an indication of a commitment to life rather than wanting to die' (Reeves and Howdin, 2010: 2). Some young people report that self-harming can be soothing and injury can cause a release of endorphins that gives a temporary sense of well-being (p. 2). However, it is important for counsellors to note that:

> People's experience of self-harm is unique and provides sometimes contradictory effects. For some people it is a confirmation of being alive, for some a distraction; for some an external expression of internal turmoil whilst for others it is a visible communication that they are struggling … being open to explore with the person what their behaviour might mean for them and what might be being communicated by it is essential. (Reeves and Howdin, 2010: 2)

Young people have reported that an obstacle to getting help is the fear that 'self-harm, the only coping strategy that had been keeping them going, might be taken away from them' (Richardson, 2012: 14). Therefore, young people need to be given support and time to gradually develop more helpful and less risky coping skills (Richardson, 2012). It is therefore important that self-harming be understood as a coping strategy, and yet also that counsellors balance risk assessment with seeking to facilitate clients 'over time to find alternative, less self-destructive ways of caring for themselves' (Reeves and Howdin, 2010: 5). O'Connor et al. (2010: 2) note that 'Irrespective of the motive(s) that underpins the self-harm episode, it is important to recognise that adolescent self-harm signals significant levels of current distress'. Counsellors are in a unique position to listen to the children and young people's stories, help them manage their distress and continue the journey with them to understanding what is happening and find new positive ways of coping.

The NSPCC (2009: 5) summarises that: 'In the majority of cases, self-harm appears to be a way of coping rather than an attempt at destroying life: it is usually intended to inflict harm rather than kill (MHF/CF, 2006)'. Choose Life (2012: 5) notes that 'Self-harm is generally a way of coping with overwhelming emotional distress. Many young people self-harm where there is no suicidal intent. However, research shows that young people who self-harm can be at a higher risk of suicide'. MIND (2013c) comments that 'The majority of people who self-harm are not suicidal, but a small minority will intentionally attempt suicide'. Therefore, counsellors should also be aware that significant self-harm can have an associated risk of death and also a person can feel so distressed or overwhelmed that their self-harm coping strategy can have the capacity to evoke suicidal tendencies and behaviours. Overdosing is more likely to indicate suicidal intent, as compared to cutting, 'which tends to be a survival response to distress and depression' (NSPCC, 2009: 5). Repeated self-harming is associated with risk of suicide (SCIE, 2005a).

Self-Harm: Prevalence

It has been reported that self-harming is prevalent and increasing and is the primary issue that young people are concerned about among their peers (YoungMinds and Cello, 2012: 14–15). Whilst it is difficult to ascertain accurate figures for the prevalence of self-harm among children and young people, one national survey found that 'the prevalence among 5–10-year-olds was 0.8 per cent among children without any mental health issues, but 6.2 per cent among those diagnosed with an anxiety disorder and 7.5 per cent if the child had a conduct, hyperkinetic or less common mental disorder' (National CAMHS Support Service, 2011: 3, citing SCIE, 2005a). It was reported that this study also noted that 'The figures increase dramatically for 11–15-year-olds, with the prevalence of self-harm at 1.2 per cent among children without any mental health issues, but 9.4 per cent among those diagnosed with an anxiety disorder, and 18.8 per cent if the diagnosis is depression'.

Although disclosures of self-harm have increased over the last decade, e.g. ChildLine reported a 65 per cent increase between 2002 and 2004, a 'heightened awareness of the issue by both young people and professionals' may explain some of the increase (National CAMHS Support Service, 2011: 3). ChildLine's (2013) report citing data for 2012/2013 indicates a 41 per cent year-on-year increase in young people talking about self-harm, mostly (where age was known) in those aged between 12–15 years. ChildLine (2013) also reports that it found a correlation between self-harming behaviours and feeling suicidal: 'During 2012/13, where suicide was the main reason for young people contacting ChildLine, 34 per cent (4,993) also mentioned self-harm' (p. 34).

Children and young people in Northern Ireland live in a context that is still experiencing the legacy of conflict and this has a negative impact on well-being. A report by the Northern Ireland Commissioner for Children and Young people (NICCY, 2007) states that children in Northern Ireland experience higher levels of suicide and abuse than in the rest of the UK. However, a number of initiatives aim to reduce the impact of the legacy of the conflict on psychological and emotional well-being in Northern Ireland. For instance, the Department of Education's iMatter programme aims to promote pupils' positive mental health and well-being, and the department funds the Independent Counselling Service for Schools which provides access to professional counselling support for young people in post-primary and special schools.

Self-Harm: Risk Factors

Research by O'Connor et al. (2010: 3) summarises that:

> The CASE [Child and Adolescent Self-Harm in Europe] studies confirm past research on clinical samples which suggest that the suicide and self-harm risk factors fall into two main clusters: i) environmental or psychosocial factors which can be thought of as external influences and adverse life events, and ii) psychological factors which include personality and psychological characteristics (de Wilde, 2002). In addition, both Hawton et al. (2002) and O'Connor et al. (2009) found evidence to suggest that social influences, such as family and friends' self-harm, are strongly associated with adolescent self-harm.

Hagell (2013) summarises research that indicates a peak of self-harm in mid-adolescence. Self-harming seems to be more prevalent in the following: older children and young people, in females and in Asian females, in young people in custodial settings, and in those who have spent time in local authority care (NSPCC, 2009: 2–3).

The majority of those who engage in self-harm are young females compared to males, although the figures for young men seem to be increasing (MIND, 2013c), and in particular, 'the rate in young men aged 15–24 years is rising more quickly than in any other group' (Royal College of Psychiatrists, 2010: 31). One study reported that 'Four times as many girls as boys self-harm up to age 16, although this ratio reduces to twice as many among 18 to 19 year-olds' (SCIE, 2005a). However, ChildLine (2013) reports a 15:1 ratio of girls to boys mentioning self-harm. In Northern Ireland, research indicates that 'One in ten young people reported that they had self-harmed at some stage in their lives with girls being 3½ times more likely to engage in self-harm than boys' (O'Connor et al., 2010: 32).

MIND (2013c) cites research indicating that 10 per cent of 15–16-year-olds have self-harmed, with such young people experiencing pressure within families, from school and among peers and being more likely to have low self-esteem, be depressed and anxious. Other risk factors include: mental health problems, dependency on drugs or alcohol, major life problems, feelings of helplessness or powerlessness with regard to their emotions (MIND, 2013c). Choose Life (2012: 10) summarises some identified vulnerable 'at risk' groups:

> adolescent females; young people in a residential setting; lesbian, gay and bisexual and transgender people; young Asian women; children and young people in isolated rural settings; children and young people who have a friend who self-harms; groups of young people in some sub-cultures who self-harm; children and young people who have experienced physical, emotional or sexual abuse during childhood.

The counsellor again must always see the child and young person as an individual and they may or not be part of one of these groups. Appropriate and comprehensive assessment and ongoing review are of vital importance.

Indicators

Warning signs may not be obvious, because self-harming is usually a somewhat secretive behaviour. However, they may include (Choose Life, 2012: 11):

- wearing long sleeves at inappropriate times;
- spending more time in the bathroom;
- unexplained cuts or bruises, burns or other injuries;
- razor blades, scissors, knives, plasters have disappeared;
- unexplained smell of Dettol, TCP, etc.;
- low mood – seems to be depressed or unhappy;

- any mood changes – anger, sadness;
- negative life events that could have prompted these feelings – bereavement, abuse, exam stress, parental divorce, etc.;
- low self-esteem;
- feelings of worthlessness;
- changes in eating or sleeping patterns;
- losing friendships;
- withdrawal from activities that used to be enjoyed;
- abuse of alcohol and or drugs;
- spending more time by themselves and becoming more private or defensive.

The diversity of indicators again indicates the importance of the counsellor using comprehensive assessment and ongoing review.

Self-Harm: Interventions

Whilst acknowledging that diverse terminologies, categorisations and perspectives exist in relation to defining and working with self-harm, Reeves and Howdin (2010: 2) emphasise that 'Working with self-harm therapeutically is ultimately about creating and maintaining therapeutic "contact" with the individual who finds self-harm to be an important aspect of their experience, rather than pathologising their behaviour'. Tackling and reducing the stigma, guilt, shame, fear and mystery that can be associated with self-harming by young people, parents and professionals is important (YoungMinds and Cello, 2012: 9).

Interventions can include increasing knowledge and awareness raising, as well as strategies to develop resilience and emotional literacy. 'There is an urgent imperative to build the emotional resilience of children and young people across society and particularly in school' (YoungMinds and Cello, 2012: 9), especially as part of a whole school approach to promoting emotional health and well-being (YoungMinds and Cello, 2012: 37; Connolly et al., 2011). It is important that such approaches to promoting pupils' emotional health and well-being are audited appropriately (Connolly et al., 2011).

The Royal College of Psychiatrists (2010: 5) recommend that 'the needs, care, well-being and individual human dilemma of the person who harms themselves should be at the heart of what we as clinicians do'. When assessing those who self-harm, 'it is important to consider how intentional the behaviour is, the lethality of the action and whether it is a one-off act or is something that a child or young person does frequently over a period of time' (National CAMHS Support Service, 2011: 2: 1.1). Assessment should also include a full assessment of family and social situation and child protection issues (NICE, 2011: 19).

> Counsellors should note that 'It may also be valuable to investigate what happened just prior to self-harming as this will enable an exploration of the intense emotions that were managed through self-harm'. (Reeves and Howdin, 2010: 3)

Counsellors working with children and young people who are self-harming need to take account of cultural aspects.

> Cultural aspects will also be important defining factors in relation to self-harm, i.e. the acceptability of behaviours will be defined as what is culturally and socially permissible. … the meaning and context of the behaviour for the client will help clarify its communication. (Reeves and Howdin, 2010: 2)

Practitioners working with children and young people who disclose self-harming have to manage various ethical aspects, as relevant to the age of clients. These include negotiating confidentiality issues and consent for treatment and for the involvement of parents and others and assessments should be underpinned by NICE Guidelines and the Common Assessment Framework (NSPCC, 2009: 8). Counsellors need to be aware of, and comply with, the legal requirements involved in working with children and young people, such as when seeking consent for counselling. 'Gillick competence is assessed to decide whether a child under 16 is able to consent to his or her own medical treatment without parental permission or knowledge: a child should fully understand the medical treatment that is proposed' (NSPCC, 2009: 8).

The NSPCC (2009: 8) summarises that

> Types of therapeutic interventions mentioned in the MHF/CF report (2006) include:
>
> - counselling that concentrates not on the injuries but the underlying problems that have triggered the self-harm
> - family therapy
> - in-patient treatment e.g. in a specialist unit
> - brief psychological therapy (problem-solving therapy)
> - crisis cards (showing the card assures the holder of quick access to mental health workers and admission to hospital in a crisis)
> - behaviour therapy involving individual therapy.

A review commissioned by the National Institute for Health and Clinical Excellence (NICE) for the purpose of developing clinical practice guidelines found that whilst 'The evidence reviewed here suggests that there are surprisingly few specific interventions for people who have self-harmed that have any positive effect … the positive outcome for adolescents who have repeatedly self-harmed receiving group therapy is encouraging', although it qualified this by stating that this research has limitations and overall, more investigation is needed (NICE, 2004: 177–8).

In a Report of the National Inquiry into Self-harm among Young People (Brophy, 2006: 11), one of the recommendations was:

> Innovative approaches to prevention and intervention should be developed and evaluated across the fields of health, education and social care. Counselling and peer support schemes in schools, exercise on prescription and creative arts approaches all appear to be worth taking further.

In the review questionnaire findings, when young people were asked what would be helpful, the most popular response was '1:1 support/counselling' (n = 121, 85%), followed by responses including: 'Group support/drop-in' (n = 101, 71.1%), 'Self-help group (facilitated)' (n = 86, 60.6%), 'Creative initiatives' (n = 85, 59.9%), 'Multimedia/internet access' (n = 81, 57%) (p. 58).

When working with clients who engage in self-harming, it is important that the counsellor can demonstrate relational competence, such as empathic congruence (Reeves and Howdin, 2010: 3). Supervision and professional self-care are also vital when working with clients who engage in self-harming (Reeves and Howdin, 2010: 4–5).

Counselling and Suicide

Suicide is a 'major public health issue' that is 'a devastating event for families and communities' (Scowcroft, 2013: 4). It has been described as a 'multi-faceted phenomenon involving the interaction between biological, psychological, sociological, environmental and cultural factors' (Devaney et al., 2012: 7). Hawton et al. (2012a: 2373) note that 'important contributors to self-harm and suicide include genetic vulnerability and psychiatric, psychological, familial, social, and cultural factors'. The World Health Organization (WHO, 2013) reports that: 'Suicide is complex with psychological, social, biological, cultural and environmental factors involved.'

The term suicide refers to 'deaths from both intentional self-harm and injury or poisoning of undetermined intent' (DH/Knowledge – Evidence and Analysis/Public Health, 2012: 4). In 2011 England, Wales, Scotland and Northern Ireland adopted a change in the classification of death statistics in line with the World Health Organization (WHO) new coding rules which means that cases of self-injury/poisoning of 'undetermined intent' are now classified as suicide (Scowcroft, 2013: 6).

Practitioners working with children and young people need to be aware that those who are feeling suicidal may have mixed feelings such as wanting to die, wanting others to understand how they are feeling, wanting help, etc., and such mixed emotions can be confusing and cause more anxiety. Suicidal feelings often arise when we feel increased hopelessness and worthlessness (MIND, 2013a).

Suicide: Prevalence

Hawton et al. (2012a: 2375) report that 'Globally, suicide is the most common cause of death in female adolescents aged 15–19 years'. The World Health Organization (WHO, 2013) reports that:

> Every year, almost one million people die from suicide; a 'global' mortality rate of 16 per 100,000, or one death every 40 seconds. In the last 45 years suicide rates have increased by 60% worldwide. Suicide is among the three leading causes of death among those aged 15–44 years in some countries, and the second leading cause of death in the 10–24 years age group; these figures do not include suicide attempts which are up to 20 times more frequent than completed suicide.

A systematic review of evidence summarised that 'Suicide is the cause of death for nearly 900,000 people every year. Non-fatal acts of self-harm are also very frequent, occurring in about 300 of every 100,000 people per year, and although such acts may or may not involve suicidal intent, deliberate self-harm is a significant risk factor for eventual suicide' (Winter et al., 2009: 4).

In the UK, ChildLine's (2013) report citing data for 2012–13 indicates a 33 per cent increase from the previous year in young people talking about suicidal thoughts and feelings. ChildLine also reports that 60 per cent of its total referrals were about young people who were actively suicidal (p.30). The Public Health Agency (PHA) noted that, after a period of relatively static figures in the latter half of the last century, between 1999 and 2008 rates of suicide in Northern Ireland increased by 64 per cent and that most of the rise was attributable to young men in the 15 to 34 age group (O'Hara, 2011).

Suicide: Risk Factors

Hawton et al. (2012a: 2375) summarise risk factors for self-harm and suicide in adolescents:

Sociodemographic and educational factors

- Sex (female for self-harm and male for suicide)—most countries*
- Low socioeconomic status*
- Lesbian, gay, bisexual, or transgender sexual orientation
- Restricted educational achievement*

Individual negative life events and family adversity

- Parental separation or divorce*
- Parental death*
- Adverse childhood experiences*
- History of physical or sexual abuse
- Parental mental disorder*
- Family history of suicidal behaviour*
- Marital or family discord
- Bullying
- Interpersonal difficulties*

Psychiatric and psychological factors

- Mental disorder*, especially depression, anxiety, attention deficit hyperactivity disorder
- Drug and alcohol misuse*
- Impulsivity
- Low self-esteem
- Poor social problem-solving
- Perfectionism
- Hopelessness*

All the factors in the panel have been shown to be related to self-harm.

*Shown to be related to suicide.

Devaney et al. (2012: 73) summarise research by Coleman and Hagell (2007: 14) and note that:

> The major risk factors for children tend to lie within chronic and transitional events, rather than in acute risks. Therefore children show greater resilience when faced with acute adversities such as bereavement, or short term illness, and less resilience when exposed to chronic risks such as continuing family conflict, long term poverty, and mult iple changes of home and school. The research highlighted in this report also confirms that it is the multiplicity of chronic adversities which are the most dangerous for children and young people.

Hawton et al. (2012a: 2373) note that: 'The effects of media and contagion are also important, with the internet having an important contemporary role.' In recent years, the media have produced guidelines and revised policy on the reporting of self-harm. For instance, 'The UK *Editors' Codebook* introduced a new rule for editors in 2006 that when reporting suicide, care should be taken to avoid excessive detail of the method used' (Royal College of Psychiatrists, 2010: 53). It has been noted that 'One in five schoolchildren with a history of self-harming questioned by researchers said they first learnt about it after seeing or reading something online, second only to hearing about it from friends' (Royal College of Psychiatrists, 2010: 52–3). Counsellors should be aware of the risks and benefits of media and internet influences and resources.

A report on UK suicide statistics by the Samaritans (Scowcroft, 2013) indicates that the suicide rate for young males is higher than that of young females. Young males generally are associated with greater rick of suicide, particularly those aged 15–25 (Reeves and Seber, 2010: 2). As well as young men, looked-after children and young people who are misusing drugs or alcohol are at risk of death by suicide and the latter 'can be particularly vulnerable in the "come down" phase' (Choose Life, 2012: 17).

Other risk factors for children and young people include: mental health problems, previous suicide attempts, having a relative or friend who has attempted or completed suicide, having been in a young offenders institution/prison, recent bereavement, recent loss of employment, in an isolated or rural community, homeless (Choose Life, 2012: 17). Other general risk factors include: social isolation, a history of sexual/physical abuse, one of various psychiatric illnesses including depression, prior attempts/history of suicide and in family, unemployed, specific plan formulated, and single (Reeves and Seber, 2010: 2; Reeves et al., 2003; Ruddell and Curwen, 2002). Repeated self-harming is associated with risk of suicide (SCIE, 2005a).

Whilst factors contributing to suicidal behaviour are multiple, complex and both personal and social, 'It is possible that when one decides to commit suicide, he/she may select one of the options available to make the act more socially and personally acceptable, and one of these may be alcohol' (Pompili et al., 2010: 1407).

In severe forms, major/clinical depression can be life-threatening (MIND, 2013b). However, counsellors should note that MIND (2013b) notes that people are more vulnerable to acting on suicidal thoughts as they start to come out of depression, rather than when it is at its most severe, possibly because people 'have more energy and motivation available at that stage'.

Hawton et al. (2012a: 2373) summarise that:

> Major challenges include the development of greater understanding of the factors that contribute to self-harm and suicide in young people, especially mechanisms under lying contagion and the effect of new media. The identification of successful prevention initiatives aimed at young people and those at especially high risk, and the establishment of effective treatments for those who self-harm, are paramount needs.

Suicide: Interventions

In a review of the evidence, it has been reported that interventions to prevent suicide and self-harm are diverse and offered across a range of levels and settings (Macdonald et al., 2012).

Effective intervention is characterised by a systemic approach that takes serious consideration of the individual child or young person's developmental context (Daniel and Goldston, 2009), cultural context (Joe et al., 2008; Goldston et al., 2008) and social context (Burrows and Laflamme, 2010). A systemic approach also aims to offer interventions organised across relevant levels, and such models include providing:

- preventative measures, early intervention, and interventions that focus on those who are engaging in self-harming or suicidal behaviour (Macdonald et al., 2012: 140) and rehabilitation (after a child is in state care and/or has complex and enduring needs) (Hardiker et al., 1991) such as is implemented in children's services in Northern Ireland (Devaney et al., 2012: 49);
- whole school/community interventions, targeting specific high-risk groups, and focusing on those showing early signs of self-harming or suicidal behaviour (Nordentoft, 2007);
- individual measures (e.g. counselling) and structural measures (restricting means, addressing social exclusion) (Nordentoft, 2007);

Hawton et al. (2012a: 2373) note that

> Prevention of self-harm and suicide needs both universal measures aimed at young people in general and targeted initiatives focused on high-risk groups. There is little evidence of effectiveness of either psychosocial or pharmacological treatment, with particular controversy surrounding the usefulness of antidepressants. Restriction of access to means for suicide is important.

Devaney et al. (2012: 50) note that:

> Arensman (2010) concluded that interventions with the best evidence for suicide prevention include:
>
> - means restriction, including identification of 'hotspots';
> - clinical guidelines for all health and social services staff to use when dealing with people who are at risk of suicide/self-harm; and
> - programmes that enhance the coping and problem-solving skills of those who self-harm, and which reduce the risk of repeat self-harm.

Counsellors should engage in assessing risk for suicide and self-harm and, as with all practice, this should be informed by the use of appropriate risk assessment tools and routine outcome evaluation. Age and ability relevant measures should be implemented and this should include outcome measures and therapeutic alliance measures; for instance using outcome and session rating scales (Duncan and Miller, 2008). In child and adolescent therapy, 'Therapists are advised to monitor alliance over the course of treatment' (Shirk and Karver, 2010: 8). The BACP's Children and Young People Practice Research Network (CYP PRN, 2013) published *A Toolkit for Collecting Routine Outcome Measures* that offers information and resources relating to evaluation and the collection of routine outcome data.

Counsellors may also be involved in appropriate post-vention responses (Choose Life, 2012: 19), for instance as part of a comprehensive community response (Forbes et al., 2012).

Counsellors should be research-informed in their practice and differentiate between evidence and myths. 'We need to be able to speak about suicide with children and young people and to dispel myths for all concerned' (Care Inspectorate, 2011: 3). Reeves and Seber (2010: 2) state that:

> There is no evidence that asking clients whether they have suicidal thoughts will put the thought into their mind if it was not there before. There is, however, a great deal of evidence to suggest that being able to talk to clients about suicide is extremely important in providing a safe space for them to explore their feelings.

NICE (2005) recommends that professionals should follow advice on consent in local legislation and government guidelines.

Devaney et al. (2012: 50) summarise that Crowley et al. (2004):

> provided a review of suicide prevention strategies specifically for young people:

> Curriculum-based suicide prevention programmes; recognition, management and prevention of youth suicidal behaviour by primary care practitioners; interventions targeting family risk factors; suicide prevention programmes for at-risk groups; potential points of access to those contemplating suicide; prevention of access to means; media restrictions; and psychosocial and pharmacological treatments for deliberate self-harm.

Hawton et al. (2012a: 2378) summarise approaches to prevent self-harm and suicide in adolescents:

Population measures

- School-based psychological well-being and skills training programmes
- Gatekeeper training (e.g., school teachers, peers)
- Screening to identify those who might be at risk
- Restriction of access to means used for self-harm and suicide

- Improved media reporting and portrayal of suicidal behaviour
- Encouragement of help-seeking behaviour
- Public awareness campaigns
- Help-lines
- Internet sources of help
- Reduction of stigma associated with mental health problems and help seeking

Measures for at-risk populations

- Psychosocial interventions for adolescents at risk of self-harm or suicide (e.g. depressed adolescents, abused individuals, runaway children)
- Screening of those at risk (e.g., young offenders)
- Psychosocial interventions for adolescents who have self-harmed
- Pharmacotherapeutic interventions for adolescents at risk of self-harm or suicide.

A Scottish practice guide on suicide prevention for looked-after children and young people (Care Inspectorate, 2011: 32) notes the importance of a 'partnership approach to protecting children and young people where at all possible from attempting or completing suicide'. This involves engaging and developing the young person's inner resources and supporting these by effective joint working and appropriate communication.

Building resilience is seen as one key factor in helping those engaging in self-harm (National CAMHS Support Service, 2011: .9: 4.1). A recent General Comment from the Committee on the Rights of the Child (2011: 26) states: 'It is of critical importance to understand resilience and protective factors, i.e. internal and external strengths and supports which promote personal security and reduce abuse and neglect and their negative impact'. Joiner et al. (2001) suggest that problem-solving treatment benefits suicidal young adults with comorbid depressive and anxiety disorders.

Supervision and professional self-care are vital when working with suicidal clients (Reeves and Seber, 2010: 5) and can help manage the effects of vicarious stress or traumatic reaction.

There are strategies, such as in England (HMG/DH, 2012), that aim to help in the prevention of suicide. These note the need to contribute to prevention by addressing the need to (HMG/DH, 2012):

- reduce suicide risk in high-risk groups such as young men and those with mental health problems, with a history of self-harm, and in contact with the criminal justice system;
- improve mental health and well-being, including of children and young people, looked-after children, those in the youth justice system, survivors of abuse or violence, ethnic minorities, etc.;

- address problems such as bullying, poor body image, low self-esteem, etc.;
- create safer online environments, including 'Recognising concern about misuse of the internet to promote suicide and suicide methods, we will be pressing to ensure that parents have the tools to ensure that their children are not accessing harmful suicide-related content online'. (HMG/DH, 2012: 8: 34)

Online resources are available, such as the Department of Health's e-portal which includes 'specific learning and professional development in relation to self-harm, suicide and risk in children and young people' (HMG/DH, 2012: 24: 2.15).

Whitlock (2010) summarises a systematic review (Hawton et al., 1999) of 23 randomised controlled trials related to deliberate self-harm in which reviewers 'concluded that the most promising approaches include problem-solving therapy, provision of emergency service contact information, long-term psychological therapy' and pharmacological treatment where appropriate.

A meta-synthesis of research (Winter et al., 2009) identified a number of themes with regard to views held concerning the *process* of counselling or psychotherapy relating to the prevention of suicide:

- *Therapeutic relationship*: indicated as important in quantitative and qualitative studies.
- *Therapist qualities*: communicating respect, understanding and being non-judgmental, were reported by clients to be important.
- *Therapy components*:
  o *Duration*: in general, clients seemed to report that therapy sessions and duration were sometimes too short.
  o *No self-harm contracts*: clients' views on the value of no self-harm contracts were mixed, and counsellors in general seemed to endorse the inappropriateness of such contracts – although both varied across theoretical modality. In insight oriented counselling, such contracts tended to be viewed as problematic, whilst in dialectical behaviour therapy (DBT), such contracts tended to be viewed as 'an effective way of reducing the therapist's anxiety to allow them to focus on teaching the skills to alleviate self-harming behaviour'. (Winter et al., 2009: 45).
- *Theoretical framework*: working within a coherent theoretical framework.
- *Therapy techniques*: group, skills training, telephone coaching.

Key recommendations of the review by Winter et al. (2009: 55) are that:

- People at risk of suicide should have access to psychological interventions, including those within the cognitive-behavioural spectrum.
- Therapies for which there have been promising findings, but which are under-researched, should be a research priority.

- Psychotherapists, counsellors and other staff working with clients at risk of suicide should be provided with specific training and support systems in relation to this work.

Counsellors can inform their practice by noting that Devaney et al. (2012: 51) summarise that:

> The key message from the research on the effectiveness of suicide prevention interventions is that there are a range of evidence-based approaches but there is no magic bullet or one size fits all approach as interventions are needed across the different levels, tiers or steps and across all aspects of life including parenting, education, employment, health and social care.

Case Study   Terry

Terry is 14. He is encouraged by his teacher to attend counselling on the school site which is linked with a family support service. The teacher is concerned that Terry has recently become very withdrawn since his brother's death in a road accident. When approached, he said he 'didn't see much point in going on now'. Terry agrees to meet the counsellor 'just to see …'.

Consider: How should the counsellor proceed?

Particularly consider:

What safeguarding issues are there and how can the counsellor manage them?

What ethical issues are there and how can the counsellor manage them?

Does the counsellor involve the teacher?

For the counsellor, the young client's welfare is the most important issue in that counselling/therapeutic space. What are the implications for practice?

Joining with the young person is key to ensuring that their issues are allowed to surface in this safe place. What are the implications for practice?

The counsellor has to be aware of their own situation and be conscious of transference/countertransference taking place. Is the young client thinking of suicide, do they have a plan? What are the implications for practice?

What are the implications for practice in relation to Gillick competency, client autonomy, and risk management?

What if the young person walks out, disengages, and what can a counsellor do in these situations?

> How might it change implications for practice if the client was being seen in the community?
>
> How might it change implications for practice if the client was of another age, gender, culture, ability, context, etc.?

Summary

Key implications for practitioners undertaking this work with children and young people include the need to:

- de-stigmatise self-harm and suicidality and dismantle misconceptions
- respect confidentiality and young people's wishes
- set the right priorities, such as minimising harm; rather than focusing on stopping it altogether without support and without establishing other coping mechanisms
- act in accordance with current law and codes of practice
- have appropriate ongoing training and supervision
- engage in early prevention and promotion of mental health, particularly in schools. (NSPCC, 2009: 12–15)

Reflective Questions

1. What therapist qualities are identified by clients as being important in the process of counselling children and young people who are suicidal/self-harming?
2. Why is self-harming more prevalent in adolescence?
3. What continuing professional development do you need in this area and what is your CPD plan of action, including identifying research, legislation and key learning that can inform your practice?

Learning Activities

1. As an individual or team consider what Gillick competency means in your practice, taking into account your contextual situation.
2. Critically evaluate some ethical issues you might encounter.
3. Identify ways of managing these, including appropriate consultation and the use of ethical frameworks and decision-making models.

Further Reading

NICE (2011) *Self-Harm: Longer-Term Management. NICE Clinical Guideline 133*. London: NICE. Available at: www.nice.org.uk/nicemedia/live/13619/57179/57179.pdf.

Royal College of Psychiatrists (2010) *Self-Harm, Suicide and Risk: Helping People Who Self-Harm: Final Report of a Working Group*. College Report CR158. Available at: www.rcpsych.ac.uk/files/pdfversion/cr158.pdf.

Online Resources

BACP website: www.bacp.co.uk/, especially the BACP Children and Young People Division and the Competences for Working with Children and Young People,

Counselling MindEd: http://counsellingminded.com.

23

Sexual, Physical and Emotional Abuse

Beverly Turner-Daly

This chapter includes:

- A brief summary of the evidence base and an outline of the general principles of working therapeutically with children who have been abused
- An overview of the legal and policy context, especially in relation to confidentiality, information-sharing and differing roles and responsibilities and how this fits within the wider 'safeguarding children' agenda
- An in-depth account of the effect of abuse on a child's sense of self, explored within a case study drawing on the author's clinical experience

Introduction

Children who have been abused experience a wide range of emotional and behavioural difficulties which sometimes result in them being referred for counselling or therapy (Allnock and Hynes, 2012; Daniels and Jenkins, 2010; Geldard et al., 2013). The effects of abuse are different for each child but in some instances, they can be enduring, lasting into adult life and impacting significantly on mental health, relationships and well-being (Davidson et al., 2010; Pritchard, 2013). Empirical studies into the efficacy of therapeutic interventions are limited due to the significant ethical and methodological challenges posed (Mudaly and Goddard, 2009); nevertheless, research in this field is progressing and it has been suggested that we are moving towards a clearer understanding of the respective merits of different forms of intervention (Myers, 2011).

Some aspects of this chapter overlap with Chapter 17, 'Law and Policy', which provides important foundation knowledge, consolidated upon here. Both chapters stand alone, however if you choose to read them together, it is recommended that you read Chapter 17 first.

Note of Caution

The case study in this chapter is fictitious but inspired by the stories of many children with whom the author has had direct or indirect contact. It has been designed to bring to life the impact of child abuse and, as such, has potential to cause distress to some readers.

General Principles for Working Therapeutically with Children Affected by Abuse

Working with children who have been abused can be daunting, and it would help therapists enormously to have access to evidence about which approaches are most effective in which circumstances. Although there is an extensive research base relating to the long-term effects of abuse on children (Cashmore and Shackel, 2013) and evidence-informed clinical excellence guidelines exist relating to specific psychiatric disorders (NICE, 2005) the comparative value of the wide range of treatment interventions on offer is still being explored (Myers, 2011).

Amongst the interventions available to counsellors are play therapy (directive and nondirective), systemic family therapy, group work and cognitive-behavioural therapy. Exponents of the latter have led the way in establishing an evidence base and research suggests that cognitive-behavioural therapy is particularly effective in reducing symptoms of post-traumatic stress disorder in children who have been abused (Deblinger et al., 2006). However, until more research becomes available, it would be unwise to rule out 'unproven' interventions and more helpful perhaps, to think in terms of key therapeutic principles that give rise to a range of possibilities. These principles are:

- Pre-requisites to working with children who have been abused
- Avoidance of 'labelling'
- Listening to children
- Managing the legal process in the best interests of the child.

Prerequisites to Working with Children Who Have Been Abused

There are several prerequisites to the provision of counselling and therapy for children and young people who have been abused. Firstly, the client ought to be living in a safe, secure environment where his/her physical and emotional needs are being met (Doyle, 2012). Supportive carers make strong allies and can have a significant impact on outcomes of therapeutic work (Sgroi, 1982). Consideration must be given to how therapy may affect ongoing legal proceedings; an issue explored in more detail elsewhere in this chapter and in Chapter 17. In the most appropriate way, children should be consulted about therapeutic options and their wishes and feelings taken into account. Empowerment is central to all interventions with children who have been abused. Some children are reluctant to attend counselling sessions (Spratt and Devaney, 2009), therefore careful thought should be given to the extent to which children are pressurised into attending against their wishes. Consideration should also be given to what else is happening in the child's life at the point of referral so that the timing of intervention is compatible with other priorities such as relationships, education and home-life (Bannister et al., 1990).

Given that resources are scarce and, in some areas, children have limited access to counselling, care must be taken to ensure the timing is right. A child may be afforded only one opportunity for therapy therefore it is essential that this is not wasted.

Labelling

Devastating though it may be, we must remember that abuse is an experience, one aspect of a child's life. Therapists and other professionals must take care not to contribute to any process through which abuse becomes part of a child's identity. Children who have been abused may find the labels 'victim' or 'abused child' hugely stigmatising (Bass and Davis, 2008). Abuse can be seriously damaging to a child's self-esteem and sense of identity (Sanford, 1991) therefore counsellors, therapists and other professionals can make an important therapeutic intervention simply by being careful not to label. By seeing beyond the abuse and emphasising that the child is so much more than their abusive experience, counsellors can begin the process of helping children to move forward. Language is vitally important in this regard. We might deliberately choose to talk about 'a child who has been abused' rather than an 'abused child' or 'victim of abuse'. We might challenge assumptions that all children who have been abused need therapy or that all children who have been abused are in some way damaged. It is not uncommon for children who have experienced abuse in its various forms to feel angry, hurt, betrayed, ashamed, guilty, frightened, sad, unlovable, unworthy and culpable, however this is not universal (Browne and Finkelhor, 1986). Labels are rarely helpful to anyone. In the case of child abuse, labels may reinforce the negative experiences and act as barriers to recovery and we should avoid them.

Listening to Children

By listening very carefully and being mindful not to judge, counsellors can empower children and lay positive foundations for future work. This is equally important whether we are involved in a counselling relationship or in any other capacity. In this author's experience, professionals sometimes recommend and advocate strongly for children to receive therapy even when there are indications that the child is not ready for this. Child abuse can make caring adults feel incredibly responsible, sometimes 'duty-bound' to do something to compensate for the harm caused by others. Pushing for a child to receive therapy can be part of this process. Sometimes, when considering the suitability of counselling or therapy for a child who has been abused, it is important to step back, reflect on our feelings and examine carefully, whose needs we are trying to meet.

The 'child protection' system, with its emphasis on gathering information and preventing further abuse, can at times be disempowering to children. Children may be worried about the consequences of telling and become overwhelmed by the impact of professional involvement in their lives. This may shed light on why so many children report abuse only to retract later, although research is needed to substantiate this hypothesis. Abuse can give rise to conflicting and ambivalent feelings (Browne and Finkelhor, 1986). Professionals may assume that thoughts and feelings relating to abuse will be uppermost in a child's mind when in fact for some, home life, hobbies, friendships and day to day stuff of life might matter more. It could be suggested that on occasion, the best intervention a professional can make is to recognise that therapy can go on hold in the short-term whilst focus is placed on supporting the child to re-adjust to post-abuse life, whatever that may involve.

Managing the Legal Process in the Best Interests of the Child

Counselling children who have been abused is particularly complex because often, not only are such children clients but they are simultaneously witnesses to a crime and, as such, may be required to give evidence in legal proceedings against the perpetrators of their abuse. In these situations, the therapeutic needs of individual children may be viewed by some professionals as secondary to the task of securing a conviction, thus protecting other children from harm. Counsellors who work in the field of child abuse need to be familiar with the legal and policy context of their work so that they are best placed to contribute to decision-making with regard to timing and nature of therapeutic interventions. The legal and policy context of counselling children who have been abused is explored below. If you have not done so already, you may find it helpful to read Chapter 17 before continuing.

Legal and Policy Overview

Comprehensive statutory guidance exists to help UK professionals understand their responsibilities in relation to safeguarding children. This guidance, contained in the document 'Working Together to Safeguard Children' (DfE, 2013) is regularly updated and regarded as essential reading for all practitioners whose work brings them into contact with children and young people who may have experienced physical, sexual, emotional abuse or neglect. 'Working Together' makes clear that all professionals have a responsibility to share safeguarding concerns (usually with the local authority or the police) and emphasises that in cases where a child may be at risk of 'significant harm', this overrides any duty of confidentiality a professional may have towards a child. As the title of the guidance suggests, an objective of this guidance is to strengthen inter-professional communication and reduce the risk of child abuse going undetected or unreported. For over 30 years, inquiries into child deaths and 'serious case reviews' have consistently highlighted weaknesses in professionals' ability to recognise indicators of abuse, exchange information and take effective action to protect children. By updating and clarifying legal and policy terms, defining different forms of abuse and recommending structures to support information sharing, the government, through 'Working Together', makes explicit its expectations of all practitioners who work with children and young people. This document, in addition to local safeguarding children board (LSCB) policies and procedures and a clear working knowledge of appropriate professional codes of practice, should provide counsellors with a good understanding of their role and responsibilities in relation to safeguarding children. Many counsellors find it helpful to supplement this knowledge by attending 'Child Protection Awareness' training offered locally by most LSCBs, where they can discuss tensions and dilemmas with other professionals and reflect on their role in this complex area of practice.

There are, without doubt, some tensions between 'child protection' and counselling/ therapeutic work and despite guidance and training, knowing what to refer on is not always clear cut. 'Significant harm' is a subjective term and safeguarding children is a complex task, characterised by uncertainty and ethical dilemmas. Despite guidance contained in codes of practice (BACP, 2010b) this issue is one that is often brought to supervision, where the 'policeman' function is often in evidence and is a space where ethical dilemmas can be explored (see Chapter 13: 'Supervision'). Counsellors should never be afraid to voice concerns about real or potential child abuse. Reflection, critical analysis and soul-searching usually results in safer professional judgements being made. Children who are/have been abused deserve nothing less.

Although statutory guidance suggests that neither the police nor Crown Prosecution Service should seek to prevent therapy from taking place prior to a trial (Crown Prosecution Service, 2001) in practice there can be disagreement as to whether therapy is appropriate and if so, when. It should also be remembered that often, children disclose abuse during the process of therapy or make additional 'fresh allegations' that have to be shared. There may be occasions where there appears to be a contradiction between what the child needs and what is needed of the child which may give rise to tensions between the various adults involved. Good working relationships, negotiation and effective planning in the best interests of the child are essential in these circumstances, as is remembering to consult the child and ensure their wishes and feelings are included in decision-making.

Issues relating to pre-trial therapy are outlined in Crown Prosecution Service guidance; essential reading for counsellors who work with children (Crown Prosecution Service, 2001). Whilst making clear that the best interests of the victim must come first, potential pitfalls of pre-trial therapy are recognised and highlighted. A key issue is the extent to which therapy may be construed as 'contaminating' a child's evidence and used to undermine the chances of a successful conviction. Where a child has received therapy prior to giving evidence in court, lawyers acting for the defendant(s) may question reliability, suggesting that talking about experiences can interfere with accurate recall. Group therapy is particularly problematic in terms of legal proceedings as children and young people hear about the abuse of others and it may be argued that personal experiences become muddled with those of others. The younger/more impressionable the child, the more problematic this becomes. Although steps are taken to shield children from the most intimidating aspects of giving evidence in court (pre-recorded evidence, video-links and informal dress) children are nevertheless subject to vigorous cross-examination; a process through which a child's true experiences can be made to appear false. When a child goes through the ordeal of giving evidence in court and the outcome is acquittal, the impact on the child can be devastating. Nothing can compensate for the message this gives to the child. Since not being believed is one of the most common strategies abusers use to silence their victims, a 'not guilty verdict' reinforces the power of the abuser and usually has a significant impact on the child's recovery process.

The problems associated with fair and ethical prosecution of child sexual abuse cases are well documented. At the time of writing, a consultation process is underway on new government guidelines (Crown Prosecution Service, 2013) issued following the high profile prosecution of several cases of child sexual exploitation. These interim guidelines suggest that where therapy is carried out in accordance with statutory guidance, therapy should not interfere with a subsequent trial, therefore where needed, pre-trial therapy or counselling should not be withheld. This guidance should strengthen the hand of counsellors who may at times have to make the case for prompt therapy, for example, where a child is showing acute signs of distress or where a delay to therapy may jeopardise a good placement. In other situations, where there is a real risk that the therapy may be used against the child, a case may be made for delaying therapy until criminal proceedings are over.

In all matters relating to safeguarding children, child-centred practice and good working relationships between professionals is fundamental to successful outcomes. In ways appropriate to their level of understanding, children and young people should be consulted in decisions about therapy and their opinions genuinely listened to. Despite the confidentiality that forms the basis of all therapeutic relationships, it is still possible for counsellors to work in partnership with children, carers and professionals to share whatever information is relevant and negotiate how best to help the child. Skilfully navigating around ethical dilemmas and avoiding polarisation or professional splitting is an essential part of a therapist's role in this area of work.

Evidence-Informed Practice

At the time of writing, a discourse of 'evidence-informed practice' is widespread, underpinned by government expectation that clinical interventions should be informed by appropriate theory and research, especially in relation to efficacy. This is more complex than it may seem. One position is that it is possible through research to demonstrate the effectiveness of some forms of therapeutic intervention in the same way one might measure the effectiveness of a drug. An alternative position is to question the reliability of the science behind such research and suggest that in a challenging economic climate, there is an inherent bias in favour of short-term, comparatively cheap methods. Counsellors need to be aware of current theory and research but be critical consumers of knowledge; exploring origins, considering ethical issues and measuring published findings against their own practice wisdom and experience. The effects of child abuse and choices of therapeutic intervention are inextricably linked however in our quest for evidence-informed practice, we must be aware of the risks of over-generalising.

Humans are infinitely complex; the unique 'product' of what they bring into the world and what is experienced from then on in. How each child or young person is affected by abuse is unique. Factors considered relevant include: nature and duration of the abuse, relationship to abuser, age, gender, physical and emotional maturity, culture, ethnicity and race (Cashmore and Shackel, 2013; Myers, 2011). There is much debate about core concepts such as attachment theory, vulnerability and resilience (Howe, 2005) although it has long been asserted that the quality of relationships with non-abusing significant adults is highly significant in outcomes for children (Wyatt and Powell, 1988). Given the complex interplay of a huge number of variables, counsellors need to be cautious in their use of theory and research and true to the principle of treating each client as an individual in their own right.

Whether they work with children, adults or both, counsellors require knowledge of the short- and long-term effects of abuse and the range of therapeutic responses and interventions that may be appropriate in different circumstances. Therapeutic need and selection of methods for intervention should be informed by theory and research whenever possible. It is also useful for therapists to have some understanding of what is known about sexually abusive behaviour, especially the 'grooming' process – the strategies used by perpetrators of abuse to intimidate, disempower and silence their victims (Finkelhor, 1984). Therapists also need to keep up to date with developments in 'child sexual exploitation' and also what is known about needs of children who harm other children.

In situations where there is uncertainty about how best to intervene, the following suggestions may be helpful. Where trauma is clearly apparent and 'symptom' reduction a priority, as in cases of post-traumatic stress, a cognitive-behavioural approach may be indicated (Deblinger et al., 2006). Where isolation and self-esteem are primary concerns, therapy within a group setting might be more effective than individual counselling (Doyle, 2012). Where trust is an issue and the client ambivalent about being referred, it may be that progress will best be achieved through a slow, careful process such as person-centred counselling or play therapy (Doyle, 2012). Therapeutic objectives are numerous and multi-faceted ranging from working through feelings (such as anger, loss, guilt and shame) to directly focussing on reducing behaviours that may be harmful. Improving self-image and self-esteem may also be valid goals as may repairing and strengthening relationships with significant others.

In reality, it is often left to each therapist to assess and provide what they believe to be appropriate which, inevitably, is influenced heavily by each therapist's training and theoretical orientation. What a child is offered will depend to a large extent on where they live, to whom they are referred and how knowledgeable and experienced the therapist is. Methods of intervention are likely to be influenced as much by cost and availability as suitability and efficacy and it is not uncommon these days for therapists to be allowed only a small number of sessions in which to work with each child.

The case study below is intended to give a flavour of the various ways in which children who have been abused might be assisted.

Sexual, Physical and Emotional Abuse   359

Case Study   Tina

When Tina was born, her mother experienced post-natal depression and was unable to bond with her. For the first eight months of her life Tina was cared for by her father, and her emotional needs in particular were neglected. She received little warmth and affection and spent many hours strapped in a buggy with a soother in her mouth. Tina's parents' relationship involved frequent episodes of domestic violence, both parents being physically and verbally abusive to one another. On more than one occasion, Tina was caught in the crossfire, once sustaining a blow to the head. This was not reported and her injury was never noticed by others. When Tina was two, her parents separated and her father went to live with another woman who was expecting his child. Soon after the baby was born, he left the area and never saw Tina again. Tina's mother became extremely bitter towards Tina's father and these feelings persisted throughout Tina's pre-school years. Tina bore a close resemblance to her father, which grew more noticeable with each passing year. Tina's mother often shouted at and insulted her, telling her she was 'an ugly pig, just like him!'

By the age of 11, Tina had two younger half-brothers, aged five and seven, whose father had left shortly after the youngest was born and had no contact with them. Tina spent most evenings and weekends looking after the boys and doing domestic chores. Her mother worked in the offices of a local taxi company and was often out during the evenings, leaving Tina to feed and supervise the boys and put them to bed. Tina loved her brothers and went to great lengths to make sure the family's domestic situation did not come to the attention of school or the local authority. Social workers had followed up anonymous referrals on two occasions but Tina and her mother had presented a united front and convinced them these referrals were malicious and without grounds. Tina stayed 'below the radar' at school, maintaining acceptable levels of attendance and avoiding attention. Tina had no friends to speak of and the only affection and happiness in her life was through the boys. Tina was afraid that she and her brothers would be taken 'into care' if details of their family life were ever to be discovered.

When Tina was 13, her mother began a relationship with Dave, a man she had met at work. Dave moved in with the family and life changed dramatically. Tina's mother was happier than Tina had ever known and the shouting and criticism that had hitherto been a constant feature of her life virtually stopped. Dave was kind to Tina and used his tips to buy her presents, which he jokingly told her not to tell the others about. No-one had ever made Tina feel special before and she came to like and trust Dave a great deal. Tina did not know that these were the beginnings of an elaborate grooming process that would eventually lead to sexual abuse.

At the age of 15, Tina was admitted to hospital having taken an overdose of painkillers with cider. Hospital records showed that she had been admitted three months earlier with a broken arm which was said to have been caused falling downstairs. During a series of interviews with a psychiatrist, Tina disclosed sexual abuse and later, in the presence of a social worker, made a formal statement to the police alleging rape by Dave over an 18-month period. Professionals learned that she had tried

(Continued)

(Continued)

unsuccessfully to draw attention to the abuse a few months earlier by throwing herself down the stairs at home. Medical examination revealed numerous scars to Tina's arms and legs that had been self-imposed. Dave had used many strategies to silence Tina, convincing her that she was to blame and that no-one would believe her if she told. On discharging her, the psychiatrist concluded that Tina's was not a serious attempt to take her own life but rather a classic 'cry for help'. The report stated that Tina had not expressed any emotions at all during her time in hospital and seemed to have 'no sense of self-worth whatsoever'.

Therapeutic Responses

The aftermath of the disclosure and ensuing child protection investigation was traumatic for Tina. Tina's mother did not believe her and refused to have any further contact with her. Tina was placed with foster-carers who lived many miles away. She was able to speak to her brothers by telephone but opportunities for direct contact were few. Initially, Dave denied the allegations. However, faced with forensic evidence, he admitted the abuse but claimed Tina had 'led him on'. Tina's mother supported Dave and agreed to cooperate with an in-depth, formal assessment to identify risks to the boys. Dave was charged and bailed awaiting trial. He was not allowed to live with the family or to make contact with Tina. He was subsequently sentenced to a term of imprisonment, something Tina felt incredibly guilty about.

A multi-agency plan was put in place to address Tina's needs. Included in the plan was a recommendation she be offered 'post-abuse counselling'. Tina found talking about the abuse very difficult and was reluctant to see a therapist but not assertive enough to refuse. During the first year following disclosure, two attempts at establishing therapeutic relationships failed, with counsellors concluding that it was the wrong time. Tina's care team prioritised her home and school life, eventually finding a foster carer, Ann, who was willing and able to commit to Tina long-term. This enabled Tina to start afresh in a new school and to experience nurture and care for the first time in her life. She lost weight, joined the school running club and began to form friendships.

Ann understood that Tina had difficulties expressing her emotions and was sensitive enough not to push this. She was respectful of Tina's privacy and personal space and noticed over time that Tina became more relaxed in her presence and more able to hold short conversations. Some members of the care team remained concerned that Tina had never talked about what Dave had done to her and felt that some of the distorted thinking and self-blame that had been evident in her sessions with the psychiatrist needed to be addressed. Encouraged by Ann, Tina agreed to give counselling another go.

Tina's counsellor, Louise, was trained in person-centred counselling and play therapy. She was creative in her methods and her counselling room was bright, cheery and had artwork and poetry on display. Louise understood the importance of establishing clear boundaries and took a lot of time explaining to Tina what counselling involved, how she worked and what to expect.

She involved Tina in negotiating a working agreement and made use of every opportunity that arose to empower Tina, knowing that feelings of powerlessness are common in children who have been abused. Although Louise did not know the details of Tina's early life, she was experienced enough to know that Tina's poor self-esteem and difficulties expressing emotion might pre-date the sexual abuse and that she should not allow assumptions to creep into her work. Although she was curious to know more about Tina's early years and her relationship with her mother, Louise trod carefully, letting Tina lead the way. Louise had to be strong and assertive over this issue. Some members of the care team did not think she could work properly with Tina without understanding what was now on record as a 'chronic history of physical, sexual and emotional abuse'. Others were concerned that the work lacked focus and that clearer objectives needed to be set in order to justify the funding. Louise trusted her instincts, refusing to allow others to set the therapeutic agenda. She relied on supervision to help her remain focused on her therapeutic process with Tina.

Over a series of 12 sessions taking place in two blocks of six with a review mid-way, Louise and Tina worked together, supported by Ann, who encouraged attendance but never asked to be told the details. Louise had warned Ann that there might be times when Tina would seem upset by the sessions or even that the sessions might seem to be making her worse. Louise prepared Ann carefully in order to reduce the risk of her undermining the process. She also did this with members of the care team, making clear that with the exception of information suggesting ongoing risk of harm, no detailed feedback would be provided on the content of the sessions. She explained that affording confidentiality gave the counselling a better chance of success.

Louise's person-centred approach enabled her to establish a working relationship with Tina. She understood that direct conversation was hard for Tina so made use of various mediums to facilitate communication. A significant breakthrough occurred when Tina was making a pebble sculpt and Louise offered her a box of buttons to supplement the stones. Tina was drawn to a particular button which she held and stared at. Tears began to pour down her face – the first show of emotion Louise had witnessed. Remaining calm and staying with the process, Louise used congruence to acknowledge what was happening and Tina began to talk in detail about her brothers and her sorrow at being separated from them. She also revealed snippets of the neglect, physical and emotional abuse that had characterised her early life.

In subsequent sessions, Tina drew pictures of herself and her brothers, representing herself as fat and ugly. She was able to tell Louise that her mother had referred to her as 'the Pig' and that she had been teased at school for being overweight and smelly. At times, Louise had to work very hard to contain her own feelings and remain focused. She longed for Tina to realise that she was in fact a very beautiful young woman and was staggered that Tina believed herself to be ugly and unlovable. She was a mother herself and could not imagine how Tina's mother could treat her own daughter in this way. She felt utter fury towards this woman who she would never meet. At times,

(Continued)

(Continued)

she fought strong urges to express this anger. Louise knew that Tina might have deep-rooted and ambivalent feelings towards her mother and that an ill-judged comment could jeopardise their working relationship. There were times during her work with Tina that Louise had a strong urge to reach out and physically comfort her.

At the start of one session, Tina asked Louise if they could play a word game she had on her mobile phone. This was slightly unconventional but Louise decided to agree and see where it went. Louise quickly realised that Tina had introduced this game so that she could talk about difficult things without needing to make eye contact. At the end of the session, she saved the game on the screen and brought it back unchanged to the next session. On the third occasion, Tina typed the word 'slut', almost inviting Louise to comment. Louise felt that a door had been opened and, taking care not to make any assumptions or judgements, she gently enabled Tina to begin talking about the sexual abuse and the impact it had had on her.

What emerged was the story of a needy, vulnerable little girl who had been desperate for affection and easy to manipulate. Dave had told Tina that she was the 'daughter he never had' and that he was going to protect and care for her the way a father should. When he had begun to sexually abuse her, he had told Tina that most fathers did this and that it was his 'job to introduce her gently to being a woman'. Tina had no friends at school and no-one to check this out with. Her mother had been less hostile towards her since Dave's arrival and Tina was terrified that talking to her would spoil everything. By the time touching turned into rape, Tina had been made to feel that she had cooperated with the abuse and had encouraged it. Dave always gave her sweets and money and made her feel that these were in payment for sex. She had thrown herself downstairs hoping that the abuse would be discovered but this did not work. Tina's overdose had been an expression of her powerlessness and self-loathing, as had been several months of self-mutilation. Louise was aware that many children who have been sexually abused feel great shame about their bodies having responded to the abuse and to it being physically pleasurable. She took great care not to say anything about how the abuse must have felt or to make any judgements about how Tina felt about Dave.

Working with Tina's new-found openness, Louise was able to help her think about what had happened to her and begin reducing the level of self-blame that had been instilled. Louise also realised that Tina might now be able to make use of a therapeutic group where more direct approaches to challenging distorted thinking could be used.

Group Work

Tina agreed to attend a therapeutic group for girls who had been sexually abused and made further progress as a result. Group leaders did not share any of the content of the sessions outside the group, although the weekly agenda and activities they used were passed on to other professionals and carers. Within this group, Tina was enabled to participate in activities that focused on body-image and self-esteem. She was shown DVDs made by other groups of girls who had 'survived' sexual abuse and, in a variety of ways, was helped to realise that she was not alone in this experience and that sexual abuse is never the child's fault. She was enabled to share some of the ambivalent feelings she had towards her abuser and non-protecting parent and to hear that this was not uncommon. Tina had hoped that if she was examined, doctors would discover she was being abused; this was because she believed that signs of sexual abuse were noticeable. Many children think they are forever damaged by abuse and have heard many myths about never being able to have children, going on to become abusers and so on. Attending the group enabled some of the myths that reinforced Tina's low self-esteem to be dispelled. It also allowed taboo subjects and some of the most embarrassing, humiliating aspects of abuse to be explored in a safe and sensitive way.

Individual and group counselling were valuable stages in Tina's 'recovery' process. However, the effects of her early abuse and neglect were not so readily addressed through therapy. Tina had two very good experiences of therapeutic relationships and, crucially, was provided with appropriate care and a place to live where she felt loved and wanted. Practical steps were taken to try and facilitate more contact with her siblings, which proved to be a very complicated process.

Tina's story is fictitious but borrows aspects from the lives of real children and young people. Although theory, research and policy differentiate child abuse into the categories of physical, emotional, sexual and neglect, the reality is that there is much overlap between them, as Tina's story demonstrates.

Despite these challenges, this is an extremely worthwhile and rewarding area to work in, having potential to make a huge difference to a child's well-being in both the short- and long-term. The theory and research in this area can be fascinating to study and there is great potential for creativity in practice, making it well worth the effort of developing the knowledge and skills necessary to be effective.

Working with children who have been abused is extremely challenging and is not for everyone. The emotional impact on the counsellor of hearing first-hand and in-depth the stories of children who have been abused cannot be underestimated. This work carries with it a significant risk of compassion fatigue (Figley, 2002) and it is essential the counsellor avails him- or herself of high quality supervision from a supervisor who is experienced in this area. It is rarely obvious at the outset what method of intervention is most likely to be successful, and sometimes it can be a struggle to establish the trust necessary to engage the client. At times it can be incredibly frustrating to witness the damage done to children both by abusers and the system around them, and to feel powerless to change this. Sometimes, through parallel process, therapists may even begin to experience some of the same feelings as their clients and it is not uncommon for them to take to supervision feelings such as anger, frustration, sorrow, fear, guilt and even shame (see Chapter 13).

Summary

- There is evidence to suggest that child abuse can have a lasting impact and that counselling and therapy may improve outcomes for children
- The research base is developing rapidly but, as yet, there is insufficient evidence to evaluate the effectiveness of all forms of therapeutic intervention
- Counsellors have a range of options open to them and should be guided by some important principles including certain pre-requisites to offering counselling/therapy, avoidance of labelling, importance of listening to children and managing the legal process in the best interests of the child
- This area of work can be very demanding and counsellors should remain alert to issues of parallel process, transference and counter-transference and compassion fatigue, ensuring they have access to an appropriately trained and experienced supervisor

Reflective Questions

1 Do you think any of Tina's experiences are likely to affect her permanently?

There is some evidence to suggest that abuse and neglect in infancy may damage the developing brain (Gerhardt, 2004). However, more research is needed in this area. In other respects, it is important to remain positive and have an optimistic outlook about the capacity of humans to survive trauma and abuse. Research in this area is inherently flawed in that we can never know how many people were abused in childhood, live full and happy lives and choose never to speak of their experiences. These people are absent from our statistics and what we have therefore may be a skewed sample of children and adults who we know about because of their struggles. Therapy is the perfect place for distorted thinking to be addressed and for clients to discover what coping strategies work for them. The survivor stories in *Strong at the Broken Places* speak for themselves (Sanford, 1991).

2 How might intervention need to be different if there was only funding for six sessions?

Where intervention is limited to six sessions, therapists have to think strategically about their chosen method. Goal-based interventions may be more realistic than the approach used in the case study. During the contracting stage, clients choose which issues they wish to work on and the counsellor helps to ensure the target is realistic. The principle of 'non-maleficence' should be applied; sometimes it is more harmful to create expectations that cannot be met and therapists must avoid this wherever possible.

3 Are there any circumstances in which therapeutic intervention should be withheld?

- Where other needs are more pressing and counselling may undermine the meeting of these, e.g. settling into a new home/school, undertaking examinations.
- Where there is a strong risk that therapy may undermine the legal process and the client's greatest priority is the conviction of the perpetrator.
- Where the client does not want therapy and the referral is driven by others (this depends on the age of the child and their ability to make an informed choice).

4 What is the ideal physical environment in which to do therapeutic work with children and young people who have been abused?

In an ideal world, therapy will take place in a purpose-built environment, equipped with resources to enable the full range of interventions the therapist is skilled to offer. In reality, such places are not always available. Each therapist needs to consider their working environment and how this matches the needs of their clients. Children who have been abused may have a great need to feel safe and to be assured of privacy and guaranteed of no interruptions. They may be more sensitive than others to the stigma attached to counselling and believe that everyone knows what has happened to them. On the other hand, some children who have been abused may feel uncomfortable or even threatened by environments that are too intimate. Therapists should be aware that some places have certain associations and where possible, seek the client's view about where and when sessions should be held. The counsellor feeling at home should always come second to finding the right environment for the client. This should be thought about as part of the referral and planning process.

5 What level of confidentiality should be offered within the counselling relationship?

The same principles of confidentiality apply to this client group as any other (see Chapters 17 and 18). Information has to be shared where the therapist is made aware that a child is at risk of significant harm. It is not unusual for children to disclose new information about abuse during therapy. The counsellor needs to be prepared for this and build into the contract what action would be taken in this event. It is unusual for children (especially older children) to 'accidentally' disclose, especially if it has been made clear to them that such information would have to be passed on. In these situations, the counsellor should empower the client by sharing information about what will happen next and allowing them choices wherever this is possible.

Learning Activities

1. Make contact with your Local Safeguarding Children Board (LSCB) and find out what relevant training is available to you. Attending events such as 'Child Protection Awareness Workshops' will give you an opportunity to think about child abuse within a multi-disciplinary forum and help you to understand how counselling fits within the wider context of safeguarding children.
2. Reflect on your theoretical orientation and preferred method of intervention and consider the extent to which it lends itself to working with children or young people who have been abused. Ask your supervisor to read this chapter, then discuss it together.
3. If you have never worked with a child who has been abused before, consider how prepared you would be if a child disclosed abuse during a session with you. Would you know how best to respond? Would you know how to respond therapeutically whilst following your agency's safeguarding procedure? (If not, the workshops outlined in point 1 above will help.)

Further Reading

Allnock, D. and Hynes, P. (2012) *Therapeutic Services for Sexually Abused Children and Young People: Scoping the Evidence Base*. London: NSPCC

Daniels, D. and Jenkins, P (2010) *Therapy with Children: Children's Rights, Confidentiality and the Law*, 2nd edn. London: SAGE.

Deblinger, E., Mannarino, A.P., Cohen, J.A. and Steer, R.A. (2006) 'Follow-up study of a multisite, randomised control trial for children with sexual abuse-related PTSD: Examining predictors of treatment response', *Journal of the American Academy of Child and Adolescent Psychiatry,* 45: 1474–1484.

Doyle, C (2012) *Working with Abused Children.* 4th edn. Basingstoke: Palgrave Macmillan.

Geldard, K., Geldard, D. and Yin Foo, R. (2013) *Counselling Children: A Practical Introduction.* 4th edn. London: SAGE.

Gerhardt, S. (2004) *Why Love Matters: How Affection Shapes a Baby's Brain.* Hove: Brunner–Routledge.

Mudaly, N. and Goddard, C. (2009) 'The ethics of involving children who have been abused in child abuse research', *International Journal of Children's Rights,* 17: 261–281.

Online Resources

Counselling MindEd: http://counsellingminded.com.

24

Eating Disorders

Erica Allan, Elizabeth K. Hughes and Daniel Le Grange

This chapter includes:

- Information about eating disorders and their presentation in children and adolescents
- Speculations about the aetiology of these disorders
- A description of the most prominent psychosocial treatments for these disorders

The authors of this chapter have experience in the assessment and treatment of young people with eating disorders. The senior author (DLG) has been working as a clinical researcher in the field of adolescent eating disorders for the past 25 years. He received his training at the Maudsley Hospital in London in the 1980s, and has since then been at the forefront of developing and evaluating psychosocial treatments for adolescents with eating disorders. The first (EA) and second (EH) authors are close research collaborators and have been working with DLG for more than three years. Together, they have been primarily involved in managing a clinical trial for adolescents who present at a tertiary educational hospital in a metropolitan area. In this role, EA and EH have been working with a large multi-disciplinary team of clinicians who run a specialist inpatient and outpatient treatment programme for adolescents with eating disorders. Through this endeavour, all three authors are at the forefront of the clinical presentation of children and adolescents with eating disorders, and evaluating the best evidence-based practice for these complex disorders.

Eating Disorders: Definitions

The Diagnostic and Statistical Manual of Mental Disorders (DSM-5) (American Psychiatric Association, 2013) describes the eating disorders as follow; anorexia nervosa (AN), bulimia nervosa (BN), binge eating disorder (BED), avoidant/restrictive food intake disorder, and other specified feeding or eating disorder. Eating disorders usually onset in early to mid-adolescence (Swanson et al., 2011), and are complex psychiatric disorders associated with significant short- and long-term physiological and psychological morbidity and high rates of mortality (Crow et al., 2010). Rates of morbidity and mortality are among the highest of any psychiatric disorder (Herpertz-Dahlmann, 2009), with the physical development of children and adolescents being affected by medical complications such as bradycardia (slow heart rate) (Misra et al., 2004), osteopenia or osteoporosis (low bone density) (Allan et al., 2010), biochemical instability, hypothermia, hypoglycaemia (low blood glucose level) (Gaudiani et al., 2012), fatigue (Bulik et al., 2005) and amenorrhoea (absence of menstrual periods) (Herpertz-Dahlmann, 2009). High rates of psychiatric comorbidity such as depression, substance abuse (Rosling et al., 2011), suicidality and suicide attempts (Swanson et al., 2011), anxiety, self-consciousness (Bulik et al., 2005), social isolation (Beumont and Touyz, 2003), and obsessive compulsive disorder (Herpertz-Dahlmann, 2009), are often experienced and can have profound impact on psychological development of children and adolescents with eating disorders (Bulik et al., 2005).

Anorexia Nervosa (AN)

Anorexia nervosa (AN) is characterised by a) inability to maintain an appropriate body weight for age and height; b) an intense fear of weight gain or becoming fat, or engaging in behaviours that prevent weight gain; and c) a distorted sense of body weight or size, or denial of the seriousness of low weight (American Psychiatric Association, 2013). It is important to note that in adolescents, there may be a failure to gain weight during a period of growth rather than weight loss (American Psychiatric Association, 2013). AN is divided into two subtypes; restricting subtype, where binge eating or purging is not the main feature, and binge-eating/purging subtype, where binge eating and/or purging is a main feature (American Psychiatric Association, 2013). AN often emerges in adolescence (Lock and Le Grange, 2005a; Golden, et al., 2008), with a median age of onset of 12.3 years (Swanson et al., 2011), and an average illness length of seven years (Beumont and Touyz, 2003). The lifetime prevalence of anorexia nervosa in adolescents has been estimated at 0.3 per cent (Swanson et al., 2011).

Bulimia Nervosa (BN)

Bulimia nervosa (BN) is characterised by frequent episodes of binge eating, followed by unhealthy compensatory behaviours aimed at preventing weight gain that occur on average once a week for three months (American Psychiatric Association, 2013) An episode of binge eating is defined as consuming an objectively large amount of food in comparison to others in a similar period of time and circumstances, and a sense of loss or lack of control, i.e., either not being able to stop or control how much is being eaten (American Psychiatric Association, 2013). Inappropriate compensatory behaviours most often include self-induced vomiting, laxative and/or diuretic misuse, excessive exercise, enemas, or fasting. Further, and like AN, BN involves an undue emphasis of body weight and shape on self-evaluation (American Psychiatric Association, 2013). Individuals with BN generally do not present as being underweight, though some patients may be at the lower range of normal (Herpertz-Dahlmann, 2009). The median age of onset for BN is 12.4 years and the lifetime prevalence of this disorder has been estimated at 0.9 per cent in adolescents (Swanson et al., 2011).

Binge-Eating Disorder (BED)

Binge-eating disorder (BED) is characterised by frequent episodes of binge eating that occur once a week for three months, and is associated with a feeling of distress (American Psychiatric Association, 2013). Further, these binge episodes are associated with three or more of the following: feelings of disgust or guilt after the episode, consuming food at a more rapid pace than usual, consuming a large amount of food though not physically hungry, eating until feeling uncomfortably full, or feelings of embarrassment over the amounts of food consumed leading to eating alone. Unlike BN, binge episodes are not associated with compensatory behaviours (American Psychiatric Association, 2013).

Avoidant/Restrictive Food Intake Disorder

Avoidant/restrictive food intake disorder is characterised by a disturbance in eating that results in reduced nutritional or energy intake and is associated with an impact on functioning, reliance on nutritional supplements, nutritional deficits, or loss of weight (American Psychiatric Association, 2013).

Other Specified Feeding or Eating Disorder

Other specified feeding or eating disorder is a heterogeneous category of eating disorders, used as a diagnosis when the full DSM-5 criteria are not met for anorexia nervosa, bulimia nervosa, or binge-eating disorder. Those falling within this category may present with aspects of AN, BN, or BED without meeting full thresholds for those disorders (Beumont and Touyz, 2003; Turner and Bryant-Waugh, 2005; Eddy et al., 2008). For example, a young person might meet all of the diagnostic criteria required for a diagnosis of AN, but may not have lost sufficient weight to put them below their expected body weight.

In a population-based survey within the United States, the prevalence of subthreshold AN in adolescents, defined as a lowest body weight of less than 90 per cent of expected body weight and an intense fear of gaining weight, was estimated at 1.6 per cent (Swanson et al., 2011). Using data from the same survey, Le Grange et al. (2012) found the lifetime prevalence rate of DSM-IV-TR Eating Disorder Not Otherwise Specified (EDNOS) in adolescents to be 4.78 per cent, which included binge eating disorder (BED), sub-threshold AN (SAN), and sub-threshold BED (SBED). These authors also reported that for those with a lifetime diagnosis of an eating disorder, EDNOS accounted for 80.97 per cent of all eating disorder diagnoses among adolescents. Although full diagnostic criteria for a specific AN or BN diagnosis may not be met, it is important not to view sub-syndromal eating disorders as any less severe than either a diagnosis of AN or BN. Several studies (e.g. Eddy et al., 2008; Peebles et al., 2010; Swanson et al., 2011) have now demonstrated that patients who do not meet full diagnostic criteria for AN or BN are both medically and psychiatrically as unwell as patients meeting full criteria for AN and BN. Moreover, mood disorders, anxiety disorders and suicide plans have been found to be more common among adolescents with a sub-threshold diagnosis than those with AN, while also reporting similar frequency of substance use and behavioural disorders (Le Grange et al., 2012).

It is important to recognise that it is sometimes difficult to arrive at a DSM-IV diagnosis of an eating disorder in many children or young adolescents. For instance, young patients may not have the cognitive maturity to express their concerns for weight gain, or they may present with a loss of appetite rather than intentional weight loss, or are prepubertal and therefore rendering the loss of menses criterion obsolete. It is for these reasons that there may be a delay in the identification and diagnosis of eating disorders in younger children. A recent opinion piece (Bravender et al., 2010), prior to the publication of DSM-5, argued for the re-evaluation of the DSM criteria for eating disorders and how these may have to be adjusted for younger patients. Consequently, the diagnostic criteria for AN, BN and EDNOS were revised in the DSM-5 manual. The changes to the AN criteria excluded amenorrhoea as a criterion for diagnosis. Criteria for BN were also amended, reducing the frequency of binge-eating episodes and compensatory behaviours from twice per week to once per week for the previous three months. In addition, BED was recognised as a stand-alone eating disorder rather than bracketed within DSM-IV EDNOS (c.f. www.dsm5.org).

Historical and Theoretical Perspectives

The diagnosis and treatment of eating disorders have changed dramatically since they were first identified and described. Although there may be earlier accounts of AN, it was not until the latter part of the 19th century that Charles Lasegue in France and William Gull in England provided the first accounts of this disorder (Habermas, 1989; Striegel-Moore and Bulik, 2007). BN was initially described by Gerald Russell at the Maudsley Hospital in London, but not until 1979 and only included in the third edition of the DSM in 1987. Early therapeutic models promoted the isolation of children and adolescents by removing them from the care of parents (Silverman, 1997). These early therapeutic models were focused on the idea that family interactions contribute to the development of eating disorders. It is now recognised that the family, especially parents, play an important positive role in the treatment of young people with eating disorders (Lock and Le Grange, 2005a; Le Grange et al., 2010).

Despite a growing body of research, the causes of eating disorders remain largely unknown. However, it is thought that genetic factors, personality traits and thinking styles, physiological changes associated with starvation, and puberty all may contribute to the development of these disorders (Herpertz-Dahlmann et al., 2011). One of the most consistent findings is that the risk of developing AN is increased in those with immediate relatives with AN (Bulik et al., 2005, 2006, 2010). Socio-cultural influences are also often cited as contributing to the development of AN as it has been found to be more common in industrialised countries, and the prevalence of eating disorders has been observed to increase with the introduction of media endorsing thin ideal body standards (Becker et al., 2002). Overall, it is thought that a combination of biological and cultural factors contributes to the development of eating disorders (Striegel-Moore and Bulik, 2007).

There is a tendency for eating disorders to be viewed as mostly occurring among females, with the majority of research, treatment models and resources, particularly for AN, focusing on females (Strother et al., 2012; Wooldridge and Lytle, 2012). Few studies have reported the incidence of AN in males (Hoek and van Hoeken, 2003), but the ratio of females developing AN in comparison to males is typically cited as 10:1 (Currin et al., 2005). Previous research has demonstrated that among males with eating disorders, AN is a more common diagnosis than BN (Norris et al., 2012).

Key Models of Engagement and Intervention

Few psychotherapeutic interventions have been systematically tested for the paediatric eating disorders population. Fewer still have proven to be efficacious (Lock and Le Grange, 2005a). In this section of the chapter, we will briefly review four treatment modalities that have received relatively robust research support for this clinical population.

Family-Based Treatment (FBT)

Family-based treatment (FBT) was developed at the Maudsley Hospital, London, as an outpatient therapy for AN in adolescents. Within this model, adolescents with AN are viewed as being 'overtaken' by their disorder and are therefore unable to make healthy decisions about their nutritional intake. Parents are guided by a therapist in restoring their child's weight to a healthy level. Treatment occurs over three phases, with the first phase concentrating primarily on weight gain, and returning the adolescent to their healthy weight. During this phase, parents are given the responsibility of making all decisions regarding food and eating. As weight steadily increases and resistance to eating sufficient amounts of healthy food required for weight gain is reduced, the family is guided into phase two. During this phase, parents are encouraged to gradually reduce their control over eating decisions and return these decisions to the young person in an age appropriate way. Phase three of FBT concentrates on adolescent developmental issues and refocusing family relationships to relevant adolescent developmental concerns, especially as the illness no longer occupies centre stage (Lock and Le Grange, 2012).

FBT for AN is typically conducted in ~20 sessions over a period of six to 12 months. The first phase would last three to five months and consists of about 50 per cent of the treatment sessions (1–10). Phase two lasts two to three months (sessions 11–16), while phase three concludes the treatment over a two-month period of sessions 17–20 usually conducted at three-weekly intervals.

There have been several studies demonstrating the effectiveness of FBT as a treatment for adolescents with AN. Overall, these studies have demonstrated that 50–75 per cent of adolescents who receive FBT respond well and achieve weight restoration, and 60–90 per cent are fully recovered at four to five year follow-up (for a summary, see Le Grange and Eisler, 2009).

Family-based treatment for BN (FBT-BN) has also been developed for adolescents with bulimia nervosa. It is a three phase treatment that does not focus on exploring the cause of the disorder, instead focusing on managing and treating the symptoms. It is recognised that the disorder has a negative effect on the adolescent's development and disempowers parents. The treatment emphasises a collaborative approach between the parents and adolescent and they are encouraged to work together to combat the symptoms of the illness. As in FBT-AN, the therapist aims to absolve the parents of any guilt associated with the perception of having caused the illness and encourages the parents to view the illness as external to their child. Parents are also encouraged to be united in their efforts to help their child recover and the therapist aims to empower them through encouraging and guiding them in making their own decisions in helping resolve the bulimia symptoms (Le Grange and Lock, 2007). FBT-BN differs from the AN version as it does not focus on weight gain, focusing instead on reducing the episodes of bingeing and purging as well as promoting regular eating (Le Grange and Lock, 2007).

Although research has primarily focused on FBT for AN adolescents, with few exceptions, the principles of FBT are similar when treating children with BN. The main difference is in phase one of FBT-BN where the therapist will provide the adolescent with more of an opportunity to participate in the decision-making around healthy eating. This principle is primarily supported by the premise that BN in adolescents is fundamentally experienced as more ego-dystonic, i.e. symptoms are experienced as unpleasant and unwanted. AN, on the other hand, is mostly experienced as ego-syntonic, i.e., symptoms are viewed with pride and any attempts at intervention are fiercely rebuffed. Therefore, an adolescent with BN, at least in part, is motivated not to engage in binge eating and purging behaviours. Starvation is almost always experienced as desirable and to be 'protected' by the sufferer. For the most, though, FBT-BN follows the same therapeutic steps as FBT-AN (Le Grange and Lock, 2007).

Cognitive-Behavioural Therapy (CBT)

Within the CBT model, extreme weight control measures are seen as being driven by shape and weight concerns (Wilson, 2005). As a treatment for BN, the aim is to reduce the emphasis that is placed upon shape and weight while also developing mechanisms to deal with situations that may lead to bingeing and purging (Wilson, 2005). The aim of CBT for AN is to improve health by addressing the irrational thoughts that perpetuate the illness and altering the way starvation and exercise are viewed (Wade and Watson, 2012). Other factors that contribute to the eating disorder, such as poor self-esteem and perfectionism, may also be attended to during CBT sessions (Wade and Watson, 2012). CBT has received little attention in adolescent eating disorders with only one published RCT for adolescent AN (Gowers et al., 2007) and one for adolescent BN (Schmidt et al., 2007). In neither of these studies did CBT prove to be more efficacious than the comparison treatments.

Other Therapeutic Interventions

Individual ego-oriented therapy, also referred to more recently as adolescent-focused therapy (AFT) (Fitzpatrick et al., 2010), is an individual therapy used to treat adolescents with AN. The primary aim of AFT is to address issues regarding identity, as well as social and emotional maturation. A recent large RCT of FBT versus AFT for adolescent AN, demonstrated similar rates of full remission at the end-of-treatment. However, FBT was superior to AFT at six- and 12-month follow-up, and those in FBT generally showing an earlier response to treatment and less likely to relapse at follow-up once fully remitted at end-of-treatment (Lock et al., 2010).

Individual supportive psychotherapy (SPT) is a treatment for BN adapted for use in adolescents from an adult version. It involves three phases, with the first phase focused on building therapeutic rapport and gaining information regarding the patient's history of her/his eating disorder, and helps the adolescent identify issues that might be related to the development of the eating disorder. Phase two focuses on exploring emotional issues and concerns, while phase three addresses preparation for treatment termination and relapse prevention, i.e. identifying potential issues that may arise in the future. In a comparison of SPT and FBT-BN, it was found that those treated with FBT-BN were able to gain symptomatic relief more quickly than those in SPT. FBT-BN was also more efficacious than SPT at end-of-treatment and at six-month follow-up (Le Grange et al., 2007).

Case Study   Belinda

Belinda is a 15-year-old female who presented to the eating disorders outpatient clinic with her parents. She was referred by her GP after her parents became increasingly concerned over her loss of weight, restrictive eating patterns and social isolation.

Belinda described a long-standing history of body dissatisfaction and concerns about her shape and weight. Although she had felt this way for several years, it was in the previous six months that Belinda had decided to 'do something about it'. Consequently, Belinda increased her exercise and reduced her portion sizes at meal times. Although Belinda originally aimed to lose a small amount of weight, she soon became driven to lose more weight and admitted that she 'could not imagine being happy at any weight'. Belinda described a gradual decrease in the portion sizes of her meals and variety of foods eaten, having become a vegetarian within the past six months. Although Belinda was actively avoiding foods she had previously enjoyed, such

(Continued)

(Continued)

as chocolate and take-aways, she described this as only occurring because she didn't want to eat unhealthy foods.

Belinda's parents, Anne and Jacob, became aware of a change in their daughter's habits in the six months prior to their presentation to the clinic. Anne had become concerned when Belinda decided to become a vegetarian but thought it might be a passing phase. However, Belinda began to further restrict both the variety and quantity of foods. When offered foods and meals that Belinda had previously enjoyed, she claimed that she no longer liked these foods or that they made her feel unwell. Further, Belinda spent many hours looking at recipe books and preparing meals for the rest of the family, unwilling to eat what Anne had prepared. Anne and Jacob became especially concerned when they observed Belinda becoming very anxious at the suggestion of having dinner at a restaurant that 'did not have healthy options'. Anne has also observed Belinda weighing herself on a daily basis and appearing to pinch her stomach, arms and thighs.

Upon examination, Belinda's extremities were cold and she described herself as feeling cold constantly. Her weight put her below 85 per cent of her expected body weight for her age and height and she expressed concern over not having menstruated in the previous four months. She denied purging or laxative misuse but became tearful when describing the guilt experienced after feeling that she had eaten too much. Although she described feeling a sense of loss of control, the amount that she categorised as being too much was not enough to constitute an objectively large amount. In fact, the portions she described as being too large were minimal.

After meeting with Belinda and her parents individually, they were delivered feedback as a family. Belinda was diagnosed as having anorexia nervosa and it was recommended that she commence family-based treatment immediately.

The family arrived for their first therapy session and Belinda's sister, Jessica, attended the session. Although initially being reluctant to be involved in the sessions, Jessica found them to be informative and helped her understand why Belinda behaved the way she did. Jessica also found it helpful to gain an understanding of her sister's troubles and how she was able to support her.

The family received 18 sessions of family-based treatment with the family-based treatment clinician over six months, receiving four sessions within the first two weeks, and then weekly sessions for the first three months of therapy. Sessions were then spaced out every two to three weeks to enable the family to prepare for the end of treatment.

Anne and Jacob chose to take time off of work during the first phase of therapy and Belinda was kept from school. Although this placed financial stress on the family, they reasoned that having the time off now might prevent them from having more time off in the future. This enabled Anne and Jacob to supervise all of Belinda's meals and support her when she became distressed. It also allowed her parents to prevent her from exercising. This enabled Belinda to gain 1 kilogram per week in the first four weeks of the intervention and her family noticed a slight decrease in her anorexic behaviours.

The next eight weeks of phase one were focused on weight gain and addressing the difficulties they encountered with re-feeding.

After three months of treatment, Belinda was allowed to return to school for half the day and was then taken home for lunch. Belinda was also allowed to prepare her own breakfast during this time and have her morning snack at school. As her weight was maintained throughout this process, Belinda was then able to return to school full time and was no longer supervised at lunch times. The family had planned that any weight loss would result in returning back to half days at school.

Throughout phase three, the focus was on a review of adolescent development, how the eating disorder impacted this process, preparation for treatment ending, relapse prevention and helping Belinda to become more independent.

Treatment was concluded within the prescribed 18 sessions. By this time, Belinda had been weight restored and had resumed exercising in a healthy way. She no longer felt the need to restrict her portion sizes and was able to eat a wide variety of foods, including meat. Although she was still adjusting to her new body shape, she did not feel that she needed to lose weight. She was no longer preoccupied by food and calories, and had become more social and actively participated in family life.

Summary

- Anorexia nervosa is characterised by: a) inability to maintain an appropriate body weight for age and height; b) an intense fear of weight gain or becoming fat; and c) a distorted sense of body weight or size, or denial of the seriousness of low weight
- Bulimia nervosa is characterised by frequent episodes of binge eating, followed by unhealthy compensatory behaviours aimed at preventing weight gain that occur on average once a week for three months
- The most common treatments for adolescents with AN and BN include family-based treatment, individual adolescent-focused therapy, and cognitive-behavioural therapy

Reflective Questions

1. Celebrations and religious festivals are usually centred around food and eating. How do you think someone with an eating disorder would cope in these situations? What strategies could someone with an eating disorder adopt to help them cope with a difficult situation such as this?

2. Eating disorders in childhood and adolescence have the potential to disrupt physical development. What do you think the social and emotional consequences of having an eating disorder during this time are? Would these create long-term problems?
3. How do you differentiate healthy exercise from exercise as a symptom of an eating disorder? How much exercise is too much?
4. How much do you think people know about eating disorders? Are there any misconceptions they might have about people who have eating disorders? How would you go about addressing these?
5. How would having a child or sibling with an eating disorder impact on the lives of family members? What are some of the difficulties family members would face?

Learning Activities

1. What factors influenced how you felt about your body as a child and then as an adolescent? How did it change as you got older?
2. How would your feelings compare with a child or adolescent with an eating disorder?
3. One of the primary aims of FBT is weight gain. Individuals with AN often perceive themselves as needing to lose weight. Imagine how someone who views themselves as needing to lose weight may react and feel when told that they need to gain weight.
4. One challenge that parents of children with an eating disorder experience is understanding the behaviour of their child in relation to food and eating. One aim of FBT is to help the parents externalise their child's illness and understand that their child's behaviour is a result of the eating disorder. How might you describe an eating disorder to parents to help them understand their child's behaviour?
5. Has your understanding of eating disorders changed after reading this chapter? If so, how has it changed?

Further Reading

Dare, C. and Eisler, I. (1997) 'Family therapy for anorexia nervosa', in D.M. Garner and P.E. Garfinkel (eds), *Handbook of Treatment for Eating Disorders*. New York: The Guilford Press. pp. 307–24.
A detailed description of family therapy for adolescent AN by the founders of this approach.

Gowers, S.G., Clark, A., Roberts, C., et al. (2007) 'Clinical effectiveness of treatments for anorexia nervosa in adolescents: Randomised controlled trial', *The British Journal of Psychiatry*, 191 (5): 427–435.

The largest randomised controlled trial (RCT) for adolescent anorexia nervosa to date. The authors demonstrate that specialist inpatient re-feeding is no better than outpatient treatment.

Le Grange, D. and Lock, J. (2007) *Treating Bulimia in Adolescents: A Family Based Approach*. New York: Guilford Press.
A detailed treatment manual for clinicians. This text is suitable for clinicians who seek guidance how to conduct a course of FBT for adolescents with BN.

Lock, J. and Le Grange, D. (2012 [2001]) *Treatment Manual for Anorexia Nervosa: A Family-Based Approach*. 2nd edn. New York: Guilford Press.
This is a detailed clinicians' manual of FBT for adolescent AN. This is the second edition of this manual, and provides detailed guidance about implementing FBT for AN.

Lock, J., Le Grange, D., Agras, W.S., et al. (2010) 'Randomized clinical trial comparing family-based treatment with adolescent-focused individual therapy for adolescents with anorexia nervosa', *Archives of General Psychiatry*, 67 (10): 1025–1032.
The largest RCT, to date, of FBT and AFT for adolescent AN. This study provides robust support of the efficacy of FBT for adolescent AN.

Russell, G.F., Szmukler, G.I., Dare, C. and Eisler, I. (1987) 'An evaluation of family therapy in anorexia nervosa and bulimia nervosa', *Archives of General Psychiatry*, 44 (12): 1047–1056.
The first RCT for eating disorders involving two psychosocial treatments. This seminal work provided the foundation for the future involvement of parents in the recovery of their ill offspring with AN.

Additional Reading

Alexander, J. and Le Grange, D. (2010) *My Kid Is Back: Empowering Parents to Beat Anorexia Nervosa*. London: Routledge.
Collins, L. (2005) *Eating with Your Anorexic*. New York: McGraw Hill.
Lock, J. and Le Grange, D. (2005) *Help Your Teenager Beat an Eating Disorder*. New York: Guilford Press.

Online Resources

BACP website: www.bacp.co.uk/, especially the BACP Children and Young People Division and the Competences for Working with Children and Young People.
Counselling MindEd: http://counsellingminded.com, especially Modules CMD 02: Participation and Empowerment; CMD 03: Legal and Professional Issues; CMD 04: Cultural Competence; CMD 05: Initiating Counselling; CMD 07: Relational Skills; CMD 08: Therapeutic Skills: CMD 10: Concluding Counselling.
A website that is educational for parents and practitioners: www.maudsleyparents.org.

Part 4

Practice Settings

25

Health and Social Care Services

Barbara Smith, Sue Pattison and Cathy Bell

This chapter includes:

- Practice and policy and the development of child-focused services
- Working with children in care including adopted children
- Child and Adolescent Mental Health Services (CAMHS)

Introduction

The work of the professional counsellor takes place in a diverse range of practice settings and covers the main modalities and interventions such as talking therapies in the client-centred/humanistic, cognitive-behavioural and psychodynamic approaches and play therapy/therapeutic play, filial therapy and other creative approaches. This chapter looks specifically at the practice contexts of health care and social services where counsellors are employed to work with children and young people, either directly through the statutory organisations, National Health Service (NHS) and local authority (LA) or sub-contracted from another service provider such as a charitable trust or agency on an employed or self-employed basis. Although the range of health and social care services are similar across the various parts of the UK, they may be organised and referred to differently in England, Northern Ireland, Wales and Scotland and be informed by country specific legislation and policies. Counsellors are advised to familiarise themselves with the policies, practices and legislation most appropriate to their context. Professional counselling bodies such as BACP are a good source of information or signposting.

As practitioners, we are familiar with a range of sub-contexts within the health and social care services, and we share with you our knowledge, skills and experience from our work with some of the most vulnerable children and young people. As authors we have learnt much about each others' career histories from the process of story sharing. Our joint career histories include counselling and psychotherapy, teaching, researching, writing, social work, nursing and health visiting. Our knowledge, skills and experience are brought to this chapter in a way that you, the reader, can find accessible and can engage with in ways that enable you to inform and enhance your own practice. The scope of 'health and social care services' is vast and it is not possible to cover it all in relation to the work of counsellors.

Practice and Policy: The Development of Child and Young Person-Focused Services

In developed countries, the notion of childhood has shifted from one of extreme vulnerability and lack of consequence to a position strengthened by human rights legislation and policy, for example, the United Nations Convention on the Rights of the Child (UNICEF, 1989). In the UK, the National Health Service (NHS) was set up to address the needs of the post-war population and included welfare strategies to enhance the physical growth, development and health needs of mothers, babies and children (Webster, 2002). Children's developmental progress became of interest to parents and professionals and could be measured and charted and used by UK Local Authorities as a yardstick for the quality of care provided by parents. Child abuse and neglect were studied and legislated for, leading to the responsibilities and powers that Local Authorities now have in relation to the welfare of children and young people. Alongside this, child guidance clinics attached to hospitals and in the community grew in number to provide for the needs of 'difficult' children and young people, those with behavioural problems and/or special educational needs such as physical or learning disabilities (Sampson, 1976). The responsibility for children and young people with 'special educational needs' developed and became part of political discourses around human rights and the concept of inclusion gained political credibility leading to the health and social care landscape of anti-discrimination, access to services for all and addressing the needs of diverse and marginalised groups (MacBeath et al., 2006).

Mention health and social care services to a counsellor working in any sector or from any modality and a variety of responses are liable to be solicited. These may range from frustrated responses such as: 'There are not enough resources, therefore, it's a postcode lottery' and 'Even though my young clients are living in extremely neglectful homes, nothing is ever done about it', to grateful comments such as: 'I'm so glad there is support out there for vulnerable young people'. The response will depend on the individual's experience, and yet when the UK National Health Service was set up in 1946 it was hailed as being free for all from the 'cradle to the grave' at the point of delivery. With health and social care being a devolved matter within the United Kingdom, despite shared values and similarities in legislation, policy and practice, considerable differences are continuing to develop within the systems of each of the four countries (nations) that make up the United Kingdom: Scotland, Wales, Northern Ireland and England.

As with any counselling context, it is useful for counsellors to have an understanding of what is meant by health and social care services. However, in view of the statutory nature of these services and their powers and responsibilities in respect of safeguarding children and young people, a good working knowledge of these services and how their work is impacted is essential for counsellors. For discussion on safeguarding see Chapter 17: Law and Policy.

Across the countries of our world, access to health care will vary. This is largely influenced by each country's social and economic condition and the health policies in place. Some countries see health care distributed among market participants, whereas in others planning is made more centrally among governments or other coordinating bodies. The four nations of the UK can be seen as microcosms in relation to global health and social care systems. According to the World Health Organization (WHO) a well-functioning health care system: 'Requires a robust financing mechanism with a well-trained and adequately paid workforce, reliable information on which to base decisions and policies and well maintained facilities and logistics to deliver quality medicines and technologies' (World Health Organization Health Systems: www.who.int/topics/health_systems/en/). For the counsellor who works with children and young people this means they would be well advised to know about and have some understanding of how the health and social care services which surround that child and their family work in order to operate safely and ethically. In order to achieve this some health and social care authorities will purchase the services of counsellors, art therapists, play therapists, music therapists and others directly to enable a useful resource to add to an existing or developing multi-disciplinary team. This approach helps to provide balance in relation to knowledge and experience. In other instances local services may be put out to public contract and counsellors and therapists could be employed by the local agency or charity in the voluntary or community sector that successfully applies for and is granted the tender for a specific service delivery. This is another service building approach that can lead to shared knowledge and experience. The lone counsellor may be vulnerable as a practitioner and their practice less encompassing in terms of knowledge and experience.

The modern approach to health and social care requires groups of trained professionals and para-professionals to come together as interdisciplinary teams in order to provide an all-round service to the child and family, known as multi-agency working (Edwards et al., 2009). The cost of providing such care can be high as the number of 'problem families' in the UK rises in relation to socio-economic factors such as high unemployment and increasing demands on health care systems due to changing demographics and greater expectations. In many nations health care alone, according to OECD data, can use up to as much as 23 per cent of a country's expenditure.

For ease of access in deciphering the maze of health and social care services within the United Kingdom and to enable international contexts to be compared by the reader, we will look at services as they fit into the categories of primary, secondary and tertiary care. Although no longer formalised categories of care in the UK NHS (now referred to as Tiers 1–4), they provide the reader with a sense of perspective across the levels of care across the range of services. Primary care is the term for those health care services which contribute to the health and well-being of the local community. It is the first stage of any journey within health and social care, the first port of call for all who use the health care system. Such professionals could be a nurse, general practitioner (GP), dentist, counsellor or play therapist depending on which services a local authority or NHS Trust offers within its primary care provision. In most areas the first contact is the GP, who is the main referral agent for children and young people outside of the school context. Within the sphere of mental health services for children and young people, formalised in the NHS as Child and Adolescent Mental Health Services (CAMHS), primary care fits with Tier 1 services (see Table 9.1). Generally, secondary care is when a patient needs to see professionals such as cardiologists, urologists and allied health professionals, for example, counsellors, and psychologists. Secondary care is often associated with hospital care yet a dietician, a counsellor or a psychiatrist may be seen in a local health centre, clinic or community centre. Secondary care is normally only accessed via a doctor's referral and in rare instances by a patient self-referral (equates to Tiers 2 and 3 in CAHMS).

Tertiary care is specialised consultative health care and includes Tiers 3 and 4 CAHMS. It is usually for inpatients and is reached by a referral from a primary or secondary health professional. Examples of this are cardiac surgery, advanced neonatal services, palliative care, and secure or other psychiatric units. It is important for counsellors to recognise that many types of health and social care interventions take place outside of health facilities. Food safety services, needle exchange services, professionals who serve in residential and community settings, self-care, home care, assisted living treatment for substance misuse are examples of such services. The counsellor may come into contact in any counselling situation with a child or young person who has input from other professionals. In the counselling room at times it will be very obvious to the counsellor that the young client has a physical disability, a communication difficulty or an illness that requires some form of health or social care support. For example, the child may be a wheelchair user or have adapted equipment to carry out everyday tasks. Some of our young clients may have a physical illness such as diabetes, asthma, epilepsy or childhood cancer. It may be useful for counsellors to be aware of any physical illness as it can have a direct impact on the counselling, for example, young people who take medication for epilepsy on a morning may be more alert in the afternoon and more able to engage with counselling. Some illnesses can cause tiredness and impact on the ability to concentrate. In our individual practices we have each had young people in the counselling room who, due to physical illness, could not have a counselling session in the afternoon as they were physically too tired. Physiotherapists, occupational therapists, specialist nurses and social workers specialising in disability could have an involvement with the young client and a team approach may (though not necessarily) be helpful. A counsellor may notice a progressive or sudden change in a young person's physical health and be required to share this information under safeguarding policies or as a specific requirement of contracts with the organisation through which they deliver counselling.

Working with Children and Young People in Care

At the present time there are about 67,000 children in England looked after by Local Authorities (Harker, 2012). Looked-after children are those young people who are subject to 'care orders' under Section 31 of the Children Act (1989) or those who are voluntarily accommodated under Section 20 of the Children Act (1989). Some children are looked after if they are involved with the youth justice system or subject to police protection. Some young people are looked after within foster families, while others are looked after by kinship carers (members of their own extended family) or in residential homes. This section addresses the particular issues and challenges for therapists working with these children and their families. What is distinct about this group of children is that by definition they have been neglected, abused, or are at least dealing with the traumatic impact of separation and loss.

Common Experiences of Looked-After Children

When we meet any child for the first time for counselling, we are curious about what brings them into our lives. What's happened? With looked-after children we can safely assume that this child has experience of social workers, maybe police officers, judges, case conferences, not to mention what went before – the reasons why these professionals became involved in their lives. Research by Cleaver et al. (2011) found that there are particular difficulties relating to parenting capacity that impact on the health and development of children at different ages. These issues are domestic violence, drug and alcohol dependency, mental illness (the toxic trio) and learning disability. They found that it is the 'multiplicative impact' of a combination of these different problems that are more likely to be harmful and that bring children into the care system. What we have learned about the impact of domestic violence on children and young people is that like other abused children, they may be dealing with symptoms of PTSD – dissociation, numbness, disturbed sleep, lack of concentration and withdrawal. They may be experiencing flashbacks, memory problems and difficulties relating to other children (Graham-Berman and Levendosky, 1998). Children unable to deal with these distressing feelings will often 'act out' all manner of behaviours in their attempt to survive, bringing them to the negative attention of teachers, police officers and other professionals. As a result, placement stability in care can be difficult, some children moving placements as many as three times in one year (Munro and Hardy, 2006). Children in care frequently suffer chronic low self-esteem and self-confidence. Fahlberg (1991) tells of the risk of problems with attachment in the early years where poor parenting through drug and alcohol use or mental illness can cause infants to see themselves as unloved and unlovable. Golding (2008) suggests an inability to regulate emotion is a consequence of a difficult infancy and early childhood, often resulting in a range of distressing emotional, psychological and behavioural problems (Golding, 2008).

Therapeutic Work with Children in Care

Given the particular levels of distress of children in care it is important for counsellors, social workers, teachers and carers to have knowledge and understanding of attachment difficulties and their ensuing problems. Gerhardt (2004) writes about what neuroscience offers in understanding the internal world of the child, promising greater insight into how we can support children's emotional life in the future. In her work on the importance of affection in shaping a baby's brain, Gerhardt (2004: 49) speaks of the powerful impact of a disapproving or rejecting look, which causes 'a sudden lurch from the sympathetic arousal to parasympathetic arousal, creating the effects we experience as shame – a sudden drop in blood pressure and shallow breathing'. Some children have been raised in cold affectionless environments and need a reparative therapeutic process to help them to heal, not just with a loving therapist, but with all adults who they come into contact with. For this reason much of the therapeutic work undertaken with children in care involves foster carers and/or perhaps birth family members. As well as the different individual play therapy approaches discussed elsewhere in this book, some authors have written specifically for children traumatised in early childhood and who have attachment difficulties. A specific role for a counsellor working with local authority personnel would be to offer consultation and training to social workers, teachers and carers. Some of the therapeutic approaches used in working with looked-after children are outlined in the following sections.

Attachment-Focused Parenting

Attachment-focused parenting, developed by Dan Hughes (2006), fosters a relationship between carer and child in which the child experiences a 'safe haven' and where the child feels physically, psychologically and emotionally safe. Hughes uses the acronym of PACE to describe his model – Playfulness, Acceptance, Curiosity and Empathy. The idea is to facilitate parents to engage the child expressively and playfully giving the child the message that the relationship is stronger than any small irritations. Hughes' model suggests that an attitude of acceptance and empathy enables the adult to co-regulate the child's emotional state, enhancing the child's own capacity for emotional regulation. An attitude of curiosity and wondering enhances the child's capacity to construct meaning (Golding, 2008). This is supported by the ground-breaking work of Schore (2010) who has integrated attachment theory and neuroscience. He describes how our right brain hemisphere regulates emotion and processes our sense of self, suggesting that what we (counsellors) communicate unconsciously is essential to our clients' recovery from early childhood trauma. The PACE model then, is based on facilitating carers to offer therapeutic environments for children in their care. Often carers have suggested that children's difficult behaviours happen suddenly 'as if a switch had been turned on' – the carer begins to recognise the onset of a child's overwhelming feelings.

Case Study   Katy

Katy, aged six, came for counselling with her grandmother, Joan, her kinship carer, because Katy would on occasions scream abuse and scratch and punch her Gran 'out of the blue'. When this happened, Joan found it difficult to deal with Katy – she was hurt and angry and would threaten that Katy would have to go and live with someone else – exacerbating Katy's anguish and insecurity. Joan's own distress was getting in the way of her helping Katy to learn how to deal with her difficult emotions. It is hard to empathise with a child who is raging at you. Using an attachment focused parenting approach Joan learns that Katy's angry displays are not about her – they are the only way Katy knows how to get through the next moment/ten minutes/hour/day. Joan needs support to stay grounded and loving when Katy is suffering in this way by learning about attachment and what is behind Katy's behaviour.

(Continued)

(Continued)

Over time, Joan came to develop the PACE skills, offering Katy a containing experience (as was offered to Joan by the counsellor) and Katy's distressing episodes became less frequent and less intense. Katy is now able to deal with her feelings by asking for her needs to be met and asking for help when she is feeling upset.

Theraplay

Another way of supporting children within their foster placements is through Theraplay, a model designed to build and enhance attachment (Booth and Jernberg, 2010). This too has a basis of playful interaction between children/young people and carers, and focuses on four essential qualities of the relationship between parent and child – structure, engagement, nurture and challenge. The notion of Theraplay was originally developed by DesLauriers and Carlson (1969) to work with children with autism. Their research focused on five severely autistic children over a one year period. Applying the method (now known as Theraplay), personality and socialisation qualities improved, as was evidenced by parent, clinic and therapist ratings. Emphasising the importance of an emotional connection between the child and parent/caregiver, the work differs from the work of Hughes (2006) in that the play is structured to attend to specific difficulties the child may be having. For example they give specific examples of ways of working with children and young people with autistic spectrum disorder, those who have experienced complex trauma and young people who have been adopted. Such specific difficulties are met with a range of specific Theraplay activities to enhance children's functioning, but particularly to enhance the young person's attachment relationships. Counsellors may work with children, carers and others involved in the Theraplay approach, both supporting and contributing to the approach.

Life Story Work

It is well documented that placement instability adversely affects the psychosocial development of children in care (Lewis et al., 2007). Furthermore, as previously mentioned, some looked-after children can have as many as three placements in the course of one year (Munro and Hardy, 2006). Shockingly, research by Ward and Skuse (2001) found that in a long stay sample of 242 children and young people, 28 per cent had three or more placements and 3 per cent had six or more. This may be because placements are often unplanned and crisis-driven, or because of a shortage of carers and unfilled social work vacancies. When a child is moved, they not only leave their placement, but they have to deal with a range of changes of school, friends or even separation from siblings. When a child has been in care for some years, particularly when they have had several placements, they can become confused about their past, and memories of different places and people become blurred. One child said 'I lived with John and Sue when I was five or it might have been when I was eight … I think I had a dog named Boudie and I think I had a sister'.

A life story book is not only a record of places, people and events in the child's life, but an opportunity to process painful feelings about incidents and endings along the way. While some people consider the life story book as an 'end product' with important factual information for the child, it can also be a therapeutic 'journey' in which the child makes sense of why they came into care and why they moved from one fostering or residential placement to another. If a child is not clear about why they have moved, they may experience a move as a rejection. The book is put together over a period of time covering the time from birth until the present day. It often takes the form of a scrap book with copies of birth certificate, photographs of birth family members and stories and photographs of foster families. Counsellors and play therapists within the local authority context, or social workers using counselling as part of their wider role may use life story work extensively to help children and young people build self-esteem and confidence, develop a sense of identity, and express and deal with difficult emotions and psychological distress.

Case Study   James

James, now aged 12, had been adopted at age two, but sadly the adoptive placement broke down because his adoptive parents could not cope with James's behaviour – biting, hitting, swearing, etc. James's infancy had been troubled, leaving him unable to regulate his emotions and with a confused sense of self. He had had numerous short-term placements in foster care and was eventually placed with long-term foster carers. It was important that James did not experience the same rejection as with his birth mother and adoptive parents, and so life story work began within a contracted counselling context. Over several months of counselling, using a child-centred approach and creative art materials, James came to understand why his birth mother had been unable to take care of him. An important piece of information for James was that while his mother struggled with addiction problems, she had fought hard to keep him. He had not been rejected! – he had been taken into care for his protection and survival. He was able to talk about his anger with his counsellor and social worker, and at the same time hear about the impact of addiction on people's ability to look after a small child. In making sense of the various moves he had been subject to, he learned the difference between short term and long term foster placements, and how those foster carers had loved and cared for

(Continued)

(Continued)

him while the social worker was finding the right long term placement for him. He was able to cry about people he missed and also talk about some that he hadn't been keen on. During this process, the counsellor listened with empathy and compassion and answered some difficult questions about adults and how they can sometimes get it wrong for children. As James began to understand more fully the reasons for the multiple moves in his young life, he came to see that there was nothing wrong with him and that his behaviours were a perfectly understandable reaction to distressing feelings that he didn't know what to do with. Making sense of his past enabled James to be more self-accepting and develop a stronger sense of identity. James regularly re-visits his life story book and will need to re-visit it with an adult, perhaps a counsellor, a social worker, or carer when his questions need to be answered in ways appropriate to his different developmental stages.

Therapy with Adopted Children

Since 2005, when the Adoption and Children Act 2002 was fully implemented, the law specified that only those therapists who are registered with Ofsted as part of an adoption support agency (ASA) can offer specific adoption services. Therefore, counsellors who work with clients for whom adoption is the main focus of therapeutic work are employed by registered adoption agencies.

Rogers (2010) highlights the work of therapists working with adopted clients. She suggests that a therapist working in the field of adoption needs 'to be able to bear the weight of all of the losses and grief of the adopted clients, adoptive parents, birth relatives and prospective adopters – and survive its enactment in the therapeutic space'. In addition, she argues, the early experience of rejection can lead the client to play out their pain in the transference relationship. Further, if and when intimacy is established, there may be a premature ending to the therapy; to risk intimacy might lead to further unbearable experiences of rejection and abandonment.

Adopted children have often had a turbulent history before being looked-after in the care system. These early traumatic experiences of loss and separation can lead to children developing attachment disorders, behavioural difficulties and developmental problems which can disturb them long into adult life. The naïve expectation that the provision of a loving home with new loving parents will lead to instant stability has long been questioned. Adopted children often believe that they are somehow fundamentally flawed. This is true for many clients from a range of backgrounds, but there is something about the experience of being adopted that gives the child hard 'evidence' that they were not wanted, not loveable enough or not good enough.

Rogers (2010) highlights the different areas of expertise required to work as an adoption therapist, including understanding issues of rejection, reunion and life story work. Themes of identity and belonging are frequently present – those often 'taken-for-granted' issues of religious background, blood relatives, cultural history and genetic and medical history cannot be assumed for many adopted children. 'It is the not knowing that results in many adoptees having burning questions about who they are; the circumstance behind their placement, their birthparent and ultimately why they were given up' (see: www.counselling-directory.org.uk/adoption.html).

Young people who have been adopted may need support in dealing with the emotional impact of tracing birth parents and the experience of reunion – both positive and negative. Birth parents may have a new family and the client has to deal with the fact that these other children were 'kept', again reinforcing long held beliefs that it is their 'badness' that made their parent give them up. As well as intense feelings of loss and grief then, strong feelings of anger and shame may also be present. Approved Adoption Counsellors are registered with Ofsted, and are subject to regular inspections. This challenging and rewarding work needs therapists who are resilient, knowledgeable, reliable and willing to commit to the 'long haul'.

The Work of Specialist Child and Adolescent Mental Health Services (CAMHS)

The information provided in the following sections on Child and Adolescent Mental Health Services (CAMHS) is as accurate as is possible in an ever-changing UK NHS environment, giving a flavour and overview of how services are organised as providers of mental health care for children and young people. CAMHS are NHS community and hospital-based mental health services for children and young people. The work of community CAMHS teams was previously undertaken by the local authority child guidance clinics, until 1995 when the *Together We Stand* document was published (NHS Health Advisory Service, 1995), offering a coherent planning, delivery and evaluation strategy for children's mental health. The document introduced the current four tier CAMHS framework.

Tier 1 is provided by universal services such as in-school counsellor, teachers, health visitors and GPs, who are not necessarily specialist mental health practitioners but may have some mental health knowledge They offer advice and support including mental health promotion and are able to signpost young people to other more specialist services. Tier 2 are those professionals working in community and primary care settings and may be counsellors, play therapists, primary mental health workers, paediatric clinics or psychologists. They may guide and support families, train Tier 1 workers and identify young people with more severe or complex needs. Counsellors may be employed by CAMHS to provide care and support in the school or CAMHS based contexts. Tier 3 CAMHS provide a multi-disciplinary approach in a community mental health clinic. The team usually consists of specialists such as psychiatrists, psychologists, family therapists, mental health practitioners, counsellors, play therapists and nurse therapists. Tier 3 services support those young people with severe, complex and persistent disorders. Typically, a Tier 3 service will take referrals from GPs, school counsellors, teachers, school nurses, social workers when young people have symptoms of mood disorders such as depression, and anxiety disorders such as social anxiety disorder, post-traumatic stress and phobias. Specialist CAMHS workers may also see children and young people who need assessment for autistic spectrum disorder (ASD), attention deficit and hyperactivity disorder (ADHD) (although this latter condition is as likely to be assessed by the community paediatric team). Tier 4 CAMHS services are for children and young people with serious mental health problems, provided by highly specialised day units, outpatient teams or inpatient units. CAMHS also offer targeted services for young people with learning difficulties, physical illness, behaviour difficulties or children in care, although the scope of provision may differ in different parts of the UK and change in response to NHS objectives. Counsellors may act as referral agents to CAMHS or be part of specialist service provision.

Working with Risk

Working with risk is relevant to all contexts of counselling children and young people (see Chapter 17: 'Law and Policy'). However, the elements of risk may be higher in children and young people who have been referred to specialist CAMHS, though this cannot be assumed. Tier 3 specialist CAMHS workers often carry a caseload of a wide range of difficulties, including young people who are persistently self-harming. This might include overdosing on medicines, using ligatures dangerously, and often cutting their skin, sometimes quite deeply. Similar risky behaviours may also be seen in other counselling contexts, for example, secondary schools.

Favazza (1989: 143) suggested that 'of all disturbing patient behaviours, self-mutilation is the most difficult for clinicians to understand and treat'. A range of negative emotions are expressed by practitioners dealing with young people who self-mutilate, but particularly powerlessness, helplessness and inadequacy (Favazza, 1989; Spiers, 2001; Sanderson, 2006). In a study undertaken by YoungMinds and Cello (2012), as many as one in 12 children and young people are believed to self-harm, inpatient admissions increasing by 8 per cent. Intensive therapeutic intervention, including outreach work and telephone contact is recommended by the National Institute for Health and Clinical Excellence (NICE) for the treatment of self-harm, particularly when a young person is at risk of repetition. They also emphasise the importance of follow-up on missed appointments to lessen risk. In the YoungMinds and Cello report, young people identified unmet needs in being able to speak openly to a range of professionals, finding support and advice from the adults around them. Although self-harm behaviours are common in other counselling contexts when working with children and young people, the severe or more dangerous types of self-harm tend to be referred to specialist CAMHS.

According to the Royal College of Psychiatrists (2012) there are a range of reasons why young people harm themselves, but essentially it is a way of coping with distressing feelings building up inside. Feeling desperate with nowhere to turn may lead a child to feel helpless. This might lead to a young person cutting themselves to relieve the tension and to feel more in control. Others have reported feeling guilt and shame; self-harm being a way of punishing themselves. Some report traumatic events where they have disconnected from their bodies, the self-harm enabling them to feel alive (Royal College of Psychiatrists, 2012). It is important to distinguish self-injury from suicidal intention, and Connors (2000) claims that self-injury has been misperceived and confused with suicidal intent. Self-injury is often indicated when young persons have a serious mental health problem, have been subject to abuse or rejection, are depressed or have an eating disorder, along with alcohol and drug problems which indicate increased risk. Often, self-harm is triggered by arguments with family or close friends (Royal College of Psychiatrists, 2012). While self-injury is often serious, it is important to know that suicide is more likely when a young person is depressed or has a serious mental illness. CAMHS practitioners assess for previous suicide attempts, and in particular if a young person has a plan about dying in a situation where they cannot be saved. Having a relative who has killed themselves also increases risk, and if a young person is intoxicated or under the influence of drugs, they are at particular risk.

Part of the care plan for young people in this category is to ascertain the level of support within the family and to help them to find new ways of expressing their distress. Advice to parents to lock away pills or sharps is part of helping to keep young people safe until the therapeutic work can get underway and until their mood improves.

Specialist CAMHS and Cognitive-Behavioural Therapy

Many of the interventions recommended by NICE include an element of cognitive-behavioural therapy (CBT). For example, depression, anxiety disorders, PTSD, ASD and ADHD. CBT theories and interventions are addressed in Chapter 4 of this volume and therefore it is not necessary to detail the approach here. However, it is important to recognise ways in which CBT is utilised within CAMHS. School age children with a diagnosis of ADHD, for example might be offered some CBT and/or social skills training, as well as parents being recommended parent training/education programmes (NICE, 2008). In addition, CBT has been shown to be feasible for children with ASD having a verbal IQ of at least 69 (Scottish Intercollegiate Guidelines Network, 2007). It is also recommended as a first-line treatment for moderate to severe depression in children and young people (NICE, 2005). Below is an account of a piece of work undertaken over three sessions with an adolescent boy who had walked with crutches or had used a wheelchair for the past 18 months, unable to walk unaided.

Case Study   Jack

Jack, aged 15, was referred from the Children's Hospital, having been admitted for a range of tests to ascertain reasons why he could not walk. He had not walked unaided for 18 months. His symptoms were not medically explained and may have been psychologically based. When he came for his first session, Jack used crutches, and leaned heavily on the walls and banister to keep him upright. He lumbered up the stairs awkwardly and appeared really sad. His parents were extremely worried about Jack, fearful that he would not be able to walk again.

On discussing Jack's 'condition' he himself suggested that it might be for 'attention'. I felt moved by Jack's 'take' on his situation and shared my own experience of the attention I had received when I used a wheelchair having fractured my foot. However, Jack's insight did not help him to get up and walk, so we agreed to take a CBT approach (Speckens et al., 1995). I asked Jack what would happen if he tried to walk without his crutches and why. He said that it was like someone had cut a tendon at the back of his knees and he would collapse. We talked about the power and strength of the muscles in our legs and about the recent achievements of Olympians. We then discussed some 'exposure' homework to do with his dad at home – a chart recording Jack's progress – day one, Jack would take three steps with the help of his dad. On day two he would take five steps, until he had done ten steps by day seven. When Jack came back the following week, I asked about the homework, but it had not been successful. They were a little despondent and feeling hopeless.

Having a background in outdoor therapy (see Chapter 8) I asked if they would be willing to come to the nearby park with me for some behavioural experiment work in the form of graded exposure. Risk was clearly an issue, as Jack could have fallen and hurt himself. However, the alternative was to refer him to Tier 4 services (hospital) and both agreed that we should head for the park, acknowledging there were risks involved.

We identified two large trees about 50 yards apart. On the first 'walk' he held on tightly to his dad's hands and staggered towards the tree leaning heavily on his father. I encouraged and supported Jack, telling him he was strong and safe. By the fourth 'walk' he was more stable, but still holding on tightly to his dad. I encouraged him to hold more lightly to his dad, which he did. As his confidence grew, Jack held more and more lightly to his dad. Then I supported Jack on his walks between the trees, inviting him each time to lean less and less on my support. On the last 'walk' Jack was just touching my finger very lightly 'like a butterfly', and I told him I was going to take my hand away. He walked confidently to the tree, then back to the office. He has not used aids since.

Case Study   Poppy

CBT was also helpful with Poppy, a little girl aged eight, who had a strong aversion to foods other than yogurt, biscuits and crisps. Poppy was a bright, articulate child, whose parents were loving and supportive, but who were increasingly concerned about Poppy's long term health and social life. She had begun to have regular blood tests to ensure that her health was not being impacted and refused to attend children's parties or family outings to restaurants. When presented with new foods Poppy would become highly anxious and get into a panic, wanting to please the adults around her, but crumbling into tears feeling bad about letting people down. She was frightened and phobic, but wanted to eat. I agreed to undertake some CBT graded exposure work with Poppy, gently exposing her to increasing amounts and a broader range of food.

Once Poppy had got to know me, I cut and pasted pictures of a range of different foods from the internet onto a large flip chart. We sat on the floor and gave each food a rating of 0–10. A score of 10 indicated food she would definitely not want to try. We identified a couple of things such as cheese and breakfast cereals and spoke about them at length. In the first 'eating' session Poppy tried the smallest piece of cheese you can imagine. She put the cheese to her lips and began to get very anxious and tearful. It is at this point that the skill of the CBT therapist prevails, resisting the temptation to say 'Don't eat it if you don't want to'. Instead gently supporting – 'It's okay sweetheart, it's just a little tiny weeny piece of cheese. It's soft like yogurt and a bit salty like crisps. Yes, that's right just put in on your tongue. Brave girl. Well done. Now, if you eat two more pieces like that you can take two of the Gogo's out of the box'. The offer of two more Gogo's (little plastic figures) was too much to resist. Poppy ate two more tiny pieces of cheese. The next week she ate some breakfast cereal, then over several weeks toast, then fish fingers at a popular fast food outlet, until she was able to eat out with her family, serve herself at the buffet on holiday and attend her friend's birthday party.

Summary

This chapter has provided the reader with:

- An overview of health and social care services beginning with a section that looked at the development of child-focused services through practice and policy
- Information and case study examples of counselling looked-after children, their life experiences and appropriate therapeutic interventions such as therapeutic parenting for Katy, aged six, and life story work for James, aged 12, to help him gain a stronger sense of identity and become more self-accepting
- An outline of the role of specialist CAHMS and the case study of Jack, aged 15, is presented to show how a CAHMS practitioner provided counselling using the cognitive-behavioural approach resulting in Jack gaining the confidence to walk again unaided
- Examples of therapeutic work, such as the work carried out with little Poppy, aged eight, which is seen to help her overcome her issues with food

Reflective Questions

1 Read and reflect upon the attachment focused work carried out by the counsellor working with Katy, aged six, in the first case study. What stands out about this approach?

The difficulty that Joan, the grandmother has in empathising with Katy when she lashes out at her is apparent and highlights the difficulties in empathising with children and young people who are raging at you. The support offered to Katy and her grandmother alongside each other is central to the therapy.

2 Read the second case study, about James, aged 12, and consider how you could incorporate life story work into your own practice with young clients.

Life story work can be incorporated into work, for example in a school counselling context, or an NHS paediatric setting with children and young people who have lost a parent to bereavement, or with a terminally ill parent.

3 How flexible do you see your practice being in terms of offering sessions to children and young people with chronic illness or chaotic lives? Reflect upon your service management and whether this would be possible.

This is a difficult issue due to the structure of many organisations offering support and services to children and young people. Some services have drop-in slots or keep a selection of appointments free for young clients.

4 What can the counsellor offer the 'looked-after' child or young person who has experience of instability and frequently changing foster placements? How might the child experience the counselling relationship?

Points to consider include the client's previous experience of relationships ending prematurely and/or badly. They may have experienced several broken relationships and have deep rooted feelings of loss. By offering a boundaried counselling relationship and a clear structure leading to the inevitable ending, offering some control and power to the child/young person, for example, in the type of ending they would like to experience, the ending may be reparative.

Learning Activities

1. Read further around attachment theory in Chapter 1 of this book and research advances in neuroscience.
2. Use creative materials, narrative and photographs to look at your own life story. You may want to carry out this activity in personal therapy if you feel that it may be painful for you.
3. Audit your practice environment to see if it is user-friendly for children and young people who may have chronic illnesses or chaotic lives.
4. Look at your own counselling practice and examine service policies around endings and boundaries with young clients.

Further Reading

Cleaver, H., Unell, I., and Aldgage, J. (2011) *Children's Needs – Parenting Capacity: Child Abuse: Parental Mental Illness, Learning Disability, Substance Misuse and Domestic Violence*. 2nd edn. London: The Stationary Office.

Gerhardt, S. (2004) *Why Love Matters: How Affection Shapes a Baby's Brain*. London. Routledge.

Golding, K (2008) *Nurturing Attachments: Supporting Children Who Are Fostered or Adopted*. London. Jessica Kingsley.

Hughes, D. (2006) *Building the Bonds of Attachment: Awakening Love in Deeply Troubled Children* 2nd edn. New York: Jason Aronson.

Improving Access to Psychological Therapies (2012) Available at: www.IAPT@nhs.uk.

YoungMinds and Cello (2012) *Talking Self Harm*. London: YoungMinds.

Online Resources

Counselling MindEd: http://counsellingminded.com, especially CM1.9: Counselling Across Services.

26

Third and Non-Statutory Sector

David Exall

This chapter includes:

- History and background
- Theoretical underpinnings
- Voluntary and statutory partnerships
- Service provision
- Organisational case study
- Research

Introduction

This chapter is an attempt to give an overview of services and practice for counsellors and psychotherapists who work, or wish to work within the voluntary and non-statutory sector with children and young people. Within this chapter this broad range of organisations and practitioners will be referred to as the third sector.

History and Background

Charity work and volunteering has a proud history. From the earliest times support for clients and patients has been delivered through philanthropic ideals. Hospitals, clinics and centres have been established over centuries that are primarily funded from trusts and philanthropy. In terms of therapeutic provision for children and young people, very often non-statutory work has been in advance of support laid down by statute – there have been many services offering parental support before CYP IAPT for example. By its nature this sector is led by individuals who have the ability to shape work as they see fit, ensuring that children and young people are involved in moulding their service and so can provide innovative approaches to counselling children. This pioneering also highlights the dangers of working without clear boundaries and having to speculate and lead the way in understanding the client/young person. Often no one has trod a particular pathway and there is a danger of stumbling in this undiscovered country.

Individuals shape and start a service but those that survive cultivate an organisational identity beyond a single person, indeed a service based upon the vision and drive of one person can flounder when that person leaves.

In the past 'counselling' has often been delivered by a range of people – some who are experienced and trained counsellors and psychotherapists, others who are trained to offer active listening, emotional support and mentoring. Very often such counselling was delivered over the telephone, in groups, home visits or in centres and was sometimes named in different ways such as helping or befriending.

Today counselling has become more professionalised and now most organisations that offer 'counselling' employ those who have core competencies and qualifications, thanks to the drive of membership organisations such as the BACP and Youth Access. Services for children and young people have been at the forefront of offering such levels of quality assurance due to the uniquely vulnerable nature of their clients. However, many organisations that have adopted counselling and psychotherapy have sprung from generic services. MIND (founded in 1946), CRUSE and RELATE have in the past, and do today, offer support for children and families. Agencies such as ChildLine and Place2Be have adapted and learnt from early pioneers to integrate specialist counselling and therapeutic services which are supported by core competencies which are added to by specialist training provided by the agency itself.

Large charities will deliver therapeutic interventions in line with their overall strategic goals. Small organisations need to consider their strategy, even when they have been established to match a perceived need and focus on the client: someone has seen that a particular approach seems to work and so builds a model from that perception. People with such insight are frequently not those with business and other skills and so in successful organisations they have gathered others around them that support these strategic goals. Overall many organisations have been initiated by a single person or small group of people with a vision. It would seem that their ability to thrive is not solely based upon the efficacy of their direct work with children but by the ability they have to inter-link with their environment, develop and adapt and to promote the work that they do.

It is not the strongest of the species that survive, nor the most intelligent, but the ones most responsive to change. (Charles Darwin)

Organisations that provide predominantly or exclusively counselling services are potentially vulnerable with some recently closing. Competitive tendering does not always suit small organisations or those with few strings to their bows. In larger services counselling has become one aspect of provision in most third-sector organisations – for example, Family Action. Many counsellors wish to offer long-term counselling as their experience and empathy is with the particular vulnerabilities of their client group and hold on to this desire as it seems to be ethical to do so. One of the strengths of counselling in the third sector is that strong individuals have been able to run counter to other prevailing trends in the landscape of mental health provision.

Theoretical Underpinnings

Much third-sector and non-statutory provision has sprung from teaching and training in a local area – having been established by counsellors and therapists whose ethical and philosophical ideas have been forged in their own training. Therefore the ethical underpinning of these agencies has run in parallel with changes in therapeutic approaches – the rise of humanistic approaches in the 1960s which enabled the empowerment of clients, the many changes in psychodynamic counselling and psychoanalytic thinking, the development and professionalisation of art, play and drama therapies and the movement towards cognitive and behavioural approaches have all caused changes that have swept the third sector in its wake.

Many organisations use psychodynamic principles to underpin their work. This theory has a focus on conflict and a long history of examining childhood to bring insight to the clinical relationship, and so it is perhaps understandable that such thinking weighs heavily in child-based therapeutic organisations. Developmental theories around children have provided an important foundation for many organisations' work and these have often grown from psychoanalytic thinking – the work of Mahler, Erikson, Piaget and Bowlby to name a few. However, services often do not offer extremely long-term work due to financial pressure, as well as high-need children being supported by the statutory sector. Few agencies – although a significant few – will offer counselling for over a year for example, although many offer ongoing differing forms of support and forward referral.

As the social agenda towards children and young people has often been on altering or managing children's behaviour – especially in early adolescence – there are many who use cognitive and behavioural approaches. This enables time-effective therapeutic work to be delivered flexibly within a range of settings. Recent developments in CYP

IAPT has supported this school of thought and the Department of Health is currently funding Wave 2 of a national roll-out.

Within and without the therapeutic field there has also been a movement in the belief in the empowerment of children and young people. Person-centred and humanistic principles have grown beyond the therapeutic world but the core conditions of genuineness, empathy and acceptance are often held as important – usually 'necessary' and sometimes 'sufficient'. Humanistic philosophies are also inclusive and so often allow for the integration of other methods and approaches to working with children and young people.

Many organisations marry different approaches in part to bring the 'best' elements of theory together to match their particular client group. Integrative practice has become the underpinning for both training institutions and their placement providers. In truth there is also a need to pursue funding that will support the ongoing existence of their organisation and so support their clients, and being linked closely to a particular therapeutic approach can make an organisation overly reliant on fewer training institutions and funding streams. Most organisations that predominantly deliver counselling and support work will have a theoretical underpinning which informs the approach to the work and provides the foundation stones that can be referred back to when liaising with partners. It is useful for organisations to consider how coherent these principles are and how transparent they appear to their service users and other partners.

The BACP has developed a Competency Framework for counsellors working with children and young people. This framework includes competencies for working within voluntary and third-sector organisations. The Counselling MindEd curriculum came online in March 2014 and is part of a broader curriculum for working with children and young people. It also has core modules related to understanding counselling in the community context and has modules that address the main theoretical concepts related to working with children and young people.

Voluntary and Statutory Partnerships

There are few counsellors and psychotherapists who have not worked at some stage in the third sector. Whatever therapeutic approach or training they may have experienced and by whatever pathway that they have come to the profession, it is rare to find an experienced therapist who has not at some stage volunteered or worked in the third sector. This vast group of small and large organisations has been the breeding ground for best practice and, on some occasions less good practice, in the field of counselling and psychotherapy. Statutory services are those services that are laid down by law (statute) and so are provided by local health and social care trusts and by the Department for Education in the case of some school-based services. Non-statutory provision has always complemented or added value to statutory provision – although in many cases it could be argued that the third sector overlaps with statutory provision, offering couns elling to children with a high threshold of need.

Organisations such as Barnardo's have been delivering therapeutic work to children and young people for years and small agencies have managed to deliver some very specific and targeted therapeutic support to children and young people – matching evolving needs in the local communities that they serve.

Statutory services will rely on the third sector to refer children and young people, such agencies being well placed to identify and work with levels of need in families and children and holding strong community links and local knowledge. Best practice will mean this will involve a discussion about the appropriate level of support for the child or family. Often this supports the statutory Child and Adolescent Mental Health Service (CAMHS) in prioritising appropriate support for other children. At times this will mean that the agency is playing a 'holding' role for the child before moving on to CAMHS intervention, where waiting times can be long. At times the therapy will coexist alongside CAMHS support. So the third sector is both alongside and separate from CAMHS, needing to understand the language and ethos of the medical profession and psychiatry. Third-sector organisations need to be able to brush up against other beasts such as the education system and still maintain their own voice and identity. The relationship between a third-sector organisation and the statutory sector is both symbiotic and parasitic in nature. The third sector cannot and should not replace statutory provision and would struggle to function without the referral channels, expertise and overview provided by those services. However, the statutory system would undoubtedly experience significant difficulties if third-sector providers were completely removed, and the emotional well-being of families, children and young people would plummet as a result.

In the midst of sometimes difficult social and economic backdrops such agencies and motivated individuals have delivered a high level of therapeutic interventions and have pioneered different models and approaches to working with young people, engaging with the diverse needs of their client group and being able to take the time to understand the full context of the client's world. Standards of professionalism are very high and poor practice rare – in part due to the 'survival of the fittest' environment of non-statutory work. Such provision is often cost-effective due to the use of volunteers and matches political agendas such as the 'Big Society'.

However, there are weaknesses in the sector. Typically third-sector provision suffers during difficult economic times – often being seen as expendable, services that can be easily and quietly cut, reliance on indirect statutory funding is risky and philanthropic capital frequently dries up during such times.

The current voluntary and non-statutory landscape looks grim:

- Loss of £3.3 billion from public funders by 2015
- Static growth in individual and corporate giving
- Voluntary services get £13.9 billion from government, 79 per cent is contracts for services

- About 3 per cent of government funds go to small/medium organisations, the rest to large charities
- Sustainability weakened – in 2009/10 voluntary organisations spent 99 per cent of all incoming resources
- Inflation biting, grants reducing, spending up
- Social investment discussed but not market-ready
- Threat to voluntary services' independence
- Five per cent reduction in staff in 2010/11
- Volunteering numbers down
- Demand for services has increased
- Big Society policies have failed to engage the voluntary sector as yet.

There are opportunities within this landscape:

- Schools: More autonomy for schools to make their own commissioning decisions
- NHS: New clinical commissioning groups
- CAMHS: Transformation, working in partnership with children and young people to shape their local services
- 'Payments by result' ethos which may suit voluntary and third-sector organisations
- Overall unified outcomes measuring and consistency through NICE guidelines.

In terms of clinical governance and quality assurance of the therapeutic work there is a wide range of practice within the sector with there being exemplars of clinical excellence and at times practice that falls short – small agencies in particular being vulnerable if, for example, they do not have robust child protection protocols or are not quality assured by professional bodies such as BACP and/or Youth Access, both requiring adherence to quality assurance standards.

There can be any number of local children's-based services in any region. Usually there are youth and children counsellors locally available, working out of small offices and therapeutic rooms. Larger agencies will have therapeutic practitioners available and there will always be private counsellors available to support children. However, there are no consistent or universal referral mechanisms for such agencies or processes that coordinate their work. These bodies may need to promote themselves and often 'piggy back' their offer as part of a larger whole – for example, working as part of a school or children's centre. There may be agencies established to support a particular part of the community, for example single-parent families. There may be services that provide for particular mental health issues such as drug and alcohol services. There may be those that work within a restricted geography that does not match local authority boundaries.

Organisations can also deliver services as part of a wider programme such as Improved Access to Psychological Therapies (IAPT) and the Children and Young

Peoples IAPT (CYP IAPT). Indeed the CYP IAPT is a 'service transformation project for Child and Adolescent Mental Health Services' and has an agenda to be 'open to voluntary and statutory services' and so is designed to bring sectors together and create coherent pathways of referral. Such programmes will have their own processes and referral systems as well as a tendering system to enable third-sector organisations to access funding. These can provide useful support for third-sector organisations but, as is often the case with commissioning processes, the organisation may need to adapt its core approach, up skill staff and systems and, more importantly, the agenda may not match the needs of the children and young people as the individual third-sector organisation sees it – therefore altering the organisation's core ethos and values. There is also the issue that these initiatives may not be permanent solutions to organisational difficulties as political imperatives change.

Service Provision

Counselling can be offered in this sector for any number of sessions – there is no typical length of counselling across all services, although there may be trends for shorter sessions in certain client groups. However, there is a strong body of third-sector organisations offering longer term and open ended support including clients that are able to return to counselling for further sessions after breaks or other interventions. This level of therapeutic support is difficult to match in the statutory sector unless there is a clear identification of high threshold need, which often needs to be supported by measurable difficulties and/or diagnostic criteria. Such diagnosis can take a long time to establish, as well as children, young people and their families often being resistant to the concept. In services that are based in schools the average number of counselling sessions rises, perhaps due to 'captive' clients, with this client group likely to have high attendance and retention rates.

Services tend toward offering a range of services – advice, guidance, support groups, mentoring, etc. – of which counselling is sometimes a small part. The *Stretched to the Limit* Youth Access report notes that 87 per cent of respondents to its online survey deliver a range of other services including educative and advocacy support. There will be referral systems that exist between those services and thoughtful discussions amongst various professionals that support a child or young person. As laid out by the Fraser Guidelines for younger children, these discussions should include the parents or carers and, if appropriate, other professionals who will be able to hold in mind the clients' individual needs with a broad range of insight and perspective. The strength of many services for older young people is founded on the ability of clients to self-refer, often without any other professional contact. If risks and needs are critical, any group of professionals and carers around a child or young person will investigate all possible channels of support for them. This may involve onward referral to CAMHS, social services, education or other statutory bodies as well as other non-statutory providers. All involved will have identical obligations in terms of protecting the mental health and safeguarding of that person, although there may be a range of ways in which the professionals interpret that duty. In therapeutic terms there is a high level of regard paid to autonomy, confidentiality and empowerment which may be at odds with other professionals' duties. The onus is on all those professionals to manage those dynamics for the welfare of the client(s). Clarity and transparency is often key. In a scoping report commissioned by BACP, *The Relationship between Specialist Child and Adolescent Mental Health Services and Community-Based Counselling for Children and Young People* (Spong et al., 2013), it was highlighted that there is 'mixed evidence about how effectively working together is achieved', but a strong emphasis from counsellors who were interviewed on the importance of communication between professionals and clear pathways of referral supported by both systems and good interpersonal relationships.

The quality assurance of counselling services delivered in the third sector is crucial. Services deliver using both volunteers and paid counsellors – but all should be professional in their approach. It is vital to have robust processes for induction, training and ongoing support for volunteers. In many ways these should mirror processes for any professionals, although there are some key differences:

- Volunteers may often be counsellors in training. While they may have a vast range of life experience they will very often need specific support in gathering skills needed for the client group of the organisation – specialist therapeutic skills and awareness that is detailed elsewhere in this book. The relationship between a placement provider and the learning institution should be one that has clear boundaries and clarifies the ethos and methods of working, as well as re-enforcing core competencies and responsibilities of the counsellor.
- Many volunteers will also be experienced therapists – perhaps looking to build therapeutic hours or grow specialist skills. These counsellors by their nature are perhaps in a position to hold a higher threshold of clinical distress in children and young people. However, care should be taken to support such volunteers to the same degree as less experienced counsellors
- Volunteers will have slightly different rights and expectations in their role. However, in terms of delivering a professional service it should always be emphasised that they are working to the same standards as any other counsellor. In most cases the client should not experience a different service to that delivered by any statutory body or fully paid professional.

Most counselling services will use volunteers and paid professionals interchangeably. By using volunteers, services can often be cost-effective – and thus more 'competitive' in service provision, often bringing in leverage funding to the local authority at significant levels. It should be recognised that by using volunteers the best possible service needs to be built that has a higher level of organisational commitment than is sometimes required for a service that exclusively uses paid staff, as follows:

- Financial and clinical cost of managing a high number of counsellors who perhaps see a small number of clients per person, especially in relation to induction training and ongoing support
- Higher levels of clinical and managerial supervision
- Higher levels of training to ensure consistency
- 'Case-working' volunteers – coordinating with learning institutions, colleges, etc.

From an organisation perspective there are additional tasks required to enable service delivery:

- Publicity
- Referral pathways, including self-referral
- Criteria for client access – notably what restrictions exist for referral
- Local knowledge and negotiation with other local agencies

It is worth noting that volunteers delivering counselling may by its nature de-professionalise counselling. Many organisations are considering how voluntary counselling should evolve towards an 'apprenticeship' model where counselling delivery is part of a vocational training placement similar to other professions, particularly those in the health care sphere.

Organisational Case Study

Place2Be and Croydon Drop In both work closely with a range of local partners who will be connected to their clients in diverse ways. However, due to the nature of these organisations they can operate differently with their clients. This is an example of different extremes of partner involvement when offering counselling.

Croydon Drop In offers counselling to a young person on a self-referral basis and can also engage with young people who are actively 'signposted' by other agencies; the core requirement is that the young person wishes to attend. For younger adolescents, i.e. if under 13, Fraser guidelines and Gillick competence are utilised to ensure that the young person can access support without parental consent. Very often there will be no contact with parents, school, police or any other professional or connected organisations, unless the young person so wishes. This brings with it many advantages in terms of empowering the young person, hearing their perspective and experience free from the potential bias of other professionals or parents and is more likely to allow the young person to feel secure in boundaries such as confidentiality. There are also risks in terms of the counsellor not having the full picture and so working in the dark around wider issues. Therefore there is greater autonomy for the young person, counsellor and the service, while still working within a structure of safeguarding and child protection but not restrained by other systems and processes. Croydon Drop In can offer 'wrap round' services such as advocacy and practical advice and deliver counselling services to secondary school pupils within similar boundaries.

Place2Be never offers therapeutic work to primary age children without explicit consent from parents and various levels of agreement from relevant professionals – especially school based colleagues. This has advantages of allowing the counsellor to work in a more systemic way with the client, supports pathways for onward referral and joins up counselling as part of a wider support package and as part of a team around the child. Therefore it is more likely that issues of safeguarding can be more quickly noted and addressed. However, there will be tensions and sensitivity around confidentiality issues and more scope for outside influences to skew the direction of the counselling work. While, with careful handling, this is not usually a major factor, it should be acknowledged that this landscape is likely to make building trust and fostering empowerment more difficult. Having aligned and linked-up structures and pathways with partner schools also provides an extra level of accessibility for clients in a different way to autonomous counselling. Ideally teachers and school staff work alongside Place2Be personnel to de-stigmatise counselling.

Both these organisations will have strong processes and procedures that ensure safety in the counselling provision. Both these organisations have referral and assessment processes to enable effective counselling delivery, strong procedures of quality assurance and are well placed to swiftly offer one-to-one counselling in conjunction with other support services and so have shorter waiting times than statutory agencies. Perhaps the most important structure is clinical supervision, which is offered in these organisations at a frequency that exceeds the minimum 1.5 hours a month recommended by BACP.

Research

Many third-sector organisations have built a strong body of practice-based evidence that can be in many ways unique to them. This provides some fascinating insights to therapeutic work but does not always support consistency and the comparing of outcomes and effectiveness and so can be detrimental to the ability of organisations to access funding and engage in the commissioning landscape. Recently the importance of evidence-based practice has become paramount such as is delivered through the CYP IAPT programme. Practice has been developed based upon evidenced interventions – in that case, as defined by the NICE guidelines. Whilst this is part of statutory provision there is a drive to include third-sector providers if possible. To add value to statutory provision third-sector providers at this time need to be able to use the same evidence and so shift to the use of evidenced-based practice as supported by evidence such as randomised controlled trials (RCTs), which are often seen as the gold standard of measuring outcomes despite being expensive and time consuming.

COREYP is seen as an effective research tool which is widely used across third-sector providers and can offer some comparison with statutory organisations – thus providing a base for demonstrating outcomes and cost effectiveness and so supporting funding and commissioning for an organisation. Such evidence can also inform the clinical and systemic approach to the work – for example, good outcomes are demonstrated after four sessions and are not significantly different after 10 sessions – that indicates that short-term work can be effective in that example. Alternatively it could be shown that counselling work is more effective (has better outcomes) if the client has received guidance or advice before the counselling intervention. All of this may shape the way a project is developed.

The recent Targeting Mental Health Support (TaMHS) Initiative was an example of counselling services being evaluated alongside and as part of other statutory provision. In that case the SDQ in full was used as the primary tool to reference outcomes and compare impact. Counselling services compared favourably to other interventions that were delivered as part of TaMHS.

Current evidence shows that children and young people receiving counselling in third-sector organisations have demonstrable improvements.

Many organisations such as Place2Be are also striving to find other ways to demonstrate impact, for example tracking if the counselling may improve capacity to access learning for a child or have wider long-term implications. If these can be demonstrated clearly then both counselling and the service itself becomes much more commissionable and service users and their families will be more likely to trust the intervention.

Many counsellors will be more interested in the use of outcome measurements to tailor what and how to deliver as part of a service rather than make that service commissionable. Good evidence offers this in an autonomous service. What intervention works best for my clients? How can I use this evidence to improve the experience of the counselling and generate better outcomes? Do we need to consider our recruitment of counsellors? Shall we change the ethos of our approach? It may be that on a small scale research will show that counsellors from a certain training institution are less effective, for example. Or it may show that offering 24 sessions is markedly more effective (in this particular service) than offering 12. These are questions that research can provide an answer to, and if organisations do not have the resources to gather this evidence they may need to find others who have considered these questions – small organisations may find the cost of gathering and analysing this data prohibitive.

Third-sector organisations will need to be innovative in proving effectiveness alongside statutory agencies. Those who are able to match systems and guidelines such as are evidenced through CYP IAPT will be well served in commissioning processes. Others – perhaps those who engage in longer-term work or innovative models – will need to ensure that their service quality is demonstrable. Tracking the current temperature of the field of therapeutic research will remain an important aspect of a thriving organisation.

A third-sector organisation is often like a child itself. Born out of need and imagination, raised by a few dedicated carers or parents and then needing to find its place alongside older and more established siblings and adults. For such a child to grow up and thrive it must learn to adapt to the realities of the current landscape, foster new skills and understanding and work alongside others without being destroyed. It will encounter tough times and conflict. There will be some who think it is not worthy. It will be asked to prove its worth. It will be asked to make sense and take responsibility for what it says and does. It must hold on to its core personality and shape but build strength in the right ways – including knowing when to speak to others and ask for help.

The evolving landscape of the world of counselling and therapy is changing as much for children and young people as with any other client group, as in the need to be ready for meeting clients in their language of communication, telephone, email and online counselling. The many challenges facing children in the 21st century all add up to an exciting and dangerous world for third-sector counsellors.

Summary

- The voluntary and non-statutory sector is a crucial aspect of mental health and counselling provision
- The third sector provides innovative and pioneering approaches and methods of counselling delivery
- The third sector is the training ground for counselling and psychotherapy
- It is important to hold in mind factors both clinical and practical when considering delivering therapeutic work in the third sector

Reflective Questions

1 For organisations:

1. What is the ethos of your counselling organisation and how does it fit into the wider systems?
2. Are you re-inventing the wheel? Can you borrow what you need from other organisations?

3. Are you strategic in your approach to the work?
4. How do you know that your organisation works for your particular clients?
5. Do your children and young people understand what you do and who you are?
6. Do you have robust quality assurance processes – would they stand comparison to statutory bodies?
7. What evidence, beyond anecdotal feedback, do you have that counselling (and your method of counselling) matches the needs of your client group?
8. What are the 'criteria' for children and young people to access your service?

2 For counsellors joining a third-sector organisation:

1. Does the organisation match your theoretical approach and ethos? What is their mission statement? How do they operate?
2. What are the support structures around the organisation – supervision, line management, continual professional development? Do they offer specific training to equip you to work with their client needs?

3 For counsellors looking to establish a service:

1. What areas of my own competence do I need to enhance, either by professional development or working with or employing others?
2. Is someone else already doing what I wish my service to do? Can I learn from them?

Learning Activities

Consider allocating resources (time and money) to build partnerships and relationships for a counselling service. How much time can you spare?

Any counselling that is delivered in the voluntary and third sector needs to be able to stand alongside other services. To this end counsellors working in this sector should not be afraid to liaise closely with local and national providers of therapeutic services. Therefore it is recommended that you match:

- Outcomes – using up-to-date tools
- Standards of practice and core competencies

(Continued)

(Continued)

- Ethical frameworks
- Induction, training and other support processes

  i. Find allies in local services that will support your work in all ways and enable a sustained service to be delivered. Find a good partnership (or several) that will work to your mutual benefit and so increase the added value to the children and young people.

  ii. Match quality assurance processes to those in the statutory sector and, if possible, exceed them.

  iii. Join third-sector forums of counselling or those that include counselling – BACP, CYP, Youth Access. Join local voluntary service groups: voluntary action (VA). If possible, create your own.

  iv. Join or create local specialist groups for agencies or individuals to work together based around shared themes: for example eating disorders, bullying, etc.

  v. Join safeguarding boards, local commissioning groups and NHS clinical commissioning groups

  vi. Map out what your service does from aims to outcomes, including a mission statement, vision and ethos behind the work

  vii. Work closely with specialist CAMHS teams, building referral pathways and good working relationships which will support the clinical work and aid with funding applications or approaches to commissioning groups.

Online Resources

BACP website: www.bacp.co.uk.

BACP Children and Young People Division.

Counselling MindEd: http://counsellingminded.com – The curriculum includes modules CMD 08: Counselling in the Community and CMD 11: Counselling and Specialist CAMHS.

Children and Young People's Improving Access to Psychological Therapies (CYP IAPT): www.cypiapt.org.

27

School and Education Settings

Peter Pearce, Ros Sewell and Karen Cromarty

This chapter includes:

- An outline of the role of counselling within a school setting
- A summary of the history of school counselling in the UK
- Details of some aspects of practice for schools counselling
- A current picture of the research on school-based counselling
- An exploration of many of the challenges and benefits of counselling provision within these settings

Introduction

Counselling in schools is a very accessible and acceptable intervention for young people and can play a key, pro-active and preventative, early intervention role. It is often a much smaller step to make contact with a school counsellor than to be referred to a service separate from the school and can mean that many young people who might otherwise not be seen, or who might only be referred when problems have become severe and entrenched, can make use of the service. In addition to this immediate, on-site response, counselling can also offer support, consultation and training to other staff in the school system.

A range of different school counselling service models currently operate within the UK which include external agencies delivering the services (for example the local authority, or a charity) and schools employing their own counsellors. These models of provision will each impact upon the service that can be provided within the school, considerations that need to be taken into account to ensure the clarity of the role and the lines of responsibility and reporting. Some services have developed along an individualised approach with a counsellor 'in the school but not of the school', and some have become more system-oriented, seeking to understand and align with the values and priorities of the school. Similarly some services have developed just to provide a one-to-one counselling service to students and some have sought to offer a whole school service which, in addition to one-to-one counselling, might include, a drop-in, group and family work, peer support, supervision and counselling skills training for teaching staff and consultation on safeguarding and policy development.

These different models might each have their relative merits – for example, at the extremes, a lone, independent practitioner might be particularly vulnerable to a funding crisis, a key 'stakeholder' staff member leaving or getting into conflict with a 'school's culture'. At the other end, an embedded, 'school-owned' service might be in danger of being seen by students as not a safe place to talk (for more details of peer support initiatives see Chapter 13: 'Supervision').

Whatever structure the counselling service takes in a particular school, it is important that the service becomes widely known and what can be offered is understood. Referrals can come through a variety of sources: from the young person themselves or a peer, through parents or carers or other family members, via outside agencies or through a staff member. A majority of referrals are likely, however, to be initiated because of a staff member's concern about a young person, maybe because they have seen them distressed or withdrawn or because they are concerned about the young person's behaviour. 'Could you see Ahmed? He's very disruptive in class and never does his homework.' Referrals are often co-ordinated through the pastoral care team with the counsellor expecting the referrer to have spoken to the young person about their concern and sought consent for the counsellor to at least see them for an initial meeting. The counsellor's role is then to offer the opportunity for the young person to decide for themselves whether a 'time to talk' in private is something that they might like to try out. In this way, within school, a timely response to issues as they arise can be offered which feels a small step for the young person and seeks to minimise stigma and pathologising. In this first session, the counsellor needs to be absolutely clear about the limits of confidentiality, in a way that is clearly understood by the client, and how any need to break this would be brokered. In this first session the client will be helped to understand how counselling is different in some ways from other parts of school life: the client may call the counsellor by their first name rather than 'Sir' or 'Miss', for example, quickly signalling how the relationship being offered may differ from that of other adults in school. One student, recognising the gift in this gesture offered by the counsellor, replied jokingly, 'and you can call me Mr Aziz', so the counsellor did, every time they encountered each other from then on. This first session also provides an opportunity to acknowledge that attendance at counselling is part of school and boundaries need to be maintained, so for example the client will be expected to turn up on time for a session and when it is over then return to their next lesson.

Frequent reasons for referral include family problems, managing anger, bereavement, peer relationship problems and bullying. These may all first come to light because of changes in the young person's behaviour within school perhaps becoming more disruptive or more withdrawn. The orientation of the counsellor may to some degree determine how these issues will be responded to and it is important for the counsellor to be able to articulate their practice clearly both to the school and to the young person themselves. However, in order to operate effectively in school, regardless of orientation, the school counsellor needs to be approachable, adaptable and sensitive to systemic complexities of this setting. The young person's behaviour is perhaps best understood as their way of trying to cope with the problem rather than as the problem itself.

History of School Counselling in the UK

School counselling in the UK underwent a period of rapid development throughout the 1960s and 1970s, which was later followed by an equally rapid decline in availability during the 1980s. This rise and fall has been variously attributed to a lack of resources, the belief that the counselling role should be more part of the school's pastoral care team role itself and to the fact that early UK counselling was not embedded sufficiently well into the culture of the school or adequately monitored (Bor et al., 2002; Baginsky, 2004; Robinson, 1996). The Children Act (1989) brought increased recognition of the rights of children and young people and with it greater demands on the pastoral care team role within schools, perhaps becoming instrumental in the reversal of this decline and renewed interest in school counselling as an accessible, acceptable and appropriate means of emotional support for young people (Mabey, 1995). Equally, the change in the devolution of school budgets, under Local Management of Schools (LMS) within the Education Reform Act (1988), gave head teachers and governing bodies in England, Northern Ireland and Wales far greater powers to 'buy in' appropriate and relevant services for their individual schools; many commissioned counselling services in both secondary and primary school settings.

In 2007, the government of Northern Ireland introduced school counselling in all post-primary schools within the province. In 2008 the Welsh government published its National Strategy for School-Based Counselling Services (following the recommendations of the Clwych Inquiry). And by 2009, all secondary schools in Wales had access to school-based services. In 2013 access to counselling for 11–16-year-olds in Wales became a statutory responsibility. A commitment to provide school counselling by 2015 was made in Scotland (Public Health Institute of Scotland, 2003). However, there has been no national overarching programme of implementation across the country.

There is now 'an excellent case for rolling out a new "school counsellor welfare support role" in all schools', according to a recent report by the influential Institute for Public Policy Research (Sodha and Margo, 2008).

The Benefits and Challenges

As there are significant differences in the respective professional 'cultures' of education and therapy it is of importance that roles and expectations are clarified in the setting up of any school counselling service. For example in one setting it was suggested that the counselling team should put up the counselling list and timetable on display in the staff room and that the counselling appointments could be read out in assembly to the whole school as this would help to remind students of their appointments. At another time there were discussions about the counselling team becoming class tutors. Whilst these arrangements may be acceptable to some teachers, the confidentiality issues and the dual roles involved would make it impossible to deliver a confidential counselling service built upon trust. It is important to remember that the culture, ethics and requirements of a counselling service may not be familiar or understood by a school who are taking on counselling as an addition to the school system. Prospective school counsellors, therefore, will need to be able to negotiate the service to fit within the school context.

This is a challenging setting for counsellors and working with young people in schools provides its own difficulties. A counsellor can find themselves encountering a client group who have not elected to have counselling or in some cases even know what is being offered. Consequently, they can be met by a range of reactions to the referral which can affect the young person's ability to engage with the counsellor. A counsellor in this setting would be well advised to have a great deal of experience in establishing a solid working therapeutic relationship before embarking on working with difficult to reach clients with complex issues.

Case Study   Jason

Jason was referred to the counselling service because he had disengaged from school, had few friends and was underachieving academically. I was told that his Mum was 'lovely' and that she had thought that counselling might be a good idea when the possibility had been suggested at a parent's evening. I was also informed that Jason had reluctantly agreed to see me, and his teachers found him aggressive and argumentative.

When I met Jason our first moments together were awkward. He sat quietly and didn't really want to engage with me. I said that I realised that he hadn't really wanted to have counselling but had agreed, which I didn't think were the same thing. From looking down at the floor this comment seemed to make him look up at me but straight back down again. I struggled to make a connection with him and he clearly showed me that he didn't really want to be there. When he first spoke he used few words and seemed quiet and aggressive in his manner. I said that I wasn't a teacher and that he didn't have to call me 'Miss' and that other people had thought he might benefit from some time to talk. He looked straight at me.

J: What would I wanna talk to you for? Why would I wanna talk to anyone in this fucking school? I hate it here . . . I hate school, I don't wanna fucking talk to no-one. You can report me if you like.

Th: Report you Jason?

J: I was swearing Miss

Th: Oh that … that's okay in here. I think I was listening to the fact that you hate school more than the swearing. … I was thinking … you know it must be a long day if you hate it.

J: Yeah, it is. (laughs)

Th: And every day Jason … you have to spend a lot of time at school.

J: That's it innit ... that's just it! Your whole life in a place you hate.

Th: *Your* whole life in a place you hate.

J: It's a thing you say innit I hate school. But me, I really *do* hate school, It's so boring. … M … I was gonna call you Miss then … what's your name?

Th: You're bored Jason

J: Yeah, and all the teachers. … I hate them as well. … They hate me too. … I'm always in trouble.

It was hard to engage Jason and there were moments where I really felt that I managed to feel connected to him, but these moments did not stay. Working with Jason, I always felt as though I needed to strive to establish and maintain a working relationship. Gradually as our therapeutic relationship developed, Jason shared more of himself and his struggle to find his place at home in a family of seven children. Jason said that although he felt loved by his parents he didn't feel as though they had the time to listen to him, and I began to realise the place of counselling in his life. He never missed a session and displayed very difficult behaviour in school if a session had to be moved or cancelled for school reasons. In the early counselling sessions, Jason would share stories about his school week and shouted and blamed others for his numerous detentions.

J: It's not fair because I put my hand up to say that I didn't understand and he kept saying 'Jason put your hand down', 'Jason put your hand down' so I'd had enough right, I just got up and went to the door. This is 'im, 'where are you going?' This is me, 'I'm bored', this is 'im, 'sit down now!' I just ignored 'im and walked out.

(Continued)

(Continued)

I took my constant struggle to offer consistent acceptance and empathy to supervision and I noticed that Jason began to process in the sessions.

J: It was jokes today. He said 'have you done your homework?' I said 'no' and he said 'well what a surprise Jason' and we both laughed. Then I said 'I tried but I couldn't do it'. He's offered to help me. I'd like help. It was different today. I usually end up shouting and then he gets cross.

Th: Something was different today Jason, you didn't end up shouting.

J: Yeah … yeah … it's better really. But it wasn't just me, he was nicer

Th: He was nicer and you were both different with each other.

As the sessions developed Jason's focus changed from how fed up he was with school to his struggle to achieve academically. I wondered whether Jason had learning difficulties and that he was bored and hated all the teachers because he could not keep up in class. As he began to gain an understanding of his experience he identified this for himself and managed to speak to his teacher about this. Things were put in place to help him to manage school. He was assessed by the educational psychologist and dyslexia was diagnosed, and consequently he was able to negotiate a shorter timetable and some help for dyslexia.

It would be easy to read this case material and to assume that once the learning difficulties had been acknowledged and help was in place that Jason's problems were sorted out. This was not the case – we continued our work together as Jason began to make sense of his experiencing and to find his own way to manage to come to school and to participate in school life whilst still hating attending.

School structures require the whereabouts of students to be known so a mechanism to inform class teachers of a pupil's absence from class will need to be brokered and schools may require appointments during some 'core subjects' to be avoided altogether. Part of the complexity of working in a school context is the need to respect the confidentiality of the young person whilst also communicating with the pastoral care team about the broader picture. Counsellors will therefore need to find a way to liaise with the pastoral care team and senior management about ongoing work in order to help the school understand the delicate balance between supporting the young person's autonomy, respecting their confidentiality and acknowledging the needs arising from the different duty of care held by the school system.

Learning to communicate in a way that is respectful of the school system and negotiating the differing needs and requirements of the two worlds of counselling and education becomes an essential competency within this setting. Counsellors can work most effectively when integrated with the whole pastoral care response of the school and also need to find a way to enshrine the independence of the service so that students can remain confident of the difference between their counsellor and other staff in this system.

Counsellors will need to consult with their external supervisor and line manager about the nature of referrals and about the limits of their competence in this setting. They will need to be familiar with the range of local services for children and young people and understand how the respective referral processes operate. Reasons for referral on will include seeking more specialist help for a particular issue, for example PTSD, lack of engagement with the current service being offered, a specific request by the client or their family and following the counsellor's own assessment of their competence with the issues involved.

Counselling in schools requires careful consideration of the potential impact of an array of additional contextual factors. As has been described, these begin with third-party referral – it's most often initially someone else's concern and they may themselves have other concerns or none, and this referrer may continue to be involved, often expecting 'results' quickly, keen to feedback to the counsellor their views of the issues. There may also be other 'stakeholders' who have a significant influence over whether the young person can continue therapy and the counselling may be taking place in the very setting in which the issues have arisen. The student and counsellor are highly likely to encounter each other around the building and see each other interacting with others in the school system – in fact some of the other 'characters' in the person's narrative may well also be known to the counsellor. Practical issues may also need careful negotiation, including rooming for the work, how the young person leaves class to come to counselling, which classes are acceptable to leave and who in the system needs to be informed that this is happening. In this setting there is no division between working therapeutically and not, as staff or students might approach us around the building to connect about a referral and it is important that the counsellor becomes proficient at managing these one-way permeable boundaries to ensure that support for the counselling work continues. The counsellor may also be the only adult who doesn't pick the student up on their uniform, lateness or behaviour as they move around the school, and this sometimes needs sensitive brokering both with a staff member seeking additional adult support and with a student given a window of freedom from the school rules but plunged straight back into them at the end of the session.

Research

Cooper, M. (2013) School-Based Counselling in UK Secondary Schools: A Review and Critical Evaluation. Available at: www.iapt.nhs.uk/ silo/files/school-based-counselling-review.pdf

School-based counselling is one of the most prevalent forms of psychological therapy for young people in the UK, with approximately 70,000–90,000 cases per year. School-based counselling services in the UK generally offer one-to-one supportive therapy, with clients typically referred through their pastoral care teachers, and attending for three to six sessions. Around two-thirds of young people attending school-based counselling services are experiencing psychological difficulties at 'abnormal' or 'borderline' levels, with problems that have often been present for a year or more. Clients are typically in the 13–15-year-old range, white, most commonly female, and presenting with family problems or, if boys, anger. With respect to effectiveness, non-directive supportive therapy is a NICE-recommended intervention for mild depression; and there is emerging evidence to suggest that school-based humanistic counselling – a distillation of common school-based counselling practices in the UK – is effective at reducing psychological distress and helping young people achieve their personal goals. School-based counselling is evaluated positively by service users and school staff and is perceived by them as an effective means of bringing about improvements in students' mental health and emotional well-being. School staff and service users also perceive school-based counselling as enhancing young people's capacity to engage with studying and learning. From the standpoint of a contemporary mental health agenda, the key strengths of school-based counselling are that it is perceived as a highly accessible service and that it increases the extent to which all young people have an independent, supportive professional to talk to about difficulties in their lives. However, there are also several areas for development: increasing the extent to which practice is evidence-informed, greater use of outcome monitoring, ensuring equity of access to young people from black and minority ethnic backgrounds, increasing service user involvement, and enhancing levels of integration with other mental health provisions. It is hoped that current initiatives in the development of competences, e-learning resources and accreditation for counsellors working with young people will help to achieve this. The conclusions of the review are that commissioners should give consideration to the utility of school-based mental health provisions and that school-based counsellors – working with colleagues in the field of child and adolescent mental health – have the potential to contribute to an increasingly comprehensive, integrated and 'young person-centred' system of mental health care.

British Association for Counselling and Psychotherapy Children and Young People's Practice Research Network (CYP PRN)

CYP PRN's mission is to promote psychological health and emotional well-being among children and young people in the UK. In supporting high-quality and rigorous research the network seeks to improve the quality and effectiveness of school and community-based counselling for the benefit of service users and to widen access to such services by influencing policy-makers and those responsible for the commissioning of services. CYP PRN aims to bring together practitioners, researchers and trainers to engage in research and evaluation in order to develop the evidence base for school and community-based counselling services for children and young people. This in turn provides opportunities to improve the effectiveness and acceptability of counselling interventions and to impact on policy decisions.

The Align Trial: A Pragmatic Randomised Controlled Trial of School-Based Person-Centred Counselling at Secondary Schools in London. Led by Peter Pearce and Ros Sewell at Metanoia Institute in collaboration with BACP and Professor Mick Cooper

This study examines the effectiveness of a term (12 weeks) of a standardised school-based counselling intervention, school-based, person-centred counselling (SBPCC). The trial builds on the protocols used for three earlier UK RCTs, increasing the control to nine months and extending follow-up to six and nine months.

Conclusion

Working as a counsellor in a school setting can be both exciting and challenging. It can feel like work that is at a cutting edge. Current research is showing that counselling can have a positive impact on young people's lives which feels like an investment for the psychological well-being of the future.

Summary

This chapter:

- Has identified some of the complex issues arising in this setting
- Suggests that particular qualities for the counsellor could be useful to develop: diplomacy, ability to communicate, enhanced counselling ability and a solid understanding of ethical considerations, to name but a few
- Identifies that it is essential to ensure supervision with an experienced supervisor who has knowledge of working in the education system. This is important as a school counsellor can spend a great deal of time in an educative role with staff and careful, ongoing, negotiation of the counsellor's role is often required.

Reflective Questions

1 What are the factors to take into account when you as a counsellor are ascertaining if a client is capable of consent to counselling? Where can guidance be sought in law?

- Age of client (over 16 generally regarded by law as being competent, unless exceptional circumstances; and unlikely that a 13-year-old would be deemed competent without involvement of parent)

- Maturity: understanding of consequences of his or her actions
- Suffering mental illness
- Under the influence of drugs including alcohol
- Conditions of Gillick Competence and Age of Legal Capacity (Scotland) Act

2 How can you as a counsellor maintain the trust of clients within an educational establishment, when you are clearly seen as a member of staff outside of the counselling room?

- Attention to detail in contracting with client, e.g. reassurance of confidentiality within usual limits of risk
- Explanation of your role in and around the educational establishment, e.g. may need to attend staff meetings or be seen talking to other staff in corridors, and confirm that these conversations are not about the content of the counselling session
- Note that although clients may know others who attend, you will not confirm their attendance with peers
- Revisit contract regularly, being actively seeking and open to questions
- Be sensitive to clients when seeing them around the site – discuss with them in session if you should acknowledge, smile, say hello, etc.
- Some establishments have policies on confidential discussions. Check to see if yours does
- Consider your attendance at public functions such as prize-givings, awards evenings, open days, etc., and if necessary explain to clients in advance that you may be attending

3 In which ways could a counsellor contribute to the institution, above and beyond their work one-to-one in the counselling room?

- Prepare regular reports for management that identify current trends in the population on the roll, e.g. bullying and substance misuse.
- Support management in the writing of policies and guidelines for specific and relevant issues such as safety online and dealing with self-harming behaviours
- Support whole school approaches such as critical incidents (e.g. death of a student or staff member)
- Provide training for staff in areas such as mental health and well-being
- Provide time in school assemblies or curriculum areas for students, e.g. informing about the counselling service, stress management during examination periods, etc.
- Attend open days/evenings to inform students, parents and stakeholders about the counselling service and being able to answer any questions they may have
- Run peer support programmes

Learning Activities

1. What are the important factors that you would want to ask about in a referral form to your counselling service? Not all will be appropriate depending on setting, but you may find it helpful to receive information on the following:

- Name and role of referrer
- Date of referral
- Name of client
- Age of client
- Year group/course studied/faculty
- Postal address
- Reason for referral
- Does the client support the referral?
- Parental permission (if appropriate) sought (how and when)
- Can the information on referral be shared with client?
- Any barriers of access for the client?
- How urgent is the referral?
- History (include any other services involved with client and any significant events, e.g. bereavement)
- Current health (physical and emotional, and including any knowledge of sleep habits/drugs/alcohol/food – including energy drinks)
- Any known details about relationships (peers/staff/family)

2. Can you devise a document that goes back to the referrer at the end of therapy, that updates them on the current situation, without breaking client confidentiality? Include:

- Thanks for the referral
- Name of client
- Its appropriateness (or otherwise)
- That therapy is over
- Client found it helpful (if this is so)
- Date
- Please don't discuss this directly with client

Do:

- Discuss this document with your client
- Agree what can and can't be said
- Regard this as a way of promoting appropriate referrals to your service

Further Reading

BACP (British Association for Counselling and Psychotherapy) (2011 [2009]) *School-Based Counselling Operating Toolkit*. Lutterworth: BACP and Welsh Assembly Government.

McGinnis, S. (2006) *Good Practice Guidance for Counselling in Schools*. 4th edn. Lutterworth: BACP.

Prever, M. (2010) *Counselling and Supporting Children and Young People: A Person-Centred Approach*. London: SAGE.

Smyth, D. (2013) *Person-Centred Therapy with Children and Young People*. London: SAGE.

Online Resources

BACP website: www.bacp.co.uk/, especially the BACP Children and Young People Division and the Competences for Working with Children and Young People.

Counselling MindEd: http://counsellingminded.com, especially Modules CMD 0104–6.

28

Extending Practice: New Horizons

Sue Pattison, Terry Hanley and Olga Pykhtina[1]

Introduction

This chapter looks at the use of technology in counselling children and young people and explores the following in relation to the authors' practice and research:

- Technology and the internet
- Online counselling
- Interactive tabletops

It is difficult to ignore the influence that modern technological developments are having upon society and their 'newness' is something which can be intimidating. However, as Douglas Adams reminds us:

> Another problem with the net is that it is still technology, and technology, as the computer scientist Bran Ferren memorably defined it, is stuff that doesn't work yet. We no longer think of chairs as technology, we just think of them as chairs. But there was a time when we hadn't worked out how many legs chairs should have, how tall they should

[1] Acknowledgement to Zehra Ersahin for case study material. Zehra is a counselling psychologist in doctoral training at the University of Manchester whose research interest is in online youth counselling.

be, and they would often crash when we tried to use them. Before long, computers will be as trivial and plentiful as chairs (and a couple of decades or so after that, as sheets of paper or grains of sand) and we will cease to be aware of the things. (Douglas Adams, *Sunday Times*, 29 August 1999)

Despite the awareness of its limitations, the majority of us still embrace technology and invite it into our homes with the hope that it will enrich our lives. Commonplace items such as cars, phones, televisions and washing machines have all become reliant upon computers to aid the tasks that they do. Unfortunately, the fact that the computer within them is still 'technology' is unavoidable and with this comes the numerous flaws and problems associated with it. However, our hunger for such devices remains unabated by such technicalities, and if computer usage continues to increase on its present trajectory it is almost inevitable that computers will become as 'plentiful as chairs'. However, although the advances (a term that could easily be contested) that we have already made are significant, the fine-tuning process still has some way to go before the title of 'technology' dissipates and is forgotten. In the meantime we are stuck in a period of transition and a phase of technological evolution.

Technology and the Internet

The Office of National Statistics reports that 61 per cent of households within the UK could access the internet from home in 2007 (National Statistics Report, 2009), a figure likely to have grown significantly since the survey was carried out. This has had an impact on a range of areas of everyday life. For example, the prevalence of the internet has inevitably begun to impact upon how people approach health care. For instance, individuals are reported to commonly use online resources to access information about health issues of interest before consulting with a professional. Interestingly, surveys suggest that such practice 'is not as common as is sometimes reported' (Baker et al., 2003: 2400), although this was in 2003 and the use of the internet is a phenomenon that is clearly on the increase. In addition to this, evidence is mounting which displays that individuals are increasingly accessing health services online. Probably the most relevant and striking statistics available are those collected by the Samaritans' (UK volunteer help and support organisation) email support service. The Samaritans received and responded to 36,500 emails in the year 2000; this increased to 72,000 during 2002 and in 2006 they received 184,000 emails (Samaritans Statistics, 2007). This phenomenal increase reflects changing attitudes to the internet as a resource, a concept that is supported by a Market and Opinion Research International (MORI) poll finding (2001) which revealed that 60 per cent of the internet users who were interviewed would seek help for mental health problems online.

Technology has impacted substantially upon the world of counselling and psychotherapy. It seems important to acknowledge that the world is changing at a fast pace and today's technologies, as suggested by Adams (above), will potentially be just part of what we do in the future. Furthermore, for those who may be a little technology averse, it may also be a bit frightening to know that it is inescapable and not always within our control. In this chapter, we discuss how technology is integrated into therapy in a number of very explicit ways. However, we pay less attention to our softer engagement (that is, peripheral use of technology, rather than direct work with clients) with such work. For instance, in Table 28.1 we outline some areas in which technology may creep into our therapeutic work, both inside (column 1) and outside (column 2) the counselling room.

Table 28.1   Some soft encounters with technology within therapeutic work.

In the counselling room	Outside the counselling room
Using a computer to find out helpful information – 'let's consider what the side effects of cannabis are…'	You have a website to attract clients
	You use a computer to book appointments and write your notes
The client shows you pictures on their phone – 'here's a picture of my dad…'	You are running late and phone to inform your client/organisation of this
The client talks about their internet habits – 'I was on Facebook last night…'	You have a phone meeting or Skype with a supervisor
The client talks about problems with cyber bullying – 'I got this horrible text message yesterday…'	Your manager calculates your effectiveness based upon outcome data using a computer software package
Using a relaxation audio recording/podcast – 'how about we use some of the session to practise relaxing?'	You complete a training programme online, for example some of the MindEd modules
You audio record the session – 'I have an assignment for a programme I'm studying for, would you mind me recording this session? …'	

If we consider the different types of technological involvement noted above, it is evident how pervasive the use of modern technologies has become.

Online Counselling

If we move to consider more explicit ways in which technology gets integrated into therapeutic work, we enter a territory that often raises anxieties within a profession that tends to prize face-to-face communication. We begin to consider the concepts of computer-delivered therapy and computer-mediated counselling. The former reflects computer programmes that have been created to support individuals in working through specific therapeutic tasks, the most notable being the development of computerised cognitive-behavioural therapy programmes, for example, Beating the Blues for issues around depression or Fear Fighter for issues around anxiety (Thase and Lang, 2006). The latter concept looks at how individuals can utilise technology to connect directly with others. Table 28.2 lists some of the different forms of one-to-one computer mediated counselling that have become relatively commonplace.

Table 28.2 Common forms of online one-to-one counseling.

Type of mediated counselling	Brief explanation
– Electronic mail (email)/Text messages	Counselling mediated through email conversations (asynchronous communication). This might be brief interchanges or work based upon longer documents.
– Internet relay chat (IRC)	Counselling mediated using real-time chat rooms (synchronous communication).
– Telephone/Voice over internet	Counselling using telephone programmes mediated through the internet.
– Tele/Videoconferencing	Counselling in which the counsellor and client can both see and hear each other on separate computers, including webinars.
– Avatar	Counselling in a space similar to a chat room. In these spaces those involved will have designed characters to converse.

Each of these forms brings with it its own nuances and complexities. They prove attractive to different groups and provide unique strengths. They also each bring with them their own challenges to overcome (see texts such as Evans (2009) and Jones and Stokes (2009) for more detailed overviews of such approaches). A common challenge to such work is the distance between the counsellor and the client, a factor that seems irreconcilable with therapeutic theory for some (see Pelling and Renard, 2000). Interestingly, however, when considering whether such methods are beneficial there is an increasing body of literature supporting the notion that online therapy can create strong therapeutic alliances (Hanley and Reynolds, 2009; Hanley et al., 2012) and result in positive change similar to the effects of face-to-face equivalents (Barak et al., 2008; Hanley and Reynolds, 2009). This has led the British Association for Counselling and Psychotherapy to conclude:

Anecdotal and empirical evidence suggests that it is not only possible to create deep, emotional relationships online but that, while not replicating them, these can closely resemble relationships formed in face-to-face therapy. (Anthony and Goss, 2009: 2)

It is important to reflect directly upon how such developments have begun to impact upon work with young people. Without a doubt this has been an enormous growth area and online counselling services for this age group have emerged in numerous countries (see Vossler and Hanley (2010) for a discussion of such services in Europe, Campbell and Glasheen (2012) in Australia and Pattison et al. (2012) for a discussion of how such practice might be utilised in Africa). These developments have reflected a broad shift in how young people appear to be accessing health care provision and the need to be more responsive to this demand. Table 28.3 outlines some of the reasons put forward by youth online counselling services for their creation.

As is evident, some of the issues noted in Table 28.3 are very practical in nature

Table 28.3 Reasons that online counselling services for young people cite for their development.

To meet the needs of young people who:

- have concerns, or fears, about approaching a face-to-face counselling service
- live in an area where they are unable to get to a face-to-face counselling service
- have a physical disability which makes it difficult/impossible for them to get to us
- have other commitments/time limits that mean they wouldn't ordinarily seek counselling
- prefer chatting online

To meet service needs by:

- reducing costs
- supporting the creation of easily accessible, thorough session notes
- creating a youth-friendly access point (e.g. see the points above when considering the needs of young people)
- potentially improving therapeutic relationships with this client group (e.g. by supporting young people to be more honest with their counsellor and reducing power imbalances present within adult–young person relationships)

while others intend to directly improve the quality of service offered to those seeking support. There is, however, a counterpoint to such positive views – for instance, regarding the former, some authors reflect upon the ethical issues or regulation of such work (Hanley, 2006) and, regarding the latter, some authors note the fear of young people utilising the internet to perpetuate their own isolation rather than connecting with others (Wolak et al., 2003). Caution should therefore be exercised before moving into such territories as a practitioner.

When considering the quality of online services for young people it is notable that the research base supporting this work is limited. However, the restricted evidence base does begin to reflect a similar picture to that of trends in adult counselling. For instance, young people who have accessed online services report doing so because they find the internet to be a comfortable and safe space to seek support (Hanley, 2011; King et al., 2006a). Furthermore, strong therapeutic alliances have been reported (King et al., 2006b; Hanley, 2008, 2011) and positive outcomes observed (King et al., 2006b). However, it is more sobering to consider that, within the King et al. study referred to above (2006b; also see Chardon et al., 2011), the alliances proved weaker and outcomes reduced when compared to telephone equivalents. With such findings in mind, it is clear that we are just at the beginning of understanding the impact of new technologies upon therapeutic work with young people. However, we should be wary of shoving our heads in the sand and ignoring these new developments. Therefore, we would argue that an open, pluralistic attitude to such work is adopted that is responsive to the client's needs when considering issues such as the psychological approach adopted *and* the therapeutic medium utilised (also see Hanley et al., 2013).

Online Counselling with Young People: A Therapist's Experience

This section reflects upon the experiences of a counsellor working online with young people as part of an online youth counselling service. The service offers therapeutic support to young people aged between 12 and 25 and uses synchronous chat, asynchronous emailing, moderated forums and a magazine to support its users. The service is free at the point of delivery and most users remain anonymous. When young people sign up to use the service, they create a profile with a user-name, age, an avatar (an image representing them), and provide the locality through which they access the service. Upon registering with the service, users are free to choose the way of support with which they feel most at ease.

On Becoming an Online Counsellor for Young People

Utilising synchronous chat can pose new challenges within counselling practice. In face-to-face counselling all therapists work with ambiguity to a certain extent, however, this can be magnified in an online medium due to the absence of verbal cues and body language of the client. In particular, the story of the blind men and the elephant springs to mind. In this story a group of men (all blind) try to work out what the object in front of them is by feeling its different parts. They fail, and it is only when they combine efforts and share experiences that they discover it is an elephant. In much a similar way, the absence of observational information can prove a major challenge to therapeutic work and the therapist can feel professionally challenged by the lack of information. They may contemplate what the young people they work with look like, what the things they want to reveal are, and what the expressions and feelings are that they hide. However, relationships with clients change as the therapist becomes more adept at using his/her other senses.

The following sections present and reflect upon therapeutic work entered into with young people and the types of issues and challenges encountered. Amended transcripts collected during a reflexive research project are used to illustrate what online work with young people might look like.

Utilising Compensatory Techniques

Some of the alternative techniques used to communicate effectively while online form part of this dialogue, where words are the only tools both therapist and client can utilise. With the aim of compensating for the lack of bodily and emotional presence, the use of emoticons (☺☺☹), acronyms (PAW: parents are watching), abbreviations (ur: your), capitalisation (SORRY), emotional bracketing (<<<concerned>>>), and words expressing physical contact ({hug}) are used. The following brief interchange with Locket (avatar pseudonym) might shed some light on the experience:

Therapist:	It seems you have been through HARD times, and still affected by this loss of {{loved}} one ☹
Locket:	yeah ... I still miss him loads ☹ ☹ ☹ and (…)

Unfortunately, although compensatory techniques can be helpful, communicative barriers commonly emerge when working using text-based approaches. For instance, typographical errors and unknown/vague written statements occur quite often. Therefore, it is the responsibility of the therapist to act upon errors and explicitly seek clarification where needed:

Therapist:	that ounds practical!
Therapist:	sounds*
Locket:	☺ BI5
Therapist:	sorry 'locket', could u explain what 'BI5' means
Locket:	awww sorry! Back In 5 mins :p

Beginnings and Endings: Negotiating Goals and Maintaining Time Boundaries

When negotiating therapeutic goals within counselling relationships, particularly where the work may be brief in nature, it is useful to work towards the articulation of such a focus in online therapy. Here is an example:

Therapist:	im curious 'lioness' … 'it sounds STUPID'?
Lioness:	just seems silly for me to find the situations so stressful and i dont even get why they do
Therapist:	hmm … what I'm hearing here is if you find the reason behind your anxiety, it will become more rational and …?
Lioness:	yeah and then I ll be able to try and avoid this or come to terms with it, but at the moment it seems to have just come over me suddenly and now i seem to panic more about panicking because Im aware of the situation happening so it makes it worse!
Therapist:	it sounds as if it's **building UP**! I'm wondering if then, this could be our goal to work on for today's session, then you may feel you are taking sth from here?
Lioness:	yes please
Therapist:	kool ☺ shall we identify our goal and start working on it?
Lioness:	yes please
Therapist:	I would also like to hear your voice 'lioness' in this goal. Would you mind paraphrasing it in terms of your focus or intention maybe?
Lioness:	yeah id say that my goal is to work out what it is that makes me anxious in these situations so that i can try to come to terms with this.

Following on from considering the focal points of the sessions it is worth being mindful of maintaining boundaries around the work where possible. In the instance below, there may be a need to end the session so as not to encroach upon another client's time:

Janedoe:	its complicated though, we have more to lose, there is more than I told you and i need to think about it
Janedoe:	but thank you
Therapist:	no worries at all! I need to close this chat quite soon. but would love to talk about it MORE … you want to meet again next week?

Entering the Black Hole: Online Silence

A final issue to raise related to developing online therapeutic work is the issue of silence – sometimes referred to as the black hole effect. Unlike face-to-face work, the power dynamic of the work can operate very differently. A young person may choose to end the contact at any point of time and this can prove quite a challenge. Below is an interchange with Feather92 which reflects how this might unfold in therapeutic work:

Feather92:	I would love him to change his mind! But deep down I know he won't! That's why I always go back to him with the hope that he will change his mind!
Feather92:	But he is losing me friends
Therapist:	You have a point there ... and yeah I have a feeling about him leaving me drained ... but I also hear it is either ur ex or ur friends ... where are 'u' in this story 'Feather92]?
	-5 mins passed...-
	Therapist: are u there 'Feather92'?
Feather92:	yes
Therapist:	sorry, did I upset u?
Feather92:	Sorry no! I was just thinking! I dunno..
-Feather92:	left the chat temporarily-
	-3 mins passed...-
-Feather92:	entered the chat-
Feather92:	Yeah exactly! I think I need to put myself first! I'm sick of not doing things I want to do to please other people! I'm just scared of upsetting anyone, I'm upsetting myself!

As is evident in this quote, the session became a little disjointed. It also raised the therapist's anxieties about what was going on for Feather92. In this instance, the session ended relatively clearly but this does not always prove to be the case. With this in mind, and in navigating such silence, supervision has proven invaluable in helping make sense and learn from such experience.

Therapeutic Use of Technology with Young Children: Digital Interactive Tabletops and Play Therapy

Although this section looks at digital technology in relation to therapeutic play and play therapy, it does not explore play therapy as a therapeutic approach (see Chapter 7 for a full account of play therapy). Lack of mental well-being can impact on children's behaviour in the classroom and on their learning (Aviles et al., 2006: 20; Wagenaar et al., 2000: 21) and may lead to offending. Over 90 per cent of young offenders have had a mental health problem as a child (Mental Health of Children and Adolescents in Great

Britain in 'Facing the Future', 2000). Half of those with mental health problems aged 26 were first identified with a mental health problem by age 15 and nearly 75 per cent had been so identified by the late teens (Healthy Lives, Brighter Future report, 2009). Therefore, there is a need for children's well-being to be promoted as well as the need for therapeutic interventions.

Technology has become a familiar medium in children's lives. Video games and virtual reality have been successfully implemented into counselling to treat a range of anxiety and panic disorders and phobias (Coyle et al., 2005). Yet, despite the rise of technology in therapies with older children, it is largely missing, or used minimally, in play therapy with children of primary school age. Mental health interventions may be of high importance for younger children as it is estimated that 80 per cent of children externalising their problems, for example challenging behaviour at the age of five, develop more serious forms of anti-social behaviour in the future if not provided with successful interventions (Mental Health of Children and Adolescents in Great Britain in 'Facing the Future', 2010).

Interactive tabletops are a new generation of computers that allow direct interaction with the multi-touch surface and they have been used to promote children's fantasy play (Mansor et al., 2009), storytelling (Cao et al., 2010), creativity (Marco et al., 2009), and interaction (Piper and Hollan, 2006). Although fantasy play, storytelling and interaction are some of the concepts play therapy is based on, there is little research on the use of interactive tabletops in child play therapy. Generally, play therapy remains embedded in traditional toys, representative objects and other creative materials, largely provided by the therapist and not rooted in firm evidence. There is no evidence base regarding the acceptability of digital technology by therapy practitioners or service providers, although such evidence is being generated by research carried out by the authors in partnership with Play Therapy UK and Place2Be.

Toys generally used in the play therapy room are not interactive or computer generated for a number of reasons. First, there is a belief that technology would interfere with the therapeutic process when the child focuses more on making the toy work rather than on expression of role or fantasy play (Carmichael, 2006). Second, frustration with the toy can lead to the loss of valuable therapy time. Finally, the child can get absorbed into playing with a toy. If the child does not communicate through words or play, 'therapy is just another play session without therapeutic value' (Carmichael, 2006: 20). However, there is little empirical evidence to support the above explanation of the absence of technology in non-directive play therapy. How does the child's engagement with traditional static toys differ from their engagement with computerised toys? If computerised games can support directive therapy (Coyle et al., 2005), what, if anything, can it offer for the non-directive approach and what is the rationale for using technology, or not?

The above questions and the children's increasing requests to bring game consoles and other digital devices into the play therapy room (Riedel Bowers, 2011) motivated a research project to examine the use of digital interactive tabletop technology in play therapy (Pykhtina et al., 2012). This aimed to understand whether interactive tabletops could be used in play therapy and how to design applications for non-directive play therapy. Technology has been introduced into children's play for a number of reasons. First, technology is present in adults' lives and this has to be reflected in the children's play through which they make sense of the world around them. Second, children enjoy interactive toys and find them entertaining. Mechanical toys can increase children's interest and engagement in play activities (Fernaeus et al., 2010). In addition to being just entertaining and engaging, play with interactive toys has been shown to have therapeutic effects. Interactive toys support social exchanges and cognitive development of children with socio-relational disturbances, learning disabilities, and autism and provide opportunities for emotionally, mentally and psychologically impacted children to fully engage in and enjoy play (Dautenhahn and Werry, 2004). One of the first designs of robotic stuffed animals was done to help children with cardiac issues to talk about their problems and cope with the situation (Bers et al., 1998). The 'Billow' system was developed for children in hospitals, who are quarantined or otherwise isolated, to play in a virtual audio-visual cloudscape using a malleable, egg-shaped input/output device. This was intended to address the children's need for increased human interaction and social development, mastery and control, comfort and security (Rueb and Wardzala, 1997).

The promotion of social exchanges through digital media has increased especially with the introduction of interactive tabletops, large horizontal displays that several users can interact with simultaneously, although in play therapy the interactions are one-to-one with the child and the therapist. Digital tabletops have been shown to promote face-to-face interaction (Hatch, 2009) and the benefit of interactive tabletops, for example in the deaf community, was shown in the study described by Piper and Hollan (2008), in which the communication between the doctor and the deaf patient was facilitated through an interactive tabletop. In addition, games on interactive tabletops have been revealed to support collaboration between the therapist and children with autistic spectrum disorder in CBT (Giusti et al., 2011).

The use of tabletops has been extended to promoting children's creativity through such play activities as storytelling (Cao et al., 2010) and fantasy play (Mansor et al., 2009). StoryMat, an application to promote collaboration through storytelling, is a quilt-like play-mat that records voice and toy movements as a story is being told. Once finished, the mat selects a similar story to be re-told from an archive, to inspire and allow for mediated collaboration (Cassell and Ryokai, 2001). StoryTable (Cappelletti et al., 2004), is a tabletop application requiring users to select information carried on virtual ladybirds to create a coherent story to support explicit storytelling. To foster children's creativity and collaboration through storytelling, a new system, TellTable (Cao et al., 2010), was designed to mix tangible objects with created virtual environments. The system allowed children to incorporate photographs of real-world objects into a story, draw on them and play back a recorded story. It has been shown to foster creativity, incorporate identity and support collaboration and interaction.

The attempts to foster children's fantasy play through the design of interactive systems on a tabletop (Mansor et al., 2009) have suggested that virtual objects can stimulate fantasy play, whenever proper interaction design allows children to engage with them.

Interactive tabletops enable play of a type that would not be available in a traditional play therapy room (such as playing with floating feathers and snowflakes, lights, fire, and ice, burning fireballs and frost frames to change picture patterns). These options support such a therapeutic factor of play as mastery (Schaefer, 1993). They contribute to the development of the child's sense of power, control and mastery of their environment, especially important for children who live chaotic, disrupted lives (Sallman, 2007). Interactive tabletops afford methods of manipulating objects and images, for example rotation and scale, that naturally mimic the way one would move a piece of paper on a tabletop. Scale is intuitive and gives the child new creativity that isn't available in the traditional play therapy room; in the real world you can't easily make a picture or object larger.

Figure 28.1 Expressing emotions on the digital tabletop

The Magic Land software (Pykhtina et al., 2012) is designed to facilitate all aspects of play therapy in young children. For example, the Water application allows the child to play with 'water', making ripples, adding pebbles and various stones, ships and shells. This was combined with the sounds of rain and thunder and corresponding visual effects created on the surface of the water to explore the possibility and potential benefits of bringing music and play therapy together. The child can also add/take away fish, which are moving around freely but can be affected by the child's touch. Water has two therapeutic advantages: it contributes to a sense of happiness and well-being and is a powerful antidote to the stress of living (Sallman, 2007).

Case Study   Dean

Dean, aged five, used the Magic Land interactive tabletop application 'Rosebush' to express his feelings. He identified himself with a picture of a sad blobby character to depict how he was feeling when his Dad threw him out of the window. Dean used options to erase a pre-set emotion on a character's face and drew a new 'happy face': 'I am happy in the warmth by the tree'. He used frost frames in the 'Flying' application to express how he felt about flying when his family were travelling overseas with a Forces placement: 'This is to make the sky cold. I don't like flying'. He chose to play with sounds of a fireball to describe his father when he was angry and whom he was scared of – 'It sounds like my Dad ... yes I'm scared of him'.

Fantasy play with superheroes was observed to encourage Dean to deal with his fear of flying. He first created two characters, one that was afraid of flying and the other one a superhero who was happy with flying. By the end of the play Dean had vanquished the scared figure off the screen and associated himself with the hero saying: 'I think I'll put myself down here by the tree where it's warm'.

It could mean that, through play with the hero, Dean was preparing himself for the flight with his family. However, could this fear of flying be connected to dealing with Dean's fear of his father and the violent episode when he was thrown out of the window? If so, Dean could be working through deep material that has multiple connections.

Summary

In this chapter we have looked at the use of computer technology and the internet to support counselling with children and young people. Several main topics were covered:

- Computers and the internet in counselling practice
- Online counselling with young people
- Interactive tabletops and play therapy with young children

Reflective Questions

1. Reflect upon the case study material provided in the chapter. How would you deal with a young client who indicated they might harm themselves?
   You would follow the ethical framework of your professional body, including taking the issue urgently to your supervisor if possible and your line manager or safeguarding officer in the organisation.
2. After reading about and perhaps looking at a few interactive tabletop video clips, how could you see this type of technology helping communication in therapy?
   The technology could provide a creative medium to enable the child or young person to communicate where words may not be possible, or to supplement verbal communication.
3. Reflect upon your own attitudes to and experiences with technology. Would there be any barriers to you incorporating technology into your counselling work with children and young people?
   This will be a personal reflection – there is no 'right' answer.

Learning Activities

1. Check out the online counselling children and young people pathway and learning resources at: https://www.minded.org.uk/totara/program/view.php?id=68.
2. There are many online counselling resources for children and young people. Use a UK Google search to locate some of these and check them out.
3. An internet search brings up several video clips on YouTube demonstrating the use of interactive tabletops in play therapy and sand-tray work. Watch one or two of these video clips and reflect on whether you would consider using this type of technology in your work with children and young people.

Further Reading

Pattison, S., Hanley, T, and Sefi, A. (2012) 'Online counselling for children and young people: Using technology to address the millennium development goals in Kenya', in D.B.I. Popoola and O. Adebowale (eds) *Online Guidance and Counselling: Toward Effectively Applying Technology*. Hershey, PA: IGI Global.

Pykhtina, O., Balaam, M., Wood, G., et al. (2012) 'Magic Land: The design and evaluation of an interactive tabletop supporting therapeutic play with children', in *DIS 2012: Proceedings of the Designing Interactive Systems Conference*. Newcastle: ACM Press.

Olga Pykhtina and Sue Pattison's Interactive Tabletop projects:

http://di.ncl.ac.uk/ilablearn/?page_id=291

http://di.ncl.ac.uk/playtherapy/

http://www.youtube.com/watch?v=Pmm6m8dRwz8

References

Ackerman, S.J. and Hilsenroth, M.J. (2001) 'A review of therapists' characteristics and techniques negatively impacting the therapeutic alliance', *Psychotherapy: Theory, Research, Practice, Training,* 38 (2): 171–185.

Adam-Westcott, J. and Isenbart, I. (1995) 'A journey of change through connections', in S. Freedman (ed.), *The Reflecting Teams in Action: Collaborative Practices in Family Therapy.* New York: Guilford Press.

Adams, J. (2012) 'Understanding grieving teenagers', *Information Sheet.* Child Bereavement UK. Available at: www.childbereavement.org.uk/Portals/0/Support%20 and%20Information/Information%20Sheets/Understanding%20Grieving%20 Teenagers.pdf.

The Age of Legal Capacity (Scotland) Act 1991 www.legislation.gov.uk/ukpga/1991/50/ contents

Ainsworth, M.S. (1989) 'Attachments beyond infancy', *American Psychologist,* 44 (4): 709.

Ainsworth, M.S. and Bowlby, J. (1991) 'An ethological approach to personality development', *American Psychologist,* 46 (4): 333.

Ainsworth, M.S., Blehar, M.C., Waters, E. and Wall, S. (1978) *Patterns of Attachment.* Hillsdale, NJ: Erlbaum.

Alexander, J. and Le Grange, D. (2010) *My Kid Is Back: Empowering Parents to Beat Anorexia Nervosa.* London: Routledge.

Allan, R., Sharma, R., Sangani, B., Hugo, P., Frampton, I., Mason, H. and Lask, B. (2010) 'Predicting the weight gain required for recovery from anorexia nervosa with pelvic ultrasonography: An evidence-based approach', *European Eating Disorders Review,* 18 (1), 43–48.

Allen, B. (2011) 'The use and abuse of attachment theory in clinical practice with maltreated children. Part II: treatment', *Trauma, Violence, & Abuse,* 12 (1): 13–22.

Allington-Smith, P. (2006) 'Mental health of children with learning disabilities', *Advances in Psychiatric Treatment,* 12: 130–138.

Allnock, D. and Hynes, P. (2012) *Therapeutic Services for Sexually Abused Children and Young People: Scoping the Evidence Base* (unpublished internal report). London: NSPCC.

Alvarez, A. (2012) *The Thinking Heart: Three Levels of Psychoanalytic Work in Psychotherapy with Children and Adolescents.* London: Routledge.

Aman, J. (2006) 'Therapist as host: Making my guests feel welcome', *The International Journal of Narrative Therapy and Community Work*, 3: 3–10.

American Psychiatric Association (APA) (1994) *Diagnostic and Statistical Manual of Mental Disorders – Fourth Edition* (DSM-IV). Washington. DC: APA.

American Psychiatric Association (2013) *Diagnostic and Statistical Manual of Mental Disorders*. Washington DC: American Psychiatric Press.

Anthony, K. and Goss, S. (2009) *Guidelines for Online Counseling and Psychotherapy*. 3rd edn. Lutterworth: British Association for Counselling and Psychotherapy.

Arensman, E. (2010) *Review of the Evidence Base for Protect Life – A Shared Vision: The Northern Ireland Suicide Prevention Strategy*. Cork: National Suicide Research Foundation.

Aristotle (1895) *The Poetics*, translated with a critical text by S.H. Butcher. London: Macmillan. Available at: http://classics.mit.edu/Aristotle/poetics.html.

Arnold, C. (2010) *Understanding Schemas and Emotions in Early Childhood*. London: SAGE.

Arrow, H., Henry, K.B., Poole, M.S., Wheelan, S.A., and Moreland, R.L. (2005) 'Traces, trajectories, and timing: The temporal perspective on groups', in M.S. Poole and A.B. Hollingshead (eds), *Theories of Small Groups: Interdisciplinary Perspectives*. Thousand Oaks, CA: SAGE.

Aviles, A., Anderson, T. and Davila, E. (2006) 'Child and adolescent social-emotional development within the context of school', *Child and Adolescent Mental Health*, 11 (1): 32–39.

Axline, V. (1947) *Play Therapy*. Boston: Houghton Miffin.

Axline, V. (1989 [1969]) *Play Therapy*. New York: Ballantine Books.

Axline, V. (1990 [1971]) *Dibs in Search of Self: Personality Development in Play Therapy*. London: Penguin Books.

Bachelard, G. (1994 [1957]) *The Poetics of Space*. Boston, MA: Beacon Press.

BACP (British Association for Counselling and Psychotherapy) (1998) *Code of Ethics and Practice for Counsellors*. Lutterworth: BACP.

BACP (British Association for Counselling and Psychotherapy) (2006) *Good Practice Guidelines for Counselling in Schools*. 4th edn. Rugby: British Association for Counselling and Psychotherapy.

BACP (British Association for Counselling and Psychotherapy) (2010a) *Counselling for Depression (CfD): General Information*. Lutterworth: BACP. Available at: www.bacp. co.uk/learning/Counselling%20for%20Depression/.

BACP (British Association for Counselling and Psychotherapy) (2010b) *Ethical Framework for Good Practice in Counselling and Psychotherapy*. Lutterworth: BACP.

BACP (British Association for Counselling and Psychotherapy) (2011 [2009]) *School Based Counselling Operating Toolkit*. Lutterworth: BACP and Welsh Assembly Government.

BACP (British Association for Counselling and Psychotherapy) (2013) *Ethical Framework for Good Practice*. Lutterworth: BACP.

BACP (British Association for Counselling and Psychotherapy) (2014) *Competencies for Humanistic Counselling with Young People.* Lutterworth: BACP. Available at: www.bacp.co.uk/research/resources/cyp_competences.php/.

Baginsky, W. (2004) *School Counselling in England, Wales and Northern Ireland: A Review.* London: NSPCC.

Bailey, S. and Shooter, M. (eds) (2009) *The Young Mind: An Essential Guide to Mental Health for Young Adults, Parents and Teachers.* London: Bantam Press.

Baker, B.L., McIntyre, L.L., Blacher, J., Crnic, K., Edelbrock, C. and Low, C. (2003) 'Pre-school children with and without developmental delay: Behaviour problems and parenting stress over time', *Journal of Intellectual Disability Research*, 47: 217–230.

Bala, P., Pratt, K. and Maguire, C. (2011) 'The needs of children and young people: Developing a new service', *Healthcare Counselling and Psychotherapy Journal*, April: 20–24.

Bandroff, S. and Newes, S. (eds) (2005) *Coming of Age: The Evolving Field of Adventure Therapy.* Boulder, CO: Association for Experiential Education.

Bandura, A. (1977) *Social Learning Theory.* Englewood Cliffs, NJ: Prentice-Hall.

Bandura, A. (2001) 'Social cognitive theory: An agentic perspective', *Annual Review of Psychology*, 52 (1): 1–26.

Bannister, A., Barrett, K. and Shearer, E. (1990) *Listening to Children: The Professional Response to Hearing the Abused Child.* Essex: Longman.

BAPT (British Association of Play Therapists) (2009) *Play Therapy – Its Relevance to 21st Century Needs of Children, Young People and Families.* Available at: www.bapt.info/downloads/NICE%20one-pager%20from%20research%20subcomm%20sep%2009.doc.

Barak, A., Hen, L., Boniel-Nissim, M. and Shapira, N. (2008) 'A comprehensive review and a meta-analysis of the effectiveness of internet-based psychotherapeutic interventions', *Journal of Technology in Human Services*, 26 (2/4): 109–160.

Barber, P. and Brownell, P. (2008) 'Qualitative research', in P. Brownell (ed.), *Handbook for Theory, Research and Practice in Gestalt Therapy.* New York: Cambridge Scholars Publishing. pp. 37–63.

Barrett, P. (2012) *Friends for Life: Group Leaders Manual.* 5th edn. Available at: www.friendsinfo.net/uk.htm (FRIENDS anxiety prevention programme).

Barrett-Lennard, G.T. (2013) 'Origins and evolution of the person-centred innovation in Carl Rogers' lifetime', in M. Cooper, M. O'Hara, P.F. Schmid and A.C. Bohart (eds), *The Handbook of Person-Centred Psychotherapy and Counselling.* Basingstoke: Palgrave Macmillan.

Baruch, G. (2001) *Community-Based Psychotherapy with Young People: Evidence and Innovation in Practice.* Philadelphia: Taylor and Francis.

Baskin, T.W., Slaten, C.D., Sorenson, C., Glover-Russell, J. and Merson, D.N. (2010) 'Does youth psychotherapy improve academically related outcomes? A meta-analysis', *Journal of Counseling Psychology*, 57, 290–296.

Bass, E. and Davis, L. (2008) *The Courage to Heal: A Guide for Women Survivors of Child Sexual Abuse, 20th Anniversary Edition*. New York: Harper Row.

Beauchamp, T. and Childress, J. (2008) *Principles Of Biomedical Ethics*. 6th edn. Oxford: Oxford University Press.

Beaudoin, M.N. (2004) 'Problem with frogs, clients and therapist: A cultural discourse analysis', *Journal of Systemic Therapies*, 23 (3): 51–64.

Beaudoin, M.N. (2005) 'Agency and choice in the face of trauma: A narrative therapy map', *Journal of Systemic Therapies*, 24 (4): 32–50.

Beck, A.T. (1963) 'Thinking and depression. 1. Idiosyncratic content and cognitive distortions', *Archives of General Psychiatry*, 9: 324–333.

Beck, A.T. (1964) 'Thinking and depression. 2. Theory and therapy', *Archives of General Psychiatry*, 10: 561–571.

Beck, A.T., Rush, A.J., Shaw, B.F. and Emery G. (1979) *Cognitive Therapy for Depression*. New York: Guilford Press.

Beck, J. (1995) *Cognitive Therapy: Basics and Beyond*. New York: Guilford Press.

Becker, A.E., Burwell, R.A., Herzog, D.B., Hamburg, P. and Gilman, S.E. (2002) 'Eating behaviours and attitudes following prolonged exposure to television among ethnic Fijian adolescent girls', *British Journal of Psychiatry*, 180: 509–514.

Behr, M., Nuding, D. and McGinnis, S. (2013) 'Person-centred psychotherapy and counselling with children and young people', in M. Cooper, M. O'Hara, P.F. Schmid and A.C. Bohart (eds), *The Handbook of Person-Centred Psychotherapy and Counselling*. Basingstoke: Palgrave Macmillan.

Beloff, Q.C. and Mountfield, H. (1994) *Joint Opinion: Sex Education in Schools*. London: Association of Teachers and Lecturers.

Bers, M., Ackermann, E., Cassell, J., Donegan, B., Gonzalez-Heydrich, J., DeMaso, D., Strohecker, C., Lualdi, S., Bromley, D. and Karlin, J. (1998) 'Interactive storytelling environments: Coping with cardiac illness at Boston's Children's Hospital', in *Proceedings of Computer-Human Interaction* (CHI'98) ACM: 603–609.

Beumont, P.J. and Touyz, S.W. (2003) 'What kind of illness is anorexia nervosa?', *European Child and Adolescent Psychiatry*, 12 (Suppl.): 20–24.

Bion, W. (1962) 'A theory of thinking', *International Journal of Psychoanalysis,* 43: 328–332.

Bion, W. (1965) *Transformations: Change from Learning to Growth*. London: Heinemann.

Bion, W. (1967) *Second Thoughts*. London: Karnac Books.

Blake, P. (2011) *Child and Adolescent Psychotherapy*. London: Karnac Books.

Blanchard, C.W. (1993) *Effects of ropes course therapy on inter-personal behavior and self-esteem of adolescent psychiatric inpatients*. PhD dissertation, New Mexico State University, Las Cruces.

Blend, J. (2007) 'Am I bovvered? A gestalt approach to working with adolescents', *British Gestalt Journal*, 16 (2): 19–27.

Blom, R. (2006) *The Handbook of Gestalt Play Therapy*. London: Jessica Kingsley.

Bolton, G. and Heathcote, D. (1999) *So You Want to Use Role Play?* Stoke on Trent: Trentham Books.

Bomber, L.M. (2011) *What About Me?* Brighton: Worth Publishing.

Bonanno, G.A. and Lilienfeld, S.O. (2008) 'Let's be realistic: When grief counseling is effective and when it's not', *Professional Psychology: Research and Practice*, 39 (3): 377–378.

Bond, T. and Mitchels, B. (2008) *Confidentiality and Record Keeping in Counselling and Psychotherapy*. London: SAGE.

Booth, P.B. and Jernberg, A.M. (2010) *Theraplay: Helping Parents and Children Build Better Relationships Through Attachment-Based Play*. San Francisco, CA: Wiley.

Bor, R., Ebner-Landy, J., Gill, S. and Brace, C. (2002) *Counselling in Schools*. London: SAGE.

Bordin, E.S. (1979) 'The generalizability of the psychoanalytic concept of the working alliance', *Psychotherapy: Theory Research and Practice*, 16: 252–260.

Bostic, J., Shadid, L. and Blotcky, M. (1996) 'Our time is up: Forced terminations during psychotherapy training', *American Journal of Psychotherapy*, 50: 347–359.

Bowlby, J. (1969) *Attachment and Loss: Attachment. Vol. 1*. New York: Basic Books.

Bowlby, J. (1973) *Attachment and Loss: Separation – Anxiety and Anger. Vol. 2*. London: Hogarth Press.

Bowlby, J. (1977a) 'The making and breaking of affectional bonds. I. Aetiology and psychopathology in the light of attachment theory. An expanded version of the fiftieth Maudsley Lecture', *The British Journal of Psychiatry*, 130 (3): 201–210.

Bowlby, J. (1977b) 'The making and breaking of affectional bonds. II. Some principles of psychotherapy. The fiftieth Maudsley Lecture', *The British Journal of Psychiatry*, 130 (5): 421–431.

Bowlby, J. (1980) *Attachment and Loss: Loss – Sadness and Depression. Vol. 3*. London: Hogarth Press.

Bowlby, J. (2005) *A Secure Base*. London: Routledge Classics.

Boyer, S. and Hoffman, M. (1993) 'Counsellor affective reactions to termination: Impact of counsellor loss history and perceived client sensitivity to loss', *Journal of Counselling Psychology*, 40: 271–277.

Bozarth, J.D. (2013) 'Unconditional positive regard', in M. Cooper, M. O'Hara, P.F. Schmid and A.C. Bohart (eds), *The Handbook of Person-Centred Psychotherapy and Counselling*. Basingstoke: Palgrave Macmillan.

BPS (British Psychology Society) (2009) *Code of Ethics and Conduct*. Leicester: British Psychology Society.

BPS (British Psychology Society) (2010) *Human Research Ethics*. Leicester: British Psychology Society.

Bråten, S. (1998) 'Infant learning by altercentric participation: the reverse of egocentric observation in autism', in S. Bråten (ed.), *Intersubjective Communication and Emotion in Early Ontogeny*. Cambridge: Cambridge University Press. pp. 105–126.

Bratton, S., Ray, D., Rhine, T. and Jones, L. (2005) 'The efficacy of play therapy with children: A meta-analytic review of the outcome research', *Professional Psychology: Research and Practice*, 36 (4): 376–390.

Bravender, T., Bryant-Waugh, R., Herzog, D., et al. (2010) 'Classification of eating disturbance in children and adolescents: Proposed changes for the DSM-V', *European Eating Disorders Review*, 18 (2): 79–89.

Brent, D., Emslie, G., Clarke, G., et al. (2008) 'Switching to another SSRI or to Venlafaxine with or without cognitive behaviour therapy for adolescents with SSRI-resistant depression. The TORDIA randomised controlled trial', *Journal of the American Medical Association*, 299 (8): 901–913.

Bright, G. (2013) 'Risk, school counselling and the development of resilience: re-imagining the empirical'. Paper presented at the Twelfth Annual European Affective Education Network Conference. York: York St John University.

Bright, G. and Harrison, G. (2013) 'Switching on your curiosity: Developing research ideas', in G. Bright and G. Harrison (eds), *Understanding Research in Counselling*. London: Learning Matters.

Bronfenbrenner, U. (1979) *The Ecology of Human Development: Experiments by Nature and Design*. Cambridge, MA: Harvard University Press.

Bronfenbrenner, U. (1986) 'Ecology of the family as a context for human development: Research perspectives', *Developmental Psychology*, 22 (6): 723–742.

Bronfenbrenner, U. (2005a) *Making Human Beings Human: Bioecological Perspectives on Human Development*. London: SAGE.

Bronfenbrenner, U. (2005b) 'Strengthening family systems', in U. Bronfenbrenner (ed.), *Making Human Beings Human*. London: SAGE.

Brophy, M. (2006) *Truth Hurts: Report of the National Inquiry into Self-harm among Young People*. London: The Mental Health Foundation and The Camelot Foundation. Available at: http://socialwelfare.bl.uk/subject-areas/services-client-groups/chil dren-mental- health/mentalhealthfoundation/1531542006_truth_hurts.pdf.

Brown, A. (2006) '"In my agency it's very clear – but I can't tell you what it is": Work settings and ethical challenges', *Counselling and Psychotherapy Research*, 6 (2): 100–107.

Browne, A. and Finkelhor, D. (1986) 'Impact of child sexual abuse: A review of the research', *Psychological Bulletin*, 99: 66–77.

Bryant, J. and Baldwin, P. (2010) 'School counsellors' perceptions of mandatory reporter training and mandatory reporting experiences', *Child Abuse Review*, 19: 172–186.

Bryant-Jefferies, R. (2004) *Counselling Young People: Person-Centred Dialogues*. Oxford: Radcliffe Medical Press Ltd.

Buber, M. (1959 [1937]) *I and Thou*. Edinburgh: T & T Clark.

Bulik, C.M., Reba, L., Siega-Riz, A.M. and Reichborn-Kjennerud, T. (2005) 'Anorexia nervosa: Definition, epidemiology, and cycle of risk', *International Journal of Eating Disorders*, 37: s2–s9.

Bulik, C.M., Sullivan, P.F., Tozzi, F., Furberg, H., Lichtenstein, P. and Pedersen, N.L. (2006) 'Prevalence, heritability, and prospective risk factors for anorexia nervosa', *Archives of General Psychiatry*, 63 (3): 305–312.

Bulik, C.M., Thornton, L.M., Root, T.L., Pisetsky, E.M., Lichtenstein, P. and Pedersen, N.L. (2010) 'Understanding the relation between anorexia nervosa and bulimia nervosa in a Swedish national twin sample', *Biological Psychiatry*, 67 (1): 71–77.

Bunting, L., Rosenblatt, B. and Wallace, I. (2010) 'Information-sharing and reporting systems in the UK and Ireland. Professional barriers to reporting child maltreatment concerns', *Child Abuse Review*, 19: 187–202.

Burrows, S. and Laflamme, L. (2010) 'Socioeconomic disparities and attempted suicide: State of knowledge and implications for research and prevention', *International Journal of Injury Control and Safety Promotion*, 17 (1): 23–40.

Butler-Sloss, E. (1988) *Report of the Inquiry into Child Abuse in Cleveland 1987*. Cm 412. London: HMSO.

Calear, A.L. and Christensen, H. (2010) 'Systematic review of school-based prevention and early intervention programs for depression', *Journal of Adolescence*, 33 (3): 429–438.

Campbell, A.F. and Simmonds, J.G. (2011) 'Therapists' perspectives on the therapeutic alliance with children and adolescents', *Counselling Psychology Quarterly*, 24 (3): 195–209.

Campbell, M. and Glasheen, K. (2012) 'The provision of online counselling for young people', in B.I. Popoola and O.F. Adebowale (eds), *Online Guidance and Counseling: Toward Effectively Applying Technology*. Hershey, PA: International Science Reference. pp. 1–13.

Campbell, V., Baker, D. and Bratton, S. (2000) 'Why do children drop-out from play therapy?', *Clinical Child Psychology and Psychiatry*, 5: 133–138.

Canham, H. (2006) 'Latency', in B. Youell (ed.), *The Learning Relationship: Psychoanalytic Thinking in Education*. London: Karnac Books.

Cao, X., Lindley S., Helmes J. and Sellen, A. (2010) 'Telling the whole story: Anticipation, inspiration and reputation in a field deployment of telltable', in *Proceedings CSCW*, ACM Press'10: 1–10.

Cappelletti, A., Gelmini, G., Pianesi, F., Rossi, F. and Zancanaro, M. (2004) 'Enforcing co-operative storytelling: First studies', in *Proceedings of the IEEE International Conference on Advanced Learning Technologies (ICALT)*, 30 August 30 – 1 September. Washington DC: IEEE Computer Society. pp. 281–285.

Care Inspectorate (2011) *Practice Guide: Suicide Prevention for Looked After Children and Young People*. Social Care and Social Work Improvement, Scotland. Available at: www.anguschildprotectioncommittee.org.uk/pdfs/suicidepreventionguide.pdf.

Carlisle, J., Shickle, D., Cork, M. and McDonagh, A. (2006) 'Concerns over confidentiality may deter adolescents from consulting their doctors: A qualitative exploration', *Journal of Medical Ethics*, 32: 133–137.

Carmichael, K.D. (2006) *Play Therapy: An Introduction*. Glenview, IL: Prentice Hall.

Carpentier, M.Y., Silovsky, J.F. and Chaffin, M. (2006) 'Randomized trial of treatment for children with sexual behaviour problems: 10-year follow-up', *Journal of Consulting and Clinical Psychology*, 74 (3): 482–488.

Carr, A. (2004) *Family Therapy: Concepts, Process and Practice*. Chichester: John Wiley & Sons.

Carroll, J. (1998) *Introduction to Therapeutic Play*. Oxford: Blackwell Science.

Carroll, J. (2002) 'Play therapy: The children's views', *Child and Family Social Work*, 7: 177–187.

Carson, D. and Becker, K. (2004) 'When lightning strikes: Re-examining creativity in psychotherapy', *Journal of Counseling and Development*, 82 (1): 111–115.

Casemore, R. (2006) *Person-Centred Counselling in a Nutshell*. London: SAGE.

Cashmore, J. and Shackel, R. (2013) 'The long-term effects of child sexual abuse', *Child Family Community Australia Information Exchange* (CFCA). Paper 11. Available at: www.aifs.gov.au/cfca/pubs/papers/a143161/cfca11.pdf.

Cassell, J. and Ryokai, K. (2001) 'Making space for voice: Technologies to support children's fantasy and storytelling', *Personal and Ubiquitous Computing*, 5 (3): 169–190.

Cassidy, J. and Shaver, P.R. (eds) (1999) *Handbook of Attachment: Theory, Research, and Clinical Applications*. New York: Guilford Press.

Castonguay, L. (2006) 'Personal pathways in psychotherapy integration', *Journal of Psychotherapy Integration*, 16 (1): 36–58.

Cattanach, A. (1997) *Children's Stories in Play Therapy*. London: Jessica Kingsley.

Cattanach, A. (2003) *Introduction to Play Therapy*. Hove: Brunner-Routledge.

Centre for Cognitive Behavioural Counselling (2014) *Child/Adolescent CBT*. Available at www.centreforcbtcounselling.co.uk/child.php (accessed 15/3/14).

Channel4News (2011) '"Poor parenting" to blame for UK riots, says exclusive poll', Channel4News. Available at www.channel4.com/news/poor-parenting-to-blame-for-uk-riots-says-exclusive-poll (accessed 24/9/14).

Chardon, L., Bagraith, K. and King, R. (2011) 'Counselling activity in single-session online counseling with adolescents: An adherence study', *Psychotherapy Research*, 21 (5): 583–592.

Charura, D. (2012) 'What's a disrupted and traumatic childhood got to do with it? Exploring therapeutic ways of working following childhood disruption with asylum seekers' concept of self and identity in adulthood'. Paper presented at the Annual Conference of the UK Oral History Society – Displaced Childhoods: Oral History and Traumatic Experiences. Solent University, Southampton, UK.

ChildLine (2013) *What's Affecting Children in 2013: Can I Tell You Something? ChildLine Review 2012–13*. Available at: https://www.nspcc/childline/can-I-tell-you-something_wda10.

Children's Legal Centre (1997) 'Offering children confidentiality: Law and guidance', *Childright*, 142: 1–8.

Choose Life (2012) *Supporting Children and Young People at Risk of Self Harm and Suicide.* Tayside Multi-Agency Guidance. Available at: www.nhstayside.scot.nhs.uk/Suicide/Suicide.pdf.

Churchill, S. (2011) *The Troubled Mind: A Handbook of Therapeutic Approaches to Psychological Distress.* Basingstoke: Palgrave Macmillan.

Ciottone, R. and Madonna, J. (1996) *Play Therapy with Sexually Abused Children: A Synergistic Clinical-Developmental Approach.* Northvale, NJ: Jason Aronson.

Clark, D.M., Fairburn, C.G. and Wessely, S. (2008) 'Psychological treatment outcomes in routine NHS services: a commentary on Stiles et al. (2007)', *Psychological Medicine,* 38 (5): 629–634.

Clarke, G., Lewinsohn, P., Hops, H. and Grossen, B. (1990) *Leader's Manual for Adolescent Groups.* Available at: www.kpchr.org/research/public/acwd/acwd.html (Adolescent coping with depression course).

Clarkson, P. (2003) *The Therapeutic Relationship.* London: Whurr Publishers.

Cleaver, H., Unell, I. and Aldgage, J. (2011) *Children's Needs – Parenting Capacity: Child Abuse: Parental Mental Illness, Learning Disability, Substance Misuse and Domestic Violence.* 2nd edn. London: The Stationary Office.

Cochran, N.H., Nordling, W.J. and Cochran, J.L. (2010) *Child-Centred Play Therapy: A Practical Guide to Developing Therapeutic Relationships with Children.* New York: John Wiley & Sons.

Cohen, J. (1988) *Statistical Power Analysis for the Behavioral Sciences.* 2nd edn. Hillsdale, NJ: Lawrence Erlbaum.

Cole, P.M., Bruschi, C.J. and Tamang, B.L. (2002) 'Cultural differences in children's emotional reactions to difficult situations', *Child Development,* 73 (3): 983–996.

Coleman, J.C. (2010) *The Nature of Adolescence.* 4th edn. London: Routledge.

Coleman, J. and Hagell, A. (eds) (2007) *Adolescence, Risk and Resilience.* Chichester: Wiley.

Collins, L. (2005) *Eating with Your Anorexic.* New York: McGraw Hill.

Committee on the Rights of the Child (2011) *General Comment No. 13: The Right of the Child to Freedom from all Forms of Violence.* Geneva: United Nations.

Connolly, P., Sibbett, C., Hanratty, J., Kerr, K., O'Hare, L. and Winter, K. (2011) *Pupils' Emotional Health and Wellbeing: A Review of Audit Tools and a Survey of Practice in Northern Ireland Post-Primary Schools.* Belfast: Centre for Effective Education, Queen's University Belfast. Available at: www.qub.ac.uk/research-centres/Centre forEffectiveEducation/Filestore/Fileutoupload,299374,en.pdf.

Connors, R.E. (2000) *Self-Injury: Psychotherapy with People Who Engage in Self-Inflicted Violence.* Northvale, NJ: Jason Aronson.

Conwell, Y. and Duberstein, P.R. (2001) 'Suicide in elders', *Annals of the New York Academy of Science,* 932: 132–147.

Cook, A., Spinazzola, J., Ford, J., et al. (2005) 'Complex trauma in children and adolescents', *Psychiatric Annals,* 355: 390–398.

Cook, J., Biyanova, T., Elhai, J., Schnurr, P. and Cones, J. (2010) 'What do psychotherapists really do in practice? An internet study of over 2000 practitioners', *Psychotherapy Theory, Research, Practice and Training*, 47 (2): 260–267.

Cooper, M. (2004) *Counselling in Schools Project: Evaluation Report*. Glasgow: University of Strathclyde.

Cooper, M. (2006) *Counselling in Schools Project – Phase 2: Evaluation Report*. Glasgow: University of Strathclyde.

Cooper, M. (2008) *The Facts Are Friendly: Essential Research Findings in Counselling and Psychotherapy*. London: SAGE.

Cooper, M. (2009a) 'Counselling in UK secondary schools: A comprehensive review of audit and evaluation studies', *Counselling and Psychotherapy Research*, 9 (3): 137–150.

Cooper, M. (2009b) *Counselling in UK Secondary Schools: A Meta-Analysis and Review of Evaluation and Audit Studies*. University of Strathclyde: Strathprints Institutional Repository. Available at: http://strathprints.strath.ac.uk/15636/1/strathprints015636.pdf.

Cooper, M. (2013) *School-Based Counselling in UK Secondary Schools: A Review and Critical Evaluation*. Available at: www.iapt.nhs.uk/silo/files/school-based-counselling-review.pdf (accessed 18/7/13).

Cooper, M. and Bohart, A.C. (2013) 'Experiential and phenomenological foundations', in M. Cooper, M. O'Hara, P.F. Schmid and A.C. Bohart (eds), *The Handbook of Person-Centred Psychotherapy and Counselling*. Basingstoke: Palgrave Macmillan.

Cooper, M. and McLeod, J. (2007) 'A pluralistic framework for counselling and psychotherapy: Implications for research', *Counselling and Psychotherapy Research*, 7 (3): 135–143.

Cooper, M. and McLeod, J. (2010) 'Pluralism: Towards a new paradigm for therapy', *Therapy Today*, 20 (9). Available at: www.therapytoday.net/article/show/2142/.

Cooper, M., McGinnis, S. and Carrick, L. (2014) 'School-based humanistic counselling for psychological distress in young people: A practice research network to address the attrition problem', *Counselling and Psychotherapy Research*, 14 (3). DOI: 10.1080/14733145.2014.929415.

Cooper, M., O'Hara, M., Schmid, P.F. and Bohart, A.C. (eds) (2013) *The Handbook of Person-Centred Psychotherapy and Counselling*. Basingstoke: Palgrave Macmillan.

Cooper, M., Rowland, N., McArthur, K., et al. (2010) 'Randomised control trials of school-based humanistic counselling for emotional distress in young people: Feasibility study and preliminary indications of efficacy', *Child and Adolescent Psychiatry and Mental Health*, 4 (12). Available at: www.capmh.com/con tent/4/1/12.

Cooper, M., Stewart, D., Bunting, L. and Sparks, J. (in press) 'Client-directed, outcome informed counselling for psychological distress in children: Outcomes and predictors of change', *Psychotherapy Research*.

Cooper, M., Stewart, D., Sparks, J.A. and Bunting, L. (2012) 'School-based counselling using systematic feedback: A cohort study evaluating outcomes and predictors of change', *Psychotherapy Research*, 23 (4): 474–488.

Corey, G. (1981) *Theory and Practice of Group Counselling*. Belmont CA: Brooks/Cole.

Corey, G. (2001) *Theory and Practice of Counselling and Psychotherapy*. 6th edn. Belmont, CA: Wadsworth.

Corsaro, W.A. (2011) *The Sociology of Childhood*. 3rd edn. London: SAGE.

Counselling MindEd (2013) Counselling MindEd website. Available at: http://counsellingminded.com/.

Cowie, H. and Wallace, P. (2000) *Peer Support in Action*. London: SAGE.

Coyle, D., Matthews, M., Sharry, J., Nisbet, A. and Doherty, G. (2005) 'Personal Investigator: A therapeutic 3D game for adolescent psychotherapy', *International Journal of Interactive Technology and Smart Education*, 2: 73–88.

Crawford, M.J. and Patterson, S. (2007) 'Arts therapies for people with schizophrenia: An emerging evidence base', *Evidence Based Mental Health*, 10: 69–70.

Crespi, B.J. (2011) 'The strategies of the genes: Genomic conflicts, attachment theory, and development of the social', in A. Petronis and J. Mill (eds), *Brain, Behavior and Epigenetics*. Berlin: Springer. pp. 143–167.

Cromarty, K. and Richards, K. (2009) 'How do secondary school counsellors work with other professionals?', *Counselling and Psychotherapy Research*, 9 (3): 182–186.

Crow, S.J., Peterson, C.B., Swanson, S.A., et al. (2010) 'Increased mortality in bulimia nervosa and other eating disorders', *American Journal of Psychiatry*, 166 (12): 1342–1346.

Crowley, P., Kilroe, J. and Burke, S. (2004) *Youth Suicide Prevention*. Dublin: Institute of Public Health in Ireland and NHS Health Development Agency.

Crown Prosecution Service (2001) *Provision of Therapy for Child Witnesses Prior to a Criminal Trial*. London: HMSO.

Crown Prosecution Service (2013) *Interim Guidelines on Prosecuting Cases of Child Sexual Abuse*. Available at: www.cps.gov.uk/consultations/csa_consultation.html.

Currin, L., Schmidt, U., Tresure, J. and Jick, H. (2005) 'Time trends in eating disorder incidence', *The British Journal of Psychiatry*, 186 (2): 132–135.

Curry, N.A. and Kasser, T. (2005) 'Can coloring mandalas reduce anxiety?', *Art Therapy*, 22: 81–85.

CYP PRN (Children and Young People Practice Research Network) (2013) *A Toolkit for Collecting Routine Outcome Measures*. Lutterworth: BACP.

Danger, S. and Landreth, G. (2005) 'Child-centred group play therapy with children with speech difficulties', *International Journal of Play Therapy*, 14 (1): 81–102.

Daniel, S.S. and Goldston, D.B. (2009) 'Interventions for suicidal youth: A review of the literature and developmental considerations', *Suicide and Life-Threatening Behavior*, 39 (3): 252–268.

Daniel, T. and McLeod, J. (2006) 'Weighing up the evidence: A qualitative analysis of how person-centred counsellors evaluate the effectiveness of their practice', *Counselling and Psychotherapy Research*, 6 (4): 244–249.

Daniels, D. and Jenkins, P. (2010) *Therapy with Children: Children's Rights, Confidentiality and the Law*. 2nd edn. London: SAGE.

Daniunaite, A., Ali, Z.A. and Cooper, M. (2012) 'Psychological change in distressed young people who do not receive counselling: Does improvement happen anyway?', *British Journal of Guidance and Counselling*, 40 (5): 515–525.

Dare, C. and Eisler, I. (1997) 'Family therapy for anorexia nervosa', in D.M. Garner and P.E. Garfinkel (eds), *Handbook of Treatment for Eating Disorders*. New York: The Guilford Press. pp. 307–324.

Dasen, P. and Mishra, R. C. (2000) 'Cross-cultural views on human development in the third millennium', *International Journal of Behavioral Development*, 24 (4): 428–434.

Dautenhahn, K. and Werry, I. (2004) 'Towards interactive robots in autism therapy: Background, motivation and challenges', *Pragmatics and Cognition*, 12 (1): 1–35.

Davenport, B. and Bourgeois, N. (2008) 'Play, aggression, the preschool child, and the family: A review of literature to guide empirically informed play therapy with aggressive preschool children', *International Journal of Play Therapy*, 17 (1): 2–23.

David, D.H., Gelberg, L. and Suchman, N.E. (2012) 'Implications of homelessness for parenting young children: A preliminary review from a developmental attachment perspective', *Infant Mental Health Journal*, 33 (1): 1–9.

Davids, F. (2011) *Internal Racism: A Psychoanalytic Approach to Race and Difference*. London: Palgrave Macmillan.

Davidson, G., Devaney, J. and Spratt, T (2010) 'The impact of adversity in childhood on outcomes in adulthood: Research lessons and limitations', *Journal of Social Work*, 10: 369–390.

Day, C., Carey, M. and Surgenor, T. (2006) 'Children's key concerns: Piloting a qualitative approach to understanding their experience of mental health care', *Clinical Child Psychology and Psychiatry*, 11 (1): 139–155.

Dearden, C. (1998) *The children's counselling service at Family Care: An evaluation*. Available at: www.lboro.ac.uk/research/ccfr.

Deblinger, E., Mannarino, A.P., Cohen, J.A. and Steer, R.A. (2006) 'Follow-up study of a multisite, randomised controlled trial for children with sexual abuse-related PTSD: Examining predictors of treatment response', *Journal of the American Academy of Child and Adolescent Psychiatry*, 45: 1474–1484.

Deci, E.L. and Ryan, R.M. (2000) 'The "what" and "why" of goal pursuits: Human needs and the self-determination of behavior', *Psychological Inquiry*, 11 (4): 227.

Deighton, J. and Wolpert, M. (2009) *Mental Health Outcome Measures for Children and Young People*, CAMHS Evidence-Based Practice Unit. Available at: www.corc.uk.net/resources/downloads/.

DeMille, R. (1997) *Put Your Mother on the Ceiling: Children's Imagination Games.* Cambridge, MA: The Gestalt Press.

DesLauriers, A.M. and Carlson, C.F. (1969) *Your Child Is Asleep: Early Infantile Autism.* Homewood, IL: Dorsey Press.

Devaney, J., Bunting, L., Davidson, G., Hayes, D., Lazenbatt, A. and Spratt, T. (2012) *Still Vulnerable: The Impact of Early Childhood Experiences on Adolescent Suicide and Accidental Death.* Belfast: NICCY.

DfE (Department for Education) (2011) *Me and My School: Findings from the National Evaluation of Targeted Mental Health in Schools 2008–2011.* Research Report DFE-RR177. London: Department for Education. Available at: https://www.gov.uk/government/uploads/system/uploads/attachment_data/file/184060/DFE-RR177.pdf.

DfE (Department for Education) (2013) *Working Together to Safeguard Children: A Guide to Inter-Agency Working to Safeguard and Promote the Welfare of Children.* London: Stationery Office.

DfE (Department for Education)/DoH (Department of Health) (2004) *Child and Adolescent Mental Health Services (CAMHS) Standard: National Service Framework for Children, Young People and Maternity Services.* London: DfE/DoH.

DfES (Department for Education and Skills) (2003) *The Children's Green Paper: Every Child Matters.* London: Stationery Office.

DfES (Department for Education and Skills) (2004a) *The Children Act.* London: Stationery Office.

DfES (Department for Education and Skills) (2004b) *Gender and Achievement Standards.* London: Stationery Office.

DfES (2008) www.standards.dfes.gov.uk/genderandachievement/goodpractice/generaladvice (accessed 26/9/08).

DH/Knowledge – Evidence and Analysis/Public Health (2012) *Statistical Update on Suicide.* London: Department of Health. Available at www.gov.uk/government/uploads/system/uploads/attachment_data/file/216931/Statistical-update-on-suicide.pdf (accessed 24/9/14).

Dighton, R. (2001) 'Towards a definition of play therapy: Part 1', *Play therapy: British Association of Play Therapists Newsletter,* 28: 8–11.

DoH (Department of Health) (2005) Research Governance Framework for Health and Social Care. Second edition. DoH: London.

DoH (Department of Health) (2008a) *Mental Health Act 1983 Code of Practice.* London: DoH.

DoH (Department of Health) (2008b) *Improving Access to Psychological Therapies Implementation Plan: National Guidelines for Regional Delivery.* Available at: www.dh.gov.uk/en/Publicationsandstatistics/Publications/PublicationsPolicyAndGuidance/DH_083150.

DoH (Department of Health) (2011) *Talking Therapies: A Four-Year Plan of Action.* London: DoH.

DoH (Department of Health) (2012) *Knowledge – Evidence and Analysis: Statistical Update on Suicide*. September. Available at: https://www.gov.uk/government/uploads/system/uploads/attachment_data/file/216931/Statistical-update-on-suicide.pdf.

DoH, HO, DfEE (Department of Health, Home Office, Department for Education) (1999) *Working Together to Safeguard Children*. London: Stationery Office.

Donaldson, M. (1978) *Children's Minds*. London: Fontana/Croom Helm.

Donelly, C. (2003) 'Pharmacologic treatment approaches for children and adolescents with postraumatic stress disorder', *Child and Adolescent Psychiatric Clinics*, 12: 251–269.

Döring, E. (2008) 'What happens in child-centred play therapy', in M. Behr and J.H.D. Cornelius-Whilte (eds), *Facilitating Young People's Development: International Perspectives on Person-Centred Theory and Practice*. Ross-on-Wye: PCCS Books.

Dowling, E. and Osborne, E. (2003) *The Family and the School: A Joint Systems Approach to Problems with Children*. London: Routledge.

Doyle, C. (2012) *Working with Abused Children*. 4th edn. Basingstoke: Palgrave Macmillan.

Drell, M.J., Siegel, C.H. and Gaensbauer, T.J. (1993) 'Post-traumatic stress disorder', in C.H. Zeanah (ed.), *Handbook of Infant Mental Health*. New York: Guilford Press. pp. 291–304.

Dryden, W. (1989) 'The therapeutic alliance as an integrating framework', in W. Dryden (ed.), *Key Issues for Counselling in Action*. London: SAGE.

Duncan, B.L. and Miller, S.D. (2008) *The Outcome and Session Rating Scales: The Revised Administration and Scoring Manual, including the Child Outcome Rating Scale*. Chicago: Institute for the Study of Therapeutic Change.

Duncan, B. and Sparks, J. (2010) *Heroic Clients, Heroic Agencies: Partners for Change*. 2nd edn. Jensen Beach, FL: Author.

Duncan, B., Miller, S. and Sparks, J. (2003) *Child Outcome Rating Scale*. Jensen Beach, FL: Author.

Duncan, B., Miller, S.D. and Sparks, J.A. (2006) *Child Session Rating Scale*. Jensen Beach, FL: Author.

Dunn, J. (2004) *Children's Friendships: The Beginnings of Intimacy*. Oxford: Wiley-Blackwell.

Dunnett, A., Cooper, M. and Wheeler, S. (2007) *A Core Curriculum for Counselling and Psychotherapy*. Lutterworth: BACP.

Durrant, M. and White, C. (1992) *Ideas for Therapy with Sexual Abuse*. Adelaide: Dulwich Centre Publications.

Eddy, K.T., Doyle, A.C., Hoste, R.R., Herzog, D.B. and Le Grange, D. (2008) 'Eating disorder not otherwise specified in adolescents', *Journal of the American Academy of Child and Adolescent Psychiatry*, 47 (2): 156–164.

Edwards, A., Daniels, H., Gallagher, T., Leadbetter, J. and Warmington, P. (2009) *Improving Inter-professional Collaborations: Multi-agency Working for Children's Wellbeing*. Abingdon: Routledge.

Egan, G. (1998) *The Skilled Helper: A Problem Management and Opportunity-Development Approach to Helping.* Pacific Grove, CA: Brooks Cole.

Elliott, R. (1999) 'Client change interview protocol', *Network for Research on Experiential Psychotherapies.* Available at: http://experiential-researchers.org/instruments/elliott/changei.html.

Ellis, A. (1994) *Reason and Emotion in Psychotherapy: Comprehensive Method of Treating Human Disturbances: Revised and Updated.* New York: Citadel Press.

Elsbree, C. (2009) 'Interview with Violet Oaklander', *International Gestalt Journal*, 32 (2): 183–213.

Emunah, R. (1994) *Acting for Real: Drama Therapy Process, Technique, and Performance.* London: Brunner-Routledge.

Erikson, E.H. (1965) *Childhood and Society.* Harmondsworth: Penguin.

Esbjørn, B., Bender, P., Reinholdt-Dunne, M., Munck, L. and Ollendick, T. (2012) 'The development of anxiety disorders: Considering the contributions of attachment and emotion regulation', *Clinical Child and Family Psychology Review*, 15 (2): 129–143.

Eubanks, C., Muran, J.C. and Safran, J.D (2010) 'Alliance ruptures and resolution', in J.C. Muran and J.P. Barber (eds) *The Therapeutic Alliance: An Evidence-Based Guide to Practice.* New York: The Guilford Press.

Evans, W. (2009) 'Telling a new story: Helping children to heal from homelessness', *The Homeless Hub Newsletter.* Available at www.homelesshub.ca/resource/telling-new-story-helping-children-heal-homelessness

Everall, R. and Paulson, B. (2002) 'The therapeutic alliance: Adolescent perspectives', *Counselling and Psychotherapy Research*, 2 (2): 78–87.

Ewert, A. (1989) *Outdoor Adventure Pursuits: Foundations, Models and Theories.* Tucson, AZ: Publishing Horizons Inc.

Facing the Future Report (2000) *Mental Health of Children and Adolescents in Great Britain.* Available at www.theplace2be.org.uk/media/uploads/page_contents/downloadables/P2B_impact_report_smSept.pdf

Fahlberg, V. (1991) *A Child's Journey through Placement.* Indianapolis: Perspective Press.

Family Futures (2014) *Comprehensive Multi-disciplinary Child Assessment.* Available at www.familyfutures.co.uk/child-assessment (accessed 15/3/14).

Favazza, A.R. (1989) 'Why patients mutilate themselves', *Hospital and Community Psychiatry*, 40 (2): 137–145.

Fearon, R.P., Bakermans-Kranenburg, M.J., Van Ijzendoorn, M.H., Lapsley, A.-M. and Roisman, G.I. (2010) 'The significance of insecure attachment and disorganization in the development of children's externalizing behavior: A meta-analytic study', *Child Development*, 81 (2): 435–456.

Feller, C.P. and Cottone, R.R. (2003) 'The importance of empathy in the therapeutic alliance', *Journal of Humanistic Counselling, Education and Development*, 42 (1): 53–61.

Feltham, C. (1997) *Time-Limited Counselling.* London: SAGE.

Feltham, C. and Horton, I. (2000) *The SAGE Handbook of Counselling and Psychotherapy.* London: SAGE.

Fernaeus, Y., Håkansson, M., Jacobsson, M. and Ljungblad, S. (2010) 'How do you play with a robotic toy animal?', in Narcís Parés (ed.), *IDC'10 Proceedings of the 9th International Conference on Interaction Design and Children.* New York: ACM. pp. 39–48.

Figley, C. (ed.) (2002) *Treating Compassion Fatigue.* New York: Brunner-Routledge.

Finkelhor, D. (1984) *Child Sexual Abuse: New Theory and Research.* New York: The Free Press.

Finkenauer, C., Engels, R. and Meus, W. (2002) 'Keeping secrets from parents: Advantages and disadvantages of secrecy in adolescence', *Journal of Youth and Adolescence*, 31 (2): 123–136.

Fitzpatrick, K.K., Moye, A., Hoste, R., Lock, J. and Le Grange, D. (2010) 'Adolescent focused psychotherapy for adolescents with anorexia nervosa', *Journal of Contemporary Psychotherapy*, 40 (1): 31–39.

Fonagy, P. and Target, M. (2002) 'Early intervention and the development of self-regulation', *Psychoanalytic Inquiry*, 22 (3): 307–335.

Fonagy, P., Target, M., Cottrell, D., Phillips, J. and Kurtz, Z. (2002) *What Works for Whom?: A Critical Review of Treatments for Children and Adolescents.* New York: The Guilford Press.

Forbes, T., Sibbett, C., Miller, S. and Emerson, L. (2012) *Exploring a Community Response to Multiple Deaths of Young People by Suicide. Report.* Belfast: Centre for Effective Education, Queen's University Belfast.

Formica, M.J. (2009) *Enlightened living: Mindfulness practice in everyday life.* Available at: www.psychologytoday.com/blog/enlightened-living.

Fraley, R.C. and Shaver, P.R. (1999) 'Loss and bereavement: Attachment theory and recent controversies concerning "grief work" and the nature of detachment', in J. Cassidy and P.R. Shaver (eds), *Handbook of Attachment: Theory, Research, and Clinical Applications.* New York: Guilford Press. pp. 735–759.

Fraser, S., Lewis, V., Ding, S., Kellett, M. and Robinson, C. (eds) (2004) *Doing Research with Children and Young People.* London: SAGE.

Freedman, J. and Combs, G. (1996) *Narrative Therapy.* New York: Norton.

Freeman, H., Epston, D. and Lobovits, D. (1997) *Playful Solutions to Serious Problems.* New York: W.W. Norton & Co.

Freeman, A., Pretzer, J., Fleming, B. and Simon, K. (2004) *Clinical Applications of Cognitive Therapy.* 2nd edn. New York: Plenum Publishers.

Freire, E.S. (2013) 'Empathy', in M. Cooper., M. O'Hara., P.F. Schmid and A.C. Bohart (eds), *The Handbook of Person-Centred Psychotherapy and Counselling.* Basingstoke: Palgrave Macmillan.

French, L. and Klein, R. (2012) *Therapeutic Practice in Schools.* London: Routledge.

Freud, A. (1928) *Introduction to the Technique of Child Analysis,* trans. L.P. Clark. New York: Nervous and Mental Disease Publishing.

Freud, A. (1946) *The Psycho-Analytical Treatment of Children*. Oxford: Imago Publishing Co.

Freud, A. (1965) 'Normality and pathology in childhood: Assessments of development', in *The Writings of Anna Freud, Vol. 6*. New York: International University Press.

Freud, A. (1974 [1927]) *Introduction to Psychoanalysis*. London: Hogarth.

Freud, S. (1953 [1900]) 'The interpretation of dreams', *Standard Edition*, 4–5. London: Hogarth Press.

Freud, S. (1953 [1905]) 'Three essays on the theory of sexuality', *Standard Edition*, 7: 136–234. London: Hogarth Press.

Freud, S. (1953 [1909]) 'Analysis of a phobia in a five-year-old boy', *Standard Edition*, 10: 1–147. London: Hogarth Press

Friedberg, R.D. and McClure, J.M. (2002) *Clinical Practice of Cognitive Therapy with Children and Adolescents*. New York: Guilford Press.

Friedberg, R.D, McClure, J.M. and Hillwig Garcia, J. (2009) *Cognitive Therapy Techniques for Children and Adolescents*. New York: Guilford Press

Friedlander, S. (1918) *Schöpferische Indifferenz*. Munich: Georg Müller.

Galbally, M., Lewis, A.J., Von Ijzendoorn, M. and Permezel, M. (2011) 'The role of oxytocin in mother–infant relations: A systematic review of human studies', *Harvard Review of Psychiatry*, 19 (1): 1–14.

Gardener, H. (1983) *Frames of Mind: The Theory of Multiple Intelligences*. New York: Basic Books.

Gass, M. (1993) *Adventure Therapy: Therapeutic Applications of Adventure Programming*. Dubuque, IA: Kendall/Hunt.

Gass, M. and McPhee, P.J. (1990) 'Emerging for recovery: A descriptive analysis of adventure therapy for substance abusers', *Journal of Experiential Education*, 13 (2): 29–35

Gass, M.A., Gillis, H.L. and Russell, K.C. (eds) (2012) *Adventure Therapy: Theory, Research and Practice*. London: Routledge.

Gaston, L., Goldfried, M.R., Greenberg, L.S., et al. (1995) 'The therapeutic alliance in psychodynamic, cognitive-behavioural and experiential therapies', *Journal of Psychotherapy Integration*, 5 (1): 1–26.

Gaudiani, J.L., Sabel, A.L., Mascolo, M. and Mehler, P.S. (2012) 'Severe anorexia nervosa: Outcomes from a medical stabilization unit', *International Journal of Eating Disorders*, 45 (1): 85–92.

Geddes, H. (2005) *Attachment in the Classroom*. London: Worth Publishing.

Geidd, J.N. (2008) 'The teen brain: Insights from neuroimaging', *Journal of Adolescent Health*, 42 (4): 335–343.

Geldard, K. and Geldard, D. (2002) *Counselling Children: A Practical Introduction*. 2nd edn. London: SAGE.

Geldard, K. and Geldard, D. (2009) *Relationship Counselling for Children, Young People and Families*. London: SAGE.

Geldard, K. and Geldard, D. (2010) *Counselling Adolescents: The Proactive Approach for Young People*. 3rd edn. London: SAGE.

Geldard, K., Geldard, D. and Yin Foo, R. (2013) *Counselling Children: A Practical Introduction*. 4th edn. London: SAGE.

Gerhardt, S. (2004) *Why Love Matters: How Affection Shapes a Baby's Brain*. London. Routledge.

Gersie, A. (1991) *Story Making in Bereavement: Dragons Fight in the Meadow*. London: Jessica Kingsley.

Gibbs, I. (2009) 'Race, culture and the therapeutic process', in M. Lanyado and A. Horne (eds), *The Handbook of Child and Adolescent Psychotherapy. Psychoanalytic Approaches*. 2nd edn. London: Routledge.

Gilliam, N.G. (1990) *A qualitative study of ropes courses in psychiatric treatment facilities*. PhD dissertation, The Union Institute, Cincinnati, OH.

Gillick v. West Norfolk AHA [1985] 3 All ER 402; [1986] AC 112.

Gillman, M., Swain, J. and Heyman, B.O.B. (1997) 'Life history or "case" history: The objectification of people with learning difficulties through the tyranny of professional discourses', *Disability & Society*, 12 (5): 675–694.

Gillon, E. (2007) *Person-Centred Counselling Psychology: An Introduction*. London: SAGE.

Gillon, E. (2013) 'Assessment and formulation', in M. Cooper, M. O'Hara, P. Schmid and A. Bohart (eds), *The Handbook of Person-Centred Psychotherapy and Counselling*. London: Sage. pp. 410–421.

Gilmore, S. (1980) 'A comprehensive theory for eclectic intervention', *International Journal for Advanced Counselling*, 3: 185–210

Giusti, L., Zancanaro, M., Gal, E. and Weiss, P. (2011) 'Dimensions of collaboration on a tabletop interface for children with autism spectrum disorder', in *Proceedings CHI*. ACM Press'11. pp. 3295–3304.

Glickman, N.S. (2013) *Culturally Affirmative Psychotherapy with Deaf Persons*. New York: Routledge.

Golden, N.H., Jacobson, M.S., Sterling, W.M. and Hertz, S. (2008) 'Treatment goal weight in adolescents with anorexia nervosa: Use of BMI percentiles', *International Journal of Eating Disorders*, 41 (4): 301–306.

Goldfinch, M. (2009) '"Putting humpty together again": Working with parents to help children who have experienced early trauma', *The Australian and New Zealand Journal of Family Therapy*, 30 (4): 284–299.

Golding, K. (2008) *Nurturing Attachments: Supporting Children Who Are Fostered or Adopted*. London: Jessica Kingsley.

Goldman, J. and Padayachi, U. (2005) 'Child sexual abuse reporting behaviour by school counselors and their need for further education', *Health Education Journal*, 64 (4): 302–322.

Goldston, D.B., Molock, S.D., Whitbeck, L.B., Murakami, J.L., Zayas, L.H. and Hall, G.C. (2008) 'Cultural considerations in adolescent suicide prevention and psychosocial treatment', *American Psychologist*, 63 (1): 14–31.

Göncü, A., Abel, B. and Boshans, M. (2012) 'The role of attachment and play in young children's learning and development', in K. Littleton, C. Wood and J.K. Staarman (eds), *International Handbook of Psychology in Education*. Bingley: Emerald House. pp. 35–72.

Goodenough, F. (1926) *Measurement of Intelligence by Drawings*. New York: Harcourt, Brace and World.

Goodman, P. (1951) 'Part two: Manipulating the self', in F. Perls, R. Hefferline and P. Goodman, *Gestalt Therapy: Excitement and Growth in the Human Personality*. New York: Delta.

Goodman, R. (2001) 'Psychometric properties of the strengths and difficulties questionnaire', *Journal of the American Academy of Child and Adolescent Psychiatry*, 40 (11): 1337–1345. Available at: www.psychologytoday.com/blog/enlightened-living/200901/the-me-in-you-parallel-process-in-psychotherapy.

Goodman, R.F. and Brown, E.J. (2008) 'Service and science in times of crisis: Developing, planning, and implementing a clinical research program for children traumatically bereaved after 9/11', *Death Studies*, 32 (2): 154–180.

Goodyer, I., Dubicka, B., Wilkinson, P., et al. (2007) 'Selective serotonin reuptake inhibitors (SSRIs) and routine specialist care with and without cognitive behaviour therapy in adolescents with major depression: randomised controlled trial', *British Medical Journal*, 335 (7611): 141.

Goswami, U. (2004) 'Neuroscience and education', *British Journal of Educational Psychology*, 74 (1): 1–14.

Gowers, S.G., Clark, A., Roberts, C., et al. (2007) 'Clinical effectiveness of treatments for anorexia nervosa in adolescents: Randomised controlled trial', *The British Journal of Psychiatry*, 191 (5): 427–435.

Graham, P. (2005) 'Jack Tizard lecture: Cognitive behavior therapies for children: passing fashion or here to stay?', *Child and Adolescent Mental Health*, 10 (2): 57–62.

Graham-Bermann, S.A. and Levendosky, A.A. (1998) 'Traumatic stress symptoms in children of battered women', *Journal of Interpersonal Violence*, 13 (1): 111–128.

Gratier, M. and Trevarthen, C. (2007) 'Voice, vitality and meaning: On the shaping of the infant's utterances in willing engagement with culture', *International Journal for Dialogical Science*, 2 (1): 169–181.

Green, E.J. and Christensen T.M. (2006) 'Elementary school children's perceptions of play therapy in school settings', *International Journal of Play Therapy*, 15 (1): 65–85.

Green, V. (ed.) (2003) *Emotional Development in Psychoanalysis, Attachment Theory and Neuroscience*. London: Routledge.

Greenberg, L.S. (2008) 'Quantitative research', in P. Brownell (ed.), *Handbook for Theory, Research, and Practice in Gestalt Therapy*. Newcastle: Cambridge Scholars Publishing. pp. 64–89.

Greenson, R. (1967) *The Techniques and Practice of Psychoanalysis, Vol. 1.* New York: International Universities Press.

Grehan, P. and Freeman, A. (2009) 'Neither child nor adult: applying integrative therapy to adolescents', *Journal of Psychotherapy Integration*, 19 (3): 269–290.

Greig, A., Taylor, J. and Mackay, T. (2007) *Doing Research with Children.* 2nd edn. London: SAGE.

Griffiths, G. (2013) *Helpful and Unhelpful Factors in School Based Counselling: Client's Perspective.* Counselling MindEd Scoping Report. Available at: http://counselling minded.com/wp-content/uploads/2013/12/griffiths_MindEd_report.pdf.

Guest, G., MacQueen, K.M. and Namey, E.E. (2012) *Applied Thematic Analysis.* London: SAGE.

Habermas, T. (1989) 'The psychiatric history of anorexia nervosa and bulimia nervosa: Weight concerns and bulimic symptoms in early case reports', *International Journal of Eating Disorders*, 8 (3): 259–273.

Hadley, S. and Yancy, G. (eds) (2012) *Therapeutic Uses of Rap and Hip Hop.* New York: Routledge.

Hagell, A. (2013) Adolescent self-harm. *AYPH Research Summary* 13 (March). Association for Young People's Health. Available at: www.ayph.org.uk/publica tions/316_RU13%20Self-harm%20summary.pdf.

Halse, C. and Honey, A. (2005) 'Unraveling ethics: Illuminating the moral dilemmas of research ethics', *Signs: Journal of Women in Culture and Society*, 30 (4): 2141–2162.

Hanley, T. (2006) 'Developing youth-friendly online counselling services in the United Kingdom: A small scale investigation into the views of practitioners', *Counselling and Psychotherapy Research*, 6 (3): 182–185.

Hanley, T. (2008) 'A five-year evaluation of the effectiveness of person-centred counselling in routine clinical practice in primary care', *Counselling and Psychotherapy Research*, 8 (4): 215–222.

Hanley, T. (2011) 'Understanding the Online Therapeutic Alliance through the eyes of adolescent service users', *Counselling and Psychotherapy Research*, 12 (1): 35–43.

Hanley, T. and Reynolds, D. Jr. (2009) 'Counselling psychology and the internet: A review of the quantitative research into online outcomes and alliances within text-based therapy', *Counselling Psychology Review*, 24 (2): 4–13.

Hanley, T., Jenkins, P., Barlow, A., Humphrey, N. and Wigelsworth, M. (2012) *A Scoping Review of the Access to Secondary School Counselling.* Manchester: School of Education, University of Manchester.

Hanley, T., Sefi, A. and Lennie, C. (2011) 'Practice-based evidence in school-based counselling', *Counselling and Psychotherapy Research*, 11(4): 300–309.

Hanley, T., Cutts, L., Gordon, R. and Scott, A. (2013) 'Research informed therapy', in G. Davey (ed.), *Applied Psychology.* London: BPS Wiley-Blackwell.

Hardiker, P., Exton, K. and Barker, M. (1991) 'The social policy contexts of prevention in child care', *British Journal of Social Work*, 21 (4): 341–359.

Harker, R. (2012) *Children in Care in England: Statistics*. London: House of Commons Library. Available at: http://www.parliament.uk/business/publications/research/briefing-papers/SN04470/children-in-care-in-england-statistics.

Harper, N.J. (2009) 'The relationship of therapeutic alliance to outcome in wilderness treatment', *Journal of Adventure Education and Outdoor Learning*, 9: 45–59.

Harrington, R. and Bailey, S. (2005) *Mental Health Needs and Effectiveness of Provision for Young Offenders in Custody in the Community*. London: Youth Justice Board for England and Wales.

Harris, B. and Pattison, S. (2004) *Research on Children and Young People: A Systematic Review*. Rugby: BACP.

Harris, N. (2011) 'Something in the air: Conditions that promote contact when meeting young people who have stories of early trauma and loss', *British Gestalt Journal*, 20 (1): 21–28.

Harrison, A. (2009) 'Setting up the doll house: A developmental perspective on termination', *Psychoanalytic Inquiry*, 29: 174–187.

Hatch, A., Higgins, S. and Mercier, E. (2009) 'SynergyNet: Supporting Collaborative Learning in an Immersive Environment'. STELLAR Alpine Rendez-Vous Workshop 'Tabletops for Education and Training'. pp. 1–2.

Hawkins, S. (2008) 'Working at relational depth with adolescents in school: A person-centred psychologist's perspective', in S. Keys and T. Walshaw (eds), *Person-Centred Work with Children and Young People: UK Practitioner Perspectives*. Ross-on-Wye: PCCS Books.

Hawton, K.K.E., Townsend, E., Arensman, E., Gunnell, D., Hazell, P., House, A. and van Heeringen, K. (1999) 'Psychosocial and pharmacological treatments for deliberate self-harm', *Cochrane Database of Systematic Reviews*, 3, Art. No.: CD001764.

Hawton, K., Saunders, K.E.A. and O'Connor, R.C. (2012a) 'Self-harm and suicide in adolescents', *The Lancet*, 379: 2373–2382

Hawton, K., Bergen, H., Waters, K., Ness, J., Cooper, J., Steeg, S. and Kapur, N. (2012b) 'Epidemiology and the nature of self-harm in children and adolescents: Findings from the multicentre study of self-harm in England', *European Child & Adolescent Psychiatry*, 21 (7): 369–377.

HCPC (Health and Care Professions Council) (2008) *Standards of Conduct, Performance and Ethics*. London: HPC.

HCPC (Health and Care Professions Council) (2010) *Standards of Conduct, Performance and Ethics*. London: HPC.

Healthy Lives, Brighter Futures Report (2009) *The Child Health Strategy*. Available at www.ncb.org.uk/media/42243/healthy_lives__brighter_futures_vcs_brief.pdf

Hedges, D. (2005) *Poetry Therapy and Emotional Life*. London: Radcliffe.

Heimann, P. (1950) 'On counter-transference', *International Journal of Psycho-Analysis*, 31: 81–84.

Herpertz-Dahlmann, B. (2009) 'Adolescent eating disorders: Definitions, symptomatology, epidemiology and comorbidity', *Child and Adolescent Psychiatric Clinics of North America*, 18 (1): 31–47.

Herpertz-Dahlmann, B., Seitz, J. and Konrad, K. (2011) 'Aetiology of anorexia nervosa: From a "psychosomatic family model" to a neuropsychiatric disorder?', *European Archives of Psychiatry and Clinical Neuroscience*, 261 (Suppl. 2): S177–S181.

Hickmon, W.A.J. (1993) *Analysis of an adventure-based marriage enrichment program.* PhD dissertation, Virginia Polytechnic Institute and State University, Blacksburg.

Hill, A., Cooper, M., Pybis, J., Cromarty, K., Pattison, S., Spong, S., Dowd, C., Leahy, C., Couchman, A., Rogers, J., Smith, K. and Maybanks, V. (2011) *Evaluation of the Welsh School-based Counselling Strategy: Final Report.* Wales: Welsh Government Social Research. Available at: http://wales.gov.uk/docs/caecd/research/111118EvalWelshSchoolCounsellingStrategyExecSummaryen.pdf.

Himebauch, A., Arnold, R.M. and May, C. (2008) 'Grief in children and developmental concepts of death', *Journal of Palliative Medicine*, 11 (2): 242–243.

HM Government (2006) *Reaching Out: An Action Plan on Social Exclusion.* London: Cabinet Office.

HMG/DH (2012) *Preventing Suicide in England: A Cross-Government Outcomes Strategy to Save Lives.* London: Department of Health. Available at: https://www.gov.uk/government/uploads/system/uploads/attachment_data/file/216928/Preventing-Suicide-in-England-A-cross-government-outcomes-strategy-to-save-lives.pdf.

HMSO (1989) *The Children Act 1989.* London: HMSO. Available at: www.legislation.gov.uk/ukpga/1989/41/contents.

HMSO (1995) *Together We Stand: Commissioning, Role and Management of Child and Adolescent Services.* London. HMSO.

HMSO (2002) *Adoption and Children Act 2002.* London: HMSO.

Hoek, H.W. and Van Hoeken, D. (2003) 'Review of the prevalence and incidence of eating disorders', *International Journal of Eating Disorders*, 34 (4): 383–396.

Hogan, D. (2005) 'Researching "the child" in developmental psychology', in D. Hogan and S. Greene (eds), *Researching Children's Experience: Approaches and Methods.* London: SAGE. pp. 22–41.

Hollanders, H. (1999) 'Eclecticism and integration in counselling: Implications for training', *British Journal of Guidance and Counselling*, 27 (4): 483–500.

Hollanders, H. and McLeod, J. (1999) 'Theoretical orientation and reported practice: A survey of eclecticism among counsellors in Britain', *British Journal of Guidance and Counselling*, 27 (3): 405–414.

Holmes, J. (1999) 'The relationship in psychodynamic counselling', in C. Feltham (ed.), *Understanding the Counselling Relationship.* London: SAGE.

Holmes, J. (2010) *Exploring in Security.* London: Routledge.

Holm-Hadulla, R., Hofmann, F. and Sperth, M. (2011) 'An integrative model of counselling', *Asia Pacific Journal of Counselling and Psychotherapy*, 2 (1): 3–24.

Hopkins, D. and Putnam, R. (1993) *Personal Growth through Adventure*. London: David Fulton Publishers.

Horne, A. (1999) 'Normal child development', in M. Lanyado and A. Horne (eds), *The Handbook of Child and Adolescent Psychotherapy*. London: Routledge.

Horne, A. and Lanyado, M. (eds) (2012) *Winnicott's Children: Independent Psychoanalytic Approaches with Children and Adolescents*. London: Routledge.

Horton, I. (2000) 'Structuring work with clients', in C. Feltham and I. Horton, *The SAGE Handbook of Counselling and Psychotherapy*. London: SAGE.

Horvath, A.O. and Luborsky, L. (1993) 'The role of the therapeutic alliance in psychotherapy', *Journal of Consulting and Clinical Psychology*, 61 (4): 561–573.

Horvath, A.O. and Symonds, B.D. (1991) 'Relation between working alliance with outcome in psychotherapy: A meta-analysis', *Journal of Counselling Psychology*, 38: 139–149.

Houston, G. (1995) *Supervision and Counselling*. London: The Rochester Foundation.

Houston, G. (2003) *Brief Gestalt Therapy*. London: SAGE.

Howe, D (2005) *Child Abuse and Neglect: Attachment, Development and Intervention*. Basingstoke: Palgrave Macmillan.

Hoyano, L. and Keenan, C. (2007) *Child Abuse: Law and Policy across Boundaries*. Oxford: Oxford University Press.

Hug-Hellmuth, H. (1921) 'On the technique of child-analysis', *International Journal of Psychoanalysis*, 2: 287–305.

Hughes, D. (2006) *Building the Bonds of Attachment: Awakening Love in Deeply Troubled Children*. 2nd edn. New York: Jason Aronson Inc.

Hughes, J. (1993) *The effects of adventure-based counselling on sensation seeking and the self-efficacy of chemical dependant males*. PhD dissertation, Mississippi State University, Mississippi.

Hunt, K. (2004) *An exploration of the experience of loss and its relationship to counselling practice*. PhD dissertation, University of Durham, UK.

Hurry, A. (1998) *Psychoanalysis and Developmental Therapy*. London: Karnac.

IAPT (Improving Access to Psychological Therapies) (2012) *Children and Young People's Project: Key Facts Briefing*. Available at: www.iapt.nhs.uk/silo/files/cyp-iapt-key-facts-briefing-29-feb-2012.pdf.

ICO (Information Commissioner's Office) (2009) *Guide to Data Protection*. Wilmslow: ICO.

Ina-Egbe, E. (2010) 'Developing a positive racial identity – challenges for psychotherapists working with black and mixed race adopted adults', *The Psychotherapist*, 44: 10–12.

Inskipp, F. and Proctor, B. (2003) BACP supervisors' workshop: Ethical Framework for Good Practice in Counselling and Psychotherapy (editor F. Shall). Apollo Print Management.

Itin, C.M. (1998) Exploring the boundaries of adventure therapy: International perspectives. *Proceedings of the Second International Adventure Therapy Conference: Perth, Australia.* Denver, CO: Association for Experiential Education.

Jenkins, P. (2007) *Counselling, Psychotherapy and the Law.* 2nd edn. London: SAGE.

Jenkins, P. (2010) 'Having confidence in therapeutic work with children and young people: Constraints and challenges to confidentiality', *British Journal of Guidance and Counselling*, 38 (3): 263–274.

Jenkins, P. (2011) *A Confidential Space: Ethical Considerations When Counselling Children and Young People* (DVD). Counselling DVDs, in association with University of Wales, Newport.

Jenkins, P. (2013a) *Exploring Children's Rights: A Participative Exercise to Introduce the Issues around Children's Rights in England and Wales.* 2nd edn. Brighton: Pavilion.

Jenkins, P. (2013b) *Children's and Young Persons' Rights to Counselling: A Participative Exercise to Introduce the Issues Around Children's Rights in England and Wales and Their Access to Counselling.* Brighton: Pavilion.

Jenkins, P. and Palmer, J. (2012) '"At risk of harm?" An exploratory study of school counsellors in the UK, their perceptions of confidentiality, information-sharing and risk management', *British Journal of Guidance and Counselling*, 40 (5): 545–559.

Jenkins, P. and Polat, F. (2006) 'The Children Act 2004 and implications for counselling in schools in England and Wales', *Pastoral Care in Education*, 24 (2): 7–14.

Jenkins, R. (2002) 'Addressing suicide as a public health problem', *The Lancet*, 359: 813–814.

Jennings, S. (ed.) (1992) *Dramatherapy: Theory and Practice, Vol. 2.* London: Routledge.

Jennings, S. (1994) *Introduction to Developmental Playtherapy.* London: Jessica Kingsley.

Joe, S., Canetto, S.S. and Romer, D. (2008) 'Advancing prevention research on the role of culture in suicide prevention', *Suicide and Life-Threatening Behavior*, 38 (3): 354–362.

Johnson, S.C., Dweck, C.S., Chen, F.S., Stern, H.L., Ok, S.-J. and Barth, M. (2010) 'At the intersection of social and cognitive development: Internal working models of attachment in infancy', *Cognitive Science*, 34 (5): 807–825.

Joiner, T.E., Voelz, Z.R. and Rudd, M. (2001) 'For suicidal young adults with comorbid depressive and anxiety disorders, problem-solving treatment may be better than treatment as usual', *Professional Psychology: Research and Practice*, 32 (3): 278–282.

Jones, A. (1970) *School Counselling in Practice.* Ward Lock Educational.

Jones, E. and Landreth, G. (2002) 'The efficacy of intensive individual play therapy for chronically ill children', *International Journal of Play Therapy*, 11 (1): 117–140.

Jones, G. and Stokes, A. (2009) *Online Counseling: A Handbook for Practitioners.* London: Palgrave Macmillan.

Josefi, O. and Ryan, V. (2004) 'Non-directive play therapy for young children with autism: A case study', *Clinical Child Psychology and Psychiatry*, 9: 533–551.

Joseph, R. (1999) *Neuropsychiatry, Neuropsychology, Clinical Neuroscience.* 3rd edn. Philadelphia: Lippincott Williams & Wilkins.

Joyce, A., Piper, W., Ogrodniczuk, J. and Klein, R. (2007) *Termination in Psychotherapy: A Psychodynamic Model of Processes and Outcomes.* Washington, DC: American Psychological Association.

Kagan, J. (2008) 'In defense of qualitative changes in development', *Child Development,* 79 (6): 1606–1624.

Kağıtçıbaşı, C. (1996) *Family and Human Development across Cultures.* Mahwah: Lawrence Erlbaum.

Kalff, D. (2003) *Sandplay: A Psychotherapeutic Approach to the Psyche.* Cloverdale: Temenos Press.

Kanner, C. and Lee, R.G. (2005) 'The relational ethic in the treatment of adolescents', *Gestalt Review,* 9 (1): 72–90.

Kanzer, M. (1981) 'Freud's "analytical pact": The structured therapeutic alliance', *Journal of American Psychoanalytic Association,* 29 (1): 69–87.

Kareem, J. and Littlewood, R. (eds) (1992) *Intercultural Therapy.* Oxford: Blackwell.

Karkou, V. (ed.) (2010) *Art Therapies in Schools: Research and Practice.* London: Jessica Kingsley.

Karpman, S.B. (1968) 'Fairy tales and script drama', *Transactional Analysis Bulletin,* 26 (1): 39–43.

Kaufman, J. (1989) *The Psychology of Shame.* London: Routledge.

Kaufman, N.K., Rohde, P., Seeley, J.R., et al. (2005) 'Potential mediators of cognitive-behavioral therapy for adolescents with co-morbid major depression and conduct disorder', *Journal of Consulting and Clinical Psychology,* 73 (1): 38–46.

Kazdin, A. and Mazurick, L. (1994) 'Dropping out of child psychotherapy: Distinguishing early and late dropouts over the course of treatment', *Journal of Consulting and Clinical Psychology,* 62: 1069–1074.

Keen, R. (2011) 'The development of problem solving in young children: A critical cognitive skill', *Annual Review of Psychology,* 62 (1): 1–21.

Kegerreis, S. (2010) *Psychodynamic Counselling with Children and Young People: An Introduction.* London: Palgrave.

Kegerreis, S. (2011) 'Taking psychodynamic thinking "home" to the workplace – how can courses manage better the impact on student and employing agency?', *Psychodynamic Practice,* 17 (1): 23–39.

Keinanen, M. (1997) 'The meaning of the symbolic function in psychoanalytic psychotherapy: Clinical theory and psychotherapeutic applications', *British Journal of Medical Psychology,* 70 (4): 325–338.

Kendall, P.C. (1991) *Child and Adolescent Therapy: Cognitive-Behavioral Procedures.* New York: Guilford Press.

Kendall, P.C. (ed.) (2012) *Child and Adolescent Therapy: Cognitive-Behavioral Procedures.* 4th edn. New York: Guilford Press.

Kendall, P.C. and Hedtke, K.A. (2006) *Cognitive Behavioural Therapy for Anxious Children: Therapist Manual.* 3rd edn. Available at: www.workbookpublishing.com/ (Coping Cat anxiety treatment programme).

Kennedy, H., Landor, M. and Todd, L. (2010) 'Video interactive guidance as a method to promote secure attachments', *Educational and Child Psychology*, 27 (3): 59–72.

King, R., Bambling, M., Lloyd, C., Gomurra, R., Smith, S., Reid, W., et al. (2006a) 'Online counselling: The motives and experiences of young people who choose the internet instead of face to face or telephone counselling', *Counselling and Psychotherapy Research*, 6 (3): 169–174.

King, R., Bambling, M., Reid, W. and Thomas, I. (2006b) 'Telephone and online counselling for young people: A naturalistic comparison of session outcome, session impact and therapeutic alliance', Counselling and Psychotherapy Research, 6 (3): 175–181.

Kirschenbaum, H. and Henderson, V.L. (eds) (1989) *The Carl Rogers Reader.* New York: Houghton Mifflin.

Klein, M. (1932) *The Psycho-Analysis of Children.* London: Hogarth Press.

Knight, P.A. and Swanwick, R.A. (1996) *Bilingualism and the Education of Deaf Children: Advances in Practice.* Leeds: Leeds University Press.

Kot, S., Landreth, G. and Giordano, M. (1998) 'Intensive child-centered play therapy with child witnesses of domestic violence', *International Journal of Play Therapy*, 7 (2): 17–36.

Krefting, L. (1991) 'Rigor in qualitative research: The assessment of trustworthiness', *The American Journal of Occupational Therapy*, 45 (3): 214–222.

Ladany, N., Walker, J.A., Pate-Carolan, L. and Gray, L. (2008) *Practicing Counselling and Psychotherapy: Insights from Trainees, Clients, and Supervisors.* New York: Taylor and Francis.

Lago, C. (2006) *Race, Culture and Counselling: The Ongoing Challenge.* Maidenhead: Open University Press/McGraw-Hill.

Lago, C. (ed.) (2011) *The Handbook of Transcultural Counselling and Psychotherapy.* Maidenhead: Open University Press/McGraw-Hill.

Lahad, M. (1992) 'Story-making in assessment method for coping with stress', in S. Jennings (ed.), *Dramatherapy Theory and Practice.* London: Routledge. pp. 150–163.

Lambert, M.J. and Barley, D.E. (2001) 'Research summary on the therapeutic relationship and psychotherapy outcome', *Psychotherapy: Theory, Research, Practice, Training*, 38: 357–361.

Lambert, M.J. and Shimokawa, K. (2011) 'Collecting client feedback', *Psychotherapy*, 48 (1): 72–79.

Laming, Lord (2003) *The Victoria Climbie Inquiry: Report of an Inquiry by Lord Laming* (Cm 5730). London: Stationery Office.

Laming, Lord (2009) *The Protection of Children in England: A Progress Report* (HC 330). London: Stationery Office.

Lampert, R. (2003) *A Child's Eye View: Gestalt Therapy with Children, Adolescents and Their Families.* Cambridge, MA: The Gestalt Press.

Landreth, G.L. (2002) *Play Therapy: The Art of the Relationship.* New York: Brunner-Routledge.

Lanyado, M. (2004) *The Presence of the Therapist: Treating Childhood Trauma.* Hove: Routledge.

Lanyado, M. and Horne, A. (eds) (2009) *The Handbook of Child and Adolescent Psychotherapy: Psychoanalytic Approaches.* 2nd edn. London: Routledge.

Law, D. (2011) *Goals and Goal-Based Outcomes (GBOs): Some Useful Information* (Internal CORC Publication). Available at: www.corc.uk.net.

Layne, C.M., Saltzman, W.R., Poppleton L., et al. (2008) 'Effectiveness of a school-based group psychotherapy program for war exposed adolescents: A randomized controlled trial', *Journal of the American Academy of Child and Adolescent Psychiatry,* 47 (9): 1048–1062.

Lazarus, A. (2002) *Dual Relationships in Psychotherapy.* New York: Springer.

Lazarus, A.A. (2005) 'Multimodal therapy', in J.C. Norcross and M.R. Goldfried (eds), *Handbook of Psychotherapy Integration.* 2nd edn. New York: Oxford. pp. 105–120.

LeBlanc, M. and Ritchie, M. (2001) 'A meta-analysis of play therapy outcomes', *Counselling Psychology Quarterly,* 12 (2): 149–163.

Lee, R.G. (1996) 'Shame and the gestalt model', in R.G. Lee and G. Wheeler (eds), *The Voice of Shame: Silence and Connection in Psychotherapy.* Cambridge, MA: The Gestalt Press. pp. 3–22.

Lee, R.G. (2007) 'Shame and belonging in childhood: The interaction between relationship and neurobiological development in early years of life', *British Gestalt Journal,* 16 (2): 38–45.

Lee, R.G. and Harris, N. (2011) *Relational Child, Relational Brain.* New York: Routledge, Taylor & Francis.

Lee, R.G., Tiley, C. and White, J. (2009) 'The Place2Be: Measuring the effectiveness of a primary school-based therapeutic intervention in England and Scotland', *Counselling and Psychotherapy Research,* 9 (3): 151–159.

Lee, V. and Das Gupta, P. (1995) *Children's Cognitive and Language Development.* Maidenhead: Open University Press.

Le Grange, D. and Eisler, I. (2009) 'Family interventions in adolescent anorexia nervosa', *Child and Adolescent Psychiatric Clinics of North America,* 18 (1): 159–173.

Le Grange, D. and Lock, J. (2007) *Treating Bulimia in Adolescents: A Family Based Approach.* New York: Guilford Press.

Le Grange, D., Crosby, R.D., Rathouz, P.J. and Leventhal, B.L. (2007) 'A randomized controlled comparison of family-based treatment and supportive psychotherapy for adolescent bulimia nervosa', *Archives of General Psychiatry,* 64 (9): 1049–1056.

Le Grange, D., Lock, J., Loeb, K. and Nicholls, D. (2010) 'Academy for Eating Disorders position paper: The role of the family in eating disorders', *International Journal of Eating Disorders*, 43 (1): 1–5.

Le Grange, D., Swanson, S.A., Crow, S.J. and Merikangas, K.R. (2012) 'Eating disorder not otherwise specified presentation in the US population', *International Journal of Eating Disorders*, 45 (5): 711–718.

Lerner, R.M., Almerigi, J.B., Theokas, C. and Lerner, J. V. (2005) 'Positive youth development: A view of the issues', *The Journal of Early Adolescence*, 25 (1): 10–16.

LeSurf, A. and Lynch, G. (1999) 'Exploring young people's perceptions relevant to counselling: A qualitative study', *British Journal of Guidance and Counselling*, 27 (2): 231–243.

Levy, S. (2000) *The Therapeutic Alliance*. Madison, CT: Psychosocial Press.

Lewin, K. (1935) *A Dynamic Theory of Personality*. New York: McGraw-Hill.

Lewinsohn, P.M., Clarke, G.N., Hops, H. and Andrews, J. (1990) 'Cognitive-behavioral treatment for depressed adolescents', *Behavior Therapy*, 21: 385–401.

Lewis, E., Rubin, D.M., O'Reilly, A.L., Luan, X. and Localio, A.R. (2007) 'The impact of placement stability on behavioral well-being for children in foster care', *Paediatrics*, 119 (2): 336–344.

Linell, P. (2007) 'Dialogicality in languages, minds and brains: Is there a convergence between dialogism and neuro-biology?', *Language Sciences*, 29 (5): 605–620.

Lines, D. (2002) *Brief Counselling in Schools: Working with Young People from 11 to 18*. Thousand Oaks, CA: SAGE.

Lock, J. and Le Grange, D. (2005a) 'Family-based treatment of eating disorders', *International Journal of Eating Disorders*, 37: 64–67.

Lock, J. and Le Grange, D. (2005b) *Help Your Teenager Beat an Eating Disorder*. New York: Guilford Press.

Lock, J. and Le Grange, D. (2012 [2001]) *Treatment Manual for Anorexia Nervosa: A Family-Based Approach*. 2nd edn. New York: Guilford Press.

Lock, J., Le Grange, D., Agras, W.S., Moye, A., Bryson, S.W. and Jo, B. (2010) 'Randomized clinical trial comparing family-based treatment with adolescent-focused individual therapy for adolescents with anorexia nervosa', *Archives of General Psychiatry*, 67 (10): 1025–1032.

Lomas, P. (1981) *The Case for a Personal Psychotherapy*. Oxford: Oxford University Press.

Lorenz, K. (2002) *King Solomon's Ring*. 2nd edn. London: Routledge.

Lowenfeld, M. (1939) 'The world pictures of children: A method of recording and studying them', *British Journal of Medical Psychology*, 18 (1): 65–101.

Lowenfeld, M. (1993) *Understanding Children's Sandplay: Lowenfeld's World Technique*. Chippenham: Antony Rowe Ltd. (Originally published as *The World Technique*, London: George Allen & Unwin Ltd., 1979.)

Lowenstein, L. (1999) *Creative Interventions for Troubled Children and Youth*. Toronto: Champion Press.

Lowenstein, L. (2011) Assessing creatively. *BACP Counselling Children and Young People*. September, pp. 27–30.

Lowndes, L. and Hanley, T. (2010) 'The challenge of becoming an integrative counsellor: the trainee's perspective', *Counselling and Psychotherapy Research*, 10 (3): 163–172.

Lussier, G., Deater-Deckard, K., Dunn, J. and Davies, L. (2002) 'Support across two generations: Children's closeness to grandparents following parental divorce and remarriage', *Journal of Family Psychology*, 16 (3): 363.

Luxmoore, N. (2000) *Listening to Young People in School, Youth Work and Counselling*. Philadelphia, PA: Taylor and Francis Group.

Lynass, R., Pykhtina, O. and Cooper, M. (2012) 'A thematic analysis of young people's experience of counselling in five secondary schools in the UK', *Counselling and Psychotherapy Research*, 12 (1): 53–62.

McArdle, P., Moseley, D., Quibell, T., Johnson, R., Allen, A., Hammel, D. and Le Couteur, A. (2002) 'School-based indicated prevention: A randomised trial of group therapy', *Journal of Child Psychology and Psychiatry*, 43 (6): 705–712.

McArdle, P., Young, R., Quibell, T. and Moseley, D. (2011) 'Early intervention for at risk children: 3-year follow-up', *European Child and Adolescent Psychiatry*, 20 (3): 111–120.

McArthur, K. (2011) 'RCTs: A personal experience', *Therapy Today*, 22 (7): 24–25.

McArthur, K. (2013) 'Change processes in school-based humanistic counselling: a qualitative interview study'. Paper presented at the 19th BACP Research Conference, Birmingham.

McArthur, K., Cooper, M. and Berdondini, L. (2013) 'School-based humanistic counselling for psychological distress in young people: Pilot randomized controlled trial', *Psychotherapy Research*, 23 (3): 355–365.

MacBeath, J., Galton, M., Steward, S., MacBeath, A. and Page, C. (2006) *The Costs of Inclusion*. London: National Union of Teachers.

McCabe, K. (2002) 'Factors that predict premature termination among Mexican-American children in outpatient psychotherapy', *Journal of Child and Family Studies*, 11: 347–359.

McConville, M. (1995) *Adolescence: Psychotherapy and The Emergent Self*. San Franscisco, CA: Jossey Bass.

McConville, M. (2007) 'Relational modes and the evolving field of parent–child contact', *British Gestalt Journal*, 16 (2): 5–12.

McCormick, B., Voight, A. and Ewert, A. (2003) 'Therapeutic outdoor programming: Theoretical connections between adventure and therapy', in K. Richards with B. Smith (eds), *Therapy within Adventure: Proceedings of the Second International Adventure Therapy Conference*. Augsburg: Zeil Verlag. pp. 155–174.

Macdonald, G., Livingstone, N., Davidson, G., Sloan, S., Fargas, M. and McSherry, D. (2012) *Improving the Mental Health of Northern Ireland's Children and Young People: Priorities for Research*. Belfast: Public Health Agency and Queen's University Belfast.

McDermott, E. (2010) *Researching and Monitoring Adolescent Sexual Orientation*. London: Equalities and Human Rights Commission.

McGinnis, S. (2006) *Good Practice Guidance for Counselling in Schools*. 4th edn. Lutterworth: BACP.

MacKay, T., Reynolds, S. and Kearney, M. (2010) 'From attachment to attainment: The impact of nurture groups on academic achievement', *Educational and Child Psychology*, 27 (3): 100–110.

McLaughlin, C., Holliday, C., Clarke, B. and Llie, S. (2013) *Research on Counselling and Psychotherapy with Children and Young People: A Systematic Scoping Review of Evidence for its Effectiveness from 2003–2011*. Lutterworth: BACP.

McLeod, J. (2003) *Doing Counselling Research*. London: SAGE.

McLeod, J. (2004) *The Counsellor's Workbook: Developing a Personal Approach*. Maidenhead: Open University Press

McLeod, J. (2009) *An Introduction to Counselling*. 4th edn. Maidenhead: Open University Press.

McLeod, J. (2010) *Case Study Research in Counselling and Psychotherapy*. London: SAGE.

McMahon, L. (2009) *The Handbook of Play Therapy and Therapeutic Play*. 2nd edn. East Sussex: Routledge.

McMahon, M. and Patton, W. (2000) 'Conversations on clinical supervision: Benefits perceived by school counsellors', *British Journal of Guidance and Counselling*, 28 (3): 339–351.

McNiff, S. (1981) *The Arts and Psychotherapy*. New York: Charles Thomas.

McNutt, B. (1994) 'Adventure as therapy: Using adventure as part of therapeutic programmes with young people in trouble and at risk', in J. Barrett (ed.), *Adventure-Based Interventions with Young People in Trouble and at Risk: Proceedings of a National One-Day Conference on Adventure-Based Interventions*, 22 April. Dumfries: Basecamp.

Mabey, J.S.B. (1995) *Counselling for Young People*. Buckingham: Open University.

Malchiodi, C.A. (2005) *Expressive Therapies*. New York: Guilford Press.

Malek, M. (1991) *Psychiatric Admissions: A Report on Young People Entering Psychiatric Residential Care*. London: Children's Society.

Malek, M. (1993) *Passing the Buck: A Summary of Institutional Responses to Controlling Children with Difficult Behaviour*. London: Children's Society.

Mallinckrodt, B. (2010) 'The psychotherapy relationship as attachment: Evidence and implications', *Journal of Social and Personal Relationships*, 27 (2): 262–270.

Mallon, B. (2011) *Working with Bereaved Children and Young People*. London: SAGE.

Mansor, A., De Angeli, A. and De Bruijn, O. (2009) 'The fantasy table', in *Proc. IDC*. ACM Press. pp.70–79.

Many, M. (2009) 'Termination as a therapeutic intervention when treating children who have experienced multiple losses', *Infant Mental Health Journal*, 30: 23–39.

Mapes, K. (2000) *Stop! Think! Choose! Building Emotional Intelligence in Young People*. Tucson, AZ: Zephyr Press.

Marco J., Cerezo, E., Baldassarri, E., Mazzone, E. and Read, J.C. (2009) 'Bringing table-top technologies to kindergarten children', *Proc. HCI*, (2009): 103–111.

Marcus, D.M. (1998) 'Manifestations of the therapeutic alliance in children and adolescents', *Child and Adolescent Social Work Journal*, 5 (2): 71–83.

Marfo, K., Pence, A., LeVine, R.A. and LeVine, S. (2011) 'Strengthening Africa's contributions to child development research: Introduction', *Child Development Perspectives*, 5 (2): 104–111.

Marscark, M. and Hauser, P.C. (2008) *Deaf Cognition: Foundations and Outcomes*. Oxford: Oxford University Press.

Martin (2001) *Harnessing the Power of Intelligence, Counter-Intelligence and Hitch-Hiking on Surprise Events*. Canada: Executive Organizational Press.

Martin, P.B. (1983) *The effect of an outdoor adventure programme on group cohesion and change in self-concept*. PhD dissertation, Boston College University, Boston, MA.

Masson, J. (2004) 'The legal context', in S. Fraser, S. Ding, M. Kellett and C. Robinson (eds), *Doing Research with Children and Young People*. London: SAGE/Open University Press. pp. 43–58.

Mayers, K.S. (1995) 'Songwriting as a way to decrease anxiety and distress in traumatized children', *The Arts in Psychotherapy*, 22 (5): 495–498.

Maynard, A.E. and Greenfield, P.M. (2003) 'Implicit cognitive development in cultural tools and children: lessons from Maya Mexico', *Cognitive Development*, 18 (4): 489–510.

Mearns, D. (1997) *Person-Centred Counselling Training*. London: SAGE.

Mearns, D. and Cooper, M. (2005) *Working at Relational Depth in Counselling and Psychotherapy*. London: SAGE.

Mearns, D. and Thorne, B. (1988) *Person-Centred Counselling* in Action. 1st edn. London: SAGE.

Mearns, D. and Thorne, B., with McLeod, J. (2013) *Person-Centred Counselling in Action*. 4th edn. London: SAGE.

Meins, E. and Russell, J. (1997) 'Security and symbolic play: The relation between security of attachment and executive capacity', *British Journal of Developmental Psychology*, 15 (1): 63–76.

Meltzoff, A.N. and Moore, M.K. (1998) 'Infant intersubjectivity: broadening the dialogue to include imitation, identity and intention', in S. Bråten (ed.), *Intersubjective Communication and Emotion in Early Ontogeny*. Cambridge: Cambridge University Press. pp. 47–62.

Mental Health Foundation (2005) *Lifetime Impacts: Childhood and Adolescent Mental Health*. London: Mental Health Foudation.

Mental Health Foundation (2013) *Mental Health Statistics: Children & Young People.* Available at: www.mentalhealth.org.uk/help-information/mental-health-statistics/children-young-people/?view=Standard.

Merry, S.N., Hetrick, S.E., Cox, G.R., et al. (2011) 'Psychological and educational interventions for preventing depression in children and adolescents', *Cochrane Database of Systematic Reviews*, 12. Art. No.: CD003380. DOI: 10.1002/14651858.CD003380.pub3.

Merry, T. (2008) *Learning and Being in Person-Centred Counselling.* 2nd edn. Ross-on-Wye: PCCS Books.

Midgley, N. and Kennedy, E. (2011) 'Psychodynamic psychotherapy for children and adolescents: A critical review of the evidence base', *Journal of Child Psychotherapy*, 37 (3): 1–29.

Midgley, N. and Vrouva, I. (eds) (2012) *Minding the Child: Mentalization-Based Interventions with Children, Young People and Their Families.* London: Routledge.

Midgley, N., Anderson, J., Grainger, E., Nesic-Vuckovic, T. and Urwin, C. (2009) *Child Psychotherapy and Research: New Approaches, Emerging Findings.* London: Routledge.

Mikulincer, M., Shaver, P.R. and Berant, E. (2013) 'An attachment perspective on therapeutic processes and outcomes', *Journal of Personality*, 81 (6): 606–616.

Miller, S. and Duncan, B. (2006) *The Outcome Rating Scale.* Chicago: Authors.

MIND (2013a) *How to Cope with Suicidal Feelings.* MIND. Available at: www.mind.org.uk/media/46938/how_to_cope_with_suicidal_feelings_2011.pdf.

MIND (2013b) *Understanding Depression.* MIND. Available at: www.mind.org.uk/mental_health_a-z/7980_understanding_depression.

MIND (2013c) *Understanding Self-harm.* MIND. Available at: www.mind.org.uk/mental_health_a-z/8006_understanding_self-harm.

Misra, M., Aggarwal, A., Miller, K.K., Almazan, C., Worley, M., Soyka, L.A. and Klibanski, A. (2004) 'Effects of anorexia nervosa on clinical, hematologic, biochemical, and bone density parameters in community-dwelling adolescent girls', *Pediatrics*, 114 (6): 1574–1583.

Mitchels, B. and Bond, T. (2010) *Essential Law for Counsellors and Psychotherapists.* London: SAGE.

Mitten, D. and Itin, C.M. (eds) (2009) *Connecting with the Essence of Adventure Therapy.* Boulder, CO: Association of Experiential Education (AEE).

Moore, B.A., Bursch, B. and Walshaw, P. (2008) 'Termination of psychotherapy with children', in W. O'Donohue and M. Cucciare (eds), *A Clinician's Guide to the Termination of Psychotherapy.* London: Routledge. pp. 251–267.

Moreno, J.L. and Moreno, Z.T. (1969) *Psychodrama, Vol. 3.* New York: Beacon House.

Morrall, P. and Hazleton, M. (2004) *Mental Health, Global Policies and Human Rights.* London: Whurr.

Mortola, P. (2011) 'You, me, and the parts of myself I'm still getting to know: An interview with Violet Oaklander', in R.G. Lee and N. Harris (eds), *Relational Child, Relational Brain.* New York: Routledge, Taylor & Francis.

Moustakas, C. (1953) *Children in Play Therapy: A Key to Understanding Normal and Disturbed Emotions*. New York: McGraw-Hill.

Mudaly, N. and Goddard, C. (2009) 'The ethics of involving children who have been abused in child abuse research', *International Journal of Children's Rights*, 17: 261–281.

Mulley, K. (2009) *21st Century Schools: A World-Class Education for Every Child, DCSF Consultation*. Action for Children. Available at: www.actionforchildren.org.uk/media/95796/action_for_children_21st_century_schools.pdf.

Munro, E.R. and Hardy, A. (2006) *Placement Stability: A Review of the Literature*. Loughborough: Centre for Child and Family Research, Loughborough University.

Muran, J.C. and Barber, J.P. (eds) (2010) *The Therapeutic Alliance: An Evidence-Based Guide to Practice*. New York: The Guilford Press.

Murray, L., Sinclair, D., Cooper, P., Ducournau, P., Turner, P. and Stein, A. (1999) 'The socio-emotional development of 5-year-old children of postnatally depressed mothers', *Journal of Child Psychology and Psychiatry*, 40 (8): 1259–1271.

Music, G. (2011) *Nurturing Natures: Attachment and Children's Emotional, Sociocultural and Brain Development*. Hove: Taylor Francis Group, Psychology Press.

Mychailyszyn, M.P., Brodman, D.M., Read, K.L. and Kendall, P.C. (2012) 'Cognitive–behavioural school based interventions for anxious and depressed youth: A meta-analysis of outcomes', *Clinical Psychology, Science and Practice*, 19: 129–153.

Myers, J.E.B. (2011) *The APSAC Handbook on Child Maltreatment*. 3rd edn. London: SAGE.

National CAMHS Support Service (2011) *Self-harm in Children and Young People: Handbook*. National Workforce Programme. Available at: www.chimat.org.uk/resource/view.aspx?RID=105602.

National Statistics Online (2004) *Mental Health: Mental Disorder More Common in Boys*. Available at: www.statistics.gov.uk. Cited in Mental Health Foundation (2013) *Mental Health Statistics: Children & Young People*. Available at: www.mentalhealth.org.uk/help-information/mental-health-statistics/children-young-people/?view=Standard.

National Statistics Report (2009) Available at http://data.gov.uk/publisher/office-for-national-statistics.

Neil, A.L. and Christensen, H. (2009) 'Efficacy and effectiveness of school based prevention and early intervention programmes for anxiety', *Clinical Psychology Review*, 29: 208–215.

Nelson-Jones, R. (2002) *Essential Counselling and Therapy Skills: The Skilled Client Model*. London: SAGE.

Newson, J. and Newson, E. (1975) 'Inter-subjectivity and the transmission of culture: On the social origins of symbolic functioning', *Bulletin of the British Psychological Society*, 28: 437–446.

NHS Health Advisory Service (1995) *Together We Stand: Thematic Review of the Commissioning, Role and Management of Child and Adolescent Mental Health Services*. London: The Stationery Office.

NICCY (2007) *The Inquiry into the Prevention of Suicide and Self Harm: Response by the Northern Ireland Commissioner for Children and Young People (NICCY).* Belfast: NICCY. Available at: www.niccy.org/uploaded_docs/Consultation%20Responses/NICCY%20Response%20to%20inquiry%20on%20suicide%20-%20Oct%2007.pdf.

NICE (National Institute for Health and Clinical Excellence) (2004) 'Self-harm: The short-term physical and psychological management and secondary prevention of self-harm in primary and secondary care', *NICE Clinical Guideline*, 16 July. London: NICE. Available at: www.nice.org.uk/nicemedia/live/10946/29421/29421.pdf

NICE (National Institute for Health and Clinical Excellence) (2005) *Depression in Children and Young People: Identification and Management in Primary, Community and Secondary Care* (Clinical Guide 28). London: National Collaborating Centre for Mental Health.

NICE (National Institute for Health and Clinical Excellence) (2008) *Attention Deficit Hyperactivity Disorder: Diagnosis and Management of ADHD in Children, Young People and Adults.* London: NICE.

NICE (National Institute for Health and Clinical Excellence) (2009) *Core Interventions in the Treatment and Management of Schizophrenia in Primary and Secondary Care: Update.* London: NICE.

NICE (National Institute for Health and Clinical Excellence) (2011) *Self-Harm: Longer-Term Management. NICE Clinical Guideline 133.* London: NICE. Available at: www.nice.org.uk/nicemedia/live/13619/57179/57179.pdf.

Nicholson, C., Irwin, M. and Dwivedi, K.N. (2011) *Children and Adolescents in Trauma: Creative Therapeutic Approaches.* London: Jessica Kingsley.

Nock, M. and Kazdin, A. (2001) 'Parent expectancies for child therapy: Assessment and relation to participation in treatment', *Journal of Child and Family Studies*, 10: 155–180.

Nordentoft, M. (2007) 'Prevention of suicide and attempted suicide in Denmark: Epidemiological studies of suicide and intervention studies in selected risk groups', *Danish Medical Bulletin*, 54 (4): 306–369.

Norris, M.L., Apsimon, M., Harrison, M., Obeid, N., Buchholz, A., Henderson, K.A. and Spettigue, W. (2012) 'An examination of medical and psychological morbidity in adolescent males with eating disorders', *Eating Disorders*, 20 (5): 405–415.

NSPCC (National Society for the Prevention of Cruelty to Children) (2008) *Evidence to Lord Laming's Review of Child Protection.* London: NSPCC.

NSPCC (National Society for the Prevention of Cruelty to Children) (2007) *Casenotes: A Series of Reports on Issues Facing Children Today.* London: NSPCC.

NSPCC (National Society for the Prevention of Cruelty to Children) (2009) 'Young people who self-harm: Implications for public health practitioners', *Child Protection Research Briefing.* London: NSPCC. Available at: www.nspcc.org.uk/Inform/research/briefings/youngpeoplewhoselfharmpdf_wdf63294.pdf.

Oaklander, V. (1979) 'A gestalt therapy approach with children through the use of art and creative expression', in E.H. Marcus (ed.), *Gestalt Therapy and Beyond.* Cupertino, CA: Meta Publications.

Oaklander, V. (1988) *Windows to Our Children.* New York: Gestalt Journal Press.

Oaklander, V. (1992) 'Gestalt work with children: Working with anger and introjects', in E.C. Nevis (ed.), *Gestalt Therapy: Perspectives and Applications.* New York: Gardner Press.

Oaklander, V. (1997) 'The therapeutic process with children and adolescents', *Gestalt Review*, 1 (4): 292–317.

Oaklander, V. (1999) Group play therapy from a gestalt therapy perspective', in D.S. Sweeney (ed.), *Group Play Therapy: Theory and Practice.* New York: Charles C. Thomas.

Oaklander, V. (2006) *Hidden Treasures.* London: Karnac.

O'Callaghan, C.C. (1996) 'Lyrical themes in songs written by palliative care patients', *The Journal of Music Therapy*, 33: 74–92.

O'Connor, R.C., Rasmussen, S. and Hawton, K. (2010) *Northern Ireland Lifestyle and Coping Survey, Final Report.* Available at: www.dhsspsni.gov.uk/ni-lifestyle-and-coping-survey-2010.pdf.

O'Connor, R.C., Rasmussen, S., Miles, J. and Hawton, K. (2009) 'Self-harm in adolescents: Self-report survey in schools in Scotland', *The British Journal of Psychiatry*, 194: 68–72.

O'Donohue, W. and Cucciare, M. (2008) *Terminating Psychotherapy: A Clinician's Guide.* New York: Routledge.

Ofsted (2004) *Special Educational Needs and Disability: Towards Inclusive Schools.* London: Ofsted.

Ogawa, Y. (2004) 'Childhood trauma and play therapy intervention for traumatized children', *Journal of Professional Counselling: Practice, Theory & Research*, 32: 19–29.

Ogilvie, K.C. (2011) *Roots and Wings: A History of Outdoor Education and Outdoor Learning in the UK.* Lyme Regis: Russell House Publishing/Institute for Outdoor Learning.

O'Hara, M. (2011) 'Sharp increase in suicide rates in Northern Ireland', *The Guardian*, 16 March.

Omizo, M.M. and Omizo, A.O. (1987) 'The effect of group counselling on classroom behaviour and self-concept among elementary school learning disabled children', *The Exceptional Child*, 34 (1): 57–64.

Orbach, I., Glaubman, H. and Berman, D. (1986) 'Children's perception of various determinants of the death concept as a function of intelligence, age and anxiety', *Journal of Clinical Psychology*, 15 (2): 120–126.

Parkes, C.M. (1986) *Bereavement: Studies of Grief in Adult Life.* 2nd edn. London: Penguin.

Parkes, C.M. (1993) 'Bereavement as a psychosocial transition: Processes of adaptation to change', in D. Dickenson and M. Johnson (eds), *Death, Dying and Bereavement.* London: SAGE.

Parkes, C.M. (1998) 'Editorial comments', *Bereavement Care*, 17: 18.

Parlett, M. (2000) 'Creative adjustment and the global field', *British Gestalt Journal*, 9 (1): 15–27.

Parry, G., Castonguay, L.G., Borkovec, T.D. and Wolf, A. (2010) 'Practice research networks and psychological services research in the UK and USA', in M. Barkham, G. Hardy and J. Mellor-Clark (eds), *Developing and Delivering Practice-Based Evidence: A Guide for the Psychological Therapies.* Chichester: John Wiley.

Pattison, S. (2010) 'Reaching out: A proactive process to include young people with learning disabilities in counselling in secondary schools in the UK', *British Journal of Guidance & Counselling*, 38 (3): 301–311.

Pattison, S. and Harris, B. (2004) *Research on Counselling Children and Young People: A Systematic Scoping Search.* Rugby: BACP.

Pattison, S., Hanley, T, and Sefi, A. (2012) 'Online counselling for children and young people: Using technology to address the millennium development goals in Kenya', in D.B.I. Popoola and O. Adebowale (eds) *Online Guidance and Counselling: Toward Effectively Applying Technology.* Hershey, PA: IGI Global.

Pattison, S., Rowland, N., Cromarty, K., Richards, K., Jenkins, P., Cooper, M., Polat, F. and Couchman, A. (2007) *Counselling in Schools: A Research Study into Services for Children and Young People.* Lutterworth: BACP.

Payne, H. (2006) *Dance Movement Therapy: Theory, Research, and Practice.* London: Routledge.

Pearson, Q. (1998) 'Terminating before counselling has ended: Counselling implications and strategies for counsellor relocation', *Journal of Mental Health Counselling*, 20: 55–63.

Peebles, R., Hardy, K.K., Wilson, J.L. and Lock, J.D. (2010) 'Medical compromise in eating disorders not otherwise specified: Are diagnostic criteria for eating disorders markers of severity?', *Pediatrics*, 125 (5): 1193–1201.

Pelling, N. and Renard, D. (2000) 'Counselling via the internet: Can it be done', *The Psychotherapy Review*, 2 (2): 68–72.

Pennells, M. and Smith, S. (1995) *The Forgotten Mourners.* London: Jessica Kingsley.

Perls, F.S. (1948) 'Theory and technique of personality integration', *American Journal of Psychotherapy*, 2 (4): 565–586.

Perls, F.S. (1969 [1947]) *Ego, Hunger & Aggression.* New York: Vintage Books.

Perls, F.S. (1970) 'Four lectures', in J. Fagan and I.L. Shepherd (eds), *Gestalt Therapy Now.* New York: Harper & Row.

Perls, F.S. (1975 [1959]) 'Resolution', in J.O. Stevens, *Gestalt Is ….* Moab, UT: Real People Press. pp. 69–74.

Perls, F.S., Hefferline, R. and Goodman, P. (1951) *Gestalt Therapy: Excitement and Growth in the Human Personality*. New York: Delta.

Perry, B.D. (2001) 'The neuro-developmental impact of violence in childhood', in D. Schetky and E. Benedek (eds), *Textbook of Child and Adolescent Forensic Psychiatry*. Washington, DC: American Psychiatric Press.

Perry, B.D. and Szalavitz, M. (2010) *Born for Love: Why Empathy is Essential and Endangered*. New York: Harper.

Pfirman, E.S. (1988) *The effects of wilderness challenge courses on victims of rape in locus of control, self-concept and fear*. PhD dissertation, University of Northern Colorado, Greeley.

Phillips, A. (2003) *Equals*. London: Faber & Faber.

Philippson, P. (2004) 'The experience of shame', in *Gestalt Therapy: Roots and Branches – Collected Papers*. London: Karnac Books. pp. 167–177.

Piaget, J. (1936) *Origins of Intelligence in the Child*. London: Routledge & Kegan Paul.

Piaget, J. (1953) *The Origin of Intelligence in the Child*. London: Routledge & Kegan Paul.

Piaget, J. (1965 [1932]) *The Moral Judgment of the Child*. 2nd edn. New York: Free Press.

Piper, A.M. and Hollan, J.D. (2006) 'Supporting medical conversations between deaf and hearing individuals with tabletop displays.'

Piper, A. and Hollan J. (2008) 'Supporting medical conversations between deaf and hearing individuals with tabletop displays', in *Proc. CSCW*. ACM Press'08. pp. 147–156.

Plotnikoff, J., and Woolfson, R. (2009) *Measuring Up? Evaluating Implementation of Government Commitments to Young Witnesses in Criminal Proceedings: Executive Summary*. London: NSPCC.

Pommier, J.H. (1994) *Experiential adventure therapy plus family training: Outward Bound schools efficacy with status offenders*. PhD dissertation, Texas A&M University, College Station.

Pompili, M., Serafini, G., Innamorati, M., Dominici, G., Ferracuti, S., Kotzalidis, G.D., Serra, G., Girardi, P., Janiri, L., Tatarelli, R., Sher, L. and Lester D. (2010) 'Suicidal behavior and alcohol abuse', *International Journal of Environmental Research and Public Health*, 7 (4): 1392–1431. Available at: www.mdpi.com/1660-4601/7/4/1392.

Ponterotto, J., Casas, M.J., Suzuki, L.A., Alexander, C.M. (2001) *Handbook of Multicultural Counselling*. 2nd edn. Thousand Oaks, CA: SAGE.

Prever, M. (2010) *Counselling and Supporting Children and Young People: A Person-Centred Approach*. London: SAGE.

Prior, S. (2012) 'Overcoming stigma: How young people position themselves as counselling service users', *Sociology of Health and Illness*, 34 (6): 697–713.

Pritchard, J. (ed.) (2013) *Good Practice in Promoting Recovery and Healing for Abused Adults*. London: Jessica Kingsley.

Pryor, A., Carpenter, C., Norton, C.L. and Kirchner, J. (eds) (2012) *Emerging Insights: Proceedings of the 5th International Adventure Therapy Conference*. Prague: European Science and Art Publishing.

Public Health Institute of Scotland (2003) *Needs Assessment Report on Child and Adolescent Mental Health*. Edinburgh: Public Health Institute of Scotland.

Pykhtina, O., Balaam, M., Wood, G. and Olivier, P. (2012) 'Magic Land: The design and evaluation of an interactive tabletop supporting therapeutic play with children', in *DIS 2012: Proceedings of the Designing Interactive Systems Conference*. Newcastle: ACM Press. pp. 136–145.

Rackett, P. and Holmes, B.M. (2010) 'Enhancing the attachment relationship: A prenatal perspective', *Educational and Child Psychology*, 27 (3): 33–50.

Radin, M.J. (1991) 'Reflections on objectification', *Heinonline*, 65: 341. Available at: http://heinonline.org/HOL/LandingPage?handle=hein.journals/scal65&div=21 &id=&page=.

Raghavan, R., and Patel, P. (2008) *Learning Disabilities and Mental Health*. London: Blackwell.

Ragsdale, K.G., Cox. R.D., Finn, P. and Eisler, R.M. (1996) 'Effectiveness of short-term specialized inpatient treatment for war-related posttraumatic stress disorder: A role for adventure-based counselling and psychodrama', *Journal of Traumatic Stress*, 9 (2): 269–283.

Raphael, B. (1984) *Anatomy of Bereavement: A Handbook for the Caring Professions*. London: Hutchinson.

Ray, D. (2011) *Advanced Play Therapy: Essential Conditions, Knowledge and Skills for Child Practice*. New York: Routledge, Taylor and Francis.

RBSCB (Rochdale Borough Safeguarding Children Board) (2012) *Review of the Multi-agency Responses to the Sexual Exploration of Children*. Available at: www.rbscb.org/CSEReport.pdf (accessed 3/11/12).

Reddrop, S. (1997) *Outdoor Programs for Young Offenders in Detention: An Overview*. Hobart: National Clearinghouse for Youth Studies.

Rees, G., Gorin, S., Jobe, A., Stein, M., Medforth, R. and Goswami, H. (2010) *Safeguarding Young People: Responding to Young People Aged 11 to 17 Who Are Maltreated*. London: Children's Society.

Reeves, A. (2013) *An Introduction to Counselling and Psychotherapy*. London: SAGE.

Reeves, A. and Howdin, J. (2010) 'Considerations when working with clients who self-harm', *Information Sheet* G12. Lutterworth: BACP.

Reeves, A. and Seber, P. (2010) 'Working with the suicidal client', *Information Sheet* P7. Lutterworth: BACP.

Regan, H. and Craig, E. (2011) 'A thematic analysis of schools' and children's experiences of the Barnardo's primary school counselling service'. 'Time 4 Me' unpublished paper, Barnardo's N. Ireland.

Reid, H. and Westergaard, J. (2011) *Effective Counselling with Young People*. London: Learning Matters.

Reid, M. (2003) 'Clinical research: The inner world of the mother and her new baby – Born in the shadow of death', *Journal of Child Psychotherapy*, 29 (2): 207–226.

Richards, K. and Smith, B. (2003) 'Therapy within adventure', *Proceedings of the Second International Adventure Therapy Conference*, University of Augsburg, 20–24 March, 2000. Germany: Zeil Verlag.

Richards, K., Harper, N. and Carpenter, C. (eds) (2011) 'Looking at the landscape of adventure therapy: Making links to theory and practice', *Journal of Adventure Education and Outdoor Learning*, 11 (2): 83–90.

Richards, K., Peel, J., Smith, B. and Owen, V. (2002) *Adventure Therapy and Eating Disorders: A Feminist Approach to Research and Practice*. Ambleside: Brathay Hall.

Richardson, C. (2012) *The Truth About Self-Harm*. London: The Mental Health Foundation and The Camelot Foundation. Available at: www.mentalhealth.org. uk/content/assets/PDF/publications/truth_about_self-harm_NEW_BRAND. pdf?view=Standard.

Richardson, G., Partridge, I. and Barrett, J. (2010) *Child and Adolescent Mental Health Services: An Operational Handbook*. 2nd edn. London: Royal College of Psychiatrists Publications.

Richardson, J. (2002) *The Mental Health of Looked-After Children. Bright Futures: Working with Vulnerable Young People*. London: Mental Health Foundation.

Rickson, D.J. and Watkins, W.G. (2003) 'Music therapy to promote prosocial behaviors in aggressive adolescent boys: A pilot study', *Journal of Music Therapy*, 11 (4): 283–301.

Riedel Bowers, N. (2011) Canadian Association for Child and Play Therapy Level II Workshop'11.

Robinson, B.D. (1996) 'School counsellors in England and Wales, 1965–1995: A flawed innovation?', *Pastoral Care in Education*, 14 (3): 12–19.

Robson, M. (2008) 'Working with planned endings', in W. Dryden and A. Reeves (eds.) *Key Issues for Counselling in Action*. 2nd edn. London: SAGE.

Rohde, P., Feeny, N.C. and Robins, M. (2005) *Characteristics and Components of the TADS CBT Approach*. Available at: www.ncbi.nlm.nih.gov/pmc/articles/ PMC1894655/ (Programme used in the Treatment for Adolescents with Depression Study – TADS).

Rogers, A., Maidman, J. and House, R. (2011) 'The bad faith of "evidence-based practice": Beyond counsels of despair', *Therapy Today*, 22 (6): 26–29.

Rogers, C. (2003) *Client Centred Therapy: Its Current Practice, Implications and Theory* (reprint). London: Constable & Robinson Ltd.

Rogers, C.R. (1939) *The Clinical Treatment of the Problem Child*. Boston, MA: Houghton Mifflin.

Rogers, C.R. (1951) *Client-centred Therapy: Its Current Practice, Implications and Theory*. London: Constable.

Rogers, C.R. (1957) 'The necessary and sufficient conditions for therapeutic change', *Journal of Consulting Psychology*, 21: 95–103.

Rogers, C.R. (1959) 'A theory of therapy, personality and interpersonal relationships as developed in the client-centered framework', in S. Koch (ed.), *Psychology: A Study of a Science. Vol. 3: Formulations of the Person and the Social Context*. New York: McGraw-Hill.

Rogers, C.R. (1961) *On Becoming a Person: A Therapist's View of Psychotherapy*. London: Constable.

Rogers, C.R. (1980) *A Way of Being*. Boston, MA: Houghton Mifflin.

Rogers, C.R. (1983) *Freedom to Learn for the Eighties*. Columbus, OH: Merrill Publishing.

Rogers, C.R. (1986) 'Rogers, Kohut and Erickson', *Person-Centred Review*, 1: 125–140.

Rogers, C.R. (2004) *On Becoming a Person*. London: Constable.

Rogers, C. and Farson, R. (1987) 'Active listening', in R.G. Newman, M.A. Danzinger and M. Cohen (eds), *Communicating in Business Today*. Lexington, MA: D.C. Heath & Company.

Rogers, M. (2010) 'The challenges of working with adoption', *The Psychotherapist*, Spring: 2–15.

Roggman, L.A., Boyce, L.K. and Cook, G.A. (2009) 'Keeping kids on track: Impacts of a parenting-focused early head start program on attachment security and cognitive development', *Early Education and Development*, 20 (6): 920–941.

Rolls, L. and Payne, S. (2003) 'Childhood bereavement services: A survey of UK provision', *Palliative Medicine*, 17: 423–432.

Rosling, A.M., Sparén, P., Norring, C. and von Knorring, A.L. (2011) 'Mortality of eating disorders: A follow-up study of treatment in a specialist unit 1974–2000', *International Journal of Eating Disorders*, 44 (4): 304–310.

Rosselló, J., Bernal, G. and Rivera-Medina, C. (2008) 'Individual and group CBT and IPT for Puerto Rican adolescents with depressive symptoms', *Cultural Diversity and Ethnic Minority Psychology*, 14 (3): 234–245.

Rowan, J. (1993) 'Counselling for a brief period', in W. Dryden (ed.), *Questions and Answers on Counselling in Action*. London: SAGE.

Rowling, J.K. (2005) *Harry Potter and the Half Blood Prince*. London: Bloomsbury.

Royal College of Paediatrics and Child Health (2012) *Looked After Children: Knowledge, Skills and Competence of Health Care Staff*. Available at www.rcpch.ac.uk/system/files/protected/page/RCPCH_RCN_LAC_2012.pdf (accessed 16/3/14).

Royal College of Psychiatrists (2004) *Mental Health and Growing Up: The Child with General Learning Disabilities: For Parents and Teachers*. London: RCP.

Royal College of Psychiatrists (2010) *Self-harm, Suicide and Risk: Helping People Who Self-harm* (Report 158). London: Royal College of Psychiatrists.

Royal College of Psychiatrists (2012) 'Self-harm in young people: Information for parents, carers and anyone who works with young people', *Mental Health and Growing Up Factsheet* (March). Available at www.rcpsych.ac.uk/healthadvice/parentsandyouthinfo/parentscarers/self-harm.aspx.

Royal College of Psychiatrists (2013) 'Depression in children and young people: information for young people', *Mental Health and Growing Up Factsheet*. London: Royal College of Psychiatrists. Available at: www.rcpsych.ac.uk/healthadvice/parentsand youthinfo/youngpeople/depressioninyoungpeople.aspx.

Rueb, T. and Wardzala, J. (1997) Billow: Networked hospital playspace for children. CHI 97 Electronic Publications: Late-Breaking/Short Talks. Available at www.sigchi.org/chi97/proceedings/short-talk/tr.htm

Russell, G.F., Szmukler, G.I., Dare, C. and Eisler, I. (1987) 'An evaluation of family therapy in anorexia nervosa and bulimia nervosa', *Archives of General Psychiatry*, 44 (12): 1047–1056.

Rustin, M. (2003) 'Research in the consulting room', *Journal of Child Psychotherapy*, 29 (2): 137–145.

Rutter, M. (1995) 'Clinical implications of attachment concepts: Retrospect and prospect', *Journal of Child Psychology and Psychiatry*, 36 (4): 549–571.

Rustin, M. and Quagliata, E. (2000) *Assessment in Child Psychotherapy*. The Tavistock Clinic Series. Kindle edition. London: Karnac.

Rutter, M., Kreppner, J. and Sonuga-Barke, E. (2009) 'Attachment insecurity, disinhibited attachment, and attachment disorders: Where do research findings leave the concepts?' (Emanuel Miller Lecture), *Journal of Child Psychology and Psychiatry*, 50 (5): 529–543.

Ryan, V. (2004) 'Adapting non-directive play therapy for children with attachment disorders', *Clinical Child Psychology and Psychiatry*, 9 (1): 75–87.

Ryan, V. and Needham, C. (2001) 'Non-directive play therapy with children experiencing psychic trauma', *Clinical Child Psychology and Psychiatry*, 6: 437–453.

Safran, J.D. and Muran, J.C. (2000) *Negotiating the Therapeutic Alliance: A Relational Treatment Guide*. New York: The Guilford Press.

Sallman, C. (2007) Play Therapy: An Overview and Marketing Plan, Kansas University thesis available at https://krex.k-state.edu/dspace/bitstream/handle/2097/363/Cyndi McNeilSallman2007%5B1%5D.pdf?sequence=1

Samaritans Statistics (2007) Available at www.samaritans.org/about-us/our-organisation/read-our-publications

Sameroff, A. (2009) *The Transactional Model of Development: How Children and Contexts Shape Each Other*. Washington, DC: American Psychological Association.

Sampson, O.C. (1976) 'Treatment practices in British child guidance clinics: An historical overview', *Educational Review*, 29 (1):13–29.

Sandel, S.L., Chaiklin, S. and Lohn, A. (1993) *Foundation of Dance/Movement Therapy: The Life and Work of Marian Chace*. Columbia, MD: Marian Chace Memorial Fund of the American Dance Therapy Association.

Sanders, P. and Wilkins, P. (2010) *First Steps in Practitioner Research: A Guide to Understanding and Doing Research for Helping Practitioners*. Ross-on-Wye: PCCS Books.

Sanderson, C. (2006) *Counselling Adult Survivors of Child Sexual Abuse*. 3rd edn. London: Jessica Kingsley.

Sanford, L.T. (1991) *Strong at the Broken Places: Overcoming the Trauma of Childhood Abuse*. London: Virago.

Saunders, J.B. and Rey, J.M. (2011) *Young People and Alcohol: Impact, Policy, Prevention, Treatment*. Oxford: Blackwell.

Schaefer, C.E. (ed.) (1979) *The Therapeutic Use of Child's Play*. New York: Aronson.

Schaefer, C. (1993) *The Therapeutic Powers of Play*. Northvale, NJ: Jason Aronson.

Schaefer, C.E. (ed.) (2003) *Foundations of Play Therapy*. Hoboken, NJ: John Wiley & Sons.

Schaefer, C.E. and O'Connor, K.J. (eds) (1983) *Handbook of Play Therapy*. New York: John Wiley & Sons.

Schmidt Neven, R. (2010) *Core Principles of Assessment and Therapeutic Communication with Children, Parents and Families: Towards the Promotion of Child and Family Wellbeing*. London: Routledge.

Schmidt, U., Lee, S., Beecham, J., Perkins, S., Treasure, J., Yi, I., Winn, S., Robinson, P., Murphy, R., Keville, S., Johnson-Sabine, E., Jenkins, M., Dodge, L., Berelowitz, M. and Eisler, I. (2007) 'A randomized controlled trial of family therapy and cognitive behavior therapy guided self-care for adolescents with bulimia nervosa and related disorders', *American Journal of Psychiatry*, 164 (4): 591–598.

Schneider, C.B. (2006) *Acting Antics: A Theatrical Approach to Teaching Social Understanding to Kids and Teens with Asperger Syndrome*. London: Jessica Kingsley.

Schore, A. (2010) 'The right brain implicit self: A central mechanism of the psychotherapy change process', in J. Petrucelli (ed.), *Knowing, Not-knowing and Sort of Knowing. Psychoanalysis and the Experience of Uncertainty*. London: Karnac. pp. 177–202.

Schore, J. and Schore, A. (2008) 'Modern attachment theory: The central role of affect regulation in development and treatment', *Clinical Social Work Journal*, 36 (1): 9–20.

Schottenbauer, M., Glass, C. and Arnkoff, D. (2007) 'Decision making and psychotherapy integration: Theoretical considerations, preliminary data and implications for future research', *Journal of Psychotherapy Integration*, 17 (3): 225–250.

SCIE (Social Care Institute for Excellence) (2005a) 'Deliberate self-harm (DSH) among children and adolescents: Who is at risk and how it is recognised', *SCARE Research Briefing* 16. Available at: www.scie.org.uk/publications/briefings/files/briefing16.pdf.

SCIE (Social Care Institute for Excellence) (2005b) 'Therapies and approaches for helping children and adolescents who deliberately self-harm (DSH)', *SCARE Research Briefing* 17. Available at: www.scie.org.uk/publications/briefings/files/briefing17.pdf.

Scocco, P. and De Leo, D. (2002) 'One-year prevalence of death thoughts, suicide ideation and behaviours in an elderly population', *International Journal of Geriatric Psychiatry*, 17: 842–846.

Scott, M.J. and Stradling, S.G. (2006) *Counselling for Post-Traumatic Stress Disorder.* 3rd edn. London: SAGE.

Scott, T., Burlingame, S., Starling, M. and Porter, C. (2003) 'Effects of individual client-centered play therapy on sexually abused children's mood, self-concept, and social competence', *International Journal of Play Therapy*, 12 (1): 7–30.

Scottish Government (2008) *A Guide to Getting it Right for Every Child.* Available at www.scotland.gov.uk/Resource/Doc/1141/0065063.pdf (accessed 16/3/14).

Scottish Intercollegiate Guidelines Network (2007) *Assessment, Diagnosis and Clinical Interventions for Children and Young People with Autism Spectrum Disorders* (Quick Reference Guide). Scottish Intercollegiate Guidelines Network Services for Bereaved Children: A Discussion of the Theoretical and Practical Issues.

Scowcroft, E. (2013) *Suicide Statistics Report 2013: Data for 2009–2011.* The Samaritans. Available at: www.samaritans.org/sites/default/files/kcfinder/files/research/Samari tans%20Suicide%20Statistics%20Report%202013.pdf.

Sgroi, S. (1982) *Handbook of Clinical Intervention in Child Sexual Abuse.* Toronto: Lexington Books.

Shakespeare, T. (2006) *Disability Rights and Wrongs.* London: Routledge.

Sharry, J. (2004) *Counselling Children, Adolescents and Families.* London: SAGE.

Shechtman, Z. and Pastor, R. (2005) 'Cognitive-behavioural and humanistic group treatment for children with learning disabilities: A comparison of outcomes and process', *Journal of Counseling Psychology*, 52 (3): 322–336.

Shedler, J. (2010) 'The efficacy of psychodynamic psychotherapy', *American Psychologist*, 65 (2): 98–109.

Sherr, L. and Sterne, A. (1999) 'Evaluation of a counselling intervention in primary schools', *Clinical Psychology and Psychotherapy*, 6: 286–296.

Sherwood, P. (2010) *The Healing Art of Clay Therapy.* Melbourne: Acer Press.

Shirk, S.R. and Karver, M. (2010) 'Alliance in child and adolescent psychotherapy', in J.C. Norcross (ed.) *Evidence-Based Therapy Relationships.* Available at: www.nrepp.samhsa.gov/pdfs/norcross_evidence-based_therapy_relationships.pdf.

Silverman, J.A. (1997) 'Charcot's comments on the therapeutic role of isolation in the treatment of anorexia nervosa', *The International Journal of Eating Disorders*, 21 (3): 295–298.

Silverman, P. and Klass, D. (1996) 'Continuing bonds', in D. Klass, P.R. Silverman and S.L. Nickman (eds), *Continuing Bonds. New Understandings of Grief.* Philadelphia, PA: Taylor and Francis.

Simpson, A.R. (2001) *Raising Teens: A Synthesis of Research and a Foundation for Action.* Boston: Center for Health Communication, Harvard School of Public Health.

Skinner, B.F. (1968) *The Technology of Teaching.* Englewood Cliffs, NJ: Prentice-Hall.

Slaughter, V. (2005) 'Young children's understanding of death', *Australian Psychologist*, 40 (3): 179–186.

Slavin, R.E. (1997) 'Cooperative learning and student diversity', in R. Ben-Ari and Y. Rich, *Enhancing Education in Heterogeneous Schools*. Ramat-Gat: Bar-llan University Press. pp. 215–247.

Smith, B. and Widdowson, M. (2003) 'Child centred counselling', in C. Lago and B. Smith (eds), *Anti-Discriminatory Practice in Counselling and Psychotherapy*. London: SAGE.

Smyth, D. (2013) *Person-Centred Therapy with Children and Young People*. London: SAGE.

Social Exclusion Unit (2004) *Mental Health and Social Exclusion*. Social Exclusion Unit Report. London: Office of the Deputy Prime Minister.

Sodha, S. and Margo, J. (2008) *Thursday's Child*. London: Institute for Public Policy Research.

Speckens, A.E., Van Hemert, A.M., Spinhoven, P., Hawton, K.E., Bolk, J.H. and Rooijmans, H.G. (1995) 'Cognitive behavioural therapy for medically unexplained physical symptoms: A randomised controlled trial', *British Medical Journal*, 311 (7016): 1328–1332.

Spiel, C. (2009) 'Evidence-based practice: A challenge for European developmental psychology', *European Journal of Developmental Psychology*, 6 (1): 11–33.

Spiers, T. (2001) *Trauma: A Practitioner's Guide to Counselling*. London: Routledge.

Spong, S., Waters, R., Dowd, C. and Jackson, C. (2013) *The Relationship between Specialist Child and Adolescent Mental Health Services (CAMHS) and Community-Based Counselling for Children and Young People*. Lutterworth: BACP/Counselling MindEd. Available at: www.counsellingminded.com.

Sroufe, L.A. (2005) 'Attachment and development: A prospective, longitudinal study from birth to adulthood', *Attachment & Human Development*, 7 (4): 349–367.

Spratt, T. and Devaney, J. (2009) 'Identifying children with multiple problems: Perspectives of practitioners and managers in three nations', *British Journal of Social Work*, 39: 418–434.

Stallard, P. (2002) *Think Good – Feel Good: A Cognitive Behaviour Therapy Workbook for Children and Young People*. Chichester: John Wiley.

Stallard, P. (2005) *A Clinician's Guide to Think Good, Feel Good: The Use of CBT with Children and Young People*. Chichester: John Wiley.

Stansfeld, S., Head, J., Bartley, M. and Fonagy, P. (2008) 'Social position, early deprivation and the development of attachment', *Social Psychiatry and Psychiatric Epidemiology*, 43 (7): 516–526.

Steen, S., Bauman, S. and Smith, J. (2007) 'Professional school counsellors and the practice of group work', *Professional School Counselling*, 11 (2): 72–80.

Stern, D. (1985) *The Interpersonal World of The Infant: A View From Psychoanalysis and Developmental Psychology*. New York: Basic Books.

Stern, D. (2004) *The First Relationship*. Cambridge, MA: Harvard University Press.

Stern, D.N., Sander, L.W., Nahum, J.P., Harrison, A.M., Lyons-Ruth, K., Morgan, A.C., Bruschweilerstern, N. and Tronick, E.Z. (1998) 'Non-interpretive mechanisms in psychoanalytic therapy: The "something more" than interpretation', *International Journal of Psychoanalysis*, 79: 903–921.

Stevens, C., Stringfellow, J., Wakelin, K. and Waring, J. (2011) 'The UK Gestalt psychotherapy CORE research project: The findings', *British Gestalt Journal*, 20 (2): 22–27.

Stewart, D. (2012) 'Giving the young client a voice: Outcome informed counselling', *British Association for Counselling and Psychotherapy Counselling Children and Young People*, September: 19–23.

Stice, E., Rohde, P., Gau, J.M. and Wade, E. (2010) 'Efficacy trial of a brief cognitive-behavioral depression prevention program for high-risk adolescents: Effects at 1- and 2-year follow-up', *Journal of Consulting and Clinical Psychology*, 78: 856–867.

Stiles, W.B. and Goldsmith, J.Z. (2010) 'The alliance over time', in J.C. Muran and J.P. Barber (eds), *The Therapeutic Alliance: An Evidence-Based Guide to Practice*. New York: The Guilford Press. pp. 44–62.

Stiles, W.B., Barkham, M., Mellor-Clark, J. and Connell, J. (2008) 'Effectiveness of cognitive-behavioural, person-centred, and psychodynamic therapies in UK primary-care routine practice: Replication in a larger sample', *Psychological Medicine*, 38 (5): 677–688.

Stokes, J., Pennington, J., Monroe, B., Papadatou, D. and Relf, M. (1999) 'Developing services for bereaved children: A discussion of the theoretical and practical issues involved', *Mortality*, 4 (3): 291–307.

Street, C. (2013) *Voluntary and Community Sector (VCS) Counselling Provision for Children, Young People and Young Adults in England*. Lutterworth: BACP: Counselling/MindEd.

Striegel-Moore, R.H. and Bulik, C.M. (2007) 'Risk factors for eating disorders', *American Psychologist*, 62 (3): 181–198.

Stroebe, M.S. and Schut, H. (1999) 'The dual process model of coping with bereavement: Rationale and description', *Death Studies*, 23: 197–224.

Stroebe, M. and Schut, H. (2010) 'The dual process model of coping with bereavement: A decade on', *Journal of Death and Dying*, 61 (4): 273–289.

Strother, E., Lemberg, R., Stanford, S.C. and Turberville, D. (2012) 'Eating disorders in men: Underdiagnosed, undertreated, and misunderstood', *Eating Disorders*, 20 (5): 346–355.

Sutton, C. (1997) 'Reviewing and evaluating therapeutic progress', in S. Palmer and G. McMahon (eds), *Client Assessment*. London: SAGE.

Swanson, S.A., Crow, S.J., Le Grange, D., Swendsen, J. and Merikangas, K.R. (2011) 'Prevalence and correlates of eating disorders in adolescents: Results from the national comorbidity survey replication adolescent supplement', *Archives of General Psychiatry*, 68 (7): 714–723.

Tervo, D. (2007) 'Zig zag flop and roll: Creating an embodied field for healing and awareness when working with children', *British Gestalt Journal*, 16 (2): 28–37.

Thase, M. and Lang, S. (2006) *Beating the Blues: New Approaches to Overcoming Dysthymia and Chronic Mild Depression*. New York: Oxford University Press.

Thompson, R.A. (2000) 'The legacy of early attachments', *Child Development*, 71 (1): 145–152.

Thompson, R.A. (2008) 'Measure twice, cut once: Attachment theory and the NICHD Study of Early Child Care and Youth Development', *Attachment & Human Development*, 10 (3): 287–297.

Thompson, W. (2013) *School-Based Counselling in UK Primary Schools*. Lutterworth: BACP/Counselling MindEd. Available at: www.counsellingminded.com.

Tracey, A., McElearney, A., Adamson, G. and Shevlin, M. (2009) 'Practitioners' views and experiences of participating in a school counselling evaluation study', *Counselling and Psychotherapy Research*, 9 (3): 193–203.

Treatment for Adolescents with Depression Study (TADS) Team (2009) 'The Treatment for Adolescents with Depression Study (TADS): Outcomes over one year of naturalistic follow-up', *American Journal of Psychiatry*, 166: 1141–1149.

Trevarthen, C. (2001) 'Intrinsic motives for companionship in understanding: Their origin, development, and significance for infant mental health', *Infant Mental Health Journal*, 22 (1–2): 95–131.

Trevarthen, C. (2011) 'What is it like to be a person who knows nothing? Defining the active inter-subjective mind of a newborn human being', *Infant and Child Development*, 20 (1): 119–135.

Trevarthen, C. and Aitken, K.J. (2001) 'Infant intersubjectivity: Research, theory, and clinical applications', *Journal of Child Psychology and Psychiatry*, 42 (1): 3–48.

Trower, P., Casey, A. and Dryden, W. (1988) *Cognitive Behavioural Counselling in Action*. London: SAGE.

Tryon, G.S. and Winograd, G. (2002) 'Goal consensus and collaboration', in J.C. Norcross (ed.), *Psychotherapy Relationships that Work*. New York: Oxford University Press. pp. 109–125.

Tsai, M. and Ray, D. (2011) 'Children in therapy: Learning from evaluation of university-based community counselling clinical services', *Children and Youth Services Review*, 33 (6): 901–909.

Tuckman, B.W. (1965) 'Developmental sequence in small groups', *Psychological Bulletin*, 63: 384–399.

Turner, H. and Bryant-Waugh, R. (2005) 'Eating disorder not otherwise specified (EDNOS): Profiles of clients presenting at a community eating disorders service', *European Eating Disorders Review*, 12: 18–26.

Twigg, E., Barkham, M., Bewick, B., Mulhern, B., Connell, J. and Cooper, M. (2009) 'The young person's CORE: Development of a brief outcome measure for young people', *Counselling and Psychotherapy Research*, 9 (3): 160–168.

Ungar, M., Barter, K., McConnell, S., Tutty, L. and Fairholm, J. (2009) 'Patterns of abuse disclosure among youth', *Qualitative Social Work*, 8: 341–356.

UNICEF (1989) *The United Nations Convention on the Rights of the Child 1989*. London: UNICEF. Available at: www.unicef.org/crc/.

UNICEF (2007) *Innocenti Research Centre Report Card 7: Child Poverty in Perspective: An Overview of Child Wellbeing in Rich Countries*. Florence: UNICEF Innocenti Research Centre.

Van der Kolk, B. (1994) 'The body keeps the score: Memory and the evolving psychobiology of post-traumatic stress', *Harvard Psychiatric Review*, 1 (5): 253–265.

Van der Kolk, B. (2005) 'Developmental trauma disorder', *Psychiatric Annals*, 35 (5): 401–408.

Van Fleet, R., Sywulak, A.E. and Sniscak, C.C. (2010) *Child Centered Play Therapy*. New York: The Guilford Press.

Van Ijzendoorn, M.H. and Juffer, F. (2006) 'Adoption as intervention. Meta-analytic evidence for massive catch-up and plasticity in physical, socio-emotional, and cognitive development' (The Emanuel Miller Memorial Lecture). *Journal of Child Psychology and Psychiatry*, 47 (12): 1228–1245.

Venable, W. and Thompson, B. (1998) 'Caretaker psychological factors predicting premature termination of children's counselling', *Journal of Counselling and Development*, 76: 286–293.

Verduyn, C., Rogers, J. and Woods, A. (2009) *Depression: Cognitive Behaviour Therapy with Children and Young People*. London: Routledge.

Vossler, A. and Hanley, T. (2010) 'Online counseling: Meeting the needs of young people in late-modern societies', in J. Leaman and M. Woersching (eds), *Youth in Contemporary Europe*. London: Routledge. pp. 133–148.

Vygotsky, L.S. (1934) *Thought and Language*, edited and translated by E. Hanfmann, G. Vakar and A. Kozulin. Cambridge, MA: MIT Press.

Vygotsky, L.S. (1962) *Thought and Language*. Cambridge, MA: MIT Press.

Vygotsky, L.S. (1978) *Mind in Society*. Cambridge, MA: Harvard University Press.

Wade, T.D. and Watson, H.J. (2012) 'Psychotherapies in eating disorders', in J. Alexander and J. Treasure (eds), *A Collaborative Approach to Eating Disorders*. New York: Routledge/Taylor & Francis. pp. 125–135.

WAG (Welsh Assembly Government) (2008) *A National Strategy for a School-Based Counselling Service in Wales*. Cardiff: DELLS/WAG.

Wagenaar, A., Harwood, E., Toomey, T., Denk, C. and Zander, K. (2000) 'Public opinion on alcohol policies in the United States: Results from a national survey', *Journal of Public Health Policy*, 21 (3): 303–327.

Walker, S. (2005) *Culturally Competent Therapy: Working with Children and Young People*. London: Palgrave Macmillan.

Walkup, J.T., Albano, A.M., Piacentini, J., Birmaher, B., Compton, S.N., Sherrill, J.T. and Kendall, P.C. (2008) 'Cognitive behavioral therapy, sertraline, or a combination in childhood anxiety', *The New England Journal of Medicine*, 359: 2753–2766.

Walsh, J. (2010) 'Definitions matter: If maternal–fetal relationships are not attachment, what are they?', *Archives of Women's Mental Health*, 13 (5): 449–451.

Wampold, B.E. (2001) *The Great Psychotherapy Debate: Models, Methods and Findings.* Mahwah, NJ: Lawrence Erlbaum Associates.

Ward, H. and Skuse, T. (2001) 'Performance targets and stability of placements for children long looked after away from home', *Children and Society*, 15: 333–346.

Warr, S. (2009) 'Counselling refugee young people: An exploration of therapeutic approaches', *Pastoral Care in Education*, 28(4): 269–282.

Washburn, C.A. (1983) *The effects of participation in high risk ropes courses on individual self-concept.* Published Doctorate of Education, Oklahoma State University.

Watson, V. (2011) 'Training for multicultural therapy: The challenge and the experience', in C. Lago (ed.), *The Handbook of Trans-cultural Counselling and Psychotherapy.* Maidenhead: Open University Press.

Webster, C. (2002) *The NHS: A Political History.* Oxford: Oxford University Press.

West, J. (1996) *Child Centered Play Therapy.* 2nd edn. London: Arnold.

Westergaard, J. (2009) *Effective Group Work with Young People.* Berkshire: Open University Press.

Westerman, G., Thomas, M.S.C. and Karmiloff-Smith, A. (2010) 'Neuroconstructionism', in U. Goswami (ed.), *Childhood Cognitive Development.* Oxford: Blackwell. pp. 723–748.

Wheeler, G. and McConville, M. (2002) *The Heart of Development. Vol. 1: Childhood.* Cambridge, MA: The Gestalt Press.

Wheeler, S. and Elliott, R. (2008) 'What do counsellors and psychotherapists need to know about research?', *Counselling and Psychotherapy Research*, 8 (2): 133–135.

White, M. (2000) *Reflections on Narrative Practice.* Adelaide: Dulwich Centre Publications.

White, M. (2004a) 'Value, resonance, and definitional ceremony', *International Journal of Narrative and Community Work* 1. Adelaide: Dulwich Centre Publications.

White, M. (2004b) *Narrative Practices and Exotic Lives.* Adelaide: Dulwich Centre Publications.

White, M. and Epston, D. (1990) *Narrative Means to Therapeutic End.* New York: Norton.

Whitlock, J. (2010) 'Self-injurious behaviour in adolescents', *PLoS Medicine*, 7 (5): e1000240. Available at: www.plosmedicine.org/article/info%3Adoi%2F10.1371%2 Fjournal.pmed.1000240.

WHO (1999) *Internal Classification of Functioning and Disability-2.* Geneva: World Health Organisation.

WHO (2001) *The World Health Report.* Geneva: World Health Organisation.

WHO (2003) *International Classification of Diseases*, Tenth Revision (ICD-10). USA: World Health Organisation Publications Centre.

WHO (2013) *Suicide Prevention* (SUPRE). Available at: www.who.int/mental_health/prevention/suicide/suicideprevent/en/.

Wierzbicki, M. and Pekarik, G. (1993) 'A meta-analysis of psychotherapy dropout', *Professional Psychology: Research and Practice*, 24 (2): 190–195.

Wilkinson, S., Croy, P., King, M. and Barnes, J. (2007) 'Are we getting it right? Parents' perceptions of hospice child bereavement support services', *Palliative Medicine*, 21: 401–407.

Willis, C. (2002) 'The grieving process in children: Strategies for understanding, educating, and reconciling children's perceptions of death', *Early Childhood Education Journal*, 29 (4): 221–226

Wilson, G.T. (2005) 'Psychological treatment of eating disorders', *Annual Review of Clinical Psychology*, 1 (1): 439–465.

Wilson, K., Kendrick, P. and Ryan, V. (2001) *Play Therapy: A Non-Directive Approach for Children and Adolescents.* London: Bailliere Tindall.

Wilson, P. (2004) *Young Minds in Our Schools: A Guide for Teachers and Others Working in Schools.* London: YoungMinds.

Winnicott, D.W. (1958) *Collected Papers: Through Paediatrics to Psycho-Analysis.* London: Tavistock.

Winnicott, D. (1965) *Maturational Processes and the Facilitating Environment.* London: Hogarth Press Ltd.

Winnicott, D. (1991) *Playing and Reality.* London: Routledge

Winsler, A., Naglieri, J. and Manfra, L. (2006) 'Children's search strategies and accompanying verbal and motor strategic behavior: Developmental trends and relations with task performance among children age 5 to 17', *Cognitive Development*, 21(3): 232–248.

Winter, D., Bradshaw, S., Bunn, F. and Wellsted, D. (2009) *Counselling and Psychotherapy for the Prevention of Suicide: A Systematic Review of the Evidence.* Lutterworth: BACP.

Wittenberg, I. (1999) 'Ending therapy', *Journal of Child Psychotherapy*, 25: 339–356.

Wolak, J., Mitchell, K. and Finkelhor, D. (2003) 'Escaping or connecting? Characteristics of youth who form close online relationships', *Journal of Adolescence*, 26 (1): 105–199.

Wolfe, B.E. and Goldfried, M.R. (1998) 'Research on psychotherapy integration: Recommendations and conclusions from an NIMH workshop', *Journal of Consulting and Clinical Psychology*, 56: 448–451.

Wood, D. (1998) *How Children Think and Learn.* 2nd edn. Oxford: Blackwell.

Wood, D., Bruner, J.S. and Ross, G. (1976) 'The role of tutoring in problem solving', *Journal of Child Psychology and Psychiatry*, 17 (2): 89–100.

Wooldridge, T. and Lytle, P.P. (2012) 'An overview of anorexia nervosa in males', *Eating Disorders*, 20 (5): 368–378.

Woolf, A. and Austin, D. (2008) *Handbook of Therapeutic Play in Schools*. Chester: A2C Press.

Worden, J. (1991) *Grief Counselling and Grief Therapy: A Handbook for the Mental Health Practitioner*. 2nd edn. New York: Springer.

Worrall, M. (2006) 'Contracting within person-centred counselling and psychotherapy', in C. Sills (ed.), *Contracts in Counselling and Psychotherapy*, 2nd edn. London: SAGE.

Wulff, R. (1996) *The Historical Roots of Gestalt Therapy Theory*. Available at: www.gestalt.org/wulf.htm.

Wyatt, G.E. and Powell, G.J. (1988) *Lasting Effects of Child Sexual Abuse*. London: SAGE.

Yalom, I.D. and Leszcz, M. (2005) *The Theory and Practice of Group Psychotherapy*. 5th edn. New York: Basic Books.

YoungMinds and Cello (2012) *Talking Self-Harm, Talking Taboos*. London: YoungMinds and Cello. Available at: www.cellogroup.com/pdfs/talking_self_harm.pdf.

Zand, D.H. and Pierce, K.J. (eds) (2011) *Resilience in Deaf Children: Adaptation through Emerging Adulthood*. New York: Springer.

Zeanah, C.H., Berlin, L.J. and Boris, N.W. (2011) 'Practitioner review: Clinical applications of attachment theory and research for infants and young children', *Journal of Child Psychology and Psychiatry*, 52 (8): 819–833.

Zilberstein, K. (2008) 'Au revoir: An attachment and loss perspective on termination', *Clinical Social Work Journal*, 36: 301–311.

Index